THE
NEW TESTAMENT
AND THE PEOPLE OF GOD

CHRISTIAN ORIGINS AND THE QUESTION OF GOD

Volume One

THE
NEW TESTAMENT
AND THE PEOPLE OF GOD

N T Wright

FORTRESS PRESS   MINNEAPOLIS

THE NEW TESTAMENT AND THE PEOPLE OF GOD

First North American edition published 1992 by Fortress Press.

Published in Great Britain by SPCK, Holy Trinity Church, Marylebone Road, London NW1 4DU

Scripture quotations, unless otherwise noted, are from the New Revised Standard Version of the Bible, copyright © 1989 by the Division of Christian Education of the National Council of Churches.

Library of Congress Cataloging-in-Publication Data

Wright, N. T. (Nicholas Thomas)
    Christian origins and the question of God / N. T. Wright. – 1st
Fortress Press ed.
        p. cm.
    Includes bibliographical references and indexes.
    Contents: v. 1. The New Testament and the people of God
    ISBN 0-8006-2681-8 (v. 1; alk. paper)
    1. God—Biblical teaching. 2. God—History of doctrines—Early
church, ca. 30–600. 3. Bible. N.T.—Theology. 4. Christianity—
Origin. I. Title.
BS2398.W75 1992
225.6—dc20
                                                92-19348
                                                 CIP

Printed in the United States of America   AF 1-2681

Typeset by Tom Wright, Oxford, using *Nota Bene* software

for Brian Walsh

CONTENTS

PREFACE

For some years I tried to write two books side by side: one about Paul and his theology, the other about Jesus within his historical context. It gradually dawned on me that the two belonged together more closely than I had realized. Both were concerned with the historical description of events and beliefs in the first century. Both emphasized a particular way of understanding the relevant texts and events. Both required a pre-understanding of first-century Judaism. Both demanded concluding theological and practical reflections. So it was that I found myself driven to think of a two-volume work on Jesus and Paul.

But the material, and the nature of the arguments I wished to advance about it, would not let me leave it at that. One of the vital questions that has to be asked as part of the search for Jesus has to do with the gospels as they stand, and the enormous problems raised there could hardly be dealt with in a single chapter somewhere within an already over-long book. Having given in, and admitted to myself that I was thus planning three volumes, it was only a short step to the realization that I was actually thinking of five: one each for Jesus, Paul, and the gospels, and an introduction (the present volume) and conclusion in which the various things that would otherwise have to be said at the beginning and end of each of the other three books could be gathered together. The result is a project which, though still focused centrally on Jesus and Paul, is also inevitably about the New Testament as a whole.

One reason for allowing the material to expand in this way is the frustrating brevity of so many one-volume, or even two-volume, 'New Testament theologies' in the present century. To compress the discussion of the parables, or of justification, into two or three pages is actually not much use either to the ordinary reader or to the advancement of scholarship. At best, all one can hope to do by that method is to set a few bells ringing and see if any listeners want to go away and work out what they might mean. I hope to do a little more than that, and actually to address substantial issues, and engage in debate with opposing views, at certain key points.

At the opposite extreme from the brief overall survey is the fragmentation which exists in so much of the discipline, whereby people spend entire professional careers specializing in one sub-area, and never try to draw together the threads of wider hypotheses. I believe it is important that the synthesis be attempted, but without false compression or over-simplification. I hope, then, to offer a consistent hypothesis on the origin of Christianity, with particular relation to Jesus, Paul and the gospels, which will set out new ways of understanding major movements and thought-patterns, and suggest new lines that exegesis can follow up. I hope to contribute to this task myself.

The phrase 'New Testament theology', which I discuss in the first chapter of the present volume, is in the present day loaded with a variety of connotations. Although in many ways what I am doing falls into the pattern of books with titles like that, I have preferred to leave the main title of the project concrete rather than abstract. One of the underlying themes throughout is the meaning of the word 'God', or for that matter 'god' (see below), and it seems to me that the early Christians, including the writers of the New Testament, wrestled with that question more than is usually imagined. The word *theos* for Greek-speakers (and its equivalents in other languages spoken in the first century) was not univocal, and the early Christians made out a fairly thorough case for understanding it in a particular sense. I am therefore not merely investigating the 'general' area of 'theology' (i.e. anything that passes for 'theological' reflection on any subject), but wish to focus particularly on 'theology' proper—i.e. the meaning and referent of the important word 'god'. This has, perhaps surprisingly, been somewhat neglected within 'New Testament theology', and it seems to me high time that the situation was rectified.

There are five matters of linguistic usage on which I must comment, and either apologize for or, perhaps, explain why apology should be unnecessary. First, I normally refer to Jesus as 'Jesus', not simply 'Christ', as did many older writers. This is not simply to avoid offending my Jewish friends, and others for whom Jesus' Messiahship is a matter of debate. It is because Messiahship is itself in question throughout the gospel story, and the task of the historian is to see things as far as possible through the eyes of the people of the time. In particular, it may serve as a reminder that 'Christ' is a title with a specific, and quite limited, meaning (see the discussions in volumes 2 and 3). It was not of itself a 'divine' title, however much it has been used as such in Christian circles, and was not in earliest Christianity reducible to a mere proper name.[1]

Second, I have frequently used 'god' instead of 'God'. This is not a printer's error, nor is it a deliberate irreverence; rather the opposite, in fact. The modern usage, without the article and with a capital, seems to me actually dangerous. This usage, which sometimes amounts to regarding 'God' as the proper name of the Deity, rather than as essentially a common noun, implies that all users of the word are monotheists and, within that, that all monotheists believe in the same god. Both these propositions seem to me self-evidently untrue. It may or may not be true that any worship of any god is translated by some mysterious grace into worship of one god who actually exists, and who happens to be the only god. That is believed by some students of religion. It is not, however, believed by very many practitioners of the mainline monotheistic religions (Judaism, Christianity, Islam) or of the non-monotheistic ones

---

[1] See Wright 1991a, ch. 3.

(Hinduism, Buddhism and their cognates). Certainly the Jews and Christians of the first century did not believe it. They believed that pagans worshipped idols, or even demons. (The question as to how Jews and Christians regarded each other's beliefs on this topic will be addressed in Part V of the present volume.)

It seems to me, therefore, simply misleading to use 'God' throughout this work. I have often preferred either to refer to Israel's god by the biblical name, YHWH (notwithstanding debates about the use of this name within second-temple Judaism), or, in phrases designed to remind us of what or who we are talking about, to speak of 'the creator', 'the covenant god' or 'Israel's god'. The early Christians used the phrase 'the god' (*ho theos*) of this god, and this was (I believe) somewhat polemical, making an essentially Jewish-monotheistic point over against polytheism. In a world where there were many suns, one would not say 'the sun'. Furthermore, the early Christians regularly felt the need to make clear which god they were talking about by glossing the phrase, as Paul so often does, with a reference to the revelation of this god in and through Jesus of Nazareth. Since, in fact, the present project presents a case, among other things, for a fresh understanding of the meaning and content of the word 'god', and ultimately 'God', in the light of Jesus, the Spirit and the New Testament, it would be begging the question to follow a usage which seemed to imply that the answer was known in advance. I think it quite likely that many of those who come to a book like this with the firm conviction that 'Jesus is God', and equally well many of those who come with the firm conviction that he is not, may hold views on the meaning of 'god', or 'God', which ought to be challenged in the light of the New Testament. The christological question, as to whether the statement 'Jesus is God' is true, and if so in what sense, is often asked as though 'God' were the known and 'Jesus' the unknown; this, I suggest, is manifestly mistaken. If anything, the matter stands the other way around.[2]

Third, some people get cross if they see the usage BC and AD in reference to dates before and after the birth of Jesus, since they take it as a sign of Christian imperialism. Others are irritated if they see Christians using the increasingly popular 'neutral' alternatives BCE ('Before the Common Era') and CE ('Common Era'), because it seems either patronizing or spineless. Similar debates rage as to whether the Hebrew Bible should be called 'Tanach' or 'Old Testament', or perhaps even 'The Older Testament' (in my view, this last is the most patronizing of all); or whether 'First Testament' and 'Second Testament' are more appropriate. It is strange that it seems to be scholars within the broad Christian tradition who are afflicted with these problems. Jewish writers do not affect 'Christian' ways of referring to dates and books, nor would I wish them to. In all these cases there is, I fear, a malaise among us, which consists of the desire to present a 'neutral' or 'objective' view as though we were all merely disinterested historians looking down from an uninvolved Olympian height. As I shall be arguing in Part II of the present volume, such an epistemology is inappropriate and indeed impossible. Therefore, mindful of

---

[2] I am encouraged to see that the usage is not entirely original: cf. Lane Fox 1986, 27; Hengel 1974, 266f.

the further impossibility of pleasing all the people all the time, I shall continue to follow the usages to which I am accustomed (AD and BC, 'Old Testament' and/or 'Hebrew Bible'), with neither imperialistic nor patronizing intent—noting, indeed, that the same usage obtains in the revision of Schürer's classic work by a team of historians from widely differing backgrounds under the leadership of Professor Geza Vermes.[3]

Fourth, we meet the currently vexed question of the gender of language about 'God', or gods. Here again we meet a puzzle. Nobody insists that a Muslim theologian should refer to the god he or she discusses as 'she'; this is just as well, otherwise Muslims would not be able to write much theology. The same would be true, I think, for all Jews until very recently, and certainly for the great majority of Jews in the present. Nobody insists that someone writing about Hindu deities should make them all indiscriminately androgynous: some are clearly masculine, others equally clearly feminine. Nor would the pagan gods and goddesses of the ancient world have been pleased if their devotees had got their genders muddled. In a work of history I think it is appropriate to refer to the god of the Jews, the gods of the Greco-Roman world, and the god of the early church, in ways which those groups would themselves have recognized as appropriate.

Fifth, I shall constantly need to refer to that part of the Middle East in which the gospel events are set. If I consistently call this territory 'Palestine' my Jewish friends may object; if I refer to it as 'Israel' my Palestinian friends may feel slighted (and, after all, most of the native Christians currently living in the area happen to be Palestinians). I shall therefore adopt no consistent policy, but wish to place on record my desire to be sensitive to the feelings, fears and aspirations of all concerned, as well as my gratitude for the wonderful welcome and hospitality I received on all sides during the time I spent in Jerusalem in 1989, working on the first three volumes of this project.

Something must now be said about the scope of this first volume. It is basically an exercise in ground-clearing, designed to enable me to engage in further work on Jesus, Paul and the gospels without begging quite so many questions as I would have done had I tried to squeeze this material into the early chapters of other books. In most of this book, then, I write as a fascinated amateur, rather than a highly-trained professional. My own specializations have been Jesus and Paul, and I have come to hermeneutical and theological theory on the one hand, and to the study of first-century Judaism on the other, as an enthusiastic outsider. Some, eager for exegesis, will find much of this book arcane and unnecessary; others, having spent their lives sifting material that I here pull together quite briskly, will suspect that important questions are still being begged. (This is particularly true of Part II.) I have found it necessary, though, to trespass on these territories, since the present climate of New Testament studies has thrown up so many confusions of method and content that the only hope is to go back to the beginning. The only way of alleviating the remaining inadequacies of the present work would have been to turn each Part into a whole book in itself.

[3] Schürer 1973–87. Cf. too Goodman 1987.

This means, among other things, that readers looking for a lengthy 'history of research' will usually be disappointed. To include that sort of material would make the project at least half as long again as it already is. I have written elsewhere about the present state of New Testament studies, and about particular issues within current research, and shall continue to do so.[4] In a work like this, however, one must be quite selective in choosing one's conversation partners, even at the risk of appearing to bypass certain questions. Those who want to check up on details or debates will find plenty of books to help them.[5] In setting out my own proposals, I am at least implicitly entering into dialogue with many more writers than are listed in the footnotes. On almost every page it would have been possible to double or treble the secondary sources referred to, but one must draw a line somewhere. I have tended to refer to recent discussions, many of which give full bibliographies of earlier works.

A word must be said here about the category of 'story', which I have found myself using increasingly frequently. It has already proved fruitful in a variety of areas in recent scholarship, not only in literary criticism but in areas as diverse as anthropology, philosophy, psychology, education, ethics and theology itself. I am well aware that some will regard my use of it as faddish, and it is of course true that 'story' is a central feature of postmodern criticism, with its rejection of the anti-traditional, anti-story attitude of the Enlightenment. But I do not wish, in using this category, to buy wholesale into postmodernism itself. On the contrary: whereas postmodernism sometimes uses 'story' as a means whereby one may talk about something other than space-time reality, I have tried to integrate it within the 'critical-realist' epistemology expounded in Part II, and to use it as a way forward in history and theology as well as literary study.

This all leads to a final word of warning. I frequently tell my students that quite a high proportion of what I say is probably wrong, or at least flawed or skewed in some way which I do not at the moment realize. The only problem is that I do not know which bits are wrong; if I did I might do something about it. The analogy with other areas of life is salutary: I make many mistakes in moral and practical matters, so why should I imagine my thinking to be mysteriously exempt? But, whereas if I hurt someone, or take a wrong turn in the road, I am usually confronted quite soon with my error, if I expound erratic views within the world of academic theology I am less likely to be convinced by contradiction. (The first person here, as sometimes in Paul, includes the generic.) We all have ways of coping with adverse comment without changing our minds; but, since I am aware of the virtual certainty of error in some of what I write, I hope I shall pay proper attention to the comments of those—and no doubt there will be many—who wish to draw my attention to the places where they find my statement of the evidence inadequate, my arguments weak, or my

---

[4] See Neill and Wright 1988; and my article on the modern Quest for Jesus, in the forthcoming Anchor Bible Dictionary.

[5] See e.g. Epp and MacRae 1989 on the New Testament material; Kraft and Nickelsburg 1986 on early Judaism.

conclusions unwarranted. Serious debate and confrontation is the stuff of academic life, and I look forward, not of course without some trepidation, to more of it as a result of this project.

Three small technical matters. First, I have adopted the increasingly popular style of bibliographical references that use author's name and date, with full details listed in the bibliography. (Where an original-language publication, or a first edition, antedates the most recent one by more than two or three years, I have indicated it in square brackets.) This allows the footnotes to remain where they belong without becoming too lengthy. Second, in quoting from biblical and other ancient sources I have frequently used my own translations. Where I have followed others it has been because they seem adequate rather than because I have a consistent policy of following one particular version, though I have tended to use the New Revised Standard Version (substituting 'YHWH' for 'the LORD') unless otherwise noted. Third, I have deliberately kept quotation of ancient languages to a minimum, and have transliterated Greek and Hebrew in as simple a way as possible.

It only remains to thank several friends who have contributed to the project by reading bits of the manuscript, criticizing and encouraging, making suggestions of all sorts, and generally enabling me to bring a large and unwieldy project to birth. Valued readers and critics of various parts have included Professors Michael Stone and the late Sara Kamin, of the Hebrew University; Professor Richard Hays, of Duke Divinity School in Durham, North Carolina; Professor Charlie Moule, formerly of Cambridge; and Professors Christopher Rowland, Rowan Williams, and Oliver O'Donovan, of Oxford. The friendship of these last three has been, for me, among the greatest blessings of living and working in Oxford. I am particularly grateful to friends who have let me see work in progress before publication; I think particularly of Dr Anthony Thiselton of St John's College, Durham, whose major book *New Horizons in Hermeneutics* I was privileged to read in typescript. I owe a further debt of gratitude to my students, both graduate and undergraduate, who have listened patiently to my ideas over the years and frequently made acute observations and criticisms. I want to thank the editors and staff of SPCK and Fortress, particularly Philip Law, for their enthusiasm for this project, the care which they have lavished upon it, and the patience with which they have waited—and are waiting!—for it. David Mackinder, Andrew Goddard and Tony Cummins all read the completed typescript and spotted dozens of ways in which it could be improved and clarified, for which I am profoundly grateful. A special word of thanks must go to the manufacturers of the superlative *Nota Bene* software, which has done virtually everything I have asked of it, enabling the book to be typeset in my own study. The remaining mistakes, of course, large and small, belong to none of the above persons, but to myself alone.

Secretarial and editorial assistance of high quality has been provided over the years of this work by Jayne Cummins, Elisabeth Goddard, Lucy Duffell, and particularly, in the later stages, by Kathleen Miles, who performed wonders of organization and clarification on a mass of unwieldy material, including compiling the indexes. In thanking these four I wish also to thank those who set up the fund through which I was able to afford to employ them, in these days of university austerity. Particular mention must be made in this connection of Paul Jenson, of Orange, California, and the Revd Michael Lloyd, of Christ's College, Cambridge, who have given, in this and in many other ways, much valued support, encouragement and practical help.

The main draft of volumes 1 and 2, and the first half of volume 3, was written while on sabbatical in Jerusalem during the summer of 1989. For this I must not only thank Worcester College and the University of Oxford for granting me leave of absence, and the Leverhulme Trust for a generous Travelling Fellowship, but also my hosts in Jerusalem, namely Professor David Satran of the Hebrew University, who organized my teaching there, and particularly the then Dean of St George's Cathedral, the Very Revd Hugh Wybrew, who gave me a marvellous *pied-à-terre* in his flat, and provided a context, both domestic and ecclesiastical, which came as close as anything I have ever found to creating the perfect conditions for writing. I am also deeply grateful to the Revd Michael Lloyd, the Revd Andrew Moore, and Dr Susan Gillingham for looking after the different bits of my job during my various absences, and to the latter two for reading parts of the text and offering comments whose searching nature reflected the best sort of collegiality. The librarians at the Hebrew University and the École Biblique were very helpful; back home, the Bodleian Library remains a congenial and privileged place to work, despite its problems with shrinking resources. The libraries of the Oriental Studies and Theology Faculties have likewise been of great help.

Pride of place in acknowledgement must go, as always, to the support of my dear wife and children, who put up with my absence in Jerusalem, and with numerous other absences and pressures in the course of the work. If hermeneutics, and indeed history itself, are inevitably a matter of interaction between reader and evidence, those who have helped the reader to be who he is, and to become what he ought to become, are to be recognized as part-architects of the reading that results.

One part-architect who in many ways has been a *sine qua non* for the whole project, and for my theological and particularly hermeneutical thinking over the last decade, is Dr Brian Walsh of Toronto. It was symptomatic of his enthusiasm for the work that he took six weeks, in the summer of 1991, to help me think through and reshape the crucial first five chapters of the present volume. The many weaknesses that the book still has belong to me alone; several of its strengths, in so far as it has any, come from this act of scholarly generosity and friendship, which is reflected, though hardly rewarded adequately, in the dedication.

N. T. Wright

Worcester College, Oxford
St Peter's Day
June 1992

Part One

Introduction

Chapter One

CHRISTIAN ORIGINS AND THE NEW TESTAMENT

1. Introduction

The land of Israel is a small country. You can walk its length, north to south, in a few days, and from its central mountains you can see its lateral boundaries, the sea to the west and the river to the east. But it has had an importance out of all proportion to its size. Empires have fought over it. Every forty-four years out of the last four thousand, on average, an army has marched through it, whether to conquer it, to rescue it from someone else, to use it as a neutral battleground on which to fight a different enemy, or to take advantage of it as the natural route for getting somewhere else to fight there instead.[1] There are many places which, once beautiful, are now battered and mangled with the legacies of war. And yet it has remained a beautiful land, still producing grapes and figs, milk and honey.

The New Testament has not been around as long as the land of Israel, but in other ways there are remarkable parallels. It is a small book, smaller than anybody else's holy book, small enough to be read through in a day or two. But it has had an importance belied by its slim appearance. It has again and again been a battleground for warring armies. Sometimes they have come to plunder its treasures for their own use, or to annex bits of its territory as part of a larger empire in need of a few extra strategic mountains, especially holy ones. Sometimes they have come to fight their private battles on neutral territory, finding in the debates about a book or a passage a convenient place to stage a war which is really between two worldviews or philosophies, themselves comparatively unrelated to the New Testament and its concerns. There are many places whose fragile beauty has been trampled by heavy-footed exegetes in search of a Greek root, a quick sermon, or a political slogan. And yet it has remained a powerful and evocative book, full of delicacy and majesty, tears and laughter.

What ought one to do with the New Testament? We may take it for granted that it will be no good trying to prevent its still being used as a battleground. No border fences would be strong enough to keep out the philosophers, the philologists, the politicians and the casual tourists; nor should we erect them if they were. There are many who have come to pilfer and have stayed to be pil-

---

[1] I owe this statistic to the Revd David Praill, formerly of St George's College, Jerusalem.

grims. To place all or part of this book within a sacred enclosure would be to invite a dominical rebuke: my house is to be a house of prayer for all the nations. Past attempts to keep it for one group only—the take-over bids by the scholars and the pietists, the fundamentalists and the armchair social workers—have ended with unseemly battles, the equivalent of the sad struggle for the control of Holy Places in the land of Israel. This book is a book of wisdom for all peoples, but we have made it a den of scholarship, or of a narrow, hard and exclusive piety.

There have been two groups, broadly, who have tried to inherit this territory for themselves, to make this book their own preserve. Like the two major claimants to the land of Israel in our own day, each contains some who are committed to the entire removal of the other from the land, though each also contains many who persist in searching for compromise solutions. We must understand something of both positions if we are to appreciate the overall task before us, let alone the smaller tasks (the study of Jesus, Paul and the gospels in particular) that fall within it.

There are those who, having seized power a century or two ago, and occupying many major fortresses (eminent chairs, well-known publishing houses, and so forth), insist that the New Testament be read in a thoroughgoing historical way, without inflicting on it the burden of being theologically normative. We must find out the original meanings of the texts, and set them out as carefully as we can, irrespective of the feelings of those who thought that a particular passage belonged to them and meant something different. There is sometimes an arrogance about this claim to power. Building on the apparent strength of history, and able to demonstrate the inadequacies of the simple way of life which preceded them, such scholars have set up concrete gun-stations where before there were vineyards, and they patrol the streets to harass those who insist on the old simplistic ways.

There are, on the other side, those who have shown just as much determination in resisting the advance of the new regime. Some still regard the New Testament as a sort of magic book, whose 'meaning' has little to do with what the first-century authors intended, and a lot to do with how some particular contemporary group has been accustomed to hear in it a call to a particular sort of spirituality or lifestyle. This phenomenon is seen most obviously within fundamentalism, but it is by no means confined to the groups (mostly in the Protestant traditions) for which that word is usually reserved. For some, the New Testament has become simply part of the liturgy, to be chanted, read in short detached snippets, used in public prayer, but not to be studied in and for itself, to be wrestled over in the hope of discovering something one did not already know. It exists, so it seems, to sustain the soul, not to stretch the mind. Such attitudes have responded to arrogance with arrogance, have tried to set up 'no-go' areas where the scholarly occupying forces cannot penetrate, have manned barricades with the stones of personal piety, and have bolstered morale with tales of scholarly atrocities.

As so often in the world of day-to-day politics, it is hard to feel that one side is totally right and the other totally wrong. The New Testament is undoubtedly a collection of books written at a particular time and by particular people, and if we were to treat it as though it fell from the sky in the King James Authorized Version, bound in black leather and 'complete with maps',[2] we would be like those in present-day Israel who are content to know nothing about what happened before 1948. We would have forgotten that there was a Bible long before 'our' Bible, that St Paul spoke Greek, not seventeenth-century English. On the other hand, to imagine that the religious, theological, and spiritual aspects of the New Testament are all side-issues, and that because there is such a thing as fundamentalism we must avoid it by embracing some sort of reductionism, would be like ignoring the present problems and tensions in the land of Israel on the grounds that the only real issue is the meaning of the book of Joshua. On the one hand, then, we have a justifiable insistence on the importance of history as giving depth and extra dimensions to contemporary awareness; on the other, a justifiable insistence that historical description by itself is incomplete. Both sides, in fact, are arguably defending comparatively modern positions: post-Enlightenment rationalism on the one hand, anti-Enlightenment supernaturalism on the other. Both sides need to reckon with the fact that there might be other alternatives, that the either-or imposed in the eighteenth century might be false.

Other oversimplifications crowd in at this point if we are not careful. Within the armies currently in the field, there are some who owe primary allegiance to older causes. The division between the academic and the popular has roots far deeper than eighteenth-century controversies between history and theology, roots which include, in their different ways, the Montanist, Franciscan, Lollard, Protestant and Quaker movements, and the reactions to them. The squabble between those who conceive of Christianity as basically a matter of outward and physical signs and those who conceive it to be a matter of an inner light is almost perennial; so is the deep mistrust that separates those who advocate simple piety from those who insist that faith must always be 'seeking understanding'. Fighters from all these wars may well have joined up in the current battles, not necessarily wishing to support the present cause to the limit, but seeing it as the nearest equivalent to their own particular *penchant*. There are also the equivalents of United Nations observers, those who (in theory at least) come to the New Testament as 'neutral' outsiders: these are the literary theorists or the ancient historians, who from time to time survey the battleground and tell the warriors that they are all mistaken. Like their secular analogues, they may sometimes be right, but they may also sometimes get in the way.[3]

What then ought to be done with this strange and powerful little book? This whole present project is designed to offer a set of answers, which may well prove controversial. But something must be said at this stage in very general terms in the hope of establishing initial, even if superficial, agreement. It is, of course, open to anyone to do what he or she likes with this or any book. A

[2] Archbishop Michael Ramsey, speaking in Cambridge in 1980.
[3] Two who have helped a good deal are Kermode (e.g. 1968, 1979) and Sherwin-White (1969 [1963]).

volume of Shakespeare may be used to prop up a table leg, or it may be used as the basis for a philosophical theory. It is not difficult, though, to see that using it as the foundation for dramatic productions of the plays themselves carries more authenticity than either of these (though of course raising further questions about whether a 'modern dress' production is more or less appropriate than a 'period' one, and so forth). There is a general appropriateness about using Shakespeare as a basis for staging plays which justifies itself without much more argument.

What might the equivalent be for the New Testament?[4] That is precisely our question. The New Testament, I suggest, must be read so as to be understood, read within appropriate contexts, within an acoustic which will allow its full overtones to be heard. It must be read with as little distortion as possible, and with as much sensitivity as possible to its different levels of meaning. It must be read so that the stories, and the Story, which it tells can be heard *as* stories, not as rambling ways of declaring unstoried 'ideas'. It must be read without the assumption that we already know what it is going to say, and without the arrogance that assumes that 'we'—whichever group that might be—already have ancestral rights over this or that passage, book, or writer. And, for full appropriateness, it must be read in such a way as to set in motion the drama which it suggests. The present volumes are an attempt to articulate a reading which does justice to these demands.

2. The Task

(i) What to Do with the Wicked Tenants

What, then, is the nature of our task? It may help if we begin with another illustration, again concerning a squabble over territory:

> A man planted a vineyard, put a fence round it, dug a pit for the wine press, and built a tower. Then he let it out to tenant farmers, and went abroad. At the appropriate time he sent a servant to the tenants so that he might receive from them some of the fruit of the vineyard. They took him, beat him, and sent him away empty-handed. Again he sent another servant to them; this one they beat over the head and abused. He sent another, and they killed him; then, many others, some of whom they beat, and some of whom they killed. He still had one other, a beloved son; and he sent him last of all to them, saying 'They will respect my son.' But those tenants said to one another 'This is the heir; come, let us kill him, and the inheritance will be ours.' So they seized him, and killed him and cast him out of the vineyard. What then will the owner of the vineyard do? He will come and destroy the tenants and give the vineyard to others. Have you not read this scripture:
> 'The stone which the builders refused has become the cornerstone;
> This was the Lord's doing, and it is marvellous to our eyes'?[5]

What might we do with a text like this? In order even to see how we might address the question, we have to be aware of the pressures upon us from our surrounding cultural confusion. We live at a time of major changes and swings

---

[4] A similar question is raised, using the analogy of musical performance, by Young 1990.
[5] Mk. 12.1–11.

of mood within Western culture: from modernism to postmodernism; from Enlightenment dualisms to 'New Age' pantheisms; from existentialism to new forms of paganism. To make things more confusing, elements of all these and more layers still coexist side by side within the same city, the same family, and sometimes even the same mind and imagination. It is important to be aware that the sorts of questions one asks depend for their perceived force on all sorts of assumptions about the way the world is and the nature of the human task within it. Since there is no prospect of agreement on such questions, the only possibility is to proceed with caution, looking, at least to begin with, in as many directions as reasonably possible.

There are, perhaps, four types of reading that might be offered, which will illustrate four movements within the history of reading the New Testament at which we will presently look in more detail. The four ways (pre-critical, historical, theological and postmodern readings) correspond very broadly to three movements within the history of Western culture in the last few centuries. The first belongs to the period before the Enlightenment of the eighteenth century; the second, to the major emphasis of the Enlightenment, sometimes known as 'modernism' or 'modernity'; the third, to a corrective on the second, still from within the Enlightenment worldview; and the fourth to the recent period, in which the Enlightenment worldview has begun to break up under questioning from many sides, and which has become known as 'postmodern'.[6]

The first way of reading the parable is that of prayerful Christians who believe the Bible to be Holy Writ, ask few if any questions about what it meant in its historical context, and listen for the voice of God as they read the text. They might, perhaps, see themselves as tenants, needing to be rebuked for their own failure to recognize the Son of God; or, in a context of persecution, they might identify themselves and their church with the prophets who are rejected by the powerful *de facto* owners, but who will be vindicated at the last. This *pre-critical* approach aims to take the authoritative status of the text seriously, but would today be criticized on (at least) three grounds, corresponding to the other three ways of reading: it fails to take the text seriously historically, it fails to integrate it into the theology of the New Testament as a whole, and it is insufficiently critical of its own presuppositions and standpoint.

Allowing each of these objections its own day in court, this brings us to the *historical* approach. Associated primarily with the Enlightenment's insistence on the importance of history, this approach will ask a range of questions. (1) Did Jesus actually tell the parable, and if so what did he mean by it? Were there other similar stories of owners and tenants in the Jewish background which help us to discover what nuances it might have carried for his hearers? (2) How did the early church use this parable in its preaching? Was it, perhaps, retold at a time when the church needed to explain why most of Jesus' Jewish contemporaries had rejected his message? What new impact might it have had in that newer context, and has it been adapted to meet different

---

[6] For analysis of the collapse of the Enlightenment worldview see e.g. Gilkey 1981; Louth 1983; MacIntyre 1985; Gunton 1985; O'Donovan 1986; Meyer 1989; Newbigin 1989; Milbank 1990; and many others.

needs, for instance by the highlighting of Jesus' divine sonship? Was it even, perhaps, created out of nothing to meet needs which remained unmet by actual sayings of Jesus? (3) How has the evangelist used the parable within his work? What new colour does it acquire from its placing at this point in the narrative, just when Jesus has performed a dramatic action in the Temple, and when the pace of the story is now quickening towards the crucifixion? Has the writer altered it and adapted it for these purposes? These three approaches correspond broadly to the questions asked by (1) so-called historical criticism of the gospels, (2) form- and source-criticism, and (3) redaction-criticism. I shall discuss them in more detail in Part IV below. Most scholars would agree that such questions are still indispensable for a serious reading of the text.

There are various further levels of historical enquiry which might also prove fruitful. If we met the parable unawares and out of context, we might treat it as a historical or quasi-historical account of a real, though somewhat improbable, incident. It would be of interest, perhaps, at the level of the social history of its period. But we would discover, by historical means, signs in the material itself that this story is not, as we say, to be 'taken literally'. Its very improbability indicates that it is being used to say more than its surface meaning might suggest. When it is placed in the context of a narrative whose central character tells many such stories; when these stories are given a genre-name, 'parable'; when we discover that the narrative stands in a tradition which already contains other similar stories (e.g. Isaiah 5.1–7); then we rightly conclude that it may best be read as a meta-story, not for its own surface meaning but for some other. All these discussions take place within the historical reading of the text, the attempt to 'place' it within its appropriate historical context.

Such a historical reading might be open to challenge on three grounds. First, it is not clear from all this how the text, thus read, can have any 'authority' for the church or world today, and it is simply the case that the great majority of people who have read the New Testament have come with some such expectation. Second, it would not at first sight raise questions about the theology of the documents; but it would now be generally agreed that such questions are both appropriate and necessary. Thirdly, it might be over-optimistic to think that we could get back to 'what actually happened', arriving finally at 'objective' historical truth. For all these reasons, historical criticism has broadened, over the last hundred years in particular, to include theological study of the texts.

The *theological* approach asks different, though overlapping, questions. What is the underlying theology of the parable? What christology is implied by the picture of the 'Son'? Where does it belong within Mark's (or Matthew's or Luke's, or the early church's) total theological statement? These questions, growing out of the 'New Testament Theology' project as conceived by Rudolf Bultmann in the middle years of the present century, have been much in vogue recently. Although they can be answered in ways which include *en route* the questions both of authority and of history, they can also neatly avoid both, relativizing a potentially 'normative' statement or a potentially 'historical' one into 'merely an aspect of Matthaean theology'. And it is not clear that this method, either, has taken seriously the charge of recent critics that it must attend more carefully to the processes involved in its own reading.

The fourth and final approach is that of the recent so-called *postmodern* literary critics. Rejecting pre-critical piety on the one hand, and the historicizing approach of the Enlightenment on the other, such criticism insists on examining the process of reading in itself. What are we doing when we are reading this text? What do I bring to the text by way of presupposition, and in what way am I changed through reading it? Though the answer to this question might depend in part on whether I think Jesus actually told the parable, that historical question would only be ancillary to the real one, which concerns me and my reading. If such questioning gains its apparent strength from the difficulty that the other projects have in proving their case, that victory is won at the cost of the natural objections: I may end up discovering what is happening to me, but I thought I was going to find out about God, or Jesus, or the early Christians. Am I simply to give up those possibilities? Can such a reading coexist with authority, history or theology? Perhaps because of these problems, postmodern literary theory has not yet made many inroads into mainline biblical scholarship, but there is every reason to suppose that it will shortly do so.[7]

The problems that arise when these different approaches are juxtaposed are often focused on to one particular point, namely, the tension between a reading that seeks to be in some sense normatively Christian and that which seeks to be faithful to history. The modern (as opposed to the postmodern) reader has been under two conflicting pressures. There is, first, the Enlightenment's insistence that all dogma be tested at the bar of history. Thus H. S. Reimarus (1694–1768), who was one of the Enlightenment's chief representatives in New Testament studies, believed that Jesus was an ordinary Jewish revolutionary, and that this fact disproved orthodox Christianity. There is, second, the Christian insistence that, so to speak, Pontius Pilate belongs in the Creed; that the events which are central to Christian belief and life are not reducible to terms of non-spatio-temporal reality, but have to do with events that occurred within the real world. The rootedness of Christianity in history is not negotiable; one cannot escape from the Enlightenment's critique by saying that history cannot question faith. (At least, attempts to do so, from early Gnosticism to the recent theologian Paul Tillich, have been widely regarded as avoiding rather than addressing the problem.)

Part of the difficulty has been, I think, that the heirs of the Enlightenment have been too shrill in their denunciation of traditional Christianity, and that Christianity has often been too unshakeably arrogant in resisting new questions, let alone new answers, in its stubborn defence of . . . what? Christians have often imagined that they were defending Christianity when resisting the Enlightenment's attacks; but it is equally plausible to suggest that what would-be orthodox Christianity was defending was often the pre-Enlightenment worldview, which was itself no more specifically 'Christian' than any other. Who are the real tenants in the New Testament vineyard? And in what does their responsibility consist? And who has the right to be seen as the band of

[7] See ch. 3 below.

prophetic figures, coming to rescue the vineyard from the ravages of the usurpers?

Here is the paradox that lies at the heart of this whole project. Although the Enlightenment began as, among other things, a critique of orthodox Christianity, it can function, and in many ways has functioned, as a means of recalling Christianity to genuine history, to its necessary roots. Much Christianity is afraid of history, frightened that if we really find out what happened in the first century our faith will collapse. But without historical enquiry there is no check on Christianity's propensity to remake Jesus, never mind the Christian god, in its own image. Equally, much Christianity is afraid of scholarly learning, and in so far as the Enlightenment programme was an intellectual venture, Christianity has responded with the simplicities of faith. But, granted that learning without love is sterile and dry, enthusiasm without learning can easily become blind arrogance. Again, much Christianity has been afraid of reducing a supernatural faith to rationalist categories. But the sharp distinction between the 'supernatural' and the 'rational' *is itself a product of Enlightenment thinking*, and to emphasize the 'supernatural' at the expense of the 'rational' or 'natural' is itself to capitulate to the Enlightenment worldview at a deeper level than if we were merely to endorse, rather than marginalize, a post-Enlightenment rationalist programme.

It is, therefore, impossible for Christianity to ignore or relativize the 'modernist' challenge of the eighteenth and subsequent centuries. This does not mean, of course, that we must simply endorse the Enlightenment critique; merely that its questions must remain on the table. And, as I shall argue later, the postmodern critique of the Enlightenment itself, while placing very necessary restraints on Enlightenment ambitions, does not (as some would like to think) invalidate the 'modern' project lock, stock and barrel. While the dispute between the tenants continues, it would be a bold person who presumed to speak for the Owner.

All this may sound very negative. Reading the New Testament seriously, at the present moment in Western culture, sounds so problematic that some may feel like giving it up. The vineyard is overcrowded and apparently unfruitful. But this response, too, would be inappropriate. Whatever one's viewpoint, this text matters. If the Christian claims for the New Testament are anywhere near the truth, we cannot see it as a safe garden into which Christians can retreat *from* their contemporary world. It must function as part of the challenge and address of the creator god *to* the contemporary world. If, however, the Christian claims about the New Testament are false, then (as critics since the eighteenth century have been saying) the sooner its deficiencies are pointed out, the better. Whether, therefore, one has a Christian or non-Christian point of view, a thorough examination of this text is a necessary responsibility.

Underneath all these puzzles, I suggest that there are two questions in particular from which we cannot escape. They are: (1) How did Christianity begin, and why did it take the shape that it did? and (2) What does Christianity believe, and does it make sense? Hence the overall title of this project: Christian Origins and the Question of God. Both these questions, obviously, take up the question of the New Testament within them. It is part of the first question that we ask why the early Christians wrote what they did. It is part of the second that we explore the dynamic relationship between what the New Testament says and what Christians believe—and the further question, of whether those beliefs are coherent.

(ii) The Questions

The two main questions which we have posed break down into more detailed ones. To begin with, there are questions to be raised about the *literary* study of these texts. What is to count as an appropriate reading of them? How might we tell? Looking at the methods of reading the New Testament that have become institutionalized and even sacralized over the years in the public and private devotion of the church, we are bound to ask whether such readings do justice to the texts: whether, for instance, a book like the Gospel according to Mark is well served by being read a dozen or so verses at a time, taken out of context. We are looking for an appropriate reading, and there is at present no agreement as to what might count. We shall continue this quest in chapter 3.

Looking next at the *historical* set of questions, we find the issues focused on Jesus, Paul and the gospels. (a) Who was Jesus, and was he in any sense responsible for the beginning of 'Christianity'? What were his aims, what did he hope to achieve, why did he die, and why did (what we now call) the church come into being? (b) Was Paul the real founder of 'Christianity', the corrupter of the original message, or was he the true interpreter of Jesus? What was the structure and content of the belief-system that motivated him to undertake such extraordinary labour? (c) Why are the gospels what they are? Where do they stand in relation to Jesus and Paul? And, in answering these three sets of questions, can we relate them to each other? Can we draw the lines of early Christian thought so that they pass in some way or other through all of them, and if so how? These are the questions—to say nothing of other important and interesting ones, such as the origin and theology of the Letter to the Hebrews, or of major non-canonical works such as the *Didache* or the *Gospel of Thomas*—which, I suggest, must be looked at. They are open to any historian, of whatever ideological or cultural background, who wishes to understand and do justice to the first century and the extraordinary phenomenon which confronts us there, namely, the rise of a new and exceedingly powerful movement which some called a religion, some a sect, and its own adherents 'the way'.

From one point of view, it is an accident that we happen to need to study the New Testament in depth in order to answer historical questions about early Christianity. It might in principle have been the case that we had excellent alternative records which would have enabled us to provide a thorough and adequate set of historical answers with only occasional recourse to the books written by Christians themselves. Some, of course, might want to object to this suggestion, and to insist that the events could only be understood through the eyes of faith, so that nothing short of the New Testament would do—and perhaps that Providence has ordered the obliteration of almost all other evidence in order to make the point clear. I think this smacks of cooking the evidence in advance, but such a retort could only properly be made when the bulk of the work is done. But whatever option we take here, this second set of questions remains firmly within what is normally thought of as 'history'. We shall look at the methodological issues raised by all this in chapter 4.

But there is a third set of questions that must also be addressed in various ways throughout this work. What is Christian *theology*? In what way ought it to be the same today as it was in the beginning? Is such continuity even thinkable, let alone possible? What counts as normative Christianity? How do we know? Is there a worldview available to modern human beings which makes sense of the world as we know it and which stands in appropriate and recognizable continuity with the worldview of the early Christians? Should we even be looking for an authoritative statement of what the true faith and life might be, and if so where might we find it? How might it be reproduced in the modern church and world? And, underneath all such questions: what should we mean by the word 'god', or 'God'?

Some people (self-styled historians, mostly) will protest that one should never muddle up this set of questions with the historical set.[8] Some theologians have taken this warning seriously and have written about Christian theology with little attention to the historical question of Christian beginnings.[9] It is, nevertheless, a matter of fact that most people who have tried to write about Christian theology have felt it appropriate to devote some space to the historical questions,[10] and that the vast majority of people who have read the New Testament seriously from a historical point of view, and who have written about it thus, have in some way or other intended to address the theological questions as well, albeit of course reaching a wide range of answers.[11] Naturally, the questions have often been confused with one another, and have interacted upon one another in ways which have produced distortion. Usually this has taken place to the detriment of history, as various theological or practical agendas have been projected back anachronistically into the first century.[12] But these risks, happily, have not prevented other people from struggling to find out whether there is an appropriate way of integrating the literature, the history and the theology—the questions, that is, of early Christian literature, of Christian origins and of the Christian god—and, if so, what that way might be.[13]

[8] e.g. Vermes 1973a; Sanders 1985.

[9] e.g. Macquarrie 1966. His more recent book on christology (1990) makes up for this in some ways, but only some.

[10] e.g. Pannenberg 1968 [1964]; Moltmann 1990.

[11] Thus, for instance, the various lines of NT scholarship, from Bultmann to Perrin and Käsemann, from Lightfoot to Dodd and Moule, from Schweitzer to Sanders, from Montefiore and Klausner to Vermes and Maccoby. On these movements, see Neill and Wright 1988, *passim*.

[12] We might cite, as extreme examples, the work of some Jewish apologists such as Rivkin 1984 and Maccoby 1986, 1991; or some would-be Christian apologists like Gerhard Kittel, on whom see MacKinnon 1979, ch. 9.

[13] For example, within the present century, Bultmann, Käsemann, Moule, Caird, Meyer, Stuhlmacher, Morgan and Dunn.

Without some such attempt at integration, the danger is always present that history and theology will fall apart. There are still plenty of people who insist that the only proper task for the New Testament scholar is 'neutral' historical description.[14] 'History' is regarded as the public task, out in the open. Anyone can engage in it, and indeed anyone might wish to, since, as Räisänen argues, early Christianity was part of a vital period in world history, and to understand it might well contribute to greater mutual understanding within our own worldwide community. Theology, meanwhile, is often seen as a private Christian game, played on a safe pitch away from serious opposition. Many Christians have in fact encouraged this conception of the task and have acted accordingly. Many will only regard historical study as 'legitimate' if its contemporary relevance is immediately obvious and accessible ('but what does that mean for us today?', said in the tone of voice which implies that failure to give a quick and easy answer will indicate that a mistake has been made somewhere).[15]

This potential mutual hostility between 'history' and 'theology' has resulted in the well-known split in New Testament studies, whereby the subject is divided into 'Introduction', conceived as a 'purely historical' task, and 'Theology', conceived less historically and more synthetically. This split is now enshrined in the rubrics of many a university syllabus, and (an even more Law-of-the-Medes-and-Persians area) in the classification systems of many a library. But this great divide, however much it is encouraged by some on either side, is neither necessary nor automatic, and is in fact highly misleading. On the one hand, studying the theology of the New Testament depends on some belief, however vague, that certain things that *happened* in the first century are in some sense normative or authoritative for subsequent Christianity. On the other hand, studying the history of early Christianity is impossible without a clear grasp of early Christian beliefs. It is notoriously difficult to go beyond these two vague statements. This, however, does not detract from, but rather emphasizes, the fact that theology, even specifically Christian theology, cannot exist in a vacuum, or in a sealed world away from public scrutiny and question. Integration, though difficult, remains an appropriate task.

While history and theology work at their stormy relationship, there is always a danger, particularly in postmodernism, that literary study will get on by itself, without impinging on, or being affected by, either of the others. The more we move towards a climate in which 'my reading of the text' is what matters, the less pressure there will be either to anchor the text in its own historical context or to integrate a wider 'message' of the text with other messages, producing an overall theological statement or synthesis. This again, as I shall argue later,

[14] See e.g. Räisänen 1990a, following the well-established path set by Wrede, on which see below.

[15] See the protest against this kind of thing in Käsemann 1980, viii: 'The impatient, who are concerned only about results or practical application, should leave their hands off exegesis. They are of no value for it, nor, when rightly done, is exegesis of any value for them.' This actually overstates the point, and needs to be balanced by e.g. Käsemann 1973, 236, where he declares that if his work were of no possible benefit to someone like Dom Helder Camara, he 'would not want to remain a New Testament scholar'.

represents an unnecessary step, though preventing it being taken is not always easy.

The present work, then, is an attempt to integrate three tasks often thought to be disparate. There will be times when we shall lean more heavily on questions of one sort rather than another. In a sense, the study of Jesus is first and foremost a matter of history, needing careful ancillary use of literary study of the texts and theological study of implications. I shall describe Jesus from the point of view of historical events which precipitated a theological and literary revolution. In a sense, the study of Paul is a matter of theology, needing careful ancillary historical and literary work. I shall discuss Paul from the point of view of a revolutionary theology which precipitated a historical achievement. In a sense, studying the gospels in their own right is first and foremost a literary task, but it cannot be done without careful attention to the historical and theological setting, context and implications. I shall analyse the gospels from the point of view of a literary achievement which embodied a revolutionary worldview (or several revolutionary worldviews?). And, as I shall argue in Part II of the book, none of these kinds of study can be done with a detached, positivistic 'objectivity'. All involve, as all knowledge involves, the knower or researcher, the student or reader. Unless we are clear about this from the start we shall be labouring under an over-simplistic conception. Things might look pleasantly straightforward to begin with, but trouble would be stored up for later on.

If we are to take this programme further forward, we must now look briefly at what has been done in the three areas under consideration, and offer some comments on each. I take them here in the order in which they have emerged as forces to be reckoned with in New Testament studies during the last century.

(iii) The History of Early Christianity

For the last two hundred years and more, scholars have busied themselves with the search for what may be called *early Christian history*. What was the early church really like? What were its main movements? How did it change, within a hundred years, from being a small Jewish sect to a large and loosely knit multi-cultural group stretching across the Roman empire?[16] We shall look at this whole area in Part IV of the present volume, and there is no need to anticipate that survey here. As we have already seen, this historical study must include what may be called *early Christian theology*; that is, a historical description of the worldviews and belief-systems of professing Christians between, say, 30 and 130 AD.[17] If this is what we want, the New Testament is obviously the main place to go, even if only for want of anything else. But a lot of reading between the lines will be needed, since the writers of the New Testament

[16] For the history of the discussion see Kümmel 1972. For a full, if controversial, modern treatment see Koester 1982b.

[17] On worldviews and belief-systems and their relation see ch. 5 below.

were not for the most part trying to give their readers this sort of information, and indeed were sometimes *combating* certain types of early Christian belief-systems. Reconstructing the theology of early Christianity will include the reconstruction of the theologies of those whose own writings (if such there were) have not been preserved. Fair enough: that sort of between-the-lines reconstruction is what historians often have to do. In principle it may be possible. Certainly a great deal of energy has been expended on it in recent decades.[18]

The great advantage of this task is that it can be seen quite clearly as a public operation. It is open to all and sundry; its methods are those of any historian reconstructing any society and its belief-systems. In addition, there is a great opportunity for this task in contemporary scholarship. New tools and texts have opened up worlds of thought and life of which our predecessors a century ago were ignorant. Studying the history of the early church, including the history of its beliefs, is possible, fascinating, and potentially fruitful.

At the same time, there are several difficulties that this task will encounter. To begin with, it shares the general difficulty of all ancient history: there is not enough material to make a thorough job. We cannot attain to as full a description of early Christian religion, and hence theology, as we would like. The documentation, not having been designed to give us this information, is inadequate. As a result there is always the danger of a vicious circle: part of the aim of historical study of early Christianity is to arrive at a vantage point from which we could survey the whole landscape, including the New Testament; but most of the material for this task is contained within the New Testament itself.

The result of this, in turn, is the possibility of endless and fruitless speculation. Extraordinary hypotheses can grow up in the night like Jonah's gourd, but no hot wind comes the next day to cause them to wither. They survive, giving shelter to various contemporary views of Christianity that do not, perhaps, deserve them. There is the 'big bang' theory of Christian origins, according to which true, pure and unadulterated Christianity appeared briefly at the beginning, and has been cooling down and getting itself muddled up ever since. There is the 'steady development' hypothesis, according to which theological and practical ideas and agendas develop in straight lines, without twists, turns or second thoughts. There is the old Tübingen hypothesis, according to which Christianity developed in two parallel and distinct ways, divided by racial background, and then came together in the second generation into the catholic church. There is a good deal to be said against each of these theories, but they continue to wield influence at a subliminal level.

A further problem with one regular conception of the task is its positivistic self-description. I shall argue in chapter 4 that all history involves selection, arrangement and so on, and that the idea of a 'neutral' or 'objective' history is a figment of post-Enlightenment imagination. If we must make any distinction here, it is better to think of 'public' and 'private' tasks, rather than 'objective'

---

[18] See e.g. Dunn 1977, and the study of (e.g.) Paul's opponents by Georgi 1987 [1964]; Barclay 1987; and others.

and 'subjective'. Yet the positivist element still remains, advocating a value-free and dogma-free historiography as though such a thing were really attainable.[19] This approach is, in a measure, self-refuting: Räisänen's own account of the history of the discipline is itself a good example of selection and arrangement on the basis of prior conceptions.

Granted that some sort of historical knowledge is possible, that we resist a slide into subjectivism as firmly as we resist arrogant objectivism, we must ask: of what *use* is this task? It is all very well to say, as some will, that history is undertaken for its own sake, to find out simply what happened. But the fact remains that all writers on the New Testament and early Christianity known to me, without exception, have come with their own ideas about the importance of the events concerned, and have not remained content with bare description. The story that is told about this bit of the past is universally perceived as having relevance for the present. So far, so good; but *how* is the history of early Christianity to be 'relevant' for the present day? At this point there is no agreement, but rather a muddle.

First, many writers of this and some other centuries have seen the religious experience of the early Christians (sometimes including their 'theology') as the normative element within Christianity. This has the apparent advantage that it enables one to conduct the 'scientific', supposedly 'objective', study of early Christian religion and theology, with the knowledge that when one has found them one is in touch with the real model of what Christianity is supposed to be like. One might then, it would be hoped, reactivate this model by preaching and prayer.[20] This achieves some integration with the agenda of Wrede and Räisänen, in that it appeals to a history which is in principle observable by all. It also fits conveniently with the programme of the so-called 'biblical theology' movement of the post-war period, which rejected the idea that the Bible was itself 'revelation' and opted instead for the idea that God reveals himself in mighty acts within history, to which the observers, specifically in this case the early Christians, bear witness, enshrining that witness in their writings.[21] On this showing, the New Testament, read historically, is 'authoritative' because it is the set of documents closest to the facts. It is therefore 'authoritative' in the same sense that Suetonius is the best 'authority' for the life of Domitian. This example, however, shows just how slippery the word 'authority' actually is. Suetonius is no more reliable than a tabloid newspaper. Mere proximity to the event is not enough.

Second, if early Christianity is to function in any way as a norm, the process will clearly involve selection—not simply the selection involved in any historical account of anything, but the selection of types of early Christianity according to a pre-arranged *evaluative* scheme. This will inevitably involve omissions. There are more types of early Christianity than can easily be

[19] See the line from Wrede (whose programmatic essay is published in Morgan 1973, 68–116) to Räisänen 1990a.
[20] This agenda loosely describes the work of Rudolf Bultmann and his school, combining Wrede's 'descriptive' programme with a theologically prescriptive one.
[21] See the famous article of Stendahl 1962 (discussed in Morgan 1987, 189; Räisänen 1990a, 74f.).

grouped together and given authoritative status. And at this point—since on the model being used the canon is of no significance—one is forced to import other criteria from outside, which will enable us to distinguish the 'right' sort of early religious experience from the 'wrong' sort. Either one must elevate the earliest period on the grounds of its being primitive and therefore purer;[22] or one will take a particular *type* of religion, described according to either its cultural provenance (Jewish or Greek) or its conformity to a theological norm (Pauline Christianity, for instance).[23] And this again seems highly problematic: where did these criteria come from? They do not seem to have come from the Bible or tradition. They can only have come from the interpreter's view of what mainstream, or 'authentic', early Christianity was really like. But in that case the would-be 'objective' study of early Christianity has been abandoned. What is being attempted instead is a far more generalized Christian theology (with a starting-point as yet undisclosed), or at least some sub-branch of New Testament theology.[24]

This problem is equally evident in the work of Räisänen, who, advocating 'objective' study of the history of early Christian belief, argues that it would be good to apply the results of New Testament study to the world, and not just to the church. This accords with the presuppositions of first-century Jews and Christians, as he correctly notes (although, interestingly, he cannot explain this phenomenon historically or theologically).[25] But this raises two difficulties. Why should anyone outside the Jewish or Christian traditions find any relevance in the retelling of a chapter in the history of those traditions? At most it would be an example of either human folly and credulity or human courage and perseverance—or, perhaps, a mixture of both. And that would hardly merit the attention that scholars, Räisänen included, still lavish on the material. In addition, Räisänen's claim to read the New Testament and find there material with which he can address modern issues leaves him with the problem of selection: where is *his* evaluative scheme coming from, to enable him to sort out the wheat from the chaff and use the former to address contemporary questions? The main message that seems to emerge from his treatment is that the early divisions between Judaism and Christianity are so muddled and confused that we would do a lot better to rethink the whole

---

[22] A good example of this may be found in Küng 1967, 180, 293–4. Another is the current attempt, by Crossan, Mack and others, to argue that Q and the *Gospel of Thomas* are the earliest sources for the life of Jesus, over against the canonical gospels (see ch. 14 below). The point here is not whether this is correct, but the assumption that the *earliest* sources are the most *authoritative*, which drives people of many shades of opinion to push their preferred material as early as possible. This differs from a prevalent contemporary Lutheran view, exemplified by Käsemann, according to whom the earliest (Jewish) Christianity was *corrected* by Paul. Here the status of Paul within one tradition is so strong as to override an otherwise powerful tendency to prefer the earliest material.

[23] The older history-of-religions school of the first half of the century (exemplified by W. Bousset and others) elevated Greek categories; the post-war history-of-religions school idealized Jewish ones. Pauline Christianity has always been at the centre of the Protestant canon, as seen recently in the work of Käsemann and others.

[24] Bultmann takes the first of these routes, Dunn the second.

[25] Räisänen 1990a, 199 n.48.

question from scratch. Similar generalized messages emerge from other recent historians who try to move from a descriptive to a normative statement.[26] An alternative method is to suggest, by historical reconstruction of Jesus and his first followers, that later Christianity has been wrong to accord them the status it has.[27]

Finally, what does this scheme do with Jesus? It is residually odd to subsume Jesus under 'early Christian experience', or theology, or religion, as though Jesus were simply the first early Christian, whose 'experience' of his god might be deemed the most normative.[28] From one perspective, as we shall see, it is of course vital to describe Jesus with as much historical accuracy as possible. But it would be quite a radical innovation to claim straightforwardly that Jesus' experience of his god ought to be that of subsequent Christians. There are, no doubt, parallels and analogies (the 'Abba' prayer, for example), and there certainly is a strand of *imitatio Christi* in the New Testament. But there is also normally thought to be a uniqueness about Jesus which would make it strange to hold up his experience, or his beliefs, as *the* normative part of early Christianity, to be copied as closely as possible by subsequent Christian generations.

For all these reasons, it seems to me clear that the simple historical description of early Christianity and its theology cannot by itself be a complete enterprise. It remains, of course, one vital part of the task. We shall see later on that, without it, the attempt to mount a successful reading of the New Testament, let alone a Christian theology, is doomed to failure. It purports to have a simple and clear-headed agenda. But the clarity is superficial, and is purchased at the cost of major difficulties elsewhere. At the theoretical level, it tends towards either positivism or idealism, or an uncomfortable alliance of the two. At the practical level, it is bogged down by two things: the apparent arbitrariness, or at least the question-begging nature, of the choice of supposedly normative samples, and the difficulties of abstracting from a first-century context, complete with all its cultural trappings, a picture of this supposedly normative Christianity that would be both adequate for the task and sufficiently transportable to be applied in other cultures and times.[29] The historical project, if it is to be successful even in its own terms, must broaden its horizons.

(iv) 'New Testament Theology'

The second model we must explore is that of *New Testament theology* proper. This phrase has come to designate, more or less, the attempt to read the New Testament from a historical point of view, and, either simultaneously or sub-

---

[26] e.g. Theissen 1978, 119; Meeks 1986, 161f.

[27] This is the line followed by e.g. Reimarus, Vermes and Sanders.

[28] See, in different ways, Kümmel, Jeremias, Goppelt and Dunn; see the discussions in Morgan 1987; Räisänen 1990a.

[29] See Meyer's criticism (1989, 63) of James M. Robinson.

sequently, to draw its major theological emphases together into a coherent statement which can then address subsequent generations, our own included.[30]

About both aspects of this two-sided term, 'New Testament theology', there are certain preliminary things that need to be said.[31] The first half (the description of the theology of the New Testament) forms, of course, a subset of the category we have just been examining: New Testament theology is one part of the theology of early Christianity, and the latter is one part of the total history of early Christianity. These things should not be confused, as they sometimes are. In addition, there can be no guarantee in advance, unless we adopt an unthinking a priori, that the theologies of the different writers will be the same, and indeed a good deal of recent writing has been devoted to demonstrating that they are not. A certain amount of precision is therefore called for in the use of the phrase.

The second half (addressing the modern world on this basis) is more complex, bringing us of course into the sphere commonly, though misleadingly, called 'hermeneutics'.[32] We need to look first at the roots of the question. Why should people think that studying the New Testament would allow a fresh word from their god to be heard?

This belief grows out of the ineradicable Christian conviction, held from very early times, that being Christian means, among other things, living, believing and behaving in some sort of continuity, in principle demonstrable, with the New Testament (and hence with the Old Testament too, though that has always raised further difficulties which need not be addressed here). This belief gained additional momentum as a result of the Protestant Reformation, when the principle of *sola scriptura* was articulated, placing the Bible (and, *de facto* at least, the New Testament in particular) in the position of supreme authority. Reading the New Testament, it has always been felt within Protestantism, is where the Christian begins, and in doing so he or she is equipped, challenged, reinforced, given a basis for belief and life.

The particular emphasis which eventually gave rise to the present meaning of the phrase 'New Testament theology' was the Protestant insistence on the *literal or historical sense of scripture* as the arbiter of the meaning of the text and hence the vehicle of its authority. This principle, originally articulated as a way of keeping allegorical fancy at bay, left residual problems within the churches of the Reformation as they struggled with what the literal sense might be and how it might function as authoritative. These problems eventually emerged, in the new situation of the Enlightenment, with the rise of the criti-

---

[30] For basic discussions of 'New Testament theology' see particularly Räisänen 1990a; Meyer 1989 ch. 3, and esp. ch. 10. See also Morgan 1973, 1977, 1987; Käsemann 1973; Strecker 1975; Stuhlmacher 1977; Dunn and Mackey 1987; Fuller 1989. For actual 'New Testament theologies', see e.g. Bultmann 1951–5; Conzelmann 1969; Kümmel 1973; Neill 1976; Goppelt 1981–2.

[31] See the nuanced statement of this in Morgan 1987, 198ff.

[32] This term is often used to refer to a process of 'application' which occurs only *after* a text has been understood historically. I shall argue against this essentially positivist position in Part II, and adopt the wider meaning common during the last two centuries, where 'hermeneutics' refers to the whole activity of understanding, including the historical reading of texts. See particularly Thiselton 1980, 1992, and, for a brief summary, Jeanrond 1990.

cal movement. The literal sense was again insisted on, but with two possible results. Either it could be shown that the historical sense of scripture was in fact false, calling the veracity of Christianity as a whole into question. Or one could explore the historical meaning in order to abstract from it timeless theological truths, hoping that these would refresh areas of contemporary life that the literal sense could not reach. It was the tensions implicit here that gave birth to the nineteenth- and twentieth-century debates about New Testament theology. Would historical exegesis provide the church with the material for its proclamation, or would it provide the problems which that proclamation would have to deal with or skirt around? How can the historical and the normative readings be combined? In other words, is 'New Testament theology' in its combined sense a viable proposition?

Two ways of making it viable which have been explored turn out upon examination to be ultimately unsatisfactory. The first, which brings together thinkers from Lessing in the eighteenth century to Bultmann in the twentieth, follows the line indicated above, of doing the historical work in order to move beyond it to an ultimate truth which is beyond space and time, outside history altogether. What then emerges is a timeless message, a timeless truth, or a timeless call to decision. This is the thing we can use today. Such a 'timeless theology' is then the real object of the historical quest. If and when we discover what the beliefs of the New Testament writers were, we can, like theological archaeologists, unearth the essential substructure of Christianity in order to carry it off and display it elsewhere, making it available for all generations in some kind of museum. 'Theology' then becomes the 'real' thing that the New Testament is 'about', the real fruit that emerges when the outer skin of historical circumstance is peeled away. This is often stated in terms of some aspects being 'timelessly true' and others being 'culturally conditioned'.

The problem with this programme is that the skin does not peel away so cleanly. It is very difficult to produce a 'theology' from the New Testament that is couched in 'timeless' categories, and if we succeed in doing so we may justifiably suspect that quite a lot of fruit has been thrown away, still sticking to the discarded skin. All of the New Testament is 'culturally conditioned': if that were to disqualify an idea or a theme from attaining 'relevance' to other periods or cultures, the New Testament as a whole is disqualified.

Two outworkings of this method, in twentieth-century scholarship, have been (1) demythologization: the attempt to move away from the culture-specific first-century forms of speech and thought in which the timeless message or call was clothed, and (2) form-criticism: the means of analysing material, which at face value offers historical narratives about Jesus, in such a way as to let it reveal the (supposedly) 'timeless' faith of the early church. Both these movements have cultural and theological roots not only in modern critical movements but in pre-modern pietistic ways of reading scripture, extracting a 'message' from passages whose literal sense might not have offered one. The whole process goes back, ultimately, to the allegorical exegesis of the Fathers.[33] Here is a not inconsiderable irony within the Bultmannian agenda,

---

[33] cf. Kermode 1979, 44: 'Allegory is the patristic way of dealing with inexhaustible hermeneutic potential'; cp. Louth 1983.

which grows out of Protestant theology, insisting on a message which breaks out of the apparent strait-jacket imposed by history and the law and offers free forgiveness, grace, a new start. In doing so, it still emphasizes the literal sense of scripture, at least in relation to the gospels—but only in order to insist that the literal sense must be transcended if the true voice of scripture is to be heard. The gospels are actually 'about' Christian faith in Jesus rather than Jesus himself. The events themselves can become relativized: notoriously, even Jesus can become simply an early preacher of the timeless message, his death a bare event that (somehow or other) set in motion the early faith of the church, that primitive 'experience' which, as expressed in the writings of the New Testament, became the really normative phenomenon.[34] This proposal is subject to the damaging criticism that it has not given to history, or creation, sufficient weight for them to be taken seriously within the reading of the New Testament, in which both seem to be enormously important. This first model, moving from history to timeless truth, brings large problems with it, and cannot any longer be affirmed without serious difficulty.

The second model was proposed by the 'biblical theology' school of the 1950s and 1960s.[35] In philosophical terms, this school opposed the idealism of Bultmann with a kind of realism. The New Testament is given authority not because it witnesses to timeless truth, but because it witnesses to the mighty acts of the creator god within history, and especially in the events concerning Jesus. The text is then revelatory, and hence authoritative, insofar as it bears witness to the 'real thing', that is, to the event(s). This model can be combined with the view of church history that sees it starting off in a 'pure' period, and thus with some of the ways in which, as we saw, the study of early Christian history can be used in a normative programme. But this in turn appears not to do justice to the Protestant insistence on the text itself as being divine revelation. Nor has this model succeeded, either in highlighting the events that are to count as revelation, or in providing a clear theological account of how such a revelation is to be conceived.

A further problem for both models is caused by the diversity of the material. In order to produce a 'normative' statement out of the New Testament it is practically inevitable that one will emphasize one part of the text at the expense of the rest. This functions, at both a scholarly and a popular level, by means of elevating certain parts of the theology of the New Testament, for instance the theology of Paul, into a 'canon within the canon'. Such a method is often justified by appeal to the principle that the harder parts of the Bible are to be interpreted in the light of the easier ones. It is remarkable just how long a life this 'principle' has had, considering the blatant subjectivism which it contains.[36] What is 'harder' or 'easier' will of course vary enormously from one

---

[34] I detect this emphasis behind the thrust, and the overall title, of such a book as Bornkamm 1969 (*Early Christian Experience*).

[35] cf. Wright 1962; Stendahl 1962.

[36] cf. Kermode 1979, 35: 'My way of reading the detail of the parable of the Good Samaritan seems to me natural; but that is only my way of authenticating, or claiming as universal, a habit of thought that is cultural and arbitrary.'

generation, and cultural setting, to another: witness he varying fortunes of 'apocalyptic' in our own century.[37] This is not to say that one should not operate with some kind of an inner canon: all interpreters do, whether they admit it or not, in that all come to the text with some set of questions that begin the encounter. The question then is: what should we do with this starting-point? Should we use it simply as a way in to the material, remaining conscious of its implicit bias? Or will it be used as a Procrustean bed by which to measure, and condemn, the other bits that do not fit? The former may be possible in theory, but the latter is very tempting.

The largest problem faced by the 'New Testament theology' project, particularly within the Bultmannian paradigm and its variations, is what to do with Jesus. 'New Testament theology', strictly speaking, does not include the teaching (or the facts of the life, death and resurrection) of Jesus, but merely the beliefs of the New Testament writers *about* Jesus, or perhaps those beliefs expressed mythologically *in terms of* Jesus-stories. It is the odd nemesis of the Protestant principle of *sola scriptura* that one of the basic models to which it has given rise has little place within its hermeneutical structure or authority-system for Jesus himself, since he was the author of no New Testament book. From this point of view, Bultmann was perfectly correct in the famous opening sentence of his *New Testament Theology*: '*The message of Jesus* is a presupposition for the theology of the New Testament rather than a part of that theology itself.'[38] Here we see the line that runs from Melanchthon to Bultmann and beyond: once we grasp the *pro me* of the gospel, the idea that God is 'being gracious to *me*', we no longer need Jesus to be too firmly rooted in history.[39] But the criticisms of Christianity put forward by Reimarus and others, not to mention the revisionist schemes of many Jewish writers in our own day, will not be satisfied with the retreat from history exemplified by Kähler, Bultmann and Tillich. Nor will the problems of the modern scholarly portraits of Jesus, such as those by Sanders, evaporate. If Jesus was as Reimarus, or Schweitzer, or Sanders, have portrayed him, then the church needs at the very least to revise its faith quite substantially.

In addition, as we will see in Part IV, there is a particular oddity about placing 'New Testament theology' as a norm over against Jesus himself, as was done classically by Bultmann. It is perfectly true that the New Testament presents us with Paul's, Mark's, Luke's, etc. theology *about* Jesus, so that Jesus' own theological beliefs cannot be read off the surface of the text. Some would

[37] On the question of the 'canon within the canon' see the classic discussions of Käsemann 1970; Schrage 1979; and now also Räisänen 1990a. On the varying fortunes of 'apocalyptic' see Koch 1972, and ch. 10 below.

[38] Bultmann 1951, 3 (italics original).

[39] An interesting example of this is the position of Tillich, nicely highlighted in his debate with C. H. Dodd, recorded by Langdon Gilkey and published in Dillistone 1977, 241–3. On Melanchthon see e.g. the statement in his *Loci Communes* of 1521: unless one knows why Christ took upon himself human flesh and was crucified, what advantage would accrue from having learned his life's history? One modern interpreter, embracing this, writes that knowing Christ is not achieved 'by an acquaintance with the historical or earthly Jesus' (Hultgren 1987, 3).

say that the real Jesus *can*not be rediscovered at all, being now so thoroughly overlaid with the evangelists' theologies; others would say that he *should* not be searched for at all, since to look for Jesus behind the evangelists is to look for a historian's construct (or another 'ideal' figure) rather than the Lord whom the earliest Christians worshipped and followed. But even to say this much implies that the New Testament writers did not think that they were setting up, by means of their writings, an authority over against that of Jesus. It has been customary to say that the New Testament writers 'did not think they were writing "scripture";' and though, as we shall see, that formulation may need to be revised, not least in the light of recent redaction-criticism, it is certainly true to the extent that for them the place where Israel's god had acted decisively for the salvation of the world was not in their taking pen and ink to write gospels, but in their god's taking flesh and blood to die on a cross. Their own work was conceived as derivative from and dependent upon that fact. Thus, while it is true that Jesus and his own belief-system is not, strictly speaking, 'part of New Testament theology', this does not mean that Jesus and his proclamation should be relativized in favour of the 'real thing', i.e. New Testament theology.[40] One might say instead, so much the worse for 'New Testament theology' itself: if it does not contain the decisive proclamation of Jesus, it cannot itself be the be-all and end-all of the divine revelation, the ultimate locus of authority, *the* 'thing' that all study of the New Testament is bent towards finding.

If the project of 'New Testament theology' is as full of problems as this, why should anyone want to continue with it? Why are we faced, in both popular and scholarly work, with frantic efforts to locate, distill, salvage or even invent something that can still be called 'New Testament theology', and that will serve as the substance of academic courses and as the starting-point for church life, preaching, mission and evangelism? The answer, I think, is threefold. First, the theological sector where this task has been carried on most urgently is Protestantism, and Protestants still regard the New Testament as in some sense or other the 'real' authority for Christians. Second, the philosophical context of much of this work has been Idealism, which has been happier with abstract ideas than with concrete history; so *theology*, seen as a set of such ideas, attains a privileged status. If the New Testament is 'authoritative', this authority has been deemed to lie in the *theology* that it contains. Third, the practical context for 'New Testament theology' has been the church's perceived task of addressing both itself and the wider world with a word from the true god. 'New Testament theology' is believed to fuel preaching. The problems which this model has run into have driven some to object that it was foolish to look for authority, coherence or even relevance in the New Testament; that objective historical study should abjure all such *a prioris*; or that the project simply collapses back into that articulated by Wrede three generations ago or Räisänen three years ago ('objective' description of religious writing in its historical context). It has caused others to try to restate a way of still doing something which can be called 'New Testament theology', which can still hold

---

[40] See the discussion in Räisänen 1990a, 114f.

on to description and prescription and have both lines running through the New Testament, or at least some of its so-called 'major witnesses'. I suspect, however, that the right way out of this jam is not backwards to Wrede (Räisänen), nor by means of a sideways expansion into a revised and post-modern Bultmannism (Morgan), but on into a wider category, with a new view of 'authority', 'theology' and 'relevance'.

Within any traditional Christian scheme—invoked here not as an *a priori* to settle historical matters, but as the necessary foundation for showing how traditional Christian judgments have in fact worked—all authority belongs ultimately to the creator god; and if (as traditional Christianity has gone on to say) this god is made known supremely in Jesus, then Jesus, too, holds an authority that is superior to all writing about him. Many, of course, will suppose this to be a false antithesis, since what we know about Jesus we know precisely in these writings. But this will scarcely hold within mainline 'New Testament theology', in which, as we have seen, it is axiomatic that the gospels do not give us direct access to Jesus, but only to the theology of the evangelists and their predecessors. If all authority belongs to the creator god, it is a matter of some delicacy to describe how such 'authority' comes to be vested in the New Testament, and what the limits of this might be.

The three approaches we have examined thus far (early Christian history, and 'New Testament theology' in two distinct forms) have continued to be pursued within the guild of New Testament scholarship. Much of the 'normal science' of New Testament studies (to use Kuhn's phrase)[41] has proceeded to fill in the paradigms represented by Wrede's historical agenda, Bultmannian 'New Testament theology', and the vestiges of the 'biblical theology' movement. It is, after all, large agendas like this that give the meaning and purpose, the sense of excitement, to the detailed activities of biblical scholars, in commentaries, articles and monographs. From the Enlightenment's thirst for history there has flowed the quest for Jesus, producing endless problems, but also possibilities, for scholar and church alike. From the Bultmannian thirst for New Testament theology there have flowed, among other things, major studies of Pauline theology and major reconsiderations of the gospel traditions. From the post-war 'biblical theology' movement there have flowed, among other things, essays on 'salvation-history'. New agendas have come into play, not least the post-war desire to free Christianity and the New Testament from the suspicion of complicity in the Holocaust (or, alternatively, to blame them for it). There has been no shortage of activity on all fronts.

It is to this range of interlocking issues that the present chapter, and indeed the present volumes, address themselves with, I hope, some new and positive proposals. We need to do both history and theology: but how? Ultimately, the present project is part of the wider task—which I believe faces modern Western culture in its entirety, not only theologians or Christians—of trying to rethink a basic worldview in the face of the internal collapse of the one which has dominated the Western world for the last two centuries or so. And it is precisely one of the features of the worldview now under attack that 'history'

---

[41] Kuhn 1970 [1962], *passim*.

and 'theology' belong in separate compartments. The challenge is now before us to articulate new categories which will do justice to the relevant material without this damaging dualism—and without, of course, cheating by collapsing the data into a monism in which one 'side' simply disappears into the other. This challenge is faced in all sorts of areas, of which the study of the New Testament is only one. But before pursuing this further we must look briefly at the third element in the study of the New Testament. If we are to be historians and theologians, we must also be literary critics.

(v) Literary Criticism

There are still some New Testament scholars for whom the phrase 'literary criticism' means the application to the New Testament of the critical questions and methods made famous in the first half of the century. Source-, form- and redaction-criticism were the order of the day, and some wish they still were. A good deal of professional New Testament studies has been concerned with such things, and, with them, the historical analysis of the intention of the writers or transmitters of the material that we now find in the New Testament.

This world, however, has changed beyond all recognition in the last few years. The rise of postmodernist literary criticism (see chapter 3) has made the essentially *modernist* disciplines—of investigating the early community that handed on traditions, of trying to uncover complex literary sources, of unpicking what precisely the evangelists were doing with those sources—look decidedly passé. The new emphasis in gospel studies is not on the creative evangelist so much as on the text in itself. The study of the phenomenology of reading, and the application of this to what happens when today's readers read the New Testament, is an increasingly popular field.[42] And it has recently been argued that, since historical criticism seems not to have produced the goods that critics were looking for, a sideways step into the world of (postmodern) literary criticism might help. Since what we are there doing is observing how readers appropriate things for themselves, maybe this will produce a new and satisfying reading of the New Testament.[43]

This provides, in effect, a new way of being Bultmannian. Instead of doing history in order to uncover timeless truths, we will study (biblical) literature to receive messages that transcend space and time. It is an attempt to accomplish, within postmodernity, what Bultmann's package failed to accomplish within modernity. As such, this proposal moves away from the sterile positivism of Wrede and Räisänen, and opens up possibilities for giving an account of how texts can speak afresh in situations other than their original ones. In particular, unlike the classic forms that Bultmannian theology has taken, this method has the inestimable advantage that it begins from and studies the known (actual texts) instead of the unknown (early Christianity as it may be reconstructed from between the lines of the New Testament).

---

[42] cf. Sanders and Davies 1989, chs. 15–16.
[43] See Morgan 1988, 199, 286, citing a good deal of recent relevant literature.

But the proposal is still faced with some serious questions. It is not clear, from within the model, why one should be reading the New Testament to achieve this effect. Why should one not read, as of equal value, the *Gospel of Thomas*, or *Pirke Aboth*, or for that matter *Pride and Prejudice*? Likewise, it is not clear what continuing status the model gives to history, nor why, within its own terms, one should focus on *literature* specifically. Why not early Christian art or artifacts? Is it just that literature is more obviously amenable to post-modern study? Or that the overshadowing of the whole area by one complex text—the New Testament—misleads us into thinking that the whole task can be undertaken in terms of texts? In particular, it is still not at all clear where Jesus might fit in to such a reading. Is it enough to say that when we read the parables we are meeting, at however many removes, a literary version of his own originally oral works of art? And, in particular, how will this method avoid the slide into subjectivism? We shall have to pursue these questions further in chapter 3.

At the same time as the postmodern shift in emphasis to reader-oriented study, historical study of the literature in its original context has continued. But it has searched for quite different phenomena from its predecessors. Biblical specialists are at last following their classical colleagues in abandoning the endless and tortuous search for exactly reconstructed sources.[44] We have seen a spate of studies recently on ancient rhetorical and literary conventions and forms, and an insistence that New Testament research should take note of these.[45] This is, from one point of view, simply filling in a new gap in Wrede's programme, attempting to place the New Testament documents on the historical map of their day. At the same time, it functions as an attempt to assess the likely reception of the writings within their own communities, which is, effectively, a modernist (historical) analysis of a postmodern phenomenon. For too long scholars have assumed that the readers of (say) Paul or Matthew were basically similar to modern readers, so that something that seems difficult to us would probably have seemed difficult to them. The study of ancient rhetoric and writing conventions exposes this sort of massive anachronism for what it is. As such it is greatly to be welcomed. Though not by itself a complete way of reading the New Testament, it can clearly make a major contribution to the overall task.

(vi) The Task Restated

We have now briefly examined the major components of the task of reading the New Testament, in terms of some modern discussions and their direction. What we now require is a creative synthesis of all of them. We must try to combine the pre-modern emphasis on the text as in some sense authoritative,

---

[44] This is of course a generalization. There are still those for whom the Quest for the Historical Q is as vital as ever. On this, see ch. 14 below.

[45] Betz 1979 is a good example. See too e.g. Stowers 1986. Bultmann himself had begun his career with this kind of work (1910).

the modern emphasis on the text (and Christianity itself) as irreducibly integrated into history, and irreducibly involved with theology, and the postmodern emphasis on the reading of the text. To put it another way, we need to do justice, simultaneously, to Wrede's emphasis on serious history (including the history of Jesus), Bultmann's emphasis on normative theology, and the postmodern emphasis on the text and its readers. Each of these, of course, is inclined to claim sole rights, and to resent sharing territory it regards as its own. But such grandiose claims should be resisted.[46]

We seem unlikely to find this way forward by the route of positivism (see chapter 2), or by the search for timeless truths, or by simply concentrating on *my* reading *now*. I suggest that the only way to combine what needs to be combined is by means of a fresh examination of what a contemporary Christian literary, historical and theological project might look like. That is the aim of Part II. In the course of this task we will tell some stories about the way these tasks are done which will, I hope, subvert some of the stories told about them elsewhere. Not to allow for this possibility would be to close the range of conceivable historical and theological answers ahead of time in a quite unacceptable fashion. In the contemporary world, with all its uncertainties about controlling paradigms, we have a chance to address these tasks in new ways. It is to be hoped that this will contribute, not merely to private edification or academic satisfaction—though these should ideally be taken care of *en route*—but to wider goals, not least advancing the 'kingdom of god'. That, however, is to run some little way ahead of the argument.

In the light of Part II, we need to advance some hypotheses about the historical situation within which the New Testament writings were born. This will involve a historical reconstruction of the Judaism and Christianity of the first century. We know a good deal more about ancient Judaism than we used to, and I shall draw on this new knowledge in some detail in Part III. The reconstruction of early church history has less frequently been attempted, and the lack of materials has resulted in a certain amount of fantasy. Our particular task, to describe Christianity between 30 and 150 AD without discussing Jesus or Paul, is somewhat artificial—rather like discussing European music from 1750 to 1850 without mentioning Mozart and Beethoven—but it must be attempted for two reasons. First, it is important to set up as clearly as possible the historical context within which the two major subjects, Jesus and Paul, may be studied. Second, virtually all our information about Jesus comes in the form of documents in which we meet traditions handed on, and eventually written down, by Christians some of whom were living in that early period and addressing its particular needs. We must therefore understand something about the early church itself in order to be able to read the gospels with proper historical sensitivity and care. This is the subject of Part IV, and will enable us to reach, in Part V, a preliminary restatement of some of the key issues. There is, of course, an inevitable circularity here, but, as I shall show in Part II, it is in no way vicious; it is the necessary circularity of all serious historical and indeed epistemological reconstruction.

---

[46] As Kermode 1979, 79f. argues, following Ricoeur.

This will set the scene for the subsequent volumes, dealing with Jesus, Paul and the gospels. In each area there have been many new waves of study and interest in recent decades; but this has not been integrated either historically or theologically. In attempting this large task, I am writing something like the 'New Testament theologies' which have been written from time to time, but am also conscious, as I argued earlier, of the differences between the classic formulations of that model and the way in which I conceive the task and goal.

This first volume, then, in one sense introduces the entire project at hand, but in another stands by itself. It argues for a particular way of doing history, theology, and literary study in relation to the questions of the first century; it argues for a particular way of understanding first-century Judaism and first-century Christianity; and it offers a preliminary discussion of the meaning of the word 'god' within the thought-forms of these groups, and the ways in which such historical and theological study might be of relevance for the modern world. And if these tasks are in one way simply preliminaries to the task of going in and possessing the land itself, that may be no bad thing. If the tenants had heeded the owner's instructions, there would have been no dispute about the vineyard. If the children of Israel had heeded the Deuteronomic warnings, there would have been more milk and honey, and less misery and injustice, when they eventually crossed the Jordan.

Part Two

Tools for the Task

Chapter Two

KNOWLEDGE: PROBLEMS AND VARIETIES

1. Introduction

We have seen that the study of the New Testament involves three disciplines in particular: literature, history and theology. They are, as it were, among the armies that use the New Testament as a battleground. Many of the debates which have occupied scholars as they have crossed the terrain of gospels and epistles have not been so much the detailed exegesis of this or that passage, but the larger issues as to which view of history, or of theology, they will take, and which pieces of territory they can then annex with a claim of justified allegiance. It is therefore inevitable—though some will perhaps feel it regrettable—that we must spend some time at this stage seeing what these large issues look like, and getting some idea as to what the options are between them. Until we do this, study of Jesus, Paul and the gospels will remain largely the projection of an undiscussed metaphysic: if we do not explore presuppositional matters, we can expect endless and fruitless debate. Those who are eager to get on with what they see as the real business are, of course, welcome to skip this section, but they must not mind if by doing so they run into puzzles at a later stage. They could always come back.

The inner rationale of this Part of the book is the sense that the problems which we encounter in the study of literature, history and theology all belong together. Each reflects, in the way appropriate to its own area, the basic shape of the problem of knowledge itself. This is scarcely surprising, but it is worth pointing out, since to address the problems piecemeal, without recognizing their broad similarities, would be to rob the whole discussion of its sense of direction. It is therefore much the best thing to deal with the wider issues first before plunging into the specifics of particular questions.

Facing such issues is even more necessary today than before. There is at the moment a much-observed and much-discussed state of crisis in the humanities. The dominant viewpoint of the last two hundred years, associated particularly with the Enlightenment, has been in a state of disarray for some while, and its so-called 'modernism' is being steadily overtaken by the somewhat unhappily named 'postmodernism'.[1] Old certainties have given way to new uncertainties,

---

[1] For description and discussion cf. e.g. Lyotard 1984; MacIntyre 1985; Appignanesi and Lawson 1989; Falck 1989; Harvey 1989; Jencks 1989 [1986]; Sorri and Gill 1989; Milbank 1990; and many other similar texts.

and in such a time it is vital that a project such as this one should show from the outset where it stands on basic questions of method. It will not be possible here to argue at great length for the viewpoint I propose to adopt. That would demand a whole book to itself; and anyway the real proof of the pudding is in the eating, that is, whether the method adopted succeeds in making more sense of the subject-matter when we get to it.[2] I intend, in any case, to return to these issues in the final volume of the project.

The basic argument I shall advance in this Part of the book is that the problem of knowledge itself, and the three branches of it that form our particular concern, can all be clarified by seeing them in the light of a detailed analysis of the *worldviews* which form the grid through which humans, both individually and in social groupings, perceive all of reality. In particular, one of the key features of all worldviews is the element of *story*. This is of vital importance not least in relation to the New Testament and early Christianity, but this is in fact a symptom of a universal phenomenon. 'Story', I shall argue, can help us in the first instance to articulate a critical-realist epistemology, and can then be put to wider uses in the study of literature, history and theology.[3]

2. Towards Critical Realism

The position which I shall here briefly outline is that which is now known, broadly, as *critical realism*.[4] This is a theory about how people know things, and offers itself as a way forward, over against other competing theories that have appeared in several fields (not least in the three with which we shall be particularly concerned) and that seem now to be in a state of collapse. To see this more clearly we need a brief and broad-brush account of these rival theories, which are, more or less, the optimistic and pessimistic versions of the Enlightenment epistemological project, or of a broad empiricism. The technical terms I shall use at this stage are deliberately general, and are of course much debated; but I hope the case is clear in outline.

On the one hand there is the optimism of the *positivist* position.[5] The positivist believes that there are some things at least about which we can have definite knowledge. There are some things that are simply 'objectively' true, that is, some things about which we can have, and actually do have, solid and

---

[2] See Crites 1989 [1971], 72 n.6: '. . . the argument is in the end circular, as any good philosophical argument is. And in the end it has only the explanatory power of this particular circle to commend it.'

[3] After I had already written a first draft of this section, there appeared Ben Meyer's book *Critical Realism and the New Testament* (1989), in which a good deal of what I was trying to say is spelled out, argued for, and given (to my mind) solid foundations. I have also been encouraged by the similarity between my broad argument and the (much more sophisticated) discussions of e.g. Torrance 1976, 2–7; Louth 1983; Gunton 1985; and Thiselton 1992.

[4] The term is used quite widely in various disciplines. It has been helpfully discussed in relation to the New Testament by Meyer 1989.

[5] On positivism, and logical positivism, see Abbagnano 1967; Passmore 1967.

unquestionable knowledge. These are things which can be tested 'empirically', that is, by observing, measuring, etc. within the physical world. Taking this to its logical conclusion, things that cannot be tested in this way cannot be spoken of without talking some sort of nonsense.[6] Though this view has been largely abandoned by philosophers, it has had a long run for its money in other spheres, not least those of the physical sciences. Despite the great strides in self-awareness that have come about through (for instance) sociology of knowledge, not to mention philosophy of science itself, one still meets some scientists (and many non-scientists who talk about science) who believe that what science does is simply to look objectively at things that are there.[7] The reverse of this belief is that, where positivism cannot utter its shrill certainties, all that is left is subjectivity or relativity. The much-discussed contemporary phenomenon of cultural and theological relativism is itself in this sense simply the dark side of positivism.

People thus assume, within the world of post-Enlightenment positivism, that they know things 'straight'. At what many regard as a common-sense level, this position may be called 'naïve realism.' Optical and other similar illusions are regarded as freaks, departures from the norm—which is presumed to be that human beings, with proper scientific controls available, have instant access to raw data about which they can simply make true propositions on the basis of sense-experience. Since it is obvious that not all human knowledge is of this type, the sorts of knowledge that break the mould are downgraded: classically, within positivism this century, metaphysics and theology come in for this treatment. Since they do not admit of verification, they become belief, not knowledge (as Plato had long ago suggested), and then meaningless or nonsensical belief (as Ayer argued). Aesthetics and ethics are reduced to functions of the experiences of one or more people: 'beautiful' and 'good' simply mean 'I/we like this' or 'I/we approve of that'. Positivism thus manages to rescue certain types of knowledge at the expense of others. There are some things, it claims, for which we have (in principle) a god's-eye view, and others for which all we have are prejudices and whims. The fact that positivism has been subjected to damaging criticism in recent decades, being drastically modified even by its leading proponents (including Ayer himself), has not stopped it from continuing to exercise an influence at the popular level, where it accords well with the prevailing Western worldview which gives pre-eminent value to scientific knowing and technological control and power while relativizing the intangible values and belief-systems of human society. One meets it among naïve theologians, who complain that while other people have 'presuppositions', they simply read the text straight, or who claim that, because one cannot have 'direct access' to the 'facts' about Jesus, all that we are left with is a morass of

---

[6] The clearest exposition of this sort of position remains that of Ayer 1946 [1936].

[7] On sociology of knowledge see Berger and Luckmann 1966; Berger 1969; Wilson 1982; and the discussion in Thiselton 1992, ch. 16 section 2. On philosophy of science see Polanyi 1958, 1966; Kuhn 1970 [1962]; Barbour 1974; Greene 1981; Newton-Smith 1981; Gerhart and Russell 1984; Yee 1987; Banner 1990.

first-century fantasy. We will meet a good deal of this sort of thing as we proceed.[8]

History finds itself stuck between the two poles. Is it a sort of 'objective' knowledge, or is it all really 'subjective'? Or is this a false dichotomy?[9] What sort of knowledge do we have of historical events? On the one hand, historical knowledge is subject to the same caveats as all knowledge in general. It is possible to be mistaken. I may think I am holding a book when it is in fact a lump of wood; I may think Caesar crossed the Rubicon, but it may in fact have been some other river; I may think that Paul founded the church in Philippi, but it is conceivable that someone else got there first. When, therefore, people talk anxiously about whether there is 'real proof' for this or that historical 'event', usually concluding that there is not, the chances are that they are at least dangerously near the edge of the positivist trap, the false either-or of full certainty *versus* mere unsubstantiated opinion. The evidence for Caesar's crossing the Rubicon is ultimately of the same order as the evidence that what I am holding is a book. Very similar verification procedures, in fact, apply to both propositions. Neither is absolutely certain; neither is so uncertain as to be useless. If we do not recognize this fundamental similarity, we may find ourselves ignoring Cartesian doubt in everyday life and embracing it uncritically for more 'serious' issues. In the New Testament field, some critics have made a great song and dance about the fact that the details of Jesus' life, or the fact of his resurrection, cannot be proved 'scientifically'; philosophical rigour should compel them to admit that the same problem pertains to the vast range of ordinary human knowledge, including the implicit claim that knowledge requires empirical verification.

The pessimistic side of the Enlightenment programme can be most clearly seen in certain more modest forms of empiricism, not least *phenomenalism*.[10] The only thing of which I can really be sure when confronted by things in (what seems to be) the external world are my own sense-data. This view, with a kind of apparent epistemological humility, therefore translates talk about external objects (this is a mug) into statements about sense-data (I am aware of hard, round, smooth and warm feelings in my hands). Positivism, at this point, would go on to infer, and if possible verify, the presence of external objects; phenomenalism remains cautious, and this caution has affected a good deal of popular speech: instead of the brash 'this is correct', we say 'I would want to argue that this is correct', collapsing a dangerously arrogant statement about the world into a safely humble statement about myself. The well-known problems with this view have not stopped it from having enormous influence, not least within some parts of postmodernism. When I seem to be looking at a text, or at an author's mind within the text, or at events of which the text seems

---

[8] The problem may be encountered in the musical sphere. Montreal has two (excellent) classical-music radio stations, one French and one English. The English announcers regularly say that the music is 'played by . . .'; the French, that it is '*interprété par* . . .' Here we have, in a nutshell, Anglo-Saxon positivism and Continental caution. On the attempt, from Descartes to Dummett, to find a 'neutral' point of view see e.g. Kerr 1989.

[9] cf. Bernstein 1983.

[10] On phenomenalism see Hirst 1967.

to be speaking, all I am really doing is seeing the author's view of events, or the text's appearance of authorial intent, or maybe only my own thoughts in the presence of the text . . . and is it even a text?[11]

A diagram may help at this point. The positivist conceives of knowing as a simple line from the observer to the object. This results in the following model:

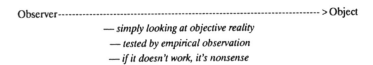

The phenomenalist, however, tries this model out and discovers that all results bend back on to the knower:

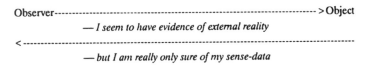

There are, of course, all sorts of variations on these themes, but they show the difference between two broad positions. They could be further characterized by an illustration. If knowing something is like looking through a telescope, a simplistic positivist might imagine that he is simply looking at the object, forgetting for the moment the fact that he is looking *through* lenses, while a phenomenalist might suspect that she is looking at a mirror, in which she is seeing the reflection of her own eye. One logical result of the latter position is of course solipsism, the belief that I and only I exist. What else do I have evidence for?

Over against both of these positions, I propose a form of *critical realism*. This is a way of describing the process of 'knowing' that acknowledges the *reality of the thing known, as something other than the knower* (hence 'realism'), while also fully acknowledging that the only access we have to this reality lies along the spiralling path of *appropriate dialogue or conversation between the knower and the thing known* (hence 'critical').[12] This path leads to critical reflection on the products of our enquiry into 'reality', so that our assertions about 'reality' acknowledge their own provisionality. Knowledge, in other words, although in principle concerning realities independent of the knower, is never itself independent of the knower.[13]

---

[11] See ch. 3 below.

[12] We should perhaps note that the adjective 'critical' in the phrase 'critical realism' has a different function to the same adjective in the phrase 'critical reason'. In the latter (as e.g. in Kant) it is active: 'reason *that provides* a critique'. In the former it is passive: 'realism *subject to* critique'.

[13] The exception that proves the rule is the special (and highly complex) case of self-knowledge.

We might, then, attempt a preliminary sketch of the shape of knowledge, according to the model of critical realism, as follows:

Observer--- >Object
initial observation

< ---
is challenged by critical reflection

--- >
but can survive the challenge and speak truly of reality

The second and third of these stages need, clearly, further discussion. Critical awareness reveals three things at least about the process of knowing, all of which challenge either a naïve realism or a mainline positivism. First, the observer is looking from one point of view, and one only; and there is no such thing as a god's-eye view (by which would be meant a *Deist* god's-eye view) available to human beings, a point of view which is no human's point of view.[14] Second, and consequent upon this, all humans inevitably and naturally interpret the information received from their senses through a grid of expectations, memories, stories, psychological states, and so on. The point of view is not merely peculiar in terms of location (I am standing on this side of the room, not that side, so my viewpoint is different from yours); it is also peculiar in terms of the lenses of my worldview (as various writers have shown, a tacit and pre-theoretical point of view is itself a necessary condition for any perception and knowledge to occur at all).[15] Thirdly, and most importantly, where I stand and the (metaphorical) lenses through which I look have a great deal to do with the communities to which I belong. Some things which I see in a particular way I see thus because I belong to a particular human community, a network of family and friends; some, because I belong to a profession; some, because I am an amateur musician; and so on. Every human community shares and cherishes certain assumptions, traditions, expectations, anxieties, and so forth, which encourage its members to construe reality in particular ways, and which create contexts within which certain kinds of statements are perceived as making sense. There is no such thing as the 'neutral' or 'objective' observer; equally, there is no such thing as the *detached* observer.[16]

All of these factors mean that any 'realism' which is to survive has to take fully on board the provisionality of all its statements. How then can it proceed?

---

[14] On the significance of different views of god/God within this argument, see ch. 5 below. It is noticeable that, for instance, in Hawking 1988 the discussion of deity assumes that the word 'God', if it has any referent, refers to the god imagined by Deism, without consideration of other possible options (e.g. the biblical one(s)). The Deist god would be the ultimate naïve realist; when the God of Abraham, Isaac and Jacob—and of Jesus—'knows' things or people there is a level of engagement, of active involvement, therein implied of which Deism knows nothing.

[15] cf. Polanyi 1958; Wolterstorff 1984 [1976].

[16] See MacIntyre 1985, 220ff. This whole critique corresponds to Ricoeur's sense of 'explanation'; see the discussion in Thiselton 1992, ch. 10.

The one thing that is not possible at this point is to revive some form of positivism, albeit in a chastened mood. That is, it will not do to say at this point that, when all the above allowances have been made, there simply are some things which can still be said, on the basis of empirical sense-data, about the world external to the observer(s). No: instead of working from the particulars of observation, or 'sense-data', to confident statements about external reality, positivistically conceived, critical realism (as I am proposing it) sees knowledge of particulars as taking place within the larger framework of the story or worldview which forms the basis of the observer's way of being in relation to the world. (I shall discuss what worldviews are, and how they work, in chapter 5.) Instead of working as it were upwards from empirical data, in however chastened and hence cautious a fashion, knowledge takes place, within this model, when people *find things that fit* with the particular story or (more likely) stories to which they are accustomed to give allegiance. I shall discuss presently the further problems to which this gives rise.

I am well aware that, by itself, this statement will sound very puzzling. It will seem as though knowledge is simply a private matter; the phenomenalists, or the subjectivists, have won after all. All I know about is something that takes place inside my own story. In order to show why this reduction is unwarranted we must look at the matter of verification. What counts as 'verifying' that which is claimed as knowledge?[17]

The usual accounts of 'scientific' method focus (with good reason, in my view) on hypothesis and verification/falsification. We make a hypothesis about what is true, and we go about verifying or falsifying it by further experimentation. But how do we arrive at hypotheses, and what counts as verification or falsification? On the positivistic model, hypotheses are constructed out of the sense-data received, and then go in search of more sense-evidence which will either confirm, modify or destroy the hypothesis thus created. I suggest that this is misleading. It is very unlikely that one could construct a good working hypothesis out of sense-data alone, and in fact no reflective thinker in any field imagines that this is the case. One needs a larger framework on which to draw, a larger set of *stories* about things that are likely to happen in the world. There must always be a leap, made by the imagination that has been attuned sympathetically to the subject-matter, from the (in principle) random observation of phenomena to the hypothesis of a pattern. Equally, verification happens not so much by observing random sense-data to see whether they fit with the hypothesis, but by devising means, precisely on the basis of the larger stories (including the hypothesis itself), to ask specific questions about specific aspects of the hypothesis. But this presses the question: in what way do the large stories and the specific data arrive at a 'fit'? In order to examine this we must look closer at stories themselves.

---

[17] On all of what follows see Barbour 1966, Part Two.

3. Stories, Worldviews and Knowledge

Stories are one of the most basic modes of human life.[18] It is not the case that we perform random acts and then try to make sense of them; when people do that we say that they are drunk, or mad. As MacIntyre argues, conversations in particular and human actions in general are 'enacted narratives'. That is, the overall narrative is the more basic category, while the particular moment and person can only be understood within that context:[19]

> Just as a history is not a sequence of actions, but the concept of an action is that of a moment in an actual or possible history abstracted for some purpose from that history, so the characters in a history are not a collection of persons, but the concept of a person is that of a character abstracted from a history.[20]

Human life, then, can be seen as grounded in and constituted by the implicit or explicit stories which humans tell themselves and one another. This runs contrary to the popular belief that a story is there to 'illustrate' some point or other which can in principle be stated without recourse to the clumsy vehicle of a narrative. Stories are often wrongly regarded as a poor person's substitute for the 'real thing', which is to be found either in some abstract truth or in statements about 'bare facts'. An equally unsatisfactory alternative is to regard the story as a showcase for a rhetorical saying or set of such sayings. Stories are a basic constituent of human life; they are, in fact, one key element within the total construction of a worldview. I shall argue in chapter 5 that all worldviews contain an irreducible narrative element, which stands alongside the other worldview elements (symbol, praxis, and basic questions and answers), none of which can be simply 'reduced' to terms of the others. As we shall see, worldviews, the grid through which humans perceive reality, emerge into explicit consciousness in terms of human *beliefs* and *aims*, which function as in principle debatable expressions of the worldviews. The stories which characterize the worldview itself are thus located, on the map of human knowing, at a more fundamental level than explicitly formulated beliefs, including theological beliefs.

The stories which most obviously embody worldviews are of course the foundation myths told by the so-called primitive native peoples of the world to explain the origins of the world in general and their race in particular. Anthropologists and others, eager to unearth vestiges of primal viewpoints now hidden from more apparently civilized gaze, study such stories as the appropriate means to this end. But modern analogues are not far to seek, for instance in the use of narrative in political debate. Stories of how things were

---

[18] On this currently much-discussed topic see in particular Frei 1974; Alter 1981; Ricoeur 1984, 1985, 1988; Funk 1988; Hauerwas and Jones 1989 (particularly the article by Crites (65–88) and the discussion between Hartt, Crites and Hauerwas (279–319)). MacIntyre 1985, particularly ch. 15, is also vital. At a late stage in the reworking of this chapter I read John Milbank's account (1990, ch. 12) of what he calls 'a true Christian metanarrative realism' (389), which, if I understand it correctly, seems to me quite close to what I am arguing, though of course much more finely tuned.

[19] MacIntyre 1985, 211.

[20] ibid., 217.

in the Depression are used to fuel sympathy for the oppressed working class; stories of terrorism are used to justify present right-wing regimes. Closer to home, stories are used in personal and domestic discourse not merely to provide information about events which have taken place, but to embody and hence reinforce, or perhaps to modify, a shared worldview within a family, an office, a club or a college. Stories thus provide a vital framework for experiencing the world. They also provide a means by which views of the world may be challenged.

The fact that stories are a fundamental characteristic of worldviews can be further illustrated in relation to the Jewish worldview and its various mutations. These can never be reduced to sets of maxims. Even at its most proverbial and epigrammatic, Jewish writing retains the underlying substructure of the Jewish story about the covenant god, the world, and Israel. For most Jews, certainly in the first century, the story-form was the natural and indeed inevitable way in which their worldview would find expression, whether in telling the stories of YHWH's mighty deeds in the past on behalf of his people, of creating new stories which would function to stir the faithful up in the present to continue in patience and obedience, or in looking forward to the mighty deed that was still to come which would crown all the others and bring Israel true and lasting liberation once and for all.[21]

Stories, never unpopular with children and those who read purely for pleasure, have thus become fashionable of late also among scholars, not least in the biblical studies guild. Within the last generation several writers have drawn on the work of folk-tale analysts such as Vladimir Propp to help them understand the structure and significance of various bits of the Bible. Instead of 'translating' narrative into something else, we are now urged to read it as it is and understand it in its own terms.[22] In both literary and theological terms, this seems to me an altogether admirable development; it needs, no doubt, some checks and balances, but in principle can be welcomed with enthusiasm.

This research has, further, examined how stories work both in themselves and in relation to other stories. At the internal level, stories have structures, plots and characters. They use various rhetorical techniques, which include mode of narration (is the narrator a character in the drama, or does (s)he have privileged insight into all the events?), irony, conflict, different narrative patterns such as 'framing', and so forth. They will quite likely have, by implication, what has been called an 'ideal reader', that is, they imply and perhaps invite an appropriate reading of a particular kind. All of these have their own effect on how their actual readers see things. We are, in other words, invited to do with a complex story what (as we shall see in the next chapter) we do with any literary criticism, that is, to study the effect created and the means by which it is created. Authorial intent should not be excluded from this process, though it

---

[21] See Part III below. Examples from our period are *Jubilees*, 4 Maccabees, Josephus. Even those writings whose *form* is not that of Story tell stories nonetheless: the Qumran commentaries on scripture tell the story of the community, its origins, struggles and destiny, under the medium of detailed *pesher* exegesis. Philo may be the exception that proves the rule, though he too used stories at certain stages, as did Plato himself.

[22] See particularly Frei 1974; Alter 1981.

often is: for instance, when dealing with ancient texts we should remember that ancient commentators on rhetoric were perfectly well aware of the varied possible effects of narratives, and we are not bound to regard all the evangelists as ignorant of such ideas. Equally, however, a writer like Mark might well have produced such effects in the same way that a 'natural' orator would do, using a variety of techniques without thinking or even knowing about them.[23]

When we examine how stories work in relation to other stories, we find that human beings tell stories because this is how we perceive, and indeed relate to, the world. What we see close up, in a multitude of little incidents whether isolated or (more likely) interrelated, we make sense of by drawing on story-forms already more or less known to us and placing the information within them. A story, with its pattern of problem and conflict, of aborted attempts at resolution, and final result, whether sad or glad, is, if we may infer from the common practice of the world, universally perceived as the best way of talking about the way the world actually is. Good stories assume that the world is a place of conflict and resolution, whether comic or tragic. They select and arrange material accordingly. And, as we suggested before, stories can embody or reinforce, or perhaps modify, the worldviews to which they relate.[24]

Stories are, actually, peculiarly good at modifying or subverting other stories and their worldviews. Where head-on attack would certainly fail, the parable hides the wisdom of the serpent behind the innocence of the dove, gaining entrance and favour which can then be used to change assumptions which the hearer would otherwise keep hidden away for safety. Nathan tells David a story about a rich man, a poor man, and a little lamb; David is enraged; and Nathan springs the trap. Tell someone to do something, and you change their life—for a day; tell someone a story and you change their life. Stories, in having this effect, function as complex metaphors. Metaphor consists in bringing two sets of ideas close together, close enough for a spark to jump, but not too close, so that the spark, in jumping, illuminates for a moment the whole area around, changing perceptions as it does so.[25] Even so, the subversive story comes close enough to the story already believed by the hearer for a spark to jump between them; and nothing will ever be quite the same again.

It would be possible, and in principle desirable, to chase this insight through various further ramifications. Societies are complex entities, and the worldviews that dominate them give rise not only to straightforward stories but also to fragmented and distorted versions of those stories, as different groups and individuals mark out their own way within a larger setting. Humans live in overlapping worlds, and, as individuals or as groups, they may well tell themselves different and overlapping, but also competing, stories. In addition, the

---

[23] On all this see ch. 3 below; and cf. Beardslee 1969; Rhoads and Michie 1982, and other recent writers. Compare also H.-D. Betz's commentary on Galatians (1979). Much recent work on the gospels as stories (e.g. Mack 1988) assumes that the 'story' phenomenon is a late development, but this is actually absurd: see Part IV below, esp. ch. 14.

[24] On the different things that stories can do, see Thiselton 1992, ch. 15, section 3.

[25] See Crossan 1988b [1975]. On metaphor see Ricoeur 1977; Caird 1980; Soskice 1985.

stories that are explicitly told by a group or individual may well be consciously or unconsciously deceitful, and will require checking in the light of actual praxis and of a wider symbolic universe. What someone habitually *does*, and the symbols around which they order their lives, are at least as reliable an index to their worldview as the stories they 'officially' tell.[26]

The result of all this in our particular field, i.e. the New Testament, is as follows. A certain group of first-century Jews, who held, and wished to commend, one particular variant of the first-century Jewish worldview (which we shall describe in detail in Part III) wished to say: the hope which characterizes our worldview has been fulfilled in these events. And they chose to say this in the most natural (and obviously Jewish) way, by telling the *story*, in order thereby to subvert other ways of looking at the world. To be more explicit: first-century Jews, like all other peoples, perceived the world, and events within the world, within a grid of interpretation and expectation. Their particular grid consisted at its heart of their belief that the world was made by a good, wise and omnipotent god, who had chosen Israel as his special people; they believed that their national history, their communal and traditional story, supplied them with lenses through which they could perceive events in the world, through which they could make some sense of them and order their lives accordingly. They told stories which embodied, exemplified and so reinforced their worldview, and in so doing threw down a particularly subversive challenge to alternative worldviews. Those who wished to encourage their fellow-Jews to think differently told the same stories, but with a twist in the tail. The Essenes told a story about the secret beginning of the new covenant; Josephus, a story about Israel's god going over to the Romans; Jesus, a story about vineyard-tenants whose infidelity would cause the death of the owner's son and their own expulsion; the early Christians, stories about the kingdom of god and its inauguration through Jesus. But one thing they never did. They never expressed a worldview in which the god in question was uninterested in, or uninvolved with, the created world in general, or the historical fortunes of his people in particular. To this we shall return.

The reason why stories come into conflict with each other is that worldviews, and the stories which characterize them, are in principle *normative*: that is, they claim to make sense of the whole of reality. Even the relativist, who believes that everybody's point of view on everything is equally valid even though apparently incompatible, is obedient to an underlying story about reality which comes into explicit conflict with most other stories, which speak of reality as in the last analysis a seamless web, open in principle to experience, observation and discussion. It is ironic that many people in the modern world have regarded Christianity as a private worldview, a set of private stories. Some Christians have actually played right into this trap. But in principle the whole point of Christianity is that it offers a story which is the

---

[26] cf. ch. 5 below. I am grateful to Professor Christopher Rowland for emphasizing this point to me.

story of the whole world. It is public truth. Otherwise it collapses into some version of Gnosticism.[27]

We can therefore draw up something of a sliding scale to show what happens when stories which one group tells about the world come into contact with stories that other groups tell. At one end of the scale there is the phenomenon of direct confirmation: the story implied by an 'object', an action, or an event fits unproblematically into my worldview. At the other end is direct confrontation: if I were to make sense of the stories I see enacted in front of me, I would have to abandon my controlling story and find a new one, which would happen not by my constructing it out of the evidence of the sense-data before me but by my overhearing some other community's story that *could*, apparently, make sense of this (at present puzzling) event.[28] The only other way of handling the clash between two stories is to tell yet another story, explaining how the evidence for the challenging story is in fact deceptive. This is a very common move in science (the experiment did not 'work'; therefore some unexpected variable must have intruded into the proceedings), history (the texts do not fit the facts; therefore, someone has distorted them), and other areas. And, in between these two extremes of confirmation and confrontation, events and 'objects' can either modify or subvert the story or stories with which we began. And, as always, the proof of the pudding remains in the eating. There is no such thing as 'neutral' or 'objective' proof; only the claim that the story we are now telling about the world as a whole makes more sense, in its outline and detail, than other potential or actual stories that may be on offer. Simplicity of outline, elegance in handling the details within it, the inclusion of all the parts of the story, and the ability of the story to make sense beyond its immediate subject-matter: these are what count.[29]

We have returned, therefore, to something like a notion of hypothesis and verification. A hypothesis (in any field) is usually held to be 'verified' if it includes the relevant data, does so with a certain sort of simplicity, and proves fruitful in areas beyond its immediate concern. What we have done, however, is to fill in the gaps in the account of what a hypothesis actually is, and of what counts as verification. A full account, it now appears, must include the following elements: question, hypothesis, testing of hypothesis.[30]

There is, first, the *question* in answer to which the hypothesis is formed. The question does not arise out of thin air: it emerges precisely from the *stories* that certain human beings are telling themselves, at whatever level. One asks questions because one's present story is in some way either puzzling or incomplete.

---

[27] See Newbigin 1986, 1989; Walsh 1989; and many other writers.

[28] My use of 'controlling stories' is similar to Wolterstorff's discussion of 'control beliefs' (1984 [1976] part I, esp. ch. 1). The question of whether one could ever in fact 'see' contradictory evidence (since it might be supposed to be 'screened out' precisely by the worldview according to which it ought not to exist) is a complex one, but I strongly suspect that the problem is really a variant on the puzzle of the hare and the tortoise. We all know that the hare does in fact overtake the tortoise; we all know that radical conversions, radical shifts of worldview accommodating new evidence, do in fact take place, though not usually without predictable trauma.

[29] See ch. 4 below.

[30] Meyer 1979, 80.

I am driving along the road, thinking about all sorts of things, but taking for granted an underlying story about cars, driving and roads. The car then begins to shudder. At once I begin to tell myself a variety of stories which might explain this phenomenon. Perhaps the council has been digging up this bit of road, and has not yet smoothed it out again. Perhaps I have a flat tyre. Perhaps there is something wrong with the suspension. These hypotheses offer themselves to me as potential missing links within the stories; when inserted appropriately, they turn my habitual stories into would-be *explanatory stories*. Where they themselves come from is difficult to describe, though it is not unimportant: they appear to arrive by a process of intuition. Then (resuming the illustration) the car behind me flashes its lights, and the driver points at one of my wheels. At once the second story looms larger. I pull over and examine the tyre, which, sure enough, is looking decidedly sorry for itself. Two further bits of data, namely, the action of the other driver and the sight of the tyre, convince me that the second story meshes with reality. One of the stories I have been telling has emerged as a *successful explanatory story*. Of course, there *may* also be something less than perfect with the road, and the suspension; but the simplest explanation is that the shuddering was caused by the flat tyre. At each stage of the process what matters can best be expressed in terms of story: the story which prompts the question, the new stories which offer themselves in explanation, and the success of one of these stories in including all the relevant data, doing so within a clear and simple framework, and contributing to a better understanding of other stories (I always was just a bit suspicious of the garage where I had bought those tyres). This description of a quite simple process of knowledge demonstrates what is involved in the 'hypothesis-and-verification' model, locating it on the map, which I shall develop more fully in chapter 5, of the nature of worldviews and of the place of stories within them. This will be extremely important in discussing history in particular (chapter 4 below), where we will also discuss some of the more fine-tuned problems about the process of 'verification'.

When, therefore, we perceive external reality, we do so within a prior framework. That framework consists, most fundamentally, of a worldview; and worldviews, as we have emphasized, are characterized by, among other things, certain types of story. The positivist and phenomenalist traditions are wrong to imagine that perception is prior to the grasping of larger realities. On the contrary, detailed sense-perceptions not only occur within stories; they are verified (if they are) within it. The crucial thing to realize is that what the positivist tradition would see as 'facts' already come with theories attached; and theories are precisely stories told as the framework to include 'facts'. What is true of 'facts' is also true of 'objects': 'objects' also carry stories about with them. The word 'cup' does not just denote an object of certain physical properties, nor when I look at or handle a cup do I merely 'see' or 'feel' those physical properties. The word, and the object itself, have to do with the set of implicit stories within which the cup can feature, whether they concern a pottery class, a family tradition, a tea-party, or the borrowing of sugar from a neighbour. In other words, we only know what objects *are* when we see them, at least implicitly, within *events*. And events have to do with (in principle) intelligible actions. The result of this is that instead of the dialogue or conversation we examined earlier, between 'observer' and 'object' as conceived within the empiricist tradition, whether in its optimistic or its pessimistic form, we have a dialogue or conversation between *humans* (not merely neutral and detached observation-platforms) and *events* (not merely detached or meaningless objects). And on both sides of this dialogue we therefore have stories: the stories that the humans are implicitly telling about the world, and the stories that are implied by events and, within them, by the 'objects' that form their component parts.[31]

We may therefore draw a modified version of the earlier diagram of critical-realist epistemology, taking account of the new details we have now introduced:

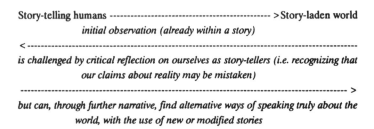

Story-telling humans --- >Story-laden world
            initial observation (already within a story)

< --

*is challenged by critical reflection on ourselves as story-tellers (i.e. recognizing that
our claims about reality may be mistaken)*

--- >

*but can, through further narrative, find alternative ways of speaking truly about the
world, with the use of new or modified stories*

This has, I think, several similarities to the hermeneutic of 'suspicion and retrieval' advocated by Paul Ricoeur, though to discuss the point here would take us too far afield.[32] It suggests that, where before the Western world has tended to divide knowledge into 'objective' and 'subjective', a less misleading way of speaking would think in terms of 'public' and 'private' knowledge. The publicness of certain sorts knowledge is not threatened, but rather enhanced, by the fact that particular people are doing the knowing.

4. Conclusion

The hard-and-fast distinction between objective and subjective must be abandoned as useless. If anyone, reading that sentence, at once thinks 'so there is no such thing as objective knowledge', that merely shows how deeply ingrained the positivist tradition has become in our culture, just at the moment when its perpetrators have finally admitted that it was wrong. What is needed, I have argued, is a more nuanced epistemology, and, subject to the confines of this book and the limitations of my expertise, I have tried to offer one. But,

---

[31] This whole paragraph is indebted to MacIntyre 1985.
[32] See Thiselton 1992, 372: 'What remains central for Ricoeur is the double function of hermeneutics: the hermeneutics of suspicion which unmasks human wish-fulfilments and shatters idols, and the hermeneutics of retrieval which listens to symbols and to symbolic narrative discourse. Where criticism operates, this is only to arrive at post-critical creativity on the yonder side of the critical desert.'

assuming for the moment a Christian worldview, to be argued in more detail on another occasion, we can at least say this: knowledge has to do with the interrelation of humans and the created world. This brings it within the sphere of the biblical belief that humans are made in the image of the creator, and that in consequence they are entrusted with the task of exercising wise responsibility within the created order. They are neither detached observers of, nor predators upon, creation. From this point of view, knowledge can be a form of stewardship; granted the present state of the world, knowledge can be a form of *redeeming* stewardship; it can be, in one sense, a form of love. (If misused, it can of course become the opposite of all those things: knowledge may be seen as a gift designed to be *used in* stewardship.) To know is to be in a relation with the known, which means that the 'knower' must be open to the possibility of the 'known' being other than had been expected or even desired, and must be prepared to respond accordingly, not merely to observe from a distance.

The critical realism offered here is therefore essentially a *relational* epistemology, as opposed to a detached one. The stories through which it arrives at its (potentially) true account of reality are, irreducibly, stories about the interrelation of humans and the rest of reality (including, of course, other humans). Furthermore, the crucial stories themselves are, of course, a vital element in the relationship both between those who share a worldview (who tell one another stories to confirm and fine-tune the worldview) and between holders of different worldviews (who tell one another stories designed to subvert one another's positions). This model allows fully for the actuality of knowledge beyond that of one's own sense-data (that which the 'objectivist' desires to safeguard), while also fully allowing for the involvement of the knower in the act of knowing (that upon which the 'subjectivist' will rightly insist). Such a model has, I believe, a lot of mileage. It may serve as something of an Ariadne's thread to guide us through the labyrinths of New Testament study.

This critical-realist theory of knowledge and verification, then, acknowledges the essentially 'storied' nature of human knowing, thinking and living, within the larger model of worldviews and their component parts. It acknowledges that all knowledge of realities external to oneself takes place within the framework of a worldview, of which stories form an essential part. And it sets up as hypotheses various stories about the world in general or bits of it in particular and tests them by seeing what sort of 'fit' they have with the stories already in place. If someone asks what knock-down arguments I can produce for showing that this theory about how humans know things is in fact true, it would obviously be self-contradictory to reply in essentially empiricist terms. The only appropriate argument is the regular one about puddings and eating. Proposing a new epistemology is, in fact, intrinsically difficult, precisely because of the difficulty with empiricism itself. It is impossible to find solid ('objective') ground to stand on: such a thing does not exist. All epistemologies have to be, themselves, argued as hypotheses: they are tested not by their coherence with a fixed point agreed in advance, but (like other hypotheses, in fact) by their simplicity and their ability to make sense of a wide scope of experiences and events. I have told a story about how humans know things. We must now exemplify and, I hope, appropriately verify this story, by seeing ways in which it can make sense of how humans know certain particular sorts of things, namely literature, history and theology.

Chapter Three

LITERATURE, STORY AND THE ARTICULATION OF WORLDVIEWS

1. Introduction

The study of early Christianity, of Jesus and Paul, and especially of the theology of the whole movement and of individuals within it, is conducted by means of the study of literature. (The only exceptions to this rule are the occasional relevant coin, inscription, or other archaeological find.) We must therefore enquire, in general terms at least, what literature does, how it works, and how best to treat it. The question, what should one do with the New Testament, is a special case of the general question, what should one do with any book. This conclusion presses particularly upon us in the late twentieth century. The tide of literary theory has at last reached the point on the beach where the theologians have been playing, and, having filled their sandcastle moats with water, is now almost in danger of forcing them to retreat, unless they dig deeper and build more strongly.

Current questions about literature have close affinities with those we have already examined.[1] We are faced once more with problems about *knowledge*, albeit highly specialized ones. First, we need to discuss the question of reading itself: what is going on when a reader encounters a text? Second, we need to ask what literature itself is; thirdly, in the light of this, what the task of criticism may be. Since this will lead us into the question of Story once more, we must then look in more detail at the way in which stories function. Finally, we must apply all of this in more detail to the New Testament.[2]

We may begin, though, with some examples that will help us along the way.

'Is there anybody there?' said the Traveller,
  Knocking on the moonlit door;
And his horse in the silence champed the grasses
  Of the forest's ferny floor.

And a bird flew up out of the turret,
  Above the Traveller's head:
And he smote upon the door again a second time;
  'Is there anybody there?' he said.

---

[1] See, for examples of this already, Young and Ford 1987, ch.5; Morgan 1988, ch.7.

[2] For background, see Beardslee 1969, 1989; Frei 1974; Alter 1981; Frye 1983; Barton 1984; Cotterell and Turner 1989; Hauerwas and Jones 1989; Sanders and Davies 1989, chs. 15–16; Warner 1990; and many others, e.g. Poythress 1978. Two of the most important recent books on the whole area of this chapter are Moore 1989 and Thiselton 1992.

But no-one descended to the Traveller;
  No head from the leaf-fringed sill
Leaned over and looked into his grey eyes,
  Where he stood perplexed and still.

But only a host of phantom listeners
  That dwelt in the lone house then
Stood listening in the quiet of the moonlight
  To that voice from the world of men:

Stood thronging the faint moonbeams on the dark stair
  That goes down to the empty hall,
Hearkening in an air stirred and shaken
  By the lonely Traveller's call.

And he felt in his heart a strangeness,
  Their stillness answering his cry,
While his horse moved, cropping the dark turf,
  'Neath the starred and leafy sky;

For he suddenly smote on the door, even
  Louder, and lifted his head:—
'Tell them I came, and no-one answered,
  That I kept my word,' he said.

Never the least stir made the listeners,
  Though every word he spake
Fell echoing through the shadowiness of the still house
  From the one man left awake:

Aye, they heard his foot upon the stirrup,
  And the sound of iron on stone,
And how the silence surged softly backward,
  When the plunging hooves were gone.[3]

What should we do with a piece of writing like this? We may content ourselves, if we wish, by commenting on de la Mare's poem in terms of literary
art, such as alliteration. The still, soft sense of the forest is conveyed by the
string of 'f's in the fourth line; the return to silence, as of a pool once disturbed
and now regaining stillness, by the 's's in the penultimate line. We observe the
effect, and explain the method. But there are broader effects worth pondering.
The title of the poem is 'The Listeners'; not, perhaps, the title we would
choose ourselves ('The Lonely Horseman', 'The Moonlight Rider'?). It throws
attention in one direction even as the introduction to the poem is pointing
elsewhere. It invites the reader to ponder: who are these phantom listeners?
What are they doing? Who made the rider promise to come back, and where is
he or she now? The tension between title and poem, only partly resolved by
the listeners becoming the subject of the second half, combines with all the
unexplained allusions ('Tell them . . . I kept my word') to create the effect of a
great and solemn mystery, to which we are nearly privy but not quite. We realize, in fact, that we are witnessing the climax of a much longer and more complex drama, pregnant, out of sight and full of significance. We are, in fact,

[3] Walter de la Mare, 'The Listeners', in de la Mare 1938, 316–17.

drawn irresistibly into the world of a *story*—and a story, moreover, which, like the modern 'short story', invites us to share its world as much by what it does not say as by what it does. The effect of the poem is more than the sum total of the rhymes, the assonance, the evocative setting. These all fall within (and of course, since the poem is a good one, they enhance) the wider effect of the story itself. Something similar, I shall suggest, is true of the gospels. And throughout these discussions we are met by the question: how open is the poem to new ways of being read? What would count as a 'correct' reading, and how important is it to try to achieve such a thing?[4]

Let us take a second example. In Thomas Mann's celebrated and alarming novel *Doctor Faustus* we are introduced to Adrian Leverkühn, a brilliant composer who has invented an entirely new method of writing music.[5] Mann alludes almost at once to the composer's Faustian pact with the Devil, and then pretends (in the person of the narrator) to be cross with himself for letting such a major theme out so soon. But the real major theme remains hidden, only surreptitiously being revealed, as the novel draws on to its stupendous climax. In parallel with the life-story of the composer is set the life-story of modern Germany, culminating in the rise of Hitler and the Second World War. Only in the last sentence of the novel is the parallel finally made explicit, as the narrator looks at the ruin of his friend Leverkühn and at the ruin of his homeland, and combines the two: 'Gott sei euerer armen Seele gnädig, mein Freund, mein Vaterland'—'God be gracious to your poor soul, my friend, my Fatherland!'[6] Here the effect is of a massive and sustained critique of twentieth-century Germany, from within, by one who has loved her and now grieves over her. The effect is achieved by large-scale juxtaposition and parallelism, never overstated, only gradually emerging from the shadows. It is, in other words, the story itself that has the effect, behind all Mann's brilliant musical reconstructions (it is a bold novelist who describes fictitious pieces of music) and characterizations. And part of the power of the story, within Western culture, lies precisely in Mann's retelling of the Faust legend in such a way as to subvert some other tellings, notably Goethe's. This, he is saying, is what the story is *really* all about.

Once again, there are remarkable similarities to all of this in the gospels. And, once again, the question presses: how much of all this can we, or must we, 'get right', and how much remains open to new readings and interpretations?

For our third example we return to territory by now familiar. In Jesus' parable of the Wicked Tenants, as told in the synoptic gospels, we find a clas-

---

[4] See Louth 1983, 103, discussing Eliot's distinction between things that can and must be 'got right' in criticism and things that must be left 'open'.

[5] Mann 1968 [1947]. Mann was forced to acknowledge in a note at the end of the book (491) that this twelve-tone row 'is in truth the intellectual property of a contemporary composer and theoretician, Arnold Schönberg'. One can understand Schönberg's annoyance at the 'borrowing' more particularly if one considers the implications of the novel as a whole: see Carnegy 1973, ch. 4 (I am grateful to my colleague Mr F. J. Lamport for this reference and some helpful discussions).

[6] Mann 1968 [1947], 490.

sic example of a subversive story. Its parallel with the vineyard story in Isaiah 5 gives us a starting-point, as Mann's conclusion gives us a fixed point from which to work back. This is the story of Israel; it was already a tragedy when Isaiah told it, but now it has become more intense, more poignant. It is now the story not only of a landowner and his tenants, but also of a father and his son. This element, too, is subversive: in the Old Testament it is Israel who is the beloved son of the creator god, and now there is apparently a son who stands both in Israel's place and over against Israel. We observe how the story is built up in stages to its climax: (1) the vineyard is prepared, (2) the owner sends the messengers, who receive increasingly rough treatment, (3) finally the son is sent, rejected and killed. There remains the conclusion: (4) the vineyard will be taken away and given to others. The dramatic sequence is complete, and (interestingly, as we will see) essentially tragic: the vocation of the tenants, taken in isolation and pushed to its limits, is the cause of their own downfall. Called to be tenants, they aspire to be owners. As in much tragedy, we have here an essentially Promethean emphasis. We can thus already see how the story works in its context; how it works within itself; and where to locate it on a general map of stories. Once again, we may ask: how important is it to get these details *right*? And a further question: what difference, if any, does it make if we read this text as part of 'holy scripture'?

2. On Reading

(i) Introduction

With these examples in mind, we turn to the question: what happens when we read? The remarks in chapter 2 about the nature of knowledge must now be applied to this specific area. What kind of 'knowledge' do we gain as we read?

Readers in the modern West are often tempted to give a naïvely realistic answer. I pick up a newspaper and read it; the authors tell me what happened in the world yesterday. The 'telescope' of the text is simply a window, gazing out on reality. I read a history-book, and so discover simply 'what happened' at some moment in the past. But then one day we read in a newspaper, or in a history-book, an account of something we know about through a different source. This makes us stop and think. All of a sudden, naïve realism looks worrying, and so we lurch instead towards a naïve reductionism along the phenomenalist model: the words are not 'about' reality, but are simply 'about' the opinions of the writer. A shift has occurred: instead of looking 'through' the writer and the words at the event, I begin to suspect that I am looking only, or mainly, at the writer. The telescope has become an angled mirror: what is seen is not an event, merely an author. This can be demonstrated diagrammatically as follows:

Reader	Text	Author	Event

naïve realist ------->   ------>   ------>
    - *reading text, gaining access to author and thence to event*

phenomenalist ------>   ------>   ------>
                                    <------
    - *reading text, gaining access to author, but event is illusory*

A good example of this shift, in a 'neutral' area, can be found in the painting of Monet. Monet began, like most painters, painting objects in the real world: bridges, cathedrals, his garden, his wife. As Impressionism became, so to say, more impressionistic, and particularly, and interestingly, as his own sight deteriorated, he began to paint more and more not so much the objects as they were but his *impressions* of the objects, so that in his middle period we find ourselves looking—often, to be sure, with great delight—not at a quasi-photographic picture but at the depiction of someone's sense-data. But, by his own account, Monet became less and less interested in the sense-data that the objects themselves were presenting to him, and more and more interested in the patterns and shapes, the colours and movement, which he was simply imagining. In his later works we find him moving towards sheer abstraction. This summary of Monet's progression is, of course, like a good deal else in this Part of the book, a gross over-simplification, but it will suffice to make the point.[7]

We may suspect, in fact, that most people lurch from one position to another depending on circumstances. English people tend to think of themselves as robust realists: we just observe the facts and describe them, we just read the text as it is. But (as we saw above) as soon as we read a newspaper report of an event we know something about, we are aware of the difference between the journalist's point of view and our own: and as soon as we engage (for instance) in personal counselling we become aware that one person can, in all apparent innocence, superimpose or 'project', on to his picture of another person, phenomena which are purely inside his own head. To revert to the example of journalism, what we often see (for instance in television documentaries, or pseudo-documentaries) appears to the reader or viewer as straightforward fact; but what is actually going on is very likely (a) the reporter's idea of what *ought* to be occurring, projected on to an apparently 'real' world, (b) this idea appearing as 'his point of view on reality', and (c) this point of view *appearing as* reality itself.[8] When you agree with the point of view, you tend to watch as a realist (this is how things actually are); when you disagree, you quickly become a phenomenalist at the author/event stage (it was just her point of view) or even a subjectivist (she simply made it all up).

All this may seem a little remote from the world of the New Testament. But in fact it strikes us in the face as soon as we pick up a modern book on the gospels. The German scholar G. Strecker has recently published a book on the

---

[7] On the development of Monet's intentions and achievements see e.g. House 1977, 3–13; on the present point, esp. 12f.

[8] On the idea of something *appearing as* something else see particularly Berger 1969.

Sermon on the Mount.[9] On the back cover we are told, with an air of triumph, that the Sermon on the Mount does not represent what Jesus said, but rather contains Matthew's own theology. That, I submit, is not primarily an exegetical or even a historical judgment: it is a philosophical one. Strecker is inviting us to move from the risky ground of making claims about Jesus himself to the apparently safer, more secure ground of saying that this is the state of Matthew's own mind.[10] We read the Sermon on the Mount and we ask 'Is there anybody there?' The answer is no: not in the sense of an original speaker, a Jesus sitting on a mountain talking to the crowds. There is only Matthew. We have jumped from realism, right over an empiricist reading (Matthew's *impression of* Jesus) and landed in phenomenalism (Matthew's *state of mind*). The apparent force of Strecker's proposal has comparatively little to do with first-century history, and a great deal more to do with late-twentieth-century habits of mind and reading.

Or take, as another example, the usual account that is given of Josephus' description of the Pharisees. He talks about them as though they were a philosophical school, with opinions about determinism and so forth.[11] Now nobody doubts that there were Pharisees, and that they did have opinions; but everybody doubts that they were really like Greek philosophers. Here we opt for a cautiously empiricist reading: Josephus, we say, is giving his perception of the Pharisees, or more accurately the perception which he knows will be comprehensible to his pagan audience. This perception is not *merely* an idea in his own mind, but nor does it correspond exactly to the way things actually were.

A third example comes from recent oral tradition, but it is interesting for all that. I am assured by several eyewitnesses, research students in a university I visited recently, that one of their professors solemnly asserted in public that Rudolf Bultmann was not influenced by theological or philosophical convictions when studying the history of the synoptic tradition, but was engaged in purely 'objective' historical research. This claim, which flies in the face of Bultmann's own account of historical and hermeneutical method, involves anyone holding it in a complex position: positivism in relation to Bultmann's writing about the early church (he just told it like it was); scepticism about Bultmann's own account of what he was doing (he said he had presuppositions,[12] but we know he didn't); and phenomenalism, according to Bultmann himself, in relation to the early church and its writings about Jesus (they wrote 'about' Jesus, but they were really, for the most part, talking 'about' their own faith).

One very important variation on these themes has been the concentration, in some parts of modern biblical study, on the *community* that may be presumed to stand behind a text. Just as, in many quarters, historical study of Jesus *via* the text has given way to study of the evangelists, so, ever since the rise of form-criticism seventy years ago, the focus has been not on a *referent*

[9] Strecker 1988.
[10] Talk about Jesus is risky philosophically, in the same way (ultimately) as it is risky to say 'I see a house': one might be mistaken. There are theological risks as well, which we shall come to later; not least the danger that if we did find Jesus we would not know what to do with him.
[11] e.g. Jos. *Ant.* 18.12–15.
[12] See Bultmann 1960, 342–51.

beyond the text but on the communities that transmitted traditions. Even where form-criticism has given way to redaction-criticism, study of the evangelists has often focused simply on their church and community setting. 'Community' has thus functioned as an alternative sort of referent, beyond or behind the text:

Reader[13]	Text	[Author]	Community
------>	-------->	------>	

This move has, for many twentieth-century theologians, more obvious hermeneutical and theological usefulness: we know (we think) what to do with a community and its theology, but an event is harder to handle. But it will soon become obvious that the ground could be cut from under even this redaction-criticism by some sort of a postmodern reading of the gospels, which would deny the propriety of finding even Matthew's own mind, let alone that of his 'community', within his gospel, and which would insist instead on the interaction between reader and text (or even between the reader and his or her own mind) as the only locus of 'meaning'. These readings are all inherently unstable: the philosophical reasons why they come into being in the first place (Cartesian anxiety about predication of actual referents) will swallow them up in their turn.

All of this means that the phenomenon of reading, at any level other than the naïve, has become very confusing. People have read great literary texts on the one hand, and the Bible on the other, in a bewildering variety of different ways. Sometimes they have been naïve realists. Shakespeare is telling a story about Julius Caesar, and that is all there is to it. Sometimes they have heard echoes of something else: perhaps he is discussing tyranny and democracy in general? Might he be using Caesar as an allegory for a tyrant closer to home? How might we tell? De la Mare is telling a story about a horseman and an empty house. Is that all? Is he perhaps 'really' talking about someone looking for 'God'? Is he talking about modern literature itself, with its sense that there used to be an author 'inside' this text, but that now there is nobody at home? How might we find out?[14] Mann is telling a story about a fictitious composer. But he is also, quite certainly, telling a story about modern Germany. In doing so, he is of course revealing his own opinions and beliefs, which are fully 'involved' in the reality of which he writes. Here, the means by which we may decide the matter is quite clear: his last sentence gives the clue, in an artistically appropriate manner (i.e. without any *deus ex machina* effect).[15] So, in the same way, Jesus tells a story about tenants in a vineyard. (Or, to put it less naïvely, the gospels tell a story about Jesus telling a story about tenants in a

---

[13] The reader, of course, is never an isolated individual: see ch. 2 above.

[14] On the strange sense of longing for something just out of reach, which pervades much of de la Mare's work, see Leavis 1963 [1932], 47–51.

[15] Here we can, as it were, 'check up on' authorial intent: Mann said himself that he wrote the last lines of the book on January 27 1947, 'as I had had them framed in my mind for a long time' (Mann 1961, 183). (The account is very stylized, however, and we may legitimately question whether Mann himself can be trusted at this point.) On the counterpoint between Germany and the composer see ibid., 107.

vineyard.) But many readers have concluded that the story which at one level is 'about' the vineyard is 'really about' 'God' and Israel. What we are faced with, I suggest, is confusion at a variety of levels:

Reader	Text	Author	Event
		------>	vineyard
----->	------>	------>	'God'/Israel
		------>	early church
		<------	

Equally, many devout readers, finding the merely historical to be hermeneutically uninteresting, have read the text as a story about themselves. How might we make sense of this? Will it do simply to say that the biblical writers were also telling the story of 'God', and, since 'God' is always the same, the story can become 'our' story today? At what point, in other words, does the analogy with Thomas Mann hold—that the writer in each case was 'really' writing about Germany/'God', and that Leverkühn/Jesus was just a (fictitious) 'vehicle' for this 'real' interest? At what point, and why, might this analysis break down? It looks as though we are here faced, in a pre-critical anticipation of some post-critical readings, with the following situation:

Reader	Text	Author	Event
------>			

devout reading of text
    <------
translated at once into message about reader
    ------> [divine inspiration]
possibly explained by postulating 'God' as the referent/source of the text

Substitute the possibility of some textual structure for 'God', and we have here a working model of some structuralist readings: take away that possibility, and we have, embedded in the pietist tradition, exactly the same account of reading as we find in the postmodernism of Barthes, Derrida, Rorty or Fish (see below). What matters is 'what the text says to me'.

Until we think clearly about this set of problems, we will not really know what is happening. Many 'critical' methods look so properly 'neutral', but in fact encapsulate whole philosophical positions which are in themselves contentious and highly debatable. All this seems to me to call for a more thorough analysis of the different stages in the process of reading texts.

(ii) 'Is There Anybody There?'

We have already seen that, while naïve realism imagines itself to have direct access to the event or object spoken of in the text, a more phenomenalist reading realizes that it can only be sure of the author's viewpoint. This is a less ambitious claim. It is harder to refute. It seems altogether safer. But it is not the end of the road. The examples just discussed deal with the relation between the text and the reality it purports to describe. The same problems occur when we deal with the relation between ourselves and the text. I said earlier that the aim of criticism is to describe the effect of a piece of writing and to show how that effect is achieved (this may of course include negative comments about either phase, effect or means). But can we say that the author 'intended' to create this or that effect? In plotting the effect that we have observed, are we reading the author's mind? 'Is there anybody there?'

The enormous debates at this point occupy whole books in themselves, and we cannot enter into it in any detail. But we may note the movement of criticism this century, and comment on it a little.[16] As an example of what has come to be known as the 'New Criticism', we may take the issues raised by C. S. Lewis in his famous debate with E. M. W. Tillyard.[17] Lewis launched a strong attack on that style of criticism which seeks to unearth, from the work under consideration, details about the life, habits, emotions and so forth of the author. That, he claimed, is not what criticism should be about. The response from Tillyard attempted to put a moderate case for retaining, within a proper criticism, some element of comment about the writer.[18] But Lewis's line won the day. Much modern study of literature has simply rejected the idea that we have access to the mind or intention of a writer. The road to hell is paved with authorial intentions: all we have is the work itself, seen as an independent entity. What matters now, it seems, is the interaction of reader and text, not of reader and author *via* text. 'Is there anybody there?' we ask, as we read our ancient text, or for that matter our modern one. But all we sometimes imagine is a host of silent listeners, who bear witness that we have kept our word, that we have returned to the overgrown and beforested text. The phantoms will know that a reading of the text has occurred, but the house itself—the private world where the writer once lived—remains locked and barred.

Lewis, of course, was not recommending this position in all its starkness. He was reacting to a particular overemphasis, and stressing (as in his *Experiment in Criticism*) the importance of the effect that the text has on the reader.[19] This points towards the modern authorless reading, but does not itself embrace it. As with so many debates, there was (or so it seems to me) right on both sides. Lewis was entirely correct to reject the idea, which is the product of a marriage between romanticism and empiricism, that criticism either could or should attempt to work out, by reading between the lines of the poem, what the author had for breakfast that morning, or whether he had just fallen in love with the housemaid. These, of course, might themselves be the subject of a poem, either explicitly or allegorically; that would be quite a different matter. Part of the difficulty, clearly, lay in the fact that many nineteenth-century poets *were* basically talking about their own states of mind and emotions, and this lured critics into imagining that to discover such things was the normal busi-

---

[16] See now especially Meyer 1989, ch. 2; Bergonzi 1990, *passim*; Thiselton 1992, *passim*.

[17] On the 'New Criticism' in general and its effects in biblical studies, see Morgan 1988, 217ff.; Moore 1989, 9–13; Thiselton 1992, ch. 2, section 2.

[18] Tillyard and Lewis 1939. The debate is discussed helpfully, and set in the wider context of the so-called New Criticism, by Bergonzi 1990, 62f. See also Moore 1989, 9–13.

[19] Lewis 1961. The almost prophetic significance of Lewis' position is also discussed by Bergonzi 1990, 64f.: Lewis was 'even hinting at the "free-floating signifiers" of poststructuralist theory'.

ness of all literary criticism. Thus was the text freed from the burden of the author:

Reader	Text	Author	Event
------>	------>		
	<-----		

I shall argue in a moment that the proper rejection of a criticism bent simply on discovering the inner life of the poet, and on reducing the 'meaning' of the poem to terms of that discovery, has pushed itself too far (in a way that Lewis, we may say in spite of the position here discussed, did not intend) when it absolutizes the poem to the extent of rejecting not only the desirability, but even the possibility, of knowing the author's intention. In biblical studies, this is the move made from 'composition-criticism' (what was Luke doing in writing his work as a whole?) to 'narrative-criticism' (never mind Luke, what is this book as a whole doing in itself?).[20] But if the focus of study now falls on the text itself, what is to be said *about* the text, if we are not to smuggle in authorial intention after all? At this point there are several possible moves, all of them with significance for biblical studies.

First, it has been a commonplace of mainline Western hermeneutics, at least since Schleiermacher, that it is possible, indeed likely, that the poet, or the evangelist, was writing at one level, of conscious intentionality, but that we can detect within the poem levels of meaning of which, in the nature of the case, the writer was unconscious. This is a grander version of the well-known phenomenon of the unintended pun, which may perhaps reveal, at a Freudian level, something of which the speaker was unconscious. It may be that we can see, with the advantage of hindsight or psychological analysis (Freud is read these days as much by literary critics as by psychologists), that he or she was internally or externally influenced without realizing it, so that the poem points in directions which have only subsequently become clear, and perhaps could not have been imagined by the writer. We may actually know more about the author than was, and that could have been, present to his or her mind at the time.[21] This, of course, is in itself a kind of pseudo- or shadow-intentionality, and may well be thought not to have escaped from the problems of the ordinary sort.

Or, second, it may be that, by projecting a similar method on to a wider screen, the poem might serve as evidence for the deep structure of all human thought, which then becomes the real object of the critical enquiry, to be organized, along with other anthropological data, into conclusions about the nature of human beings and their societies. This is the way in which the move-

[20] See Moore 1989, 4–13.

[21] One example of this in modern biblical studies is the technique known as *Sachkritik*, the criticism of a writer on the basis of the inner logic of his or her own ideas. This is what is going on, for instance, when someone relativizes a section of Paul (as Bultmann does with Romans 9–11) on the grounds that if Paul had thought through his ideas properly he would not have put it like that. It is also what is going on when people accuse Bultmann of not following his own theology through far enough, and still holding on to the historicity of the cross. On this see Wright 1991a, 4, 6.

ment known as 'structuralism' proceeds: from text to deep structures of thought, and thence to conclusions about a reality which lies beyond ordinary consciousness. Such structuralism appears as one of the modern versions of Platonism—the attempt to get behind the phenomena to analyse what is 'really' there.[22] The attraction of such a movement may perhaps lie partly in the fact that it appears to avoid the problems which beset much biblical exegesis of a certain type, namely, the problems of always going behind the text (either to the 'events described' or to the author's mind) in order to get at the real meaning. How much better, more 'scientific', if the universalizable meaning is contained deep within the text itself. Authorial intention got in the way of universalizability; deep structure is much more effective.[23] For these and other reasons, a whole range of writers, especially in North America, have tried to look at the texts in this new way.[24] In these works we see the reintroduction into biblical studies of a question which should have been asked all along, but which has been bracketed out for most of the modern critical movement. Critics have tended to ask two sorts of questions: (a) What event does the text refer to, and what do those events mean? (b) What theological ideas did the author of this text have? 'Meaning' is located, in these models, in the one case in the events themselves, in the other in the beliefs of the writers. The newer formalist or structuralist literary criticism, however, looks for meaning in neither of these, but in the literary form or structure itself.[25] How might we find 'meaning' there, and what might we do with it when we had found it?

Third, there is an analogy between this level of enquiry and the suggestion, sometimes made within more traditional biblical exegesis, that there exists, over and above the author's meaning, a *sensus plenior*, by which an 'inspired' text actually says more than the author realized at the time, with the Holy Spirit filling in the blank of authorial ignorance, or bringing about an 'unintended' prophecy by which (for instance) Caiaphas speaks a word of the Lord even when intending to say something else. The recognition of such a sense, and the possibilities for allegorical and other exegesis which it opens up, have at various stages of the church's reading of scripture been ways of allowing for the experience of Christians that the biblical text 'speaks' to them in ways that the author might not have imagined.[26] We thus have a new range of possibilities:

[22] So Caird 1980, 222f. Meyer 1989, 28 describes structuralist analysis, along with various other current options, as 'the contemporary flight from interpretation'.

[23] See Thiselton 1992 on the reasons for structuralism, which arose as part of the desire in the post-war period for a quasi-objective goal in literary studies, once authorial intention had been declared invalid. But, for biblical studies at least, part of the proof of this pudding is in the eating. Structural analysis of the biblical text has so far failed to resonate with the power and promise that many readers still instinctively find there. Can one preach week by week from deep structures?

[24] Beardslee 1969; Johnson 1976; Polzin 1977; Patte 1976, 1978, 1983; Petersen 1978, 1985. See the discussions in Barton 1984, chs. 8–9; Tuckett 1987, ch. 10; Sanders and Davies 1989, ch. 15; and Thiselton 1992.

[25] On all this, see Petersen 1978, 20f.; Galland 1976, 3f.

[26] On allegorical and other pre-critical exegetical and hermeneutical methods, see Louth 1983; Thiselton 1992, chs. 4–5.

Reader	Text	non-authorial meanings
------- >	------- >	'more than the author intended'
	------- >	deep structure
	------- >	*sensus plenior*

Such proposals—the last of which, clearly, is found within the New Testament itself—are ways of ensuring that meaning is not *limited to* authorial intention. Whether or not we go the route of structuralism, we have to make allowance for a *je ne sais quoi* which lies beyond what the author explicitly had in mind at the time. It does not take much thought to see that criticism cannot shut the door on such a possibility, even though it may find it hard to handle either descriptively or hermeneutically. But (just in case someone might think that this has landed us back in the subjectivist's reading of the text) this does not mean that authorial intention is unimportant or, in the last resort, indiscoverable. A complete account of intention is of course impossible. Knowledge of entire motivation, such as was dreamed about by early behaviourists, recedes like a rainbow's end the closer we get to it.[27] But, as has often been pointed out, it is still very difficult to maintain a 'pure' subjective reading. Even ardent structuralists would want to maintain that they are talking about something, and that their books, however 'open', mean and intend certain things and not certain other things. It remains, at least in principle, possible to know an author's basic intention, and to know that one knows it; for instance, by checking one's reading with the author in person (one thinks of Barth's approving comments on Hans Küng's attempt to read his mind on the subject of justification).[28] There is nothing odd about saying 'the government intended this legislation to have the effect x, but in fact the effect was y', when x and y are clearly incompatible; there is nothing in principle odd in saying that an author intended effect x (shall we say, high tragedy) but achieved effect y (uproarious farce) instead; but we have thereby directly accused the government, or the author, of incompetence or failure. But in a book that we mean to take seriously, it amounts to a fairly serious criticism to say 'the author intended x, but the book means y'. To suggest that such a comment is irrelevant is like insisting that the hare cannot in fact overtake the tortoise because, as is well known, he merely keeps on halving the distance between them into ever-smaller portions. The philosophical tricks by which authorial intention has been dismissed from the reckoning are in the last analysis no more impressive than the well-known mathematical trick which keeps the hare in permanent pursuit.

One problem with the attempt to provide an analysis which goes beyond the text but not to the author is the lack of *control*. There is little agreement between structuralists as to what will count as the deep structure of a passage or book, and how we might know when we had found it. And, as the Reformers argued, though there may indeed be a *sensus plenior* to Holy Writ, it is difficult to tell the difference between that and the projection on to the

---

[27] So, in relation to biblical studies, Moore 1989, 174.

[28] Küng 1964 [1957], xvii: Barth, in his preface, writes that 'your readers may rest assured ... that you have me say what I actually do say and that I mean it in the way you have me say it'.

text of a theological idea or belief acquired by some other means. If one then appeals to the 'literal sense' as the control, has one really learnt anything new from a passage by the *plenior* method?

The difficulties with all of these potential models for getting 'beyond' the text *without going through the author's mind* have meant that many critics, as we saw, have insisted on bringing the focus of attention back simply to the text itself. But, once we have made that move, why should we stop there? Does not the same thing apply at the first stage? The naïvely realistic view of that stage—the 'reader' simply reading the 'text'—can itself be made to collapse: in good phenomenalist style, all I am really aware of in the presence of this text is my own sense-data. The whole thing 'deconstructs' into the feelings, thoughts, and impressions I have in the presence of the text:

Reader	Text	Author	Event
--------->			
<---------			

—so that there is not only no event, not only no author with an intention, but now not even a text. And this will result in a multiplicity of possibilities of 'reading', with endless and often minute analysis at which those outside the game may well look with considerable scepticism.[29] This position, which might seem the death of all reading or criticism, has of course in turn become the jumping-off point for whole new schools of literary criticism, of which 'deconstructionism' proper is only one: Stephen Moore, in his recent book, plots stages in recent criticism that can be labelled by such writers as Kermode, Fish and ultimately Roland Barthes and Jacques Derrida.[30] The idea of this school, put absurdly simply, is that the only thing to do with a text is to play with it for oneself: I must see what it does to me, and not ask whether there is another mind out there behind the text.[31] And of course if that is so there is not much point discussing the text with someone else. There will be no 'right' or 'wrong' reading; only my reading and your reading.[32]

I think it will be clear just how well this latter position will appeal to many elements in contemporary consciousness. We live in a relativistic and pluralistic age, an age which places self-fulfilment above the integration of self

[29] cf. Meyer 1989, 87: 'Without human authenticity, interpretation trails off into the capricious, thwarted by absorption in pretentious or unpretentious trivia . . . This includes, on the part of literary scholars who for whatever reason find themselves with nothing very compelling, or even very definite, to do, a misplaced hankering to break out into creativity and inventiveness. There follow declarations of independence from the tyrannies of philology and history, from the merely intended sense of the text, and finally from the text itself. But faddism, and particularly the faddism that hinges on forms of alienation, is notoriously ineffective occupational therapy.'

[30] Moore 1989, chs.7–8. On Barthes, and his 'infinite plurality of meanings', see Thiselton 1992, ch. 3 section 3; on Derrida, *ibid.* ch. 3 section 5, and Bergonzi 1990, ch. 8. For a thorough critique of Fish (and Rorty) see Thiselton 1992, ch. 14; cf. Moore 1989, ch. 7.

[31] See Taylor 1982, 114, speaking of reading in terms of autoeroticism. This is not far from Roland Barthes' phrase about the reader 'taking his pleasure with the text', where the emphasis is on *his*; see Moore 1989, 144. See the criticism of this by Lundin in Lundin, Walhout and Thiselton 1985.

[32] This sharp point has broadened out in recent biblical studies, in what is called 'reader-response' criticism; see Sanders and Davies 1989, ch. 16.

with other selves. There are, of course, many different criticisms that could be advanced against this whole view of the world. It traces its philosophical and indeed literary ancestry through Foucault and Nietzsche in particular, and shares with them something of the nihilism that is (in my opinion) the twin ugly sister of the positivism that still clings to some parts of contemporary culture. I shall, however, save such criticisms for different contexts, for one reason: that, so far, deconstructionism in all its strange glory has not yet really burst upon the world of New Testament studies, and so falls strictly outside our purposes here. There have been some attempts to introduce it, notably in the various works of the brilliant writer J. Dominic Crossan.[33] Crossan, despite being read quite widely, has not been followed by many others as yet, perhaps because, as Moore has pointed out, his work subverts itself through his insistence on trying, at the same time as he is deconstructing the texts, to discover the historical Jesus through and behind them.[34] The way is hard that leads to genuine deconstructionism, and those who follow it consistently are few.

Most Bible-readers of a conservative stamp will look askance at deconstructionism. But its proposed model is in fact too close for comfort to many models implicitly adopted within (broadly speaking) the pietist tradition. The church has actually institutionalized and systematized ways of reading the Bible which are strangely similar to some strands of postmodernism. In particular, the church has lived with the gospels virtually all its life, and familiarity has bred a variety of more or less contemptible hermeneutical models. Even sometimes within those circles that claim to take the Bible most seriously—often, in fact, there above all—there is a woeful refusal to do precisely that, particularly with the gospels. The modes of reading and interpretation that have been followed are, in fact, functions of the models of inspiration and authority of scripture that have been held, explicitly or (more often) implicitly within various circles, and which have often made nonsense of any attempt to read the Bible historically. The devout predecessor of deconstructionism is that reading of the text which insists that what the Bible says to *me, now*, is the be-all and end-all of its meaning; a reading which does not want to know about the intention of the evangelist, the life of the early church, or even about what Jesus was actually like. There are some strange bedfellows in the world of literary epistemology.

Often, of course, practice has been better than theory, and a word from the readers' god has been heard despite the awful muddle that readers and interpreters have got themselves into. That simply shows, if anything, that this god is gracious, and perhaps has a sense of humour. It does not excuse a failure to think, or to work out more carefully what is, or ought to be, happening when

[33] See e.g. Crossan 1976, 1980, 1988b.

[34] See Moore 1989, 143–6; and cf. Wilder 1982, 29–33; Thiselton 1992, ch. 3 section 6; and now Crossan 1991. The 'Jesus' whom Crossan wants to find is far more gnostic than the picture one would get from the synoptic tradition; hence his preference for the *Gospel of Thomas* and a reconstructed (and reinterpreted) 'Q' as the favoured sources (see ch. 14 below). But can one, as a good deconstructionist, ever hope to find *any* historical referent, even another deconstructionist (as Crossan supposes Jesus to have been)?

people read the gospels. But to take such a discussion further at this point would require a consideration of the sorts of reading that are appropriate for different sorts of writing, and for the gospels as a special case; and that must be deferred until considerably later.

Protests, then, against the postmodern readings of the Bible are likely to be ineffectual. Unless, that is, those who care about serious reading of the gospels set about exploring ways in which to articulate a better epistemology, leading to a better account of what happens when a text is being read, a better account of what happens when a *sacred* text is being read, a better account of what happens when *a sacred text which purports to be historical* is being read, leading to a better account of what happens when the gospels themselves are being read. Any philosophically minded literary critics looking for a worthwhile life's work might like to consider this as a possible project. I would not pretend that I am sufficiently competent to attempt it myself, nor would I have the time and patience. But, since this chapter is already turning into a *tour de force* of areas where I am not (to say the least) totally competent, I ought to say how I think such a project might proceed.

(iii) Reading and Critical Realism

What we need, I suggest, is a *critical-realist account of the phenomenon of reading, in all its parts.*[35] To one side we can see the positivist or the naïve realist, who move so smoothly along the line from reader to text to author to referent that they are unaware of the snakes in the grass at every step; to the other side we can see the reductionist who, stopping to look at the snakes, is swallowed up by them and proceeds no further. Avoiding both these paths, I suggest that we must articulate a theory which locates the entire phenomenon of text-reading within an account of the storied and relational nature of human consciousness.

Such a theory might look something like this. We (humans in general; the communities of which you and I, as readers, are part) tell ourselves certain stories about the world, and about who we are within it. Within this storytelling it makes sense, it 'fits', that we describe ourselves as reading texts; as we have already seen, even deconstructionists themselves write texts which they want others to read to discover what they, the deconstructionists, intend to say.[36] Within this text-reading activity it makes sense, it 'fits', that we find ourselves, at least sometimes and at least in principle, in contact with the mind

---

[35] I am here conscious of an ongoing debt to Meyer 1989; cf. also his articles of 1990, 1991b.

[36] Compare the point (made by Meyer 1991b, 10 drawing on Bergonzi 1990, 111): 'the followers of Nietzsche and Foucault are passionately persuaded that truth is a mere rhetorical device employed in the service of oppression, and say so at length. What, then, is the status of their saying so? We should give them their choice. Is it false? Or in the service of oppression?' See too Moore's criticisms (1989, 145f.) of Crossan. Moore himself, though in many ways an advocate for a postmodern reading of texts, has provided an essentially *modern* reading of the writers he discusses. See, finally, Norris' critique of Rorty, discussed in Thiselton 1992, ch. 11 section 3.

and intention of the author. Discussing the author's mind may or may not be an easy task; it is in principle both possible and, I suggest, desirable.[37] I for one shall never be convinced that de la Mare did not intend the obvious 'surface' effects of his poem, even though the deeper meanings are, as we have seen, a matter of speculation, hypothesis and discussion. He might, for instance, have written about them elsewhere himself.[38] Nor can I believe that the parallel between Leverkühn and Germany never occurred to Mann while he was writing his novel.

At the same time, it is important to stress that both of these authors wanted their readers to think about the subject-matter of their works, not about them as authors for their own sakes. Their work points neither back to the reader nor inside their own heads. They are constructing neither mirrors nor kaleidoscopes. They are offering telescopes (or perhaps microscopes, which are really the same thing): new ways of viewing a reality which is outside, and different from, reader, text and author alike, though of course vitally related to all three. It thus 'fits' with the story we tell about ourselves and the world that texts and authors should point to realities in the world, to entities beyond themselves. Only a very naïve reader would suggest that the only referent of the poem was a horseman and an empty house in a wood, that the only thing described by Mann's novel was a demon-possessed composer, or that the only reality portrayed in the parable was a tragic everyday story of the grape-farming community. Describing the real referents in such cases is the complex task of serious literary criticism, to which I shall shortly turn.

What we need, then, is a theory of reading which, at the reader/text stage, will do justice *both* to the fact that the reader is a particular human being *and* to the fact that the text is an entity on its own, not a plastic substance to be moulded to the reader's whim. It must also do justice, at the text/author stage, *both* to the fact that the author intended certain things, *and* that the text may well contain in addition other things—echoes, evocations, structures, and the like—which were not present to the author's mind, and of course may well not be present to the reader's mind. We need a both-and theory of reading, not an either-or one.[39] Similarly, we need a theory which will do justice, still at the text/author stage, *both* to the fact that texts, including biblical texts, do not normally represent the whole of the author's mind, even that bit to which they

---

[37] See the staunch defence of this in Meyer 1989, xif., and esp. 17–55. Cf. too Young and Ford 1987, 137: '. . . progress in understanding is a real experience. Meaning is in principle determinable, even if in practice we have to live with large areas of uncertainty, and even if we refuse to restrict it to authorial intention. Debates about meaning are not always settleable, but they are debates about objective realities. There is a difference between eisegesis and exegesis, and the more informed we are, the more it is possible to sense where the line is to be drawn.'

[38] Since we are talking about German ideologies, we might compare the task of interpreting Wagner's operas by means of his little-known prose works, as has been done by Dr Margaret Brearley (1988).

[39] See Funk 1988, 298: 'I share the conviction that the interplay of texts is inevitable and perpetual, but I am also convinced that humankind, on rare occasions, catches glimpses of reality aborning, of fellow men and women without disguises, of the "beyond" of texts.' On this possibility even in modern and postmodern theory, see the discussion of Heidegger's notion of an 'opening' in Thiselton 1992, ch. 3 section 5.

come closest, *and* to the fact that they nevertheless do normally tell us, and in principle tell us truly, quite a bit about him or her. Finally, we need to recognize, at the author/event stage, *both* that authors do not write without a point of view (they are humans, and look at things in particular ways and from particular angles) *and* that they really can speak and write about events and objects (in the full sense of event and object explored in chapter 2) which are not reducible to terms of their own state of mind.

There is a sense, which we cannot explore in detail here, in which this demands a full theory of language. We need to understand, better than we commonly do, how language works. Words which describe events function regularly and properly on all sorts of levels, because events themselves function on all sorts of levels. What a Martian might have seen was human beings putting pieces of paper in little tin boxes; what the politicians at the time saw was a tense election in progress; what the historians will see is the turning-point at which a country moved from one era to another. Language is regularly used to refer to all three levels of 'event'—physical actions, significance perceived or imagined at the time, and significance perceived later—in all sorts of subtle ways, through metaphor, symbol, image and myth. This is inescapable, and needs no apology.[40] And such language itself performs many extra functions: it edifies, annoys, amuses, evokes associations, creates new possibilities of understanding, and so on. The danger is that we set up some sort of reductionism. We might imagine that what we call 'significance' is something artificially 'added on' to the actions (in fact, nobody would have bothered to stuff paper into the boxes if they had not thought they were doing something with wider significance); or that words which invest physical actions with their significance are thus simply decoration or embroidery, to be seen as 'mere metaphor'. (Alternatively, of course, the event can be lost in the significance.) This alerts us once more to the fact that there is no such thing as a 'bare event', as we shall see in the next chapter when discussing history. And if all this is true of language in general, there are special rules and cases within historical writing; within systems of religious language, other special cases; within sacred texts, special cases within special cases; within the gospels, which combine all these and more besides, a highly complex set of questions and problems. Even to begin to address these issues here would take us too far afield.

I suggest, then, that the epistemology which I outlined earlier—that which sees knowledge as part of the responsibility of those made in the image of the creator to act responsibly and wisely within the created world—results, at the level of literature, in a sensitive critical realism. We must renounce the fiction of a god's-eye view of events on the one hand and a collapsing of event into significance or perception on the other. Until we really address this question, most of the present battles about reading the gospels—and most past ones too, for that matter—will be dialogues of the deaf, doomed to failure. But, for a

---

[40] On the importance of metaphor see particularly Ricoeur 1977, discussed helpfully in Thiselton 1992, ch. 10 section 2; Soskice 1985; the suggestive essay of White 1982; and particularly Caird 1980.

start, I suggest a possible hermeneutical model, to be explored more fully on another occasion. It is a hermeneutic of *love*.

In love, at least in the idea of *agape* as we find it in some parts of the New Testament,[41] the lover affirms the reality and the otherness of the beloved. Love does not seek to collapse the beloved into terms of itself; and, even though it may speak of losing itself in the beloved, such a loss always turns out to be a true finding. In the familiar paradox, one becomes fully oneself when losing oneself to another. In the fact of love, in short, both parties are simultaneously affirmed.[42]

When applied to reading texts, this means that the text can be listened to on its own terms, without being reduced to the scale of what the reader can or cannot understand at the moment. If it is puzzling, the good reader will pay it the compliment of struggling to understand it, of living with it and continuing to listen. But however close the reader gets to understanding the text, the reading will still be peculiarly that reader's reading: the subjective is never lost, nor is it necessary or desirable that it should be. At this level, 'love' will mean 'attention': the readiness to let the other *be* the other, the willingness to grow and change in oneself in relation to the other. When we apply this principle to all three stages of the reading process—the relation of readers to texts, of texts to their authors, and beyond that to the realities they purport to describe—it will be possible to make a number of simultaneous affirmations. First, we can affirm *both* that the text does have a particular viewpoint from which everything is seen, *and* at the same time that the reader's reading is not mere 'neutral observation'. Second, we can affirm *both* that the text has a certain life of its own, *and* that the author had intentions of which we can in principle gain at least some knowledge. Third, we can affirm *both* that the actions or objects described may well be, in principle, actions and objects in the public world, *and* that the author was looking at them from a particular, and perhaps distorting, point of view. At each level we need to say both-and, not just either-or.

Each stage of this process becomes a *conversation*, in which misunderstanding is likely, perhaps even inevitable, but in which, through patient listening, real understanding (and real access to external reality) is actually possible and attainable.[43] What I am advocating is a critical realism—though I would prefer to describe it as an epistemology or hermeneutic of love—as the only sort of theory which will do justice to the complex nature of texts in general, of history in general, and of the gospels in particular. Armed with this, we will be able to face the questions and challenges of reading the New Testament with some hope of making sense of it all.

---

[41] I am well aware—and to be aware of such things is part of the model itself—that this word has various other shades of meaning elsewhere: see Barr 1987.

[42] A similar possibility is discussed by Thiselton 1992, ch. 16 section 2.

[43] On the question of whether the 'conversation' model is adequate for this task—a question which goes back to Schleiermacher at least—see now Thiselton 1992, ch. 10 section 3, ch. 11 section 3, discussing Gadamer and Tracy.

3. On Literature

If, then, we may agree that such a thing as literature exists, and that we can read it and talk sense about it without having our words collapse back upon themselves, it is important that we ask, albeit briefly, what literature itself is, and what we ought to do with it. (I take 'literature' here in a fairly broad sense, including most writings of most human beings, but perhaps stopping short of telephone directories, bus-tickets and the like, however valuable they may be as cultural symbols.) Here the now familiar story of modern epistemology repeats itself again, except that examples of the extreme viewpoints might be hard to find. At the extreme positivist end, literature might be conceived simply as the 'neutral' description of the world; the bizarre attempts in some earlier generations to flatten out poetry by reducing metaphor to plain unadorned language seem to have been labouring under this misapprehension. At the other end of the scale, literature has been regarded (and perhaps, as we saw, the Romantic poets encouraged us to regard it[44]) as a collection of subjective feelings.

As the alternative to both these extremes, I suggest that human writing is best conceived as the articulation of worldviews, or, better still, *the telling of stories which bring worldviews into articulation.* This of course happens in a wide variety of ways. Some are quite obvious: the novel, the narrative poem, and the parable all tell stories already, and it is not difficult to describe the move that needs to be made from the specific plot in question (or its sub-plots) to the kind of worldview which is being articulated. Others are not so obvious but just as important in their own way. The short letter to a colleague reinforces our shared narrative world in which arrangements for next term's teaching have to be made in advance, and thus reinforces in turn the larger world in which we both tell ourselves, and each other, the story of universities, of the study and teaching of theology—or, if we are cynical, the story of having a job and not wanting to lose it. The love-letter, no matter how ungrammatical and rhapsodic, tells at a deeper level a very powerful story about what it means to be human. The dry textbook, with its lists and theorems, tells the story of an ordered world and of the possibility of humans grasping that order and so working fruitfully within it. Short poems and aphorisms are to worldviews what snapshots are to the *story* of a holiday, a childhood, a marriage. And so on.

Part at least of the task of literary criticism is therefore, I suggest, to lay bare, and explicate, what the writer has achieved at this level of implied narrative, and ultimately implied worldview, and how.[45] This task can be done even if the writer remains unknown (which is just as well in view of the anonymity of a great many works, not least in the New Testament). But it may be helped on its way by some consideration, even at a hypothetical level, of what the writer

---

[44] See above, p. 55f.

[45] See, for a fascinating description of the analogous task within a very different sphere, that of music, Menuhin 1977, 182–9. 'Like a biochemist discovering that every human cell bears the imprint of the body it belongs to, I had to establish why these notes and no others belonged to this sonata; and it was important that I do it myself, no more accepting ready-made explanations than I would consider myself acquainted with someone at second hand' (184).

was *trying* or intending to do. Here again we have the familiar dichotomy. The positivist critic will say that the purpose of criticism is to establish the 'right' or 'true' meaning of the text, and will assume that there is such a thing and that it can in principle be found. The phenomenalist reader—who in this case might well turn out to be a deconstructionist—will move towards saying that no such thing exists. There is only my reading, your reading and an infinite number of other possible readings. In reply to both extremes, a critical-realist reading of a text will recognize, and take fully into account, the perspective and context of the reader. But such a reading will still insist that, within the story or stories that seem to make sense of the whole of reality, there exist, as essentially other than and different from the reader, texts that can be read, that have a life and a set of appropriate meanings not only potentially independent of their author but also potentially independent of their reader; and that the deepest level of meaning consists in the stories, and ultimately the worldviews, which the texts thus articulate.

Thus the positivist critic, reading the parable of the Wicked Tenants, will seek to locate the parable within a particular historical context, whether the life of Jesus, the preaching of the early church, or the writing of one of the gospels. He will attempt a full and 'objective' description of what it meant at the time. The apparent success of such a project may lure the unwary into thinking that positivism has proved its point—until other commentaries are consulted, where equally 'objective', but quite different, accounts are offered. These may, of course, enter into dialogue with each other. But once they start doing so they are already admitting that positivism is not as simple as it looks, and that perhaps a different model of knowing is to be preferred.

The phenomenalist, by contrast, reads the parable and finds herself addressed by it. Though she realizes that it may have a historical context, what matters is what it says to her today. This account, as we observed earlier, fits to some extent both the fundamentalist and the deconstructionist. What cannot be done with this sort of reading, however, is to claim any normativity for it: just because the text says this to *me*, there is no reason why it should say it to *you*. If we are not careful, the claim 'this parable tells me that I must face up to my god-given responsibilities' or 'this parable speaks of Jesus dying for me' will collapse into statements of no more public significance than 'I like salt' or 'I like Sibelius'. The phenomenalist purchases the apparent certainty and security of her statements in relation to the text at the high cost of forfeiting public relevance.

Critical realists, however, will attempt to avoid both pitfalls. We must be aware of our own viewpoint. Readers of texts about masters and servants may well have instinctive sympathies on one side or the other; readers of texts about fathers and sons, likewise; readers of texts that they take to be in some way normative (or that they know others regard in this way) come with certain hopes and, perhaps, fears. We read this story, in other words, in the light of all sorts of other stories that we habitually carry about with us—that is to say, in the light of our fundamental worldview. Nevertheless, it is precisely part of the story that we continually tell ourselves, as making most sense of our being in the world, that there exist, in addition to our own private stories, *other* stories, other texts, including those found in the New Testament, and that these stories may, if we attend to them, reaffirm, modify, or subvert some or all of the stories we have been telling ourselves. There are other worldviews; they are expressed in works of literature; and they interact with our own. Critical-realist reading is a *lectio catholica semper reformanda*: it seeks (that is) to be true to itself, and to the public world, while always open to the possibility of challenge, modification, and subversion.

We therefore read the text, examining it in all its historical otherness to ourselves as well as all its transtemporal relatedness to ourselves, and being aware of the complex relation that exists between those two things. When we come to the parable, we read it as a story which already has a history; a story about Israel which is receiving a new and worrying twist; a story about Israel which turns out to be a story about Jesus; a story which will have meant one thing in the ministry of Jesus and something rather different in its retelling by the early church, just as a book about a novel is a different sort of thing from the novel itself. And, even though as part of our overall (and in principle subvertible) story we may believe that we can, again in principle, achieve some sort of historical accuracy in these readings, the 'meaning' that the parable *continues to have* will in several important respects remain open. There will be an appropriateness about certain potential meanings, and an inappropriateness about others. Discussion of where different suggested 'meanings' come on this scale of appropriateness can and must take place; this is not a private game. And the test for new proposed meanings will have to do with their demonstrable continuity with the historical meanings. As to what counts as continuity, that must itself remain open for the moment. The point at issue here is that the story has brought a worldview to birth. By reading it historically, I can detect that it was always intended as a subversive story, undermining a current worldview and attempting to replace it with another. By reading it with my own ears open, I realize that it may subvert my worldview too.

Applying all this on a wider front to Jewish and Christian literature of the first century, we discover without difficulty that the great majority of the material has an easily discernible story-form, either on the surface of the text or not far beneath it.[46] But there are, in both religious traditions, two observably different types of stories. There are, first, stories which embody and articulate a worldview even though it is clear that the stories do not refer to events which happened in the public world. The parables obviously fall into this category; so within Judaism, does a book like *Joseph and Aseneth*.[47] There are, second, stories which embody and articulate the worldview by telling what *has* (more or less) actually happened in the public domain, *since that is what the worldview purports to explain*. Within Judaism, this is obviously the case with books like 1 and 2 Maccabees, and with Josephus' *Antiquities* and *Jewish*

---

[46] In the case of Paul, this has been argued most persuasively by Hays 1983 (who lists among his predecessors Via 1975) and Petersen 1985; see ch. 13 (b) below.
[47] Charlesworth 1985, 177–247.

War. Josephus is well aware of the charge that he made it all up, and it clearly matters to him to assert that he did not.[48] Within Christianity, the issue is of course much controverted. The book that professes most loudly that it was written by someone who knew what he was talking about (John's gospel, cf. 21.24) is the one most usually regarded as a story of the first rather than the second type. A similar irony is found in the work of some critics who regard the 'Gnostic' gospels as being stories of the second type, closer up to the events, and the synoptics as stories of the first type, aetiological myths for a brand of Christianity out of touch with its founder.[49] We will have to examine these issues further in Part IV below. But we can at least say this: within the Jewish worldview, it mattered vitally that certain events should happen within public history, precisely because the great majority of Jews believed, as we shall see, that their god was the creator of the world who continued to act within his creation. Though they were quite capable of expressing all or part of their story in narratives without actual historical referent, such stories are therefore essentially derivative, designed to draw out, reinforce, or perhaps subvert the emphasis of stories of the second type. A story about a god who did not and would not act in history would subvert the basic Jewish story so thoroughly that there would be nothing left. That is what Marcion and the Gnostics did; interestingly, those modern movements that are closest to Gnosticism are also the loudest contemporary voices urging the de-Judaization of the Jesus-tradition.[50]

At this point I suggest that the critic who wishes to do justice to the texts themselves, rather than deconstructing them beyond recognition, must come to terms with the need to speak of matters in the extra-linguistic world if what is said about the linguistic world is not to lapse into incoherence. This case is one of the main arguments of Anthony Thiselton's recent work.[51] Drawing on the speech-act theory propounded by Searle, and the philosophical arguments of Wolterstorff, Habermas and above all Wittgenstein, Thiselton argues convincingly that for a great many speech-acts there is a vital and non-negotiable element, which consists of the 'fit' between what is said and events in the extra-linguistic world. Though much of his attention is directed to speech-acts which have to do with present and future non-linguistic events, he also includes explicitly the point I here wish to highlight: that a vital part in appropriating at least *some* biblical texts is the work of historical reconstruction.[52] That such

---

[48] cf. *Apion* 1.53: '. . . it is the duty of one who promises to present his readers with actual facts first to obtain an exact knowledge of them himself, either through having been in close touch with the events, or by inquiry from those who knew them. That duty I consider myself to have amply fulfilled in both my works.' Cf. too his polemic against historical fiction in 1.293. The fact that modern critics have little difficulty in criticizing Josephus (or the books of the Maccabees) by these standards does not mean that Josephus did not know what he was talking about. See the discussion of historiography in the next chapter.

[49] See e.g. Mack 1988; Crossan 1991, and ch. 14 below.

[50] See particularly Mack 1988, and the work of the Claremont school of which that book is a characteristic product.

[51] Thiselton 1992, especially chs. 8 and 16.

[52] Thiselton 1992, ch. 15 section 1. See too Ricoeur 1978, especially 191, on the way in which historical narrative, though emphatically not to be conceived positivistically, nevertheless includes a referent outside the world of the text itself.

reconstruction is possible as well as desirable I shall argue in the next chapter. I have come to the view that arguments against its possibility can often be reduced to arguments against its desirability. The philosophical worldview which makes it undesirable offers at the same time tools with which to render it apparently impossible. This whole Part of the book is designed to subvert such a worldview. The literary critic working on documents from first-century religious movements must therefore draw out and make explicit the story which the writings are telling or to which they are, in their varied ways, contributing. This analysis of worldview-by-means-of-story is central to the task. In doing this it is of course also necessary to examine the story or stories that the writings are themselves addressing, reinforcing, subverting or whatever. And, just as the critic at work on de la Mare or Mann must also show *how* the texts in question achieve the function they *do* achieve, and must also, perhaps, enquire whether this is the function the author intended, so the New Testament critic must study the parts in the light of the whole, drawing out the relation between form and content, structure and impact, art and effect. There is, no doubt, much more to be said on this whole subject. But we have at least created some space in which we may take our stand and proceed with the task. Before we move on to the major components of the New Testament's subject-matter, history and theology, we must look in more detail at the central category which we are using all along. We have seen throughout our argument that one of the most basic themes in human consciousness is that of *story*. In addition, it is beyond question that a good part of the New Testament (and of the Jewish literature that forms part at least of its proper context) consists of actual stories. We must therefore look more closely at what stories are, and how they work.

4. The Nature of Stories

(i) The Analysis of Stories: Narrative Structure

The way in which stories possess the power they do, by which they actually change how people think, feel and behave, and hence change the way the world actually is, can be seen more clearly by means of an analysis of the essential components which they (stories) contain. Among the many features which have been studied in recent years are: narrator, point of view, standards of judgment, implied author, ideal reader, implied reader, style, rhetorical techniques, and so on. About all this there is a good deal that could be said for which there is here neither time nor space.[53] Much attention, however, has been focused on one element in particular, namely, the narrative structure of stories and how it operates; and this element will form a vital part of several arguments I shall advance later in the book. I here follow, more or less, the

---

[53] See the literature already cited, especially the works of Patte, Petersen, Funk and Thiselton; and compare Rhoads and Michie 1982.

analysis of stories which was worked out by A. J. Griemas, following the pioneering work of Vladimir Propp.[54] About this a few preliminary remarks seem necessary.

Griemas' work has often been incorporated into biblical studies during the last twenty years, in (for example) the work of D. O. Via and J. D. Crossan, discussed briefly above. Generally, this has been done in the service of a formalist and/or structuralist approach, which as we saw has been a way of reading the text, and perhaps attempting to say something 'objective' about it,[55] as distinct from an approach which attempted to locate the text within the history of an author or a community, or to use it as the basis for historical reconstruction. It might be thought, therefore, that to use Griemas is of itself to buy into a structuralist model which is already somewhat *passé* and is in any case decidedly anti-historical. Against this, and in favour of a cautious use of Griemas-like narrative analysis within the present project, I suggest that the recent emphasis on narrative, within the theories of epistemology, hermeneutics (see chapter 2 above) and historical study (chapter 4 below) demands that we seek an understanding of how narratives work, and that we reuse Griemas within this setting—not to follow him slavishly or in a formalist setting, but within the service of a broader historical and hermeneutical programme. Griemas' method is doubtless not foolproof, and I shall not here enter into the debates about it.[56] As usual, the proof of the pudding will be in the eating.

Griemas' scheme can best be seen in a series of diagrams. The complexity of these, particularly to those unfamiliar with Griemas and his designs, may seem forbidding, as though one were explaining an unknown by an unknowable.[57] But the point of what might seem tortuous analysis will, I hope, gradually become apparent. Without close attention to the different phases of how the story actually works, the interpreter is almost bound to jump too quickly to this or that (probably wrong) conclusion, particularly when the story in question is over-familiar through frequent retelling. The requirements of the method force us to slow down and attend carefully at every stage to what is in fact going on. I shall suggest later that failure to attend to the actual story told by Jews and Christians alike—i.e., the story of the Old Testament—was the basic charge that the early church levelled at Judaism. It might also be suggested that a similar failure on the part of contemporary Christians is widespread, and is moreover at the root of a great deal of misunderstanding of the Christian tradition in general and the gospels in particular.

---

[54] See Griemas 1966, 1970; Propp 1968. On these, see especially Galland 1976; Patte 1976, 1978. For an application of the method to Pauline exegesis, see Hays 1983, 92–103; Wright 1991a, ch. 10; and, for other uses of recent literary theory in Pauline exegesis, Moore 1989, xx n.18.

[55] See Thiselton 1992, ch. 13 section 4; and cf. above, p. 57.

[56] See e.g. Thiselton 1992, ch. 13 section 3.

[57] See Moore 1989, xix, for a description of one scenario: 'The structuralist would lumber along, laden down with some massive Griemasian ... apparatus to arrive at some conclusion where, almost invariably, the unencumbered historical exegete would be waiting, having already attained it by means of a few economical strides.'

A basic and typical story may be divided up into three moments. There is the *initial sequence*, in which a problem is set up or created, with a hero or heroine entrusted with a task which appears difficult or impossible; the *topical sequence*, in which the central character tries to solve the problem thus set and eventually manages to do so; and the *final sequence*, in which the initial task is finally completed. Thus:

> *a.* initial sequence: Little Red Riding-Hood is given some food by her mother to take to her grandmother, but is prevented by the wolf from doing so;
> *b.* topical sequence: rescue eventually comes in the form of the woodcutter;
> *c.* final sequence: Little Red Riding-Hood is thus able to deliver the food to her grandmother after all.

These sequences can be set out in helpful diagrams, using the following scheme:

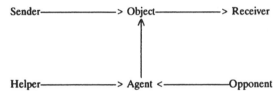

The 'sender' is the initiator of the action, who commissions the 'agent' to perform it, i.e. to take or convey the 'object' to the 'receiver'. The 'agent' is prevented from doing what is required by a force or forces, i.e. the 'opponent', and is, at least potentially, helped by the 'helper'. In the initial sequence, obviously, the opponent (which might simply be a defect of character in the agent) is more powerful than the agent and any available helpers. There would otherwise be no story, only a sentence: 'Little Red Riding-Hood was sent by her mother to take some food to her grandmother; she did so and they were all happy.' This might be charming, but it is hardly a story. It has no plot. It does not embody a worldview, except possibly an extremely naïve one. Thus:

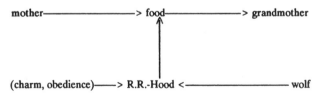

For all her charm and obedience—the only things she can rely on—the heroine is not able to prevent the wolf thwarting the plan, eating the grandmother, and threatening to eat her too. The mother's plan of providing food for the inhabitant of the cottage in the wood is receiving a nightmarish twist. But then the topical sequence provides help, as it must if the story is not again to be aborted: 'Little Red Riding-Hood took some food to her grandmother, but a wolf ate them both'; this again is not a story in the full sense. In the topical sequence, importantly, the agent of the initial sequence becomes the receiver, since she is the one who now needs something, namely, help to get out of the mess. There is no apparent 'sender' in this particular instance, as in many sequences in many stories. This poses no problem, and in fact often lends an air of highly effective mystery, as in Tolkien's *The Lord of the Rings*, where the reader is always aware that even the seldom-seen leaders on either side themselves represent powers which stand beyond and behind them.

Topical sequences take the same form as initial sequences: but in the nature of the case the 'Agent' of the first scheme is the 'Receiver' of this one, since the agent now needs rescuing or helping. A new 'Agent' is therefore required, to bring a new 'Object'—which will have something to do with releasing the Agent from her plight—to the rescue. More opponents might or might not be added at this stage, too. Thus:

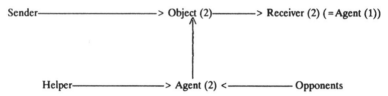

When we apply this to the topical sequence of the folk-tale, this is what we find:

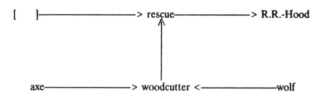

The axe is too powerful for the wolf; the unfortunate girl is rescued; grandmother, having been delivered from the wolf's stomach (at least in some versions of the story), receives the food at last. The final sequence thus repeats the initial sequence, with the important difference that it is now successful:

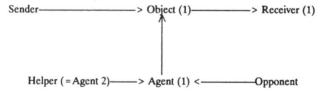

So, applying this to our heroine and her gallant rescuer:

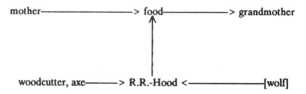

John Barton, one of the clearest recent exponents of different methods of biblical study, makes the point that the story demands such an ending: if the woodcutter had freed the wolf and married Red Riding Hood, an entirely different worldview would be brought to birth.[58] That is of course possible: one can imagine a disciple of Sartre propounding such a thing; but it is not what the story was pointing to all along.[59] This is the syntax of folk-tales: this is simply how they work. If this syntax is altered, a powerfully subversive movement of thought is brought to expression.

We must of course recognize right away that most stories are far more complex than this one. They usually contain subdivisions, plots within plots, and so forth; we shall see in a moment a well-known biblical story that has essentially one plot within another. And it must also be said that a major division of narrative, namely, tragedy, does not fit so obviously into the scheme. In folk-tales, things tend to work out well in the end: this no doubt has a lot to do with the functions that they are designed to serve. I think tragedy can be given an outline of its own, which fits Griemas' scheme in its own appropriate way. The story I shall presently tell will illustrate this too.[60]

As we shall see, the many twists and turns of the plot of a story, which will mostly fall in subdivisions of the 'topical sequence', exhibit miniature sequences of the same form, often right down to small details. Such minute analysis has in fact been practised already on the gospels,[61] with the text being put under the microscope to see what is in fact 'going on' behind a narrative whose outward features are often so well known that they prohibit, rather than encourage, fresh understanding. Although this exercise sometimes seems so dense that it becomes in its turn a new barrier to understanding, in principle it can and often does enable us to sort out, for example, where the main emphases of a narrative lie (they may not be at all where 'normal' readings of the text have conditioned us to look), and how the diverse parts relate to the whole. There is urgent need for better control within the practice of this method, for finding some ways of assessing the respective assertions of critics who have used it.[62] I believe, for instance, that many of those who have practised such analysis have come with unexamined presuppositions about the subject-matter of the text which ought to be challenged.[63] But in principle narrative analysis is more than just a useful exercise. In an (academic) world that has largely forgotten what stories are, and are for, it is a necessary task if we are to recapture important dimensions of the text.

---

[58] Barton 1984, 116, referring to Propp and others.

[59] Though on Sartre see Meyer 1991b, 9f., arguing that Sartrean novels are ultimately self-contradictory: 'an authentically Sartrean novel would be a chaotic muddle. But novelists, including Sartre, labor under a first commandment, Thou shalt not be dull.'

[60] 4 Ezra and 2 Bar. might be considered examples of a still more tragic story: see Part III below.

[61] Marin 1976a, 1976b; Chabrol 1976; Patte 1978, ch. 3; etc.

[62] See Patte 1978, ch. 4.

[63] e.g. Marin 1976b, 74, assuming that the story is simply about 'God' and 'Man' (i.e. not about Israel specifically).

(ii) The Analysis of Stories: The Wicked Tenants

As an example, let us briefly look at our old friend, the parable of the Wicked
Tenants (Mk. 12.1–12 and parallels). Here we find a clear enough structure,
which turns out to be a plot inside a plot, the inner plot being essentially
tragic. The story begins with the owner planting a vineyard, in order (as it
appears) to get fruit for himself, using tenants as his agents, despite (as it
appears) their greed:

1. *Initial Sequence*

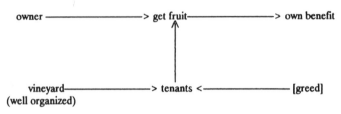

So far, so good. The owner sends messengers to the tenants to get the fruit;
this is the first move of the inner story. The tenants, however, turn out to be
not only the object of the messengers' journey but also the opponents to the
plan; this precipitates the tragic nature of the inner story, the fact that its conclusion will carry a sad irony.[64]

2. *Topical Sequence (1)* [= *new Initial Sequence for inner story*]

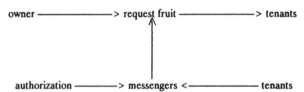

This initial move having failed, the owner sends his son to take the place of the
messengers:

3. *Topical Sequence (2)* [= *Topical Sequence of inner story*]

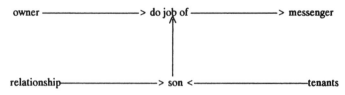

There are now two things that remain to be done if the original plan is to
succeed. As the tragic climax of the inner story, the tenants must reap the fate

---

[64] This reflects the same concern that we see in Tannehill 1985b, though I do not agree with
Tannehill's assessment of Luke-Acts as a whole.

they have sown for themselves. And, as the successful climax of the outer story, the original plan must somehow be accomplished despite the rebellion of the tenants. Thus, first, the owner comes in person and destroys the tenants:[65]

4. *Topical Sequence (3)* [= *Final Sequence of inner story*]

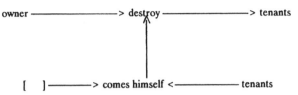

(We will see shortly that the blank in the 'helper' position is significant.) Finally, he installs new tenants who will produce the fruit he requires, thus returning at last to the initial sequence.[66] But instead of the same tenants finally doing what they were supposed to, like Little Red Riding-Hood finally delivering the food to her grandmother, the tragic nature of the inner story means that the original agent must be supplanted by a new one:

5. *Final Sequence of Main Story*

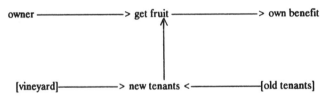

What do we learn about the story by this means? Much in every way. For a start, I think we are bound to highlight (more than we might otherwise do) the question of the owner's intentions. Clearly, they have to do with something beyond the life of the vineyard itself. The vineyard is there for a purpose. Within the historical settings of the parable (i.e. the obvious setting within the work of the evangelists, and the hypothetically historical one within the life of Jesus) the vineyard is pretty certainly Israel; and the story presupposes that Israel is not called into being for her own benefit, but for the purposes of her covenant god, purposes which stretch beyond her own borders.

Second, the role of the son is more limited than it might be thought to be by a less careful reading, over-conscious of a later christology. There is nothing in the death of the son that suggests anything other than the failure of sequence (3), no suggestion within the narrative possibilities that somehow this death might be the means of the story's turning the corner—except in the negative sense that, having nothing else left to do, the owner must now come and sort out the mess. Within the drama of the story, the son is basically the last, and

---

[65] In the Matthaean account (21.41) this part of the story is added by the hearers in response to Jesus' question as to what the owner will now do.

[66] It is only Matthew (21.41) who makes explicit the fact that the new tenants will give him the fruit, but this is clearly implicit in the other accounts.

most poignant, failed messenger. After his failure, there can be nothing but disaster to follow.

Third, we note that in sequences (2) and (4) the tenants appear in two different positions. This may perhaps be part of the essence of tragedy: that characters in the story who are designed to be involved in some other role, as receivers or subjects, turn up in the same story as opponents. (The ambiguous role of the disciples in the gospels, taken as wholes, ought to be considered from this point of view.) Unless another sub-plot intervenes through which they are removed from this category, their part of the story is bound to end in disaster.

Fourth, within the story's function in its historical contexts, the new tenants who appear as agents in sequence (5) cannot be identified (as one might at first have thought) simply as Gentiles. The owner's intention was to achieve something *through* the tenants, and this 'something', as becomes clear in various ways in the gospels' overall narratives, seems to be the *blessing* of the Gentiles.[67] The 'new tenants', through whom this is now to be achieved, cannot therefore themselves be Gentiles *per se*, but must be a new group of Jews through whom the purpose will be fulfilled.[68]

Fifth, the blank under 'helper' in sequence (4) may hide a significant implication. Blanks in stories are usually pregnant, as we saw in relation to the 'Sender' in *The Lord of the Rings*, and as might be seen in the unmentioned 'Object' in de la Mare's 'The Listeners'. Within the contexts of the story (this comes out clearest in Luke, but is implicit in Matthew and Mark as well) the means by which the owner (Israel's god) will come himself and destroy the tenants will turn out to be military action taken by Rome. This prepares the way, within the larger narrative of the gospels, for the denunciation of the Temple and the prophecy of its downfall (Mark 13 and parallels).

In addition to these exegetical points, though, there is an issue of much wider significance which this analysis has in principle opened up. The parable, like most of Jesus' parables, tells the story of Israel—that is, it sets out the Jewish worldview in the regular appropriate manner—but gives it a startling new twist. Once we grasp the storied structure of worldviews in general, and of the Jewish worldview in particular, we are in possession of a tool which, though not often used thus, can help us to grasp what was at stake in the debates between first-century Judaism and first-century Christianity. It was not just a matter of 'theological' debate, in the sense of controversy over a few abstract doctrines. Nor can the problem be reduced to terms of social pressures and groupings, in the sense of a controversy between Jews and non-Jews or between observant and non-observant Jews. It was, at a much more fundamental level, a controversy about *different tellings of the story of Israel's god, his people, and the world*. And it is in principle possible to plot these different tellings on grids such as those we have just used, to lay out in detail the ways in which the stories were being told, and so to grasp what was really at issue in

---

[67] See chs. 13–15 below.

[68] This could be queried on the basis of Matthew's explanatory note (21.43), where the vineyard is given to a nation (*ethnos*) that produces the fruits. This cannot be discussed here.

the first century. Tasks of this nature will be one feature of the remainder of this book and, indeed, of the whole project.

One final reflection. This analysis of the parable opens a window on the way in which stories in the gospels, and the story of the gospel itself, characteristically articulate tragedy within comedy, the failure of one set of agents within the 'success' of the overall plan.[69] The story of Jesus himself, of death and resurrection, suffering and vindication, has this shape; so does the story told by Christians about Israel, the people of the creator god. The story of the Wicked Tenants thus brings to birth the same narrative structure as some of the major presentations of the early Christian worldview.

(iii) Jesus, Paul and the Jewish Stories

The parable of the Wicked Tenants, obviously, does not stand alone. Telling stories was (according to the synoptic gospels) one of Jesus' most characteristic modes of teaching. And, in the light of the entire argument so far, it would clearly be quite wrong to see these stories as mere illustrations of truths that could in principle have been articulated in a purer, more abstract form. They were ways of breaking open the worldview of Jesus' hearers, so that it could be remoulded into the worldview which he, Jesus, was commending. His stories, like all stories in principle, invited his hearers into a new world, making the implicit suggestion that the new worldview be tried on for size with a view to permanent purchase. As we shall see in the next Part of the book, Israel's theology had nearly always been characteristically expressed in terms of explicit story: the story of the Exodus, of the Judges, of David and his family, of Elijah and Elisha, of exile and restoration—and, within the eventual Hebrew canon, the story of creation and the patriarchs overarching all the others and giving expression to their perceived larger significance. Jesus was (in this respect) simply continuing a long tradition.

If it is true that all worldviews are at the deepest level shorthand formulae to express stories, this is particularly clear in the case of Judaism. Belief in one god, who called Israel to be his people, is the very foundation of Judaism. The only proper way of talking about a god like this, who makes a world and then acts within it, is through narration. To 'boil off' an abstract set of propositions as though one were thereby getting to a more foundational statement would actually be to falsify this worldview at a basic point. This is not to say that we cannot use shorthand phrases and words to refer, in a few syllables, to a complex story-form worldview which it would be tedious to spell out each time. Thus the phrase 'monotheism and election' (see chapter 9 below) does not refer to two abstracted entities existing outside space and time. It is a way of summoning into the mind's eye an entire worldview. In this, as we shall describe presently, Israel told and retold the story of how there was one god, the creator, and of how he had chosen Israel to be his special possession, and of how therefore he would eventually restore her fortunes and thereby bring his

[69] cf. the remarks of D. O. Via in the foreword to Beardslee 1969, vi; and Via 1967, *passim*.

whole creation to its intended fulfilment. To provide the whole explanation each time would be impossibly wordy. It would also, in any case, be unnecessary—provided one remembers that, like so many theological terms, words like 'monotheism' are late constructs, convenient shorthands for sentences with verbs in them, and that sentences with verbs in them are the real stuff of theology, not mere childish expressions of a 'purer' abstract truth.

What *sort* of stories are most characteristic of Jews in this period? As we have already suggested, stories of all sorts can express the set of beliefs held by most Jews, including the belief that their god was the creator of the world; but this belief (unlike various forms of dualism, for instance) most naturally and characteristically comes to birth in stories about *events in the real world*. That is, when creational and covenantal monotheists tell their story, the most basic level of story for their worldview is *history*. To say that we can analyse stories successfully without reference to their possible public reference, and therefore that we cannot or should not make such a reference, is to commit the kind of epistemological mistake against which I have been arguing in the last two chapters. It is to deny referent by emphasizing sense-data. If we fail to see the importance of the actual historical nature of some at least of the stories told by Jews in this period, we fail to grasp the significance, in form as well as content, of the stories themselves. It is only if we insist on reading Jewish stories within a set of cultural assumptions alien to their worldview and underlying story that we can imagine them to be talking either about a god who does not act within history or who will one day, with a sigh of relief, bring history to a full stop.[70] But this is already taking us too far off our present target.

What is true of pre-Christian Jewish stories is also true of early Christian ones. If Jesus or the evangelists tell stories, this does not mean that they are leaving history or theology out of the equation and doing something else instead. If, as we have seen, this is how Israel's theology (her belief in the creator as the covenant god, and vice versa) found characteristic expression, we should not be surprised if Christian theology, at least in its early forms, turns out to be very similar. What we have to do, as historians, is to find out how to call up the ancient worldview to modern gaze, so that it can be discussed clearly, and so that new moves that were occurring within it may be plotted with historical accuracy. We have, in other words, to learn to read the stories with our eyes open. That part of the historical task which deals with the worldviews of the societies and individuals under scrutiny must involve itself with the careful investigation of the stories, implicit and explicit, which they told to one another and to the world outside.

Thus, as we will see in Part IV, when the early church told stories about Jesus these stories were not, as might be imagined, mere random selections of anecdotes. They were not without a sense of an overall story into which they might fit, or of a narrative shape to which such smaller stories would conform. From the smallest units which form-criticism can isolate to the longest of the early Christian gospels, the stories that were told possess a shape which can in principle be studied, plotted, and compared with other tellings of the Jewish,

---

[70] On this point see Pannenberg 1970, 15–80, esp. 77–80; and chs. 8–10 below.

and the Christian, story. These somewhat obvious tellings of the Jesus-story will form an important part of our later argument.

But what about Paul? Surely he forswore the story-form, and discussed God, Jesus, the Spirit, Israel and the world in much more abstract terms? Was he not thereby leaving behind the world of the Jewish story-theology, and going off on his own into the rarefied territory of abstract Hellenistic speculation? The answer is an emphatic no. As has recently been shown in relation to some key areas of Paul's writing, the apostle's most emphatically 'theological' statements and arguments are in fact expressions of *the essentially Jewish story now redrawn around Jesus.*[71] This can be seen most clearly in his frequent statements, sometimes so compressed as to be almost formulaic, about the cross and resurrection of Jesus: what is in fact happening is that Paul is telling, again and again, the whole story of God, Israel and the world as now compressed into the story of Jesus. So, too, his repeated use of the Old Testament is designed not as mere proof-texting, but, in part at least, to suggest new ways of reading well-known stories, and suggest that they find a more natural climax in the Jesus-story than elsewhere. This whole theme must of course be fully explored later; here I simply mention it in case anyone should think that Paul was in fact an exception to the rule I am formulating. In fact, he is an excellent example of it.

Our task, therefore, throughout this entire project, will involve the discernment and analysis, at one level or another, of first-century stories and their implications. Stories, both in the shape and in the manner of their telling, are the crucial agents that invest 'events' with 'meaning'. The way the bare physical facts are described, the point at which tension or climax occurs, the selection and arrangement—all these indicate the meaning which the event is believed to possess.[72] Our overall task is to discuss the historical origin of Christianity, and, in complex relation to that, the theological question of 'god'; and the thicket where the quarry hides, in each case, may be labelled Story. For the historian, trying to understand the worldview, mindset, motivation and intention (see chapter 4 below) of Jesus, of Paul and of the evangelists, to hunt for the quarry means not least to understand the stories the characters were telling, both verbally in their preaching and writing, and in action in the paths they chose to tread; to see how these stories worked, where their emphases lay, and particularly where they constituted a challenge, implicit or explicit, to the stories told in the Judaism and paganism of the day. We must give, as we have seen, particular attention to the difference, as well as the similarity, between the stories they told which functioned without relation to possible referents in the public world, and those that would lose their point unless they concerned historical reality. And, in attempting this complex task, the theologian will find that the question of 'god' cannot fail to be addressed at the same time.

I am not here concerned to discuss what label we should assign to this composite task (Literary Criticism? History? Theology?). That it faces the his-

---

[71] See Hays 1983, 1989; Fowl 1990; Wright 1991a, ch. 10; and ch. 13 below.

[72] As a good example, see Caird 1980, 211, listing ten different ways in which the NT writers describe the death of Jesus.

torian and theologian as a necessary task, in principle a possible task, and in the current state of scholarship a vital and timely task, I am quite certain. And it is surely obvious where we must look next. Having examined knowledge and literature, we are now in a position to examine one particular sort of knowledge, one particular sort of literature. We must move inwards, from story to history.

Chapter Four

HISTORY AND THE FIRST CENTURY

1. Introduction

Historical knowledge, I suggested in chapter 2, is indeed a kind of *knowledge*. We need to make this point clearly, not least after the last chapter. In a good deal of modern literary criticism, as we have seen, there is so much emphasis on the text apart from the author, and indeed on the reader apart from the text, that any idea that one might be reading a text which referred to something beyond itself looks so wildly ambitious that it is left out of consideration entirely—at least in theory, and at least when convenient. But this seems to me fundamentally counter-intuitive. The most convinced deconstructionist will still trace back the ancestry of this movement to Foucault, Nietzsche, Saussure or whoever. And to those for whom the study and writing of history is their everyday concern, the qualms of postmodernism will seem incredibly, almost impossibly, over-cautious, shy and retiring. We simply *can* write history. We can know things about what has happened in the past.

But what kind of knowledge is this? There is, of course, no room here for a complete discussion of the nature of history itself.[1] I shall confine myself to some broad general discussion to begin with, arguing for a 'critical realist' theory of what history is and does, and then apply this position to the major historical problems that await us in the body of the project. Throughout, however, we will discover that the more we look at 'history' in itself, the more we realize that history cannot exist by itself. It points beyond. In our specific area, it is impossible to talk about the origin of Christianity without being confronted by the question of god, just as, when considering theology, we will discover that the converse is also true. History, we will see, is vital, but by itself it is not enough.

We begin, then, with a brief account of what history is. The word 'history' is regularly used in two quite different but related ways, to refer to (1) actual happenings in the real world and (2) what people write about actual happenings in the real world. Although the second of these is technically the more correct (it is the only meaning in the *Concise Oxford Dictionary*) it is important

---

[1] Among the important works that can only be mentioned, not discussed in detail, are those of Collingwood 1956 [1946], 1968; Butterfield 1969; Elton 1984 [1967]; and Doran 1990. I have found particularly helpful Carr 1987 [1961] (on which, however, see Elton 24–8); Fornara 1983; Meyer 1989, *passim*; Gilkey 1976, part 1; Florovsky 1974, 31–65; and Caird 1980, ch. 12.

to recognize the presence of the other, at least in popular speech: it is not obviously self-contradictory to say 'I know it isn't written down anywhere, but it actually happened *in history*'. To confuse these two meanings, history-as-events and history-as-writing-about-events, as is often done, provides scope for a good deal of frustrating misunderstanding. I shall be focusing attention for much of this chapter on the latter, but in such a way as to include, not exclude, the former: history, I shall argue, is neither 'bare facts' nor 'subjective interpretations', but is rather *the meaningful narrative of events and intentions*.

The human activity of writing, including the writing of history, is itself an actual happening in the real world. As a result, the confusion between history-as-event and history-as-writing can become greater still; but recognizing this fact is also one way out of the difficulty. It is when historians write as if they did not have a point of view, as if they themselves were ahistorical observers, that the trouble starts. And that is where we ourselves must begin.

2. The Impossibility of 'Mere History'

There is not, nor can there be, any such thing as a bare chronicle of events without a point of view.[2] The great Enlightenment dream of simply recording 'what actually happened' is just that: a dream. The dreamer is once more the positivist, who, looking at history, believes that it is possible to have instant and unadulterated access to 'events'. At a naïve level, this results in the pre-critical view:

Observer   Evidence   Past Event
--------->   ---------->
simply looking at the evidence . . . and having direct access to the 'facts'

At a more sophisticated level, awareness that evidence can mislead gives rise to a chastened positivism: the observer sifts the evidence, and reckons that, though some of it is more or less worthless, other bits give the desired direct access.[3] This is the analogy of the positivistic rejection of metaphysics in favour of supposedly 'hard' scientific knowledge:

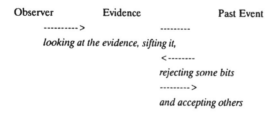

----

[2] cf. Carr 1987 [1961], *passim*.
[3] There is more than a hint of this in Sanders 1985, 321–7.

But (to repeat my opening assertion) this dream of finding bare and unvarnished facts does not correspond to waking reality. This fairly obvious point may be spelled out briefly as follows.

At a general level, it is clear from a moment's thought that all history involves selection. History shares this with other knowing. At any given waking moment I am aware of a vast number of sense-impressions, out of which I make a very limited selection for my current focus of attention and interest. (One of the reasons why art, or for that matter falling in love, are what they are, may perhaps be that they involve the heady experience of a wider-than-usual set of simultaneous selections.) At the most trivial level, any attempt to record 'what happened' without selection would fail, for the sheer overwhelming volume of information—every breath taken by every human being, every falling leaf, every passing cloud in the sky. *Some* human breaths might be worth recording: that of a person thought to be dead, for instance. Some falling leaves and passing clouds might suddenly attain significance, depending on the context (consider the small cloud which Elijah's servant saw from the top of Mount Carmel). But even a video camera set up at random would not result in a completely 'neutral' perspective on events. It must be sited in one spot only; it will only have one focal length; it will only look in one direction. If in one sense the camera never lies, we can see that in another sense it never does anything else. It excludes far more than it includes.

In order, then, to make any statements about the past, human beings have to engage in a massive programme of selection. We do this all the time, and become quite good at it, swiftly selecting tiny fragments of our lives and arranging them into narratives, anecdotes, family legends, and so on. And such a process inevitably involves a major element of *interpretation*. We are trying to make *sense* of the world in which we live. If we do not we are being bathsponges, not humans. All knowing and understanding has to do with reflection on the part of human beings: all knowledge comes *via* somebody's perceptions and reflections. As we saw in chapter 2, the legacy of positivism often seduces us into imagining that a 'fact' is a 'purely objective' thing, unalloyed by the process of knowing on anybody's part.[4] But in reality what we call 'facts' always belong in a context of response, perception, and interaction—a process which is both complex and continuing. Stories, as we have seen, are more fundamental than 'facts'; the parts must be seen in the light of the whole.

This becomes more obviously true, and at a more serious level, when we try to talk about events in the past. Suppose, for example, we try to make a small

---

[4] See Florovsky 1974, 34ff. A good example of the view I am criticizing can be found in Nineham 1976, 187f.: 'Because the early Christians belonged to a period before the rise of scientific history, and were mostly unlettered men at that, they not only mingled history and story inextricably together, but it must be confessed they sometimes allowed the demands of the story to modify the details of the history. It may be worth repeating that there was no intent to deceive in this; at that period it seemed perfectly natural . . . to modify a historical narrative in such a way as to bring out the place of the incident in the total story . . . This does mean that it is very often impossible for us to get back to the history . . .' This patronizing positivism is interestingly self-contradictory. In telling the story he wants to tell, Nineham (as we shall see) is actually falsifying the history of historiography.

but central claim about Jesus.[5] If we say 'Christ died for our sins', it is not too difficult to see an obvious element of interpretation: 'for our sins' is a theological addendum to the otherwise 'historical' statement. But even if we say 'Christ died', we have not escaped interpretation: we have chosen to refer to Jesus as 'Christ', ascribing to him a Messiahship which neither his contemporaries nor ours would universally grant. Very well: 'Jesus died'. But we still have not escaped 'interpretation', and indeed at this point it looms larger than ever: three people died outside Jerusalem that afternoon, and we have chosen to mention only one. For that matter, thousands of Jews were crucified by the Romans in the vicinity of Jerusalem during the same century, and we have chosen to mention only one. Our apparently bare historical remark is the product of a multi-faceted interpretative decision. Nor is this unusual. It is typical of all history. All history involves selection, and it is always human beings who do the selecting.

According to one popular 'modern' view, it is only in the last two hundred years that we have discovered what 'history' really is, while writers in the ancient world were ignorant about these matters, freely making things up, weaving fantasy and legend together and calling it history. There is a high irony about this view, since it is itself a modern myth, legitimating the cultural imperialism of the Enlightenment without having any basis in the real history of the ancient world. In fact, the contemporary historians of the ancient world knew what history is as well as we do, and often a lot better.[6] They were under no illusions about merely observing facts and recording them. Herodotus arranged events in such a way as to set forth his theory about how history operates—namely, that it is all a matter of the outworking of human jealousy and greed. He criticized some of the tales he recorded from other people on the grounds that they betrayed too much of the observers' (presumably eccentric) points of view. He does not say they should not have a point of view, only that he has reasons for thinking that theirs has resulted in distortion of actual events. Like all the major historians in the ancient world, Herodotus knew the difference between History proper and mere horography, the attempt to record 'what happened' from one day to the next.[7] At the same time, he knew as well as we do that there are such things as actual events, and that it is the business of the historian to write about them, discounting ones which he thinks incredible.[8]

Similarly, Thucydides held a doctrine of *anangke*, necessity, in accordance with which cause and effect take place in the historical realm. Although he lived close enough to the events of the Peloponnesian War to be able to know pretty accurately 'what happened', he did not pretend, and we should not imagine, that his account is therefore 'unbiased'. Indeed, as a sacked general watching the fortunes of the country that rejected him, that could hardly be expected. Yet, precisely from this point of view, he had the opportunity to

[5] On this see Caird 1980, 209–14.
[6] On this whole paragraph see especially Fornara 1983; cp. Hemer 1989, ch. 3.
[7] Fornara 1983, 16ff.
[8] Fornara 1983, 163.

write with both involvement and detachment: to select and arrange, of course, but also to give his readers actual knowledge of actual events. Similar things could be said, *mutatis mutandis*, about Livy and Josephus, about Caesar and Tacitus, and even, to some extent, about Suetonius. The fact that a human mind has to organize and arrange the material does not 'falsify' the history. This is simply what 'history' is. At the same time, Thucydides and the rest were every bit as aware as we are of the historian's solemn duty to strive towards intellectual honesty and severe impartiality.[9]

It is not the ancients who were deceived about the nature of history, living in a pre-modern age and not knowing what critical thought consisted of. It is we who, in the Enlightenment's rejection of reliance on *auctores*, 'authorities' in a multiple sense, have come to imagine ourselves to be the first to see the difference between subjects and objects, and so have both misjudged our forebears and deceived ourselves. Inventing 'history' by a backwards projection of ideology is as much if not more a modern phenomenon as it is an ancient one. It is something from which New Testament scholars themselves are not exempt.

Thus, on the one hand, ancient historians as well as modern ones were aware of the historian's obligation to do his best not to stand in his own light: Tacitus' famous *sine ira et studio*, honoured of course in the breach rather than the observance, is sufficient evidence of that.[10] On the other hand, no modern historian has escaped the inevitable necessity of selection, and selection cannot be made without a point of view. No point of view, in turn, can be held without being selected, at least subconsciously. The myth of uninterpreted history functions precisely *as* a myth in much modern discourse—that is, it expresses an ideal state of affairs which we imagine erroneously to exist, and which influences the way we think and speak. But it is a 'myth', in the popular sense, for all that.

It is therefore chasing after the wind to imagine that anyone, ancient or modern, could or can 'simply record the facts'. In my youth it was notorious that the newspaper which claimed to 'give you the facts, straight' was the official propagandist organ of the British Communist Party. One learns to suspect people who claim to be the only unbiased voice on their subject; normally this simply means that their agenda is so large that, like a mountain which blots out the sky, they forget that it is there at all. There is no such thing as a point of view which is no-one's point of view. To imagine, therefore, as some post-Enlightenment thinkers have, that we in the modern world have discovered 'pure history', so that all we do is record 'how it actually happened', with no interpretative element or observer's point of view entering into the matter—and that this somehow elevates us to a position of great superiority over

---

[9] Fornara 1983, 99–101; cf. the discussion of Josephus above, p. 68. Fornara's chapter on the recording of speeches (142–68) should be of interest to all New Testament scholars. He sums up as follows (168): 'We may certainly assert that the record of the speeches of the Romans and their opponents is substantially trustworthy from the time of the Second Punic War to the end of the fourth century AD.'

[10] Tacitus, *Annals*, 1.1: 'I shall write without indignation or partisanship.' Cf. too Cicero's mention of the 'laws of history', cited by Fornara 101.

those poor benighted former folk who could only approximate to such an undertaking because they kept getting in their own light—such a view is an arrogant absurdity. It would seem odd even to have to refute it, had it not had such a large influence in precisely the area of our chosen subject-matter.

All history, then, consists of a spiral of knowledge, a long-drawn-out process of interaction between interpreter and source material. This is true whether the would-be historian is a Christian, writing about Jesus and Paul with some sort of prior commitment to them, or a non-Christian, writing about them with the expectation that they were misguided. At this point Rudolf Bultmann and Bertrand Russell stand on the same ground.[11] This process of interaction is not a strange or unusual phenomenon, but a perfectly ordinary human one. Every time I pick up a telephone and hear a voice I form a judgment, a hypothesis, as to whose it might be. Sometimes I am right; sometimes—even when the person reveals his or her name—I am wrong. In the latter case one is compelled to go round the spiral several more times, leading eventually, one hopes, to identification. One can then concentrate on the next spiral of knowledge (which may already have begun), that of actually having a conversation in which one or both partners may not always understand what is being said straight off. It is not the case that one is simply a neutral listener, recording whatever is said on to a mental blank tape. Interaction takes place. In principle history is no different, except that source materials are usually more complicated than telephone callers.

When the historian's source material consists of the literature of early Christianity, the situation is of course further complicated. As we have already discussed in chapter 1, many readers of the New Testament come with the assumption that it is in some way or other *authoritative*. It is as though one were to pick up a telephone expecting to hear a voice telling one what to do. The ordinary process of the spiral of knowledge would still go on, but this time it would be overlaid, and perhaps confused, by a different set of questions. In the case of the gospels, matters are yet worse. It is now as though the voice on the line, which is presumed to be authoritative, gives no instructions, barks no orders, but rather *tells a story*. It is not surprising that those who have claimed scripture as their authority have had difficulty working out what to do with the gospels. Historians have struggled to break free from the assumption that the story is authoritative; theologians, sometimes, from the recognition that this authority comes in story-form. The same double problem meets us in the epistles. How can these historical documents possibly function as authoritative? The *prima facie* impression of the epistles, that they are easier to use as authority because they are actually telling people what to believe and how to behave, may in fact be misleading. What if Paul is telling the Galatians to avoid being lured into Judaism and telling the Romans to avoid being lured into anti-Semitism? How can a note telling a friend that Paul is hoping shortly to come and stay with him be 'authoritative' for the church in a subsequent generation? Nor is it clear from the surface of the text how a discussion of

[11] See Russell 1961 [1946], 311ff. See also the much less cool and detached account in Russell 1967 [1957].

meat offered to idols is to become relevant to the twentieth-century church. Even when the voice on the line actually seems to be giving instructions, how can we be sure that they are meant for us? And, conversely, if we are determined to use the epistles as in some sense authoritative, how can we do that without leaving history out of consideration, as has notoriously happened in much study of Paul?

There are, then, at least three separate sorts of exercise involved when we read the gospels and epistles, and they frequently appear to get in each other's way—added, of course, to the fact that the caller is speaking in a foreign language and from a very different culture. There is listening, pure and simple; there is interaction; and there is readiness to respond appropriately (or, intent to avoid making such a response). These have to do with matters wider than simply history, and they thus guarantee that the task of the historian can never be simply observing and recording 'what actually happened'. Even those who do not regard the texts as in any way authoritative must face the fact that their reading of them is inevitably conducted in dialogue with other readers, ancient and modern, who *have* regarded them in this way, and that some at least of the questions discussed by those at this end of the telephone line have been shaped down the years by that perspective.[12] And, further, even those who like to think of themselves as rugged individualists will have to face the fact that they share the telephone with others. The alternative is simply to be unaware of the other conversationalists and so unable to engage in dialogue with them. Studying history, it seems, is not such a simple task as is sometimes imagined. And reading the New Testament from a historical point of view is even less so.

There are two areas of special historical concern for the student of the New Testament. These will occupy us later in the present volume. Both provide classic examples of the way in which interpretative presuppositions have inevitably interacted with the handling of the data.

First, the study of ancient Judaism has long been bedevilled by a reading which 'knew', in advance, that Judaism was the wrong sort of religion, the dark backdrop to the glorious light of the gospel. We are now in a period of sharp, and largely justified, reaction against this. Such reaction, however, brings its own problems: there is now an atomistic, non-theological reading of Judaism, which splits it up into its different expressions and forswears any coherent synthesis except the most generalized.[13]

Second, and similarly, the study of early Christianity has for generations been dogged by the need that most writers have felt to organize the material in a theologically desirable way, squeezing the data into a quite spurious shape. The early Christians *must* have been a certain sort of people: we need them to have been, to sustain our view of what Christianity is. This has produced, as is

---

[12] cp. the remarks of Carr 1987 [1961], 13f., on the way in which our impression of the Middle Ages as a period in which people were deeply concerned with religion is irrevocably derived from the fact that the sources on which we depend were all written by people who were themselves deeply concerned with religion.

[13] See Part III below.

now commonplace to remark, 'the Myth of Christian Beginnings'.[14] As with Judaism, reaction has set in, and atomism is currently on the increase.[15]

In both cases one can feel some sympathy for the modern movements. As we shall presently see, there are two tasks facing the historian: the data must be included, and an overall simplicity must emerge. But these tasks must be held in the proper balance. If simplicity (of a spurious kind) has ruled for too long, producing the Myth of a Gloomy Judaism or the Myth of a Fresh-Faced Early Christianity, it is time that unsorted data were given a fresh hearing. But there is a counter-myth present here too, the Myth of Objective Data or of Presuppositionless History, and the purpose of my present argument is to challenge it: there is in fact no such thing as 'mere history'. There are data. Manuscripts exist, even very ancient ones. Coins and archaeological data are available. From these we can know quite a lot about the ancient world, with as good a knowledge as we have of anything else at all. But in order even to collect manuscripts and coins, let alone read, translate, or organize them into editions or collections, we must already engage in 'interpretation'.[16] There are of course disciplines which have developed around all such activities, which are designed precisely to prevent such tasks lapsing into arbitrariness. My present point is simply that all history is interpreted history.

3. This Does Not Mean 'No Facts'

(i) Critical Realism and the Threat of the Disappearing Object

The sheer complexity of the historian's task, and its manifest difference from 'mere observation', might lead, and has led some, to the conclusion that there are therefore no such things as 'facts'. If everything is coloured by someone's perspective, then everything can be reduced to terms of that perspective. This is the historian's analogue for a phenomenalist epistemology:

Observer	Evidence	Past Event
- - - - - - - - - >	- - - - - - >	
looking at evidence	*which seems to offer access to events*	
	< - - - - - -	
	but which may only be evidence about itself	
< - - - - - - - -		
or which in fact is only evidence about the observer's point of view		

So frequent is this assumption that we daily meet examples of reductionism based solely on the mistaken belief that only a 'pure' or 'neutral' point of view

[14] See the book of this title by R. L. Wilken (1971).

[15] See Part IV. A good example of the fragmented nature of the current picture of early Christianity may be found in Koester 1982b.

[16] See Carr 1987 [1961], 14f., pointing out the needless worry of Lord Acton that the pressure to write history was threatening 'to turn him from a man of letters into the compiler of an encyclopedia'. Carr goes on to speak (16) of a 'nineteenth-century fetishism of facts'.

will be of any use to anyone. 'You only say that because you're a pessimist' might or might not be a telling rejoinder to a claim that the present fine weather would not last. The 'pessimist' might have heard an accurate weather forecast. Similarly, 'you only say that because you're a mathematician' has no force whatever in dismissing the idea that two plus two equals four. In this case, as in several others, the qualification adduced as the reason for the reduction should work the other way: the fact that the person addressed is a mathematician is a *good* reason, not a bad one, for believing their statement if it concerns mathematics.[17] The equivalent in the reading of the gospels in the twentieth century has been the apparently 'scientific' statement that 'Every text is first and foremost evidence for the circumstances in and for which it was composed.'[18] The critic then responds to the evangelists: 'you only say that (this story about Jesus, this word or saying) because you're a Christian.' True enough in some ways, but manifestly not enough in others. If being a mathematician might entitle somebody to a hearing on the subject of numbers, being a Christian *might* mean that someone should be given a hearing on the subject of Jesus. If we followed the reductionist line to the end—and some today are trying to do that—we would land up, as we saw in chapter 2, with the normal phenomenalist's cul-de-sac: solipsism. One only knows about oneself, about one's own sense-data. Mark only knew about his own theology, not about Jesus.

It may help to go back for a moment to the theory of knowledge. The fact that *somebody*, standing *somewhere*, with a particular *point of view*, is knowing something does not mean that the knowledge is less valuable: merely that it is precisely *knowledge*. There is no need, despite the assertions of many empiricists of a former age and some phenomenalists in more recent times, to reduce talk about objects external to ourselves to talk about our own sense-data, so that instead of saying 'this is a desk' I should really only say 'I am aware of sensations of hardness, flatness and woodenness such as I usually have when I sit here', or possibly, to get rid of the suggestion that I have illicitly imported a reference to an actual object, namely myself, 'there is here a sensation of hardness, flatness and woodenness'—or perhaps, more simply, 'hardness—flatness—woodenness!'. The fear that 'actual events' will disappear beneath a welter of particular people's perceptions is a fear of this sort, and is to be rejected as groundless. As a particular example, it must be asserted most strongly that to discover that a particular writer has a 'bias' tells us nothing whatever about the value of the information he or she presents. It merely bids us be aware of the bias (and of our own, for that matter), and to assess the material according to as many sources as we can. 'Intellectual honesty consists not in forcing an impossible neutrality, but in admitting that neutrality is not possible.'[19] Similarly, the fear of 'objectivization' which so affected Rudolf Bultmann's theology may be laid to rest. Bultmann, within his neo-Kantian philosophical heritage, was anxious about seeming to talk of objects or events

---

[17] The latter example is adapted from Lewis 1943 [1933], 62f.

[18] Perrin 1970, 69.

[19] Holmes 1983a, 131.

other than by talking of them in relation to the observer. He therefore insisted (among other things) on doing theology by doing anthropology, following Feuerbach in collapsing god-talk into man-talk.[20] We simply do not have to accept such false dichotomies. It is not the case that some things are purely objective and others purely subjective, or that one must reduce either to the other. Life, fortunately, is more complicated than that.

The discovery, therefore, that someone has a 'point of view', or has selected or arranged material, or has a characteristic style or turn of phrase, does nothing whatever to tell us whether what the writer is talking about (if he or she purports to be describing events) actually happened or not. There are such things as events in the external world. Many of them can be described, more or less. But a writer can no more describe them without selecting them according to a point of view than he or she can watch them without using his or her eyes.

The point may be made this time with the help of a visual metaphor. If I am presented with a telescope, supposing myself never to have seen such a thing before, I may eventually find out that if I lift it to my eye I can see things at the other end which I did not expect. All sorts of thoughts might then come into my mind. If I have met kaleidoscopes in the past, I might suppose this to be a variation on the theme, and try twisting the far end to see if the interesting picture, which I assume is somehow inside the opposite end of the instrument, will change. It might actually do just that, due to my altering the focus; my (wrong) suspicions will have been (wrongly) confirmed, and I will have to make several twists of the spiral of knowledge, as well as of the telescope, before I eventually discover the truth. Or I might imagine that there was an angled mirror at the other end, giving me information about something external to the telescope but adjacent to myself. So we could go on. But the fact remains that, even though I am looking through a particular lens, there are objects out there in the real world (as all but the most dyed-in-the-wool solipsist is bound to admit), and I am really looking at them, albeit of course (a) from my own point of view and (b) through a particular set of lenses.

So it is with history. The telescope of one particular piece of evidence—a book, let us say, of Thucydides' history—contains particular lenses, arranged in a certain fashion. No doubt there are things outside its range. No doubt there are things which, because they are far apart from each other, cannot be seen through it at the same time. But Thucydides as he writes, and we as we read, are not looking into a kaleidoscope at a fictitious landscape. Nor are we looking through a slightly angled mirror which merely reveals where Thucydides, or we ourselves, happen to be standing. We are looking at events. The lens may distort, or the fact of looking with only one eye may lead us into errors of perspective; we may well need other lenses and viewpoints to correct such errors; but we are looking at events none the less. Critical realism, not the abandonment of knowledge of the extra-linguistic world, is required for a coherent epistemology.[21]

---

[20] See the criticisms of Bultmann in e.g. Thiselton 1980, 205–92, and the summary on 444. On the familiar question, whether Bultmann should have gone even further and demythologized the kerygma itself, see now Moore 1989, 175.

[21] See Thiselton 1980, 439f.

As applied to the gospels, this clearly means that, although we must read them with our eyes and ears open for the evangelists' own perspective, and must be aware too that part of that perspective is their wish to involve their readers in the material itself (they are no mere cool, detached observers, and nor do they wish us to be), this of itself in no way cancels out the strong possibility that they are describing, in principle, events which actually took place. If we reject this or that event, we must do so on quite other grounds from those regularly advanced or hinted at, namely that the evangelists are not 'neutral', that their work reveals their own theology *rather than* anything about Jesus.[22] We might apply the same point to the vexed question of Pauline theology. The discovery that Paul was addressing a particular situation, and looking at it in a particular light, is frequently hailed as indicating that the passage in question is therefore purely situational, and does not express or embody a basic theology, or worldview. This is simply bad logic. It is a false either-or, typical of the traps into which biblical scholarship regularly falls.

In particular we must note that the answer to the question 'what is a historical question?' is not 'a question about mere facts'.[23] History is primarily the history of human beings, and it attempts to plot, uncover, and understand from the inside the interplay of human intentions and motivations present within a given field of initial investigation. What a positivist would call 'the facts' are part, and an inseparable part, of a much larger whole. The move from 'fact' to 'interpretation' is not a move from the clear to the unclear: events are not mere billiard-balls cannoning into one another, to which different 'meanings' or 'interpretations' can be attached quite arbitrarily, according to which game is being played. Some 'meanings' or 'interpretations' will be, as we shall see presently, more appropriate than others. This point affects the study of the New Testament in all sorts of ways. Attempts to split off two levels of questions (first we ask when, where and by whom a book was written, then we ask what it says) are actually absurd, for all their popularity. In order to address either set of questions we must integrate it with the other. This will require that we produce historical hypotheses which take into account the complexities of human motivation, which in turn need an exploration of the worldviews and mindsets of the communities and individuals involved.

As I just hinted, this argument should not be taken to mean that all angles of looking at events are equally valid or proper. As critical realism gets to work, it is discovered that some angles of vision do less justice to the information than others. Arguably, the *Gospel of Thomas* presents a considerably more distorted angle on Jesus of Nazareth than does the Gospel according to Mark; and even those who disagree, and who would put the matter the other way

---

[22] One might consider at this point the question: are historians thus in some sense 'priests', mediating the 'truth' to the faithful? The correct answer, I think, to such an idealist viewpoint is that which goes back to the OT, and is highlighted by Caird, 1980, 217f.: historians are in some sense or other prophets, offering a perspective on events which is both their own and (in aspiration at least) that of God. If this brings home to the historian the dangers and responsibilities of the task, so be it.

[23] See Florovsky 1974, 40–4; Collingwood 1956 [1946], 42ff. See too Meyer 1989, 62, etc.

around,[24] would agree that some accounts are closer to the events they purport to describe than are others. All accounts 'distort', but some do so considerably more than others. All accounts involve 'interpretation'; the question is whether this interpretation discloses the totality of the event, opening it up in all its actuality and meaning, or whether it squashes it out of shape, closing down its actuality and meaning. To return to our billiard-balls: a Martian, observing a game of billiards, might guess that these strange humans were testing the ballistic properties of some new weapon. A human observer who had seen snooker played, but never billiards, might imagine that billiards was a poor attempt to play snooker with limited equipment and a good many mistakes. Both 'interpretations' of the data would distort, closing down the event and rendering many aspects of it incomprehensible. The watcher who knew what billiards was all about would, in one sense, likewise distort: he would at once limit the range of possible interpretations, and if by chance the players *were* after all testing a new weapon he would come to the correct interpretation long after the Martian. But in principle his interpretation would disclose more than it concealed, opening up the event so that more and more of it fitted. His story would be more complete and satisfying. The historical analogue for this is the account which not only describes 'what happened' but which, as we shall see, gets to the 'inside' of the event.

(ii) The Causes of the Misconception

Why then the problem? In particular, why have so many scholars been coy, to say the least, about 'events' in the gospels being actual events, rather than simply fictions in the mind of the evangelists?

It is sometimes thought that the real reason is the rejection of the 'miraculous', and hence the felt impossibility of using the gospels as serious history. About this I shall have more to say later, when writing about Jesus.[25] But a basic point must be made here. Accounts of strange happenings in any culture or tradition are of course subject to legendary accretions. But one cannot rule out *a priori* the possibility of things occurring in ways not normally expected, since to do so would be to begin from the fixed point that a particular worldview, namely the eighteenth-century rationalist one, or its twentieth-century positivist successor, is correct in postulating that the universe is simply a 'closed continuum' of cause and effect. How can any scientific enquiry not allow for the possibility that its own worldview might be incorrect? (If it is replied that certain types of argument and enquiry would cut off the branch on which the worldview was sitting, the counter-reply might be that, if that is where the argument leads, you had better find yourself another branch, or even another tree.)

[24] e.g. Mack 1988.
[25] Where it will also become clear why I wish to put 'miracle' and its cognates into inverted commas.

This is emphatically *not* to say that the *pre*-Enlightenment worldview was after all correct. Why, once we challenge the prevailing dualisms, should there only be two possibilities, the 'pre-modernist' and the 'modernist' ones? To say that the gospels cannot be read as they stand because their view of the 'miraculous' conflicts with the Enlightenment worldview does not of itself mean that they can only be read as they stand from within a pre-critical Christian faith. There might be plenty of other worldviews, not necessarily Christian ones, within which one could read the gospels without being offended by the 'miracles'. Nor is it to say that if we are to read the gospels as they stand, 'miracles' and all, we must frankly admit that we are ceasing to do 'history' and are now doing something else, namely 'theology', or a kind of meta-history. Only if we have devalued 'history' so that the word now *means* 'the positivist recounting of those sorts of events which fit with an eighteenth-century worldview, and which seem to have actually happened', would we need to think that. My whole argument here has been that 'history' ought to mean more than this, namely the meaningful narrative of events and intentions; and it is vital that we do not foreclose too soon on the possibility of 'meanings' other than we had originally envisaged. The closed mind is as damaging to scholarship as the 'closed continuum' idea is to history itself. If we are committed to history, there is always the possibility that when, after several trips around the hermeneutical spiral, we find certain places to stand from which we can see the material in an appropriate light, we will find that some of those places are something like Christian faith. This is not a certainty before we start. Nor would it necessarily be the case that the sort of Christian faith that we might discover in practice to be such a vantage point would look at all like what is, or what has been, thought of as orthodoxy.

The problem about 'miracles' may have been a proximate cause of the desire on the part of some theologians (Reimarus, Strauss, Bultmann, etc.) to read the gospels in a non-historical way. I do not think it was the only, or even the most pressing, reason. There were deeper reasons, lying not in the eighteenth century (when 'miracles' began to be perceived as a problem) but earlier. Many critical methods were devised not in order to do history but in order *not* to do history: in order, rather, to maintain a careful and perhaps pious silence when unsure where the history might lead. As a child in a fairground might stick out her foot to prevent herself from sliding down a ramp too fast and out of control, so many theologians have refused to abandon themselves to the changes and chances of the historical enterprise, and have either kept the brake firmly on or, in extreme cases, simply refused to join in the fun at all. Or, to change the metaphor, they are frightened of history as a walker is of a swamp: one might sink without trace.[26] If there is a convenient bridge, so much the better. If the swamp won't hold us, so much the worse for the swamp; we shall decide not to cross it at all.

[26] The metaphor is taken from an actual debate, in Bonn in 1987, in which several theologians present urged more or less the view I am attacking, using the swamp-and-bridge illustration. I find this very perplexing. After centuries of insisting that what one must do is historical criticism, history is being abandoned just when, at last, it is (arguably) actually getting us somewhere. See, for an explicit statement of this, Morgan 1988, 199.

One particularly prevalent form of this argument is the suggestion, most appealing in Lutheran circles, that to base one's faith on history is to turn it into a 'work', and thus of course—within that confessional perspective—to falsify it. That is at least part of the reason, along with the neo-Kantian rejection of 'objectification', for Bultmann's adoption of this perspective. But this argument would only hold if it were the case that early Christianity held a thoroughly non-Jewish, perhaps a Gnostic, premise (which was of course precisely what Bultmann then argued at a history-of-religions level; this argument has recently been given a new lease of life)—a premise, that is, that true religion was to be found by abandoning history and finding salvation in a realm completely outside it.[27] But using such an argument is not only totally untrue to the thought of the early church, which as a whole (Paul and John included) remained far more Jewish than Bultmann ever imagined: it is also confused as to the nature of faith. Faith may be the opposite of sight. It is also, in some important senses, the opposite of doubt. To say that basing one's faith on events is to turn it into a 'work' (as though one were oneself responsible for those events!) is to be justified not by faith but by doubt. This of course begs the question of what an 'event' *is*. As we shall see when considering Jesus' life, and particularly his death, an event is a highly complex thing, being not merely a set of happenings in the public world but the focal point of a variety of human intentionalities. Within those intentionalities—themselves the proper object of a certain type of historical questioning, however difficult—there may (or may not) be found what is sometimes thought of as significance or meaning. Again I must stress: the only sense in which this kind of understanding is inaccessible to the historian is if by 'historian' we mean 'someone holding an eighteenth-century European worldview, and committed to the belief that significance is not to be found within ordinary events'.

There is another related reason why some biblical scholars, within post-Bultmannian theology at least, have wanted to reduce the telescope provided by the gospels to either a kaleidoscope or an angled (and distorting) mirror. This reason is the desire for relevance, perceived in terms of universalizability. How can the teaching of Jesus, and the events of the gospel narratives, have 'meaning' for those outside that time and place? If we are merely looking at events in the life of Jesus, they cannot have anything to say to us. They must just be examples of the higher truth which they embody, mere manifestations or examples of the 'real thing'; it was perhaps wrong-headed or even dangerous to write them down, because people might mistake them for the real thing; maybe it shows a failure of nerve on the part of the early church, who should have been looking to the living Lord of the present and the coming Lord of the future, not to the Jesus of Nazareth of the past. We must not (this view continues) be deluded into thinking that the events themselves are important. Thus it is that parables which originally contained Jesus' message to

---

[27] Bultmann, of course, retained 'history' to the extent that the cross remained central for him. But even there he insisted that it could not be 'objectified': see Thiselton 1980, 211. On the new Bultmannian school see Part IV below.

Israel are made to contain instead a universally relevant message.[28] The Procrustean bed of the 'timeless Jesus' myth is then used as the measure for lopping off all the bits which do not fit, and we are reduced to a 'historical Jesus' who just happens to have lost all his main connections with his own actual historical place and time. We shall address these issues in their proper place; for the moment we note them as a further problem in one common would-be 'historical' reading of the gospels.

We must therefore challenge several of the assumptions which have commonly been made about history in general and the gospels in particular. First, we must reject the idea, common since Reimarus, that 'real' history will undermine the 'interpretative' and particularly the 'theological' elements in the gospels. All history involves interpretation; if the evangelists offer us a theological one, we must listen to it as best we can, and not assume that our own, especially a 'neutral' or positivist one, will automatically be right. It could just be that at the end of the day some 'interpretation'—or perhaps more than one—might after all bring out as well as seems possible the full significance of the events. To rule out such a possibility *a priori* would be an odd way of striving after 'objectivity'. History does not rule out theology; indeed, in the broadest sense of 'theology' it actually requires it.

Second, as the mirror-image of this point, we must insist that the gospels, though they are (as redaction-criticism has emphasized) theological through and through, are not for that reason any the less historical. The fact of their being interpretations does not mean they are not interpretations *of events*; if it did, there would be no events, since as we have seen all events in history are interpreted events.[29] Theology does not rule out history; in several theologies, not only some Christian varieties, it actually requires it.

Third, we must note in a preliminary way (we shall return to the point later) the multiple possibilities inherent in the word 'meaning' as applied to history. At its basic level, the 'meaning' of history may be held to lie in the intentionalities of the characters concerned (whether or not they realize their ambitions and achieve their aims). Caesar's crossing of the Rubicon 'meant' that he intended to set himself up above the law of the Republic. At another level, 'meaning' may be held to lie in the contemporary relevance or consequence of the events. Those who farmed on the Italian side of the Rubicon would have said that Caesar's crossing 'meant' certain things in terms of the subsequent state of their land. Again, the fact that we have uncovered a certain set of human motivations may suggest parallels in other historical events, including those contemporary with ourselves, where a similar set of intentionalities may be present, and from which we may deduce a 'meaning' in terms of our own world.[30] Caesar's crossing of the Rubicon 'means' that would-

---

[28] See the next volume, *Jesus and the Victory of God*. It is sometimes claimed, moreover, that this process begins in the NT itself (Dodd, Jeremias).

[29] See Hooker 1975, 36, criticizing Norman Perrin.

[30] There is a similarity between this suggestion and Troeltsch's famous principle of analogy (we only have historical knowledge of events that are analogous to events that we ourselves know of), with the all-important difference that now it is set within a critical-realist framework of what 'history' actually is.

be tyrants are to be watched carefully when they make vital symbolic moves. At yet another level, 'meaning' may be attributed to events on the grounds that they reveal the *divine* intention, and thus speak powerfully, whether to the ancient or the modern world, pagan as well as Jewish or Christian, of the nature and/or purposes of 'God', or a god. Caesar's eventual fate 'means' that his hubris did not go unnoticed, or unpunished, by divine vengeance.

Granted, then, that we are interested in 'what actually happened', we (and by 'we', I here mean historians in general) are also interested in *why* it happened. That question, in turn, opens up to reveal the full range of explanations available within any given worldview, including (in the case of answers available within first-century Judaism) the intentions not only of humans but of Israel's god. If we are to understand how things looked in the first century, and how things look to us, this full range of explanation must be kept open. We shall explore these various aspects of the subject more fully in the next chapter.

(iii) Wanted: New Categories

What we find, in short, is that the epistemological tools of our age seem inadequate for the data before us. One of the present ironies, typical of movements within the fashions of scholarship, is that some philosophers are today moving away from materialism, or even a moderate realism, and back towards idealism, just as the theologians, kept prisoner for so long in idealist strongholds, are finally rejoicing to discover some form of realism. These debates may serve to keep checks and balances alive within a discipline. But I suspect that the idealist-realist distinction is itself ultimately misleading; and swings from one to the other are not much help in terms of an actual historical investigation such as ours.

What we require, I believe, is a set of tools designed for the task at hand, rather than a set borrowed from someone who might be working on something else. Just as the gospels and epistles embody genres somewhat apart from their closest non-Christian analogues, so the study of them, and of their central figures, are tasks which, though they possess of course several analogies with other closely related disciplines, require specialized tools, that is, a theory of knowledge appropriate to the specific tasks. That is what I am trying to provide in this Part of the book. If, moreover, the Christian claim were after all true—and it would be foolish to answer that question either way in advance when dealing with preliminary method—we might perhaps expect that in studying Jesus himself we would find the clue to understanding not only the object we can see through the telescope, the voice we can hear on the telephone, but the nature of sight and hearing themselves. Studying Jesus, in other words, might lead to a reappraisal of the theory of knowledge itself.[31]

---

[31] Some such thing seems to have been envisaged by Paul in 1 Cor. 8.1–6: cf. Wright 1991a, ch. 6.

I have already suggested in barest outline some ways in which this enterprise might proceed, and I hope to return to the point at the end of this whole project. For the moment we can say: the 'observer', from whatever background, is called to be open to the possibility of events which do not fit his or her worldview, his or her grid of expected possibilities. Or, as I would prefer to say it, it is appropriate for humans in general to listen to stories other than those by which they habitually order their lives, and to ask themselves whether those other stories ought not to be allowed to subvert their usual ones, that is, to ask whether there really are more things in heaven and earth than are dreamed of in their little philosophies. Taken at one level, this might sound simply like a plea for 'modernist' Christians, or non-Christians, to be 'open to the supernatural'—a plea, in other words, for an old-fashioned conservatism or fundamentalism to be given its day in court. Against this, let it be said at once that it is often precisely the 'ordinary Christian' of this sort who needs to be open to the possibilities of ways of reading the New Testament, and ways of understanding who Jesus actually was, which will call his or her previous stories into serious question. I hope it is also clear that, just as I reject the subjective/objective distinction, so I reject the nature/supernature distinction which is equally a product of Enlightenment thinking. Indeed, it is precisely the stories that are modelled on these distinctions, whether in a 'conservative' or a 'liberal' manner, that I believe will be subverted by the story which I propose to tell.

The tools of thought which we need, then, cannot be those of premodernism any more than those of modernism. To what extent the ones I am offering belong to 'postmodernism' is a matter that does not much concern me. Diversity is, after all, a necessary feature of postmodernism. To proclaim the death of the Enlightenment worldview is not yet to announce what will rise to take its place. It may be that the study of Jesus, which cannot but focus on questions of death and resurrection, will have something to say on the matter.

If we are eventually to mount a new theory of knowledge itself, we will also need a new theory of being or existence, that is, a new ontology. In this case, too, we find ourselves in a chicken-and-egg situation: we need to know the new theory before we can study the material, but it is in studying the material that the new theory will emerge. I am therefore content, at this stage, to outline the way I think the argument might run, and to let it be modified as we go along. It seems to me, picking up a point from the last paragraph, that ontologies based on a nature/supernature distinction simply will not do. 'The world is charged with the grandeur of God', and to reject that premise by opting in advance for *either* materialism *or* 'supernaturalism' is always to run the risk of what seems to me an untenable ontological dualism. How, at an initial level, might we escape from this?

At this point, inescapably, the interpreter must declare his or her hand. I find myself driven, both from my study of the New Testament and from a wide variety of other factors which contribute to my being who I am, to tell a story about reality which runs something like this. Reality as we know it is the result of a creator god bringing into being a world that is other than himself, and yet which is full of his glory. It was always the intention of this god that creation should one day be flooded with his own life, in a way for which it was prepared from the beginning. As part of the means to this end, the creator brought into being a creature which, by bearing the creator's image, would bring his wise and loving care to bear upon the creation. By a tragic irony, the creature in question has rebelled against this intention. But the creator has solved this problem in principle in an entirely appropriate way, and as a result is now moving the creation once more towards its originally intended goal. The implementation of this solution now involves the indwelling of this god within his human creatures and ultimately within the whole creation, transforming it into that for which it was made in the beginning. This story, whose similarity to the parable of the Wicked Tenants is scarcely accidental, obviously attempts to ground ontology, a view of what is really there, in the being and activity of the creator/redeemer god. It has, in my own case, already succeeded in subverting all sorts of other stories (including several 'Christian' ones) that I used to tell myself about reality. I find that it 'fits' with far more of the real world than the usual post-Enlightenment ones. To pretend that this were not the case—to abandon this story in favour of reducing everything to 'mere history', just when that Enlightenment-style project is collapsing like the Berlin Wall—would be as dishonest as it would be foolish.

What then is the proper method for the historian? It has recently been argued with some force that history consists of the process of hypothesis and verification.[32] Since in many respects I agree with this proposal, to the extent that I believe that this (or some modification of it) is in fact what all historians do anyway, it is vital that we explore just what might be meant by it, and how in particular the 'normal critical methods' associated with contemporary New Testament study stand up within it.

4. Historical Method: Hypothesis and Verification

(i) Introduction

There is an important sense in which historical method is just like all other methods of enquiry. It proceeds by means of 'hypotheses', which stand in need of 'verification'. As we saw earlier, a better way of putting this (avoiding certain epistemological pitfalls) is to say that human life is lived by means of implicit and explicit stories; that these stories throw up questions; that humans then advance explanatory stories to deal with these questions; that some of these stories attain a degree of success. I shall continue to use the convenient terms 'hypothesis' and 'verification', but shall use them with these overtones.

---

[32] See Meyer 1979, ch. 4 for what is probably the finest statement on historical method by a practising contemporary New Testament scholar; further valuable material is in Meyer 1989. Sanders 1985, 3–22, is also clear and helpful, though not as philosophically grounded or nuanced as Meyer. For the background philosophical debates see e.g. Toulmin 1958.

Despite this similarity with other fields of enquiry, there will also be significant differences. Hypotheses in different fields will need different sorts of strengths, and will have different appropriate verification-systems. The rules for what will count as a worthwhile, let alone a successful, explanatory story will be subtly different when we are dealing with different subject-matter. We must therefore enquire as to what makes a good *historical* hypothesis as opposed to any other sort. There will be analogies and similarities with the criteria for good hypotheses in other spheres of knowledge, but what has been said already in this chapter about the nature of historical knowledge will come into play, and produce significant differences.

A hypothesis, as we saw, is essentially a construct, thought up by a human mind, which offers itself as a story about a particular set of phenomena, in which the story, which is bound to be an interpretation of those phenomena, also offers an *explanation* of them. I see a police car tearing down the wrong side of the road with its sirens blaring. Because I tell myself an underlying story about the normal state of our society, I am faced with a question: something out of the ordinary is afoot. I guess that a crime has been committed, or perhaps that there has been an accident. This is a historical hypothesis, which now requires to be tested against more evidence. The stages of testing, and ultimately of verification, may be illustrated by pursuing the analogy, and perhaps the police car. I subsequently hear a fire-engine in a neighbouring street, and see a cloud of smoke arising close by. At once I change my hypothesis: the appearance of new data has helped me clarify matters. Of course, it could still be the case that the police car is chasing a thief, and knows nothing of the fire; but the probability remains high, because of the inherent simplicity of the hypothesis and its inclusion of the data, that the events belong together. I prefer my simple story to potential complex and disjointed ones. I then remember that I heard an unexplained explosion ten minutes before. Again, this could be unrelated, but a picture is coming together with an essential simplicity, and is starting to reach out and explain more data that I had not originally connected with the event. By the time I catch up with the police car, my journey around the spiral of understanding has brought me, literally and metaphorically, to the scene of the fire. And, when I begin to ask this historian's real question, 'why', in relation to all these events, I need look no further than the action which, perhaps despite its intention, caused the fire, and the intention of police- and fire-officers to do their job in relation to the catastrophe.

(ii) The Requirements of a Good Hypothesis

There are thus three things that a good hypothesis (in any field) must do. Each of these needs further discussion, but it is important to get the shape clear at this stage.

First, it must include the data. The bits and pieces of evidence must be incorporated, without being squeezed out of shape any more than is inevitable, granted that I am looking at them through my own eyes, not from a god's-eye-view. It will not do to pretend that the smoke was a low cloud, or to imagine that the 'explosion' was simply the slamming of a large door nearby.

Second, it must construct a basically simple and coherent overall picture. It *could* be that neither the explosion, the smoke, the fire-engine nor the police car had anything to do with each other, but until we collect more data, such as observing the police car going away from the fire and towards a bank which is being robbed, it is simpler to suggest that they are parts of the same reasonably straightforward whole.

These first two aspects of a good hypothesis—getting in the data, and simplicity—are always, of course, in tension with each other. It is easy to create simple hypotheses at the expense of some of the data; it is easy to suggest explanations for all the data at the cost of producing a highly complex and convoluted hypothesis. Both these alternatives are encountered frequently within New Testament studies, not least the study of Jesus. 'Jesus the simple Galilean peasant' is straightforward, but ignores a good deal of the evidence, and the hypothesis is not noticeably strengthened by the addition of all kinds of speculations which purport to account for how the rest of the data were dreamed up by imaginary groups in the early church. Conversely, most 'conservative' readings of Jesus include all the data, because that is their aim, but without any historically cogent account of Jesus' aims and intentions during his ministry.

In any given field, it is quite likely that there will be several possible hypotheses which will include more or less all the data, and do so with reasonably simplicity. There is therefore a third thing that a good hypothesis must do if it is to stand out from the others. The proposed explanatory story must prove itself fruitful in other related areas, must explain or help to explain other problems. In my original example, other problems would include the explosion, and extra things to which I had not originally paid much attention, such as the fact that a side-road I passed earlier had been closed off.

When we apply these criteria to hypotheses about Judaism, Jesus, or to the whole business of the origin of Christianity, we find that the problems are naturally somewhat more complex than a city fire. First, we find that the stack of data to be included is vast and bewildering. In a historical hypothesis the data are of course source materials: in the ancient period this means written documents mainly, but there are also inscriptions, artifacts, archaeological evidence and so forth. A mass of material has to be assembled, and the historian who wishes for simplicity will find plenty of temptation to leave out half the phenomena in the interests of coherence.[33] The Jewish sources alone are a lifetime's study; the gospels present a range of problems quite unique in themselves; the forms of speech and writing the early Christians used, not least the apocalyptic imagery so familiar to them and so strange to us, will constantly lead us astray unless we keep on our guard. And, as always with ancient history, sources have a habit of not telling us what we really wanted to know. They do not explain something which they could take for granted; we may

---

[33] cf. Carr 1987 [1961], 14–16.

have to reassemble it painstakingly.[34] We are like paleontologists struggling to piece together a set of bones which a dinosaur had used all its life without even thinking about it. Simply seeing and assembling the data is a monstrous task.

Second, and consequently, the construction of an essentially simple historical hypothesis is likewise a major problem. It involves keeping all the key questions about Jesus in mind continually, and refusing to admit a solution in one area which leaves the rest in turmoil and disorder. It is at this stage, as we shall see later, that some New Testament scholars have evolved highly sophisticated ways of getting off the horns of the dilemma posed by these two criteria. If parts of the data do not fit the simple hypothesis (e.g. that Jesus expected the end of the world very shortly, and therefore had no time to think of founding a church), then we have ways of dealing with the recalcitrant data: there are several tools available which purport to show that it comes, not from Jesus himself, but from the later church. The data thus disappear from the picture of Jesus, but at a cost.[35] And the cost is the resultant complexity of the picture of the church and its creative activity and traditions. Anyone who has studied modern traditio-historical criticism of the gospels knows just how intricate that can be, and how few fixed points there really are. What we are seeing in such a situation is the high degree of implausible complexity in *detail* that is the purchasing price of simplicity, in *outline*, either of a portrait of Jesus, or of the picture of the early church and its hypothetical development, or for that matter of Pauline theology. It is only when we keep in mind the importance of the essential simplicity of the whole jigsaw that we become dissatisfied (intellectually; we may well feel other sorts of dissatisfaction with the present state of tradition-criticism) with results of this sort.

The third criterion (making sense of other areas outside the immediate chosen field) obviously has to do, in the case of work on both Jesus and Paul, with the wider jigsaw of the first century as a whole. In particular, large problems have been raised about the relation between our two main subjects themselves, and any hypothesis about the one which makes good sense as it points towards the other must have a decided advantage over one which leaves the two simply poles apart. It is when scholars try to keep Jesus and the early church at arm's length from each other that extra phenomena are imported, such as Paul's supposed Hellenization of the original Jewish gospel. This saves the phenomena, and deals with the wider issues, at the cost, once again, of simplicity.

We have so far omitted one criterion which regularly plays a part in historical hypotheses about the New Testament. I refer to the contemporary prac-

---

[34] This task is that which Anthony Harvey (1982) described as the plotting of 'Historical Constraints'. I find this to be a helpful and useful notion, though it needs more fine-tuning. I shall be conscious of my debt to Harvey, and my use of his model, at various stages: see Wright 1986a.

[35] The same trick can be played on Paul, and is there given the name *Sachkritik*, the process by which the critic understands Paul's thoughts better than Paul did himself, and can relativize some parts of his thought in the light of others. See Morgan 1973, 42–52, and Meyer 1989, 59–65, esp. 63–4.

tical relevance, actual or imagined, which the hypothesis may have. We have seen a little of this already, in chapter 1, and will look at the particular forms it has taken in the introductory chapters to successive volumes. Here the point to be made is quite simple, though at this point the effects on Jesus-study and Paul-study divide.

Few people, faced with the uncomfortable fact that Jesus did not after all underwrite their favourite project or programme, are prepared to say 'so much the worse for Jesus'. That, after all, was what his contemporaries did, and we have become used to criticizing them for it. This was why, as George Tyrrell said, the nineteenth-century liberal 'lives of Jesus' succeeded only in seeing the reflection of their own faces at the bottom of a deep well.[36] Thus the many highly varied models of Christianity currently available, all of which have some sort of a place for Jesus, strongly resist any change in their own version of his portrait, since, as they rightly perceive, this might have considerable and perhaps unwelcome effects in other areas of life and thought. This innate conservatism has of course meant that the average churchgoer (and many theologians are, or were at one time, average churchgoers) has an inbuilt resistance to mere innovation or silliness. It also means that serious and well-founded suggestions for modifying the picture of Jesus are sometimes wrongly dismissed out of hand. Such a process of rejection operates (as of course do innovative proposals) at a variety of levels, which it would take a sociologist or psychologist to explore.

What about Paul? We have already mentioned the way in which the portraits of Judaism, and of the early church, have been bent to suit the requirements of contemporary hermeneutical schemes. Sometimes, the Jews are the villains; sometimes, the tragic heroes. Sometimes, the earliest Christians are the noble pioneers; sometimes, the peculiar primitives. When we turn to Paul, as a special case within the early church, we discover a rather different phenomenon. It is common for people to say, in effect, that Paul believed *x* but we believe *y*, which is incompatible with it. Plenty of people still want to have Paul as an ally, but, perhaps understandably, there are far fewer scholars who are committed to this position than there are who want to keep Jesus on their side. One might have thought that this would have meant a greater degree of 'objectivity' in the results: if we are free to disagree with Paul, we are also free to let him be himself. Things are not, alas, as easy as that. What quite often happens in Pauline scholarship is that Paul is assumed to hold a view credited to him by some of his expositors, and a scholar who disagrees with that view criticizes Paul as though he were responsible for it. Two good examples are Schoeps' scolding of Paul for being a Lutheran, and Maccoby's even less temperate dismissal of him as a Hellenistic Gnostic.[37] Alternatively, some scholars come from traditions (some English ones, for instance) in which it has long been fashionable to be somewhat patronizing and dismissive

---

[36] Tyrrell 1963 [1909], 49, referring particularly to Harnack (though McGrath 1986, 86 disputes the applicability of the point to Harnack himself). Harnack, in fact, had said that a life of Jesus could not be written: see McGrath, 61.

[37] Schoeps 1961; Maccoby 1991.

of Paul: a fine fellow, no doubt, but a bit muddled and over-dogmatic, and in short not quite the sort of theologian one would care to have around in polite society. It then becomes important to find enough points of agreement to retain credible continuity with him, and enough points of criticism to avoid being tarred altogether with the Pauline brush.

It is of course part of a coherent epistemology, as I argued in chapter 2, that the knower cannot know without being involved. Positivism is no better when studying history than at any other time. In addition, as I suggested in chapter 1, the fact that the controlling story of some people's lives includes Jesus, and perhaps Paul, in a highly positive light means that there need be no pretence of 'neutrality', which is often simply a smokescreen for unexamined prejudice. But if the *controlling* criterion for a particular story is its ability to legitimate a particular stance, whether Christian or not, we have collapsed the epistemology once more in the opposite direction, that of phenomenalism. The historical evidence is only to be used provided it functions as a mirror in which we can see ourselves as we wanted to see ourselves. And this would be to deny the possibility of new stories, of subversion or modification to the stories we already tell ourselves. That way, philosophically, lies solipsism, as we have already seen; that way, historically, lies the closed mind. That way, theologically, lies fundamentalism, the corporate religious solipsism that cannot bear the thought of a new, or revised, story.

Thus, if the proposed hypothesis turned out to point us towards a form of Christianity which some people found unacceptable, or if it suggested the abandonment of Christianity altogether, it would be open to anyone to propose going over the argument again to see if a mistake had not been made. But one could not use the perceived unacceptability as a ground *in itself* for rejecting the historical hypothesis.[38] If we are to test the hypothesis, we must proceed strictly on the stated grounds: getting in the data, achieving appropriate simplicity, and proving fruitful in other fields. Of course, such 'verification' consists of humans telling stories perceived to be successful explanatory stories, and this will always involve interaction between knower and data. But one must not allow that inevitability to lure one into simply projecting on to the material either the position one wants to embrace or the position one desires to reject.

History, then, just like microbiology or indeed anything else, proceeds by hypothesis and verification. This, I suggest, is how it has always been, even with the study of Jesus and the gospels and Paul and the epistles. Schweitzer, Bultmann, and the rest, including the 'New Quest' practitioners who argued so long about appropriate criteria[39]—all of them were appealing tacitly to this scheme of thought. All had in mind some hypothesis, some controlling story, which they were defending by the claim that they were dealing with the data, operating with as simple a scheme as possible, and trying to see how this would shed light on other surrounding material. The trouble has been that this

[38] This would not, of course, be the counter-argument usually advanced; but it might well be the real one, hidden behind learned rhetoric.

[39] See Neill and Wright 1988, 288–91, 379–401.

method, though used in fact, has often been unacknowledged, and so has not always operated properly; bad arguments have passed unnoticed because attention was diverted away from the danger signs (carelessness about data, or happy acceptance of unnecessary complexity) which would have warned that all was not well. In particular, scholars have worked with dominant but misleading models of the early church, which as we shall see have exercised a major though often unnoticed influence on the study of Jesus and Paul.

As an example of the latter phenomenon, we may consider Wrede's celebrated hypothesis about the so-called 'messianic secret'.[40] First there was Jesus, who in no way thought of himself as Messiah. Then there was the early church, who hailed him as such (why?) despite his innocence of the idea. Then there was the ingenious and anonymous hero who, faced with this anomaly, invented the explanation that Jesus *had* after all spoken of himself as Messiah, but had always kept the matter strictly secret. Then there was Mark, who took this scheme and deliberately embodied it in a continuous narrative. Even he did not do such a good job, since there are still oddities, such as those times in the gospel when it seems as though the secret is being let out too soon. And all this is supposed to have happened within forty years. This is not to say that quick and dramatic theological development is impossible. It quite often happens, and the first century is a good example. But development of this oddity and complexity, for which complex and bizarre motivations have to be invented, stage by stage, out of thin air—this is asking us to believe quite a lot. A hypothesis which explains the data without recourse to this kind of thing is always going to prove more successful, and rightly so. Wrede paid dearly for the simplicity of his basic (and simple) idea—that Jesus did not think of himself as Messiah—at the cost of ultra-complexity everywhere else, and even then there was a lot of data which still refused to fit. It is no good cleaning out under the bed if the result is a pile of junk under the wardrobe.[41]

(iii) Problems in Verification

There is currently much proper and necessary discussion, for instance among philosophers of science, as to (a) the relative weight to be attached to the different criteria used in the verification or falsification of hypotheses, and (b) the proper working out, in any particular field, of what will count as satisfying each criterion in itself. These are important problems, and we must examine them more closely.

It is clear that the sort of balance required between inclusion of data on the one hand and simplicity on the other will vary according to the subject-matter. The paleontologist has a skeleton to fit together. If she creates a beautifully simple structure which omits a few large bones, her colleagues may accuse her

---

[40] Wrede 1971 [1901]. See the discussion in ch. 13 below.

[41] A modern example of a hypothesis which constantly dismembers the evidence in the interests of a broad overall scheme is Mack 1988. For my own view of secrets, messianic and otherwise, in the ministry of Jesus, see the next volume.

of satisfying the second criterion at the expense of the first, and will take with a pinch of salt her theory that the other bones belong to the animal who was eating—or perhaps being eaten by—the one now constructed. Simplicity has been achieved at the cost of getting in the data. If, however, a second paleontologist produces a skeleton which cunningly uses up all the bones but has seven toes on one foot and eighteen on the other, the opposite conclusion will be drawn: the data have been included, but simplicity abandoned, and distrust will this time be levelled at any bizarre evolutionary explanation of the new story. But which of the two theories will be preferred? On balance, I think, the former: it is harder to imagine the peculiar mutation ever really existing than it is to suspect that a few extra bones may have intruded into the pile. But this victory of simplicity over data (which only means that one story is better than the other, not yet that it is the best possible one, nor yet that it is true) cannot be assumed to hold in all fields of enquiry, and human history is a case in point. The very subject-matter of history is unruly, and all attempts to reduce it to order by a sort of intellectual martial law are suspect. The more one knows about any event, the more complex one realizes it to be. Simplicity is much easier to project on to events when little evidence is to hand. Thus, though there will be an eventual or ultimate simplicity about a good historical hypothesis, and though one should not rest content with odd complexities, inclusion of data is ultimately the more important of the first two criteria.

But what precisely counts as inclusion of data? The details of this as applied to the gospels will be worked out later. But for the moment we must at least say that this aim, the first goal of any hypothesis, must be achieved by treating the evidence seriously on its own terms. A literary text must be treated as what it is and not as something else. The present debates about the genre and intention of the gospels are particularly germane to this. Likewise, a paragraph in a gospel must be studied as what it is and not as something else, and new directions in form-criticism may have something to say about that. We have seen far too much would-be historical reconstruction of Jesus in which tools of thought and criticism have been used in an *ad hoc*, indiscriminate fashion. First we take some inconvenient passage in the gospels and dismiss it as evidence for Jesus by treating it casually as an early church production. In doing so, we quietly ignore, or postpone, the ever-increasing set of traditio-historical problems thus created at the 'early-church' point of the jigsaw: how can we explain such complex material being produced by the early Christians, if it does not go back to Jesus? In addition, we quietly ignore the actual nature of the material itself.[42]

At this point in the historical study of the New Testament some pressure is regularly exerted within the guild to show how 'critical' one's scholarship really is—i.e. to show whether or not one really belongs to the post-Enlightenment club of historical scholarship—by demonstrating one's willingness to jettison this or that saying or incident in the gospels, or this or that paragraph in Paul,

---

[42] Thus, for instance, Sanders (1985) is sometimes guilty of using Bultmann to help him get rid of this or that passage, despite the fact that his whole book utterly rejects the methods, scheme, hypotheses and results that Bultmann used and proposed (see his pp. 26–30).

in the interests of a particular hypothesis. This pressure acts (among other things) as a sort of guarantee that one is not after all a fundamentalist in disguise. But this legitimate desire for serious historical and critical reading of the sources, and the proper refusal to go back behind Reimarus to a day when such questions could not be raised, is perverted if it leads us to ignore the fact that, in history, it is *getting in the data* that really counts. And we need at this point to reopen the question, often closed this century: does it really count as 'getting in the data' to say 'this is a creation of the early church'? It might, if we could produce a really workable hypothesis about the early church which would *support* this theory, but in my judgment such a story has not yet been suggested. Study of the actual history of the early church is in its infancy, but already the young child is showing signs that it will soon become vigorous enough to attack the speculative hypotheses that have for so long usurped its place in the family (see Part IV).

A good deal of New Testament scholarship, in fact, and within that a good deal of study of Jesus, has proceeded on the assumption that the gospels cannot possibly make sense as they stand, so that some alternative hypothesis must be proposed to take the place of the view of Jesus they seem to offer. It has been assumed that we know, *more or less*, what Jesus' life, ministry and self-understanding were like, and that they were *un*like the picture we find in the gospels.[43] But hypotheses of this sort are always short on simplicity, since they demand an explanation not only of what happened in the ministry of Jesus, but also of why the early church said something different, and actually wrote up stories as founding 'myths' which bore little relation to the historical events. We may grant, of course, that the truth in these matters is likely to be very complex. But we are faced with three factors which militate against *this* sort of complexity. There is, (on any showing) the comparative chronological closeness of the gospels to the subject-matter they purport to describe.[44] There is, second, the high probability that the earliest Palestinian Christianity continued in many important respects the sort of ministry in which Jesus himself had engaged.[45] There is also the fact that we have available within current scholarship several quite plausible hypotheses about Jesus which include whole reams of data that it was formerly thought impossible to include.[46] As a result, the position of those who insist that the story of the gospels cannot be taken in any sense as history begins to look like that of the paleontologist who, finding a skeleton actually preserved all together, insists that there was not and could not have been an animal like that, and that it must somehow therefore have been put together at a later date (perhaps by Theissen's 'committee for misleading later historians').[47] As soon as a simpler hypothesis turned up—or even before that!—it would be a bold scientist who continued with such an argument. It is my contention, in the field of the historical study of Jesus, that

[43] Thus Bultmann 1968 [1921], *passim*: e.g. 145, 262, etc.
[44] We might contrast, for instance, Livy's account of the Punic Wars, or Josephus' of the Maccabaean uprising.
[45] See Theissen 1978, 4, 121; Borg 1984, 132f., 190.
[46] See, once more, Neill and Wright 1988, 379–403.
[47] Theissen 1987, 66.

the present state of traditio-historical study of the gospels has reached this sort of point, and that a simpler hypothesis, doing more justice to the data as a whole, is within reach.

The same, once more, is true of hypotheses about Paul's thought. There are several hypotheses on offer which achieve an apparent simplicity at the cost of either stripping away several verses as later accretions—i.e. *removing* evidence—or suggesting that many of the major themes and passages are actually self-contradictory and incoherent—i.e. admitting *intractability* of evidence. There is, of course, such a thing as later glossing of old texts. There is also, of course, such a thing as incoherence, and it is possible, in principle as well as in practice, that any writer, ancient or modern, may be guilty of it. But one should never suggest removing evidence which does not fit the theory unless there are good arguments for doing so on quite other grounds.[48] And the latter possibility—the admission that the evidence seems intractable—must be considered very carefully, both in itself and in its damaging effects on the hypothesis which contains or requires it, before being adopted. Such a position positively invites a new proposal for a clear solution which resolves the difficulty.

Granted all this, what is to count as satisfying the criterion of simplicity? Historians, as we suggested above, need to take care at this point. Scholars who enjoy tidiness, perhaps for quite other reasons, may well inflict their desire for order on to the material, leaving the historical workshop so tidy that no-one can find where anything is. History is not about tidiness, but, most often, about the odd, the unrepeatable and the unlikely. It is therefore important to state that not all forms of simplicity are of equal value. If we are to attempt to distinguish, in the limited field of history, between different types of simplicity (or, negatively, between different types of complexity), we might do so as follows. The areas where simplicity might count strongly are in human aims and motivations, in *the continuity of the person*. Granted that human beings are highly complex entities, living in a highly complex world, and very often failing to achieve a high level of behavioural consistency, there is still nevertheless such a thing as coherence and stability of character, so that unusual or abnormal behaviour (that is, behaviour unusual or abnormal *for that person*, granted what else may be known about him or her) invites special investigation and explanation. In the same way, actions and events simply do have consequences and sequels. An apparently odd jump or break in a chain of events invites similar investigation. Here we are justified in looking for simplicity: can we understand something at least of how the central actors in the drama were motivated and behaving, and of how, as a result, events took the course they did?[49] It is precisely because this sort of simplicity is important

---

[48] A good example of a case being made on the basis of evidence outside the text may be found in Fee's argument (1987, 699–708) for the non-originality of 1 Cor. 14.34–5.

[49] For a recent argument using exactly this criterion in the field of synoptic studies, cf. Downing 1992, 34f.: 'The simplicity of an hypothesis about literary interdependence cannot be assessed solely on the basis of the number of conjectural sources involved. Goulder's hypothesis [about Luke's use of Matthew] has fewer documents than has Streeter's. But to justify it there are innumerable hypotheses about what was going on in Luke's mind . . .' On the importance of examining 'what happened next' as part of the historical task, see Meyer 1979, 252f., following

that the major questions we shall raise about Jesus in volume 2 are what they
are. The complexity of many hypotheses at just these points is one of their
major undoings. Once again, the same would be true of Paul. Any hypothesis
which can display an overall consistency of thought, provided that the data are
retained and enhanced, and provided that there is at least the promise of
coherence with wider fields of study, will always be preferable to one which
leaves the writer as a scatty individual, chopping and changing his mind at
every turn.[50] The same would in principle be true if we were studying Aristotle,
Athanasius, Beethoven or Barth.

There is a different sort of simplicity, however, which has been very attractive to New Testament scholars, but whose value is extremely questionable.
Many hypotheses have been constructed whose simplicity lies in straightforward 'movements', and in the unilinear developments of great ideas.
Christianity, it is imagined, began very simply, and then developed into
increasing complexity.[51] But this is just not true of ideas and how they work. If
anything, the 'simpler' form is likely to be the developed and polished result of
many years of work whereby a complex phenomenon has been patiently tidied
up and made more manageable. Another example is the scheme proposed last
century by F. C. Baur, which still exercises a good deal of influence in some
quarters today. How simple, how tidy, to have Jewish Christianity developing
this way, Gentile Christianity developing that way, and then the two joining
together to make Early Catholicism![52] To object that such a scheme smells of
Hegel is to miss the serious point. Nor will it do to suggest that the scheme
cannot be true because it began as an intellectual construct (in the mind of
F. C. Baur) and was only subsequently worked out in its details. It is not a valid
criticism to say that the hypothesis was the beginning, rather than the end, of a
large study of the data. All hypotheses, as we have seen, work like this. They
all begin either as a modification of a story already told by a group or individual, or as the story at which, by an intuitive leap, the researcher arrives.
Rather, such a scheme fails as *history*, because—as can be seen in the havoc it
makes of the actual data—history simply does not seem to have moved like
this, in neat unilinear patterns. We find regress as well as progress. There is
downright change, not simply smooth observable development. People and
societies retrace steps, try different paths. They do not always march forward
in a straight line. This is not to deny that there are such things as movements
of thought. I have elsewhere tried to describe some that are going on at the
present time among New Testament scholars.[53] But, as has been shown powerfully in recent years, the simplicity of Baur's idealist scheme was deceptive.
The time available for it to have taken effect is simply too short; there is too

Kant; Neill and Wright 1988, 399.

[50] See Wright 1991a, ch. 1.

[51] This idea is thoroughly debunked by Wilken 1971.

[52] On Baur, see Neill and Wright 1988, 20–30.

[53] See Neill and Wright 1988, ch. 9; and the introductions to the next two volumes in the present series. That these accounts, too, are oversimplified may be taken for granted.

great a multitude of data to which it has to sit loose (the fact, for instance, that our main evidence for 'Jewish Christianity' as such is late, and for 'Gentile Christianity' very early); and its pet theories about history-of-religions derivations, especially in the area of christology, have collapsed entirely. There is a tidiness proper to full human life. There is also the tidiness of the graveyard.

The final problem about hypotheses is that, when all is said and done, there may be more than one possible hypothesis which fits the evidence. The question may, in technical language, be underdetermined. This is particularly likely in ancient history, where we have so little data to work with, in comparison with what we have for, say, the sixteenth century.[54] We are inevitably, to some extent, like the paleontologist who 'reconstructs' the brontosaurus from half a dozen small bones. Perhaps after all it was a mastodon. The theoretical possibility of two or more equally good solutions is, however, a problem that most historians are happy to live with. Since it is extremely difficult, to put it mildly, for any one of the guild to hold *all* the relevant data in his or her head at one time, we need each other, and should welcome, in the best scientific tradition, having our attention drawn to bits of evidence we had overlooked, to unnecessary complexities in the hypothesis, or to parts of neighbouring subject-areas where the hypothesis seems to create new problems instead of solving old ones. As to what happens when we finally arrive at two or more significantly different hypotheses which both seem to meet all the criteria equally adequately—well, we will cross that bridge when we come to it. I do not expect that to be soon.

5. From Event to Meaning

(i) Event and Intention

History, then, is real knowledge, of a particular sort. It is arrived at, like all knowledge, by the spiral of epistemology, in which the story-telling human community launches enquiries, forms provisional judgments about which stories are likely to be successful in answering those enquiries, and then tests these judgments by further interaction with data. But there are three more levels of understanding, proper to history in particular, at which we must now look.

To begin with, history involves not only the study of 'what happened' in the sense of 'what physical events would a video camera have recorded', but also the study of *human intentionality*. In Collingwood's language, this involves looking at, or at least for, the 'inside' of an event.[55] We are trying to discover what the humans involved in the event thought they were doing, wanted to do, or tried to do. The apparently obvious counter-example proves the point: when historians try to write about pre-human or non-human history they regularly

[54] See again Carr 1987 [1961], ch. 1.
[55] Collingwood 1956 [1946], *passim*. See the illuminating discussions in Meyer 1989, chs. 2 and 3.

invoke some idea of purpose, whether that of the cosmos, of some sort of guiding life-force, or even some sort of god. The argument for total randomness becomes harder and harder to sustain. Odd things happen, but as soon as they happen somebody starts to ask 'Why?' And (to return to ordinary, human, history), the answer to the question 'Why?' normally involves not only the physical properties of the 'objects' involved (the vase broke *because* it was made of glass and came into contact with a hard floor) but also the aims, intentions, and motivations of human beings and how these affected the observable events. The vase broke because (a) part of my overall aim is to live in a beautiful house, and I perceive that if I encourage my children to decorate it with flowers this will be a means to achieve this aim; (b) my intention was to hand my daughter a vase to put flowers in, and (c) I was motivated to do so at that moment; but (d) she was not expecting me to let go of it when I did (we might perhaps speak of my *inappropriate motivation*), and so there came a time when nobody was holding the vase, and it fell to the floor. The 'outside' of the event is that the vase broke. The 'inside' of the event is a story, not only about the physical properties of vases and floors, but more particularly about human aims, intentions, motivations and consequent actions. About these we must say a few more words of explanation; this is an area where important points will be made later on.[56]

By *aim* I mean the fundamental direction of a person's life, or some fairly settled subset of that fundamental direction. This aim is thus the directional aspect of an individual's *mindset*, by which I mean the individual subset of, or variant on, the *worldview* held by the society or societies to which the individual belongs.[57] Talking about the 'aim' enables talk about worldviews and mindsets to be given its proper directional aspect (i.e. the sense that they involve purpose and movement) without which they might collapse back into an apparently static form, in which humans were simply machines which, once programmed, stayed in the same place performing the same mental or physical operations. This, I believe, would be fundamentally counter-intuitive. When, therefore, we ask about someone's 'aim', we are going 'inside' an event to the point where some of the most basic questions are to be found.

By *intention* I mean the specific application of the 'aim' in a particular (and in principle repeatable) situation. Obviously, the line between the two is fairly arbitrary, and it might even be possible to reverse the two words without doing violence to the English language. But some such division is often helpful. It was Paul's 'aim' that he announce Jesus as Messiah and Lord in cities and towns around the Mediterranean world. It was his 'intention', as one result of this aim, that he should work his way around the Aegean seacoast, and, having finished there, move on to Rome. When we look at Jesus' 'intention' in going

---

[56] See ch. 5 below. I am conscious that many different categorizations could be made at this point, of which Aristotle's (in the *Nic. Eth.*) is only one. My adoption of technical terms in the next paragraphs is purely heuristic: I do not intend to import into the discussion layers of meaning from other spheres of discourse, but only to give convenient and, in a measure, arbitrary labels to things that seem to me to need distinguishing when discussing the 'inside' of historical events.

[57] On 'worldviews' themselves see ch. 5 below.

to Jerusalem for his last and fateful Passover, we must see it in the light of his overall 'aim': how did his intention on this occasion relate to the underlying aims and goals which motivated him throughout his ministry?

By *motivation* I mean the specific sense, on one specific occasion, that a certain action or set of actions is appropriate and desirable. Jesus' aim was (we may say) to inaugurate the 'kingdom of God'; his intention, towards the end of his life, was to go to Jerusalem; within both of these, he was motivated on one particular day to go into the Temple and set about overturning tables. Within Paul's general aim and intention, he was motivated on one particular occasion to debate with philosophers in the Athenian market-place; on another, to write a highly rhetorical letter to Corinth; on another, to initiate a collection on behalf of the church in Jerusalem.

It is, of course, quite possible that particular motivations will conflict with aims and intentions: Aristotle devoted a sizeable discussion to this problem, and he was by no means the last to do so.[58] It is one of the problems of discussing (say) Judas Iscariot that we find it difficult to discern a motivation, for his crucial action, that makes sense in itself and in relation to the aims and intentions that we must assume for him during the time of his following Jesus. But in a great number of cases we can see at least a broad fit between aim, intention and motivation. I aim to become a Cabinet Minister; I intend to become master of my corner of the political world; having a spare weekend, I am motivated to read up a new part of my field, or make the acquaintance of some useful contacts. If, granted the presence of suitable opportunities, I am never sufficiently motivated to do these things, it is appropriate to question the truth of the claim about my aims and intentions. Weakness of will (what Aristotle called *akrasia*) does of course occur, so that the challenge might be resisted; but it makes sense to offer it.

History, then, includes the study of aims, intentions and motivations. This does not mean that history is covert psychology. It is no doubt possible in principle to move beyond the three aspects already studied, and to ask, of particular characters, *why* they had *that* particular set of aims or intentions; or why, on that particular occasion, they were clearly motivated to act (as we might say) 'out of character'. Possible in principle, maybe; very difficult in practice. As anyone with any counselling experience knows, it is difficult and delicate to ask these questions of a friendly, honest and outgoing individual who, sharing the same culture as ourselves, is sitting with us and co-operating in the process. Much harder with a depressed, confused or hostile subject; harder still with a subject of whom we only know what history has happened to leave behind. We *might* be able to make intelligent guesses at the psychological state of Napoleon, or Martin Luther, or even Jesus; but to do so is to face enormous difficulties. We must insist, however, that to study the 'inside' of an event does not mean going that far. We can say, as historians, that King David chose Jerusalem as his capital because (a) his aim was to unite the twelve tribes of Israel, (b) his intention was to find a capital that would not obviously 'belong' to any one of them and thus be suspect, and (c) his motivation, at a particular

---

[58] Aristotle, *Nic. Eth.* book 7; cf. Hare 1963, ch. 5.

moment, was to take Jerusalem, as being an obvious and well-situated case in point. We can say, as historians, that Augustus Caesar's aim was to bring peace and stability to the Roman world, that his intention was to do this by means of securing power for himself and settling problems around the frontiers of (what became) the empire, and that his motivation was to confirm Herod in power in order to keep Palestine in good order. I think we can say, of the Teacher of Righteousness, that his aim was to found the community of the True Israel over against the usurpers in Jerusalem, that his intention was to do so by giving his followers a solid basis of biblical exegesis and a community rule, and that his motivation was, on particular occasions, to write *this* text *now*. We can say similar things, as I shall argue later, about Jesus and Paul. In no case does this involve us in psychological speculation. It involves the historical study of worldviews, mindsets, aims, intentions and motivations. We are on ground which can be debated without necessarily having to invoke Freud or Jung, and without pretending that we can see, in the case of a subject from the distant past, what would be hard enough to see in a co-operating contemporary.

Finally, if history involves all these things it must clearly involve them not just at the level of individuals, whose *mindsets* are involved directly, but also of societies, whose *worldviews* are at stake.[59] But how do we study societies and their worldviews? By means of their *symbols*, their *characteristic behaviour*, and their *literature*, particularly the stories they tell explicitly and implicitly. Societies and cultures reveal their worldviews by the cultural objects they produce, from banknotes to bus-tickets, from skyscrapers to subway cars, from pottery to poetry; from temples to Torah scrolls, from military emblems to funerary monuments, from gymnasia to amulets. Symbols provide the interpretative grid through which humans perceive both how the world is and how they might act within it: they provide a vision *of* reality and a vision *for* it.[60] Symbols cluster around the *characteristic behaviour* of a society, and vice versa: the celebration of festivals, the regular means of dealing with dissonance, the rituals associated with birth, puberty, marriage and death. And, in many cultures, symbol and characteristic behaviour are also focussed in *literature* of all sorts. It is by studying these things that the historian can uncover the *worldview* of another culture, and thus set the stage for enquiring about the *mindsets* of individuals within that society.[61]

The task of the historian is thus to address the question 'Why?' at all possible levels, down to its roots in the way the people under investigation perceived the world as a whole. But if this is so it will not do to answer the question simply by listing various antecedent circumstances in any particular order. The historian's job is to examine the balance of factors and reach a conclusion which sets out the connected train of events, giving them their appropriate weighting.[62] How is this to be done?

---

[59] On this whole point see ch. 5 below.
[60] I owe this shaping of the point to Dr Brian Walsh.
[61] See further ch. 5 below.
[62] See Carr 1987 [1961], ch. 4.

(ii) History and Narrative

The task of the historian is not simply to assemble little clumps of 'facts' and hope that somebody else will integrate them. The historian's job is to show their interconnectedness, that is, how one thing follows from another, precisely by examining the 'inside' of the events. And the model for such connections is not simply that of random atoms cannoning into one another. It is that of the interplay of fully human life—the complex network of human aims, intentions and motivations, operating within and at the edges of the worldviews of different communities and the mindsets of different individuals. To display this, the historian needs (it will come as no surprise) to tell a story.[63]

This is the point at which the historian needs to use an intuitive or imaginative construction. As I argued in chapter 2, this is something that binds the historian to all other disciplines. All knowledge proceeds by the telling of new stories, and these stories make their way by the process of verification discussed earlier. But the historical hypothesis itself, like all steps forward in knowledge (once naïve realism has been abandoned), comes from within the historian, and thus from the resources of story-telling inherent in his or her direct or second-hand experience. This may include analogy, the recognition of similar patterns of events in two different periods, but may well go beyond it. I have frequently asked my students why Rome was especially interested in the Middle East. Few of them come up with (what seems to me) the right answer: that the capital needed a constant supply of corn; that one of the prime sources of corn was Egypt; and that anything which threatened that supply, such as disturbances in neighbouring countries, might result in serious difficulties at home. (It is the more surprising that this story does not come readily to mind, considering the obvious analogies with late-twentieth-century politics: substitute oil for corn, certain other countries for Rome on the one hand and Egypt on the other, and the equation still works.) But this account of how things were—of why, for instance, someone like Pontius Pilate was in Palestine in the first place—is not read off the surface of one particular text. It is a story told by historians to explain the smaller stories they *do* find on the surface of their texts. Reaching even so simple a story requires controlled and disciplined imagination, but imagination none the less.

It is important to stress this because, as we shall shortly see, a great many people within the guild of New Testament specialists have written very little history as such. Attention to particular problems, yes; attempts to write the connected history of even part of the first century, no.[64] There are few books in the field which correspond to (say) J. B. Bury's *History of Greece*, or even Bertrand Russell's *History of Western Philosophy*.[65] More characteristic of the discipline as it has been practised, since the First World War at least, are com-

---

[63] On this whole point see Elton 1984 [1967], 160–77.

[64] This is perhaps due to the belated influence in the field of Lord Acton's principle, that one should study problems not periods: see Elton 1984 [1967], 161.

[65] See Bury 1951 [1909]; Russell 1961 [1946]. Exceptions include the *New Testament Historys* of Filson 1965; Bruce 1972; and parts of Koester 1982a. Other possible candidates will be discussed in Part IV.

mentaries on particular books, detached studies of smaller-scale problems, and exegetical notes on detailed texts. There is no recent work which does for the early church, or yet for Jesus, what the new edition of Schürer's classic *History of the Jewish People in the Age of Jesus Christ* does for its subject-matter, showing *en route* that despite the fears of New Testament scholars first-century history is alive and well.[66] Anyone who doubts whether one can write actual history based on sources most of which were written from positions of faith (not Christian faith, as it happens, but positions of faith none the less) should read the first volume of Schürer and observe the critical sifting of sources, the narrative construct in which the writers project themselves by sympathetic imagination into the worldviews and mindsets of the characters involved, and the synthesis which results.[67] The result is a narrative, a story, in which the data are contained, for the most part, within a comparatively simple scheme, which contributes substantially to our knowledge of events in other areas as well. This is what history—real history, not some strange figment of the critical imagination—looks like. Thus, even if no recent comparable work on early Christianity has yet been written, there is no good reason in principle why it should not be. We have, granted, no Josephus for early Christianity. But the other sources for Jewish history are no more or less scattered and fragmentary, no more or less biased and partial, than the Christian ones, and the task of reconstruction is no more or less hazardous and (in the senses discussed already) 'subjective'.

The trouble is that when New Testament scholars are faced with page after page of historical description and narrative, albeit peppered with explanatory footnotes and discussions of tricky points, they feel uncomfortable—especially when the subject is Jesus. They feel sure that questions must be being begged, that unwarranted harmonization must be going on somewhere. I submit that this fear is unnecessary. Of course there is to be harmonization. All serious historical writing presupposes that a sequence of events did actually take place, a sequence which has an 'inside' as well as an 'outside'. A good historical account offers precisely a harmonious treatment of the whole; that, as we have seen, is one of its tasks if it is to be taken seriously as history.

That is not to say, of course, that a harmonious account is necessarily correct. It could not be: Meyer, Harvey, Borg, Sanders, Horsley, Crossan and many others in the last fifteen years have stood out against the general trend and written internally harmonious accounts of Jesus—and they all disagree with each other at various points. They cannot all be right all of the time.[68] Harmonious accounts must be tested like any other hypothesis. But it is to say that a harmonious account is not by its very nature *in*correct. Certain events did happen, and it is in principle possible to work towards finding out what they were, and to improve on previous attempts at the task. It is this sort of

---

[66] Schürer 1973–87.

[67] On all this see Part III below. The three stages of historical work—sifting sources, imaginative reconstruction, coherent synthesis—are set out by Neill in Neill and Wright 1988, 304. The whole passage (304–12) repays close attention.

[68] See Meyer 1979; Harvey 1982; Borg 1984; Sanders 1985; Horsley 1987; Crossan 1991. On the first four see Neill and Wright 1988, 379–96.

exercise that will be attempted in Parts III and IV of the present volume, and throughout the next one.

One important aspect of the narrative is the *sequel*. It is one of the problems about studying 'contemporary history' that one has no sequel to work with; and where a sequel is lacking, an appeal, perhaps tacit, can be made to ideology to fill up the vacuum.[69] There is, of course, a great danger about sequels. 'Hindsight' tends to be an abuse word when we are analysing a period: we want to see and feel *what it felt like at the time*. But it is equally true that the full story of the 'inside' of an event may only be unfolded gradually, in the light of subsequent and consequent events. It was only in the years after the Second World War, as the truth about the 'Final Solution' came to be known, that one could really understand what had been going on all along in Germany in the 1930s. There are, of course, such things as effects which are intended by no-one. There are also effects which are intended by someone, or some group, and which only gradually come to light. As Albert Schweitzer saw, we need to understand something of the second generation of the Pauline communities in order to understand fully just what Paul himself was up to.[70] As Ben Meyer argues, it may be 'in the tradition generated by Jesus that we discover what made him operate in the way he did'.[71] The narrative must therefore point forward beyond itself to embrace the future. And in doing so historians find themselves, from time to time, using the word 'meaning'. This causes problems of its own.

(iii) History and Meaning

It is within this framework that we can at last approach the vexed question of 'meaning'. There has been a well-known debate about the meaning of meaning running in philosophical circles for some time, and, like a good deal else in this volume, we cannot pursue it here.[72] It is, however, necessary that I should offer at this stage a brief account of what I at least understand by the concept. It may be clearest if we work up from the smallest units to the largest.

First, the meaning of a word (following Wittgenstein) I take to be its use in a context, or an implicit context; that is, its use or potential use in a sentence or potential sentence.[73] If I say 'book', the meaning of this is in doubt until I form a sentence: 'I am going to book the tickets'; 'The book is on the desk'; 'The criminal was brought to book.' Even where a word is clearly univocal, we can never rule out possible metaphorical meanings, and in any case we only

[69] cf. e.g. Carr 1987 [1961], ch. 5; Barraclough 1967 [1964], 14f. A similar point could be made, of course, about thinkers who collapse the past into the present: see Thiselton 1992, ch. 16 section 3, criticizing Thomas Groome. Barraclough rightly points out, however, that one of the greatest historians, Thucydides himself, was writing 'contemporary history'.

[70] Schweitzer 1968b [1931].

[71] Meyer 1979, 253; a controversial claim, of course, which we will discuss in vol. 2.

[72] See Thiselton 1980 *passim*.

[73] Wittgenstein 1961 [1921], 14: 'only in the nexus of a proposition does a name have meaning' (n.b. 13: 'in a proposition a name is the representative of an object').

know the univocal meaning through experience of sentences in which it has become plain.

Second, the meaning of a sentence is its place in a story or implicit story.[74] 'The book is on the desk', spoken by my assistant, carries a different meaning (a) in an implicit story in which I have been searching my shelves in vain for a particular book, and (b) in an implicit story in which I had intended to hide the book before the next person entered the room. 'Jesus was crucified' carries different meanings in the story told by the centurion as he reported back to Pilate, in the story told by the disciples to one another the same evening, and in the story told by Paul in his mission preaching.

Third, the meaning of a story is its place in a worldview. (This assumes, no doubt, several intermediate stages, in which lesser stories acquire meaning within larger ones, and so on.) As we have seen frequently, stories relate in a variety of ways to worldviews: they articulate them, legitimate them, support them, modify them, challenge them, subvert them, and even perhaps destroy them. The same story can have different meanings in relation to different worldviews. The parable of the Good Samaritan, told to an ardent Jewish lawyer, would be bound to threaten or subvert his worldview. The same story, told to an ardent Samaritan nationalist, might reinforce his. The story of the collapse of the Berlin Wall is already being widely used to reinforce the Western liberal-capitalist worldview. The same story is being used by neo-Marxists to subvert older Marxist theory: that experiment failed, but we will get it right next time. The stories that historians tell gain their meaning from an overall worldview. In the introduction to the second edition of his book on the nature of history, E. H. Carr faces the possibility that the story of events between the first and second editions might subvert his worldview, his belief in progress, and then advances other arguments to suggest that he can still retain it after all.[75] And it is quite clear, as we suggested a moment ago, that the question of *sequel* looms large in these discussions. If things really turn out differently in the end, the meaning of a story, including the early parts, will be different. If the owner of the vineyard had returned, ignored the tenants' behaviour, and let them keep the vineyard in perpetuity, the meaning of all the earlier events would have to be seen in a different light. The ending of a story or play, being the sequel to the main part of the action, forces us to look back on earlier scenes with new eyes: is *The Merchant of Venice*, when all is said and done, really a comedy, or is it in fact a hidden tragedy?

What is true of stories is emphatically true of events. The meaning of an event, which as we saw is basically an acted story, is its place, or its perceived place, within a sequence of events, which contribute to a more fundamental story; and fundamental stories are of course one of the constituent features of worldviews. The fall of Jerusalem possessed one meaning for the writer of 4 Ezra, who saw it as an unmitigated disaster, subverting his expected story as thoroughly as the hypothetical ending to *Little Red Riding-Hood* which had the woodcutter freeing the wolf and marrying the heroine. It had a radically dif-

---

[74] See MacIntyre 1985 [1981], ch. 15.
[75] Carr 1987 [1961], 3–6.

ferent meaning for Josephus, who tried at least to make out that he saw it as the result of Israel's god going over to the Romans, thereby perhaps tacitly revising his worldview to take account of the new situation. It had yet another meaning for the author of Mark 13, where it is seen as the destruction of a neo-Babylon. Thus, at every level with which the historian is concerned, from individual words right up to whole sequences of events, 'meaning' is to be found within a context—ultimately, within the context of worldviews.

Does this mean that 'meaning' must always remain private? Have we, by implication at least, moved so far away from a positivistic idea of 'meaning', from the belief that there is a 'real' or 'true' meaning somehow 'out there', waiting to be discovered, that we have collapsed the whole scheme into a solipsistic phenomenalism? By no means. Two counter-arguments may be advanced.

First, events and their sequels are essentially public. Though the historian (and, for that matter, the lawyer, and a good many private individuals) wants to know about the inside of the event, the event itself is public property. The worldview of the Flat Earth society is progressively undermined by each round-the-world sailing, each photograph from space; when Guildenstern says to Rosencrantz that he doesn't believe in England, the response ('The conspiracy of the cartographers?')[76] loses its plausibility when they eventually arrive (or do they)? If events are public, they can be discussed; evidence can be amassed; and some worldviews become progressively harder and harder to retain, needing more and more conspiracy theories in order to stay in place, until they (sometimes) collapse under their own weight. We have witnessed this on a grand scale in recent events in Eastern Europe.

Second, worldviews, though normally hidden from sight like the foundations of a house, can themselves in principle be dug out and inspected.[77] Reaching them is signalled by some such sentence as 'that's just the way the world is'. When someone else says 'no, it isn't', either the conversation stops or battle is joined; and the battle consists of each side telling stories designed to subvert the other or to reinforce itself. And, in this discussion, what is really at stake is precisely the *adequacy* or *appropriateness* of the meanings assigned to a variety of stories and events within the worldview itself. This process, then, which belongs fairly obviously to the critical-realist epistemology I have been advancing all through, guarantees in principle that, though 'meaning' can never be separated from the minds of humans who suppose it, nor can it simply be reduced to terms of those humans themselves, whether individuals or groups. Dialogue is possible. People can change their beliefs; they can even change their worldviews. At the beginning of John 20 Thomas would have assigned one meaning to the crucifixion. By the end he had assigned it another. Conversion happens: Saul becomes Paul; Francis embraces a new vision of what it might mean to be human. 'Meaning', like events, is ultimately a matter that comes into the public sphere.

---

[76] This response, in Stoppard's film, is an addition to the stage play (Stoppard 1967, 89).
[77] On worldviews see further ch. 5 below.

(iv) Conclusion

Practice without theory is blind, but theory without practice is dumb. It is nearly time to leave the theory and get on with the practice. We have, I believe, laid foundations strong enough to sustain the major work of this project, which involves the study of early Jewish and Christian literature and the attempt to write history on the basis of them. I have argued that a critical-realist reading of history, paying due attention to the worldviews, mindsets, aims, intentions and motivations of the human beings and societies involved, is a proper and, in principle, a possible task. I have set out a method by which one might attempt it. This clears the ground for the study of early Judaism and Christianity, and, within them, the study of Jesus and Paul.

One more preliminary task remains, and that is that we tease out more fully the other area of concern, namely theology. But before turning to this it will be as well, in summing up this chapter on history, to look at what will be involved in the study of the two major first-century religious movements that will be our chief focus.

6. Historical Study of First-Century Religious Movements

(i) Introduction

The main focus of this project is nothing more nor less than the history of certain first-century religious movements. That description is, I think, as little likely to mislead as any other catch-all heading. When we are dealing with Jesus and his significance, with Paul and his, with the gospels and theirs, we are in the first instance studying people and movements whose worldviews (and consequent aims, intentions and motivations) included, at a high-profile level, elements that are today known as 'religious'. They believed, that is, in a god who was actively involved in their personal and corporate lives, who had intentions and purposes and was capable of carrying them out through both willing and uncomprehending human agents as well as (what we would call) 'natural forces'. We are therefore studying human history, in the recognition that the actors in the drama, and hence in a sense the drama itself, can only be fully understood when we learn to see the world through their eyes. We shall here glance at the two main areas to be addressed, which will be discussed in more detail in Parts III and IV.

(ii) Judaism in the First Century

Recent study of first-century Judaism has rightly stressed its pluriformity. This has been necessary in a climate where, for many centuries, traditions of understanding Judaism at both the scholarly and the popular level had operated with simplistic models which failed lamentably to do justice to the evidence.[78] Scholarship is now in the full swing of producing excellent new editions of, and commentaries upon, very different sorts of texts from the period. We have learned to distinguish not just aristocrats from revolutionaries,[79] and Pharisees from Sadducees, but also apocalyptists from Rabbis, and both from the schools of thought represented by Philo and *The Wisdom of Solomon*.

But this readiness to accept pluriformity can degenerate, and in my opinion sometimes has degenerated, into a kind of atomistic positivism. There are several scholars whose work seems to consist simply of studying one small area, saying certain things about it, and leaving it at that. As I argued in the previous section, this is not yet history in the full sense. It is all too easy to look at a text for its own sake, to ask questions about it within its own world of thought and vision, and to fail to relate it at more than a superficial level to the larger world within which it finds its wider meaning. We have learned that we must not glibly pass over differences of setting and time, imagining continuity of thought between documents of different provenance. But there is an equal and opposite danger against which we must also guard. A narrowly focused study can ignore the fact that events (including literary events) need to be examined from as fully historical a viewpoint as possible; and this means looking at their 'inside', at the range of motivations and understandings within which, and only within which, they can make sense. And at this level we cannot escape the constant task, important in the study of second-temple Judaism as much as anywhere else, of reconstructing the worldview which informed and underlay not only this or that particular writing but the society as a whole. We need to plot, and understand, the stories that Jews of the period were telling themselves and one another about who they were, about what their god was up to, about what the meaning of it all might be. There can be no going back to the cheap generalizations that characterized earlier scholarship. But nor should we shrink back from referring to, and indeed giving a detailed account of, the prevailing strands that went to make up the complex entity that may yet be called the overall first-century Jewish worldview. Such study is part of history itself. Not to undertake it is to risk making strictly unhistorical assumptions.

(iii) Christianity in the First Century

The same problem at the level of historical method can be witnessed in relation to first-century Christianity. Once again, there has been a recent tendency towards atomism in the wake of previous shallow generalizations. Here, however, there has been a complicating factor. A good deal of twentieth-century scholarship has indeed attempted to get to the 'inside' of events, writings and movements in the primitive church, but the tool it has employed to do this has been extremely blunt. I refer to the attempt to understand early

---

[78] See Part III below. If the point is now commonplace in NT studies, the credit for this belongs to a large extent to E. P. Sanders (1977). See Neill and Wright 1988, 371–8.

[79] *Pace* Goodman 1987; see Part III below.

Christianity in terms of its expectation of the imminent end of the world and/or its anxiety and change of mood when this expectation was disappointed. I shall argue later that this whole perception is grossly distorted, and I shall offer alternative hypotheses for a different 'inner' story that will replace it within the (perfectly valid) scheme of searching for the inner story of first-century Christian history. And, as with Judaism, we must remember that, though in many ways early Christianity appears to the post-Enlightenment world as a 'religion', within first-century categories it certainly did not. The early Christians were dubbed 'atheists'. They offered no animal sacrifices. What they did in their communal meetings bore some resemblances to non-Christian religious practices, but it was the differences that stuck out. The main thing that would have struck observers of early Christianity was not its 'religious' side, nor indeed its early doctrinal formulations, but its total way of life. When, therefore, we look at the history of (what we call) first-century religious movements such as Judaism and Christianity, it is vital that we look for the 'inside' of the events: the aims, the intentions and the motivations—and the self-perceptions—of the people involved. It is equally vital that we bear in mind the risks inherent in using post-Enlightenment categories. There is such a thing as cultural imperialism, and modern study of first-century history has not always avoided it.

In seeking to be obedient to this last demand of historical rigour, it is vital that we examine in more detail the subject-matter which, fairly obviously, stands at the centre of the first-century Jewish and Christian worldviews. We must look at Theology.

Chapter Five

THEOLOGY, AUTHORITY AND THE NEW TESTAMENT

1. Introduction: From Literature and History to Theology

It should be clear by now that the task of reading the New Testament can never be a matter of 'purely literary' or 'purely historical' study, as though either of these could be removed from wider considerations of culture, worldviews, and especially theology. The model of 'mere history', in particular, is inadequate for a full appreciation of any text, and particularly one such as the New Testament. Equally, we suggested in the first chapter that a serious reading of the New Testament must show how this book, read in appropriate ways, might function with the authority which it has been deemed to have by the great majority of its readers down the years; but we also saw that the pre-critical and 'modern' ways of articulating this have not met with success. The aim of this chapter is to suggest what might be involved in a 'theological' reading that does not bypass the 'literary' and 'historical' readings, but rather enhances them; and to explore one possible model of letting this composite reading function as normative or authoritative. I am well aware that there are large areas of possible discussion left untouched here. The aim is not to provide an exhaustive account of the nature of theology, but to draw out some salient points about how the discipline works.

We have already seen that, beyond any cavil, all reading involves the reader as an active participant. To say that one is merely studying objective history, without other presuppositions, is no longer an option:

> In every piece of work done according to the norms of historical science, the writer and the reader should be aware that a historical sketch can only take shape in the mind of a historian, and that in this process the historian himself, with all his intellectual furniture, is involved.[1]

There are therefore two levels at which we pass beyond 'mere history'. First, in order to answer the question 'Why?' in relation to the past, we must move from the 'outside' of the event to the 'inside'; this involves reconstructing the worldviews of people other than ourselves. Second, in doing this we cannot stand outside our own worldviews, any more than we can see without our own eyes. At both levels the reader must be clear about the worldviews involved,

---

[1] Schlatter 1973 [1909], 125f.

and must be on the lookout for potential peculiarities, inconsistencies or tensions. To this we shall return.

There is an irony here, in relation to our particular field, which should not escape us. It is a solidly established datum of history that Jews and Christians in the first century regarded the actual events in which they were taking part as possessing, in and of themselves, ultimate significance. They believed strongly that the events concerning Israel and her fate were not 'bare events', but possessed an 'inside', a 'meaning', which transcended mere chronicle. And, since their interpretative grid for understanding the inside of events had to do with belief in a creator god and the fulfilment of his purposes for the whole world by means of actions concerning his covenant people, they believed, oddly from the perspective of modern Western positivism, that the events in question were charged with a significance that related to all humans, and all time.[2] Whatever we think of their particular viewpoint, we must say that they understood more about the real nature of history, that is, about the complex interaction of 'event' and 'meaning', than has been grasped by the ardent proponents of 'scientific history' in comparatively recent times.

But how are we to address historical questions in a more holistic manner, avoiding the reductionisms which have plagued scholarship? To answer this we must examine two categories that we have already invoked at various points, namely, 'worldview' and 'theology'.

2. Worldview and Theology

The dimension which positivistic historiography has often lacked may be described in terms of *worldview*, and we must look at this concept first. I shall then argue that worldviews are in fact, from one point of view, profoundly *theological*, and we must therefore examine the meaning of 'theology' within this context. This will lead us to a consideration of *Christian* theology in particular, which will in turn prompt some reflections on theology in relation to the study of the New Testament.

(i) On Worldviews

Worldviews have to do with the presuppositional, pre-cognitive stage of a culture or society.[3] Wherever we find the ultimate concerns of human beings, we find worldviews. From that point of view, as the echo of Paul Tillich in the phrase 'ultimate concern' will indicate, they are profoundly theological, whether or not they contain what in modern Western thought would be

---

[2] So, rightly, Nineham 1976, 188; Räisänen 1990, 199. Both writers see this belief as typifying the sort of view that is impossible for us today.

[3] On worldviews see especially Geertz 1973; Holmes 1983b; Walsh and Middleton 1984; Olthuis 1989 [1985]; and particularly Marshall, Griffioen and Mouw 1989.

regarded as an explicit or worked-out view of a god-figure.[4] 'Worldview', in fact, embraces all deep-level human perceptions of reality, including the question of whether or not a   or gods exist, and if so what he, she, it or they is or are like, and how such a being, or such beings, might relate to the world. Though the metaphor of sight can over-dominate (world*view*), the following analysis should make it clear that worldviews, in the sense I intend, include many dimensions of human existence other than simply theory.[5]

There are four things which worldviews characteristically do, in each of which the entire worldview can be glimpsed. First, as we have seen throughout this Part of the book, worldviews provide the *stories* through which human beings view reality. Narrative is the most characteristic expression of worldview, going deeper than the isolated observation or fragmented remark.

Second, from these stories one can in principle discover how to answer the basic *questions* that determine human existence: who are we, where are we, what is wrong, and what is the solution?[6] All cultures cherish deep-rooted beliefs which can in principle be called up to answer these questions. All cultures (that is) have a sense of identity, of environment, of a problem with the way the world is, and of a way forward—a redemptive eschatology, to be more precise—which will, or may, lead out of that problem. To recognize this in relation to cultures can be as enlightening as to recognize that another human being within one's own family or circle of acquaintance has a different personality-type from one's own. It liberates all concerned from the constricting assumption that we all are, or should be, exactly alike.

Third, the stories that express the worldview, and the answers which it provides to the questions of identity, environment, evil and eschatology, are expressed (as we saw in the previous chapter) in cultural *symbols*. These can be both artifacts and events—festivals, family gatherings, and the like. In modern North America, the New York victory parade after a successful war brings together two of the most powerful symbols of the culture: the towering skyscrapers of business-orientated Manhattan, and the heroes of battle. Both, in their own fashion, demonstrate, promote and celebrate The American Way. In first-century Palestine, celebrating the Passover functioned similarly, with Jerusalem and the Temple taking the place of Manhattan, and the Passover sacrifice and meal taking the place of the victory parade. The buildings, instead of speaking of economic/ethnic goals, spoke of religious/ethnic ones; instead of the celebration speaking of triumph achieved over the forces of

---

[4] For a recent assessment of Tillich, see Kelsey 1989; as he says: '[Tillich] has added a religious term to the English language: "ultimate concern" has become a common term in secular discourse to designate "the religious dimension" as vaguely as possible' (148).

[5] On this whole problem see particularly Rowe 1989. My use of the term is close to the use of 'symbolic universe' in e.g. Berger and Luckmann 1966.

[6] See Walsh and Middleton 1984, 35; I have turned the singular form of their questions into the plural. Cp. the questions which Vatican II suggested were common to all humans: 'What is man? What is the meaning and purpose of life? What is upright behaviour, and what is sinful? Where does suffering originate, and what end does it serve? How can genuine happiness be found? What happens at death? What is judgment? What reward follows death? And finally, what is the ultimate mystery, beyond human explanation, which embraces our entire existence, from which we take our origin and towards which we tend?' (Flannery 1975, 738).

darkness, it spoke of vindication yet to come. All cultures produce and maintain such symbols; they can often be identified when challenging them produces anger or fear. Such symbols often function as social and/or cultural *boundary-markers*: those who observe them are insiders, those who do not are outsiders. And these symbols, as the acted and visible reminders of a worldview that normally remains too deep for casual speech, form the actual grid through which the world is perceived. They determine how, from day to day, human beings will view the whole of reality. They determine what will, and what will not, be intelligible or assimilable within a particular culture.

Fourth, worldviews include a praxis, a way-of-being-in-the-world. The implied eschatology of the fourth question ('what is the solution?') necessarily entails *action*. Conversely, the real shape of someone's worldview can often be seen in the sort of actions they perform, particularly if the actions are so instinctive or habitual as to be taken for granted. The choice of a life-aim—to make money, to raise a family, to pursue a vocation, to change society or the world in a particular way, to live in harmony with the created order, to develop one's own inner world, to be loyal to received traditions—reflects the worldview held; and so do the intentions and motivations with which the overall aim goes to work.[7] Inconsistency of aim and action does not invalidate this, but merely shows that the issue is complicated, and that the answer to the third question ('what is wrong?') should certainly include human muddledness.

Worldviews are thus the basic stuff of human existence, the lens through which the world is seen, the blueprint for how one should live in it, and above all the sense of identity and place which enables human beings to be what they are. To ignore worldviews, either our own or those of the culture we are studying, would result in extraordinary shallowness.

We may set out the interacting functions of worldviews as follows:

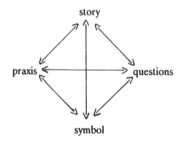

There are various broad terms that we will do well to plot on this grid. To begin with, we may say that *culture* denotes particularly the praxis and symbols of a society, both of which are of course informed by the controlling story, and reflect particular answers to the worldview questions. Second, the slippery word *religion* likewise focuses upon symbol and praxis, but draws more specific attention to the fact that symbol and praxis point beyond themselves to a controlling story or set of controlling stories which invest them with wider sig-

[7] On aims, intentions and motivations see pp. 109–12 above.

nificance. Third, *theology* concentrates on the questions and answers, and focuses specifically on certain aspects of them. I shall argue in this chapter that it is bound to integrate these with the controlling stories, and that it will be wise if it goes about this task fully conscious of the interrelation between questions and stories on the one hand and praxis and symbol on the other. Fourth, *imagination* and *feeling* can be plotted on the line between story and symbol, giving depth in different ways to praxis and questions. Fifth, *mythology* is, in many cultures, a way of speaking which reflects 'a conception of reality that posits the ongoing penetration of the world of everyday experience by sacred forces';[8] that is, a way of integrating praxis and symbol with story and, at least implicitly, with answers to the key questions. Finally, *literature*, which at the level both of reading and of writing is of course part of praxis, is a complex phenomenon in which, both explicitly and implicitly, stories are told, questions are raised and answered, praxis is exemplified, and symbols are either discussed directly or, more likely, alluded to in metaphor and other ways. Literature is, obviously, closely linked with culture, imagination and feeling, and also frequently with religion and theology. Literature itself can then create or become a new symbol: poetry, bookshops, and theatrical performances, for instance, possess symbolic value in a culture. Thus many of the vital elements of historical and literary study can be plotted accurately and interestingly on the worldview model I have suggested.[9]

Worldviews, as I said earlier, are like the foundations of a house: vital, but invisible. They are that *through* which, not *at* which, a society or an individual normally looks; they form the grid according to which humans organize reality, not bits of reality that offer themselves for organization. They are not usually called up to consciousness or discussion unless they are challenged or flouted fairly explicitly, and when this happens it is usually felt to be an event of worryingly large significance. They can, however, be challenged; they can, if necessary, be discussed, and their truth-value called into question.[10] Conversion, in the sense of a radical shift in worldview, can happen, whether in the case of a Saul on the road to Damascus or in the case of a member of a North American Indian or Inuit people who moves to the city and adopts the Western way of life. But worldviews normally come into sight, on a more day-to-day basis, in *sets of beliefs and aims* which emerge into the open, which are more regularly discussed, and which in principle could be revised somewhat without revising the worldview itself. Modern Western materialists hold a worldview of a certain sort, which expresses itself in basic beliefs about society and economic systems, and in basic aims about appropriate employment and use of time. These beliefs and aims are, as it were, shorthand forms of the stories which

[8] Berger and Luckmann 1966, 110.

[9] I have refrained from attempting to plot *ideology* on this grid, not least because of the large number of possible meanings the word currently bears (cf. Eagleton 1991, esp. ch. 1). It can mean something close to 'worldview' itself; it can also mean a much more specifically articulated corpus of beliefs; or it can denote the interaction between either or both of these and social reality. It can also, of course, carry pejorative overtones which make it even more slippery as a technical term.

[10] So, rightly, Meyer 1979, 17, 255 n.12, against Bultmann.

those who hold them are telling themselves and one another about the way the world is.[11] It is perhaps possible for someone to become convinced that some of these basic beliefs and aims are misguided, and so (for instance) to change from being a Conservative Western materialist to being a Social Democrat Western materialist, or vice versa, without any fundamental alteration of worldview.

These *basic beliefs* and *aims*, which serve to express and perhaps safeguard the worldview, give rise in turn to *consequent beliefs* and *intentions*, about the world, oneself, one's society, one's god. These, in their turn, shade off in various directions, into opinions held and motivations acted upon with varying degrees of conviction. Many discussions, debates, and arguments take place at the level of consequent belief and intention, assuming a level of shared basic belief, and only going back there when faced with complete stalemate. Much political discussion, for instance, assumes not only a worldview, but also the set of basic beliefs and aims which are held to follow from that worldview. It takes place, not at those more fundamental levels, but at the level of the consequent beliefs, or the specific proposals for action (the 'intentions' in my scheme) which are held by some to be appropriate. This can be set out schematically:

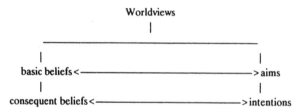

So much, for the moment, for worldviews. How do they relate to, or include, what is normally thought of as 'theology'?

(ii) On Theology

Theology, as we saw briefly a moment ago, turns the spotlight on certain particular dimensions of the worldview, of any worldview.[12] It is possible to suggest a sharply focused definition of theology: theology is the study of gods, or a god. It is also possible, and today quite common, to work with a more wideranging definition, interacting with elements of the worldview-pattern: theology suggests certain ways of telling the story, explores certain ways of answering the questions, offers particular interpretations of the symbols, and suggests and critiques certain forms of praxis. This is what Norman Petersen is getting at in his analysis of theology and the 'symbolic universe':

[11] Compare once more the notion of 'control beliefs' expounded by Wolterstorff 1984 [1976].

[12] It is of course out of the question to attempt more here than a bald and inadequate summary of many hugely complex issues. I shall interact in more detail with contemporary theological debate elsewhere. On the whole area see particularly Ford 1989.

> From the perspective of the sociology of knowledge, theology and symbolic universe are distinguished as representing two different kinds of knowledge . . . Theology . . . is for the sociology of knowledge a kind of knowledge that is the product of systematic reflection upon a symbolic universe, and indeed of reflection that serves to maintain that universe when it is in some kind of jeopardy, as for example from the threats of doubt, of disagreement, or of competing symbolic universes . . . For this reason we can speak of a symbolic universe as a primary (pre-reflective) form of knowledge and theology as a secondary (reflective) form that is dependent on it.[13]

Thus, for instance, we saw in chapter 3 that many stories have a sense that the hero (the 'agent' in Griemas' scheme) has been 'sent' on a 'mission', but it is not clear who did the sending. There is often a blank in the 'sender' category, as we saw in the case of Tolkien, and of de la Mare's 'The Listeners'. This reflects the widespread human consciousness of a purpose which comes from 'beyond', from 'above', or possibly from 'within'. If pressed, some human communities would explicate this blank in terms of one or other of the traditional views of a god. Others would fill it in in terms of 'forces of nature'. Others would speak in terms of mythology, psychology and/or sociology. All of these responses, and other possible ones, are essentially *theological*.

Theology thus tells stories about human beings and the world, stories which involve either a being not reducible to materialist analysis or at least a provocative space within the story-line where such a being might, by implication, be located. In the light of this story-telling activity, theology asks questions, as to whether there is a god, what relation this god has to the world in which we live, and what if anything this god is doing, or will do, about putting it to rights.

These questions obviously interact with the four major worldview questions. An atheist answers the theological questions with a negative to the first, leaving the rest untouched: there is no 'god', therefore there is no being to be in relation to the world or to deal with its evil; but the reply is still profoundly theological, and the answers then given to the other worldview questions reflect what, from a theological point of view, still count as a kind of theology. Materialism or totalitarianism, for instance, still have a recognizable theological shape, and such views could hold a meaningful debate with various orthodox theologies (e.g. Jewish or Christian ones) as to which of them is the original and which the parody.[14]

Theology's story-telling and questioning activity is regularly focused in symbols, whether they be objects or actions. A Torah scroll, a wooden cross, a manual act, a procession, are all capable of evoking powerfully a whole set of stories and questions-and-answers. They can, of course, become flat and lifeless, though even when this happens they are often capable of remarkable recovery. But in principle theology has to take account of symbols, not least because, as we saw, the symbols of a society or culture may sometimes tell a truer story about the actual worldview than the 'official' stories or the 'authorized' answers to questions. If symbol and story do not fit each other, it

---

[13] Petersen 1985, 29f.; cf. 57–60, 200–2, and Berger and Luckmann 1966, 92–128.
[14] See Pannenberg 1971, ch. 6.

is part of the task of theology to ask why, and to offer a critique of whichever partner is out of line.

Likewise, theology must take account of praxis. Prayer, sacraments, liturgy; almsgiving, acts of justice and peacemaking; all these integrate with story, question and symbol to produce a complete whole. Once more, while it may be tidier and easier to deal with official statements in the question-and-answer or story form, praxis may offer a truer account of how things actually are. Again, theology has the responsibility to offer a critique in such cases.

Theology is thus integrated closely with worldviews at every point. But what is theology talking *about*? Is it simply a meta-language, a fanciful way of attempting to invest reality with a significance not always perceived? Or does it refer to real entities beyond space-time reality? At this point, we must again invoke critical realism. Debates about the referent of god-language have a familiar shape: it is that which we have already studied in our discussions of epistemology, literature and history.

Pre-critical speech about gods, or a god, often seems to take it for granted that such a being, or such beings, exist, and that ordinary human language refers to this being or these beings without more ado. It is fairly clear, actually, that in every age sophisticated thinkers have been perfectly well aware of the problematic nature of this language and its referent, so that the phrase 'pre-critical' here refers, not to a period of history before the Enlightenment, but to a stage of (or perhaps a lack of) human awareness which can and does exist in every period of history, not least our own. Perhaps particularly our own, in fact: one distressing modern phenomenon is the spectacle of a would-be Christian positivism which imagines that god-language is clear and unequivocal, and that one can have the kind of certainty about it which Logical Positivism accorded to scientific or even mathematical statements. This sort of fundamentalism is simply the upside-down version of A. J. Ayer's *Language, Truth and Logic*.

But it is surely clear that language about a god, or gods, is not simply and uncomplicatedly referential in the positivist's sense. There is no straight line that leads from humans to some sort of revelation and thence to unambiguously true statements about divine being(s):

humans   revelation   god(s)
        ----------->   ---------->
simply observing revelation . . . and speaking truly about god(s)

On the contrary. In our day we have seen both halves of the sequence strongly challenged. Marx, Nietzsche, and Freud persuaded a whole generation to be sceptical of revelation, and to see it not as pointing beyond itself to a divine reality but as pointing back to other aspects of human individual and/or corporate existence and identity. A strong hermeneutic of suspicion was thus introduced into modern reflection, suggesting that god-language could be reduced to terms of economic, political or sexual agendas:

humans   revelation   god(s)

---------->

apparent revelation of the divine

   <----------

shown up as revelation of structures of human existence

Equally, where this critique has been held at bay, theologians have not found it at all easy to move beyond a belief in revelation itself to actual statements about the divine. Such statements all too easily collapse into restatements of the revelatory mode itself. Analysis of the actual being of a god, of 'divine substance', is conceived as highly problematic; all we can apparently talk about is what this god *does*, i.e. the revelation in action:

humans   revelation   god(s)

---------->   ---------->

witnessing a real revelation, which seems to be about the divine,

        <----------

but which only shows the effects of the divine, not the divine in itself

Against these reductions, however, I propose a critically realist account. Language about religion and revelation does indeed reflect many elements in human consciousness, and can indeed be used as a weapon of oppression. But this does not vitiate all such language. Post-Nietzschean, post-Freudian and post-Marxian humans—artists, writers, musicians, lovers, as well as religious persons—still tell stories about aspects of reality that transcend power, sex and money. These aspects appear, for some, in the Bible and the Christian (or other religious) stories; for others, in the beauty of creation; for others, in other human beings; for others again, deep within themselves. This gives rise, of course, to enormous problems, about natural theology, revelation and reason, and so on. But these stories suggest that we must, however critically, recognize the presence of something we may as well call 'revelation':

humans   revelation

-------------------->

initial signals of transcendence

<--------------------

subject to reductionist critique

---------------------->

but telling stories that still affirm transcendence

So, too, to reject the simplistic notion that revelation simply gives us access to the very being of a god does not mean that all we are aware of is revelation itself. Once again Story comes to the rescue. Recognition of god-language as fundamentally metaphorical does not mean that it does not have a referent, and that some at least of the metaphors may not actually possess a particular appropriateness to this referent. In fact, metaphors are themselves mini-stories, suggesting ways of looking at a reality which cannot be reduced to terms of the metaphor itself. As has become more widely recognized in recent writing, such metaphors and stories are in fact *more* basic within human consciousness than apparently 'factual' speech, and recognizing the essentially storied nature of god-talk is therefore no bar to asserting the reality of its referent. Indeed, within the Jewish and Christian worldviews, human speech, as the words spoken by those who are themselves made in the image of the creator, may be seen as in principle not just possibly adequate to the task of speaking of this god but actually appropriate to it. Of course, this will depend on whether the Jewish and Christian accounts of humans, and human speech, might turn out to be correct. If Deism were after all correct, the unknowable remote god it postulates would not readily be described in human language. But this debate cannot, obviously, be decided here.[15]

This leaves us with the following picture:

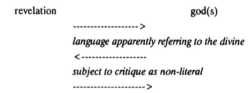

revelation   god(s)

------------------- >

language apparently referring to the divine

< -------------------

subject to critique as non-literal

--------------------- >

in principle reaffirmed as having potential referent via metaphor and appropriate story

The *possibility* of god-talk having a referent does not mean, of course, that any and all talk about god, or God, is thereby legitimated *as true*. It is put, in principle, on the same footing as language about anything else. Once the possibility of a referent is recognized, the conversation can be opened up fruitfully. But if this language is not simply self-justifying, neither does it consist of private signals, referring simply to the inside of the speakers' heads. This language belongs in the public domain. It is possible, as we have seen, to discuss worldviews, to see how they differ, and to change from holding one worldview to holding another; and it is quite possible to discuss the claims made about god(s), to assess their respective merits, to tell stories about divine being and behaviour which subvert one another, and to discern by this means which possibilities are serious contenders for truth. Critical realism can thus affirm the right of theological language to be regarded as an appropriate dimension of discourse about reality.

To sum up, then: 'theology' highlights what we might call the god-dimension of a worldview. Many thinkers, politicians and even biblical scholars notoriously dismiss 'theology' as if it were simply a set of answers that might be given to a pre-packaged set of abstract dogmatic questions, but it cannot possibly be reduced to that level. It provides an essential ingredient in the stories that encapsulate worldviews; in the answers that are given to the fundamental worldview questions; in the symbolic world which gives the worldview cultural expression; and in the practical agenda to which the worldview gives rise. As

[15] On metaphor and god-language see Ramsey 1964a, 1964b; Ricoeur 1977; Soskice 1985.

such it is a non-negotiable part of the study of literature and history, and hence of New Testament studies.

This discussion has, thus far, been deliberately unspecific about the actual content of what is asserted about god(s). We could, of course, introduce several variables into the scheme by examining some more specific sets of beliefs and claims. Thus, it would be quite possible for a critical realist to be an atheist, acknowledging that language could in principle refer to a being such as a god but claiming that in fact no such being exists. That is what one might say, in another sphere, about dragons. A Deist, believing in a distant god, detached from the world, inaccessible and remote, might be content to describe such a being in reasonably abstract and theoretical terms. A pantheist, believing that the word 'god' refers to everything that exists, and investing that 'everything' with the status of divine power and honour, would effectively draw the spirals of knowledge tighter and tighter until the difference between language about revelation or god and language about oneself and/or one's own context were reduced to nothing. Whatever the system, theological or quasi-theological, we would discover that the god-language in question, and the place for it within the worldview, formed a vital part of the relevant culture.

But what about Christian god-language? Clearly, if we are to understand the language that the New Testament writers used, we need to understand the specific nature of early Christian (and, *a fortiori*, first-century Jewish) theology. Equally, if we are to understand what it might mean today to speak Christianly about the New Testament, or about the god whom Christians worship, some attempt must be made to see how such language might be held to function.

(iii) On Christian Theology

What then might a specifically *Christian* theology be? More, I take it, than simply an account of what Christians have believed in the past, or believe in the present, though those tasks will always be part of the whole. That whole includes a necessarily normative element. It will attempt not just to describe but to commend a way of looking at, speaking about, and engaging with the god in whom Christians believe, and with the world that this god has created. It will carry the implication that this is not only what *is* believed but what *ought to be* believed. To the relativist's response, that this will seem very arrogant, Christian theology will reply that it can do no other. If it is not a claim about the whole of reality, seen and unseen, it is nothing. It is not a set of private aesthetic judgments upon reality, with a 'take-it-or-leave-it' clause attached. Even the relativist, after all, believes that relativism is universally true, and sometimes seeks to propagate that belief with missionary zeal. Christian theology only does what all other worldviews and their ancillary belief-systems do: it claims to be talking about reality as a whole.

How should one set about doing 'Christian theology'? Two ways have been popular over the last two centuries. The first offers a rearrangement of timeless truths or propositions. It collects and reorders the material arranged by previous workers in the field. Its only point of reference beyond itself is the overarching system (in some cases, a philosophical model) according to which the selection and arrangement is made. This model has some uses, not least in attaining greater clarity of discourse, but in general it seems to me quite sterile, and unlikely to engage with the sort of issues raised within the present work.[16] The second way of doing 'Christian theology' seeks actively to engage with current concerns in the world, whether through confrontation or integration.[17] This seems in some ways more fruitful for a project of the sort I am engaged upon, but there are pitfalls here too. I propose to follow a rather different path, in line with the model of epistemology developed thus far, and thus working in line with some recent studies in narrative theology.[18] Unlike most 'narrative theology', however, I shall attempt to integrate this approach with a historical focus. And this combined approach grows out of the analysis offered above of worldviews and how they work.

First, Christian theology tells a story, and seeks to tell it coherently. We have already summarized this story, and can do so again briefly. The story is about a creator and his creation, about humans made in this creator's image and given tasks to perform, about the rebellion of humans and the dissonance of creation at every level, and particularly about the creator's acting, through Israel and climactically through Jesus, to rescue his creation from its ensuing plight. The story continues with the creator acting by his own spirit within the world to bring it towards the restoration which is his intended goal for it. A good deal of Christian theology consists of the attempt to tell this story as clearly as possible, and to allow it to subvert other ways of telling the story of the world, including those which offer themselves as would-be Christian tellings but which, upon close examination, fall short in some way or other.

Second, this story, as the fundamental articulation of the worldview, offers a set of answers to the four worldview questions. We may set these out as follows, noting as we do some of the alternative views that are thereby ruled out. These, it should be noted, are at the present stage of my argument simply descriptive of what goes to make up the Christian worldview, not yet an argument that this worldview should be adopted.

(1) Who are we? We are humans, made in the image of the creator. We have responsibilities that come with this status. We are not fundamentally determined by race, gender, social class, geographical location; nor are we simply pawns in a determinist game.

(2) Where are we? We are in a good and beautiful, though transient, world, the creation of the god in whose image we are made. We are not in an alien world, as the Gnostic imagines; nor in a cosmos to which we owe allegiance as to a god, as the pantheist would suggest.

---

[16] An example of this sort of work is Berkhof 1941.

[17] e.g. the work of Moltmann (e.g. 1974, 1985, 1990).

[18] See ch. 3 above. On narrative and theology see particularly Goldberg 1982; Stroup 1984; Tilley 1985.

(3) What is wrong? Humanity has rebelled against the creator. This rebellion reflects a cosmic dislocation between the creator and the creation, and the world is consequently out of tune with its created intention. A Christian worldview rejects dualisms which associate evil with createdness or physicality; equally, it rejects monisms that analyse evil simply in terms of some humans not being fully in tune with their environment. Its analysis of evil is more subtle and far-reaching. It likewise rejects as the whole truth all partial analyses, such as those of Marx or Freud, which elevate half-truths to the status of the whole truth.[19]

(4) What is the solution? The creator has acted, is acting, and will act within his creation to deal with the weight of evil set up by human rebellion, and to bring his world to the end for which it was made, namely that it should resonate fully with his own presence and glory. This action, of course, is focused upon Jesus and the spirit of the creator. We reject, that is, solutions to the human plight which only address one part of the problem.

These four answers constitute an articulated ground-plan of the mainline or traditional Christian worldview. Many branches of Christianity, we should note, have not adopted precisely this ground-plan. In much post-Enlightenment thinking, for instance, many 'conservative' and 'liberal' Christians have shared the belief that the answers to (3) and (4) had to do with the problem of physicality and the means of escaping into a pure spiritual sphere. But a good case can be made out, I think, for this pattern as an overall account.

Third, this worldview has been given expression in a variety of socio-cultural symbols, both artifacts and cultural events. Churches and their furniture have articulated the worldview in soaring stone and decorated glass, expressing the majesty attributed to the creator and his transcendent presence within his world. Liturgy and para-liturgy (from processions to prayer meetings) have celebrated and enacted the worldview, becoming variously normative in different groups. A large variety of activities, from icon-painting to street evangelism, from the study of scripture to the setting up of sanctuaries and refuge homes for society's casualties, have attained the status of symbols. Sometimes, as in any worldview and its symbolic expression, the symbols can be challenged. It is now widely recognized that the Crusades, though they were undertaken as a symbol of the victory of the gospel, in fact symbolized a message rather different from, and actually incompatible with, that of Jesus of Nazareth. But in principle the Christian worldview, like all others, has its symbols which enable its adherents to order and direct their lives appropriately, and to view the world and their tasks in it with some degree of coherence.

Finally, the Christian worldview gives rise to a particular type of praxis, a particular mode of being-in-the-world. Actually, this might be better expressed, in the Christian case, as being-*for*-the-world, since in the fundamental Christian worldview humans in general are part of the creator's designed means of looking after his world, and Christians in particular are part of his

---

[19] cf. Lucas 1976, 136: 'I do not believe in Marx or Freud. Money and sex are important, but not all-important.'

means of bringing healing to the world. As with all other worldviews, of course, its adherents are not noticeably successful in attaining a complete correlation between their statements about their own being-in-the-world and their actual practice. This is in no way fatal to the theory; it merely means that Christians, like everybody else, are often muddled, mistaken, foolish and wayward, and are probably trying to ride at least one other horse at the same time as the Christian one. But in principle the Christian worldview supplies its adherents with a sense of direction, namely, the vocation to work in whatever way may be appropriate for the glory of the creator and the healing of his world.

This fundamental Christian worldview, expressed in the four ways outlined (story, answers to questions, symbols and praxis), gives rise in its turn to a system of *basic beliefs*, held at a more conscious level than the worldview itself. At this point more diversity appears, as different Christians in different cultures and contexts have addressed different issues in different ways, and have sought to emphasize now this, now that facet of Christian truth to make a particular point. But certain topics of belief are common to most branches of Christianity, while not forming a necessary part of the worldview itself: beliefs about the Christian god, about Jesus, beliefs about the divine spirit, beliefs about revelation, the Bible, tradition, the church. Some of these, like the traditional doctrines of trinity and incarnation, are perceived to serve as lock-nuts keeping aspects of the basic worldview in place: unless one believes something like this, it is felt, the worldview will collapse into a less desirable alternative. Debate then occurs as to whether this is in fact the case—whether, for instance, one can suspend belief in the traditional trinitarian dogmas while still holding firmly to something that remains recognizably Christian.

From these basic beliefs there will also follow certain *consequent beliefs*, which will vary more widely, but whose adherents will regard them as compatible with, or actually entailed by, some aspect of the basic beliefs. Thus a Christian individual or group might express its unseen and assumed worldview in a set of basic beliefs, say a credal formula. This can be discussed; sermons can be preached on it; it is public and observable. The group may well also hold a set of consequent beliefs: for instance, a particular view of scripture, or a particular way of articulating atonement-theology. Some in the group may come to regard these formulations as themselves 'basic beliefs': others will be more wary. The question of the status of different beliefs is itself a matter of some debate from time to time within the church: in the sixteenth century it was sometimes a matter of life and death.[20] That there are different levels, however, seems to me manifestly the case. The overall point here is that a good deal of what is called 'Christian theology' consists of discussions and debates at the level of basic belief or consequent belief, not necessarily at the level of the Christian worldview itself. If theological study is to be fully aware of its own nature, however, it must include study of the whole range, from worldviews to every level of belief. This large theological task remains a necessary part of the literary and historical study of early Christianity.

[20] See Wright 1978, 75-7.

From all this it should by now be clear that, like all worldviews, the Christian worldview is not simply a matter of a private language, a secret or arcane mystery which is of interest only to those who themselves profess the Christian faith. All worldviews, the Christian one included, are in principle public statements. They all tell stories which attempt to challenge and perhaps to subvert other worldview-stories. All of them provide a set of answers to the basic questions, which can be called up as required from the subconscious, and discussed. All commit their hearers to a way of being-in-the-world or being-for-the-world.

But the Christian claim in particular is committed to its own irreducible publicness. It claims to be telling a story about the creator and his world. If it allows this to collapse for a moment into a story about a god who is rescuing people *out of* the world, then it has abandoned something extremely fundamental in the worldview. Many of the early Fathers saw this very clearly; that is why they rejected Gnosticism. In fact, even if Gnostic dualism were true, the story would still be public, since, if the world is a place of ruin and there exists a god who can save people from it, this is news that ought to be shared. But if this dualism is avoided (as it has not always been in various forms of post-Enlightenment Christianity, not least fundamentalism) the publicness of the Christian claim is the more manifest.[21]

To what sort of speech, then, is Christian theology (whether in the first or the twenty-first century) committed? Christians find themselves compelled to speak of the creator and redeemer god as God, the one God: not a Deist god, an absentee landlord, nor one of the many gods that litter the world of paganism, nor yet the god who, in pantheism, is identified with the world; but the God who made and sustains all that is, who is active within the world but not contained within it. Christians are committed to speaking of this God in appropriate ways, namely, by stories which reflect and bring into articulation the basic Christian worldview-story. And, as we have already noted, metaphors are mini-stories, inviting the hearers into a world where certain things can be seen more clearly through this lens. They are not the icing on the cake, the embroidery around the edge of the picture, which could be removed without substantial loss. From the point of view of a Christian critical realism, we must say that story and metaphor, including myth, are ways in which, despite the almost boundless human capacity for self-deception, words in relation to the creator and redeemer God can be truly spoken.[22]

These will be words appropriate to the God of whom they speak. They will thus include, at a basic stage, praise and worship, and proclamation. They will also include the discussion of theology, since, at the level of basic or consequent belief, there will be stories to be told in order to articulate the basic worldview, support it, modify it where necessary, and subvert attractive but misleading alternatives. They will also address the questions raised by all worldviews, and do so by means of theological discussion. Again, they will explicate the symbols in which the culture finds expression, just as in Judaism

[21] On this whole topic see particularly Newbigin 1989.
[22] See particularly Caird 1980, chs. 12–14.

the celebration of the Passover is *explained*, in answer to the question 'Why is this night different from all other nights?'

In addition, they will be words about *history*. The Christian is committed to the belief that certain things are true about the past.[23] This does *not* mean that the Christian historian is committed to finding material which 'proves' Christianity 'true', or to finding in the New Testament, as an earlier generation of exegetes tried to do, advance statements of highly developed points of Christian doctrine. Rather, it means doing serious history in the belief, which Christians share with some others, that the creator of the universe is also the lord of history, and in the further belief, peculiar to Christianity, that he has acted climactically, *and not merely paradigmatically*, in Jesus of Nazareth; that he has implemented that climactic act in the gift of his own spirit to his people; and that he will complete this work in the final renewal of all things. This belief will drive the Christian to history, as a hypothesis drives the scientist to the laboratory, not simply in the search for legitimation, but in the search for the modifications and adaptations necessary if the hypothesis is to stand the test of reality. The appeal to history with which the Enlightenment challenged the dogmatic theology of the eighteenth century and after is one which can and must be taken on board within the mainline Christian theological worldview. As Paul put it in a slightly different context, if we are deceived about these things we are of all humans the most to be pitied.[24]

If the Christian theologian is committed to speaking true words about the past, he or she is also committed to speaking true words about the present and the future. This means that a proper concern for history will be balanced by a proper concern for justice and peace. Though it is impossible to explore this theme further here, history and justice belong together, as humans are called to bring the divinely intended order to birth through their speech-acts. Words about the past and the future must all alike be used in the service of truth of every sort.

Finally, the Christian theologian is committed also to speaking true words about his or her own condition in engaging in these activities. One must speak of provisionality and partial insight, of truth to which one is totally committed but which can only be stated provisionally.[25] Hence the need, within the worldview itself and the aims and intentions to which it gives rise, for faith, for hope, and (since agreement will always be difficult to attain) for love.

What will be the criteria according to which theological statements are to be judged? This again raises huge issues into which we cannot go here, but something at least may be said as the alternative to leaving a puzzling lacuna. If theology is not to be just a private game, in which the players agree on the rules while outsiders look on in perplexity, it must appeal to some sense of fittingness, or appropriateness. There must be, as in a scientific theory, a sense of clean simplicity, of things fitting together and making sense. A historical construct can present itself as more fitting and appropriate than some other con-

---

[23] See again Caird 1980, ch. 12.
[24] 1 Cor. 15.19.
[25] See McManners 1981, 230.

struct, without appealing to any external *a priori* of a particular agenda which would thereby be legitimated or reinforced. A good example would be the arrangement of Monet's eleven paintings of Rouen Cathedral in the 1990 Royal Academy exhibition. If, in other words, a particular way of approaching the historical and theological task results in a new coherence in the material itself, it may commend itself not only to those within the tradition from which the historian or theologian comes, but also to those outside it.

(iv) Worldviews, Theology and Biblical Studies

It will by now be clear that all study, all reading of texts, all attempts to reconstruct history, take place *within* particular worldviews. This could appear to force interpreters into a difficult choice, between (shall we say) a post-Enlightenment, modernist, Western worldview and a postmodern one, or between either of these and an overtly Christian one. Within that context, many have felt the pressure in recent decades to engage in scholarly work, including specialist study of the Bible, from within the post-Enlightenment modernist perspective, putting specifically Christian opinions on hold while the exercise is going on. This has been helped by the impression which is given, precisely within the post-Enlightenment worldview itself, that matters of religious opinion are simply private options which do not engage with the public world.

It should be clear, further, that this way of conceiving the problem is based on a mistake. All worldviews, including both the modernism of the Enlightenment and Christianity, claim to be public and comprehensive. They must therefore offer some account, along with everything else, of what the adherents of other worldviews are 'really' doing. To that extent, they overlap. The question is, whose account of everybody else makes most sense? Enlightenment modernism tries to subsume Christianity within it, by claiming that Christianity is simply a private religious option; but Christianity has a reply ready to hand: that it in turn can look the Enlightenment questions full in the face, can take them on board and work with them. If Christianity is committed to history, as I have argued, then it not only can but must work at history to meet the Enlightenment's demand—not, indeed, the demand for 'neutral' or 'objective' history, which as we have seen is a positivist fantasy, but the desire for genuine historical reconstruction of actual events in the past, of the 'inside' of events as well as the 'outside'. Christianity has nothing to fear from the appeal to history. It makes the same appeal itself.

Theology and biblical studies therefore need each other in a symbiotic relationship. (I deliberately refer to biblical studies in general, because I believe the wider point to be vital, even though I shall only here discuss the relation of this to the New Testament.) There are three points to be made here.

(1) Biblical studies needs theology, because only with theological tools can historical exegesis get at what the characters in the history were thinking, planning, aiming to do. This is to say no more than that if we were to write the his-

tory of the Greek philosophers we would need to study philosophy to understand what it was they were trying to say, and perhaps how their social and political actions reflected their discussions. Early Christianity cherished certain beliefs and aims, which can be traced back to their underlying worldview(s); New Testament readers are committed to studying the 'inside' of events in the first century, which includes finding what made early Christians tick; *ergo*, New Testament readers need to study theology. This becomes very important (for instance) when we consider the nature of Pauline theology: one cannot study Paul seriously without enquiring as to his worldview, mindset, basic and consequent beliefs, and practical aims and intentions.[26]

(2) Biblical studies needs theology, because only with the help of a fully theological analysis of contemporary culture can those who read the Bible be aware, as they need to be, of their own questions, presuppositions, aims and intentions. If anyone thinks that he or she comes without presuppositions, that the questions they ask are 'neutral', the study of worldviews and theology should disabuse them of the idea. Conversely, Christian theology can offer, in ways that I have outlined above, a set of aims and intentions which take up within themselves the aims and intentions contained within other projects, such as the Enlightenment one. Invoking 'theology' does not therefore mean summoning up a complete scheme of ready-made answers which will short-circuit the process of serious historical and critical exegesis, as is sometimes feared. On the contrary, it will set the historical critic free to work with clarity of aim and purpose.

(3) At the same time, theology—any theology—needs biblical studies, since the claims of any theology must sooner or later come into contact, perhaps conflict, with the stories contained in the Bible, and if a worldview of any sort is to be sustained it must be able to meet the challenge posed by its rivals. Hindus, Muslims, Deists and pantheists will therefore study the Bible to understand how Christianity works from within, in the hope that their own stories will be able to subvert the Christian one, or at least withstand its potential challenge, and establish themselves as a more adequate account of reality. How much more, though, does *Christian* theology need biblical studies. To be truly Christian, it must show that it includes the story which the Bible tells, and the sub-stories within it. Without this, it lapses into a mere *ad hoc* use of the Bible, finding bits and pieces to fit into a scheme derived from elsewhere. If finding a proof-text, or even a proof-theme, from the Bible, is what counts, then theology is simply reproducing the worst phenomenon of an earlier proof-texting biblicism, while often lacking the robust and courageous faith that frequently characterized such movements.

To be Christian, then, theology needs to tell the stories of Jesus and Paul, of the early church, and much besides. However difficult the task of reading the New Testament may be, it is harder still to conceive of the project of Christian theology in any meaningful sense without some articulable place for the New Testament and its writers, and without a clearly defined place for the Jesus of

---

[26] See Wright 1991a, chs. 1 and 14.

whom they speak. And about this topic—the place of Jesus within a Christian theology—we must offer some further reflections.

Granted the state of New Testament historical work in the last few decades, it is not surprising to find that systematic theologians are unsure which Jesus to choose to weave into their work. Most, equally unsurprisingly, choose a Jesus who just happens to fit the programme that was desired on other grounds. But at this point it is vital to remain within the boundaries of serious historical work. True, there will always be room for manoeuvre within certain rather narrow limits. But there is simply no point using the word 'Jesus' at all within theology unless one intends to refer to the Jesus who lived and died as a Jew of the first century. Unless quite strict controls are in place here, a whole range of theological debates wander off into pointlessness. And such controls are, I suggest, in place when we attempt serious 'Christian theology'.

I am therefore proposing, as a way of conceiving the task that lies before us, that to study the world of the first century, and within that to study Jesus, Paul and the gospels, does not require that we adopt wholesale and uncritically either the Enlightenment worldview or any other that may be on offer within contemporary secular culture. This does *not* mean that we are to retreat, either into a pre-modern rejection of historical criticism, or (as the positivist will imagine) into a private sphere away from potential disagreements and alternative readings. Christian theology, if conceived in the way I have suggested, offers a perspective from which the issues addressed by the Enlightenment may be handled appropriately; the Christian historian need not pretend to be something else, as though being a Christian, or operating as such, would somehow invalidate the research. The Christian reader of the New Testament is committed to a task which includes within itself 'early Christian history' and 'New Testament theology', while showing that neither of these tasks, which I set out in chapter 1 above, can be self-sufficient. And this fuller reading of the New Testament neither 'excludes' nor 'contains' Jesus, nor does it merely presuppose him. Rather, it includes as one vital part of itself the task of *telling the story of Jesus*, with the assumption that this story took place within public history.

If it is thus possible to join together the three enterprises of literary, historical and theological study of the New Testament, and to do so in particular by the use of the category of 'story', what might become of the widespread belief that the New Testament is to be regarded as in some sense 'normative'? Will this be a contradiction in terms, or at least in methods?

3. Theology, Narrative and Authority

I shall now argue that the conception of the task, the way of reading the New Testament, for which I have been arguing in the last three chapters, enables us to do what pre-modern Christian readers assumed they could do without difficulty, and what the 'modernists' found so many problems with, namely, to use the New Testament as in some way authoritative. This is not to go back to pre-

modernism. We have abandoned biblicistic proof-texting, as inconsistent with
the nature of the texts that we have (and anyone who thinks that this means
abandoning biblical authority should ask themselves where the real authority
lies in a method that effectively turns the Bible into something else). Nor can
it easily be done within modernism itself. For better or worse, there has
existed within the world of modernistic New Testament studies a kind of practical agreement to split off 'descriptive' and 'normative' readings of the Bible
from one another. If we choose to move from an 'is' to an 'ought', from description of the past to authoritative statement, that is a choice made, it is felt,
from outside the historical task itself. But need this in fact be so? Is there
another model, consistent with serious literary, historical and theological
study, which will result in the New Testament exercising that authority which
Christians from the beginning have accorded to it?

Here I have a suggestion to make, which seems to me fairly obvious though
not often explored. Since (a) stories are a key worldview indicator in any case,
and (b) a good part of the New Testament consists of stories, of narratives, it
might be a good idea to consider how stories might carry, or be vehicles for,
authority. Stories may seem at first unpromising as a starting-point for authoritative exegesis. But we may be able to conceive of a working model which
would make the point clear.[27]

Suppose there exists a Shakespeare play, most of whose fifth act has been
lost. The first four acts provide, let us suppose, such a remarkable wealth of
characterization, such a crescendo of excitement within the plot, that it is
generally agreed that the play ought to be staged. Nevertheless, it is felt
inappropriate actually to write a fifth act once and for all: it would freeze the
play into one form, and commit Shakespeare as it were to being prospectively
responsible for work not in fact his own. Better, it might be felt, to give the key
parts to highly trained, sensitive and experienced Shakespearian actors, who
would immerse themselves in the first four acts, and in the language and culture of Shakespeare and his time, *and who would then be told to work out a fifth
act for themselves.*

Consider the result. The first four acts, existing as they did, would be the
undoubted 'authority' for the task in hand. That is, anyone could properly
object to the new improvisation on the grounds that some character was now
behaving inconsistently, or that some sub-plot or theme, adumbrated earlier,
had not reached its proper resolution. This 'authority' of the first four acts
would not consist—could not consist!—in an implicit command that the actors
should repeat the earlier parts of the play over and over again. It would consist
in the fact of an as yet unfinished drama, containing its own impetus and forward movement, which demanded to be concluded in an appropriate manner.
It would require of the actors a free and responsible entering in to the story as
it stood, in order first to understand how the threads could appropriately be
drawn together and then to put that understanding into effect by speaking and
acting with both innovation and consistency. This model could and perhaps
should be adapted further: it offers quite a range of possibilities.

---

[27] I have already published a version of this suggestion in Wright 1991b.

This might provide, in our present context, a different account of authority, both in general and in relation to the New Testament, from the various ones normally imagined. We saw in chapter 1 some of the different ways in which 'authority' has been extracted from historical description(s) of the New Testament: we can make some aspect of Early Christianity normative; we can select certain theological themes within the New Testament writings themselves as central (the kingdom of god, justification by faith, or whatever); or we can include certain strands of the New Testament within a theological scheme whose beginning and end lie elsewhere. If, however, we take the model of the authority of the unfinished play, a different set of possibilities emerges. As we saw, part of the initial task of the actors chosen to improvise the new final act will be to immerse themselves with full sympathy in the first four acts, but not so as merely to parrot what has already been said.[28] They cannot go and look up the right answers. Nor can they simply imitate the kinds of things that their particular character did in the early acts. A good fifth act will show a proper final development, not merely a repetition, of what went before. Nevertheless, there will be a rightness, a fittingness, about certain actions and speeches, about certain final moves in the drama, which will in one sense be self-authenticating, and in another gain authentication from their coherence with, their making sense of, the 'authoritative' previous text.[29]

Some notes about this model are worth making before we apply it briefly to our own subject-matter.[30] First, it provides an analogy for the way in which any story, or any work of art, may possess in itself a kind of authority, particularly when in a state of needing completion. At this level, of course, the idea of the work being a play in five acts, with actors, is an unnecessary refinement: a symphony would do just as well, and the task of completion could be entrusted to a composer, not necessarily an improvising performer. Second, however, the model as I have outlined it provides a more direct and specific analogy to illustrate what I take to be at issue within the story of the creator and the creation as seen by the biblical writers, or at least some of them. This is where the idea of five acts, and of actors who are required to complete the work in their own improvisation, fits (I think) so well. The first use of the model, then, could be achieved without the second; that is to say, the model illustrates well the general point about unfinished works of art; but the second requires the first as its framework.

Among the detailed moves available within this model, which I hope to develop further elsewhere, is the possibility of seeing the biblical story as itself consisting of five acts. Thus: 1–Creation; 2–Fall; 3–Israel; 4–Jesus. The writing of the New Testament—including the writing of the gospels—would then form the first scene in the fifth act, and would simultaneously give hints (Romans 8,

---

[28] This illustration could of course run away with itself, but it is perhaps worth noting that among the actors' tasks would be to decide, for instance, whether the production was to be 'safe' or 'relevant', 'authentic' or 'contemporary', and so forth—and also to take proper account of the context in which the production was to take place . . .

[29] On the notion of 'fittingness' as a technical criterion in aesthetics see Wolterstorff 1979, 1980.

[30] I owe these thoughts to the wisdom of Professor Oliver O'Donovan.

1 Corinthians 15, parts of the Apocalypse) of how the play is supposed to end. The fact of Act 4 being what it is shows what sort of a conclusion the drama should have, without making clear all the intervening steps. The church would then live under the 'authority' of the extant story, being required to offer an improvisatory performance of the final act as it leads up to and anticipates the intended conclusion. The church is designed, according to this model, as a stage in the completion of the creator's work of art: as Paul says in Ephesians 2.10, *autou gar esmen poiema*, we are his artwork.

If we apply this to the problem of 'New Testament theology' as normally conceived, and as discussed in chapter 1, such immersing of oneself in the extant material will require a differentiation between different levels of material. As scholars and others have become aware of a necessary distinction between the Testaments, especially when one is addressing the church or the world, so we may discover other differences. Though Bultmann was wrong in thinking he could effectively truncate Act 4, and, for that matter, a good deal of Acts 1–3 as well, he was right in discerning a difference between Act 4 (Jesus) and the beginning of Act 5 (the New Testament)—even though his drawing of the distinction actually distorted both. It matters that the story of Jesus, i.e. the story of Act 4, was written by the early church as part of its appropriate task in Act 5.[31]

Indeed, it might appear that the retelling of the story of the previous acts, as part of the required improvisation, is a necessary part of the task all through. The Israelites retold the story of creation and fall. Jesus retold, in parable and symbol, the story of Israel. The evangelists retold, in complex and multi-faceted ways, the story of Jesus. This may suggest, from a new angle, that the task of history, including historical theology and theological history, is itself mandated upon the followers of Jesus from within the biblical story itself.

In addition, the notion that the writers of the New Testament were in some senses instituting a historical movement in which subsequent Christian generations may follow[32] gives to the task of hermeneutics an angle and emphasis quite different from any of the regular options which we described earlier. We are not searching, against the grain of the material, for timeless truths. We are looking, as the material is looking, for and at a vocation to be the people of God in the fifth act of the drama of creation. The church inherits, at the end of the story, the task of restoring to the owner the fruits of the vineyard. If Act 3 is essentially tragic, the total play is to be the kind of comedy that triumphs over tragedy.

One or two objections might well be lodged at this point. Can we be sure that anyone would ever understand Acts 1–4, or indeed the beginning of Act 5, well enough to make all the required moves in the later parts of Act 5? The answer must surely be no. Certainty on such matters is precisely what we do

---

[31] That the early Christians saw history in something like this differentiated way (distinguishing between the time of Jesus and their own time) is asserted, from very different standpoints, by Nineham 1976, 188f., and Lemcio 1991, *passim*. See Part IV below.

[32] The question, whether the NT writers imagined that there would be any subsequent generations, Christian or otherwise, will be addressed in Part IV below.

not have. That is why faith, and obedience, remain essentially risky. Church history, and for that matter the stories of Israel, and of the disciples during Jesus' ministry, are in fact littered with examples of individuals, groups and movements whose improvisations turned out to be based on a misreading of the story so far (though the question of which groups come into such a category would itself, obviously, be a matter of risky debate). But this does not mean that the overall task is impossible; merely that the actors remain fallible. The ultimate result is guaranteed, within the story itself, by the playwright's gift of his own spirit to the actors, but this cannot be taken to validate in advance all that they do or say.

Another objection would be: surely, in the Christian story, Act 4 (Jesus, and particularly his death and resurrection) is so climactic and conclusive that there is little left to do in Act 5? There are two possible replies to this.

First, we should stress that part of the task of Act 5—the task begun in the earliest post-Easter church, and including the writing of the gospels—is to reflect on, draw out, and implement the *significance* of the first four Acts, more specifically, of Act 4 in the light of Acts 1–3. What is more, Act 4 positively demands such further work. Such reflection and action is not simply a matter of reading ideas off the surface of the fourth-Act story, which in any case was of course itself written in Act 5. Faithful improvisation in the present time requires patient and careful puzzling over what has gone before, including the attempt to understand what the nature of the claims made in, and for, the fourth Act really amount to.

Second, I suggest that the question assumes what needs to be demonstrated, i.e. that the life, death and resurrection of Jesus really does have such a climactic sense as to leave no room for any further work. I suspect that this belief comes from a latent anti-historical tendency, within some branches of modern scholarship, rather than from the text. Certainly Paul, our earliest witness to Christianity, continually couples the work of the spirit in the present with the achievement of Jesus in the past.

To sum up: I am proposing a notion of 'authority' which is not simply vested in the New Testament, or in 'New Testament theology', nor simply in 'early Christian history' and the like, conceived positivistically, but in the creator god himself, and this god's story with the world, seen as focused on the story of Israel and thence on the story of Jesus, as told and retold in the Old and New Testaments, and as still requiring completion. This is a far more complex notion of authority than those usually tossed around in theological discourse. That is, arguably, what we need if we are to break through the log-jams caused by regular over-simplifications.

4. Conclusion

It is not easy to see at a glance what this model will mean in practice. That will have to wait until the substantial historical and theological exploration of Jesus, early Christianity and the New Testament has been undertaken. There are other elements that should be remembered, even though they cannot be included within the present project: the overall task implies a discussion of Old Testament theology, and a consideration of the world outside the Judaeo-Christian tradition, both of which are usually left out of consideration in New Testament study.[33] But for the moment the task is clear. Literary, historical and theological exploration of the New Testament, and particularly of Jesus and Paul, is our goal. And if that is to be even a possibility, it is vital that we set out the historical context of the investigation as clearly as possible. We must therefore spend the next two Parts of this volume studying, first, the Judaism from within which Christianity came to birth, and, second, early Christianity itself, as the context not only of Paul and his writings but as the world within which people remembered, and wrote about, Jesus.

---

[33] Thus meeting Räisänen's objection: 1990, 137–41.

Part Three

First-Century Judaism
Within the Greco-Roman World

Chapter Six

THE SETTING AND THE STORY

1. Introduction

(i) The Aim

We have no reason to think that Middle Eastern politics were any less complicated in the first century than in the twentieth. On the contrary, there is every reason to suppose that there were just as many tensions, problems, anomalies and puzzles then as now—just as much reason for some to throw up their hands in despair, for others to grit their teeth and forge ahead, and for others again to try to forget the whole 'situation' in the struggle to survive. Being a tenant of the vineyard was hard and depressing work.

Yet we cannot bypass the attempt to understand ancient Judaism as a whole if we are to make any sense of the new movement which was conceived, born and initially nurtured in its midst during the first century AD. To understand the origin of Christianity, and the terms in which the question of god was posed and addressed within it, and to do so in obedience to the demands of what constitutes a good hypothesis, we must gain as accurate an understanding as possible of the Judaism(s) in which Jesus and Paul grew up, and to which they related in various ways during their active ministries. We must understand the worldview(s) and self-understanding(s) held by Jews of the time, and, within that task, must attempt to grasp Judaism's sense of its own history, its belief in its covenant god, its aspirations, frustrations, hopes and fears.[1] Looking wider, we must also understand something of the cultural milieu in which Israel, and Judaism at large, found itself, i.e. the Greco-Roman world of the first century of the common era. That was the world primarily addressed by Paul and at least two of the evangelists.

The task of describing early Judaism is both easier and harder now than ever before. Easier, because we have a plethora of modern works to help us, written and edited by experts who have devoted themselves to this study over

---

[1] Though we may rightly speak of the 'Judaisms' of this period, it is often easier linguistically to refer to the singular 'Judaism' as the generic entity to which they all belong. The period is regularly known as 'second-temple Judaism', indicating the time roughly from the fourth century BC to the second century AD (even though the second Temple itself had been destroyed in AD 70), or occasionally 'middle Judaism', indicating the time between 'early Judaism' (the pre-exilic period) and the 'later Judaism' of the rabbis and beyond.

many years, and who have come from a wide variety of religious and cultural backgrounds.[2] Harder, because with knowledge comes complexity. It is far more difficult to complete the jigsaw of first-century Judaism when it suddenly turns out to contain not two hundred pieces but two thousand.

The problem is all the more acute when Western Christian scholarship is in the middle of a long-drawn-out process of repentance for having cherished false views about Judaism. Scholars and preachers tumble over one another to say that they were misguided, that they misjudged the Pharisees, that Jesus and his first followers had no quarrel with the Jews, that it was only later that the evangelists, under pressure, produced the caricatures of Jesus' opponents that we find in the gospels. How long it will be before things settle down again it is difficult to say.

In so far as the present phase is a reaction, it is a necessary one. Western Christianity lived with its misconceptions about Judaism for a long time, and allowed them to lull it into passivity at a moment of great and tragic need. It may now require at least a generation to exorcize them properly. But we will do ourselves a grave disservice if we think that simple reaction will do any lasting good. The historical task cannot be accomplished by the back-projection of modern guilt-feelings, any more than it was advanced by the back-projection of later theological controversy or prejudice.

This means that we must look with great care at the actual shape and nature of the Judaism of the first century, taking pains to listen to what is being said by scholars from all backgrounds who have really soaked themselves in the sources. This is not a task for the faint-hearted. The issues are complex and controversial. What I have to offer, however, is what seems to me a fairly mainline view, based on my own reading of the sources and of the most modern and thorough studies known to me. No doubt objections will be raised to this or that part of it, to my interpretations of this or that text or theme. But I think that the reconstruction I offer here is coherent within itself and with the sources, and that it will stand scrutiny from all sides.

In line with the proposals made in the previous chapters, I shall be attempting to uncover the *worldview* of second-temple Judaism by means of a study of its key aspects: the regular practical day-to-day life, the physical symbols such as the Temple, the retellings of the nation's story, and in particular the belief-system, the set of basic answers to basic questions that can be securely inferred from the mass of data at our disposal. From this vantage point we will be in a position to explore more particularly the detailed *beliefs* and *aspirations* of Israel, which may be loosely referred to as her 'faith' and 'hope'. These constitute, in line with the argument of Part II above, the 'inside' of the complex historical events which the present chapter will describe.

What emerges from this study may be outlined in advance as follows. The main feature of first-century Judaism, within Palestine at least, was neither a

---

[2] See the new Schürer; the *Compendia*; Nickelsburg 1981; Sanders 1990a, 1992; the new editions of texts in e.g. Charlesworth 1983, 1985; Sparks 1984; and see also e.g. Hengel 1974; Rowland 1985, parts I and II; Kraft and Nickelsburg 1986, 1–30; Ferguson 1987, ch. 5; Cohen 1987; the many works of Neusner; etc.

static sense of a religion to which one adhered, nor a private sphere of religion into which one escaped, but a total worldview, embracing all aspects of reality, and coming to sharp focus in a sense of longing and expectation, of recognition that the present state of affairs had not yet (to put it mildly) seen the full realization of the purposes of the covenant god for his people. The Jewish people of the first century, like all peoples, told themselves stories which encapsulated their worldview. One of the major differences between them and some other cultures, however, was that their controlling stories had to do with actual events in history: they were waiting for the last chapter in their story to begin. Jesus, as I shall argue in the next volume, addressed that sense of expectation and aspiration, even though arguably he was redefining it. Paul, too, claimed to be fulfilling the hopes of Israel, and, as we shall see in volume 3, he can only be understood in terms of a redefinition of Jewish theology. We must therefore see as clearly as possible what the basic Jewish worldview, controlling story, and belief-structure consisted of, how the Jewish hope functioned, what it was based on, what characteristic expressions it received, and what sort of controversies it engendered.

This statement of intent will perhaps look to some like a determination to 'read back' Christian ideas or modes of thought into Judaism. In response, I must say four things.

First, as I argued in Part II, the present mood in the study of first-century Judaism is in my view overly atomistic and positivistic. In so far as my suggestion clashes with current fashions, the conflict arises more from my concern for a fully historical approach (by which I mean a critical-realist approach) than from the reading back of any later patterns of thought, Christian or otherwise.

Second, the atomistic readings which I am implicitly criticizing are themselves just as much 'interpretations' as my own. Atomism and positivism are perhaps a necessary reaction to dogmatism, but they cannot stand for ever. Their implicit interpretations of the 'inside' of first-century Jewish history must be subjected to scrutiny, and must compete with more thoroughgoing interpretations which attempt to do justice to the underlying structures of belief and aspiration, and above all to the symbolic world which gave meaning to Jewish life.[3] It is an interpretation of this sort that I intend to offer in this part of the book.

Third, as a matter of fact the boot is on the other foot. I intend to describe the authentic first-century Jewish worldview, so often obscured in subsequent Christian reflection, in order thereby to correct some normal 'Christian' understandings of Jesus, Paul and early Christianity. Many 'Christian' readings of the gospels have screened out the political overtones of Jesus' proclamation of the kingdom; a fresh examination of the Jewish background will put that straight. Monotheism and election have not usually been regarded as the centre of Paul's thought; reassessing the structure of the Pharisaic worldview will open up new possibilities for such a reading. My aim is therefore precisely not to project non-Jewish ideas on to Judaism, but to achieve a critical-realist reading of first-century Judaism, including its beliefs and aspirations, in its own

---

[3] It is on such grounds that Sanders 1990a, chs. 3–5, mounts his criticisms of Jacob Neusner.

terms, which will then shed unexpected light on the rise of Christianity. This, as I argued earlier, is what history is all about.

In fact (this is the fourth point), first-century Judaism and Christianity have a central worldview-feature in common: the sense of a story now reaching its climax. And, most importantly, *it is the same story*. It is the story of Abraham, Isaac and Jacob; of Moses and the prophets; of David, Solomon, and the monarchy of Israel; and especially of exile and restoration—or rather, of puzzlement as to whether the exile was really over or not. Christians, of course, soon told the story with a rather different emphasis. But Jews and Christians continued to regard the story of Israel as the earlier chapters of their own story. It is here that fundamental continuity is to be sought; and this legitimates the attempt to study Judaism in such a way as to shed light on emerging Christianity.

It might be desirable in principle to study the individual writings and groups of writings first, and to work up slowly to generalizations about 'what Jews believed'; but there are seven reasons for not doing that here. First, the problem of space is acute: one would need another whole volume. Second, it has been done quite thoroughly in very recent scholarship, and it seems otiose to go over ground already well covered (though I shall challenge received opinion here and there, and suggest some possibilities not usually noticed).[4] Third, we are often reminded today that writings possessed by contemporary scholars are not necessarily representative of what the average first-century Jew thought. This is no reason for not studying the ones we have, of course, but it is a reason for exercising caution in basing judgments on them and them alone, or in imagining that once one has analysed the available writings one has completed the necessary task. Fourth, I think, and hope to demonstrate, that it is in fact possible to make certain substantial generalized points which are no less forceful for having a wide base.[5] Fifth, I shall argue later that Christianity's link with Judaism is not with one particular sub-group and set of literary remains, but with Judaism *as a whole*, whether in reaffirmation, confrontation or redefinition. And Judaism as a whole is seen as much if not more in its symbolic world and political movements as in its (possibly idiosyncratic) literary remains.[6] Sixth, the atomistic study of individual texts can sometimes function as a smokescreen behind which certain a priori approaches can be hidden, which then continue to determine the shape of the overall reading. The critical realism I am advocating must go beyond any merely inductive approach. The circle of literature, history and theology can be broken into at any point. Seventh, following from this, literature itself is (as we saw earlier) part of a wider circle which includes symbol, story, question and praxis. There is therefore a good deal to be said for studying it as part of that larger whole rather than in a position of privileged priority.

---

[4] See Sanders 1977; Schürer vol 3; Stone 1984; Nickelsburg 1981, pointing out (1–5) the importance of this method.

[5] Similar attempts are made by Goodman 1987, ch. 4; Sanders 1991b, ch. 5; 1992, chs. 13–14.

[6] See Horsley and Hanson 1985, xvi–xvii.

We are, then, looking for the self-understanding, the beliefs and hopes of an embattled little nation at a particularly tense and fateful moment in its history. This means, to return to the beginning, looking at the Jewish *worldview*, and the various aims and beliefs that brought it to expression. This must be done by examining the surface events, the symbols and stories that gave them depth, and the intentionalities of the characters and groups involved. In the present chapter we will review the basic historical story; in the next, we will discuss the developing diversity within Judaism in this period. We will then (chapter 8) examine the symbols that provide the clues to the main Jewish worldview. This will enable us to sketch the beliefs (chapter 9) and the hopes (chapter 10) which characterized Jews of this period. First, though, in order to do any of this, we must note where the main sources for the task are to be found. Though, as noted above, we cannot here study them in detail, it is important to be aware of what and where they are.

(ii) The Sources

The sources which are particularly relevant for our purposes are those which reflect the situation in Palestine before the two great rebellions of AD 66–70 and 132–5, and particularly before the first of these. The most important non-Christian source is of course Josephus, whose two great works *The Jewish War* and *The Antiquities of the Jews* dominate the landscape, and whose shorter autobiographical *Life* and defence of Judaism *Against Apion* also constitute valuable material.[7] Behind Josephus there stand the first two books of the Maccabees, and the two subsequent books which continued to retell the same story from different perspectives, and which thereby reveal something both of the events to which the books purport to refer and of Jewish attitudes at the time of the retelling.[8] The rabbinic literature, which all comes from a later period when circumstances had changed dramatically from those which obtained in the middle of the first century, contains much valuable material which, when carefully processed, tells us a good deal about the period before AD 70. But in its present form it reflects the culture and agendas of a much later time. As Jacob Neusner says:

> From the rabbinic traditions about the Pharisees we could not have reconstructed a single significant, public event of the period before 70—not the rise, success, and fall of the Hasmoneans, nor the Roman conquest of Palestine, nor the rule of Herod, nor the reign of the procurators, nor the growth of opposition to Rome, nor the proliferation of social violence and unrest in the last decades before 66 AD, nor the outbreak of the war with Rome . . .[9]

---

[7] On Josephus see the recent works of Cohen 1979; Broshi 1982; Rajak 1983; Attridge in Stone 1984, ch. 5; Feldman 1984; Schürer 1.43–63; Bilde 1988; and now especially Mason 1991.

[8] On 1 and 2 Macc. see Schürer 3.180–5, 531–7; Attridge in Stone 1984, ch. 4 (171–83); Nickelsburg 1981, 114–21. On 3 Macc. see Schürer 3.537–42; Nickelsburg 1981, 169–72, and in Stone 1984, 80–4; on 4 Macc. Schürer 3.588–93; Gilbert in Stone 1984, 316–19; Nickelsburg 1981, 223–7.

[9] Neusner 1971, 3.304.

It is wise, therefore, to treat the rabbinic tradition with great caution in reconstructing pre-70 history, and indeed this is the line taken by most scholars today.[10] We are on safer ground by far in using the apocrypha and pseudepigrapha, and the Scrolls, as witness to Jewish attitudes in our period; though of course with those too we must constantly remind ourselves that by no means all Jews knew and read them, and that those who did might well have disapproved of them.[11]

When it comes to reconstructing the 'inside' of the events of the first century, the works referred to are the vital initial sources. At the same time, we must never forget that the one book with which all Jews were familiar was of course the Bible. Not that we can easily use the Old Testament as it stands as evidence for 'what Jews believed', or what they hoped for, in this period. It was read in particular ways, seen through particular grids of interpretation and anticipation.[12] The Targums, translating the archaic Hebrew into a contemporary Aramaic, and adding some explanatory material as they did so, eventually became a fixed tradition in their own right. A good many of the apocryphal and pseudepigraphical works, and of the Scrolls, consist in large part of new ways of reading the same old texts, of making them available to address the needs of a new generation. The grids of interpretation thus offered constitute the key variations in the first-century Jewish worldview. This worldview was expressed in stories told and retold, symbols acted out and lived out, agendas taken up, tasks attempted, and (in a few cases) books written. The study of the literature leads us to the study of the history, which in turn opens up to reveal the available worldviews, and the beliefs and aims in which they were expressed. But before plunging into this history we must sketch the wider world in which the Jews found themselves.

2. The Greco-Roman World as the Context of Early Judaism

It is both impossible and unnecessary to engage in a lengthy description of the world of late antiquity within which Judaism, and, within that, earliest Christianity, found itself. The task has been well done often enough,[13] and our main focus of attention, at least for the moment, must be Judaism itself. But some account is necessary of the basic political and religious world in which we shall be moving for the next little while.

The Greek empire of Alexander the Great, whose youthful megalomania led him to attempt extraordinary feats of conquest and whose military genius enabled him to carry them out, meant that from the end of the fourth century

[10] On the rabbinic literature see Schürer 1.68–118, and especially Safrai 1987; the many works of Neusner, e.g. 1971, 1973; and now Strack and Stemberger 1991 [1982]. For similar notes of caution, see e.g. Goodman 1987, 23f.; Saldarini 1988, 7–10.

[11] See the texts in Charlesworth 1983, 1985; Vermes 1987 [1962]; and the discussions in Nickelsburg 1981; Schürer vol. 3; Stone 1984.

[12] See Mulder 1987; Barton 1986; Fishbane 1985; Chilton 1983, 1984; and chs. 8–10 below.

[13] See e.g. *CAH* vols. X, XI; Salmon 1968 [1944]; Wells 1984; Millar 1981 [1967]; Garnsey and Saller 1982.

BC the Middle East found itself more or less at the centre of a vast area which spoke (or which did its best to speak) a single language, and which was unprecedentedly culturally unified. The broad name for this unifying culture is of course Hellenism, which denotes a pervading pattern, embracing different strands and streams of thought and life, and tracing itself to the Greek culture which included Homer as a virtual holy book and the philosophy of Plato as a guiding influence. It expressed itself in Greek language and customs, in religious observance and custom, in the style of coinage, in literary and theatrical conventions, as well as in a wide variety of philosophies, some of which were more explicitly Platonic in the sense of embracing a dualism between the world known by the senses and that known by the mind. Hellenism was everywhere, and everything was Hellenistic—more or less.[14] After Alexander conquered Palestine in 332 BC, in all sorts of ways things were never the same again. For a full three hundred years before the birth of Jesus of Nazareth, Greek influence had been everywhere. Greek was everybody's second language, everybody's second culture. Loan words were symptomatic of other more subtle borrowings. Even those who resisted were living in the new world: Hellenism had set the agenda, and the terms of the debate. The Maccabees, who ousted Hellenistic pagan worship, set up a dynasty (the 'Hasmoneans', so called after an ancestor) whose outward trappings were themselves thoroughly Hellenistic.[15] The Qumran sect, who set themselves apart from all things pagan (and a good many things Jewish, too) used language and ideas which themselves borrowed from a variety of Hellenistic sources.[16] Any idea of a hidden curtain between Judaism and Hellenism, in the sense of a geographical line at which it might be said that the one stopped and the other began, must be completely rejected.

When the Roman empire took the place of the Greek, Seleucid and Ptolemaic ones that preceded it, it brought, by the end of the first century BC, blessing and bane for the average Palestinian Jew. Blessing, in that the world was basically at peace. This did not merely mean that the menfolk were not being called up, fighting as mercenaries, etc. It meant no extra war-levies, no troops marching through the land *en route* for somewhere else, no soldiers billeted on villages. It meant that trade and travel could thrive, that communications were as good as they had ever been in the ancient world (especially once the Romans had largely wiped out the pirates that used to make travel on the Mediterranean sea multiply dangerous). It meant that there was a unified

[14] On the nature of Hellenism and its spread in Palestine see especially *CHJ* vol. 2; Hengel 1974, and esp. 1989a; Schürer 2.29–80; Tcherikover 1961; Flusser 1976; Goldstein 1981 (including a useful set of definitions of Hellenism, 67); Koester 1982a, *passim*, esp. 39f., 153ff.; Cohen in Kraft and Nickelsburg 1986, 42f.; Rajak 1990. A good example of the phenomena in question is the temple of Augustus at Caesarea Philippi, on which see Jos. *Ant.* 15.363f.; Schürer 2.169; Hengel 1989 [1961] 102.

[15] Schürer 2.52f. For the view that the Hasmoneans were as much zealots for Torah, in their way, as were their opponents, see Goldstein 1989, 350f.

[16] So, arguably, the Essenes' 'War of the Sons of Light against the Sons of Darkness'. On this, see Schmidt 1982, 164–5. See also Hengel 1974, 1.218–47. For other examples of the same phenomenon see Goodman 1987, 17; Momigliano 1984, 337f., arguing that this penetration included the rabbinic schools.

system of justice which prided itself on its high standards, so that in theory at least one was not at the mercy of local officials who might or might not be open to inducements: a creaky system, perhaps, but it was at least *de jure* in place.[17]

But with these blessings there went bane. Rome kept the peace by means of military might, crushing dissent and resistance with ruthless efficiency. Taxes had to be paid to Rome as well as to one's local country, taxes which were used to keep Rome in luxury while her massive empire continued in relative or actual poverty.[18] The official Roman religion was normally imposed on local areas. Perceiving that the Jews would rather die *en masse* than offer pagan worship, the pragmatic Romans permitted them instead to sacrifice to their own god on the emperor's behalf. Even so, the Roman standards with their blasphemous inscriptions were quite enough to make a pious Jew shudder.[19] Rome needed Palestine for part of her corn supply, and as a safeguarding of the larger supplier, Egypt; the whole area also provided, for Rome, a Middle-Eastern buffer zone against the major threat of Parthia. Palestine was not just a backwater of the empire. It was important to Rome strategically, militarily, and economically.

Turning to the religion of the Roman world, we find the basic landscape dominated by paganism.[20] This took many forms, but certain general statements can safely be made. There were still many devotees of the old gods of the Greco-Roman pantheon, Zeus/Jupiter and his entire troupe, though there was also a fair amount of educated disbelief or lip-service. In many localities people worshipped eponymous gods or goddesses, of whom Roma and Athene are the obvious examples. Sometimes the old pantheon itself provided a special link with one place, as in the case of Diana/Artemis, in whom the Ephesians had a special interest (or perhaps she in them). There were nature-deities, such as Attis or Isis from Egypt, whose worship might include various nature-rituals or fertility-cults. There was the popular cult of Mithraism, evidence of which is found as far afield as army camps in Britain. The Roman emperors added to the pantheon by their strategic insistence on having their predecessors installed into it. From this it was only a short step to anticipating *post mortem* divinization and claiming divine honours for oneself during one's lifetime. This is, after all, what most totalitarian states do sooner or later.

---

[17] See e.g. the eulogy of the *pax Romana* in Epict. 3.13.9.

[18] See Borg 1984, ch. 2; though see the cautionary note in Sanders 1992, ch.9: one must not over-stress the over-taxing. At the same time, note such remarks as that attributed by Tacitus to the Briton Calgacus: 'they [the Romans] make a wilderness and call it peace' (*Agricola* 30.6; the whole passage is significant).

[19] On the question of the Roman permission of Jewish worship (the so-called *religio licita* status) see Schürer 1.275, 378f.; Sanders 1992, 212; Jos. *Ant.* 14.213–16, 241–61. On Roman respect for the Jewish cult see Goodman 1987, 15. On the Jewish protest about Roman standards, cf. Jos. *Ant.* 18.55–9, and below.

[20] For this paragraph, see Koester 1982a, 164–204; MacMullen 1981; Lyttleton and Forman 1984; Lane Fox 1986; Buckert 1985; Ferguson 1987, ch. 3; Martin 1987, *passim*. On the easy transition in our period from older forms of paganism to the newer emperor-worship see Hengel 1989 [1961], 99f.

The prevalence of all these deities meant that the average town or city was full of reminders of the pagan way of life: temples, shrines and altars; sacred pillars and cult-objects, some shocking to a Jewish conscience; sacred prostitution everywhere; sacrificial animals being taken for slaughter, their meat to be offered for sale in the markets. Pagan religion in one form or another was taken for granted. The Jewish (and then the Christian) protest that there was one god, who required none of these things and indeed hated them, came as a major challenge to a long-established worldview.

By the first century AD the mobility of some of the population and the ease of communications meant that different cults were being fused together in syncretistic blends.[21] It did not take intelligent pagans long to spot that one cult was remarkably like another, and to suggest that they could easily be combined without offence to any of the deities concerned. Since paganism basically deified different parts of, or forces in, the natural order, it was not an odd step either for some, such as the Stoics, to see all the parts coming together and producing pantheism, in which god is everything because everything is god. One of Stoicism's major competitors, the philosophy of Epicurus, moved in a different direction: the gods exist, but they live a life of blessedness removed from the world inhabited by humans. Epicureanism, at the theological level, thus offers a kind of proto-Deism.[22] These and other philosophical schools stood behind the hurly-burly of popular religion, and somewhat aloof. To be sure, one could be a philosopher and still worship the old gods, or indeed vice versa; but the Stoic and the Epicurean, the Pythagorean and the Cynic, gave higher allegiance elsewhere (in so far as it makes any sense to talk of the Cynic giving allegiance anywhere). There are several interesting parallels between Paul and the Stoics, but none that suggest direct borrowing either way. The recent suggestions that Jesus was some kind of a Cynic are (to say the least) highly controversial.[23]

If some of the ancient religious tendencies affirmed the goodness of nature, others, such as Zoroastrianism, emphatically denied it. Several of the mystery religions promised escape from the ordinariness of the present world and initiation into a higher state of being. There may have been some before the time of Jesus who claimed to possess special 'gnosis', a knowledge which set them aside from ordinary folk and marked them out for a heavenly destiny. The evidence for this is found not least in some passages in Paul's letters (e.g. 1 Corinthians 8.1–4), and it may well be that Paul faced opponents whose theology was a blend of Jewish wisdom-teaching and Hellenistic philosophy and who claimed 'a higher, non-rational knowledge of truths profounder than those apprehended at the level of simple faith'.[24] The larger question, though,

---

[21] See Martin 1987, 10–11.

[22] See Ferguson 1987, 281–302; Koester 1982a, 145–53; and ch. 9 sect. 2 below.

[23] On Stoicism see e.g. Koester 1982a, 147–53; on occasional parallels with Paul see Meeks 1983, 98, 165; Malherbe 1987. Instructive examples which show both the similarity and the fundamental difference, include the parallels between Epict. *Disc.* 2.26.1ff. and Rom. 7.13–20 (cf. below, p. 406 n.114); Epict. *Frag.* 18 and 1 Cor. 1.12. On Jesus and the Cynics see e.g. Downing 1988a; Mack 1988; and the discussion in the second volume of the present project.

[24] Chadwick 1966, 7f.

concerns the extent to which a serious systematic Gnosticism already existed prior to the rise of Christianity. A hypothesis to this effect used to be widely believed, and was the basis for much of Rudolf Bultmann's reconstruction of early Christianity. It has come under severe attacks in the last forty years, and many have abandoned it; but there are signs that it is making a comeback, and one aspect of this will be discussed later.[25]

Religion, culture and politics were not sharply divided in the ancient world. One practised one's religion either as a member of a private club, such as a mystery cult, or as part of the formal requirements of the state, or quite likely both. In the former case a certain amount of popular culture would be bound up with one's devotion; in the latter, a certain amount of political belief, adherence and activity. Ancient society was not compartmentalized after the manner of modern Western society, nor half so private an affair. What one did in any sphere of life was both observed and, in principle, integrated with other aspects.

In such a context, we should not be surprised that the Jews were regarded as atheists.[26] That, one may surmise, was probably the reaction of the Roman general Pompey when he entered the Holy of Holies in the late autumn of 63 BC and found *no image* there. He was, we may assume, disappointed; he had presumably gone in not just out of curiosity but to confront the Jews' god with the fact that the goddess Roma had just worsted him or her in a straight fight.[27] And if the Jews had no image of their own god, how much less would they worship those of others. The Jews thus appeared as a strange race, who kept to their own ancestral customs even when away from their land, and who were potentially a danger or threat to society.[28] For their part, the Jews regarded paganism as the parent of the ugly sisters, idolatry and immorality, and there was no shortage of corroborating evidence for the charge. The pagans were, it seemed, calling down upon themselves judgment from the true god, who regarded their idolatry and consequent immorality as defacing his human image and who therefore allowed them to reap the rewards of their own ways.[29] In Palestine, of course, it was exceptionally galling for the Jews to find themselves confronted with paganism being practised on their own territory,

---

[25] See ch. 14 below. Cf. Bultmann 1956, 162ff. Against: e.g. Wilson 1968; Layton 1980, 1981 (see the remark by Henry Chadwick in Layton 1981, 586: 'Perhaps any time after the middle of the second century, Gnosticism existed in time and space'); Martin 1987, 134–54; Yamauchi 1973. For more general material on Gnosticism: Jonas 1963 [1958]; Rudolph 1975, 1983 [1977]; Logan and Wedderburn 1983; Ferguson 1987, 237–51; Koester 1982a, 381–9, with fuller bibliography; Rowland 1985, 294–6. For recent attempts to argue for a Jewish (and possibly pre-Christian) origin for Gnosticism see Pearson 1980; Rudolph 1983 [1977], e.g. 308, 367 (though very cautiously); Koester 1990, 83f.

[26] See e.g. Jos. *Apion.* 2.148; cf. *War* 3.536; Tac. *Hist.* 5.2–4; 13.1. On this charge, and its potential consequences, see Sevenster 1975, 98–102; MacMullen 1981, 40, 62f.; Goodman 1987, 237.

[27] The incident is recounted in Tac. *Hist.* 5.9.1; cf. also Jos. *Ant.* 14.69–73, which emphasizes the restraint Pompey showed in his actions. Cf. the parallel with Titus in *Apion* 2.82 and *War* 6.260.

[28] On the importance of the land see ch. 8 below. For an example of Roman attitudes to Jews see Tac. *Hist.* 5.1–13.

[29] e.g. Wisd. 13–14 (and e.g. Rom. 1.18–32).

and this inevitably fuelled anger and resentment against all who were seen as representatives of Hellenism.[30] In our period this of course meant Rome, who was thus perceived by the Jews to be oppressing them in every possible way—militarily, economically, politically, culturally and religiously.[31]

This was the world in which all varieties of first-century Judaism lived, moved and had their being. We must now retrace our steps, and look at the same world from the point of view of the Jews' own story.

3. The Story of Israel, 587 BC—AD70

(i) From Babylon to Rome (587–63 BC)

The story of second-temple Judaism is one of tension and tragedy.[32] The Babylonians had destroyed the first Temple in 587 BC. Ever since then, those who looked to Jerusalem, and its Temple, as the centre of their homeland, and as their very *raison-d'être* as a people, had been faced with the mounting tension between the faith they professed and the facts they perceived. The exile had not only uprooted them from their land; it had placed a great question mark against the pre-exilic faith in the ancestral god. When the great moment had come, and Babylon had been destroyed, Israel did not become free, mistress in her own land: the Persians, who had crushed Babylon, were generous overlords to the Jews, but overlords none the less. As we have already seen, Alexander the Great swept through the old Persian empire and beyond, painting the map a new colour and imposing a new culture. The two subsequent overlordships, by Egypt in the third century and Syria in the second, make the story more complex but do not alter the basic fact that the world was now Greek. By the time of the first century, if Jesus had wanted to take his disciples to see Euripides' plays performed, he might have only had to walk down the road from Capernaum to Beth Shean. When Paul was kept prisoner in Caesarea Maritima, he would probably have been able to hear, from his prison cell, the shouts of the crowd in the large amphitheatre, or the applause of the audience in the theatre beside the shore. Nearby there was also a temple to Caesar, a Mithraeum, and probably shrines to other pagan gods. Herod had shrewdly made the town a bottleneck through which the major trade routes had to pass.[33]

This Hellenistic cultural setting formed a perpetual cultural and religious threat to the Jews, every bit as powerful as the political one (and actually not

---

[30] See now particularly Kasher 1990.

[31] On pagan attitudes to Jews and vice versa see Sevenster 1975; Stern 1976; Gager 1983, esp. ch.3; Whittaker 1984, part I; Gager in Kraft and Nickelsburg 1986, 105–16; Ferguson 1987, 341–3, with bibliography; Schürer 2.81–4.

[32] For fuller details than are possible here, see *CHJ*, vol. 2; Schürer, vol. 1; Cohen 1987, 27–59; Ferguson 1987, chs. 1–2. A list of key dates and people can be found in the Appendix (below, pp. 477ff.).

[33] On Beth Shean (= Scythopolis) see Flusser 1976, 1065ff.; Schürer 2.38 (temples), 48 (theatre), 142–5; on Caesarea Maritima (= Strato's Tower) see Schürer 1.306, 2.115–18.

distinguishable from it to the naked eye at the time, but only to the atomistic analysis of modern Western thought-forms). The self-understanding of Jews at this time was determined by the pressing question as to whether they should attempt to be distinct from this alien culture, and if so how. Pressure to assimilate was strong in many quarters, as is suggested by the evidence for Jews attempting to remove the marks of circumcision.[34]

The question of identity was forced upon Palestinian Jews in a variety of ways. But it was under the Syrian rule that there occurred the event which became, I suggest, dangerously determinative for the self-understanding and aspiration of Jews, and the new focal point of their beliefs, up to the time of Jesus and beyond.[35] The megalomaniac Syrian ruler Antiochus Epiphanes, wanting to use Judaea as a buffer state against Egypt, tried to gain Jewish support through the usurping high priest Menelaus. After the Jews, not least the ousted Jason, had reacted angrily against Menelaus,[36] Antiochus decided (this was not an odd thing to do at that period) to ensure their loyalty by changing the function and direction of their central religious symbol, so that it ceased to make them think independently and turned them in the direction of service to himself. He took over the Temple on December 25, 167 BC. Deliberately desecrating it so that Jews would no longer think of it as the place where they were reaffirmed as a unique people, he established worship of himself there instead. Very often in the ancient world such moves would have worked quite satisfactorily, at least from the conqueror's point of view. But Antiochus had not reckoned on the tenacity (he would no doubt have called it fanaticism) of some of the Jews. Some refused to break the ancestral laws, and died rather than submit, bequeathing a memory of martyrdom-for-Torah that was kept fresh right through our period. Others, having escaped, believed that their covenant god would act in a new way. He would vindicate his own name, his chosen place, his sacred turf, and his holy law—and his faithful people, provided they remained faithful to him and to his symbols no matter what happened to them.

People who believe this sort of thing tend to act with desperate daring.[37] One strand of Jewish self-understanding, belief and hope coalesced into a single movement. Judas Maccabaeus and his companions accomplished the

---

[34] On removing the marks of circumcision see 1 Macc. 1.11–15; 2 Macc. 4.11–17; Jos. *Ant.* 12.241; *T. Mos.* 8.3; see Schürer 1.148–9, and n. 28, for full discussion. For the wider issue of Jewish interaction with Hellenism see Hengel 1974, and his article on the subject in *CHJ*, vol. 2; and e.g. Goldstein 1981. 1 Macc. 1 provides a good perspective, albeit from one side, on the whole question.

[35] On this whole episode see 1 Macc.; Jos. *War* 1.31–40; *Ant.* 12.246–331; Diod. Sic. 34/5.1.1–5 (commenting on Antiochus' magnanimity and mild manner!); cf. Schürer 1.125–73, with Mørkholm 1989 and Goldstein 1981, 1989. On its continuing significance for Jewish self-understanding see Farmer 1956, esp. ch. 6. Farmer's book strikingly anticipates by two or three decades the historical concerns which have finally come to the fore in the modern study of Jesus: see e.g. his preface (vii–x) and ch. 8.

[36] On Menelaus see Schürer 1.149f.

[37] That the motivating goals of the revolutionaries, in the second century BC and the first century AD, were substantially religious and not just those of secularized self-interest (as Josephus sometimes suggests) is established by Farmer 1956, ch. 5; and see chs. 7–10 below.

unthinkable, and organized a guerrilla revolt that drove out the tyrant. Three years to the day after the Temple's desecration (December 25, 164 BC) Judas cleansed and reconsecrated it. A new festival (Hanukkah) was added to the Jewish calendar. The Maccabaean revolt became classic and formative in the same way as the exodus and the other great events of Israel's history. It powerfully reinforced the basic Jewish worldview: when the tyrants rage, the one who dwells in heaven will laugh them to scorn.[38] YHWH had vindicated his name, his place, his land, his law—and his people.

The ambiguity of the subsequent years, in which the heirs of the successful revolutionaries ruled as priest-kings, did not dim the sense of the victory of their god, but created the same sort of puzzle that was left after the so-called 'return from exile': a great vindication had occurred, but it now seemed as though there must be yet another one still to come. By no means all Jews were happy with the new situation. Getting rid of the tyrant and his idolatrous practices was one thing, but was the new (Hasmonean) regime what the covenant god actually wanted?[39] Was it not in its turn heavily compromised with Hellenism, and riding roughshod over the religious sensibilities of the Jewish people by, for instance, combining the offices of king and high priest? Some opposed it bitterly and, as we shall see, set up alternative communities. Some stuck it out, but grumbled and tried to reform from within.[40] Others played the power game to win. Most Jews—the ones who wrote no literature, led no marches, had no voice—struggled to maintain their livelihood and their loyalty, their allegiance to national and cultural symbols, as best they could, always under the social pressures of warring theologies. It was this pluriform response to the ambiguities of the second century BC that created the pluriform Judaism known by Jesus and Paul.

(ii) Jews under Roman Rule (63 BC—AD 70)

Pompey's arrival in 63 BC found Judaism in a certain amount of confusion, and created yet more.[41] If the covenant god had defeated the tyrant Antiochus Epiphanes when he presumed to desecrate the Temple, how could Pompey walk right in to the Holy of Holies and escape unscathed? From that moment there were bound to be Jews who would identify the Romans as the new great enemy, the Kittim, the power of darkness ranged against the children of light.[42] They were now seen as the archetypal idolaters, and would eventually reap the fruit of their wicked and blasphemous ways. When Pompey died thirty years later in another campaign and another place, there were Jews watching who

[38] Ps. 2.4. See again Farmer 1956, 132–58.

[39] On the name 'Hasmonean', traced back to an ancestor of the Maccabee family, see Jos. *Ant.* 12.265, etc. and Schürer 1.194 n.14.

[40] On all this see Schürer 1.200–80; Saldarini 1988, 85–95.

[41] cf. Jos. *War* 1.133–54; *Ant.* 14.37–79; Dio Cass. 37.15.2—16.4.

[42] The word 'Kittim' is used in e.g. Daniel and Qumran as a generic term for the new pagan enemy, Rome.

were ready to celebrate the downfall that had been coming to him all along.[43] The Romans inherited the odium of Babylon, of Antiochus, of the whole encroaching Hellenistic culture. They managed to make matters still worse by ruling (so it seemed to most Jews) with an insensitive arrogance that constantly bordered on provocation to rebellion.[44]

But no new Judas Maccabaeus arose to lead Israel's faithful heroes in another holy war. Instead, his heirs and successors compromised (or so it seemed to rigorists) with the faithless, played the political game, rendered unto Caesar (more or less) what Caesar thought was due to him, and gave to their god what was left. The Romans, meanwhile, oversaw Palestine from their base in the province of Syria, ruling the country through the Hasmonean, and then the Herodian, dynasties. The Temple became, *de facto*, the cultic shrine organized by those who had made a somewhat unsteady peace with Rome, while the rigorists, looking on in impotent anger, determined that they at least would be faithful to the covenant god, by keeping his covenant charter to the utmost of their ability. If anyone was to be vindicated when the covenant god finally acted, it would surely be those who had thus demonstrated their unswerving loyalty to him.

Granted this mood, it was perhaps inevitable that Herod the Great (37–4 BC) would never be accepted as the genuine king of the Jews.[45] He made every effort to legitimate himself and his successors as genuine kings: he married Mariamne, who was the granddaughter of Hyrcanus II and thus a Hasmonean princess; above all, he set in motion the rebuilding of the Temple, as the true coming king was supposed to do.[46] But his actions had the opposite effect from that intended. The rigorists saw the new Temple as thoroughly ambiguous, and never accepted any of Herod's successors as the genuine heaven-sent leader for whom some of them persisted in waiting. This rejection of Herod and his ways found various expressions, which we shall study presently. A mood of revolt was not far below the surface, and emerged particularly upon Herod's death in 4 BC.

Revolution remained in the air during the early years of the new century, and, after the revolt led by Judas the Galilean in AD 6, Rome deemed it safer to make Judaea a province in its own right. From then on a succession of

---

[43] *Ps. Sol.* 2.25–31, referring to Pompey's death in 48 BC (see the summary in Schürer 3.193f.). See Goldstein 1989, 349f.

[44] See MacMullen 1967, 83–7, 145–9; 1974; Rhoads 1976; Kraft and Nickelsburg 1986, 43f.; Koester 1982a, 396; Schürer 1.336–483; Goodman 1987, 1–3, 9–11. For the details of movements of revolt, see ch. 7 below.

[45] On Herod and his dynasty see the classic work of Jones 1967 [1938]; and Schürer 1.287–329. Herod was elevated by the Romans, at the expense of the last Hasmonean king, Antigonus, after Herod had helped the Romans to regain the losses suffered in the Parthian invasion. Cf. Jos. *Ant.* 14.470–91; Dio Cass. 49.22.6, with the interesting comment that the Roman general Sosius had Antigonus bound to a cross and flogged before being killed—a punishment, says Dio, which no other king had suffered at the hands of the Romans.

[46] See ch. 10 below. The Temple, begun in 19 BC (cp. Jn. 2.20), was consecrated in 9 BC, and the whole building eventually finished in AD 63, seven years before its destruction (*Ant.* 20.219–20). On Herod's posing as the new Solomon see *Ant.* 15.380–7, and 15.421–3, which echoes 1 Kgs. 8.1–5, and notes that the inner sanctuary was completed, no doubt by a well-designed coincidence, on the anniversary of Herod's accession. Cf. too Jacobson 1988.

'prefects' or 'procurators'[47] governed with more or less crass folly. Pontius Pilate, the third of the Judaean prefects (AD 26–32), was one of a line, perhaps no worse but certainly no better than most of the others. Isolated protests were put down with sporadic violence, and the embers of potential rebellion smouldered on, ready to be fanned into flames of expectation and aspiration. Sooner or later the covenant god would act once more to vindicate his name, to restore the symbols (particularly the Temple) which expressed his covenant with Israel, and of course to liberate Israel herself.

It was this hope, to be studied more fully in chapter 10 below, that led to the great rebellion of AD 66. The complex of motivations determined both the form of the revolt and, in large measure, its result. Belief that the covenant god would step into history and act to vindicate himself and his people is not necessarily the most efficient basis on which to plan a military uprising. It led to a fissiparous situation in which different factions, each believing that they were the true chosen warriors, fought against each other with as much or more violence as against the Romans.[48] As more than one would-be prophet had predicted, the Romans were bound to be the eventual winners. The Temple was burned, and the city taken, in AD 70; Masada followed in 74.[49] The Kittim triumphed. The covenant god did nothing. It was a very different Judaism that then reconstructed itself, with grief and pain and a sense not only of crushing disaster but of belief overturned and hope dashed. It was as though (as one of them said) an iron wall had gone up between the covenant god and his people.[50]

(iii) Judaism Reconstructed (AD 70–135)

The period after AD 70 was, obviously, of great significance for the future direction of Judaism. It has also often been regarded as of great significance for the development of early Christianity. A good many theories about the way in which Christianity developed, particularly about how it came to break finally with Judaism itself, have hinged on the belief that in the post-destruction period certain events took place which introduced a new factor into the equation. The new rabbinic movement, bitter and grieving over the loss of Jerusalem and the Temple, organized itself (so this view holds) into a great Synod at Jamnia and introduced measures which effectively excluded Christians.[51] The young church, flexing its muscles, responded to polemic with polemic. Sayings, many of them bitterly hostile to Judaism, were put in the

---

[47] On the considerable confusion surrounding these terms, see Schürer 1.358–60.

[48] On the details of the war, and the different parties, see Schürer 1.484–513; Hengel 1989 [1961], 343–76; Goodman 1987, *passim*. This war, and that of 132–5, are among the events for which we have numismatic as well as literary evidence; see Meshorer 1986.

[49] On the date of the fall of Masada (Jos. *War* 7.401) see Schürer 1.512–5.

[50] bBer. 32b; the saying is attributed to Rabbi Eliezer ben Hyrcanus. Cf. Bokser 1982/3. See the account of the people's despondency at the cessation of the daily sacrifice, Jos. *War* 6.94 (compare mTaan. 4.6); and the great lamentations of 4 Ezra and *2 Bar.* (e.g. *2 Bar.* 10.5–19).

[51] 'Jamnia' is variously spelled: variants include 'Jabneh', 'Javneh', 'Yavne', etc.

mouth of Jesus, even though they reflected the conditions in the 80s and 90s rather than the period of Jesus' own ministry or the first generation of the church. A sense that the gospel and the Torah were incompatible grew up for the first time. In many works that have taken this line, there is the constant implied suggestion: if only we could get back to the pure early period, prior to such hostility, how much happier things would be.[52]

Sadly for that noble hope, history simply does not support what has recently been called 'the "Council of Javneh" Myth'.[53] This myth, I suggest, has become a negative equivalent of those myths about Jesus which Albert Schweitzer exposed. The scholarly world has become (or thinks it has become) too sophisticated to fall any longer for the trick of projecting its highest ideals back on to Jesus; instead, it has projected its *bêtes noires* on to a generation that can then be safely dismissed. This is, in effect, a scholarly form of scapegoating. The elements in early Christianity which are least acceptable to a certain form of contemporary scholarship are placed on the head of a generation for whose views we have very little evidence; that generation is then driven off into the hermeneutical wilderness, never to be seen again. No-one wants to set up the Christianity of AD 70–135 as normative for all time.

The myth has been easy to perpetrate, because of our comparative ignorance about the two generations between 70 and 135, on either the Jewish or the Christian side. Josephus' account runs out soon after the end of the war and the destruction of Masada, and the story of subsequent Judaism must be pieced together with labour and sorrow from rabbinic writings of several generations later, together with bits and pieces of Roman historians such as Appian and Dio, and Christian writers like Ignatius, Justin, Origen and Eusebius.[54] When we attempt this task strictly on the basis of the sources, we find a picture very different from the popular one imagined by recent apologists. It looks roughly as follows.[55]

The destruction of the Temple created, not one reaction, but a variety. It is over-simplistic to think that all forms of Judaism were wiped out except Pharisaism, which then, transmuting itself into rabbinism, grew and developed in a new way, unhindered by Sadducean pressure on the one hand or revolutionary fervour on the other. We must, instead, envisage a Judaism which comprehended at least three strands: (a) the anguish of 4 Ezra and 2 Baruch, lamenting the fall of the Temple as if their hearts would break; (b) the pragmatism of Johanan ben Zakkai, calmly recognizing that Hosea 6.6 had long ago spoken of Israel's god desiring deeds of lovingkindness rather than sacrifice; and (c) the smouldering fire of rebellion, crushed once again by pagan might but seeking nevertheless the way by which to reverse the

[52] A recent example is Davies and Allison 1988, 133–8, which in turn is dependent on Davies 1964, 256–315.

[53] Aune 1991a. For what follows, see, in addition, Lewis 1964; Schäfer 1975; Stemberger 1977; Katz 1984; Cohen 1984; Gafni 1987, 14–20; and the other literature cited below. I agree broadly with Dunn 1991, 232.

[54] Compare the list of sources in Schürer 1.534.

[55] See particularly Schürer 1.514–57; Neusner 1970, 1979; Gafni 1984, 1987. Compare too Saldarini 1975.

catastrophe and to build the true Temple.[56] (We might also include (d) the young Christian church, still thinking of itself as in some way part of a wider 'Judaism' but interpreting the fall of Jerusalem in the light of its own theology.) To what extent these three main points of view overlapped, and to what extent they stood in continuity with various movements from before the destruction, must remain in question for the moment. What matters is that we recognize the non-monolithic nature of the new situation in Judaism.

It is highly probable that Johanan ben Zakkai, regarded uniformly by much later Rabbinism as the new founder of Judaism, established an academy at Jamnia, a small town near the coast about fifteen miles south of modern Tel Aviv and about twenty-five miles east of Jerusalem. The legends that grew up around his move from Jerusalem, however, have little basis in probable historical fact. Gradually—it can only have been a gradual process—this academy began to exercise an authority over Jews still living in Palestine comparable with that held by the old Sanhedrin in Jerusalem.[57] By the time of the mid-second century, the geographical location of this new Sanhedrin had shifted north, to Usha and thence to other locations, while the disastrous Hadrianic war (132–5) had wiped out many Jews and caused others to emigrate, many of them to the increasingly large community in Babylon.[58] But, despite the move (which created problems, because the rabbis were aware of the symbolic value of being close to Jerusalem), the academy and its court retained the authority which had begun gradually under Johanan and was consolidated under his successor Gamaliel II.[59]

By no means all those present accepted the views, or the authority, of Johanan himself. Centres other than Jamnia were established.[60] Another leading figure, Eliezer ben Hyrcanus, originally a pupil of Johanan, disagreed with him on a number of vital issues, and was finally excommunicated.[61] One possible way of reading these disputes is to see Johanan, and his successor Gamaliel II, as representing the scribal tradition of pre-70 Judaism, according to which the study and practice of Torah could function as an effectual *replacement for* Temple-worship, meaning that there was no need for Judaism to attempt to do other than find a *modus vivendi* with the ruling Roman authorities; and to see Eliezer, and perhaps others, as representing the pre-70 Pharisaic attitude according to which the study and practice of Torah func-

---

[56] On 4 Ezra see Schürer 3.294–306; Metzger in Charlesworth 1983, 416–559; and particularly Stone 1990; Longenecker 1991. On *2 Bar.* see Schürer 3.750–6; Klijn in Charlesworth 1983, 615–52. On Johanan ben Zakkai see especially Neusner 1970, 1979, and also Saldarini 1975; Schäfer 1979. On the continuing desire for revolt see Gafni 1984, 31, against Cohen 1987, 216. Cohen's argument seems to me to ignore the fact of Akiba, on whom see below.

[57] Compare mKel. 5.4, mPar. 7.6, mBek. 4.5, 6.8. The new assembly is mentioned as consisting of 72 members, reflecting a desire either on the part of Jamnia itself or later tradition to evoke memories of the original Sanhedrin: see mZeb. 1.3, mYad. 3.5, 4.2, and cf. Gafni 1987, 15.

[58] Gafni 1987, 21f., with references.

[59] On the succession see the discussion of various views in Gafni 1984, 29f., agreeing with Safrai against Alon that Gamaliel, because of his dynastic links, could not have attained power until after the death of Domitian (not 'Diocletian' as Gafni, 29 n.162!) in 96.

[60] Gafni 1987, 19.

[61] Schürer 2.373–5, with references.

tioned as an effectual *imitation of* Temple-worship, resulting in a much greater sense of loss over the Temple, and committing its adherents to the attempt to restore it as soon as possible.[62] It is only a short step from here to suggesting that the major disputes in this period between what came to regard themselves as the houses of Hillel and Shammai had their origin in this question: whether to go with the live-and-let-live policy of Hillel and his followers, in other words with the scribal tradition that was content to live under Rome as long as it could study and practice Torah, or to follow the Shammaite rigorists who wanted to pursue a hard-line and at least potentially anti-Roman policy. One difference at least between the pre- and post-70 Torah scholars may consist in this: that, before the destruction, the Shammaites had the upper hand, whereas after the destruction, and particularly after the Bar-Kochba rebellion of 132–5, the Hillelites naturally increased their authority. AD 70 and 135 were large nails in the coffin of revolutionary hopes.[63]

It was within this pluriform and complex context that, according to later tradition, some steps were taken to tighten up the boundaries of acceptable Judaism. As we noted earlier, this possibility has been seized upon in recent years as providing a setting for the division between Judaism and developing Christianity. The theory has been advanced that Jamnia propounded a modification of the twelfth clause within the ancient prayer known as the 'Eighteen Benedictions', which invoked a curse on heretics in general and Christians in particular and thus made it impossible for Christians to continue worshipping in synagogues, which, according to this theory, many of them had been happily doing until this point. However, though there is good reason to trace the developing story of worsening Jewish–Christian relations along a line which, beginning very early, sooner or later intersects with the promulgation and popularity of such an anti-heretical 'benediction',[64] it must also be noted most clearly that 'there is little evidence for "witch-hunting" in general and anti-Christian activity in particular' in the period between 70 and 135.[65] Instead, it is probable both that the 'heretics' in view included many groups of whom the Christians were only one, and that the measure taken against them did not necessarily extend to expulsion.[66] The commissioning of a new Greek translation of the Hebrew Bible (that of Aquila) may reflect frustration at the

[62] So Neusner in many works, conveniently summarized in his 1979 article.

[63] On these debates see further ch. 7 below.

[64] So Horbury 1982. Among the evidence for early, though not systematized, hostility between the communities cf. the letters of Paul, e.g. Gal. 1.13; 4.29; 1 Thess. 2.14–16; and also perhaps 1 Cor. 12.1–3 (see Derrett 1975). Cp. Robinson 1976, 72–81.

[65] Cohen 1984, 50, cf. 41f.; Cohen adds in a footnote: 'In other words, there is little evidence for the activity most often ascribed to the Yavneans.' See also esp. Katz 1984, 48–53, 63–76, arguing that any strictures were directed 'against all Jews who after 70 were not in the Pharisaic/rabbinic camp', and that 'the *Birkat ha-Minim* did *not* signal any decisive break between Jews and Jewish Christians' (76 n.128: italics original).

[66] Cohen 1984, 41–2. Cohen's overall thesis is that the Jamnia period saw the rise of an explicitly and intentionally pluriform Judaism which rejected 'sectarian', one-sided readings of its heritage. The sages 'created a society based on the doctrine that conflicting disputants may each be advancing the words of the living God' (51). I suspect that this, too, is an idealized picture, albeit drawn to a different ideal; but that it can even be suggested shows the frailty of the normal understanding of Jamnia.

widespread use of the old Septuagint by the early Christians, but does not itself amount to a formal separation between the two communities.[67] Among other arguments, the fact that some of the later Christian Fathers felt constrained to warn their congregations against attending the synagogue makes it very unlikely that an anti-Christian prayer formed a regular part of the synagogue liturgy.[68] Some of Kimelman's conclusions are worth quoting in full, since in the decade since his article was published they have not had their full impact even though they have never been refuted:

> There is no unambiguous evidence that Jews cursed Christians during the statutory prayers.
> There is abundant evidence that Christians were welcome in the synagogue.
> Thus *birkat ha-minim* does not reflect a watershed in the history of the relationship between Jews and Christians in the first centuries of our era.
> Apparently, there never was a single edict which caused the so-called irreparable separation between Judaism and Christianity . . .[69]

What, then, was the significance of the Jamnia period for the newly emerging form of Judaism, and for its daughter religion, Christianity? It seems that the period was as much a time of uncertainty for those who lived through it as it has proved for the scholars who have attempted to reconstruct it. For Jews, the attempt to reconstruct and maintain an authentically Jewish way of life in the absence of the Temple produced, as we have seen, a variety of responses ranging from revolutionary determination to the study and debating of Torah. For much of Christianity, which by 70 had spread far beyond the borders both of Palestine and of the Jewish communities of the Diaspora, there were pressing questions and issues quite other than that of relationships with the synagogue community. It was a period of transition, when many ambiguities lived side by side; and many, on both sides of what was to become the great divide, seemed content to let it be so. We should not forget that early Christianity, claiming the high ground of Israel's heritage, was first and foremost a movement that defined itself in opposition to paganism, and only secondarily in opposition to mainline Judaism itself.

This period of transition came to an abrupt and bloody end with the rebellion against the emperor Hadrian in AD 132–5.[70] Hadrian had passed a law forbidding circumcision as a barbaric practice (the Jews were not the only people who practised the custom, but the ban struck them especially due to the centrality of circumcision within their worldview). He had also founded a pagan city, Aelia Capitolina, on the site of ruined Jerusalem, with an altar to Zeus on

---

[67] See Gafni 1984, 29f.

[68] So Kimelman 1981, 239f.; see Ign. *Mag.* 8.1; 10.1–3; *Philad.* 6.1. Ignatius could scarcely have written as he did (in about 110/115 AD) if a binding anti-Christian decree had already been in force in the synagogue community (as is envisaged in many recent writings) for twenty or thirty years.

[69] Kimelman 1981, 244.

[70] For the details, see Dio Cass. 69.12.1—14.4; Schürer 1.534–57, Gafni 1987, 20ff., and the further discussions in e.g. Isaac and Oppenheimer 1985; Reinhartz 1989; Schäfer 1990, and the other literature there. I pass over here the anti-Roman rebellion of Jews in Egypt, Cyrene and Cyprus in 115–17, on which see Schürer 1.529–34.

the site of the Temple itself. These provocations, more serious still than those of the procurators in the 50s and 60s, and comparable to those of Antiochus Epiphanes much earlier, called forth rebellion. Simon ben Kosiba began a revolt which quickly roused the whole land. He himself was hailed as Messiah by the great rabbi Akiba, among others, and given the title Bar-Kochba, 'Son of the Star' (referring to the prophecy of Numbers 24.17).[71] Not everyone agreed with this designation: some sages controverted Akiba, perhaps for reasons of speculative chronology, while the Christians resident in the area, recognizing a rival to Jesus, refused to join in the movement and (according to Justin and Eusebius) were accordingly subjected to fierce persecution. Documents and coins from the period indicate both that ben Kosiba and his followers saw the start of the revolt as the beginning of the long-awaited new age, and that he was as concerned with the maintenance of Jewish religious duty as with revolution against Rome.[72] Nearly seventy years had passed since the destruction under Vespasian; perhaps this was the moment when Israel's god would at last liberate his people.

The hope was dashed. Despite inflicting heavy losses on Hadrian's army, the Jews were decimated. Many who survived were sold into slavery in large numbers. Jerusalem became a fully pagan city, and the ban on Jewish customs strictly enforced. Not until the twentieth century could the idea of a self-governing Jewish state in Palestine be spoken of once more as anything other than the remotest possibility.

(iv) Conclusion

This, in brief, is the story of the Jews in the period which was formative both for them and for the new movement that arose in their midst. But, as we saw when discussing history in the abstract, the story of 'what happened' can only be fully grasped when we ask the question 'why'. Why did the Jews of this period do what they did? In order to answer this question we must first fill in the story by examining the growing diversity within Judaism (chapter 7). We will then be able to examine the underlying Jewish worldview, by means of its symbols (chapter 8), its basic beliefs (chapter 9), and the hope to which these beliefs gave rise (chapter 10), a hope which, variously reinterpreted, has given shape and colour to Judaism and Christianity from that day to this.

---

[71] On Akiba see Schürer 1.544, 552; 2.377f.; and the literature there cited.
[72] Schürer 1.543–5.

Chapter Seven

THE DEVELOPING DIVERSITY

1. Introduction: The Social Setting

The period between the Babylonian exile and the destruction of the second Temple by the Romans saw the birth of a fascinating and complex variety of expressions of Jewish identity and life. It is vital that we gain a clear idea of this variety, upon which depends a good deal of our understanding of Jewish history in itself, and of the rise and development of the early church.

The event which precipitated all the major trends in first-century Judaism was, as we have seen, the Maccabaean crisis. It was, first, the backward reference-point for continued speculation about Israel's eventual deliverance from pagan rule. The annual celebration of Hannukah meant that the unlikely triumph of the little band of rebels against the might of paganism was kept before the public eye, much as centuries-old events in Northern Ireland are ceremonially recalled in the present day, and with very similar effect in the maintenance of old loyalties and the stirring up of old hostilities. As we shall see in chapter 10, most Jews of the period cherished the hope that the covenant god would again act in history, this time to restore the fortunes of his internally-exiled people. But the Maccabaean crisis was also, second, the cause of some of the divisions within Judaism. Dissatisfaction with its outcome was the reason for the rise and agenda of at least some of Judaism's different parties.

These two effects of the crisis (the renewed enthusiasm for liberation, and the splitting into parties) were of course closely related. How and when Israel's god would rescue his people were questions whose answers, in reflecting different perceptions of what it meant to be the people of the covenant god, divided one Jewish group from another. It is at this point that we begin to speak, with many modern scholars, of the plural 'Judaisms'.

But questions of belief and aspiration were not the only reasons for diversity. Geographical factors were of some weight. There were considerable differences between the pressures upon, and consequent cultural, social and religious needs and viewpoints of, Jews in the Jerusalem area on the one hand and Jews in Galilee on the other.[1] The former could focus attention most naturally on the Temple, on the problems of pagan overlordship and the threat to

[1] On all this see Freyne 1980, esp. chs. 7–8.

the sanctity of the capital, and on the maintenance of cult, liturgy and festival as symbols of a *de jure* national independence in the face of *de facto* subservience. The latter, Galilee, was three day's journey away from Jerusalem, with hostile territory (Samaria) in between. Surrounded and permeated as it was by paganism, Galilean Jewry naturally looked, more than its southern compatriots needed to, to the symbols of distinctiveness which mattered in the local setting. The Torah assumed new importance in border territory. As we shall see, it acquired some of the functions and attributes of the Temple itself.[2] And the features of Torah which loomed largest were those which functioned specifically and obviously as cultural, social and religious boundary-markers, i.e. sabbath, food-laws and circumcision.

Adherence to Torah was obviously even more significant when Jews were living away from the land of Israel, among aliens and pagans in the Diaspora.[3] There, and in Galilee, Jewish life centred on the local community, and its worship and institutions assumed an importance which, closer to Jerusalem, were overshadowed by the Temple itself. If we had to guess where one would be most likely to encounter Jewish violence directed at other Jews who seemed to be compromising Torah, we should not look in the first instance at Jerusalem, but at Galilee, and perhaps even more those parts of the Diaspora where Jewish communities felt themselves under threat from local pagans. Those who live on the frontiers get into trouble if they do not keep the boundary fences in good repair.

So it was that the maintenance of traditional Torah-based boundary-markers in Galilee, or in the Diaspora, had little to do with a detached theology of *post mortem* salvation, let alone the earning of such a thing by one's own religious or moral efforts, and a great deal more to do with the preservation of traditional Jewish identity. In so far as there was an eschatological note attached to such observances, it would be the sense that, when Israel's god finally acted to redeem his people, those who would benefit would be those who had in the mean time kept the covenant boundaries intact, whereas those who had led Israel astray and had gone after foreign gods would forfeit their right to be considered part of the people of the true god.[4] The choice between loyalty and assimilation faced Jews in the ancient no less than in the modern world. Those who took the easy route of compromise with paganism were seen as fraternizers with the enemy, whose ever-present threat continued to break out in sporadic pogroms and persecutions.

Geographical diversity was as nothing, however, compared with socio-economic diversity, and in this we find some of the seeds of the trouble that plagued Judaism throughout our period. Palestine, though in principle a potentially productive and fruitful region, contained a few who were rich and many who were at least comparatively poor. Towns tended to be associated

---

[2] See ch. 8 below.

[3] On the complex questions of Diaspora Judaism, which embraced such diverse places as Babylon, Egypt and Rome, as well as Asia Minor and Greece, see Safrai and Stern 1974, chs. 3, 4, 13; Schürer 3.1–176.

[4] See further ch. 10 below.

with the rich, countryside with the poor. There were rich landowners who controlled a good deal of the means of production; there were artisans, farmers, fishermen and others who maintained a moderate though not luxurious existence; and there were many who struggled, as day-labourers, smallholders, or whatever, to avoid being crushed between the two millstones of local exploitation and foreign overlordship. Stories about landlords and tenants, and potential disputes between them, would have a highly familiar ring.[5] Some of the party divisions in first-century Judaism clearly reflect socio-economic divisions directly, with theological debates as fairly obvious rationalizations.[6]

Among the pressing economic issues, the problem of debt grew to chronic proportions. It is not insignificant that when the rebels seized power at the beginning of the war in AD 66 one of their first acts was to burn the records of debts.[7] Hatred of Rome was not the only anger that characterized many Jews of the period: hatred of the wealthy aristocracy sometimes became more important.[8] From all this we can sense the tensions that ran throughout the Jewish society of Jesus' and Paul's day. Any suggestion, even by implication, that Jews led untroubled lives with leisure to discuss the finer points of dogmatic theology must be rejected. Jewish society faced major external threats and major internal problems. The question, what it might mean to be a good or loyal Jew, had pressing social, economic and political dimensions as well as cultural and theological ones. It is within this context that we can understand the frequency, throughout our period, of the movements of revolt which form such an important feature of the landscape.

A great deal has been written on the subject of diversity within first-century Judaism, and it is not part of my purpose to review, or to debate with, all who have put their hands to this task. What I do hope to achieve, however, is a sense of emphasis and mood. The parties are usually discussed, as Josephus himself discusses them, in a fairly detached way, as isolated phenomena, following private agendas of a somewhat abstract kind. Seen like this, the revolutionary movements stand out as being somewhat odd. I suggest that more clarity is gained by beginning at the other end. From our review of the historical situation in the previous chapter it appears that the pressing needs of most Jews of the period had to do with liberation—from oppression, from debt, from Rome. Other issues, I suggest, were regularly seen in this light. The hope of Israel, and of most special-interest groups within Israel, was not for

[5] Mk. 12.1–12 and pars. On the economic condition of Palestine in this period see particularly Applebaum 1976, esp. 656–64, 691–2; Oakman 1986, chs. 1–2; Sanders 1992, ch. 9. On the social groupings see Saldarini 1988, chs. 3–4.

[6] Thus, for instance, the Sadducee's aristocratic rejection of the (potentially seditious) Pharisaic doctrine of resurrection: see ch. 10 below.

[7] Jos. *War* 2.427–9. On the poorest class as the likely recruits for revolt, see e.g. *War* 7.438. Josephus' concern to blame the lower orders for everything should not blind us to the likelihood that he is here telling the truth. Sanders 1992, ch. 9 argues against the extremely bleak picture painted by some others, but there is no doubt that times were felt to be extremely hard. Brigandage on the scale we find in Josephus (even allowing for exaggeration) does not spring up easily in a time of moderate prosperity.

[8] Especially if, as Goodman argues (1987), the aristocracy from the time of Herod until AD 70 consisted of nonentities promoted to power solely by Herod and the Romans.

post mortem disembodied bliss, but for a national liberation that would fulfil the expectations aroused by the memory, and regular celebration, of the exodus, and, nearer at hand, of the Maccabaean victory. Hope focused on the coming of the kingdom of Israel's god.[9] I shall therefore begin by looking at the movements of revolt that characterize the period, and then assess the place of the different 'parties' in the light of the more general aspiration. We will thus, I believe, approach a more complete and rounded understanding of the worldviews, aims and belief-systems which were held by Jews within this period as a whole.

2. Movements of Revolt

To begin our consideration of groupings within first-century Judaism by looking at movements of revolt is to start on solid historical ground. If we were to sketch a map of events in first-century Palestine for which we have good evidence (mostly of course known from Josephus), many of those events would involve revolutionary activity.

Once again the story starts with the Maccabees. They set the context, and provided the model, for a tradition of movements which sought to overthrow oppression and bring about the divinely intended kingdom for Israel. Fidelity to Torah, readiness for martyrdom, resistance to compromise, and resolute military or para-military action: that was the combination that would win the day. But in the first period of relevance for us, between the Maccabees' victory (164 BC) and the arrival of Rome on the scene (63 BC), this precipitated an irony. The successful revolution created new conditions of oppression, real or perceived. The next movements of revolt after the Maccabaean uprising were launched not against an outsider, but against those who, on the strength of their victory, presumed to establish a dynasty of priest-kings as though they were the rightful heirs of both the Davidic and the Aaronic houses. There therefore arose movements in whose eyes Jerusalem was the centre of a corrupt and illicit regime. The Essenes, claiming (most likely) to be the real heirs of the Zadokite priestly line, refused to have anything to do with the 'cleansed' Temple, and established their own community elsewhere. The Pharisees worked within the system, but constantly reminded those in official power of the ancestral traditions which they were in danger of flouting, and reinforced their reminders with the threat implicit in their popular backing. At least twice (see below) they stood up to pressure and refused to swear allegiance to rulers of whom they disapproved. There are dark rumblings of discontent which come through to us from surviving tracts, denouncing the Hasmonean regime in stern apocalyptic language and imagery.[10] Although much later generations would look back on the Hasmonean period as a rare moment of Jewish independence, it is clear that at the time many Jews were deeply suspicious of the new dynasty.

---

[9] On the national hope see further ch. 10 below.

[10] e.g. *T. Mos.* 5.1–6; *Mart. Isa.* 3.10, referring back to Isa. 1.10.

Things could only deteriorate when the Romans took over in 63 BC. Economic pressure created a new class of brigands, desperate bands of Jews who found no way forward from their poverty except by living outside normal society and sustaining themselves through raids on those who still had property that could be stolen. As we shall see, such brigands were not simply anarchists. A fierce belief in the justice of their cause, and in divine backing for it, sustained them in their desperate lifestyle.[11] By the middle of the first century BC the problem of brigandage had become so acute, helped no doubt by the power vacuum while Rome was occupied with civil war and the threat from Parthia, that it was a major achievement to bring it under some sort of control, albeit temporary. Credit for this was given to Herod the Great, whose rise to power in the 40s BC was marked by his putting down of serious brigandage, notably killing the *archilestes* ('chief brigand') Hezekiah, whose family (arguably) continued the struggle in later generations.[12] This in turn provoked a reaction from the Pharisee Samaias, who objected to Herod's fierce treatment of those whom many Jews seem to have regarded as fighting their cause.[13] Herod himself, perhaps as a result, incurred the same apocalyptic denunciation as had his Maccabaean predecessors.[14] Throughout the first century BC the hardship of many Jews increased, as the existing economic constraints were overlaid with the problems and perils of living in a country beset with internal dissent and civil strife. This hardship, coupled with Herod's wanton flouting of many Jewish conventions, explains the consistent opposition to him on the part of the Pharisees, which we will study presently.

But it was between the death of Herod the Great and the destruction of Jerusalem (4 BC to AD 70) that movements of revolt came to a head, creating problems for governments at the time and headaches for scholars two millennia later. That there was widespread disaffection and readiness to revolt in this period is not in question. Exactly which groups were involved, however, has provoked considerable controversy. Disentangling different factions, parties and leaders sometimes seems almost impossible. In what follows I shall try to keep the main lines clear despite the virtually limitless possibilities for debate.

We begin with our main source, Josephus. As is well known, he tries hard to shift the blame for the eventual catastrophe of AD 70 on to one particular rebel faction, exonerating the rest of the Jewish people. The Romans formed a major part of his intended audience, and Josephus hoped that they would look with clemency on the post-destruction Jews as the innocent victims of the violence of the few. Despite this clear agenda, however, Josephus continually reveals that resistance to Rome was far more widespread than just one rebel

---

[11] On brigandage see particularly Horsley 1979a, 1981; Horsley and Hanson 1985; Crossan 1991, ch. 9. The technical term for 'brigand' or 'bandit' is *lestes*, often wrongly translated 'robber' or 'thief' in the NT (e.g. Jn. 18.40 in the AV and RSV): see Hengel 1989 [1961], 24–46. Josephus identifies the Sicarii, the 'dagger-men', as *lestai* (e.g. *War* 4.198), and aligns *lestai* with *goetes* ('seducers', i.e. those who lead the people astray) in e.g. *Ant.* 20.160.

[12] See *Ant.* 14.158–60, 420–30; Schürer 1.275. On the problems of connecting Hezekiah with later movements see below.

[13] *Ant.* 14.172–6; *War* 1.208–15.

[14] *T. Mos.* 6.2–6.

faction. The famous line in Tacitus, 'under Tiberius things were quiet', simply means that there was no major uprising or war, such as eventually engulfed the region; there was, for instance, no border struggle with Parthia, as there had been in the previous century.[15] However, not only under Tiberius but also under Augustus, Gaius, Claudius and Nero there was a continual stream of events which foreshadowed the eventual result. It may be useful to list them briefly before analysing them in more detail. Even so short an account as this may serve to evoke the turbulent flavour of the period, without which contemporary scholarship all too easily lapses into anachronistic assumptions that treat first-century Jews as though they were twentieth- (or even sixteenth-) century theologians.

We begin with the swift sequence of events that took place in 4 BC. As Herod lay dying, a group of hotheads pulled down the ornamental eagle he had caused to be placed over the Temple gate. They were egged on by two respected teachers of the law (Judas ben Sariphaeus and Matthias ben Margalothus), with the suspected collusion of the high priest.[16] This incident was punished severely by Herod in one of his last acts. Then, immediately after Herod's death, a fuller revolt took place in Jerusalem at Passover, taking its origin from protests over the treatment of the ringleaders in the previous incident. It was suppressed brutally by Herod's son Archelaus.[17] Archelaus and his brother Antipas then went to Rome to argue their respective right to the succession before the emperor, being followed by a Jewish embassy pleading for autonomy because of the brutality of Archelaus and his father.[18] In the absence of the would-be rulers a new revolt took place, which was crushed by Varus, the Roman general in charge of the province of Syria. Varus left in place an interim procurator, Sabinus, whose actions in turn provoked fresh serious riots during the feast of Pentecost, which he was unable to quell, although in the attempt the Roman soldiers looted the Temple, thus further angering the Jews.[19]

These events in Jerusalem were paralleled by a revolt among Herod's veterans,[20] and a serious revolutionary movement in Galilee, where Judas ben Hezekiah, the brigand chief killed by Herod in the 40s BC, led a revolt which Josephus describes as the most serious incident of its kind between Pompey's conquest of Palestine (63 BC) and Titus' destruction of the Temple (AD 70).[21]

[15] Tac. *Hist.* 5.9: 'sub Tiberio quies'. This scarcely warrants the placid picture of the period AD 6–44 sketched by Barnett 1975, 566–71. Sanders 1992, ch. 4, tries to tone down the impression given by some others of constant revolutionary fervour. Certainly one should not imagine that the middle years of the century were perceived, by those who lived through them, in the way we now see them, i.e. as the prelude to a major war. But even Sanders agrees that 'insurrection was never very far from the surface' (36).

[16] *Ant.* 17.149–66; *War* 1.648–55.

[17] *Ant.* 17.206–18; *War* 2.1–13. Josephus describes the rebels as 'the revolutionary party of the exegetes' (*stasiotai ton exegeton*).

[18] It is often pointed out that this sequence, documented in *War* 2.80–100 and *Ant.* 17.219–49, 299–323, lies underneath Luke 19.12, 14 and 27; cf. e.g. Evans 1990, 668f.

[19] *Ant.* 17.250–64; *War* 2.39–50.

[20] *War* 2.55; *Ant.* 17.269f.

[21] *Apion* 1.34; cp. the rabbinic tradition discussed in Schürer 1.534f. The revolt itself is described in *Ant.* 17.271–2; *War* 2.56, and will be discussed further below.

Varus returned from Syria, settled the Galilean rebellion brutally, relieved Sabinus in Jerusalem, and crucified some two thousand insurgents.[22]

At the same time as these events there were two would-be messianic movements. These involved respectively one Simon, an ex-slave of Herod who was proclaimed king before being killed by the Romans, and a shepherd called Athronges, who gave himself royal airs and organized his followers into brigand bands before being captured by Archelaus.[23]

This flurry of rebellions in 4 BC was clearly occasioned by the proximity, and then the fact, of Herod's death, which allowed the persistent hope for a new order of things to come to the surface. This illustrates one main principle of Jewish revolt: the seething unrest which was normally held down tightly by repressive government and brute force could boil over when a power vacuum appeared. It is, in addition, significant for the whole story that several such movements often took place specifically at times of festival, when Jews were thronging Jerusalem to celebrate their god-given status as free people.[24] Other regular elements in the pattern include the frequency with which such movements were led by messianic or quasi-messianic figures, and the repression of revolts in general by means of crucifixion.[25]

Another main principle, which of course overlaps with this, was that under certain circumstances provocation by those in power could become so acute that revolt would follow, whether or not it appeared to have a chance of success.[26] This was illustrated by the events a decade after Herod's death, i.e. in AD 6. To begin with, the Jews appealed to Rome against Archelaus, who had succeeded his father Herod in Judaea, Samaria, and Idumaea. His subjects went over his head to Rome and had him removed.[27] The second, more serious, incident was occasioned by the imposition of a Roman census, whose implications were not merely economic but, to a Jew, theological: enrolling in Rome's system meant admitting that the land and people were not after all sacred to Israel's god. Judas 'the Galilean', whom we will consider further presently, led the revolt which, according to Josephus, was the founding act of the sect that became responsible for the major war two generations later.[28]

Most of the revolutionary activity during the next sixty years was of the latter type, i.e. response to perceived provocation. The removal of Archelaus

---

[22] *Ant.* 17.286–98; *War* 2.66–79.

[23] *Ant.* 17.273–7 and 278–84; *War* 2.57–98 and 60–5.

[24] cf. Jos. *War* 1.88, pointing out that *stasis* (insurrection) is most likely to occur at festivals; and *Ant.* 17.213–18, explicitly linking the riots that followed the eagle-incident to the meaning of the Passover festival.

[25] On crucifixion see particularly Hengel 1977.

[26] It is possible as well that chronological speculations, based on the prophetic literature, and in particular the hope of release after seventy years of 'exile' (Dan. 9.2, 24; Jer. 25.12; 29.10; 2 Chron. 36.21f.; cp. *Ant.* 10.267; 11.1) may have fuelled hopes of sudden deliverance in the periods of 4 BC and AD 6 (roughly 70 years after the initial Roman invasion), AD 66–70 (roughly 70 years after direct Roman rule began) and AD 132–5 (70 years after the first destruction). See Beckwith 1980, 1981; Cohen 1987, 34. See p. 312f. below.

[27] *Ant.* 17.342–3; *War* 2.111–13. See the discussion of Archelaus in Schürer 1.353–7.

[28] *Ant.* 18.4–10, 23–5; cf. *War* 2.118. Ac. 5.37 claims that Judas was executed by the Romans. For this incident, and an account of other revolutionary activities between AD 6 and 66, see Rhoads 1976, ch. 3.

meant that Judaea became a Roman province in its own right rather than a client kingdom overseen from neighbouring Syria. Successive 'procurators' acted in more or less crass and heavy-handed style, which naturally had the effect of inciting Jews towards revolt. We know of at least seven such incidents in the ten years of Pontius Pilate's procuratorship (AD 26–36):

(i)   Pilate tried to bring Roman standards into Jerusalem, but backed down after a mass protest.[29]

(ii)   He used money from the Temple treasury to build an aqueduct, and crushed the resistance that this action provoked.[30]

(iii)   He sent troops to kill some Galileans while they were offering sacrifices in the Temple, presumably because he feared a riot.[31]

(iv)   He captured and condemned to death the leader of an uprising that had taken place in Jerusalem, involving murder; he then released the man as a gesture of goodwill during the Passover feast.[32]

(v)   At the same Passover, he faced a quasi-messianic movement, having some association with resistance movements; he crucified its leader along with two ordinary revolutionaries.[33]

(vi)   He provoked public opinion by placing Roman votive shields, albeit without images, in the palace at Jerusalem, which according to Philo annoyed Tiberius almost as much as it did the Jews.[34]

(vii)   Finally, he suppressed with particular brutality a popular (and apparently non-revolutionary) prophetic movement in Samaria. For this he was accused before the Roman legate in Syria, who had him sent back to Rome.[35]

Worse was to follow. The megalomaniac emperor Gaius, incensed by an anti-Roman incident at Jamnia, tried to insist on a huge statue of himself

---

[29] *Ant.* 18.55–9; *War* 2.169–74; see Schürer 1.381, 384. A similar incident occurred when Vitellius was sent to fight Aretas in AD 37: see *Ant.* 18.120–3.

[30] *Ant.* 18.60–2; *War* 2.175–7; Euseb. *HE* 2.6.6–7; see Schürer 1.385.

[31] Lk. 13.1.

[32] Lk. 23.18–25. Luke's description of Barabbas' activities (committing murder (*phonos*) during an insurrection (*stasis*) in the city (*polis*)) reads just like a sentence from Josephus.

[33] On Jesus of Nazareth see vol. 2. Josephus' account in *Ant.* 18.63–4 is notoriously controversial (see the discussions in Schürer 1.428–41; Baras 1987), but it seems to me that some parts of it at least are likely to be original. The crucial sentence *ho christos houtos en* does not mean, as is usually supposed, 'this man was the Messiah', but, because of the position of the article, ' "the Messiah" was this man'. The implication is that Josephus expects his readers to have heard of someone who bore, almost as a nickname, the title '*ho christos*' (cf. Suet. *Claudius* 25, *impulsore Chresto*), and is simply identifying this person with the one he is now describing. On Jesus' followers: it is highly likely that some at least of Jesus' disciples believed themselves to be involved in a movement of national liberation. The title of one of them, Simon *ho Kananaios* (Mk. 3.18) or Simon 'called *Zelotes*' (Lk. 6.12) probably indicates known revolutionary tendencies. See Hengel 1989 [1961], 69, note. On Jesus' identification with the *lestai* see e.g. Mt. 26.55 and pars., and vol. 2 in the present series.

[34] Philo *Leg.* 299–306. This incident (which happens to be recorded through Philo's work), and those in the gospels, suggest that there may well have been several more such happenings which Josephus has passed over.

[35] *Ant.* 18.85–9.

being placed in the Temple in Jerusalem, in deliberate contravention of Jewish law and scruple. It was this move that drew the long and reasoned protest from the philosopher Philo.[36] Gaius was adamant, however, and only his early death forestalled the blasphemous act and its horrendous possible consequences.[37]

A brief respite from continual provocation occurred during the reign of Herod Agrippa, a grandson of Herod the Great, whom the Romans allowed to rule in place of the procurators from 41 until his early death in 44. His apparent piety, and his care to avoid offending Jewish scruples, held revolutionary tendencies at bay.[38] But with the resumption of procuratorial rule we hear of renewed insurgent movements. Tholomaeus, a 'brigand chief' (*archilestes*), was executed by Cuspius Fadus in the mid-40s, during the course of a large operation against brigandage in general.[39] Around the same time a leader named Theudas, claiming to be a prophet, led a movement which aroused enough popular support to gain mention in Acts as well as Josephus. It too was put down by the Romans, and Theudas himself was executed.[40] We then hear of the two sons of Judas the Galilean, Jacob and Simon, being crucified under the procuratorship of Tiberius Alexander (46–8),[41] and of subsequent revolts under his successor Cumanus (48–52), including a riot at Passover in which perhaps 20,000 Jews were killed, attacks by brigands on Romans, and further looting of the Temple by Roman troops.[42] Cumanus over-reacted to a subsequent incident, whose complexity nicely illustrates the problems of the time. Some Galileans were murdered on their way through Samaria to Jerusalem for a festival. The Jews took violent revenge on Samaria. Cumanus responded with even more violence, out of all proportion to the original incidents. The Jews then successfully accused Cumanus before Claudius, the emperor, of having favoured the Samaritans.[43] The ringleaders of the Jewish fighters, Eleazar ben Deinaeus and Alexander, were finally captured by Cumanus' successor Felix (52–60), who proceeded, as Fadus had done in 44–6, to purge the country of *lestai*, crucifying a considerable number.[44]

The purge was only short-lived. Josephus says that around this time (the late 50s and early 60s) there arose the group he called Sicarii, the 'daggermen'.[45] In addition, groups to whom Josephus refers as 'false prophets' were

---

[36] Philo *Leg.*

[37] *Ant.* 18.302–8; *War* 2.203. On the incident see Schürer 1.394–8.

[38] On his reign and its effects see Schürer 1.442–54.

[39] *Ant.* 20.5.

[40] *Ant.* 20.97–9; Ac. 5.36, where Luke allows the incident to be placed in company with the movements led by Judas the Galilean on the one hand and Jesus of Nazareth on the other.

[41] *Ant.* 20.102; cf. Schürer 1.457.

[42] *Ant.* 20.105–12; *War* 2.224–7; *Ant.* 20.113–17; *War* 2.228–31.

[43] *Ant.* 20.118–36; *War* 2.232–46. On the details of the incident, and the problem over Tacitus' account (*Ann.* 12.54), see Schürer 1.459f.

[44] *War* 2.253.

[45] *Ant.* 20.185–7; *War* 2.254; cf. Tac. *Ann.* 12.54. On the Sicarii see particularly Hengel 1989 [1961], 46–53; Horsley 1979b.

operating in the Judaean desert.[46] An Egyptian Jew led a mass movement which assembled on the Mount of Olives, and promised them that the city walls would fall down and allow them to enter in triumph. His followers, numbering thousands (precisely how many differs widely in our sources) were cut down by the Romans, while he himself escaped and was not heard of again.[47] There were also riots over Jewish social status at Caesarea, and plenty of further evidence of brigand activity.[48] Among the first acts of Felix's successor as procurator, Porcius Festus (60–2), was to execute an 'imposter' who had promised his followers 'salvation and rest from troubles',[49] and to deal with a strange itinerant Jew who had been arraigned before Felix on a charge of inciting riots by offending Jewish scruples.[50] Despite further executions of *lestai*,[51] movements of revolt spread faster, fanned by the insensitive actions of Festus' two successors, Lucceius Albinus (62–5) and the notorious Gessius Florus (65–6), who, being unable to control the brigands, actually gave them support and, according to Josephus, shared their plunder.[52]

This brief list of movements of revolt in the years preceding the war gives, I think, sufficient indication of the mood of the country as a whole. It supports the fairly obvious conclusion: Josephus has thoroughly falsified his own suggestion that one single party, begun by Judas the Galilean, was responsible for the entire drift towards the war with Rome which broke out in AD 66. Revolution of one sort or another was in the air, and often present on the ground, both in Galilee and (particularly) in Jerusalem, throughout the period of Roman rule. It was not confined to one group, whether the Zealots properly so called, the Sicarii, or any other. Whenever it was suppressed in one place it sprang up in another.[53] The same seems to have been true even after the devastation of the war. Certainly when bar-Kochba was proclaimed Messiah large numbers from the whole country were ready to rise and attempt once more to throw off the Roman yoke.

This broad base of revolutionary activity is particularly the case in the main Jewish War itself (AD 66–73). The history of this war is bewilderingly complex, not least because it was as much a *civil* war as a war of resistance against Rome. Groups and factions formed, fought one another, regrouped, held different bits of Jerusalem at different times, called themselves and one another

---

[46] *War* 2.258–60. Cf. too the 'imposters and brigands' of *War* 2.264–5.

[47] *War* 2.261–3 (30,000 followers); Ac. 21.38 (4,000).

[48] *Ant.* 20.173–7; *War* 2.266–70.

[49] *Ant.* 20.188.

[50] Ac. 25.1–12.

[51] *War* 2.271.

[52] *Ant.* 20.252–7. This may, of course, be an exaggeration on Josephus' part. But it is not in itself implausible, if some at least of the brigands were sufficiently desperate to make temporary alliances with a Roman official in order to prosecute their struggle, which was as much with their richer Jewish neighbours as with Rome. On the widespread anger against Florus himself, see e.g. *War* 2.293, 403.

[53] I am thus at this point in substantial agreement with Goodman 1987, 108: 'There was no separate anti-Roman movement in first-century Judaism; rather, anti-Gentile attitudes which originated long before AD 6, perhaps in Maccabaean times, inspired many different groups, permeating the whole Jewish population and varying only in their intensity.' See too Horsley and Hanson 1985, xv.

by different names, and generally made life as difficult for the historian as they made it miserable for their contemporaries. Three figures especially stand out. John of Gischala came to Jerusalem from Galilee and led the Zealots, properly so called, in the revolt. He was eventually captured at the end of the war and condemned to life imprisonment.[54] Menahem, a descendant of Judas the Galilean, was the would-be Messianic figure from the Sicarii who came to Jerusalem from Masada. After a brief appearance dressed in royal robes, he was murdered by a rival group.[55] Simon ben Giora was a rebel leader who seems to have been regarded both by his followers and by the Romans as the most serious would-be 'king of the Jews'. His royal career ended in humiliation and death in Vespasian's triumph in Rome.[56] Even looking no further, we again find that Josephus' own overall statements, blaming the 'lower orders' for the entire conflict, are extremely misleading and inadequate.

But who, then, constituted these movements? Here there is no agreement in sight. We may distinguish three broad strands of interpretation that have been taken in recent scholarship. These are (a) a pan-Zealot theory; (b) a theory that blames the aristocrats for being the real trouble-makers; (c) a theory that sees several quite diverse groups.[57]

First, there is the case for an overall unity of movement and ideology, a broad stream of resistance which, begun (as Josephus says) by Judas the Galilean, continued among his family and related groups until it reached its nemesis in the war. This position, massively argued by Martin Hengel, has a great deal to be said for it.[58] True, we must grant that the title 'Zealot' itself was used, as its own self-designation, by one particular group during the factional fighting in the war itself. This group, moreover, appears to have come into existence only at that stage. But it is also clear that the noun 'zeal' and the adjective 'zealous' were used widely to refer to more general anti-Roman attitudes and activities. From this it appears that the group in question were, in so naming themselves, hijacking a word to which many others would have laid claim, rather than initiating a new idea altogether.[59] Even the usage of Josephus himself, whose writing is the basis for the claim that the Zealots were a small party newly formed in the 60s, allows for some whom he calls 'zealots'

---

[54] On John of Gischala, see *War* 2.590–632; 4.98–577; 5–6, *passim*; 7.118, 263–4.

[55] *War* 2.433–49.

[56] *War* 5–6, *passim*; 7.25–36, 153–4. On Simon's would-be 'Davidic' monarchy see Horsley and Hanson 1985, 119–27.

[57] This inevitably involves a certain amount of over-simplification of highly complex issues. I shall not, for instance, discuss further views like those of Cohen 1987, 27–34, who follows Josephus' 'official' position in minimizing the anti-Roman rebellious tendencies of Jews during the century. On the details of the whole struggle see Rhoads 1976, ch. 4. Rhoads lists (148f.) no fewer than ten distinct reasons for intra-Jewish factional disputes. On the modern Christian study of the Zealots see the interesting article of Schwartz 1992, ch. 8.

[58] Hengel 1989 [1961]. Cf. too Hayward in Schürer 2.598–606; Stern 1973.

[59] See, among many possible references, *T.Levi* 6.3; *T.Jud.* 9.2ff.; *Jub.* 30.18; 1QH 2.15; and, in Christian texts, Ac. 21.20; 22.3; Rom. 10.2; Gal. 1.14; Phil. 3.6. Hengel's discussion of these and others (1989 [1961], 177–83) is perhaps too careful to separate Paul from the movements he is describing elsewhere; after all, Paul's 'zeal', by his own account, led to actions of violence against those he saw as compromising with paganism. 'Zeal' cannot simply be reduced to piety.

who are not part of this small group.[60] And there seems no reasonable doubt that the general aim of resistance to Rome, in one way or another, summed up a good deal of the national mood which, looking back to the Maccabees, looked to the great day when the prophecies would be fulfilled and their god would rule his people without the aid of pagan overlords.[61]

Second, a parallel case has been made out by Martin Goodman, who agrees with Hengel that there was widespread resistance to Rome, but claims that the initiative and leadership in such movements came almost entirely, not from the lower orders of society as is usually supposed, but from the ruling class of the Jews.[62] They, according to Goodman, constituted a puppet oligarchy put in place by the Romans after the decline of the Herodian dynasty, against the wishes and greatly to the dislike of the people as a whole. It was they, he suggests, who provoked the war in the first place and gave it its vital leadership, contributing to the general chaos by factional rivalry between themselves, for which there is earlier evidence as well.[63] This case conflicts with the normal view, that the aristocracy would resist rebellion, since they had the most to lose. Goodman argues cogently that, once it became clear that war was likely, the aristocracy threw in their lot with it, seeing a better chance of retaining power if they were regarded by the Jews as their national leaders than if they were seen to side with the Romans. Even if the Romans won, a local oligarchy that had failed to prevent revolt would not be regarded with much favour.

It seems to me, however, that Goodman goes further than the evidence allows when he suggests that all the major leaders during the war itself were actually part of the aristocracy. His arguments about the background of Simon ben Giora, for instance, prove at the most that we may not know as much about Simon as is usually thought, not that he was an aristocrat.[64] Conversely, Goodman consistently minimizes the 'bandit' or 'brigand' involvement in insurrection, and hypothesizes aristocratic involvement where there is little or no actual proof.[65] It seems to me unlikely that *all* of Josephus' references to

---

[60] Thus (a) *War* 2.444, where the would-be Messiah Menahem goes to the Temple in royal robes accompanied by 'armed zealots', *zelotas enoplous*; Thackeray in the Loeb edition translates this 'armed fanatics', though admitting in a note that the Greek seems more specific. (b) *War* 2.564 speaks of Eleazar the son of Simon 'and the zealots under his command'; the phrase *tous hyp' auto zelotas* is translated 'his subservient admirers' by Thackeray, but this seems to me less likely. (c) *War* 2.651 has 'zealots' in Jerusalem already before the war, and before the arrival of the eventual 'zealot' leader, John of Gischala (so Donaldson 1990, 34, noting this as an exception to Horsley's case: see below). (d) *War* 4.225 speaks of Eleazar ben Gion (or Simon) and Zacharias ben Amphicalleus as leaders of the Zealots. On all this see Hengel 1989 [1961], 380–404. For the use of similar language about Mattathias, the original Maccabaean leader, in *Ant.* 12.271, see Hengel 155.

[61] See further ch. 10 below.

[62] Goodman 1987.

[63] Compare Josephus' remarks about the Sadducees, that, whereas the Pharisees are affectionate to one another, the Sadducees are boorish and arrogant both to one another and to outsiders: *War* 2.166.

[64] Goodman 1987, 202–6.

[65] e.g. 167ff. on the minimal brigand involvement; 170ff., suggesting (with no solid evidence) that Eleazar, the son of the ex-high priest Ananias, was one of the perpetrators of the 'joke' against Florus that helped to spark off the war.

brigandage, to *lestai*, are simply a fictitious cover-up for the rebellion of his own class. Goodman provides, in short, the mirror-image of Josephus' own picture; if Josephus has blamed rabble-rousers in order to exonerate his own class, Goodman has turned incidents of revolt into aristocratic plots, and has turned known aristocrats into revolutionaries, to inculpate those Josephus had defended.

Third, a case has been made for a much more diverse account. Richard Horsley, in a string of articles and two books, has argued for the distinctiveness of several groups, with different social backgrounds and agendas.[66] He distances ordinary brigands (the *lestai*) from 'Zealots' proper, the distinct group who came into being at the start of the war in 66, and both of these from the 'Sicarii', who were a group of terrorists with a different agenda, whose origins are found in a more learned and scribal background. He argues that Hengel has subsumed all these groups too readily under one broad generalized account, and attempts not only to distinguish them but also to rehabilitate one of them (the 'Zealots', strictly so called) as responding commendably or at least comprehensibly to their social and cultural plight.[67]

It is important to give Horsley his due. The great majority of references to 'zealots' do indeed refer to one particular group, that which Josephus describes in *War* 4.130–61, to whom John of Gischala joined himself after a trick (4.208–23). And it is a different group, the Sicarii, based on Masada during the war, that has a clear dynastic link with Judas the Galilean at the beginning of the century.[68] Horsley succeeds, I think, in showing that the start of the war was not due to the work of a single organized and long-standing Jewish resistance movement, but rather came about through the confluence of many streams. But this scarcely warrants his remarks about 'the demise of "the Zealots" concept'[69] or his frequent suggestion that the real impetus for revolution came from social rather than theological factors.[70] Such an antithesis is, as

[66] Horsley 1979a, 1979b, 1981, 1984, 1985 (with Hanson), 1986a, 1986b, 1987.

[67] 1986b, 158–61, 190–2. Horsley's account is supported, with an important modification, by Donaldson 1990; and by Crossan 1991, chs. 6–10.

[68] See e.g. *War* 7.253f., 262, 324. I fail to see the significance of Horsley's triumphant 'demolition' of the idea of Masada as 'the Zealot's last stand' (Horsley and Hanson 1985, xv): it seems to have been the last stand of the Sicarii, and on Horsley's own showing they were the group with more of a claim to continuity with earlier resistance movements. Hengel argues (1989 [1961], xvi–xvii) that the 'Sicarii' did not call themselves by that name, but regarded themselves as the true 'zealots', of whom other parties were parodies. It is as hard to disprove as to prove this suggestion.

[69] 1986a, 3; cp. 1981, 409; 1984, 472.

[70] The split is in any way misleading, not least since one of the reasons for revolution was the problem about pollution of the Land, which is itself both a social and a theological issue. In 1986b, 158 Horsley shows some of the hermeneutical assumptions of his arguments: Hengel's construct was (he says) useful in the 1960s to those who wanted to create a picture of Jesus as the prophet of non-resistance, and needed a historical foil for this. (So too Horsley and Hanson 1985, xiii–xvi.) This may or may not be the case; history is not well served either by such agendas or by their mirror-images (1986b, 192). In any case, even if Horsley were fully correct in restricting the use of the word 'Zealot' to the 60s of the first century, this would still not mean (as he implies in 1986b, 161) that there were no advocates of violent resistance in the time of Jesus, or that some of Jesus' teaching could not have been directed against such movements. On this see e.g. Borg 1971; 1984, chs. 2–3. The question then becomes, not whether there were advocates of violence in the time of Jesus, nor by what name they were called, but what attitude Jesus took to

we saw in Part II, quite dangerous in historical work in general, and never more so than when we are dealing with a culture like that of first-century Judaism. And there is no doubt, as Horsley himself admits, that revolution was far more widespread than simply the 'Zealot' party properly so called;[71] or that the words 'zeal' and 'zealous' were regularly used in connection with all sorts of Jews who were zealous for God and the Torah, and some of whom carried that 'zeal' to the lengths of violence.[72] Such groups or individuals may not have been connected with the 'zealot' party as we know it from Josephus, but it is risky to drive a strong ideological wedge between them. In any case, Horsley's case is at risk methodologically. He tries to isolate 'the Zealots' as a group by basing himself on a close reading of Josephus. At the same time he is rightly critical of Josephus—precisely because he isolates one party as the group solely responsible for the war.

It seems to me, in conclusion, overwhelmingly historically likely that there were, throughout the first century, many movements which laid claim to the tradition of active 'zeal', a tradition that went back, through the Maccabees, to the memory of Phineas and Elijah. (Though these figures, in their own contexts, undoubtedly represent different strands of Jewish life, they were brought together within the folk-memory as people who, in various ways, had acted out of 'zeal' for their god.[73]) One of these groups, the Sicarii, seems to have sustained some kind of a dynasty from the middle of the first century BC to the fall of Masada, beginning with the *archilestes* Hezekiah, killed by Herod, and continuing with his son Judas, the leader of a revolt after the death of Herod, and quite possibly the same person as the leader of the anti-census riots in AD 6.[74] As we saw, the sons of Judas the Galilean were crucified under Tiberius Alexander in the mid-40s, and another descendant, Menahem, became the would-be messianic leader of the Sicarii on Masada during the war, was then killed in Jerusalem, and was succeeded by his nephew Eleazar the son of Jairus. There is no reason to think that members of this group were regarded by any other as the natural leaders of revolt, but nor is there good reason to drive a sharp ideological wedge between them and any other party or band.[75] These groups, no doubt with considerable social and organizational diversity, shared to a lesser or greater extent a background of socio-economic depriva-

---

them. This will concern us in the next volume.

[71] So Horsley and Hanson 1985, xxi.

[72] Horsley 1979a, 58 admits that the 'bandits', whom he distinguishes sharply from 'official "zealots" ', i.e. resistance fighters, were nevertheless themselves inspired by 'zeal'. See too Ac. 22.3; Gal. 1.14; Rom. 10.2; Phil. 3.6.

[73] cf. Hengel 1989 [1961], 146–83, and the numerous references there.

[74] The identification of these Judases is sufficiently uncertain for the two Loeb editors to disagree, with Wikgren in favour (ad *Ant.* 17.271) and Thackeray against (ad *War* 2.118). Hengel (1989 [1961], 293, 331) supports the identification, perhaps predictably, as do e.g. Kingdon 1972/3, 80 and Stern 1973, 136; Horsley, equally predictably, rejects it (1984, 485, followed by Donaldson 1990, 24). Other details in Schürer 2.600, n.12.

[75] Against Horsley, whose all-important split comes between the Zealots (narrowly defined), of whom he more or less approves, and the Sicarii, of whom he disapproves.

tion, and, most importantly, a common stock of theological symbols and ideas. We shall explore these areas more fully in subsequent chapters.[76]

If revolution was in the air throughout this period, how did that fit in with the agendas of the other groups of whose existence we know? The most important of these groups for our purposes is undoubtedly the Pharisees, and we must turn to them now.

3. The Pharisees

(i) The Sources

It is of course impossible to offer here a full history of the Pharisees. Others have laboured, and I have entered into their labour.[77] My purpose here is to plot the main agenda of the Pharisaic movement in the last hundred years or so before the destruction of the Temple. About some other vexed questions, including the origin of the movement and the meaning(s) of its name, I have nothing new to say. It is vital, though, that we spend some time on this group, because whatever is said about them will affect the way in which we later discuss both Jesus and Paul.

The sources for the study of the Pharisees are, as is well known, full of problems. (1) Josephus, who is normally thought to have claimed to be a Pharisee himself, writes about them both explicitly and implicitly, describing them as a political group wielding considerable *de facto* power in the last two centuries BC, and fading out of consideration (or at least out of his narrative) thereafter.[78] (2) The cryptic references to the Pharisees in the Qumran scrolls are sufficient to confirm that the Pharisees held considerable influence at least in the latter half of the first century BC, and that they were regarded as a

[76] I thus agree broadly with the outline of Hengel's work, while wishing to find different terminology in many cases and to maintain more distinctiveness than he does between some of the different groupings. Horsley's reliance at certain points on articles by M. Smith (e.g. Smith 1977 [1956], 1971) seems to me ill-founded. Borg 1971 rightly stresses the limitations of the word 'Zealot' in Josephus, but then equally correctly concludes (511f.) that one cannot question the reality for which the term 'Zealot' is commonly used, namely widespread religiously inspired resistance to Rome, and that such resistance was not the prerogative of one group only, but 'involved elements from all the major groups'. This means, too, that I wish at least to modify Goodman's thesis: one cannot blame the aristocracy for everything.

[77] See particularly, among the welter of recent literature, the many works of Jacob Neusner; Porton 1986; and Saldarini 1988; Sanders 1990a, 1992; and now especially Mason 1991, which came to hand at a late stage in the redrafting of this chapter, and which seems to me most important. Cf. too Schürer 2.322–403 (bibliography, 381f.) and Gafni 1987.

[78] Josephus' basic statements are in *War* 1.110; *Ant.* 17.41; 13.297, describing the Pharisees as experts in Torah; *War* 2.162–3; *Ant.* 13.172; 18.12–15, where he presents quite stylized pictures of the Pharisees as though they were a Hellenistic philosophical school (compare *Life* 12, where the Pharisees are somewhat like the Stoics!). His remarks about his own relation to the Pharisees are in *Life* 12. He stresses their importance in earlier periods in *Ant.* 13.288 (where the Hasmonean dynasty acknowledges their authority), 13.298 (where the masses are said to favour them), and 18.17 (according to which the Sadducees submit to Pharisaic teaching for fear that otherwise the common people will resist them: cf. bYom. 19b, bNidd. 33b). For discussion of these, see below.

dangerous rival by a group which was itself manifestly an independent sect at the time.[79] Several scholars hold that this group, referred to cryptically in the Scrolls, is identical with the Pharisees, though some are more cautious.[80] The execution of some of this group at the hands of Alexander Jannaeus is apparently approved by the Essenes on the grounds, we may suppose, that the Pharisees are regarded as compromisers.[81] (3) The rabbinic evidence is massive, scattered, and highly complex, and taken by itself suggests a picture of the Pharisees as a group concerned above all else with purity, especially the kosher requirements: they are seen as the direct precursors of the rabbis themselves, and their disputes are recalled within the context of debates whose immediate relevance is to the very different situation of Judaism after the destruction.[82]

There is then the New Testament evidence. (4) The writings of Paul make some mention of his Pharisaic background, and it is often suggested that even his Christian theology owes something to the shape and content of his earlier training. If this were all we had to go on, we would have a view of the Pharisees as strict interpreters of Jewish ancestral traditions, mastered by a zeal for their god which sometimes led them to acts of violence.[83] (5) The gospels and Acts offer a picture of Pharisaic activity in Galilee and elsewhere, in which the Pharisees appear as the guardians of the strict interpretation and application of the ancestral laws.[84]

There are, of course, problems with using each of these sources. Particularly in his early work, the *Jewish War*, Josephus seems clearly motivated to exonerate the Pharisees (and almost everyone else except the lowest orders) from blame for the war. It has often been supposed that this is a pro-Pharisaic bias, reinforced from a different angle by his longer account in the *Antiquities* which, despite letting the mask slip a little as regards the Pharisees' involvement with revolution, stresses how influential the Pharisees always were. It is usually thought that Josephus was bent on persuading the Romans to entrust the Pharisees' successors, the rabbis, with ruling what was left of Judaism. The anti-Pharisaic tone of many of these passages is a problem for the theory, which has often been evaded by ascribing the relevant portions to Josephus' supposed source, Herod's court historian Nicolas of Damascus.[85] However, a different and very attractive hypothesis has now been proposed by Mason, as follows: (a) Josephus did not claim to be a Pharisee, but to have decided as a

---

[79] See particularly 4QpNah, and 4QMMT, on which see Baumgarten 1991, 112, 117f. The crucial phrase is 'those who seek smooth things', on which see Sanders 1992, 532 n.1; cf. too 1QH 2.15, 32, and CD 1.18.

[80] In favour of the identification are e.g. Schürer 1.225 n.22; Dimant 1984, 511f.; Baumgarten 1991, 117; returning an open verdict, Saldarini 1988, 278ff. See further the discussion in Stemberger 1991, 103ff.

[81] cf. 4QpNah 1.6f.; 2.2, 4; cp. Jos. *War* 1.97; *Ant*. 13.380; and Sanders 1992, 382.

[82] For a different reading of the rabbinic sources, based on (what seems to me) a somewhat arbitrary principle of selection, see Rivkin 1969–70.

[83] Gal. 1.13–14; Phil. 3.4–6; cf. Rom. 10.2–3.

[84] See the well-known passages in e.g. Mk. 2.16ff.; 3.6; 7.1ff., etc., and their parallels; and Ac. 5.34; 15.5; 23.6–9; 26.5.

[85] So Schwarz 1983; see Schürer 1.28–31.

matter of expediency rather than conviction that, upon entering public life (as a young aristocrat in his own right), he would follow their general line;[86] (b) Josephus did not like the Pharisees at all, but regarded their popularity as an unpleasant fact of life; (c) it is Josephus himself, not a source, who is responsible for vilifying the Pharisees, though when he discusses them as a 'school' he does so, as with the others, without obvious denigration. Mason's reading of the evidence is impressive, and may prove to alter the balance of scholarship decisively.[87] Whichever of these positions is adopted, though, Josephus' own bias means that he must be treated with a fair degree of caution. He will often be as useful in his indirect statements as in his direct ones.

The rabbinic literature is of course a mine of information and a minefield for the unwary. As we noted earlier, Neusner has pointed out that if we were dependent upon the rabbis for information about the pre-70 period there are a good many things which we take for granted of which we would have no knowledge at all.[88] The rabbinic material was not collected in fixed form until the end of the second century AD, with the compilation of the Mishnah, and consists for the most part of reported debates on the minutiae of Torah-observance, often between the 'houses' or 'schools' of the great teachers of the Herodian period, Hillel and Shammai. To argue from the silence of the rabbis is precarious in the extreme.[89]

Not only is the rabbinic literature thus limited in scope. We also have evidence that the debates which were remembered many generations later had subtly changed their meaning in the process. What started off (for instance) as a discussion of the biblical canon, with Shammai taking the stricter line (Ecclesiastes is not part of scripture) and Hillel the more lenient (Ecclesiastes is included), turns up as a discussion about *purity*, since if a book belongs to the canon it 'makes the hands unclean', i.e. one must wash after touching it. From that perspective, Shammai appears to have taken the more lenient line (one may touch Ecclesiastes without having to wash afterwards) and Hillel the stricter.[90] The Mishnaic period thus 'remembered' the earlier Pharisees as the great teachers of purity, even though several of them, including the great Akiba himself, were quite clearly political and revolutionary leaders of the first rank. We can watch this process of 'translation' at work, similarly, between Josephus' account of incidents and later rabbinic ones.[91] We thus have the unsurprising problem that traditions which originally meant one thing are now quoted because they mean another, making it hard to reconstruct original meanings except by inference.

In addition, the ascendancy of the school of Hillel in the post-70 period means that, as Neusner says, 'it is as if one cannot mention Shammai without

---

[86] On *Life* 10–12 see the detailed study of Mason 1989, and other literature cited there; also Mason 1991, ch. 15.

[87] Sanders' reply to Mason (1992, 532–4) does not seem to me to have damaged his case.

[88] See Neusner 1971, 3.304, summarized again in 1991, 79.

[89] Though it is still attempted: e.g. Smith 1978, 157.

[90] cf. mYad. 3.5, mEduy. 5.3. See now Safrai 1987, 189f.

[91] See e.g. Cohen 1984, 36f., one example being the different stories about the riot against Alexander Jannaeus (*Ant.* 13.372 with tSukk. 3.16).

denigrating him'.[92] Shammai, who was quite clearly a major figure in his day (the late first century BC), is presented either as too extreme to take seriously, or he is presented as agreeing with the school of Hillel over against—the school of Shammai![93] By contrast, no story out of the vast collection of material about Hillel is unfavourable to him: 'Hillel was everywhere claimed as the major authority—after Moses and Ezra—for the oral Torah.'[94] For these reasons, therefore—incompleteness, change of meaning, and evident bias—the rabbinic traditions about the pre-70 Pharisees cannot be pressed too firmly into service.

When we come to the New Testament, it is clear that we are faced with a more acute form of the same problem. If Shammai never appears in rabbinic traditions without being denigrated, the same almost always seems to be true of the Pharisees in general in Paul and the gospels. There are exceptions. Jesus accepts dinner invitations from Pharisees in Luke 7.36ff., 11.37ff., and 14.1, and in Luke 13.31 some Pharisees warn Jesus of Herod's desire to kill him. Gamaliel the Pharisee is the hero of the hour in Acts 5.34–40. In the one passage where he mentions the word 'Pharisee' itself (Philippians 3.5) Paul regards his membership of the group as something which had been a matter of 'gain' to him. Yet in no case is there any question of the Pharisees' position being affirmed or supported. The Pharisees are seen as enemies of the gospel—not the only ones, but enemies none the less. The stories in the synoptic tradition were similarly handed on in a context (whichever that may have been) which highlighted this emphasis. Such a perspective, like the rabbinic view of Shammai, makes it very difficult to use the New Testament as basic material in our reconstruction of the Pharisees. Indeed, some have doubted Paul's credibility as a Pharisee, labelling him instead a Gnosticizing Hellenist.[95]

(ii) The Identity of the Pharisees

Faced with these problems at the level of the sources, it is not surprising that a wide variety of hypotheses has been offered as to who exactly the Pharisees were, what their aims may have been, the extent of their influence, and many other things. Considerable confusion has existed on all fronts, not least because of the difficulties involved in lining up the Pharisees both with their would-be successors, the rabbis, and with various other groups who flit in and out of the literature: the scribes, the 'wise' (*hakamim*, possibly rendered into Greek by *sophistai*), the 'pious' (*hasidim*), and above all the 'associates' (*haberim*), the members of dining-societies that observed strict versions of the purity laws.

---

[92] Neusner 1971, 1.208.
[93] Neusner 1971, 1.210f.
[94] Neusner 1971, 1.300, cf. 294ff. On the meaning of oral Torah see ch. 8 below.
[95] See Maccoby 1986, 1991.

Taking first this issue of identity, and the reference of particular technical terms, it is now generally recognized that, though many Pharisees were scribes, and vice versa, there were probably many who belonged to only one of the two groups.[96] The term 'wise', which can be used with a sense of opprobrium (e.g. *Against Apion* 2.236), but can equally be neutral, is so generalized as to be difficult to pin down, but in some of its occurrences in Josephus it looks as though the people referred to are Pharisees.[97] The *hasidim*, again, may merge into the Pharisees, but the category remains imprecise, referring originally to the followers of Judas Maccabaeus but quite possibly admitting of a wider reference later on.[98] As for the *haberim*, they have sometimes been identified with the Pharisees,[99] and sometimes with a smaller, more intense group for whom the Pharisees and their successors laid down regulations: all *haberim* were Pharisees, but not all Pharisees were *haberim*.[100] *Haberim* may thus have been groups of Pharisees meeting to celebrate special meals in a context of purity that was normally impractical. Or they may have comprised the majority of Pharisees, providing tight-knit groups which would give local reality to one's adherence to a widespread movement. Or they may have been regarded by Pharisees in general as a kind of elite corps, much as Epictetus, a practical street-level Stoic, regarded the Cynics—the real out-and-out hard-liners.[101] The continuing uncertainty on this point constitutes, in fact, one of the central problems in using the rabbinic material as a source for the pre-70 movement.

Finally, the name 'Pharisee' itself is a matter of considerable controversy, not to be resolved here;[102] though Baumgarten's case for the meaning 'accurate, sharp' (sc. in interpretation and application of Israel's laws) remains attractive.

(iii) The Agenda and Influence of the Pharisees

The major questions about the Pharisees in current debate concern two closely related areas: what was their agenda, and how widespread was their influence?

---

[96] cf. Saldarini 1988, 241–76. His conclusion is that scribes 'were varied in background and allegiance and were individuals filling a social role in different contexts rather than a unified political and religious force' (276). For an attempt to link them closer, see Rivkin 1978; Kampen 1988 (e.g. 219ff.).

[97] See e.g. *Ant*. 17. 152, 155; *War* 1.648. The description of Judas the Galilean as a *sophistes* in *War* 2.118, 433 may belong here also, despite Josephus' attempt in this account to keep Judas' movement separate. Cp. Hengel 1989 [1961], 83, 86f., 227, 333. This shows again that the categories of Pharisee and *sophistes* probably overlap, without becoming identical (against Rivkin's close identification: 1969–70). For the use of 'sages' rather than 'rabbis' in the later period see Safrai 1987, xv, and of course Urbach 1987 [1975, 1979].

[98] 1 Macc. 2.42; 7.12f.; 2 Macc. 14.6. See Davies 1977; Blenkinsopp 1981, 16–19, 23f.; Saldarini 1988, 252; Kampen 1988, *passim*.

[99] e.g. Jeremias 1969a, 246–67.

[100] e.g. Rivkin 1969–70, esp. 245f.; Sanders 1977, 154f., following Moore 1927–30, 3.26 and others; see too Sanders 1985, 186ff., and, more cautiously, 1990a, 250. See also Goodman 1987, 82–5. The opposite view is taken in e.g. Schürer 2.398–400.

[101] Epict. 3.22.

[102] See Schürer 2.396–8, and particularly Baumgarten 1983.

Obviously, a group concerned simply with the internal operation of a private club for the maintenance of its own members' ritual purity is unlikely to be particularly concerned with major questions of public policy. At the same time, it is quite feasible that the Pharisees held grandiose ambitions about influencing the course of political events, but could not implement them due to their lack of real power. Or we might hold that they combined various different ambitions: just as the Sicarii on Masada maintained strict ritual purity as part of their holy resistance against Rome, so the Pharisees may well, looked at simply from an a priori standpoint, have held together a deep concern for purity with a radical longing for political change. Where in all this does the truth lie?

Josephus, as we noted above, emphasizes in his later writings that the Pharisees hold considerable *de facto* power in the early part of the first century BC. When it comes to the first century AD, things are not so clear. At one extreme (now normally abandoned) they have been held to be virtually the ruling party in Judaism, obeying strictly all the Mishnaic rules for *haberim* and enforcing them on as many Jews as they were able to.[103] Another possibility is the view that, though the Pharisees may still have been quite numerous in the first century AD, their focus of interest had shifted, in Neusner's phrase, 'from politics to piety', so that Josephus' picture of the Pharisees intervening in major social and political events is anachronistic if applied to the generation before the destruction of the Temple.[104] Sanders' current position is defined, in a complex way, by his disagreements with both of these. Over against Jeremias' view of the Pharisees' widespread authority, he suggests that, in the first century AD, the Pharisees were a small group, based only in Jerusalem, with little political significance, following their own limited agendas and without taking much interest, at least *qua* Pharisees, in the major movements of the day.[105] Over against Neusner, however, he contends that the Pharisees continued to concern themselves with matters other than merely the maintenance of private priest-like purity.[106]

I wish to suggest a different combination of elements within a historical account of the Pharisees and their agenda. Briefly, I shall argue (i) (with Sanders) that the Pharisees, though never a Jewish 'thought-police' in the first or any other century, did concern themselves with matters wider than private or ritual purity; (ii) (against Sanders) that these concerns often embraced political and revolutionary action, such that the idea of a self-contained Jerusalem-based group with little influence, and not much interest in who was doing what elsewhere, is out of the question; (iii) (between Neusner and Sanders) that the purity codes were a vital part of pre-70 Pharisaism, function-

---

[103] This is the view that Sanders attributes to Jeremias (see now Meyer 1991a and Sanders 1991a); and see Rivkin's view (1969–70, 1978) of the Pharisees supplanting the priests as official teachers of Torah, a view firmly (and in my view rightly) criticized by Mason 1988; Sanders 1992, ch. 10.

[104] Neusner 1973, 1991.

[105] So Sanders 1985, following Smith 1977 [1956]; in 1992, chs. 18–21, he seems to have softened this line somewhat.

[106] Sanders 1990a, esp. chs. 3 and 5.

ing in close symbolic relationship to the wider political agenda. I shall set out this position in relation to the four key periods, i.e. the Hasmonean period (164–63 BC), the Roman period to the destruction of the Temple (63 BC–AD 70), the period between the two revolts (AD 70–135) and, for completeness, the period after AD 135.

1. It is beyond a doubt that for quite some time before 63 BC there existed a pressure-group, known at least by its enemies as 'Pharisees'. This group, not necessarily numerous, seems to have arisen around or after the time of the Maccabaean revolt, though its connections (if any) with that event are impossible to trace with any accuracy. These Pharisees exercised considerable influence over some of the subsequent Hasmonean rulers, not least Salome (76–67 BC), the widow of Alexander Jannaeus. Even if Josephus exaggerates when he says that the Pharisees ruled Salome as she ruled Israel,[107] or that they incurred protests by their virtual ruling of Jerusalem,[108] it remains clear that they were a *de facto* power in the land. And the power they wielded, though in modern terms 'religious' in origin and intent, was emphatically 'political' in effect. Whatever the disputes about details, it is clear that the great issues of the day had to do with the proper stance for a Jew to take up when faced with (what seemed to them to be) the encroachments of non-Jewish ways of life. The Pharisees saw themselves as standing firm for the old ways, the traditions of Israel, against paganism from without and assimilation from within. Their extreme focus on Torah makes perfect sense within this setting; and so does the increasing concentration, in this and the subsequent periods, on issues of purity.

For an overall view of the Pharisees, both in this period and subsequently, it is not absolutely vital that we discover precisely which purity laws they obeyed and which they felt able to circumvent at which period.[109] What matters is the ideology that motivated them to focus so strongly on purity and to relate it in any way to the purity demanded in the Temple. Here the most attractive thesis seems to me the following: faced with social, political and cultural 'pollution' at the level of national life as a whole, one natural reaction (with a strong sense of 'natural') was to concentrate on personal cleanness, to cleanse and purify an area over which one did have control as a compensation for the

---

[107] *War* 1.112. Sanders 1992, 382f., thinks that Josephus is accurate at this point.
[108] *Ant.* 13.416.
[109] See Sanders 1990a ch.3, and the reply of Neusner 1991, esp. 89f. Neusner seems to me, despite his polemic, to admit the force of at least part of Sanders' point, when he says that, according to the Mishnah (referring particularly to mHag. 2.5—3.3, a passage whose relevance is denied by Rivkin 1969–70), the Pharisees 'are persons who eat unconsecrated food in a state of cultic cleanness, *or, more accurately, within the hierarchy of states of cultic cleanness...*' (my italics). In other words, a distinction is made between the broadly-stated position often taken as Neusner's, that Pharisees (or possibly *haberim*) ate their food in the purity appropriate for priests in the Temple, and the nuanced position here articulated, in which Pharisaic purity is *of a different degree within the same scale* as that which applied to those working in the Temple. Cf. too the story of Johanan ben Gudgada (mHag. 2.7) who is mentioned, as though he were an exception to the general rule, as having always eaten his regular food according to the second most stringent code for priests, i.e. that for those who 'eat of hallowed things'. To the extent that Sanders is challenging Neusner's broader point (see e.g. 1990a, 248) he is surely correct.

impossibility of cleansing or purifying an area—the outward and visible political one—over which one had none. The intensifying of the biblical purity regulations within Pharisaism may well therefore invite the explanation that they are the individual analogue of the national fear of, and/or resistance to, contamination from, or oppression by, Gentiles.[110] Ceremonial purity functions almost as a displacement activity when faced with the apparent impossibility of national purity. Just as, for the Maccabaean martyrs, refusing to eat pork and refusing to obey the pagan ruler were one and the same thing, so the concern for purity functioned as a means of symbolically enacting that resistance to pagan rule which was nursed secretly and maintained in readiness for revolutionary opportunities, whenever they might be afforded. At the same time, this concern could lead, and after 135 certainly did lead, to the setting up of an alternative world, the world (broadly speaking) of the Mishnah, in which the concern for private purity dominated, and the hope for national restoration took the form of mourning for the disasters suffered and a long-range hope that Israel's god would one day restore the fortunes of his people. It is interesting that Josephus does not attempt to describe the purity regulations of the Pharisees, though his mention of their 'avoiding luxury'[111] is perhaps a coded and Hellenized reference to this feature.

It is this socially and even psychologically complex situation that enables the 'translation' of what later generations would classify as a 'political' issue into a 'purely religious' one, even though the distinction would have been, I suggest, meaningless to most people for most of the time between the Maccabees and (at least) AD 70. The Mishnah itself, of course, belongs to a time when the possibility of a real change in political fortune had receded from view altogether. As we noted in a previous section, even the out-and-out revolutionaries saved their main efforts for times when it seemed as though they might have a real chance of success.

During the Hasmonean period, therefore, we may take it as read that the Pharisees existed *both* as a political pressure-group *and* as a group concerned for the maintenance of a purity which reflected in some degree, even if it did not imitate exactly, that purity proper to priests serving in the Temple. The first of these features is witnessed to by various incidents, including their standing up to what they saw as the illegitimate government of John Hyrcanus (134–104 BC). Josephus tells this story as if it were a matter of one recalcitrant Pharisee, Eleazar, but his description of the incident as a *stasis*, i.e. a civil disturbance or revolt, suggests that it was on a larger scale.[112] We might cite, again, the Pharisees who advised the people to open the gates to Herod when he marched on Jerusalem: this is not to be seen as a pro-Herodian stance, as

---

[110] See Goodman 1987, 99f., following Mary Douglas; Saldarini 1988, 286.

[111] *Ant.* 18.12.

[112] *Ant.* 13.288–98, and 299, on which cf. Sanders 1992, 380. For the possibility that Pharisees were involved in the riot against Jannaeus (*War* 1.88f.; *Ant.* 13.372f.) cf. Sanders 381f. The fuller statements on the Pharisees in the *Ant.* cannot simply, in this light, be a later pro-rabbinic exaggeration (against Goodblatt's following of Smith's bald assertion: Goodblatt 1989; Smith 1977 [1956], see the proper critique of this position in Mason 1990, 367–71, and Stemberger 1991, 23). On Pharisees and Hasmoneans cf. Schwartz 1992, ch. 2.

their subsequent behaviour indicated, but as an anti-Hasmonean act, aimed at getting rid of Antigonus.[113] The second feature—their concern for piety—is an inference from both the rabbinic literature and the New Testament, each of which bodies of literature envisages the Pharisees as concerned with questions of purity and sabbath, which, as we shall see in chapter 8, functioned as powerful symbols of national identity.

It is vital, however, that even in this period, at the height of their influence, we do not imagine the Pharisees acting, or even thinking of themselves, as a kind of secret thought-police. They were not an official body. They were not even the official teachers of Torah: that was one of the functions of the priesthood, both in Jerusalem and in the local community.[114] They only obtained power if they colluded with or influenced another group who already possessed it. Two examples from the New Testament, in the Roman period, make the point. In the gospels, the Pharisees plot with the Herodians against a perceived common threat; thus, too, the Pharisee Saul of Tarsus sought and obtained authority from the chief priest to persecute the young church. Without that, he could legally have done nothing.[115] It is unlikely that these examples present a picture any different from what would have been the case under the Hasmoneans. The Pharisees sought to bring moral pressure to bear upon those who had actual power; to influence the masses; and to maintain their own purity as best they could. Their aim, so far as we can tell, was never simply that of private piety for its own sake. Nor (one need scarcely add) was it the system of self-salvation so often anachronistically ascribed to them by Christians who knew little about the first century but a lot about the Pelagian controversy. Their goals were the honour of Israel's god, the following of his covenant charter, and the pursuit of the full promised redemption of Israel.

2. The arrival of Roman rule in 63 BC, and the rise of Herod in the late 40s and early 30s, curtailed the possibilities of the Pharisees exerting actual power either in any official capacity or through exerting influence on those with *de jure* power. The Hasmonean rulers had endeavoured to maintain at least some appearance of ruling in accordance with Israel's heritage, and had therefore been susceptible to pressure from a group claiming to speak for that heritage. Neither the Romans nor Herod were particularly interested in following the ancestral traditions, and hence were in no need of advice or support from the Pharisees. There is no evidence, though, that the group either died out or changed its ambitions. On the contrary, we hear of the Pharisees' refusal to swear allegiance to the new rulers—hardly the action of a group which had given up politics and turned to an inner piety.[116]

The Pharisaic agenda remained, at this point, what it had always been: to purify Israel by summoning her to return to the true ancestral traditions; to restore Israel to her independent theocratic status; and to be, as a pressure-group, in the vanguard of such movements by the study and practice of Torah.

---

[113] *Ant.* 15.3. That this was not a pro-Herodian act is clear from *Ant.* 14.172ff., esp. 176.
[114] See Mason 1988; Sanders 1992, ch. 10.
[115] Mk. 3.6; Ac. 9.1–2.
[116] See Gafni 1987, 9f., and below.

This means that we must understand the Pharisees, during the Roman period, even if not, or not to the same extent, under the Hasmoneans, as moving towards an identity which can be called 'sectarian'.[117] Claiming to speak for Israel and her genuine tradition, they maintained a polemic against the ruling élite in Jerusalem and, though continuing to worship at the Temple, regarded its present officials and guardians as dangerously corrupt. Increasingly, like other Jewish sects of the period (including the Essenes and the early Christians) they regarded themselves and their own groups as in some sense or other the replacements or the equivalents of the Temple.[118] They also appear to have regarded themselves in some sense as prophets, whose traditional role always included speaking out on 'political' issues.[119]

As a result, their agenda always pushed in one of two related and parallel directions. Either they would make common cause with the out-and-out rebels, continuing the tradition of 'zeal' which we examined earlier. Or they would withdraw into the deeper private study and practice of Torah, creating an alternative mode of Judaism which achieved its liberation from Rome, and from corrupt Judaism, by living in its own world where neither pagan nor renegade could corrupt it. It seems to me highly likely that these two options, the sword and the ghetto, were among the real points at issue between the Pharisees of different schools in the Roman and Herodian periods, even though later memory depoliticized the controversy and, in a period when revolt had been abandoned as having twice led to disaster, translated it into the less threatening debate between stricter and more lenient understandings of the Torah's code of purity.[120]

Thus it appears that at least one strand of Pharisaic opinion and activity maintained a political role, and often an active revolutionary one, during the Roman period. This is by no means as widely recognized as it should be, and the evidence must be amassed step by step, as follows.

(i) Two Pharisaic leaders, Pollio and Samaias, stood out against the oath of loyalty to Herod, and won their point.[121] A larger number apparently refused

---

[117] See Cohen 1984, esp. 42ff., and Neusner 1991, 92f., against Sanders (see next note). It all depends, of course, on how one defines 'sect': see Blenkinsopp 1981, 1f.

[118] Sanders (e.g. 1990a, 248) has challenged this view in terms of its detail: the Pharisees did not attempt to live in all respects like priests, but merely made some symbolic gestures in that direction. Cohen's argument (1984) is more a priori, and powerful in establishing the *mood* of Jewish sectarianism: in setting itself up as a sect, a Jewish group was automatically staking a claim for itself over against the Temple. Here is the rationale for at least a symbolic gesture towards imitating the priests' Temple-based purity codes.

[119] e.g. *Ant*. 15.4; 17.41–4. On their veneration of prophets, Mt. 23.29–31. See Webb 1991, 326–32, showing the essentially political (and potentially eschatological/messianic) dimension of Pharisaic prophecy.

[120] See the discussions of this sort of position in Goodman 1987, 107f., 209f. The possibility of a split within Pharisaism is, surprisingly, not discussed by Sanders 1992.

[121] *Ant*. 15.370. Samaias had spoken out against Herod at his trial for killing the brigand Hezechias (*Ant*. 14.172–6) On the possible identity of this Samaias with the great teacher Shammai see Gafni 1987, 10; there is no need to link this with a possible identification of Pollio, Samaias' companion, with Hillel, and indeed this political action is far more likely to have been carried out by Shammai and a close associate, not his arch-opponent.

to take the oath of loyalty to Caesar, carrying some others with them and incurring punishment.[122]

(ii) Around the same time (though the incidents are hard to separate out and date properly), some Pharisees predicted that Herod's power would pass to his brother Pheroras. Such a treasonable statement was not the action of a group devoted to private piety: Herod killed many of his own family on lesser grounds.[123]

(iii) The incident of the removal from the Temple of the golden eagle in 4 BC definitely involved some Pharisaic teachers.[124] Josephus' description of the leaders, Judas and Matthias, as 'most learned' and 'unrivalled interpreters of the ancestral laws',[125] as well as the designation *sophistai*, 'sages',[126] indicates clearly enough that they were Pharisees, as does a comparison between this passage and those relating to the refusal of the oath to Caesar.

(iv) The rebellion of AD 6 is again to be associated with Pharisaic activity.[127] Comparison between Josephus' two accounts of this incident is instructive. In the earlier passage (*War* 2.118), he is very anxious to blame what he calls the 'Fourth Philosophy' for all Israel's troubles, and attributes the revolt to Judas the 'Galilean', describing him as a *sophistes* who 'founded a sect of his own, having nothing in common with the others' (i.e. the Pharisees, Sadducees, and Essenes). In the later account (*Antiquities* 18.23), he is more relaxed about this propaganda, and openly admits that Judas acted in close collaboration with Saddok, a Pharisee (18.4f.). The word *sophistes* itself, as we saw, may well link Judas with at least a broad stream of Pharisaic piety and aims.[128] The generalized account of revolutionary activities that follows in Josephus' longer version (*Antiquities* 18.6–10) is scarcely to be confined either to the revolt of AD 6 or to the war of 66–70. Granted the ever-fresh memory of the Maccabees, the continuing restlessness under the procurators, and the other factors to be discussed in chapters 8–10 below, it seems clear that revolt against Rome, when opportunity or incitement was offered, was a not unimportant part of the Pharisaic agenda.

(v) As we have just noted in passing, Josephus himself, when writing perhaps less guardedly, links the Fourth Philosophy closely with the Pharisees. The difference, it appears, was not one of underlying ideology or long-term

---

[122] *Ant.* 17.41–5; *War* 1.571–3. These passages are discussed by Schwarz 1983 (attributing the anti-Pharisaic statements to Nicolas); Baumgarten 1991, 119f.; Sanders 1992, 384 and 532 n.5 (suggesting that the two accounts of oath-refusal are doublets, with the latter the more accurate); and now Mason 1991, *passim*. For the Pharisees' generally negative attitude towards Herod see e.g. Alon 1977, 37–40. On the significance of the *Ant.* passage for the size of the Pharisaic party, see below.

[123] *War* 1.567–72; *Ant.* 17.41–5.

[124] *Ant.* 17.149–67; *War* 1.648–55; see p. 172 above. See Stern 1973, 144, linking this movement both with the later revolt and with the House of Shammai; Sanders 1992, 384f.

[125] *Ant.* 17.149.

[126] *Ant.* 17.152.

[127] *Ant.* 18.4–10; *War* 2.118. See p. 173 above.

[128] cf. too *War* 2.433, where he is describes as *sophistes deinotatos*, 'a most forceful teacher'. The description of someone as *deinos kai sophos*, 'skilful and wise', goes back at least as far as Herodotus (5.23) and Sophocles (*Philoctetes* 440). On Pharisaic involvement with revolt at this stage and subsequently see Schürer 2.603 n.36 (written by C. T. R. Hayward); Sanders 1992, 385.

aims, but of the lengths to which one was willing to go to propagate them. If we agree with the majority of scholars that Josephus had a general desire to screen the Pharisees from criticism, this comment is extremely revealing. If we agree with Mason that he was trying to blacken their character, this still does not mean that he was making it up.[129] Josephus may have been quite well aware of the range of views within the Pharisaic movement.

(vi) At this point belongs the testimony of an ex-Pharisee, Saul of Tarsus. By his own account he had himself persecuted the church, 'being extremely zealous for the traditions of my fathers'.[130] Here we have exactly the mixture of elements which, I suggest, characterized one branch at least of Pharisaism in this period: study of the ancestral traditions, 'zeal', and physical violence directed against a deviant group. If, as we shall see later, this marks Saul of Tarsus out against some other Pharisees from the 30s and 40s, this indicates a division within the movement rather than an inaccuracy within the sources.[131]

(vii) Josephus records a strange incident during the reign of Herod Agrippa (AD 37–44). A devout Pharisee, one Simon, denounced Agrippa (in his absence) as being unclean and hence not worthy to enter the Temple.[132] Agrippa showed him extraordinary kindness and forbearance. Josephus has probably exaggerated this element, but has again included, against the grain of his normal agenda, this story about a Pharisee who, 'with a reputation for religious scrupulousness', acted on this basis in what could well, in other circumstances, have turned into some kind of revolt.

(viii) Another odd incident relates to the time of the procurator Felix (AD 52–60).[133] Josephus, having described the activities of the Sicarii or 'dagger-men', then mentions another group of 'evil men' (*poneroi*), who have 'purer hands but more evil thoughts' (*cheiri men katharoteron, tais gnomais de asebesteron*). It is impossible to be sure who this group were, who with revolutionary intent and prophetic fervour led a group into the wilderness in the hopes of there receiving 'signs of freedom' (*semeia eleutherias*), and who were cut down by Felix's soldiers. But the description of their 'clean hands' cannot but raise suspicions that they were Pharisees.[134]

(ix) It seems likely that those who complained to Agrippa II about the killing of James at the instigation of Ananus the high priest, during the interregnum between the procurators Festus and Albinus (i.e. AD 62), were also Pharisees.[135] Josephus describes them as 'those of the city who were considered the fairest-minded, and who were strict concerning the law', the latter

---

[129] Mason 1991, 282–5, suggests that the association of Pharisees with the revolt is a 'wild insinuation' designed to blacken their reputation. This seems to me to carry Mason's revisionist thesis too far. I here prefer Sanders 1992, 408f.

[130] *Gal.* 1.13–14.

[131] On the possibility that Saul was a Shammaite see below.

[132] *Ant.* 19.332–4. According to a variant reading, the charge related to Agrippa's part-Edomite descent. See Feldman's note in the Loeb edition of Josephus, 9.370f. The point is irrelevant for the present discussion. There is no good reason to doubt that this Simon really was a Pharisee (see Goodblatt 1989, 27).

[133] *War* 2.258–9.

[134] So Hengel 1989 [1961], 233, following Zeitlin.

[135] *Ant.* 20.200–2; the description of the protesters is at 201. See Baumgarten 1983, 413f.

phrase echoing other descriptions of Pharisees. While this incident does not of itself link the Pharisees with revolution, it certainly stands against any attempt to claim that by this stage the party had long since become concerned only with private piety and devout table-fellowship. They were capable of making their voices heard on a sensitive political issue.

(x) When we reach Josephus' account of the war itself, we find one leading Pharisee, Simon ben Gamaliel, who turns out to be a close associate of one of the key popular leaders, John of Gischala.[136] Although he is mentioned as opposing the 'Zealots', this relates to the party that assumed that name rather than to the anti-Roman movement itself, in which of course John was one of the leaders. Clearly Simon's Pharisaism was no bar to his taking part in revolutionary activities.

(xi) Further direct evidence of Pharisaic involvement in the war comes with the mention of Ananias ben Sadok.[137] Hengel sees his agenda as an example of the synergism of the Pharisees (the compromise position between determinism and free will: see below) being 'transferred to the plane of eschatological hope'.[138] It seems to me more likely that Josephus' description of 'synergism' as a philosophical doctrine held by the Pharisees is his own transferring of an essentially political doctrine (that humans must work for freedom as well as waiting for it, even though it comes ultimately from above) into the 'safe' sphere of philosophical discussion.

(xii) One small piece of evidence from the period of the war indicates that Pharisaic piety and revolutionary fervour did indeed continue to go hand in hand. Excavations on Masada have revealed that the ritual bathing-pools, the *mikvaot*, were built to Pharisaic specifications; and other signs of Pharisaic piety are visible as well. Hengel's conclusion is quite justified: 'at least some parts of the Pharisaical party were closer to the fourth sect in its hostility towards the Romans than the later rabbinic tradition [and, we might add, Josephus] would have us believe'.[139]

(xiii) We shall presently examine evidence in two final areas which conclude this argument about the political stance of the Pharisees in the main Roman period: I refer (a) to the continuing revolutionary tendencies of some at least of the Pharisees' would-be successors after AD 70, and (b) to the significance of the Pharisaic prayers, beliefs and practices.

We may sum up the position so far as follows. We have found that in the period between the arrival of the Romans in 63 BC and the fall of Jerusalem in AD 70 there is a good deal of evidence for continuing political and revolutionary activity on the part of the Pharisees—evidence which Josephus has included in his account despite his clear wish to exonerate the party as a whole. Equally, it is clear from the broad drift of the post-70 accounts of pre-70 Pharisees that there were major divisions within the movement, and it is

---

[136] *War* 4.159 (where he is called Symeon); *Life* 189–98. For the suggestion that John too was a Pharisee see Roth 1962, 69, with Jos. *Life* 74–6.

[137] *War* 2.451; he is mentioned as a Pharisee in *Life* 197, 290.

[138] Hengel 1989 [1961], 123.

[139] Hengel 1989 [1961], 88, with details; cp. also 401f., and esp. Sanders 1992, 224–9, 407ff. There is a photograph of the Masada bathing-pools in Stern 1973, 140.

highly likely that one of the key issues concerned precisely the extent to which involvement in practical politics in general, and in revolution in particular, was appropriate for members of the movement. We may hypothesize that the arrival of Roman power, and the rise of Herod and his house, projected the Pharisees into a new situation, different from that which they had faced under the Hasmoneans, and one which produced a wide range of responses.

We may safely assume that, though some Pharisaic opinion may have been polarized, there will have been something of a continuum of Pharisaic response to the new situation. At one point on this continuum we find Hillel, with his successors being Gamaliel in the 40s AD and Johanan ben Zakkai after 70. Each, it seems, was prepared to argue against revolution and in favour of retreating from the political sphere into the world of Torah study. (This too, of course, is a 'political' stance.) Let the Romans rule the world, as long as we can study and practise Torah. Here, if anywhere, we find a move towards the position of the later (i.e. post-135) sages. We also find, interestingly, a pointer in the direction of Josephus' own position, that Israel's god has gone over to the the Romans. Evidence for this more open Pharisaic stance may also be provided by the Pharisees mentioned in Luke 7.36ff., 11.37ff. and 13.31f.

At quite another point on the continuum we find Shammai and his house, advocating some kind of revolutionary 'zeal'.[140] Although the discussions at Jamnia moved rabbinic Judaism firmly towards Hillelite rulings, we have every reason to think that up until 70 it was the Shammaites who dominated, and that they may have continued to be a vocal and sometimes victorious presence in the period between 70 and 135.[141] The Pharisaic movement as a whole was dominated in this period by those at this point on the spectrum of opinion, whose inclinations brought them near to, and quite possibly right within, the revolutionary movements which, though coming to fullest expression in 4 BC, AD 6, 66–70 and 132–5, smouldered ceaselessly throughout the period. If we recall, as we saw at the start of the present chapter, the basic difference between the wealthier city-dwellers and the poorer folk in the countryside, it should come as no surprise to find hints that the Hillelites tended to be city-dwellers while the Shammaites enjoyed support from rural areas.[142]

When did this split within Pharisaism arise? Alon suggests[143] that the two strains, one pro-zealotry, the other ready to accept Roman rule, arose in the time after the reign of Agrippa I and before the war (i.e. between 44 and 66).

---

[140] See Gafni 1987, 11, citing mShabb. 1.4; tShabb. 1.16–20; yShabb. 1, 3c; bShabb. 13b. These passages discuss the '18 decrees', which enforced a stricter separation between Jews and Gentiles; the Shammaites imposed these, against Hillelite opposition, not long before the outbreak of war in 66. Cf. Cohen 1979, 218 n.73; Hengel 1989 [1961], 200–6: Hengel speaks of a 'deep inner division within the Pharisaical party, in which the more radical Shammaitic wing was relatively close to the Zealot movement' (206, cf. 334f.).

[141] So Hengel 1989 [1961], 334, following Finkelstein, Moore and Schlatter. See particularly e.g. mShabb. 1.4, with its 'patriotic undertones' (Roth 1962, 78).

[142] So Finkelstein 1962 [1938], 619f., discussed in Hengel 1989 [1961], 333f. See too Schäfer 1990, 296, arguing that between 70 and 135 there existed a large number of Jews who had assimilated to Roman culture, and who were predominantly city-dwellers.

[143] Alon 1977, 43f., 47.

He also suggests the existence of a third party in the middle, represented by Simeon ben Gamaliel, who took what Alon regards as the classical Pharisaic position, only joining the armed struggle when there was good opportunity for success and no other alternative. I am not sure that we have enough evidence to say precisely when the split(s) occurred, except that it was at some stage between 63 BC and AD 66; I think it most likely happened when Herod took over from the Hasmoneans. This fits perfectly with the likely date for Hillel and Shammai as the founders of two new 'schools' within Pharisaism.

We have every reason, further, to suppose that with these political concerns went a concern for the maintenance, within and perhaps beyond the group, of certain purity codes. Sanders has shown just how difficult it is to be absolutely sure precisely which bits of later purity laws were observed by Pharisees in this period. But that they tried to maintain purity at a degree higher than that prescribed in the Hebrew Bible for ordinary Jews under ordinary conditions is not in question. And it seems most likely that, whether in great detail or in symbolic gestures, their purity codes bore some familial relationship to the purity codes required for priests when on duty in the Temple. As we shall see later, the Temple functioned as the controlling symbol for Pharisees no less than for other Jews; and the purity codes functioned as a key means of granting to ordinary domestic life, and in particular the private study of Torah, the status that would normally only accrue to those who were serving in the presence of Israel's god within his Temple.

How much influence did the Pharisees seek, and how much did they actually wield, during this period? The question needs to be approached from both ends. (a) Josephus (and/or his sources) may have exaggerated the extent to which they had influence with the masses and the government under the Hasmoneans, but the arguments in favour of this look considerably weaker since the publication of Mason's recent book, and there is no reason to think that the Pharisees had no influence at all in that period. (b) It is clear that some at least of the Pharisees' successors came to hold positions of authority, both *de facto* and *de jure*, in the post-70 period. Therefore, (c) it is probably easier to postulate a continuum once more, in which the Pharisees still held influence in the period 63 BC to AD 70, albeit of a modified sort, rather than to assert, as has been popular recently, that they neither sought nor wielded any influence beyond their own ranks. The level of such influence is impossible to gauge accurately, but the fact that some Pharisees at least were clearly respected political figures (Gamaliel, Simon ben Gamaliel, and others during the war) should incline us to think that they were not without a voice in the official councils of state; and, *a fortiori*, it is highly likely that their influence as *de facto* teachers of the masses (even though the priests remained the *de jure* teachers) will have remained considerable. Certainly the burden of proof now rests, I suggest, on any who wish to argue the opposite.[144]

As to their geographical spread and numerical strength: it has recently been asserted that in the time of Jesus the Pharisees were a small group, numbering

---

[144] See now, rightly, Mason 1990, and esp. 1991, 372f., against Smith and his followers.

a few thousand at most, and based almost entirely in Jerusalem.[145] The arguments advanced in support of this turn out to be extremely slender. On the matter of their location, that their base was in Jerusalem is not surprising (John 4.1–3 indicates as much); that they had representatives in most areas, Galilee included, is highly likely.[146] We have already seen that the revolution of Judas the Galilean was in all probability closely bound up with the Shammaite wing of the Pharisees. The story of Johanan ben Zakkai, who represented the other extreme of the movement, denouncing the Galileans as Torah-haters[147] may well show that the Galileans as a whole did not follow the Pharisees, but if anything it proves (not least in view of the parallel with Matthew 11.20–4) that there had been considerable Pharisaic activity there; and in any case the story may be a reflection of Hillel/Shammai polemic rather than the denunciation of non-Pharisees by Pharisees.[148] It is not without interest that among the mentions of Pharisees in this period (apart from those in the gospels) there are four occasions when they are sent, with higher authority, from Jerusalem (or, in the last case, Jamnia) on missions to the north, to sort out trouble in Galilee or further afield.[149] The question we might ask is not, whether Pharisees became involved in such missions; the question is, what sort of issues might call them forth. Discussion of that must be postponed for the moment.

As to their numbers, the only figure we have is the 'over 6,000' mentioned in *Antiquities* 17.42 as refusing to take the oath to Caesar. But this figure, coming most likely to Josephus from Nicolas of Damascus, and referring to an event which took place in Jerusalem in the latter years of Herod's reign (roughly 10 BC), can scarcely be used to give an accurate assessment of the number of Pharisees in Jerusalem, let alone in the country as a whole, let alone spread across Judaism in the Diaspora, half a century later—especially when that half-century had contained at least two major revolts which might

[145] Sanders 1985, e.g. 194–8, 292; 1992, 14, 398, 412, etc., following Smith 1977 [1956], 1978, 153–7. Sanders' new book (1992), however, makes no mention of the geographical point on which he laid such stress in 1985.

[146] See e.g. Dunn 1988, esp. 280f.; Goodman 1987, 73ff.; Freyne 1988, 200ff. Dunn notes in particular the incident in *Ant.* 20.38–48, involving a Pharisee from Galilee named Eleazar. In addition to the arguments presented by Dunn, we might consider passages such as mYad. 4.8, which describes a dispute between Pharisees and 'a Galilean heretic'; and the evidence for a strong hasidic movement in Galilee (see Gafni 1987, 13, citing Safrai).

[147] yShabb. 16.8 (15d end).

[148] Against Smith 1978, 157. Freyne (1980, 341 n.74) dismisses the possibility, suggested by Finkel and Abrahams, of Shammai himself being a Galilean. See Neusner 1970, 47 for Johanan's residence in Galilee for eighteen years, probably between AD 20 and 40, and ibid. 47, 51 for Hanina ben Dosa also living in the area. For the possibility that Johanan had been part of the delegation sent to Josephus, see Roth 1962, 72f. Smith's idea that the Pharisees sent as a delegation to Galilee after the start of the war 'had been chosen to impress the Galileans by their rarity' (Smith 1978, 157) is faintly ridiculous.

[149] Saul of Tarsus, Ac. 9.1f.; Josephus, *Life* 62ff.; Jonathan, Ananias, Jozar and Simon (the latter from the high priestly family, the rest being Pharisees), *Life* 196ff.; one of Johanan's pupils, sent to investigate a strange holy man who was living at Beth Rama, probably in Galilee (Freyne 1980, 316).

well have encouraged others to join the movement.[150] To be sure, this does not mean that we must go back to the former days of imagining the Pharisees to be a large, ubiquitous and all-powerful group. But it does mean that they were, in this period, in all probability reasonably numerous, reasonably widespread, and reasonably influential.

3. We now turn to the period from AD 70 to 135. It might be thought that the events of AD 70 would have brought about that great change from political involvement to pious devotion that has been postulated to explain the difference between Josephus' Pharisees and those of the Mishnah.[151] But there is evidence of continuing Pharisaic involvement in revolution in the next period too, up to the events of 132–5. First, Eliezer ben Hyrcanus, one of the great rabbis of the so-called Jamnia period, is reported to have spoken of the destruction of Rome as the precondition of the kingdom of Israel's god, as predicted in Zechariah.[152] Eliezer's excommunication by the more moderate Gamaliel II[153] may well have had more to do with major differences on matters of political stance than with detailed debates about Torah; in such matters, it is clear that considerable debates could rage without one side ever excommunicating the other. It looks as though the different strands in pre-70 Pharisaism, witnessed to in the debates between Hillel and Shammai and their respective followers, continued to be a feature of the post-70 reconstruction period. It has even been speculated that the revolt in 132 was itself one result of the achievement of Jamnia: the Jews felt sufficiently united and consolidated to risk a further engagement with Rome.[154]

The second, most obvious, example of a post-70 sage who clearly stood in continuity with the Pharisaic tradition, and equally clearly supported active anti-Roman revolution, is of course Akiba himself, the best-known of the generation who grew up under the Jamnia regime.[155] His hailing of Simeon ben Kosiba as Messiah was opposed by some of his contemporaries, but the reasons given have to do with chronology rather than ideology: Akiba has got his arithmetic wrong, and he will be dead and buried long before the Messiah

---

[150] Josephus' figure of 'over 6,000' has been greatly over-used in modern discussion, and sometimes distorted (Freyne 1988, 200, says *'no more than* 6,000'; my italics).

[151] On this point see now Stemberger 1991, 129–35.

[152] MekEx. on 17.14 (1.2.158). On Eliezer see Schürer 2.373–4, and particularly Neusner 1973 (for the Shammaite influence on Eliezer, cf. Neusner 1973, vol.2, index s.v. Shammai, House of; Neusner notes (e.g. 2.307–10) that the later rabbinic traditions by no means uniformly support the view that Eliezer was a Shammaite, but this is most likely a later toning down of a problematic tradition); and Hengel 1989 [1961] 108f. I think Hengel in turn tones down unnecessarily the possibility that Eliezer himself, whom he describes as 'a "Zealot" among learned Jews', may have been active in promoting, and not merely hoping for, revolution. See too Neusner 1979, arguing (23–30) that Eliezer represented a post-70 continuation of pre-70s Pharisaism, though not in a slavish fashion, while Johanan ben Zakkai represented the old scribal tradition (ibid., 37ff.).

[153] See Neusner, 1973, 1979.

[154] See the discussions in Gafni 1984, 31; Schäfer 1990, who argues that the bar-Kochba revolt was led by priests and supported by rural folk still loyal to Torah (297).

[155] On Akiba see Schäfer 1978, 65–121; 1980; 1981; Schürer 1.543f., 552 n.173; 2.378–8; Urbach 1987 [1975], 673f. Alon 1977, 45f. argues strongly that 'the majority of the Pharisees were in agreement with R. Akiba and Bar Kokhba'.

comes.[156] No-one dared to suggest that the expectation of a warlike Messiah who would liberate Israel from Rome ran counter to received wisdom. Akiba, regarded in some later traditions as the 'father of the Mishnah', remains both in his enthusiasm for bar-Kochba and in his noble martyrdom a clear example of the continuing marriage of politics and piety which had been evident, so far as we can tell, from the very beginning of the Pharisaic movement.

Between 70 and 135, then, the two strands we have already observed remained, but no longer as 'Pharisees'. It is important to note the full complexity of the situation. (a) The two 'houses' are both regarded by the rabbinic sages as their spiritual ancestors, even though after 135 the political aspect was firmly submerged and the pious agenda exalted. The sages of Jamnia and afterwards were not coterminous with the Pharisees before 70, nor were they the descendants of one party within Pharisaism. They represented a variety of positions, many of which could trace some roots in the variety of pre-70 Judaism.[157] (b) It is not simply the case that Hillel and his house represent 'piety', and Shammai and his house 'politics'. It is only when the revolutionary option has finally and visibly been excluded—i.e. after 135—that an actual split between 'politics' and 'piety' begins to make some sense (despite the anachronisms of those who try to push such a split back not only before 70 but into the Hasmonean period).[158]

Rather, those who were happy to focus their whole attention on the scribal interpretation of Torah were able to do so, under the leadership of Johanan ben Zakkai and subsequently Gamaliel II. Those who followed the stricter old Pharisaic agenda, and clung to the hope of revolution, included Eliezer ben Hyrcanus and, a little later, Akiba. But there remained debate and flexibility within and between the two positions, so that, just as Saul of Tarsus was able to take a very different line to that of his teacher Gamaliel, Nehunya (see below) was able to promulgate the opposite view to that of his teacher Akiba.

Whether we follow Neusner and see Johanan's tradition as 'scribal' and Eliezer's as strictly 'Pharisaic', or whether we speculate that the debate between Johanan and Eliezer was the sharp focal point of the long-running debate between the houses of Hillel (Johanan) and Shammai (Eliezer), is therefore probably a matter of words rather than substance. A great transition had been effected, and the new groupings reflected different reactions to the new situation as much as continuity with different pre-70 strands of Jewish piety and tradition. In any case, we may assume that between 70 and 135 the situation remained far more fluid than the later rabbinic traditions admit. Had

---

[156] yTaan. 68d, with the objection coming from R. Yohanan ben Torta: see Beckwith 1981, esp. 536–9. For the view that the objection concerns bar-Kochba's not coming from Davidic stock, see Urbach 1987 [1975], 674. Even in this case, the objectors would still have been happy in principle with the idea of a nationalist, Davidic Messiah who would come to lead Israel in a war of liberation (against Schäfer 1990, 290ff., who sees Akiba as perhaps in a minority; this seems unlikely in view of the veneration of Akiba in later Judaism despite the rejection of his political stance).

[157] Sanders 1992, 412 repeats the usual view, that the post-70 rabbis are the direct heirs of the pre-70 Pharisees.

[158] Notably, of course, Rivkin 1978. See the criticisms by Cohen 1980 and Baumgarten 1991, 110–14. As we saw earlier, to retreat from active 'political' life is itself a 'political' decision.

the house of Hillel prevailed as thoroughly as those writings suggest, there would have been no support for bar-Kochba's rebellion. As it was, it was supported by Akiba himself, who in retrospect is perhaps the greatest transitional figure of them all: clearly standing in the line of the politically active and revolutionary-minded Pharisees from the days of the Hasmoneans and Herod, he is then looked back to and reverenced as a great Torah-teacher by those who, in a drastically changed situation, highlighted concerns of which he would undoubtedly have approved but which he would have set in a completely different context.

4. After the second revolt there began the period which marked the real beginning of what we know as rabbinic Judaism. From then on revolutionary talk was taboo. It was rabbi Nehunya ben ha-Kanah, a disciple of Akiba, who gave voice to the changed mood: 'He that takes upon himself the yoke of the Law, from him shall be taken away the yoke of the kingdom and the yoke of worldly care,' and vice versa. In other words, study of Torah means that one need not be concerned about political power.[159] Here Nehunya is closer to Johanan ben Zakkai than to Eliezer or his (Nehunya's) teacher Akiba. Those who study Torah in that mood will not need a Temple: Torah will do instead, as is said in the very next Mishnah saying, ascribed to rabbi Halafta ben Dosa, a sage of the second half of the second century: 'If ten men sit together and occupy themselves in the Law, the Divine Presence rests among them': in other words, study of Torah has the same effect as worship in the Temple. In either case one is in the presence of the Shekinah, the localized dwelling-place of Israel's god.[160] From this point of view anything that might be gained by revolution—and the chief thing to be gained by Jewish revolution was always the proper and divinely sanctioned rebuilding of the Temple—was pushed into the distant future. Energy which had previously been directed into revolutionary politics was now to be channelled into revisionist scholarship. Modern Judaism had come to birth.

We may now stand back from this chronological sequence and observe two vital features which we have not yet discussed. I refer to prayer and theology.

First, if we know anything about the Pharisees we know that they prayed, and we know more or less what they prayed for. They prayed the *Shema*; they prayed the *Shemoneh Esreh*, the Eighteen Benedictions. But these prayers, in their origin, are very far from being the articulation of an escapist piety. The *Shema*, in claiming Israel's god as the one god of all the earth, sustains the belief that this god will vindicate his people. It is no accident that Akiba was reciting the *Shema* as the Romans tortured him to death.[161] The Eighteen Benedictions include such ideas as the bringing of a redeemer to Israel, the resurrection of the dead, the proclamation of liberation with a great trumpet, and the gathering of the dispersed Israelites, the destruction of Israel's

---

[159] mAb. 3.5. Murphy 1985 has argued that *2 Bar.* represents a similar position.

[160] mAb. 3.6. The discussion goes on to assert that the same is true where five study; where three; where two; and even where one studies alone.

[161] See Schürer 2.454–5; on Akiba see bBer. 61b. Even if this account is wholly legendary it supports the basic point about the link between this prayer and revolutionary aspirations. For the *Shema* as a proclamation of the kingdom of god see Hengel 1989 [1961], 92–9.

enemies, the restoration of Jerusalem and the Temple, and the coming of the Messiah.[162] It would be a bold historian who, faced with the actual events of the period between the Maccabees and bar-Kochba, undertook to argue that those who prayed these prayers day and night never understood them in a literal sense, and never sought to act as the agents of Israel's god in bringing to pass, through political and revolutionary action, the blessings for which they were asking. These prayers, of course, continued to be prayed after 135. But from then on, as the saying from R. Nehunya demonstrates, they were systematically reread in relation to the new world order which was experienced by those who gave themselves to study of Torah. And in this world order, as one of its most notable modern exponents has insisted, theology and history have nothing to say to each other.[163]

The second more general consideration concerns the Pharisaic belief-system. Josephus' account of this gives prominence to the idea of resurrection.[164] This belief, however, is not merely to do with speculation about a future life after death. As we can see from some of the early texts which articulate it, it is bound up with the desire for a reconstituted and restored Israel.[165] This, as we shall see later, is probably the real reason why the Sadducees rejected it.[166] The last thing they wanted was a major upheaval which might well snatch away their precarious power.

The other Pharisaic belief to which Josephus draws attention is the idea of providence or fate.[167] The doctrine of the Essenes, he says, 'is wont to leave everything in the hands of God';[168] the Sadducees, on the other hand, believe that everything comes down to the exercise of human free will.[169] The Pharisees take a middle position, believing that, though everything is brought about by providence, humans still possess free will.[170] Josephus in these passages is once more clearly 'translating' the actual points at issue into Hellenistic philosophical language, using standard phrases to give his Roman audience the impression of the Jewish sects as Greek-style philosophical schools, sitting around debating abstract issues. It is not difficult to see through this disguise to the socio-political reality behind it. The Essenes proclaimed by their very mode of existence that, though they longed for the liberation of Israel, they were simply going to wait and allow Israel's god to bring it to pass

---

[162] See Schürer 2. 455–63, and the discussion in Hengel 1989 [1961], 107f. On these and other prayers as evidence for a concrete hope of national redemption see Urbach 1987 [1975], 653–60.

[163] Neusner 1991, 83f. Freeman 1986 includes an appendix on the political concepts latent in liturgical sources.

[164] *War* 2.162–3; *Ant.* 18.14 (on which see Feldman's note in the Loeb of Josephus, 9.13); compare *War* 3.374; *Apion* 2.218, both of which seem to have 'translated' the Jewish doctrine of resurrection into almost Stoic terms. See too Ac. 23.6–8, mSanh. 10.1. See the full discussions in Schürer 2.539–47; Mason 1991, 156–70, 297–300; and ch. 10 below.

[165] See e.g. Ezek. 37.1–14; 2 Macc. 7.7–40.

[166] *War* 2.165; *Ant.* 18.16; Mt. 22.23 and pars.; Ac. 23.6–8; and ch. 10 below.

[167] On this, see now Mason 1991, 132–56, 293–7, 384–98.

[168] *Ant.* 18.18.

[169] *War* 2.164f.

[170] *War* 2.162f.; *Ant.* 13.172, 18.13.

in his own time. The Sadducees proclaimed by their very existence that they believed in seizing and maintaining political power for themselves. This much is clear from what we know of the Essenes and Sadducees. Reasoning in parallel, we may take it that the Pharisees' belief was as follows: Israel's god will act; but loyal Jews may well be required as the agents and instruments of that divine action. This fits completely with all the other evidence we have studied, and indeed hints at the further debate within Pharisaism itself, with Hillel (and Gamaliel, as in Acts 5.33–9) inclining more in the direction of leaving the issue to Israel's god, and Shammai (and Saul of Tarsus) wanting to act as the means of that divine intervention. Behind Josephus' unthreatening depiction of philosophical debate there stands the turbulent world of first-century political and revolutionary struggle.[171]

We may therefore sum up this discussion of the Pharisees as follows. Having begun as a religious/political pressure-group at the time of the Maccabees, the Pharisees attained their greatest *de facto* power under the later Hasmoneans. The rise of the Herodian dynasty, and the rule of the procurators, did not in principle dampen their ardour for Israel's freedom from pagan practices and pagan rule, and many of them continued to be active in movements for revolt right up to 135.[172] At the same time, we cannot simply agree with the idea that a shift from politics to piety took place, as described by Neusner and his followers in relation to the time of Hillel, and then transfer such a shift from this period to the time after 135. It is likely that the two 'houses' of Hillel and Shammai already represented two alternative ways of being Pharisees. Both were concerned with Israel's liberation, and with the maintenance of purity on the part of those committed to this cause. But the former was happier to leave the issue to Israel's god, and the latter eager to become the zealous agent of the divine action. Both were devout; both were, in the senses already described, 'political'; they simply had different ways of putting the two things together.

Two final notes. Disputes between the different Pharisaic schools are the stuff of which the Mishnah is made up. These debates were conducted over several generations, at various levels. The detailed debates about purity almost certainly carried, for the debaters, echoes of the larger issues, much as a small debating point in contemporary politics will generate heat because all sides know the larger issues which remain unmentioned but powerfully symbolized. There is a vital difference between debates like this, with all parties regarding one another as fellow-Pharisees,[173] and disputes between Pharisees in general and non-Pharisees, such as Sadducees, Christians, or Essenes. We have, in fact, some reason to think that even the intra-Pharisaic debates were not carried on simply in the later Mishnaic mood of tolerance and banter, but

---

[171] See Hengel 1989 [1961], 122f.

[172] We have thus followed up and substantiated the suggestions made in Hengel 1989 [1961], 228, 334; Saldarini 1988, 285–7; Rhoads 1976, 38f.; and Sanders 1990a, 242–5, against Smith 1977 [1956]; Neusner 1973 (and elsewhere); Levine 1978. Berger 1988 is, I think, right in seeing the Palestinian Pharisees as remaining a political grouping, but almost certainly wrong to drive a wedge (261) between this stance and the 'religious' stance of Diaspora Pharisees.

[173] So Finkelstein 1962 [1938], 334.

sometimes involved, in the pre-70 period, violence and threats.[174] Contemporary analogies suggest that when a nation or group is in a tight corner, small issues acquire huge symbolic significance and evoke passion. Even after 70, one side was capable of excommunicating a leading member of the opposition, as in the case of Eliezer ben Hyrcanus.[175] When even sharper issues were involved, in which the entire Pharisaic programme was called into question, we have evidence quite apart from the New Testament to suggest that the Pharisees (or some of them at least) were not slow to respond.

Second, and finally, this account of the Pharisees enables us to understand the way in which our various sources have come to be what they are. (1) Josephus is concerned in the *War* to minimize the Pharisees' involvement in revolution, and to present them as a Hellenistic philosophical school. In the *Antiquities* he allows a different view to come into sight.[176] Reading him critically, he remains of the greatest value. (2) The cryptic references in the Scrolls tell us enough to satisfy us that the Pharisees were regarded as a rival sect by the writers of the Scrolls in the first century BC. (3) Paul reflects the 'zeal' of the Shammaite, despite attempts to make him into a Hillelite;[177] that after his conversion he changed in several notable respects, becoming in some ways apparently closer to Hillel, is scarcely surprising. His prime concern now was the admission of Gentiles into the one covenant people of Israel's god, and his argument was not that paganism was after all to be validated, but that Gentile converts to Christianity were no longer pagans. Paul saw himself as remaining true to Israel's covenant heritage in the light of the new situation: Israel's god had finally acted to liberate his people.[178] (4) & (5) The blocks of evidence from the gospels and from the rabbinic literature are both slanted, but in different directions. The gospels read the debates between Jesus and the Pharisees as foreshadowings both of the 'trial' of Jesus himself and of the missionary concerns of the early church; as we shall see later, the synoptic disputes concerning sabbath and food have to do not with an inner-Pharisaic problem but with the mutual self-definition of two (in some respects) sectarian movements. The rabbis of the Mishnah and afterwards understood the Pharisees as forerunners of their concern for purity, a concern that had turned in on itself and created its own shut-in world after the crushing defeats of 70 and 135. They therefore translated the political debates of their putative predecessors into the language of purity, just as Josephus had translated them into the language of philosophy.

At no point in these sources are we able to read a picture of the Pharisees straight off the text. But at no point are we forced, as some reconstructions

---

[174] See Goodman 1987, 74f.

[175] See above, p. 163.

[176] I thus side firmly with e.g. Schwarz 1983 and Mason 1990, 1991 (their own debate about Nicolas notwithstanding) against e.g. Smith 1977 [1956] and Goodblatt 1989. Even if it were true that in *Ant.* Josephus overstressed the Pharisees' real power, this would not mean that we should ignore evidence from *Ant.* in favour of the abbreviated (and itself highly prejudiced) account in *War*.

[177] See Jeremias 1969b, opposed by e.g. Bruce 1977, 51.

[178] On Paul see further Wright 1991a, and vol. 3 in the present series.

have been, to eliminate altogether, or for that matter to elevate to a position of infallible 'objectivity', any one strand of the evidence. The Pharisees remain a complex and elusive group. But this has not prevented us from sketching in some basic historical probabilities about them, which will enable us in subsequent chapters to show how their worldview and belief-system formed an important variation within the broad spectrum of options open to first-century Jews. These are, as we shall see, of considerable interest and value as part of the whole picture of Judaism and Christianity in the first century of the Common Era.

4. The Essenes: Spotlight on a Sect

Scholars will, no doubt, continue to debate whether or not the Pharisees were a 'sect'. There can be no such debate about the group that lived at Qumran, by the north-west shore of the Dead Sea. If ever there was a sect, this was it: isolated from the rest of Israel geographically and theologically, claiming to be the true heir of all the promises and the scriptures, regarding even devout Jews of other persuasions as dangerous deceivers. They were the Sons of Light, so they thought, and all others, not just the pagans, were the Sons of Darkness. This group is, in fact, one of the clearest examples known to us of what a sect looks like.[179]

But if there is no debate about that, there is plenty about almost everything else to do with Qumran. The first wave of Scrolls studies, between their discovery (1947) and the publication of the section on the Scrolls in the revised Schürer (1979), seemed to have arrived at a solid conclusion about the origin and history of the community: they were the Essenes, of whose existence we had known from Philo, Josephus and Pliny.[180] But the last decade or so has seen this consensus under increasingly heavy fire. The double equation 'Qumran community = Essenes = writers of the Scrolls' is no longer held across the board. Many now argue that those who lived at Qumran were a subgroup, perhaps a splinter-group, of a much wider Essene movement, or perhaps the original group from which that wider movement grew. Detailed study of the Scrolls themselves indicates that they come from subtly but significantly different communities: the *Damascus Document*, in particular, represents a different community and organization from the *Community Rule*.[181] It has even been argued, though most would still regard this as unlikely, that the Scrolls themselves were not written at Qumran at all, but were simply taken there for

---

[179] Davies 1990, 513 defines 'sects' as 'socially closed systems governed by non-conformist ideologies'. See Sanders 1992, 352: the group that wrote 1QS is a sect, that responsible for CD is not.

[180] Philo, *Quod Omn.* 12 (75)–13 (91); *De Vit. Contempl.*; Jos. *War* 2.119–61; *Ant.* 13.171–2; 18.11, 18–22; Pliny the Elder, *Nat. Hist.* 5.15/73. For full details and discussion see particularly Vermes 1977; 1987 [1962], 1–57; Schürer 2.555–90; Dimant 1984; Calloway 1988; Schiffman 1989. See most recently Sanders 1992, chs. 16–17.

[181] See esp. Davies 1982; 1987; 1990; following, in part, Murphy-O'Connor in a series of articles, esp. 1974. See also Charlesworth 1980, and, for a different view, Wacholder 1983.

safe keeping with the approach of war in the mid-60s AD.[182] Like the Delphic oracle, the caves, in revealing their secrets, have created more questions.

Fortunately for our present purpose, which is to examine the Judaisms which form the matrix of early Christianity, these questions do not need to be settled. However many groups or individuals may have written this or that scroll, or part of a scroll, what is interesting for our purposes is *how some Jews thought, lived and prayed in the period*, that is, what options were open, under certain circumstances, in terms of new ways of reading scripture, organizing community, expressing faith and hope. Whereas with the Pharisees we are dealing with a movement which early Christianity regarded as a rival, and which Paul in particular knew as his own background, with the Essenes and/or the Qumran community and/or the writers of the Scrolls we have no good evidence, despite the occasional flurry of journalistic activity, to connect any or all of them directly with either Jesus, Paul, or the early church. Anticipating our later conclusion, we may suggest that they can be seen as a cousin of early Christianity: sharing the same ancestor (pre-Maccabaean Judaism), exhibiting some family similarities, but without direct derivation or even visible links.

We may therefore embark on a brief general account of the Scrolls, designed to highlight certain features which will be particularly interesting for various aspects of our later study. They are arguably the work of (some part or parts of) a multiform Jewish sectarian group, the Essenes, which seems to have come into existence some time in the second century BC, or possibly somewhat later, and who, according to Philo and Josephus, numbered over 4,000.[183] Through all the recent debates, it still remains moderately likely that the issue which brought the movement into existence was the Maccabaean crisis and its aftermath, in which the older high-priestly group were ousted in favour of the new Hasmonean priest-kings. The subsequent development of the movement, including its possible split or change of direction, can probably be traced in relation to the continuing story of the Hasmonean house. At each hypothetical stage, those who wrote the Scrolls saw themselves as the true representatives of Judaism over against the group then in power, i.e. the Hasmoneans.[184] It is possible—no more than that—that the movement may have had a similar or even identical ancestor to the Pharisees, namely, the shadowy *hasidim* of the late third and early second century BC;[185] and it is also possible that some disaffected Pharisees joined the movement around the start of the first century BC.[186] The site at Qumran was then vacated in the last third of the first century BC, reinhabited early in the first century AD, and finally taken over and destroyed by the Romans in about AD 68. If it is true that the Qumran com-

---

[182] See Golb 1985; 1989; and the full critique of his views in Garcia-Martinez and van der Woude 1990, 526–36.

[183] *Quod Omn.* 75; *Ant.* 18.20. It is not clear which period Josephus is referring to. What is clear is that the monastery at Qumran could never have accommodated more than a small fraction of that number.

[184] See the attractive solution of Garcia-Martinez and van der Woude, that the references to a 'wicked priest' are *generic*, capable of being reapplied to successive Hasmonean high priests.

[185] See Davies 1977.

[186] So Charlesworth 1980, 223f., following Milik and Murphy-O'Connor.

munity, and/or those who wrote the Scrolls, were part of a wider Essene movement, we have no evidence for the continuation of such a movement after the fall of the Temple.[187]

Using the model we developed in Part II, we may now outline the worldview which the Scrolls reveal to us. In order to avoid begging the questions noted above, I shall refer to those who adhered to the Scrolls (including both the *Damascus Document* and the *Community Rule*, except where noted) by the vague terms 'the group' or 'the movement'. It is important to remember that those of whom we thus speak saw this 'group' as a tight-knit one, a 'unity' (Hebrew *yahad*), and this 'movement' as the spearhead of the divine purpose for the world. Membership was not a dilettante hobby. It was a matter of life and death, for oneself, for Israel, and for the world.

First, the symbolic world of the group was focussed on its own existence as the rightful heir of Judaism. The focal points of its own life, seen as the fulfillment of prophecy and the means whereby the divine purpose would finally be realized, became its central symbols. The council meetings of the community were solemn religious occasions; the mealtimes, sacred festivals. Communal life was governed by strict laws of purity, and the calendar was arranged in such a way as to enable festivals and sabbaths to be kept 'properly', i.e. on different days from one another.[188] Not least in symbolic importance were the implements of study and writing. Pen and ink (some of which have been found by archaeologists) were used in the service of Israel's god. Even the scroll jars themselves acquire, particularly in retrospect, a profound symbolic value: these writings are to be kept safe through the present tribulation, so that when the day of vindication dawns they may again be read. Not for nothing did the modern Israeli government place the Scrolls, discovered within a few months of the founding of the modern State of Israel, in a museum built as a gigantic replica of a scroll jar.

Of the regular praxis of the community, one feature in particular deserves special comment: the community described in the *Community Rule* (as opposed to that in the *Damascus Document*) offered no animal sacrifices.[189] Building on this, and piecing together the ideology of the movement from hints and statements, we reach the clear conclusion that at least one branch regarded itself not just as the true Israel but as the true Temple.[190] The existing Temple might have been 'cleansed' by the Maccabaean revolt, but it was still polluted as far as this group was concerned.[191] Just as the Pharisees and their putative successors developed an alternative to the Temple, offering 'spiritual sacrifices' through prayer, fasting and almsgiving, so the group that practised the *Community Rule* developed a theology in which Israel's god had called them into being as an alternative Temple. Their devotion was accept-

[187] Except, that is, for the writings of Josephus, who treats them as if they were still in existence at the time of his writing of the *Antiquities* (18.18–22).

[188] For a convenient summary, cf. Sanders 1992, 360f.

[189] As noted by Jos. *Ant.* 18.18–19.

[190] e.g. 1QS 8.5–11; 1QH 6.25–9; cf. Sanders 1992, 352–63. Among older literature see particularly Gärtner 1965; Klinzing 1971.

[191] cf. e.g. CD 5.6–7; and cp. Evans 1989a, 1989b.

able in the place of that which was still being offered a few miles away, and a few thousand feet higher up, on Mount Zion itself.

It is clear that the praxis of the group did not involve participation in active revolt. The time for fighting would come when Israel's god sent the Messiah to lead the holy war, and not until. This is the socio-political reality behind Josephus' description of the Essenes as believing in fate rather than free will.[192] Nevertheless, one tell-tale Essene, clearly not a member of the Qumran group, appears in Josephus' account of the war, and we must not suppose that positions were completely hardened one way or another.[193] As to their political involvement, it seems to have been limited to prophetic announcements, such as that which foretold that Herod would become king. According to Josephus, Herod was sufficiently impressed by the Essenes to allow them exemption from the oath of loyalty to himself. One explanation for the site of Qumran being vacated in the latter years of the first century BC is that during Herod's reign the community lived in Jerusalem itself, in the so-called 'Essene quarter', enjoying political favour and (no doubt) hoping for Israel's redemption.[194]

The stories that the group told reveal, as well and as clearly as any community's stories do, the nature of the worldview they espoused. It was, of course, Israel's story; but, like all retellings of Israel's story in this period, it had a twist to its tail. The scriptures were searched, read, prayed over, studied, copied out—all with the focus on the present and immediately future moment. Israel's history had entered a bottleneck. The return from exile had not yet really happened. This little group was the advance guard through whom it would come about. Thus the prophecies written before the exile, predicting a future return and restoration, were in fact starting to come true in the history of the group itself. The story of Israel had turned into the story of the group.

If we press this group for answers to the basic worldview questions, they are not slow in coming. Who are we? We are the true Israel, the heirs of the promises, ignored at present but with a great future before us. We are the elect ones of Israel's god, the bearers of Israel's destiny. Where are we? We are in exile, situated (whether actually, at Qumran, or metaphorically, in one of the other Essene groups) away from the rest of Israel, demonstrating by our wilderness existence the fact that the promises of restoration and redemption are yet to be fulfilled. What is wrong? Clearly, that Israel is still unredeemed; that the wrong people are in power, the wrong high priests are ruling the Temple, and Israel as a whole is blind, without knowledge and insight, deaf to the call of her god. What is the solution? Israel's god has begun to act. In calling this movement into existence he has prepared the way for the final showdown with his enemies. Soon he will send his anointed ones, a king and a priest, who will be Israel's true rulers and will lead the Sons of Light in a great war against the Sons of Darkness. Not only the Gentiles, but also all renegade Jews, will be defeated; and the Sons of Light will reign for a thousand generations. Then,

---

[192] *Ant.* 13.172; 18.18.

[193] 'John the Essene': *War* 2.567; 3.11, 19.

[194] See *Ant.* 15.371–9. On the 'Essene quarter' in Jerusalem see *War* 5.145, and Pixner 1976; Capper 1985, 149–202.

and only then, will true worship be restored, as a new Temple is built in place of the present corrupt one, to be the dwelling-place of Israel's god for all generations. In the mean time we, the advance guard, must stay at our post in prayer and purity.

This outline of the group's worldview is not, I think, controversial at any point. Detailed discussions of emphasis abound, of course, and there are endless questions as to the meaning of particular texts, especially the many tiny fragments that are now gradually coming to light after their second burial on the desks of scholars. And from this worldview we can read off a clear statement of theology, as clear as anything from the second-temple period.

First, there is one god, the god of Abraham, Isaac, Jacob and the prophets. The keen interest in angelology shown in the Scrolls (and reported by Pliny) in no way detracts from this emphasis; nor does the odd suggestion of Josephus that the Essenes worshipped the sun, which more likely reflects two things, their habit of facing east for morning worship and their adoption of a solar rather than a lunar calendar.[195] The purposes of this god, though mysterious, were revealed long ago to his prophets, and are now made known to the group through the inspired teachers, notably the so-called 'Teacher of Righteousness'.[196]

Second, Israel is the chosen people of this god, not simply for her own sake but in order to be his means of furthering his work for the reordering of his world. This election of Israel, of which the covenant is the instrument, has now been focussed on the group, who collectively form the people of the new covenant, the new elect. It should be noted at this point that discussions of 'predestination' can throw the emphasis of such a view of 'election' in the wrong direction, evoking questions of *individual* election which are quite foreign to concerns expressed in the Scrolls. The emphasis, rather, is that what was true of Israel as a whole—she was the elect people of the one true god—is now true of the group. This positive identification of the group as the elect carries, of course, a strong negative corollary: those who are not part of the group are not part of the elect, whatever status they may have in contemporary Jewish society. We may strongly suspect a particular target to be the present ruling high-priestly family, and other competing pressure-groups such as the Pharisees.

Third, the badges of membership in the renewed covenant were clearly the piety and purity enjoined by the community's rules. Acceptance of this discipline was the sign that one belonged; rejection of it would incur penalties, the severest being expulsion (which could have fatal consequences for one who had sworn solemn oaths to eat no food except that of the community). Two points need to be made here. (a) It is quite clear from the content of the

---

[195] *War* 2.128; cf. Sanders 1992, 245f., following Smith in suggesting that some actual sun-worship may have been practised.

[196] I have no special theory as to the identity of the Teacher, about whom debate continues to rage. See the interesting suggestion of Davies 1985, 54: the *Damascus Document* (6.11) predicted the coming of such a Teacher, and the Qumran group, under the leadership of one who claimed to be the Teacher, announced itself as the fulfilment of recent, as well as ancient, prophecy.

group's devotional literature that this piety and purity were not regarded as 'earning' membership, or salvation. They merely expressed it.[197] (b) The purity regulations of the group give several indications that they regarded themselves as *in some senses* analogous to, or on a par with, priests in the Temple. Obviously they could not, and did not, reproduce all the features of Temple-piety. But what they did is sufficient to show that, just as the Mishnah would argue that studying Torah is the equivalent of being in the Temple in Jerusalem, so those who framed the rules in the Scrolls regarded those who kept them as having similar privileges—and responsibilities.[198]

Finally, eschatology. It has long been common to see the Scrolls as representative of 'apocalyptic', and in part this is justified. We should not, however, make the mistake of seeing 'apocalyptic' as marking out a special type of Judaism.[199] As I shall argue in chapter 10, 'apocalyptic' is a type of literature which was *both* available to all in principle as one way of saying things that might be difficult to say otherwise, *and* most likely cherished and read, in the case of individual writings, by a comparatively small group. That is, any Jew *might* read, say, *1 Enoch*, and might find there meanings of which he or she could approve; but the chances are that most Jews, including many who cherished wild dreams about the future, did not in fact know most of the works now collected in Charlesworth's *Pseudepigrapha*, and that many Jews, if they had come across such literature, would have regarded it with great suspicion. That is why one cannot base an account of Judaism on such writings, but must always start at least with the things we know to have been common to all Jews.

The eschatology of the group who produced the Scrolls, while sharing some common features with other 'apocalyptic' writings, must not, then, be read simply as 'dualistic', or as expecting 'the end of the world'. Sanders seems to me exactly right: 'From the Scrolls, we learn that the sect looked forward to a dramatic change in the future, which modern scholars often call "the eschaton" . . . , which is slightly misleading, since *like other Jews the Essenes did not think that the world would end*.'[200] Rather, the exalted language about a coming great day was intended to refer to the time when Israel's god would act *within* history to redeem his people and re-establish them *as* his people, within his holy Land and worshipping in a new Temple. The hope, however exalted, retained its essentially this-worldly base. When Israel's god acted, he would send the true anointed priest, and the true Davidic king, to be the Messiahs of his people. This belief in *two* Messiahs may be startling to those accustomed to think of Jews as expecting 'the Messiah' simply, but it is perfectly consistent with the group's firmly held belief in a renewed Temple. It would be quite wrong for a Davidic king, descended from Judah, to preside over the true Temple; only a descendent of Levi, Aaron and Zadok would do. The Epistle to the Hebrews faced exactly the same problem, and simply solved it in a dif-

---

[197] As argued repeatedly by Sanders: see now 1992, chs. 16–17, esp. 375f.
[198] So Sanders 1992, 357–77, esp. 359, 362, 376f.
[199] So rightly Sanders 1992, 8f.
[200] Sanders 1992, 368 (my italics); cp. 456f., and ch. 10 below.

ferent way (Hebrews 5–7).[201] The royal Messiah would lead the group in their holy war against the enemy, after which Israel's redemption would be complete, and the true Israel would rule in peace and righteousness for ever. It has been interestingly argued that the group's chronological calculations may have led it to hope that the Messiahs would appear around the time of the death of Herod the Great.[202]

The sect thus held a form of what later scholarship has called 'inaugurated eschatology'. Most Jews in our period seem to have believed that their god would act in the future to liberate Israel from her continuing exile. The group whose writings were found at Qumran believed that this god had already begun the process, secretly, in and through them. What would happen in the future would be the dramatic unveiling of what had already been started, just as what had already been started was the fulfillment of prophecies hidden from long ago. At the moment, the rest of Israel would look and look, but never see; the day would come when the righteous would shine like the sun in the kingdom of Israel's god.

5. Priests, Aristocrats, and Sadducees

We could quite easily imagine first-century Judaism without Essenes or Scrolls. The same is emphatically not true of the priests in general and the chief priests in particular. Josephus, writing at the end of the first century AD, says that there were at least twenty thousand priests, far more than the figures given for the party of the Pharisees (6,000) or the sect of the Essenes (4,000).[203] Their role, often overlooked in accounts of first-century Judaism, must be put back where it belongs.[204]

The great majority of the priests were not aristocrats, or particularly wealthy. They, and the Levites who served as their assistants, were dependent on the tithing practised by the rest of the population. Most of them lived away from Jerusalem, going there in groups, by turn, for the performance of the regular rituals. For the rest of the time, they functioned in a way which has, again, often been ignored: they were the main teachers of the law, and the group to whom ordinary Jews turned for judgment and arbitration in disputes or legal problems.[205] It should be no surprise that Jesus tells the cleansed leper to 'show himself to the priest' (Matthew 8.4 and parallels). That would have been normal practice. The priests were the local representatives of mainline 'official' Judaism, as befits those who had both studied Torah themselves and, from time to time, had the privilege of serving Israel's god in his Temple.

---

[201] On Messiahship at Qumran see particularly VanderKam 1988; Talmon 1987; and other literature cited by both.

[202] See Beckwith 1980, 1981.

[203] For the priests: *Apion* 2.108. This is clearly very much a round figure: he says that there were four priestly clans, each with 'more than five thousand' members. On the Pharisees' and Essenes' numbers, see above.

[204] See particularly Sanders 1992, ch. 10.

[205] Sanders 1992, ch. 10.

At the top of the priestly tree, so to speak, we find the chief priests. As far as we can tell from our sources, they formed in the first century a kind of permanent secretariat, based in Jerusalem, wielding considerable power. They belonged to a small group of families, tight-knit and inbred, who seem on several occasions to have engaged in serious factional disputes among themselves.[206] They, unlike the ordinary priests, formed the heart of Judaism's aristocracy; there were undoubtedly lay aristocrats as well, but the chief priests have the highest profile. It was with them, and particularly with the high priest who was chosen from their number, that the Roman governors had to deal in the first instance, holding them responsible for the general conduct of the populace.[207]

This aristocracy, both clerical and lay, had no solid ancestral claim to its prestige. Goodman has argued convincingly that the Romans chose to elevate, and work with, local landowners, who were thus given a position for which their family status would not have prepared them. Herod, in addition, had carefully disposed of the Hasmonean dynasty, and, since there was no question of becoming high priest himself, he took care that the office should be held by people who posed no threat to him personally, as a dynamic or well-born high priest might easily have done.[208] Thus, by the time Judaea became a Roman province in AD 6, the ruling high-priestly family was firmly established, but without any solid claim to antiquity. Their interests thus lay in keeping the peace between Rome and an often discontented people. If this meant pacifying the Romans, they did so. When it became apparent that peace was gone beyond hope, they chose to side with the rebels, intending no doubt to retain their status as leaders, and their property as landowners, after what might have been a successful revolt.[209]

The central symbol of the priestly worldview was obviously the Temple. It represented, no doubt, different things to different priests. To the country priest, living for most of the time in comparative poverty, teaching in his local village and settling local disputes, the regular visit to the Temple, and the chance to take part in its ritual, was the high point of his year, or even of his life. Everything he did away from Jerusalem gained meaning and depth because of the Temple. As we shall see in the next chapter, it drew together the entire theology and aspiration of Israel. To the Jerusalemite priest, and particularly to the chief priests, the Temple was in principle all of that, but more besides: it was their power-base, the economic and political centre of the country. It was because they controlled the Temple that they were who they were. It gave powerful religious legitimation to the status which they had been granted under the Romans and Herod.

For this reason, our sources are surely right to represent the chief priests as fundamentally conservative. They, and the leading aristocracy, seem mostly to

---

[206] See particularly Goodman 1987. This is presumably what Josephus means in his descriptions of them as being boorish and rude (*War* 2.166; cf. *Ant.* 20.199).

[207] Sanders 1992, chs. 15, 21.

[208] On Aristobulus III, the young Hasmonean who was high priest for a while until murdered on Herod's orders (*Ant.* 15.23–41, 50–6), see Schürer 1.297.

[209] See Goodman 1987, *passim*.

have belonged to the party we know as the Sadducees. Unfortunately, there is not much more that we know about this party, other than their conservatism, and their apparently perpetual dogfight with the Pharisees. What we can trace in more detail may briefly be described as follows.[210]

According to Josephus, the Sadducees believed in free will. Just as I am inclined to think that Josephus' description of the Pharisaic blend of free will and fate is a depoliticized code for their balance between waiting for Israel's god to act and being ready to act on his behalf if necessary, so I am inclined to think that the Sadducean belief in free will has little to do with abstract philosophy and a great deal to do with the politics of power: Israel's god will help those who help themselves.[211] This is a comfortable doctrine for those in power, who maintain themselves there by taking whatever measures seem necessary, just as its mirror image, belief that divine action can only be awaited, not hastened, is a consoling doctrine for those out of power, who see no hope of regaining it by their own efforts (see above, on the Essenes).

Second, the Sadducees had no time for laws other than those in the Bible (or possibly, other than those in the Pentateuch). This viewpoint is set over against those who follow 'the traditions of the elders', a pretty clear reference to the Pharisees, who, though their elevation of such traditions to the status of absolute law may be doubted,[212] certainly maintained, and applied to themselves at least, a large body of such traditions. Here again we see the Sadducees as an essentially conservative body, unwilling to allow (what could be seen as) mere innovation. In the political realm, this is again a useful doctrine for those in power to hold if their innovating opponents are engaged, as we have seen some at least of the Pharisees were, in revolutionary activities.

Third, the Sadducees denied the doctrine of the resurrection.[213] It should not need saying, but probably does, that this has nothing to do with the post-enlightenment rationalism or 'liberalism' that doubts whether such things are possible. The best explanation for the Sadducees' view seems to me, again, the holistic one that combines theology, society and political reality. By the first century, 'resurrection' had functioned for a long time as a symbol and metaphor for the total reconstitution of Israel, the return from Babylon, and the final redemption. Ezekiel 37 spoke of the return in terms of Israel being awakened out of the grave; the Maccabaean martyrs, as presented in 2 Maccabees (written in the late second or early first century BC),[214] spoke of their own forthcoming resurrection in the context of claiming that their god would vindicate his people against the tyrant. Although the first-century aristocrats were in one sense the heirs of the Hasmoneans whose vindication 2 Maccabees envisaged, the boot was now on the other foot: resurrection, in its metaphorical sense of the restitution of a theocratic Israel, possibly under a Messiah, would mean the end of their precarious power. At the same time, we

---

[210] See Sanders 1992, 332–40; Saldarini 1988, chs. 5–6, 8–10 and esp. 13.
[211] See *War* 2.164f.; *Ant.* 13.173.
[212] See Sanders 1990a, ch. 2, esp. 125–30.
[213] *War* 2.165; *Ant.* 18.16.
[214] So Attridge 1984, 177; Schürer 3.532.

should not suppose that the only meaning of Josephus' statements is to be found at the political level. If the Sadducees concentrated, for reasons of political necessity, on the affairs of the world, they, unlike the poor and marginalized for whom the hope for restitution had to be projected forwards on to the life to come, may have quite genuinely had less concern for doctrines about the afterlife itself.[215]

The influence of the aristocrats in general and the Sadducees in particular has been controversial, for the same underlying reasons as the question of the influence of the Pharisees. Goodman, McLaren and Sanders, in their different ways, have all argued strongly that the aristocracy held considerable *de facto* as well as *de jure* power.[216] This is at first sight out of line with Josephus' assertion that the Sadducees could accomplish practically nothing, since the masses held the Pharisees in high honour.[217] Josephus is then thought to have misleadingly presented the Pharisees as the most influential party in order to persuade the Romans to accept the present Jewish regime, which purported to be the inheritor of the Pharisaic tradition, as the one which could offer best hope of influencing the people. In the light of Mason's arguments, however, I am inclined to accept Josephus' verdict, with modifications: in terms of party effectiveness, the Pharisees were far more successful in persuading the people of their views than the Sadducees were. That is, the majority of the people believed in resurrection (most probably in both the literal and the metaphorical senses); the majority of people went on believing that their god would intervene in history, that matters did not lie solely in human hands; and the majority of people were prepared to take at least some of the Pharisaic traditions with at least some seriousness. On all these points, if there was a Sadducean agenda, it was not followed.

But was this what Josephus meant? Not entirely, I suspect. His own agenda was probably not the lauding of the Pharisees; if it had been, he went about it in a very odd way.[218] His agenda, more likely, was the exoneration of the aristocracy, i.e. of his own party. If he made bald statements about Pharisaic domination which make it look as though (in Sanders' phrase) 'they ran everything', the chance is that he did so in order to give the impression of a noble and well-meaning aristocracy whose hands were tied by populist movements beyond their control. Behind this we can trace the more complex reality:

i. a good many aristocrats were in fact involved in anti-Roman sedition, though on their own terms and with motives very different from the Zealots or other groups (Goodman);

ii. the Pharisees continued to enjoy widespread popular support (Mason, and now, cautiously, Sanders);[219]

[215] On belief in resurrection see ch. 10 below.

[216] Goodman 1987; Sanders 1992, chs. 15, 21; McLaren 1991.

[217] *Ant.* 18.17; cf. 13.298.

[218] See above, on the Pharisees in Josephus.

[219] See Sanders 1992, 386: 'The chief priests and "the powerful" obviously realized that a revolutionary government needed the co-operation of the leader of *a more broadly based party than their own*' (my italics); 388: 'they could always raise a fair following'. On 398, Sanders, in saying (surely rightly) that we must doubt whether the Pharisees ran all the synagogues, clearly allows for the possibility that they ran some, perhaps quite a lot. See esp. 402–4.

iii. in many matters of ordinary practice, not least in the Temple cult, the priests may well have followed Pharisaic regulations (Mason), though neither the priests in general nor the chief priests in particular needed the Pharisees to teach them the basics of their craft (Sanders);

iv. in serious politics, what mattered was what the Roman governor and the chief priests did and said. Obviously, it was in their interests to work with rather than against a populace that was disposed to be restive, and to that extent they took the Pharisees, as populist leaders, into consideration; but they were quite prepared, when it was necessary or convenient, to ignore anybody and everybody, Pharisees included (Sanders).

(v) Josephus' main aim was to exonerate his own party, the aristocracy, and he did so by emphasizing Pharisaic influence and his own annoyance with it.

This, I think, makes sense of the data and gives a coherent historical picture. It remains to state the sequel: the aristocracy were either wiped out in the war (many of them at the hands of Jewish revolutionaries with different motives), or they assimilated, like Josephus himself, in varying degrees, into the general Greco-Roman society around them. We hear nothing of them in the period of Jamnia. Their worldview, whose central symbol was the Temple, and whose central story concerned an Israel with themselves as its rulers, had been destroyed beyond trace.

6. 'Ordinary Jews': Introduction

I have dealt thus far with what may be considered 'specialist' branches of first-century Judaism, because I think it important to get as clear a historical picture as possible before plunging into a more general account of the Jewish worldview of the first century. Others have gone about the task the other way round;[220] there may not be a lot to choose between the two approaches. But now, as we prepare to look at that which the great majority of first-century Jews held in common (chapters 8–10), we must first consider who it was that made up the majority of the population of Palestine.

We may begin by summarizing part of Sanders' recent argument. It is often thought that the majority of Jews in the period were regarded by the Pharisees, and perhaps by themselves, as 'sinners'. Equally, it is often thought that the Pharisees controlled every aspect of everyday life. Sanders has pointed out that these two ideas are mutually contradictory, and that in fact neither represents the true state of things. If most Jews were 'sinners', none of the ordinary Jews would have been able to go and worship at the Temple, since they would have been debarred by impurity. We have no reason for thinking, either, that strict Pharisaic laws were widely observed, and plenty of reasons for thinking that they were observed only by the Pharisees themselves. Thus it remains likely that the great majority of Jews cared sufficiently about their god, their scriptures and their Jewish heritage to take a fair amount of trouble

[220] e.g. Sanders 1992.

over the observance of at least biblical law. They prayed, they fasted, they went to synagogue, they travelled to Jerusalem for the regular feasts. They did not eat pork, they kept the sabbath, they circumcised their male children. Equally, they paid sufficient attention to the Pharisees as respected, though unofficial, teachers to ensure that some of these basic duties were carried out in a more or less Pharisaic fashion.

Were they, then, the people described often enough in rabbinic literature as 'the people of the land'? Most likely. But we should not downgrade that group by treating them uniformly as 'sinners', or imagine that they, or the Pharisees, could not distinguish between an ordinary law-abiding Jew of the sort just described, even if he or she did not keep to the entire Pharisaic code, and a Jew who deliberately broke the sabbath, who ate pork, who tried to remove the marks of his circumcision, or who engaged in prostitution, extortion, murder and the like. As Freyne says, ' "people of the land" may well have become a pejorative religious term in later rabbinic circles, but that should not lead us to the erroneous conclusion that the country Jews were unconcerned about the essentials of Jewish faith'.[221]

We may therefore take it that the majority of Jews in Palestine during the Roman period kept more or less to their biblical laws, prayed to their ancestral deity, and regulated their lives so as to emphasize the regular feasts and fasts of the calendar. They were not likely to have been deeply reflective theologians (even Josephus, who had studied a good deal, was clearly not that), but their symbolic world and their regular praxis give us a first-rate insight into the theology to which, however inarticulately, they gave allegiance. They also project us forward to examine the hope which they cherished, which brings us back full circle to the history of the period with which we began. Our study of the variety within Judaism in this period thus sets the agenda for chapters 8, 9 and 10, to which we proceed without more ado.

---

[221] Freyne 1988, 200, revising his earlier opinion in which he had followed Oppenheimer 1977.

Chapter Eight

STORY, SYMBOL, PRAXIS: ELEMENTS OF ISRAEL'S WORLDVIEW

1. Introduction

Within the turbulent history described in chapter 6, and amidst the pressure of parties described in chapter 7, there lived the ordinary Jews of the first century. It is difficult to tell what books, if any, such people read (other than their Bible, and not everyone would have been able to read that for themselves). What we do know, however, is that they shared to a lesser or greater extent in the worldview which, beneath the party differences, united the great majority. We can plot this worldview with some accuracy through studying, initially, three of the four worldview-components that we discussed in chapter 5: the stories which were told and retold, which embodied and integrated, as only stories can, the varied aspects of the worldview; the symbols to which all except the most non-observant would have attached themselves in some ways;[1] and the praxis, closely integrated with those symbols, which would have characterized the great majority.

2. Stories

(i) Introduction

We saw in chapter 3 that stories are important as an index of the worldview of any culture, and that it is crucial, if we are to understand them, to read their many dimensions with accuracy. Some cultures keep their characteristic stories subtly hidden. First-century Judaism is an excellent example of a culture which quite obviously thrived on stories, which we may for simplicity divide into two categories: the basic story, told in the Bible, of creation and election, of exodus and monarchy, of exile and return; and smaller-unit stories, either dealing with a small part of the larger story, or running in parallel to some or all of it. In each case, we gain a powerful index of the Jewish worldview, which then opens up to create the context for the symbols and the praxis.

---

[1] See Millar 1990, 379f.

(ii) The Basic Story

The foundation story of Judaism, to which all other stories were subsidiary, was of course the story in the Bible. Israel had told this story, one way or another, pretty much as long as she had been Israel. As the biblical tradition grew and developed, the stories it contained, and the single story which holds them all together, grew with it, and the different elements interacted upon one another in a multitude of ways.[2] Seen from the perspective of a first-century Jew, innocent of critical questionings about the origins of the different traditions, the basic story concerned the creator god and the world, and focused upon Israel's place as the covenant people of the former placed in the midst of the latter.

Thus, the call of the patriarchs was set against the backcloth of creation and fall. As we shall see in the next chapter, Abraham was seen as the divine answer to the problem of Adam. The descent into Egypt and the dramatic rescue under the leadership of Moses formed the initial climax of the story, setting the theme of liberation as one of the major motifs for the whole, and posing a puzzle which later Jews would reflect on in new ways: if Israel was liberated from Egypt, and placed in her own land, why is everything not now perfect? The conquest of the land, and the period of the Judges, then formed the backcloth to and preparation for the next climax, the establishment of the monarchy, and particularly of the house of David. David was the new Abraham, the new Moses, through whom Israel's god would complete what was begun earlier. Again came the puzzle: David's successors were (mostly) a bad lot, the kingdom was divided, the prophets went unheeded, and Judah eventually went into exile.[3] Promises of a new exodus arose naturally in such a context, and led to the ambiguous new beginnings (or were they false dawns?) under the Davidic ruler Zerubbabel and the high priest Joshua, and under Ezra and Nehemiah.[4] The biblical period (normally so-called) runs out without a sense of an ending, except one projected into the future. This story still needs to be completed.

The point can be made graphically by considering the juxtaposition of two of the great story-telling psalms (remembering, of course, how prominent the psalms were in Israel's worship, and how powerful therefore their tellings of Israel's story must have been in shaping the first-century Jewish worldview). Psalm 105 retells, in classical style, the story of the patriarchs and the exodus, concluding with no ambiguity but only a continuing task: Israel must therefore praise YHWH and keep his commandments.[5] But Psalm 106 tells the story differently: the exodus was itself an ambiguous time, with much disobedience and judgment on Israel herself, and the period of living in Canaan, similarly, was deeply flawed, and resulted in exile. Nevertheless, Israel's god remembered the covenant and caused her captors to pity her; but the story was not yet com-

---

[2] See Koch 1969; Fishbane 1985, esp. 281–440.
[3] This puzzle is stated at its starkest in Ps. 89.
[4] cp. the enthusiasm for these two in Zech. 3–4, which seems to have waned in Zech. 9–14.
[5] Ps. 105.1–6, 44f.

plete. 'Save us, O YHWH our God, and gather us from the nations, that we may give thanks to your holy name and glory in your praise.' Until that happens, the great story is not yet complete, is still full of ambiguity.[6]

The great story of the Hebrew scriptures was therefore inevitably read in the second-temple period as a story in search of a conclusion. This ending would have to incorporate the full liberation and redemption of Israel, an event which had not happened as long as Israel was being oppressed, a prisoner in her own land. And this ending would have to be *appropriate*: it should correspond to the rest of the story, and grow out of it in obvious continuity and conformity. We can see what this appropriateness might mean by taking an example of its opposite. Josephus' retelling of the entire story, in the *Antiquities*, provides an ending which destroys the narrative grammar of the rest: Israel's god goes over to the Romans, Jerusalem is destroyed, Judaism dispersed. That is like retelling the story of *Jack and the Beanstalk* in such a way that Jack's mother murders her returning son, takes the gold and goes off to marry the giant himself. If Josephus still believed in a future ending in which everything would again be reversed, he kept it very much to himself.

A different, and in some ways more orthodox, reading of Israel's story is given in Sirach 44–50, written around the start of the second century BC. 'Let us now sing the praises of famous men, our ancestors in their generation', the passage begins (44.1), and in one sense the whole section is a general account of Israel's ancestors such as might win admiration from a non-Jewish reader.[7] But it is still Israel's story that is being told. And the passage ends (50.1–21) with a glowing portrait of one who was not an ancestor at all, but most likely a contemporary of the writer: the high priest Simeon II, son of Jonathan ('Onias' in the Greek), who held office from 219–196 BC. The message is clear: Israel's story finds its perfect conclusion in the splendid and ordered worship of her god in the Temple. This fits perfectly with the theology of chapter 24 (the divine Wisdom coming to dwell, as the Shekinah, in Zion, and turning out to be identified with the Torah itself), and more or less obviates the need for eschatology, whether political or otherwise.[8] Israel's story has arrived where it should be.

This settled and quietly triumphant retelling of the story could not last, of course, when confronted with the ravages of Antiochus Epiphanes. The Maccabees thereupon offer another example of Israel's story with a new ending. Their attempt to tell their own story as the triumphant conclusion to the whole story of Israel (particularly in 1 Maccabees) was a *coup d'état* in some ways as daring and successful as the one they launched against Antiochus Epiphanes: they hijacked the story-line of Israel's future hope, and claimed that this hope had been achieved through them. The ambiguities inherent in their regime were enough to cause other groups to retell the story differently: the Has-

---

[6] Ps. 106.47. The final verse (48) of the canonical psalm rounds off the story, and the fourth 'book' of the Psalter, in a way that, though justified by the strength of the hope, must not be allowed to obscure the puzzle and the longing of the rest of the psalm.

[7] See Frost 1987; Lane 1991, 2.316f.

[8] Sir. 50.23f. may be an exception, but it looks more like a traditional and generalized prayer rather than an organic part of the writer's thought.

monean regime was corrupt, and Israel's god would overthrow it and set up the right one instead.[9]

These three examples of the many different retellings of Israel's story show that Jews of the period did not simply think of the biblical traditions atomistically, but were able to conceive of the story as a whole, and to be regularly looking for its proper conclusion. Summary forms of the story are found in many biblical passages, as well as in many second-temple works;[10] and some whole books retell the story, or foundational parts of it, in such a way as to point up both the sense of its not having reached its proper conclusion and the urgency of living appropriately while waiting for this ending to come.

Thus, for example, the book of *Jubilees* tells the story of the patriarchs with an eye to Israel's future, warning the writer's contemporaries in the second century BC that they should keep strictly to the sabbaths, the festivals, the practice of circumcision and the solar calendar (as opposed to the lunar one then current in mainstream Judaism). If they do this, the story will reach its true ending. Isaac addresses Esau and Jacob in the following words:

> Remember the Lord, my sons, the God of Abraham your father, and how I too made him my God and served him in righteousness and joy, that he might multiply you and increase the number of your descendants till they were like the stars of heaven, and that he might establish you on the earth as the plant of righteousness which will not be uprooted for all generations for ever.[11]

Israel must remain faithful to all the requirements of the covenant. Only then will the story which began with Abraham and Isaac reach its proper conclusion.

The same story is told from a very different perspective, and in a very different style, by chapters 10–19 of the (roughly contemporary) Wisdom of Solomon. The thrust of this retelling is that Wisdom, who was given to the first humans (10.1–4), was then specifically active in the history of Israel, from the time of the patriarchs (10.5–14), and in the events of the exodus (10.15—11.14, 16.1—19.22). These accounts are full of hints as to how the writer thinks the heirs of this tradition should live as a result: they should avoid that paganism which mirrors the practices of both Egypt and Canaan (11.15—15.19). This paganism, of course, was designed to correspond to that which was faced as a pressing problem by the Jews of the second-temple period.

The book of *Pseudo-Philo*, which belongs in genre somewhere between *Jubilees* and apocalyptic, and in time to the first century AD, tells the same story, but brings it up as far as the death of Saul.[12] Once again there is a strong

---

[9] On retellings of the story within the NT see Part IV below.

[10] Compare the summary 'histories of Israel' in e.g. Dt. 6.20–4; 28.5–9; Josh. 24.2–13; Pss. 78, 105, 106, 135, 136; Neh. 9.6–37; Ezek. 20.4–44; Jud. 5.5–21; 1 Macc. 2.32–60; 3 Macc. 2.2–20; Wisd. 10.1—12.27; Jos. *Ant.* 3.86f.; 4.43–5; *War* 5.379–419; CD 2.14–6.11; 4 Ezra 3.4–36; 4.29–31. Cf. too Mk. 12.1–12; Ac. 7.2–53; 13.16–41; Rom. 9–11; Heb. 11.2—12.2 (on whose parallels with Sir. see Frost 1987, and ch. 13 below); Jas. 5.10–11. I owe some of these references to (an earlier version of) Hill 1992, 100, as also the further ref. to Holz 1968, 100f.; and some others to Skehan and Di Lella 1987, 499f.

[11] *Jub.* 36.6 (tr. Charles, rev. Rabin, in Sparks 1984).

[12] The book may be found in Charlesworth 1985, 297–377 (tr. D. J. Harrington).

moralizing tone, as the readers maintain their obedience while waiting for the day of deliverance to dawn, as it surely will.[13] Hannah, Samuel's mother, rejoices over the birth of her child not just for his own sake but because of the coming kingdom:

> Behold the word has been fulfilled,
> and the prophecy has come to pass.
> And these words will endure
> until they give the horn to his anointed one
> and power be present at the throne of his king.[14]

A different perspective again is provided by the various apocalyptic writings, which we will study in more detail in chapter 10. Here world history, and particularly Israel's history, is arranged into epochs, with the last epoch about to dawn. In this, as in many things, 'apocalyptic' is not to be marked off from the much wider Jewish tradition. The apocalyptic picture of Israel's suffering and redemption, though often drawn in lurid colours, remains thematically a direct linear descendant of the exodus tradition. On virtually all sides there is a sense that the history of the creator, his world and his covenant people is going somewhere, but that it has not yet arrived there. The creator will act again, as he did in the past, to deliver Israel from her plight and to deal with the evil in the world. The multiple tellings of this basic story witness powerfully to every aspect of the Jewish worldview.

(iii) The Smaller Stories

Within this tradition of telling the large story, letting it point forwards in various ways to its own conclusion, there was a rich Jewish tradition of sub-stories. These can be seen in two forms, which criss-cross and overlap. On the one hand, there are explicit tellings of one small part of the larger story, often extensively elaborated, and designed to function as a paradigm or example of a general principle which may be abstracted from the main story. This is a process which takes place within the biblical narratives themselves, as we see in the obvious example of the book of Ruth, which falls within the period of the Judges. On the other hand, there are stories which form little or no part of the biblical story, but are loosely attached, and gain their thrust not from explaining something in the Bible but from their underlying narrative structure and meaning.

An example of the first type of story is *Joseph and Aseneth*, a work probably from the second-temple period.[15] This book recounts, in the form of a theological romance, the betrothal and marriage of Joseph to the daughter of

---

[13] See Nickelsburg 1984, 108f.

[14] *Ps-Philo* 51.6. In the light of this passage, and of the way in which the book leads up to the death of Saul (i.e. the prelude to David's becoming king), I find it difficult to agree with Harrington (in Charlesworth 1985, 301) that the book is uninterested in the future Messiah.

[15] Charlesworth 1985, 177–247 (tr. C. Burchard).

the pagan Egyptian priest Potiphera.[16] The subject is 'historical', but the message is reasonably clear. Israel and the pagans are totally distinct: intermarriage, or even lesser contact, can only take place if the pagan in question converts. The book explains a puzzle in the Bible: how could a good and wise Jew like Joseph marry a pagan girl? At the same time, it addresses its contemporaries with a message about their own covenant loyalty and hope.

A whole genre devoted to the first type of sub-story is of course the Targumim.[17] These Aramaic paraphrases of the Hebrew Bible are, in their present form, much later than our period, but it is increasingly thought that parts of them at least go back to earlier, quite probably first-century, prototypes. Certainly some Targumic activity is early, as fragments from Qumran attest. The necessity for an Aramaic version of scripture in the first century is as obvious as the need for modern translations of the Bible in the twentieth; and, though some of the Targums stuck quite close to the original text, others were very free in their midrashic adaptation of it, applying the biblical story to issues relevant in much later periods.[18] The evident popularity of the Targumim is further demonstration that retelling bits of the Jewish story was widely practised as an effective way of reinforcing the basic worldview.

An example of the second type of sub-story, a non-biblical tale which nevertheless exemplifies the narrative grammar of the biblical story and stories, is the apocryphal book of Susannah. The heroine is threatened by lustful Jewish elders, who place her honour and her life in jeopardy. Daniel comes to her rescue, and, in a dramatic lawcourt scene, Susannah is vindicated and rescued from her enemies, who are themselves killed in her place. The book thus shares the pattern of the stories in the book of Daniel, to which it is attached in the Septuagint: Jews under threat will be vindicated against their enemies.[19] The twist to this tale is that here the enemies are not pagans: they are elders of Israel. This turns the normal Jewish anti-pagan polemic against Jews themselves, as can be seen when Daniel rounds on one of the elders with 'You offspring of Canaan and not of Judah.'[20] Nickelsburg suggests that the book reflects the pressures and temptations that could arise within a Jewish community of the period, and this of course may well be true.[21] But the storyline is deeper than a mere moralistic tale. It is the regular story of Israel, persecuted but vindicated, but now told as the story of *a group within Israel*, here 'represented' in the literary sense[22] by a single individual, persecuted by those in power precisely within Israel, but finally vindicated. It is, in other words, the

---

[16] cf. Gen. 41.45; he is called Pentephres in *Jos. & As.* 1.3, etc.

[17] See Schürer 1.99–114; 2.339–55 (on expansion of biblical teaching in general); and now esp. Strack and Stemberger 1991 [1982].

[18] An extreme example is the Targum of Pseudo-Jonathan on Gen. 21.21, mentioning the names of Muhammad's wife and daughter.

[19] See ch. 10 below. As Nickelsburg 1984, 38 points out, this pattern, of the persecution and vindication of the wise or righteous one, is a regular theme in works as diverse as Gen. 34, Esther, Ahikar and Wisd. 2–5, and has also informed the passion narratives in the gospels, and the story of Stephen's martyrdom in Ac. 6–7. We might add 2 Macc. 7 and other passages.

[20] Sus. 56.

[21] Nickelsburg 1984, 38.

[22] See ch. 10 below.

sort of story which would powerfully reinforce the worldview of a Jewish sect or party: Israel's present leaders are corrupt, and no better than pagans, but we are the true Israel who will be vindicated by our god and, perhaps, by a new Daniel. The book of Daniel itself, with its story of Jewish vindication after oppression at the hands of pagans, would be read at the time of the Maccabees as providing powerful support for the Hasmonean regime. The story of Susannah, when attached to the book of Daniel, subverts this message. The new rulers are themselves becoming paganized, and are oppressing the real faithful Israelites.

(iv) Conclusion

How then does the basic Jewish story 'work', in terms of the analysis of stories outlined in chapter 3? As we shall see in the next chapter, the focal point of the worldview is clearly the creator's covenant with Israel, and hence, in a period of political oppression and tension, his rescue of Israel. This is common to all the retellings of the Jewish story that come from such a context. But the stories diverge, characterizing the different groups and sects, when they come to the question: how is rescue to be accomplished?

One basic form of the Jewish story would look like this:

Initial Sequence:

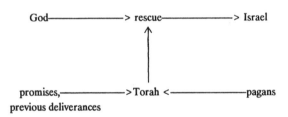

God has given Israel his Torah, so that by keeping it she may be his people, may be rescued from her pagan enemies, and confirmed as ruler in her own land. This, substantially, is how the story of the book of Joshua works; it is likely that a good deal of the rest of the Bible would also have been read in this way in the first century. It is certainly how the stories of Esther and of the Maccabees, celebrated at Purim and Hannukah, work: those who are faithful to the covenant god and his Torah will be rescued from their enemies. Some of the post-biblical writings, such as Judith, have substantially this shape, too. We have seen that the same pattern could be repeated with a dark and potentially tragic variation: Israel's rulers appear under the category of 'opponents' in Susannah, and of course in the implicit story told throughout the Essene writings.

The problem in the first century was that Israel had now been waiting a long time for rescue, and it had not been forthcoming. How, then, could Torah be made to do the job it was supposed to be doing? How could it be helped in its work of rescuing Israel? The answer is that it was to be intensified, by this or that programme:

Topical Sequence:

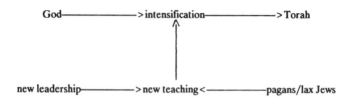

The last line allows for various options.[23] The Essenes believed that Israel's god had provided the means for the true intensification of Torah in their new community: this was how Israel would finally be rescued. The Pharisees believed that their brand of fidelity to the traditions of the fathers was the divinely appointed programme of Torah-intensification, and thus the means of Israel's rescue. No doubt other schemes would fit in here as well, not least the explicit revolutionary movements. Messianic hopes could easily become part of this scheme, as in the Scrolls. The result would be the final achievement of Israel's aspiration:

Final Sequence

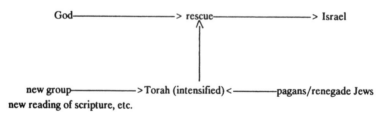

This was the resolution of the story as seen by some Jews of Jesus' day, not necessarily of course so clearly, but under the guise of various stories, and of poetry, prophecy, dreams and less articulate hopes and longings. It is this story, basically, that is articulated in apocalyptic, in legend, in tales of martyrs, in festival and symbol. Such Jewish stories served to encapsulate the worldview. Israel is the people of the creator god, in exile, awaiting release; Israel's god must become king, and rule or judge the nations; at that time, those who remain faithful to this god and his Torah will be vindicated.

There are, of course, all sorts of other dimensions to the story. It is never quite as simple as a single diagram. There is, in particular, the question of the long-term purpose of Israel: why was she called into being in the first place?

---

[23] For details, see ch. 7 above.

What was the creator up to in calling Abraham? If this purpose relates to the rest of the world, to the other nations, how is this relation to be conceived? There is, behind the story which focuses on Israel's rescue, a sense of an older and more fundamental story, which goes like this:

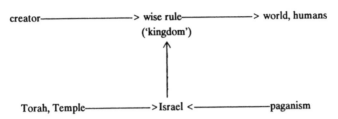

Israel is to be the creator's means of bringing his wise order to the created world. In some Old Testament passages, this is expressed, as we shall see, in terms of a pilgrimage of nations to Zion. During the period we are considering, it finds expression in terms of the defeat and punishment of the nations (e.g. the *Psalms of Solomon*). The world was made for the sake of Israel;[24] Israel is to be the true humanity, the creator's vicegerent in his ruling of the world. When YHWH becomes king, Israel will be his right-hand man. In so far as this wider story-line was in the mind of Jewish thinkers of the period, the sequence we sketched above must be seen as subsidiary. The overall plan has gone wrong, and the hero of the larger story (Israel) has been imprisoned by the villain (paganism). The rescue of the initial hero must now become the new major story-line. The larger story remains in view, but usually only in terms of the world being brought into subjection to the divine rule, probably mediated through Israel and/or her Messiah. For many Jews, however, it was the smaller story that occupied their minds: they did not need to think beyond the rescue and restoration of which some of their key stories, such as the Passover haggadah, reminded them year by year.

Israel's stories are therefore to be understood, at their deepest level, not merely as moralistic tales or pious legends designed to glorify heroes and heroines of old. They embody, in a rich variety of ways, the worldview which in its most basic form remains anchored to the historical story of the world and Israel as a whole. The creator has called Israel to be his people. She is at present suffering, but must hold fast to his covenant code, and he will rescue her. There will come a time when, in a final recapitulation of the smaller stories, Israel will arrive at the conclusion of the larger one. This analysis of the Jewish story-line is not only of interest in itself. In helping us to understand how the first-century Jewish worldview functioned, and how the biblical stories which reinforced it would have been heard, it also gives us a grid against which we can measure the alternative stories told, implicitly and explicitly, by Jesus, Paul and the evangelists, and to see their points of convergence and divergence.

[24] e.g. 4 Ezra 6.55.

3. Symbols

(i) Introduction

The stories which articulate a worldview focus upon the symbols which bring that worldview into visible and tangible reality. There is no problem in identifying the four key symbols which functioned in this way in relation to the Jewish stories. At the heart of Jewish national life, for better or worse, stood the Temple. All around, looking to the Temple as its centre, lay the Land which the covenant god had promised to give to Israel, which was thus his by right and hers by promise. Both Temple and Land were regulated by the Torah, which formed the covenant charter for all that Israel was and hoped for, and whose importance increased in proportion to one's geographical distance from Land and Temple. Closely related to all three was the fact of Jewish ethnicity: the little race, divided by exile and diaspora, knew itself to be a family whose identity had to be maintained at all costs. Temple, Land, Torah and racial identity were the key symbols which anchored the first-century Jewish worldview in everyday life.

(ii) Temple

The Temple was the focal point of every aspect of Jewish national life.[25] Local synagogues and schools of Torah in other parts of Palestine, and in the Diaspora, in no way replaced it, but gained their significance from their implicit relation to it.[26] Its importance at every level can hardly be over-estimated:

> In the eyes of the people it constituted primarily the divine dwelling-place of the God of Israel which set them apart from other nations ... the offering of the sacrifices and the ritual cleansing involved atoned for the individual's transgressions and served as a framework for his spiritual elevation and purification ... The Temple, its vessels and even the high priest's vestments were depicted as representing the entire universe and the heavenly hosts ... With the destruction of the Temple the image of the universe was rendered defective, the established framework of the nation was undermined and a wall of steel formed a barrier between Israel and its heavenly Father.[27]

The Temple was thus regarded as the place where YHWH lived and ruled in the midst of Israel, and where, through the sacrificial system which reached its climax in the great festivals, he lived in grace, forgiving them, restoring them, and enabling them to be cleansed of defilement and so to continue as his

---

[25] See esp. Safrai 1976b; Barker 1991; Sanders 1992, chs. 5–8. Among older works cf. e.g. McKelvey 1969, chs. 1–4. On the role of the Temple in Jewish economic life cf. e.g. Broshi 1987.

[26] Safrai 1976b, 904f. This means that synagogues, like the Temple itself, were as much local socio-political meeting-places as purely 'religious' ones: cf. e.g. Jos. *Life* 276–9.

[27] Safrai, ibid. Although some of the evidence for these beliefs is Talmudic, enough is found in Josephus and Philo to make the summary of great value for our purposes. See too Neusner 1979, 22 on the Temple as the vital nexus between God and Israel.

people.[28] Defilement, of course, was not a matter of individual piety alone, but of communal life: uncleanness, which could be contracted in a large number of ways, meant disassociation from the people of the covenant god. Forgiveness, and consequent reintegration into the community of Israel, was attained by visiting the Temple and taking part in the appropriate forms of ritual and worship, and it was natural that the Temple should thus also be the centre of communal celebration.

But the Temple was not simply the 'religious' centre of Israel—even supposing that a distinction between religion and other departments of life could make any sense at the period in question. It was not, shall we say, the equivalent of Westminster Abbey, with 'Buckingham Palace' and the 'Houses of Parliament' being found elsewhere. The Temple combined in itself the functions of all three—religion, national figurehead and government—and also included what we think of as the City, the financial and economic world.[29] It also included, for that matter, the main slaughterhouse and butcher's guild: butchery was one of the main skills a priest had to possess. Allowing for the fact that the Romans were the *de facto* rulers of the country, the Temple was for Jews the centre of every aspect of national existence. The high priest, who was in charge of the Temple, was as important a political figure as he was a religious one. When we study the city-plan of ancient Jerusalem, the significance of the Temple stands out at once, since it occupies a phenomenally large proportion (about 25%) of the entire city. Jerusalem was not, like Corinth for example, a large city with lots of little temples dotted here and there. It was not so much a city with a temple in it; more like a temple with a small city round it.

For all these reasons, it is not surprising that the Temple became the focus of many of the controversies which divided Judaism in this period. An extreme position is represented by the Essenes, who probably had a community in Jerusalem at some stages, as well as at Qumran.[30] As we have seen, they rejected the post-Maccabaean Temple regime as illegitimate in theory and corrupt in practice, and looked forward to the day when a new Temple, officiated over by a properly constituted high priest, would be built according to the proper specifications.[31] The Pharisees objected in principle to the Hasmonean priesthood and its successors, but were prepared to tolerate it for the sake of being able to continue with the prescribed Temple rituals, as is clear from the fact that they, unlike the Essenes, continued to attend.

Dissatisfaction with the first-century Temple was also fuelled by the fact that, although it was certainly among the most beautiful buildings ever constructed, it was built by Herod.[32] Only the true King, the proper successor of

---

[28] On Temple-worship and its significance see now particularly Sanders 1992, chs. 5–8.

[29] This is illustrated in e.g. Pss. 46, 48. Readers from outside England can, I hope, translate the symbols I have used into their own equivalents: for the USA, the White House, Capitol Hill, the National Cathedral and Wall Street are the obvious start.

[30] Josephus mentions the 'gate of the Essenes' in *War* 5.145.

[31] See ch. 7 below. On evidence for, and attitudes to, corruption in the Temple in this period see particularly Evans 1989a, 1989b.

[32] On Herod's rebuilding of the Temple, see Jos. *Ant.* 15.380–425, and Schürer 1.292, 308f.; 2.57–8.

Solomon the original Temple-builder, had the right to build the Temple (see chapter 10 below); and whatever Herod was, he was not the true King. The last four prophetic books in the canon (Zephaniah, Haggai, Zechariah and Malachi), and in its own way the work of the Chronicler, all point to the restoration of the Temple under the leadership of a royal (Davidic), or possibly a priestly, figure.[33] Only when this work was done would the new age arrive. Conversely, if the new age was not yet present, as it was not (or else why would the Romans still be ruling the Land, and why had the Messiah not come?), any building that might happen to occupy the Temple mount could not possibly be the eschatological Temple itself. There was therefore a residual ambiguity about the second Temple in its various forms. Many Jews regarded it with suspicion and distrust. It nevertheless remained, *de facto* at least, the focal point of national, cultural and religious life.

The Temple thus formed in principle the heart of Judaism, in the full metaphorical sense: it was the organ from which there went out to the body of Judaism, in Palestine and in the Diaspora, the living and healing presence of the covenant god. The Temple was thus also, equally importantly, the focal point of the Land which the covenant god had promised to give to his people.

(iii) Land

The virtual absence of the Land as a major theme in the New Testament has led most New Testament scholarship to bypass it as a topic for full discussion.[34] But if we are to understand first-century Judaism we must rank Land, along with Temple and Torah, as one of the major symbols. It was YHWH's Land, given inalienably to Israel. The Romans had no more right to be ruling it than did any of their pagan predecessors. The Land was, of course, not only a symbol: it was the source of bread and wine, the place to graze sheep and goats, grow olives and figs. It was the place where, and the means through which, YHWH gave to his covenant people the blessings he had promised them, which were all summed up in the many-sided and evocative word *shalom*, peace. It was the new Eden, the garden of YHWH, the home of the true humanity.

And it was now being laid waste. Young men were driven off ancestral property because heavy taxation prevented them from making a living.[35] Alien cultural institutions (gymnasia, schools, pagan temples, Roman standards) were being set up in it. Although, as we shall see, 'the kingdom of god' had as its primary referent the *fact of* YHWH's becoming King, this social context

---

[33] See Juel 1977; Runnals 1983. The Chronicler so emphasizes David's responsibility for the building of the original Temple, and Solomon's actual building of it, as to point forward into the future from his own perspective with the hope that another son of David might arise to rebuild and restore it once more.

[34] Notable exceptions are Davies 1974; Freyne 1980, 1988. See too Brueggemann 1977.

[35] Sanders 1992, ch. 9 argues that this fact is often exaggerated; but, even if he is right, the ordinary Jewish family still had to bear a fairly substantial burden of taxation.

meant that the idea of divine kingship also carried the notion of the Land as the *place where* YHWH would be ruler. He would cleanse his holy Land, making it fit again for his people to inhabit, ruling the nations from it.

Jerusalem was obviously the major focal point of this Land. But the holiness of the 'holy Land' spread out in concentric circles, from the Holy of Holies to the rest of the Temple (itself divided into concentric areas), thence to the rest of Jerusalem, and thence to the whole Land.[36] And 'Galilee of the Nations', on the far side of hostile Samaria, surrounded by pagans, administered from a major Roman city (Sepphoris), was a vital part of this Land. It was, moreover, a part of it which was always suspected to be under pagan influence, and which needed to be held firm, with clear boundary-markers, against assimilation.[37] The question of whether a potentially seditious Galilean teacher showed his loyalty to Jerusalem by paying the Temple-tax is exactly the sort of issue we should expect to see raised in this period and this place.[38] If Israel's god claimed the whole Land, loyal Jews needed to make sure that they—and their compatriots—were keeping in line. This meant, among other things, making the appropriate tithes to show that they still regarded the produce of their fields as covenant blessings, so that they could demonstrate their link with the centre of covenant blessing, Jerusalem and the Temple itself, and thereby with the covenant god who had placed his name there.[39] It also meant, when necessary, cleansing the Land from pollution, in order to 'turn away wrath from Israel'.[40]

The fortunes of the Land, obviously, expressed the whole theme of exile and restoration, which we shall study in detail in the following chapters. The Land shared the ambiguity of the Temple: that is, it had been repossessed by those who returned from Babylon, but the repossession had been partial, and Israel did not in fact rule it herself except as a puppet (Roman troops were not, as is sometimes imagined, everywhere in evidence, but they were near enough to be called upon if movements towards independence reared their heads).[41] Control and cleansing were what was required, and as long as Rome was policing and polluting YHWH's sacred turf it was obvious that neither had happened.

(iv) Torah

The Torah was the covenant charter of Israel as the people of the covenant god. Temple and Torah formed an unbreakable whole: the Torah sanctioned

---

[36] cf. Ezek. 40–8.

[37] See Freyne 1988, ch. 6.

[38] Mt. 17.24–7; cf. Horbury 1984. We may compare Jos. *Life* 104–11, in which Josephus, having come from Jerusalem, attempts to dissuade Galilean rebels from their sedition.

[39] See Sanders 1992, 146–57.

[40] 1 Macc. 3.8; *Ant.* 12.286 (both referring to the activity of Judas Maccabaeus).

[41] Between 63 BC and AD 66 there were Roman troops stationed at Caesarea Maritima, and small garrisons in Jerusalem and a few other towns, e.g. Jericho: see, with the evidence, Schürer 1.362–7. The centurion at Capernaum (Mt. 8.5 and pars.) was presumably stationed there because it was near the border between Galilee and Philip's territory of Gaulanitis. Customs were levied there since at least the break-up of Herod's kingdom (Schürer 1.374).

and regulated what happened in the Temple, and the Temple was (in much of this period) the practical focal point for the observance of Torah, both in the sense that much Torah-observance actually consisted of Temple-ritual, and in the sense that the Temple was the major place for study and teaching of Torah.[42] So, too, Torah and Land formed a tight bond. The Torah offered the promises about the Land, the blessings which would be given in and through it, and the detailed instructions as to the behaviour necessary for blessing to be maintained. After all, the reason that YHWH had driven out the previous occupants of the Land was precisely their idolatry and immorality. Israel had to be different if she was not going to suffer the same fate.[43]

At the same time, ever since the exile it had been possible to study and practise Torah (or, at any rate, that which came to be seen as Torah) even without the Temple and the Land. In the exile, of course, there was no Temple. This, naturally, constituted part of the problem of how to be a Jew in Babylon, how to sing YHWH's song in a strange land. But in the Diaspora, then and subsequently, the study and practice of Torah increasingly became the focal point of Jewishness. For millions of ordinary Jews, Torah became a portable Land, a movable Temple.[44] The Pharisees in particular, in conjunction with the burgeoning synagogue movement, developed the theory that study and practice of Torah could take the place of Temple worship. Where two or three gather to study Torah, the Shekinah rests upon them.[45] The presence of the covenant god was not, after all, confined to the Temple in Jerusalem, which was both a long way off and in the hands of corrupt aristocrats. It had been democratized, made available to all who would study and practise Torah.

The sanctity and supreme importance of Torah, seen from this perspective, can hardly be exaggerated. Those who kept it with rigour were, in some ways though not all, as if they were priests in the Temple.[46] Not that the Pharisees, until the destruction actually happened, ever imagined a Judaism without Temple and Land altogether. In the Diaspora they still looked to Jerusalem; after the destruction, as we saw, many of them yearned and agonized for the Temple to be rebuilt. But Torah provided, in both cases, a second-best substitute which, in long years without the reality, came to assume all its attributes. In later Judaism, the ideologies proper to Temple and Land were fused together into the central symbol of Torah.[47]

With natural logic, the sacrificial system was also translated into terms of Torah. One cannot go to Jerusalem to offer the sacrifices on a regular basis if one lives in Babylon or Rome, in Athens or Alexandria, as a large number of

---

[42] On the relation between Temple and Torah see Freyne 1988, 190f.

[43] Gen. 15.16; Lev. 18.24–8; Dt. 9.4–5; 18.12, etc.

[44] See Sanders 1990a, chs. 2–3: without travelling to the Temple, Jews would be technically unclean most of the time.

[45] mAb. 3.2.

[46] See ch. 7 above on Pharisees and Essenes, and esp. Sanders 1990a, ch.3; 1992, 352–60, 376, 438–40.

[47] See again chs. 6 and 7 above. The synagogue itself, as the focus of the teaching of Torah, also came to function as a major Jewish symbol. See Gutmann 1981; Levine 1987; Sanders 1990a, 67–81; 1992, 198–202. On the question of the antiquity of the building and use of synagogues cf. Shanks 1979; Kee 1990; and Sanders 1990a, 341–3, notes 28, 29.

would-be observant Jews did. Observance of key Torah commandments will do instead. 'Spiritual sacrifices' are thus offered when one gives alms, or prays, or studies Torah, or fasts.[48] It is difficult to tell how far this had been taken by the time of Jesus, but the progression is natural and clear. In the eyes of its adherents, Torah had come to assume the status of the Temple, and, with that, to take on divine qualities.[49] In the presence of Torah one was in the presence of the covenant god. Thus, what became true for all of Judaism after 70 and 135 was anticipated in the necessities of Diaspora life.

And the Torah, especially in the Diaspora, but also anywhere where Jews felt themselves beleaguered, as they mostly did in one way or another, could be seen as focusing on those things which distinguished Jews from their (potentially threatening) pagan neighbours: circumcision, the keeping of the sabbath, and the purity laws. With these we move into the closely related world of praxis, where the symbols come to life on a daily basis. We shall examine this presently.

If Torah is to be kept in every detail of everyday life, it must be applied to those details in a way that was clearly not done in the Pentateuch itself. The Bible instructs Israelites to dwell in booths when they celebrate the feast of Tabernacles. But what counts as a 'booth'? One must debate, and get it right; not to do so would be to treat Torah flippantly.[50] So, too, the Bible prescribes a ceremony to be used when the brother of a dead man refuses to discharge his obligation by marrying the widow: but how precisely is the ceremony to be performed?[51] These are two tiny examples of an enormous phenomenon, as a result of which there grew up a large body of what is in effect detailed case law. In the first century, this was not written down, nor officially codified, but passed on from teacher to pupil by repetition. The Hebrew for 'repetition' is *Mishnah*: thus, quite naturally, was born one of the basic genres of Jewish literature.

The 'Mishnah' itself was not written down until around the start of the second century AD. But, as we saw in the previous two chapters, many of its debates reflect, even if they distort, earlier debates and controversies. Since these took place in the oral, not the written, mode, we are faced with the question of 'oral Torah'. It has sometimes been claimed that the Pharisees created a large body of oral Torah well before the turn of the eras, and that they valued this oral Torah higher than the written Torah. The former was, after

---

[48] e.g. Pss. 40.6–8; 50.7–15; 51.16f.; 69.30f.; 141.2. See Millgram 1971, 81–3, 254, 361. For the details: on prayer, bTaan. 2a, bBer. 32b (R. Eleazar); on acts of mercy, Aboth de Rab. Nathan 4; on study of Torah (making one equivalent to a high priest), Midr. Pss. 1.26, 2.300; on fasting, bBer. 17a. These later texts embody, to be sure, a post-destruction rationalization; but they pretty certainly also reflect the reality of pre-destruction Diaspora life.

[49] cf. Sir. 24.1–23, where Wisdom is identified with the clouded Presence (24.4; cf. Ex. 14.19f.), with Shekinah (24.8–12) and then with Torah (24.23); Jos. *Apion* 2.277 ('our Law at least remains immortal'); Bar. 4.1f. ('She is the book of the commandments of God, the law that endures forever. All who hold her fast will live, and those who forsake her will die. Turn, O Jacob, and take her; walk towards the shining of her light'); 4 Ezra 9.26–37; mSanh. 10.1.

[50] For the command: Lev. 23.42; cf. Neh. 8.17f. For the discussion of valid booths, mSukk. 1.1–11. For the desire to 'get everything just right', cf. Sanders 1992, 494.

[51] Dt. 25.7–9; cf. Ruth 4.1–12; mYeb. 12.1–6.

all, somewhat esoteric: anybody could read the written Torah, but the oral Torah was the special prerogative of those to whom it had been entrusted. It was given the status of antiquity through the pious fiction of being ascribed, like the written Torah, to Moses himself.[52]

This view of an early and high-status oral Torah has been subjected to damaging criticism, and cannot now be maintained as it stands.[53] The view just outlined corresponds, in fact, more closely to the secret teachings of the Essenes: they, it appears, really did possess secret laws which they regarded as equivalent to, and as coming from the same source as, the written Torah itself. The Temple Scroll carries this to its logical conclusion, being written in the first person, as though coming direct from YHWH himself. But the Pharisees on the one hand, and ordinary Jews on the other, while they undoubtedly had case law which enabled them to apply the Torah to particular situations, did not claim for this a status exactly equivalent to the written Torah itself. They interpreted, they applied, they developed Torah. They had to. But they knew when they were doing it.

It is important to see what they were thereby achieving. The alternatives to developing some system of oral Torah (without capital letters) was to abandon the Torah itself. Case law was a way of preserving the Torah as a symbol. It could not be abandoned without giving up one major part of the worldview. Torah was interwoven with covenant, promises, Land and hope. Admit that one has abandoned Torah, and one admits to being a traitor to Israel. The detailed discussions of how Torah should be kept on a day-to-day basis are therefore ways of maintaining the vital symbol while making it relevant, while turning it into praxis. This illustrates a vital point about the elements of worldviews. A symbol that loses touch with either story or praxis becomes worthless. The Pharisees and their would-be successors developed ways of ensuring that this did not happen.

(v) Racial Identity

The question of who was actually a pure-bred Jew became one of the large issues among those who returned from Babylon in the period known, however misleadingly, as 'the return from exile'. The long genealogies that open 1 Chronicles, and that characterize Ezra and Nehemiah,[54] bear witness to the strongly felt need in the newly founded community to make good its claim to be the children of Abraham, Isaac and Jacob. Just as the Temple formed the inner circle of the Land, so the Priests formed the inner circle of Israel, and their genealogies were particularly important.[55] As the returning Israelites retold the stories of their forefathers, they were reminded of the events which had brought (in their prophetic interpretation) catastrophe upon Israel: inter-

---

[52] For this view of oral Torah see e.g. Rivkin 1978.
[53] Sanders 1990a, ch. 2.
[54] 1 Chron. 1–9; Ezra 2, 8, 10; Neh. 7, 12.
[55] cf. Ezra 2.59–63.

marriage with non-Israelites had precipitated a slide into paganism. This rereading in turn prompted anxiety, in that the same phenomenon was occurring again, and one of the focal points of Ezra's work, according to the book that bears his name, was to insist upon Israelite men separating from pagan wives.[56] Unless this was done, the 'holy seed', which seems to have functioned as an evocative synonym for 'the remnant', would be polluted.[57] Israel's god has further purposes for this 'seed', and it is therefore vital that it be kept pure. Not only intermarriage, but also the practice of allowing foreigners into 'the assembly of God', was prohibited.[58] Josephus, reflecting on this whole episode, and particularly Ezra's banning of foreigners, from his position in the late first century, remarks that Ezra thus 'purified the practice relating to this matter so that it remained fixed for the future'.[59] The book of Esther, too, stands as powerful testimony both to early anti-Semitism and to the response: the Jews must stay together and refuse to compromise with pagans.

With this fifth-century background (remembering that what matters for our present purpose is not what actually happened at that period, but how the story was being retold in the post-Maccabaean period), it is scarcely surprising that we find the issue of racial purity maintaining its significance. The fifth-century Jews had been surrounded by hostile forces who resented the re-establishment of a Jewish state, and were faced with a special problem in the form of those who became known as the Samaritans.[60] This sense of being beleaguered on all sides increased, as we saw, under Syrian rule, and by the first century BC the ideology which preserved the Jewish race intact was simply taken for granted. The covenant sign of circumcision marked out the Jews as the chosen people; sexual relations, and the begetting of offspring, was appropriate for Jews within the context of that people, but not outside.

We thus find, in works from the Hasmonean and Roman periods, an emphasis on the race as the true people. The Testament of Dan urges the Jews to 'turn from unrighteousness of every kind and hold fast to the righteousness of the law of the Lord; and your race will be kept safe for ever'.[61] The apocryphal book of Baruch urges Jews:

Do not give your glory to another,
or your advantages to an alien people.

---

[56] Ezra 9–10.

[57] Ezra 9.2; cf. Isa. 6.13; Mal. 2.15. The latter verse is difficult (cf. Smith 1984, 318–25; Fuller 1991, 52–4), but I suggest that it should be read: 'Did not he [i.e. God] make one [i.e. man and woman in marriage]? And the remnant-of-spirit [i.e. the true family, returned from Babylon] is his [i.e. God's plan for renewing Israel is in hand]. And why [did he make you] "one"? Because he intends to produce "seed-of-God" [not just "godly children", but the true "seed", through whom the promises will find fulfilment].' The problem seems to be that Jews who had earlier married Jewish wives had then divorced and married pagans. This, the prophet says, is not only covenant-breaking, but is putting in jeopardy the long-term purposes of Israel's god.

[58] Neh. 13.1–3.

[59] *Ant.* 11.153, reading *monimon*, 'fixed', with the Loeb, rather than the variant *nomimon*, 'statutory'. The difference is immaterial for our purposes.

[60] On the Samaritans see Schürer 2.16–20.

[61] *T.Dan* 6.10 (tr. M. de Jonge in Sparks 1984, 566). The last clause is missing from one MS, and is not even noted by H. C. Kee in Charlesworth 1983, 810.

Happy are we, O Israel,
for we know what is pleasing to God.[62]

Even Josephus, in his eagerness to present the Jews as accommodating and hospitable to pagans, makes it quite clear that the welcome goes so far and no further:

> To all who desire to come and live under the same laws with us, he [i.e. Moses] gives a gracious welcome, holding that it is not family ties alone which constitute relationship, but agreement in the principles of conduct. On the other hand, it was not his pleasure that casual visitors should be admitted to the intimacies of our daily life.[63]

The *Letter of Aristeas* proves the same point: Jews must set a good example to the world, but at the same time must remain clearly distinct.[64] The most notable sign of an emphasis on racial purity is of course the notice in the Temple which forbade non-Jews to penetrate further than the 'court of the Gentiles'.[65] Though of course Jews who lived in day-to-day contact with Gentiles, as many of them did even in Palestine itself, had no choice but to mix with them regularly and quite freely, the literature gives us a fairly clear sense that Gentiles were presumed to be in principle idolaters, immoral and ritually impure.[66]

Jewish racial identity remained, throughout our period, a cultural and religious symbol every bit as vital as Temple, Land and Torah, and indeed thoroughly linked with all of these. We will see presently the way in which this symbol gave rise to particular forms of praxis, and the ways in which it was reinterpreted in borderline cases.

(vi) Conclusion

The four symbols we have studied in this section clearly dovetailed completely into the story-themes we examined earlier. Symbol and story are mutually reinforcing: those who adhere to the first are implicitly telling the second, and vice versa. The symbols therefore provided fixed points which functioned as signals, to oneself and to one's neighbour, that one was hearing the story and living by it. They became in themselves stories in stone, in soil, in scroll, or in flesh and blood—just as the stories, and the fact of their retelling, were themselves symbolic. But stories and symbols must be integrated into the praxis which brought them alive. To this we now turn.

---

[62] Bar. 4.3f.

[63] Jos. *Apion* 2.210 (cf. *Ant.* 13.245, where the key word is *amixia*, 'separateness'). Thackeray's note ad loc., suggesting a reference to Passover, as in Ex. 12.43, is hardly relevant to *daily* life (so, rightly, Sanders 1990b, 183). Cp. too the prohibitions of intermarriage in *Jub.* 30.7, 14–17; *Ps-Philo* 9.5, etc.

[64] *Ep. Arist.* 139 (in its context), etc.

[65] See *War* 5.193f.; 6.125f.; and Schürer 1.175f., 378; 2.80, 222, 284f.

[66] See further section 4 (iv) below.

4. Praxis

(i) Introduction

It is commonly said that Judaism is not a 'faith', but a way of life. This is at best a half-truth. But it is true that Judaism gives 'theology' a lower place in its regular discussions than it does to the question: what ought one to do? If one is to keep the symbols alive, one must quite simply live by them. And the chief symbol by which one lives is of course Torah.

But the daily keeping of Torah was by no means the long and the short of first-century Jewish praxis. The high points of praxis in any one year were the major festivals, which both retold Israel's story and highlighted her key symbols. Second, there was the actual study of Torah: if one is to practise, one must first learn. It is in that context that we will consider, third, the day-to-day practice of Torah and what it involved.

(ii) Worship and Festivals

We have already seen that the Temple and the synagogue were far more than institutions where an individual might pursue his or her private religion in company with like-minded others, away from ordinary life. Temple and synagogue were vital social, political and cultural institutions just as much as 'religious' ones (such distinctions are of course anachronistic anyway in our period). There were daily as well as weekly services in both. Regular prayers were taught for private as well as public use, for the family (especially at meals), and for special occasions. The average Jew would grow up knowing the basic prayers, and a good many psalms, at least as well as, and probably much better than, the average child in a churchgoing family today knows the Lord's Prayer, several hymns, and—to grasp at a secular equivalent—the regular jingles of television advertisements. What (some) first-century Jews may have lacked in literacy they will more than have made up for in memory.[67]

Sabbath services in particular were a major social focus, a vital sign of loyalty to Israel. The regular prayers—the *Shema* and the Eighteen Benedictions being of course central features[68]—sustained and rejuvenated the Jewish self-consciousness, reinforced the worldview and the hope. There was one god, Israel was his people, and he would deliver them soon. In the mean time they must remain faithful.

The same message, heightened in emotional and cultural impact by the excitement of going on pilgrimage (if one could afford the time or money), and by the development of local equivalents (if one could not),[69] was undergirded

---

[67] See W. D. Davies 1987, 19-21; on the obligation even for children to recite certain prayers see mBer. 3.3. For the praying life of Jews as part of the whole culture see e.g. Sanders 1990a, 331; 1992, 195-208. See further below, on the use of the Bible.

[68] Schürer 2.447-9, 454-63; Sanders 1992, loc. cit.

[69] On the celebration of festivals outside Palestine see Schürer 3.144.

by the major festivals which brought Jews in their thousands to Jerusalem three or more times a year.[70] The three major festivals, the high holy days, and the two additional festivals of Hanukkah and Purim, summed up a good deal of the theology and national aspiration we have been studying, and celebrated it in great symbolic actions and liturgies.[71] These festivals and fasts thus gave both reinforcement and reality to Israel's theology.

The three major festivals were of course intimately connected with agriculture (Passover, with barley harvest; Pentecost, with wheat harvest and the bringing of first-fruits to the Temple;[72] Tabernacles, with the grape harvest). They thus symbolically celebrated the blessing of Israel's god upon his Land and his people, and thereby drew together the two major covenantal themes of Temple and Land. In addition, Passover celebrated the exodus from Egypt; Pentecost, the giving of Torah on Sinai;[73] Tabernacles, the wilderness wandering on the way to the promised land. All three therefore focused attention on key aspects of Israel's story, and in the retelling of that story encouraged the people once again to think of themselves as the creator's free people, who would be redeemed by him and so vindicated in the eyes of the world. This theme was amplified in the prayers appointed for the different occasions.[74]

The two extra festivals made substantially the same point, though without the agricultural connection. Hanukkah, commemorating the overthrow of Antiochus Epiphanes by Judas and his followers, underlined the vital importance of true monotheistic worship and the belief that when the tyrants raged against Israel her god would come to the rescue. Purim, celebrating the story found in the book of Esther, re-enacted the reversal of Haman's plot to destroy the Jews in the Persian empire; it drove home the same message.[75] Together the five feasts ensured that any Jew who made any attempt to join in—and by all accounts participation was widespread—would emerge with the basic worldview strengthened: one God, Israel as his people, the sacredness of the Land, the inviolability of Torah, and the certainty of redemption. Even the regular monthly festival of the New Moon reinforced the last point, as the new shining after a period of darkness symbolized the restoration of Israel after her period of suffering.[76]

The same message, too, was driven home by the regular fasts. Zechariah 8.19 lists four such fasts, taking place in the fourth, fifth, seventh and tenth months. All four were in fact linked to events connected with the destruction of Jerusalem by the Babylonians; keeping them was a reminder that Israel was

---

[70] Schürer 2.76.

[71] See Millgram 1971, chs. 8 (199–223), 9 (224–60), 10 (261–88). On the high holy days see ch. 9 below.

[72] Described in mBikk. 3.2–4.

[73] Not mentioned in this connection in the OT, but clearly a pre-rabbinic tradition, with echoes in the NT. See *Jub.* 1.5; 6.11, 17; 15.1–24; bPes. 68b; and Ac. 2.1–11; Eph. 4.7–10, etc. (see Caird 1964; Lincoln 1990, 243f., citing also evidence from the later synagogue lectionary). The addition of Simchat Torah to Tabernacles is a later innovation.

[74] Millgram 1971, 214.

[75] On Hanukkah see Schürer 1.162-3; on Purim, 2.450.

[76] So Millgram 1971, 265.

still waiting for her real redemption from exile.[77] The same point, of course, was made most strikingly for both individual and nation in the high holy days. The passage in Zechariah, interestingly, speaks of the four fasts being turned into feasts. How could this prophecy be fulfilled, except by the real return from exile—which, by implication, had still not taken place at the time when Zechariah 8 was written?[78]

Feasts and fasts thus enacted the entire Jewish worldview, and gave regular reinforcement to the fundamental Jewish hope. Temple, Land, Torah and racial identity were encapsulated in symbolic actions and memorable phrases, all of which gave expression to the Jewish belief in one god and his election of Israel, and the hope to which this twin belief gave rise.

(iii) Study and Learning

The context of Torah-study must be understood as the resolute application of passages such as these:

> The law of YHWH is perfect,
>   reviving the soul;
> the decrees of YHWH are sure,
>   making wise the simple;
> the precepts of YHWH are right,
>   rejoicing the heart;
> the commandment of YHWH is clear,
>   enlightening the eyes;
> the fear of YHWH is pure,
>   enduring forever;
> the ordinances of YHWH are true
>   and righteous altogether.
> More to be desired are they than gold,
>   even much fine gold;
> sweeter also than honey
>   and drippings of the honeycomb.
>
> Oh, how I love your law!
>   It is my meditation all day long.
>
> Consider how I love your precepts;
>   preserve my life according to your steadfast love.
> The sum of your words is truth;
>   and every one of your righteous ordinances endures for ever.[79]

If Torah was a symbol which encapsulated the Jewish worldview, it was necessary that some Jews at least be committed to a serious programme of study. The only way in which one could become a master of Torah was to

---

[77] Millgram 1971, 275ff.; Safrai 1976a, 814-6; Schürer 2.483f. Zech. 7.3f. mentions the fasts of the fifth and seventh months as being kept during the time of the exile. There were of course extra fast-days added in case of particular calamities; see Schürer 2.483f.; Safrai loc. cit.; and e.g. Jos. *Life* 290.

[78] See ch. 10 below.

[79] Pss. 19.7–10; 119.97, 159f.

spend hours and days becoming familiar with it. Nor was this study undertaken in (as we might say) a 'purely academic' way. If to study the Torah is the equivalent to being in the Temple, in the presence of the Shekinah, then studying becomes in itself a 'religious' activity, picking up these themes from the psalms. In this spirit the pious Jews of the second-temple period went to their work. At one extreme, of course, this was simply a necessary function of a society: there has to be a group who know their way about the law and can see that it is put into effect. But at the other extreme there was a sense, as in these psalms, of delighting in it for its own sake, as one of the key places where the covenant god had agreed to meet with his people. The priests were the great teachers and guardians of Torah; but there grew up alongside them, at what period it is hard to say with precision, a corps of lay scribes and teachers, who appear in the work of Ben-Sirach (early second century BC), where we meet the blend of study and piety just noted. After pointing out that all kinds of professions are necessary, as we say, 'to make the world go round' (38.1–34a), he proceeds:

> How different the one who devotes himself
>   to the study of the law of the Most High!
> He seeks out the wisdom of all the ancients,
>   and is concerned with prophecies;
> he preserves the sayings of the famous
>   and penetrates the subtleties of parables . . .
> He sets his heart to rise early
>   to seek the Lord who made him,
>   and to petition the Most High;
> he opens his mouth in prayer
>   and asks pardon for his sins . . .
> The Lord will direct his counsel and knowledge,
>   as he meditates on his mysteries.
> He will show the wisdom of what he has learned,
>   and will glory in the law of the Lord's covenant.[80]

Or, as one of Akiba's disciples, Rabbi Meir (second century AD), put it:

> Engage not overmuch in business but occupy thyself with the Law; and be lowly in spirit before all men. If thou neglectest the Law many things neglected shall rise against thee; but if thou labourest in the Law He has abundant reward to give thee.[81]

The study of Torah was thus revered and institutionalized within second-temple Judaism. It was not one profession among others; nor, as in some modern countries, was study discounted as an irrelevance within a hard-headed practical world. It was, after priesthood itself, the supreme vocation, and commanded the highest respect:

> In the study of the Law, if the son gained much wisdom [the while he sat] before his teacher, his teacher comes ever before his father, since both he and his father are bound to honour the teacher.[82]

---

[80] Sir. 38.34b–39.8.
[81] mAb. 4.10.
[82] mKer. 6.9; cp. mBMez. 2.11.

Study of Torah, as a key feature of first-century praxis, thus acquired a symbolic as well as a practical function; and it integrated into the story-line of the worldview. Israel's god gave his Torah to Moses, and one of the most characteristically Jewish activities is to study it, both for its own sake and so that one may bring oneself, and those whom one can influence or teach, under the leading of that which has been identified not only with the divine wisdom but with the tabernacling presence of YHWH himself.[83] But this then leads to the other side of the same coin. How did Torah work out in practice?

(iv) Torah in Practice

If Torah was a vital symbol within first-century Judaism, it was a severely practical one. At a time when Judaism's distinctive identity was under constant threat, Torah provided three badges in particular which marked the Jew out from the pagan: circumcision, sabbath, and the kosher laws, which regulated what food could be eaten, how it was to be killed and cooked, and with whom one might share it. In and through all this ran the theme of Jewish 'separateness'.

Within an all-Jewish or mostly-Jewish society, circumcision could be assumed, and the manner of its keeping was (more or less) uncontroversial: a male was either circumcised or he was not.[84] But, even within such societies, the keeping of sabbath was a matter of dispute: what counted and what did not?[85] The maintaining of purity was even more uncertain: what rendered one unclean and what did not?[86] Debates about sabbath and purity, therefore, occupied an immense amount of time and effort in the discussions of the learned, as we know from the Mishnah and Talmud.[87] This was not, it should be stressed, because Jews in general or Pharisees in particular were concerned merely for outward ritual or ceremony, nor because they were attempting to earn their salvation (within some later sub-Christian scheme!) by virtuous living. It was because they were concerned for the divine Torah, and were therefore anxious to maintain their god-given distinctiveness over against the pagan nations, particularly those who were oppressing them. Their whole *raison-d'être* as a nation depended on it. Their devotion to the one god was enshrined in it. Their coming liberation might perhaps be hastened by it, or conversely postponed by failure in it. If one's basic categories of thought were

---

[83] Sir. 24.10–12, 23.

[84] Circumcision was prohibited under Antiochus Epiphanes, and then again under Hadrian: see 1 Macc. 1.14f.; *Jub.* 15.33f.; and Schürer 1.155, 537–40. Some Jews attempted at various times to remove the marks of circumcision (ch. 6 above). Though the necessity of circumcision was sometimes debated, it was basically regarded as vital for full conversion to Judaism (see the debate over the conversion of Izates in the mid-first century: Jos. *Ant.* 20.38–48; and the discussion of circumcision of refugees in *Life* 112f.).

[85] See Sanders 1990a, 6–23; 1992, 208–11.

[86] Sanders 1990a, chs. 3–4, modified somewhat by 1992, 214–22.

[87] Sabbath: mShabb., mErub., *passim*, and frequently elsewhere. Purity: Tohoroth (the 6th division of the Mishnah), *passim*.

monotheism and election, creation and covenant, it is hard to see how at this period one could think differently.

To a Palestinian Jew of the first century, particularly to a Pharisee, therefore, maintaining the marks of Jewish distinctiveness was quite simply non-negotiable. One could debate the details of *how* these marks should be maintained; *that* they should be observed was not to be questioned. A challenge at this point was like an axe laid to the roots of the tree. Particularly in territory under threat or pressure, Jews who did not observe sabbath and purity were like someone in modern Montreal who puts up an English shop-sign, or like someone in any country who tears down the national flag. They were traitors to the national symbols, to the national hope, to the covenant god.

Torah thus provided the vital covenant boundary-marker, especially in those areas where it seemed important to maintain Israel's distinctiveness. That this was the case in Galilee ought to go without saying. If one were in Jerusalem, the Temple (still governed by Torah, but assuming the central role) was the dominant cultural and religious symbol. It was around this that Israel was organized, it was this that the covenant god would vindicate. But away from Jerusalem (in Galilee, or in the Diaspora) it was Torah, and particularly the special badges of sabbath and purity, that demarcated the covenant people, and that therefore provided litmus tests of covenant loyalty and signs of covenant hope.[88]

This conclusion, as we shall see later, is a point of peculiar significance for understanding both Jesus' controversies and Pauline theology. The 'works of Torah' were not a legalist's ladder, up which one climbed to earn the divine favour, but were the badges that one wore as the marks of identity, of belonging to the chosen people in the present, and hence the all-important signs, to oneself and one's neighbours, that one belonged to the company who would be vindicated when the covenant god acted to redeem his people. They were the present signs of future vindication. This was how 'the works of Torah' functioned within the belief, and the hope, of Jews and particularly of Pharisees.[89]

To what extent, then, did this practice of Torah mean that Jews were committed to a policy of non-contact with Gentiles? It is often assumed that Jews simply had no dealings with Gentiles (perhaps on the basis of a tacit *a fortiori* from their well-known policy of having no dealings with Samaritans);[90] but this is misleading. Even in Judaea and Galilee Gentiles could not be avoided; in the Diaspora only the most sheltered ghetto-dweller could avoid daily contact, and quite likely dealings, with Gentiles.[91] The fact that the Mishnah devotes an entire tractate (*Abodah Zarah*) to the question of how not to partake in Gentile idolatry shows the theological dimension of the question: but the trac-

---

[88] cf. *Apion* 2.277.

[89] See ch. 10 below. This is, more or less, what Sanders means by his phrase 'Covenantal Nomism' (see now 1992, 262–78), and I think he is here substantially correct. On 'works of Torah' in Paul see Dunn 1990, 216–25; Westerholm 1988, 109-21, etc.

[90] Sir. 50.25f. (the position of this statement, in the middle of the book's peroration, is strikingly emphatic); Jn. 4.8, etc. In mBer. 7.1, however, it is presupposed that one might eat with a Samaritan.

[91] So, rightly, Sanders 1990b, 179.

tate also shows that business with Gentiles was the norm, and that abstaining from it (e.g. before a pagan festival) was the exception.[92] The question then becomes: how were these dealings regulated? What counted as assimilation, and what as a necessary evil?

Sanders has argued that Jews in this period would not object in principle to associating with Gentiles, or even to eating with them, but that there would have been a general sense that one ought not to do these things too much.[93] This seems to me on the right lines, but I think if anything Sanders errs on the side of emphasizing Jewish openness to associating with Gentiles. Granted that ordinary life, especially in the Diaspora, was impossible without some such association, and that eating with Gentiles was not expressly forbidden anywhere (though eating their food, and drinking their wine, was ruled out),[94] there still seems to me very good warrant for believing that most Jews most of the time felt that fidelity to Torah implied non-association as far as one could manage it.

In his natural eagerness to exonerate first-century Jews from the charge of being arrogantly exclusive and stand-offish towards Gentiles,[95] Sanders seems to me to have made two unjustified moves. First, he argues (rightly) that one cannot retroject later rabbinic passages into the pre-70 period, but implies (surely incorrectly) that the pre-70 period would have been less likely than the post-70 period as a setting for anti-Gentile codes.[96] This is surely unwarranted. 'Pre-70', we should not forget, means 'post-167' and 'post-63' (both of course BC). The doctrine of *amixia*, 'separatedness', is asserted by Josephus to be well in place even before the Maccabaean revolt, and even if this is anachronistic it certainly shows what could be presupposed in the first century AD.[97] We also have evidence of the promulgation of strict codes, forbidding mixing with Gentiles, precisely from the pre-war period.[98] The codes were undoubtedly not to everyone's liking; especially in the Diaspora, regulations that may have been workable for pious circles in Jerusalem were perceived as impracticable.[99] Yet there was clearly a strong body of opinion, throughout the period from the Maccabees to bar-Kochba, that Gentiles were basically unclean and that contact with them should be kept to a minimum. Here, as elsewhere, we should think of a continuum both of theory (e.g. between Shammaites and Hillelites, and between both of them and assimilated Jews in the Diaspora) and of prac-

[92] mAb. Zar. 1.1–3, 5.

[93] Sanders 1990b, esp. 185f.

[94] See Jos. *Life* 14: some priests on their way to Rome only ate figs and nuts. This introduces a moderating note into Sanders' criticism of Bruce (1990b, 188 n.20).

[95] Sanders 1990b, 181f. The charge was made in antiquity: Tac. *Hist.* 5.5; Diod. Sic. 34/5.1.1–5, speaking of the Jewish laws as *ta misoxena nomima*, 'the hating-foreigners statutes'; Juv. *Sat.* 14.103f. See Schürer 3.153.

[96] Sanders 1990b, 172f.

[97] *Ant.* 13.245–7, esp. 247: '[the Jews] . . . did not come into contact with other people because of their separateness (*amixia*)'. See the note of Marcus in the Loeb, ad loc.; and cp. *Apion* 2.210.

[98] See the full discussion in Hengel 1989 [1961], 200–6, including a discussion of non-mixing with Gentiles in the Hasmonean period.

[99] See Hengel 1989 [1961], 203.

tice (some Jews will have had minimal contact, others a good deal).[100] But to say, as Sanders does, that 'the full expression of antipathy to Gentiles' cannot safely be retrojected earlier than 135 is to go against all we know of Judaism between the Maccabees and bar-Kochba. No doubt the post-135 rabbis added anti-Gentile sentiments of their own. But they added them to a collection that was already well established.[101]

Second, Sanders' argument seems to slide from his demonstration that contact with Gentiles was not ruled out into the suggestion that eating with Gentiles was equally permissible. He does this by the argument that all Jews were impure in any case most of the time, unless they were about to go into the Temple, and hence that even if Gentiles did partake in impurity no-one would worry, since everyone with whom one had contact was impure anyway.[102] This seems to me to cut loose from the actual socio-cultural context into a world of pure legal formality which Sanders himself has elsewhere demonstrated to be an inadequate reading of Mishnaic Judaism. The rabbinic dictum that Gentiles' houses are unclean, with the presupposition that this is because they throw miscarriages or deliberate abortions down the drains,[103] seems to indicate that there was a general *mood*, a fixed though often incoherent belief, that Gentiles were unclean and contact with them undesirable, even if when pressed the reason given was lame. Like so many quasi-theological arguments, the reason given is a manifest rationalization of a preceding and presupposed socio-cultural phenomenon, but in this case what matters is the contemporary phenomenon. Jews may not have had a good explanation for it, but ever since the exile, and increasingly since the Maccabaean revolt and the subsequent arrival of the Romans, Gentiles were the hated enemy, and serious fraternization with them was stepping out of line. To object that legally a Gentile was no more a polluting agent than one's ordinary (and usually, technically speaking, 'unclean') Jewish neighbour is, I think, to miss the point. The racial barrier cannot be reduced to terms of legalistically conceived ritual purity alone.[104] As in other areas, the tradition has altered the *focus* of a piece of teaching. We saw earlier that a debate about canonicity was turned into a debate about purity;[105] here we see an equally obvious move from a question of social policy to a question of purity.

[100] I think Sanders (1990b, 173f.) is thus a little unfair to Alon 1977, 146–89. Alon is not *simply* tracing later codes back to hypothetical early roots. The question of how long a Gentile is unclean after becoming a proselyte (mPes. 8.8 [not 8.1 as in Sanders 1990a, 284; 1990b, 174]) is not to the point; upon conversion the person becomes a Jew, and enters a new world with new regulations.

[101] See ch.7 section 2 above. We need only cite 2 Maccabees and the Psalms of Solomon. Schiffman 1983 has shown that the regulations on relations with Gentiles in CD 12.6–11 are closely parallel to the later Tannaitic material.

[102] 1990a, 284; 1990b, 174ff.

[103] mOhol. 18.7, with Danby's note; cf. mNidd. 3.7. The latter passage includes a saying by Rabbi Ishmael (a contemporary of Akiba); the former is not ascribed. On this, see Alon 1977, 186, demonstrating his awareness of the way in which traditions and explanations changed meaning over time.

[104] See Alon 1977, 187, 189, recognizing that though the idea of Gentile uncleanness goes back at least before the time of Herod, there was always a wide variety of actual practice.

[105] Above, p. 183.

The actual practice of Torah, then, no doubt varied greatly from one Jewish community to another, especially when one went outside the borders of the Land and entered the problematic world of the Diaspora. Nevertheless, difficulty (for the Jews of the time) in deciding how Torah should be kept, and difficulty (for the scholar today) in deciding who did what under what circumstances, should not be allowed to obscure the more fundamental point. Unless they intended to assimilate completely into Gentile culture, Jews in general and the stricter of them in particular regarded the day-to-day praxis of Torah as a vital badge of their Judaism, that is to say, as a vital part of their entire worldview. If a Jew removed the marks of circumcision, or ostentatiously went about his normal business on the sabbath, or organized her kitchen in flagrant disregard for the kosher laws, or treated Gentile acquaintances exactly the same as Jewish ones—any such praxis would make a clear socio-cultural and religious point. Two at least of the symbols (Torah and racial identity) were being challenged. A flag was quietly being run down, a story given a new ending.

5. According to the Scriptures: The Anchor of the Worldview

There are many threads which run throughout the entire tapestry of first-century Judaism, through its stories, its symbols and its daily life. Perhaps the most obvious one, which we may highlight in conclusion, is the centrality of scripture. The average Jew would hear a lot of scripture read aloud or sung, and might well know large amounts by heart.[106] The synagogue had a central part (not only in 'religion', but also) in the total life of a local community, and words heard often in that context, especially if they were understood to be promising liberation, would be cherished lovingly. In particular, the psalter, with its continual emphasis on the importance of the Temple and on the promises made to David, would have formed an important part of the mental furniture of the average Jew.[107]

In this context, it was natural that, as well as turning to the Bible for the raw material for worship and for everyday living, Jews would look to it for signs of the future. Direct predictions of the return from exile were of course grist to their mill, but many other passages could be pressed into service as well.[108] We shall see in chapter 10 how some groups used a book like Daniel, but this was only one of many possible sources of hope. The Scrolls contain plenty of exegesis applied to the immediate present and future, and so of course do the 'apocalyptic' works. We can be reasonably certain that the great books of Isaiah, Jeremiah and Ezekiel would all have been well known; and the no less powerful shorter books of Zechariah and Malachi, with their emphasis on the rebuilding and purifying of the Temple, would not have been far behind.

---

[106] Schürer 2.419, etc.

[107] This would have been particularly true of the Hallel psalms (113–18, and the 'great Hallel', 136), and the psalms of ascent (120–34).

[108] Barton 1986, chs. 6–7.

When we set this awareness of scripture in the context of the prevailing second-temple belief that the real return from exile had not yet occurred,[109] the idea of scriptural fulfilment takes on a meaning which transcends the mere proof-texting of which first-century Jews have often been accused.[110] It was not simply a matter of ransacking sacred texts for isolated promises about a glorious future. The entire story could be read *as* Story, namely, as the still-unfinished story of the creator, the covenant people, and the world. In that context, an event that happened 'according to the scriptures' would be an event that could be claimed as the next, perhaps the last or the penultimate, event in the story itself. The explicit prophecies of the great age to come fitted into the broader pattern. Scripture as the story, creating the context for the present, and scripture as Torah, creating the ethic for the present, both undergirded scripture as Prophecy, pointing forward to the way in which the story would reach its climax—for those who were faithful to Torah.

In this light, we can understand some of the methods that were used to bring the message of scripture as it were 'up to date'. How can an ancient text become authoritative for the present? The different answers that were given reflect, revealingly, the different perspectives of those who gave them. For Philo, the strange old stories could come to life through allegory. For the later rabbis, and probably their first-century predecessors, some form of oral Torah enabled the written code to be applied to new situations. In apocalyptic writings, scriptural imagery was reused, sometimes in bizarre fashions, and characters from the ancient story were used as mouthpieces for fresh words of warning and hope. Within ordinary synagogue teaching, the use of midrash and targum employed expanded paraphrase to ram home the relevance of the word for the present. And within the Essene community, the *pesher* method took prophecies line by line and claimed that the events of the present were the real fulfilment of what was spoken many generations before. There is an underlying logic to this: it was agreed on all sides that the prophecies had not yet been fulfilled; the sect believed that they were living in the days of fulfilment; therefore the scriptures must somehow refer to them—whatever their 'original' meaning may have been.[111] After all, Habakkuk had said that his writings were for many days hence, after an evident delay.[112] Even the retellings of bits of the story practised in very different ways from all these by Josephus, the Wisdom of Solomon, 4 Maccabees, and Paul, show that their authors were concerned to relate the biblical tradition to their own new context.

---

[109] cf. chs. 9–10 below.

[110] The 'proof-text' method, at least in its modern forms, stems (I think) from the typical eighteenth-century Deist 'proof' of, e.g., Jesus' Messiahship—and the equally typical eighteenth-century 'refutation' of such a proof. Neither has much to do with the historical actuality of the first century.

[111] See Brooke 1985; Mulder 1987, ch. 10 (M. Fishbane); Schürer 2.348, 354, 580, 586; 3.392, 420–1. In terms of 'original' meanings, Moule is right to stress the 'sheer arbitrariness' of the method (1982 [1962], 77–84). But I hold to my suggestion that, as far as the sect was concerned, the story of Israel had taken a turn which somehow justified this reading.

[112] Hab. 2.3; cf. 1QpHab 7.9–14.

What is important is to realize that all these different 'techniques' were ways of maintaining vital contact with the stories and the symbols that indicated one's continuing loyalty to the Jewish heritage. As we saw in relation to oral Torah, it was essential for Jews, particularly those with new or rigorous agendas, to be able to satisfy themselves and their followers that they were in proper continuity with the story-line of Israel, and were paying the symbols proper respect. As we shall see in looking at the early Christian movement, their retellings of the same story can without difficulty be plotted on the same grid, and can be shown to reflect exactly the new situation in which they believed themselves to be living.

6. Conclusion: Israel's Worldview

Story, symbol and praxis, focused in their different ways on Israel's scriptures, reveal a rich but basically simple worldview. We can summarize this in terms of the four questions which, as we argued in chapter 5, are implicitly addressed in all worldviews.

1. Who are we? We are Israel, the chosen people of the creator god.

2. Where are we? We are in the holy Land, focused on the Temple; but, paradoxically, we are still in exile.

3. What is wrong? We have the wrong rulers: pagans on the one hand, compromised Jews on the other, or, half-way between, Herod and his family. We are all involved in a less-than-ideal situation.

4. What is the solution? Our god must act again to give us the true sort of rule, that is, his own kingship exercised through properly appointed officials (a true priesthood; possibly a true king); and in the mean time Israel must be faithful to his covenant charter.

The differences between different groups of Jews in this period can be plotted quite precisely in terms of the detail of this analysis. The chief priests would not have agreed with (2)–(4) as stated. They were in the Temple, which was all in order; the problem was the recalcitrance of other Jewish groups, and the solution was to keep them in their place. Essenes would have modified (4): our god has already acted to call us to be the advance guard of the age to come, and he will act again to vindicate us. And so on. But in principle these four answers to the basic questions remain constant for the majority of our literature, and, so far as we can tell, for the majority of the non-literary people, throughout the period, and come to expression in story, symbol and praxis. Together they point forward. The history we have already sketched, and the worldview we have now outlined, formed the context for and indeed helped to generate a passionately held theology, and a hope that refused to die.

Chapter Nine

THE BELIEFS OF ISRAEL

1. Introduction

What did first-century Jews actually believe, at a conscious or subconscious level, that enabled them to survive where so many other nations had failed to do so? What was the set of convictions which continued to feed the hope that one day the covenant god would act to vindicate himself and them? Here we are asking, in the final analysis, about the fourth element of the Jewish worldview: we have studied symbol, praxis and story, and have made some deductions at the level of the question-and-answer pole. This in turn opens up into the question of theology, of basic beliefs and consequent beliefs.[1]

Here we are walking, of course, into a minefield. We have already seen that the one thing we can safely say about first-century Judaism is that there is no such thing as first-century Judaism, and that it may be best to speak of 'Judaisms', plural.[2] Even among particular groups within ancient Judaism there is no guarantee of uniformity: as Schechter remarked, the rabbis had many faults, but consistency was not one of them.[3] Nor were the rabbis innovators, introducing an unsystematic approach to a previously ordered world; within the Hebrew scriptures themselves there is an observable development and dialogue rather than a tidy system with everything laid out in neat rows. But, even granted this proper caution, made all the more necessary by the enormous range of primary and secondary material now available, there are still several things that can and must be said about first-century 'Judaism' as a whole. There is a basic worldview, which we can plot, that lies at a deeper and more fundamental level than these variations.

The attempt of some scholars to highlight the variety to the detriment of any underlying unity, then, goes too far.[4] No-one, of course, would deny that different texts have different emphases and points of view. I simply wish to follow the many Jewish and other writers who have recognized that behind the

---

[1] See chs. 3, 5 above.

[2] e.g. Neusner *et al.* 1987.

[3] Schechter 1961 [1909], 46. See too Ginzberg 1928, 92: 'The most characteristic feature of the rabbinical system of theology is its lack of system.'

[4] See ch. 7 above, on diversity and unity in historical description. This is a case where a proper concern for differentiated description can obliterate the equally proper task of overall synthesis—an endemic problem in work such as Neusner's.

great variation there is a broad family resemblance.[5] It is vital that we understand this belief-structure. It informs so much else in Judaism, even though, because it is usually taken for granted, it is not often discussed—unless and until someone challenges it, especially if the challenge comes from within the system. And it is the argument of my whole project that two people in particular, Jesus and Paul, while claiming to speak from within the system, provided exactly that sort of challenge and redefinition. We cannot therefore ignore the question: what was the basic Jewish belief?

Another way of stating the problem facing anyone who wants to plot the belief-system of Jews is as follows. Jews do not characteristically describe the nature of Judaism in terms of 'beliefs'. Indeed, Judaism often contrasts itself with Christianity at this point, to the latter's supposed disadvantage.[6] Nevertheless, it is not difficult to show, as many writers have done, that within the varieties of Judaism there is a set of *basic beliefs* which are more or less common to all groups, and that there are various *consequent beliefs* which, though they bear a family likeness to one another across the groups, exhibit more variety. Thus we may grant the point that we do not find, certainly in the first century, non-Christian Jewish works which have the form we now associate with a work of 'theology', that is, an abstract discussion of a point, or system, of belief; but this should in no way prevent us from producing, ourselves, a description and analysis of basic and consequent beliefs, not least now that we have set out the context of symbol, praxis and story which show how these beliefs come to expression. Such an account can in principle be done perfectly well without anachronism or Christian 'borrowing'. It does not mean, as the previous chapter has made clear, that we are imagining Judaism to be *merely* a 'faith', a system of beliefs. To call Judaism 'a faith' is actually, in one sense, a piece of Christian cultural imperialism, imagining that because Christianity thinks of itself as a 'faith' other peoples do the same. Judaism characteristically thinks of itself as a *way*, a *halakah*, a life-path, a way of being-in-the-world.[7] Nothing that I have said or will say is meant to contradict

---

[5] For the family resemblance, and the underlying view, see e.g. Schechter 1961 [1909]; Moore 1927–30, etc., and Kadushin 1938, e.g. 6ff.; Millgram 1971, ch. 15 (391–436), and e.g. 260: at the end of the Yom Kippur rite, the worshippers recite three sentences from the Bible 'whereby they rededicate themselves to the essential theological doctrines of Judaism', which of course focus on Jewish-style monotheism. Cf. the debate between McEleney 1973 and Aune 1976, with the latter concluding that Judaism does indeed have a belief-system, but that (10) this belief system was 'subordinate . . . to Jewish traditions of ritual practice and ethical behaviour'. This is not far from my distinction between worldview (ch. 8 above) and belief-systems (the present chapter). See now Sanders 1992, ch. 13 (241–78) and 413–9, esp. 416f. on discovering the *presuppositions* of Pharisaic attitudes.

[6] e.g. Millgram 1971, 416: 'the concept of a creed as the essence of a religious community is, as far as Judaism is concerned, as unreal as a disembodied spirit'—sounding almost as if he were quoting Jas. 2.26. Cf. Shechter 1961 [1909], 12: 'the old Rabbis seem to have thought that the true health of a religion is to have a theology without being aware of it'. One might ask: will any theology do? Supposing it is the *wrong* theology?

[7] There are of course several examples of Judaism picking up the language of 'faith' from Christians. The *Jerusalem Post*, on Independence Day 1989, ran a leading article called 'Keeping the Faith'.

that basic self-perception. There are none the less two reasons for focusing on the belief-system, and ultimately the worldview, of Judaism in this period.

First, as a matter of phenomenological analysis, it is simply the case that underlying worldviews are more fundamental than even the most ingrained habits of life. Underneath the basic Jewish praxis there lies the belief that Israel is the people of the creator god. If this were not so, the *halakah* would lose its point, or at least radically change its character. If one said to an articulate first-century Jew 'Why do you keep Torah?', the ultimate answer would be 'Because I am part of Israel, the chosen people of the creating and redeeming god.' For the question and answer to run the other way would be irreducibly odd: 'Why do you believe in the creating and redeeming god?' 'Because I keep Torah.' The fact of the creating and redeeming god is the greater whole, which gives meaning and purpose to the individual expression—which is not to deny that *faith in* this god may be strengthened, or even come to birth, in the context of or even as a result of Jewish attempts to keep Torah. It is therefore necessary to go deeper than the day-to-day expressions of Judaism, and to follow its own expositors into the main lines––which are not particularly controversial—of what may be called, with due caution, 'Jewish theology'.

Second, as I mentioned above, we must focus on the Jewish worldview and belief-system because this was the feature of Judaism that was radically redefined by Jesus and Paul. To be more precise: Jesus, I shall argue, redefined the *hope* of Israel in such a way as to call in question the normal interpretation of Jewish *belief*; Paul, seeing the hope thus redefined in practice around Jesus, completed in principle the task of the redefinition of belief. And both, in their own ways, demonstrated what this would mean at the level of *halakah*, of way-of-life. It is vital, therefore, to examine belief and hope as carefully as possible. We are not thereby imposing an alien set of thought-forms or categories on to first-century Judaism; we are simply concerned to draw out fundamental presuppositions.[8] Otherwise, all we would see in the challenge of Jesus and Paul would be a challenge to *halakah*. This is, actually and perhaps inevitably, all that some Jewish interpreters *have* seen.[9] But to take that standpoint is, I shall argue, to miss the real thrust of what was going on.

What I offer in this and the following chapter, then, is a hypothesis about the 'inner' history of first-century Judaism, in the sense explored in Part II above. I am trying to plot the worldview(s) of Jews in the time of Jesus and Paul. This hypothesis gains its strength not by being the sum-total of a list of parts obtained by atomistic analysis of the relevant texts, but by providing a point of view from which we can see *why* people wrote what they did—and why the great majority of Jews, who wrote nothing, behaved as they did, in the ways we have examined in the preceding three chapters.

[8] As Sanders has demonstrated quite thoroughly (1977, 420f.), the covenant is rarely mentioned explicitly, but remains absolutely fundamental to all the regular explicit statements of what makes Judaism Judaism: see below, pp. 260ff.

[9] cf. the works of H. Maccoby.

We may begin this account of Jewish belief with some obvious fixed points.[10] No Jew imagined that there were five gods. No Jew imagined that the Egyptians were the chosen people of YHWH. No Jew thought that god and the world were the same thing,[11] or that the world was made by a god other than Israel's god. At least, any Jew who thought any of these things knew that at a major and fundamental point he or she was stepping outside the normal boundaries of Jewish thought.[12] There is then, across the range of Jewish writing that we possess, solid unanimity on certain major and vital issues; and we have already seen good reason to suppose that this unanimity was equally strong among those who wrote nothing and read little. There is one god, who made the entire universe, and this god is in covenant with Israel.[13] He has chosen her for a purpose: she is to be the light of the world.[14] Faced with national crisis (and the story of second-temple Judaism is, as we have seen, one of semi-permanent crisis), this twin belief, monotheism and election, committed any Jew who thought about it for a moment to a further belief: YHWH, as the creator and covenant god, was irrevocably committed to further action of some sort in history, which would bring about the end of Israel's desolation and the vindication of his true people. Monotheism and election lead to eschatology, and eschatology means the renewal of the covenant.

We are today comparatively familiar with this set of beliefs. We must not, however, allow this fact to blind us to its importance as an underlying worldview, a way of perceiving all reality, a grid through which all experience of the world was mediated. Nor must we underestimate the enormity of the claim thereby made. Again and again in the Pentateuch, the psalms, the prophets, and the subsequent writings which derive from them, the claim is made that the creator of the entire universe has chosen to live uniquely on a small ridge called Mount Zion, near the eastern edge of the Judaean hill-country. The sheer absurdity of this claim, from the standpoint of any other worldview (not least that of Enlightenment philosophy), is staggering. The fact that Assyria, Egypt, Babylon, Persia, Greece, Egypt again, Syria and now Rome had made implicit and explicit mockery of the idea did not shake this conviction, but only intensified it. This was what Jewish monotheism looked like on the ground. It was not a philosophical or metaphysical analysis of the inner being of a god, or the god. It was the unshakeable belief that the one god who made the world was Israel's god, and that he would defend his hill against all attackers or usurpers. To the extent that Israel thought of her god in 'universal' terms, this universal was from the beginning made known in and

---

[10] For a similar brief account, see Riches 1990, ch. 2.

[11] Evidence for Jewish pantheism may, no doubt, be found here and there. But generally the statement holds true.

[12] Josephus says that Israel's god had transferred his affections to the Romans (*War* 5.411 ff.), and claims Daniel as his authority for saying that god intended Rome to take Jerusalem (*Ant.* 10.276–80). But (a) this is most likely a clear currying of favour with his new masters, and (b) he must have been aware of the boundary-breaking significance of such a move.

[13] We should perhaps add that the word 'covenant' here is used strictly in the first-century Jewish sense, which is not that of sixteenth-century Calvinism, nor exactly that of the 1950s 'Biblical Theology' movement. See below.

[14] cf. below, pp. 267f.

through the particular, the material, the historical. To the extent that forms of Judaism diverged from a main path (as, arguably, and for discernible historical reasons, Philo's thought did),[15] this is the main path from which they diverged.

2. First-Century Jewish Monotheism

All accounts of Jewish theology rightly focus on monotheism, but many give quite misleading accounts of it. In what follows I shall try to make some necessary distinctions, so that the true lines of what was believed may stand out clearly.[16]

'Hear, O Israel: YHWH our God, YHWH is one.' The *Shema*, the most famous Jewish prayer, which goes back to the days of Deuteronomy at least,[17] was burned into the consciousness of Judaism in the first century. It was not the result of speculative metaphysical enquiry, but the battle-cry of the nation that believed its god to be the only god, supreme in heaven and on earth:

> Great is YHWH, and greatly to be praised;
>   he is to be revered above all gods.
> For all the gods of the peoples are idols,
>   but YHWH made the heavens . . .
> Say among the nations, 'YHWH is king!'[18]

This is a fighting doctrine, a cause of celebration for the beleaguered little nation that went on singing these psalms and praying the *Shema* through thick and thin. The nations must know that Israel's god is the true and only god, and that the beings they mistakenly worship are non-gods, mere human inventions. This already gives us the flavour of Jewish monotheism. In order to understand it more fully we must examine its three main aspects.

(i) Creational Monotheism

First, Jewish monotheism was what we may call *creational monotheism*. It spoke of a god who had made the world, and who was thus to be distinguished

---

[15] On Philo see Schürer 3.809–89; Borgen 1984. Philo is the exception that proves the rule, because of his deep dependence on Plato, as a result of which he dehistoricized and hence de-eschatologized the whole Jewish worldview; though his innate Jewish sensibilities prevented him from going the whole way.

[16] It is quite remarkable that the only entry to 'monotheism' in the index of the revised Schürer is to the discussion of the *Shema* (2.454f.), where there is no discussion of the belief itself. The most recent discussions of the subject (Sanders 1992, 242–7; Dunn 1991, 19–21) are helpful as far as they go, particularly in showing that some Jews were prepared to try and accommodate some features of paganism within their monotheism; but they do not seem to me to go nearly far enough in analysing precisely what monotheism *meant* in this period.

[17] Dt. 6.4. On older forms of monotheism and its predecessors, see e.g. Rowley 1946, ch.5; Eichrodt 1961, 220–7; von Rad 1962, 210–12; Lang (ed.) 1981.

[18] Ps. 96.4–5, 10. Examples could be multiplied dozens of times, especially from the Psalms and from Isa. 40–55.

from four other conceptions of the divinity which might claim to be 'monotheistic', and at least one which would not.

To begin with, creational monotheism rules out *henotheism*, the belief that there are indeed other gods, but that Israel will worship only her own god. It is a matter of debate whether, and if so for how long, the ancestors of first-century Jews had held some such belief.[19] Rejection of henotheism means, in practical terms, that Israel was committed to seeing her god as ontologically (and not merely practically) superior to the gods of the nations, and hence was committed to certain beliefs about her own place and purpose, which we will discuss presently. The gods of the nations are not 'real' gods; they are idols.

Second, creational monotheism rules out *pantheism*. This is really a sophisticated form of paganism, and asserts that there is only one god, or deity, namely the deity that permeates and characterizes the whole of reality. Pantheism is best known in the ancient world within the prevalent Stoic philosophy.[20] The problem with pantheism is, of course, its apparent belittling of evil.[21] All one can do about apparent evil is to rise above it, to deny its existence (a good part of Epictetus' advice can be summed up as 'Don't hope for what you can't be sure of having; don't dislike what you can't avoid').[22] Within Stoicism, the world is involved in an endless cycle of life, and if one finds oneself sufficiently alienated from it the answer is simple: suicide.[23]

Third, creational monotheism rules out *Deism*. I use this eighteenth-century term for an older reality which was known in the ancient world, not least in the belief-system of the Epicureans: the gods exist, but they live in a world of bliss quite removed from the present world, and do not intervene in our world at all. (Hence the need for the interesting theories of physics developed by Epicureans: if the gods do not intervene in the world, why do things happen like they do?[24])

Fourth, Jewish-style creational monotheism rules out *Gnosticism*, which responds to paganism and pantheism by maintaining that the physical world was made by a supernatural being completely distinct from the true high god or sovereign god. The one true god thus remains unimplicated in evil at the cost of remaining uninvolved with the real world. An appearance of monotheism is saved at the cost of distancing this god from the ordinary world.[25]

Creational monotheism avoids these four (in some ways) 'monotheistic' alternatives. It thus commits itself to the difficult task of maintaining that the present world, as a totality, was made by the one and only true god, that evil,

---

[19] See Lang (ed.) 1981, etc.

[20] See e.g. Epict. *Disc.* 1.14.10; *Frags.* 3–4 (perhaps quoting Musonius Rufus); Cic. *De Natura Deorum* 2.38f.

[21] See below. A good example is Epict. *Ench.* 27: nothing that is by nature evil can arise in the cosmos.

[22] e.g. 4.1.75; 4.4.33; 4.10, *passim*.

[23] Epict. *Disc.* 1.25.18; 2.15.6; 3.13.14 and frequently; Socrates, though of course not himself a Stoic, and not strictly a voluntary suicide, was often held up as the great example (1.29.29).

[24] See Epict. *Disc.* 1.12.1.

[25] On the nature and rise of Gnosticism see ch. 6 above, and ch. 14 below. On 'Jewish Gnosticism' see Pearson 1980, 1984.

though real and important, is not a necessary constituent part of it, and that the one god remains sovereign over it.

Fifth, creational monotheism obviously rules out *paganism*, the belief that the universe is populated by a fairly large number of divine beings, who oversee different nations, different aspects of the created order (the sea, fire, etc.), and/or different human activities (war, sex, etc.). Paganism can, obviously, avoid the problem of charging the supreme god with responsibility for the way things are, since the pagan lives in a confusing world where at any moment some deity may choose to act in a capricious or malevolent way.[26]

Over against all of these, first-century Jews maintained their belief: there was one god, and this god had made the world. Moreover, he remained active within it. This leads to the second aspect.

(ii) Providential Monotheism

So far as we can tell, most Jews of our period cherished the belief which comes to quite full expression in Josephus: Israel's god, the creator, works in and through what may be called 'natural events'. He may well work through (what we would call) 'supernatural' events, too: there are some such in Josephus,[27] but these would be equally compatible either with various sorts of paganism or with a belief in a normally-absent deity who 'intervened' from time to time in a way that was discontinuous with the usual working of the world. And, just as Jews had rejected paganism, so they rejected an 'absentee landlord' form of deism, such as was found in some more sophisticated versions of ancient paganism.[28] This is important, since in the modern Western world a good many people use the word 'god' or 'God' imagining it to be univocal *and to refer to a Deist's absentee-landlord divinity*, so that discussions of ancient theology are often bedevilled by anachronistic semantic attachments. It is quite clear that Josephus believed, and intended his readers to believe, that Israel's god was every bit as much at work in the 'human' and 'natural' events of recent history—in such things as the rise of Rome, the fall of the Temple, or the accession of Vespasian—as in occasional 'supernatural' happenings. The facts of recent history were then explained in terms of divine punishment for evil, or the strange outworking of long-term divine purposes whose future end remained for the moment obscure.

It is important to stress that first-century Jews did not believe that their god was intrinsically remote and detached, or that he had become so of late. This idea, which has been popular for a long time and still occurs here and there, is quite off target.[29] Belief in the existence of angelic and other mediators says

---

[26] Lane Fox 1986, chs. 3–5.

[27] e.g. *War* 6.288–300.

[28] This belief (that of the Epicureans) was often flagged by the phrase *to theion*, 'the divinity', in an abstract sense. Some pagans could look at Jewish monotheism and assume that this was what it was talking about (e.g. Hecataeus *Frag.* 13); some Jews wanted to agree with them (e.g. *Ep. Arist.* 16).

[29] e.g. Charlesworth 1983, xxxi. For the argument against: Urbach 1987 [1975, 1979], 133f.

more about the attempt of some Jewish writers to speak meaningfully about their god's *involvement with*, not detachment from, his creation, than about a proto-Deist theology such as was held by some in the pagan world.[30] Belief in a first-century Jewish idea of a remote god, in turn, owes more to a post-Enlightenment myth about the significance of Jesus' proclamation (that he announced the 'near God')[31] than to a clear reading of first-century Jewish evidence.

But is it enough to speak of creation and providence? Clearly not. Josephus attempted to explain that whatever happens, happens according to the divine will; many Jews then and now regarded this as a simplistic capitulation, halfway at least to assimilation. Though there are 'strong' biblical statements of divine involvement in everything that happens, good and bad alike (e.g. Isaiah 45.7; Amos 3.6), this is a difficult doctrine to maintain, and we find 'softer' versions in the idea, for instance, that Israel's god uses and directs the actions of wicked persons within his own purposes (e.g. Isaiah 10.5–15). Providence by itself is not enough to explain the way in which belief in one god, the creator, and recognition of the radical nature of evil, can be held together. The aspect of Jewish monotheism which attempts this task, and which Josephus significantly downplays, is the third vital element within this basic belief: election and the covenant.[32]

(iii) Covenantal Monotheism

Within mainline Jewish thought over a long period, the problem of evil within creational and providential monotheism was not addressed by means of extended discussions of its origin. There are isolated statements, which borrow from one or other of the two classic texts, Genesis 3 (evil comes through wrong human choice) and Genesis 6 (evil comes through the malevolent influence of fallen angels).[33] But for the most part the question is focused on the present and the future: granted the presence of evil in the world, what is the creator going to do about it? The answer given by a wide range of Jewish writers from the redactor of Genesis to the late rabbis is clear: he has called Israel to be his people. 'I will make Adam first,' says Israel's god in the midrash on Genesis, 'and if he goes astray I will send Abraham to sort it all out.'[34] The creator calls a people through whom, somehow, he will act decisively within his creation, to

[30] See below, p. 258f., and now also the helpful discussion in Chester 1991, 47–65. The tendency may also have sometimes been the product simply of fertile imagination. From the pagan point of view, see the discussion of different theological possibilities in Epict. *Disc.* 1.12.1–3.

[31] e.g. Bultmann 1958 [1934], ch. 4, esp. 150ff.

[32] Sanders, in following Josephus closely, has in my view allowed himself to loosen the connection between monotheism and election: 1992, ch. 13, and esp. 1991, ch. 5.

[33] Thus e.g. Sir. 25.24; 4 Ezra 7.46–56; 2 *Bar.* 17.3; 19.8; 23.4, etc., emphasizing the Gen. 3 tradition (2 *Bar.* 54.15, 19 suggests, however, that 'each of us has become our own Adam'). Following the Gen. 6 tradition are *1 En.* 6–19; 64; *Jub.* 4.15, 22; 5.1–7; CD 2.17–21 and other passages. For helpful discussions of the latter theme see Alexander 1972; Bauckham 1983, 50ff.

[34] Genesis Rabbah 14.6. Further discussion of this is in Wright 1991a, 21–6, and below.

eliminate evil from it and to restore order, justice and peace. Central to this ongoing plan of action, then, is the call of Israel. When the creator acts to restore and heal his world, he will do so through this people.

We shall explore this covenant theology in more detail in due course. Within our discussion of monotheism, however, we must notice at once the effect of adding 'covenantal' to 'creational' and 'providential' as modifiers of 'monotheism'. This move shifts the large theological question, of the coexistence of a creator god and an evil world, on to a different plane. The question is no longer a static one, as though the world simply existed in a settled state; it is dynamic and relational. If there is an answer to the problem of evil it will include divine action within history, more specifically, within the history of the world as it has been affected by evil. Abraham's people are to be the means of undoing primeval sin and its consequences. This belief is a basic assumption throughout the Jewish literature of our period. And one thing that it finally rules out is any suggestion of radical dualism. Evil exists; it is real, potent, and dangerous; but it does not have the last word. The creator actually *uses* evil to cleanse and purge his creation and his people.[35] If creational monotheism entails an eschatology (the creator must restore that which he made), covenantal monotheism intensifies this eschatological entailment: the creator remains committed to giving order and peace to his world, and as the covenant god he remains committed to doing so *through Israel*. But before we can explore this any further we must look more closely at the notion of 'dualism', and see just what it is that is ruled out by this threefold Jewish monotheism.

(iv) Types of Duality

It is often said that some types of Judaism are characterized by 'dualism', or are in danger of falling into it.[36] 'Apocalyptic' is still often spoken of in this way; it is thought to be pessimistic, envisaging the only hope for the world in terms of a coming cosmic catastrophe; to have a distant view of Israel's god which needs to be filled out by the presence of angelic mediators; and to divide the world into two, in the style of the Qumranic 'War of the Sons of Light against the Sons of Darkness' (1QM). Further, it used to be said, and still is in some quarters, that all this shows a derivation from the dualism of ancient Iranian Zoroastrianism.[37]

The problem with this is that the word 'dualism' is used in several quite different senses, by no means always differentiated.[38] Furthermore, the word

---

[35] e.g. Isa. 10.5–9; 45.7; Amos 4.13; 5.8f.; 9.5f.

[36] e.g., recently, Hayman 1991; Sanders 1992, 249f.

[37] An example almost at random: Conzelmann 1969, 24; cf. Sanders 1992, 249. Sometimes quoted in this connection is 4 Ezra 7.50: 'the Most High has made not one world but two'. See below, category (9).

[38] The fullest brief account I know in relation to our literature is that of Charlesworth 1969, 389 n.1, distinguishing ten types which correspond quite closely with those below, which I worked out independently before coming across his article. Sanders (1992, 523 n.21) says that he has discussed the relation of monotheism and dualism in his forthcoming *Anchor Bible Diction-*

'dualism' itself is heavily loaded in some circles, often indicating disapproval; but several of the things which are asserted to be 'dualistic' are perfectly normal features of most if not all biblical theology, and we must make a careful distinction between that which the great majority of Jews accepted as normal and that with which some, exceptionally, flirted. I propose therefore that, to begin with, we refer to 'dualities', rather than 'dualisms', and save the latter term for certain specific dualities. There are at least ten types of duality, as follows.

1. Theological/ontological duality. The postulation of heavenly beings other than the one god, even if these beings exist at his behest and to do his will. This belief is called 'dualism' in some recent scholarship.[39]

2. Theological/cosmological duality. If pantheism is a classic form of monism, the differentiation between the creator god and the created order is often seen as itself a sort of 'dualism'.[40]

3. Moral duality. The positing of a firm distinction between good and evil, e.g. in the realm of human behaviour. Most religions maintain some such distinction, but some forms of pantheism have tried to remove it, not least by labelling it 'dualism' and associating it with other dualisms that are deemed to be unwelcome.

4. Eschatological duality. The distinction between the present age and the age to come, usually reckoning the present age as evil and the age to come as good.[41]

5. Theological/moral duality. Expressed classically in Zoroastrianism and some forms of Gnosticism, this view postulates that there are two ultimate sources of all that is: a good god and a bad god. In 'hard' versions, the two are locked in struggle for ever; in 'soft' versions, the good one will eventually win.[42]

6. Cosmological duality. The classic position of Plato: the world of material things is the secondary copy or shadow of the 'real' world of the Forms, which are perceived by the enlightened mind. In many different versions, this view filtered down as a mainline belief of the Greco-Roman (and the modern Western) world: that which can be observed in the physical world is secondary and shabby compared with that which can be experienced by the mind or spirit. (In some modern versions the order is reversed, putting the material first and the spiritual second.)[43]

7. Anthropological duality. The human-centred version of cosmological dualism. Humans are bipartite creatures, a combination of body and soul,

---

ary article on 'Sin/Sinners (NT)'. In his present work he uses 'dualism' in a variety of senses in the same passage.

[39] See again Hayman 1991.

[40] e.g. Schürer 3.881, referring to Philo.

[41] See von Rad 1965, 301ff. This feature is referred to as 'dualism' in e.g. E. Isaac's introduction to *1 En.* (in Charlesworth 1983), 9f.

[42] cf. Perrin 1983 [1974], 128; Charlesworth 1985, 48 (on *Jubilees*). It is sometimes said that the Scrolls exemplify this sort of 'dualism': e.g. Schürer 2.589; Urbach 1987, 162f. For a sensitive discussion of this see Charlesworth 1969.

[43] For the (standard) use of 'dualism' here; cf. e.g. Urbach 1987, 26, 75, etc.; and cp. Nickelsburg 1984, 216 on *1 En.* 42.

which are arranged in a hierarchy: soul ahead of body in many religions and philosophies, body ahead of soul in many political agendas.[44]

8. Epistemological duality. The attempt to differentiate sharply between that which can be known by means of human observation and/or reason and that which can be known only through divine revelation.

9. Sectarian duality. The clear division of those who belong to one socio-cultural-religious group from those who belong to another.[45]

10. Psychological duality. Humans have two inclinations, a good one and a bad one; these are locked in combat, and the human must choose the good and resist the evil.[46]

Where did first-century Judaism stand in relation to these bewildering and often-confused types of duality? There are at least four types that are embraced by most Jews of the period, and at least three that are usually rejected, with possibility of debate about the other three.

We have already made it clear that in rejecting pantheism Judaism embraced the distinction between the creator god and the created world (type 2). This reveals itself in the normal biblical language about heaven and earth: heaven is created by the one creator in order to be the location of himself and his entourage, whereas earth is where humans live. This is not, however, to be equated with cosmological duality (type 6), on which see below. It is, further, clear throughout Judaism that a distinction was maintained between good and evil in the realm of human actions: even Josephus, with his strong doctrine of divine providence, clearly thinks that some humans act wickedly (type 3).[47] Many if not most Jewish writings of the period show a belief in angels and other 'supernatural' beings (type 1). Virtually all second-temple Jews, with the possible exception only of the aristocracy, believed that they were living in a 'present age' which was a time of sorrow and exile, and which would be succeeded by an 'age to come' in which wrongs would be righted and Israel's god would set up his kingdom (type 4). If any or all of this deserves to be called 'dualism', then most first-century Jews (and most early Christians) were dualists.

However, I think this would be a confusing conclusion. The word 'dualism' has obtained its primary force in modern discussion from three of the other types, which were emphatically rejected by most Jews of the period. In respect of type 5, we will search for a long time through first-century Jewish literature without finding any evidence of the belief that there is an evil force which is equal in power to the creator god, and when we do find such evidence we are justified in supposing that the majority of Jews would have regarded the idea as outside the limit of legitimate speculation.[48] Type 5 is thus widely rejected.

---

[44] The first of these is the classic Gnostic account of anthropology.

[45] e.g. C. Burchard in Charlesworth 1985, 190f.

[46] Charlesworth 1969, 389. This may apply in particular to the 'two spirits' doctrine in 1QS (discussed, but rejected, in ibid., 395f.); it certainly applies to the 'two inclinations' doctrine of the rabbis (cf. Schechter 1961 [1909] chs. 15, 16; Urbach 1987 [1975, 1979], 471–83).

[47] e.g. the 'two ways' scheme in 1QS.

[48] See the discussion in Rowland 1982, 92, with *Mart. Isa.* 2.4; 4.2 as examples of passages which perhaps go beyond this limit.

Equally, Philo again provides the exception that proves the rule when it comes to types 6 and 7: Jews in general did not divide the world rigidly into the physical and the noumenal/spiritual, and even Philo himself shows at various points that, even if the 'real meaning' of a passage of scripture, or a Jewish ritual, is to be found in a spiritualized sphere, the material sense and performance are by no means to be despised or neglected.[49] He thus offers a soft version of types 6 and 7; most Jews would have rejected both in favour of a more integrated cosmology and anthropology. Most Jews would have held that heaven and earth, though themselves distinct, both reveal the divine glory; humans, though thoroughly at home in the space-time universe, are also open to the world of heaven, to the presence and influence of the divine. Worship and prayer are not attempts to reach across a void, but the conscious opening of human life to the god-dimension which is ever-present.[50]

The remaining three types are harder. With reference to epistemological duality (type 8), it is clear that many Jews of this period did make a fairly sharp distinction between what can be known by human observation and/or reason and what can only be known by divine revelation. This distinction has a long history, going back (for instance) to the story of Joseph in Genesis 41.14–28. An apocalypse claims to unveil secrets otherwise unknowable; a *pesher* commentary, the 'true' hidden meaning of a biblical prophecy; a discussion of *halakah*, that which was given orally by Israel's god to Moses on Mount Sinai; a Philonic allegory, the secret hidden meaning of the text. Even Josephus appears to place considerable value on the ability to foretell the future, an ability which he claimed for himself as well as for others. Yet many Jews, such as Josephus himself, make the attempt to see what Israel's god is doing *within* the ordinary world of observation, and devise logical rules whereby, with the aid of human reason, truth and holiness can be perceived. We will therefore probably not go far wrong if we postulate a wide spectrum of opinion on type 8. Similarly, sectarian duality (type 9) is obviously embraced by some, notably the Essenes and, to some extent, the Pharisees, and is rejected by those Jews who were in favour of a relaxed attitude towards their pagan neighbours.[51] Finally, psychological duality (type 10) was held by the rabbis, with their doctrine of the two 'inclinations'. But there is little early evidence for it.

These distinctions between different types of duality, and the analysis I have suggested, is not simply undertaken out of curiosity or for the sake of intellectual tidiness. It is most important in understanding the theological options that lay before first-century Jews, and the close interrelation of those options with the socio-political reality that they faced.[52] It may therefore help if we set out these types of duality in their three columns. Those on the left are more or less normal to all mainline Judaism; those on the right, definitely marginal. Those in the centre are held by some, but not all. It is only those on

---

[49] e.g. *de Migr.* 89–93, discussed in this context by Borgen 1984, 260f.
[50] A good example of this belief in the immediate presence of the god-dimension of reality is 2 Kgs. 6.17.
[51] See above, p. 239–41.
[52] See Segal 1986, 178: 'the issue of monotheism was parallel to the issue of community composition.'

the right, I propose, that deserve the title 'dual*ism*' proper; only they posit a radical split in the whole of reality.

regularly accepted	*possible*	*marginal*
1. theological/ontological		5. theological/moral
2. theological/cosmological		6. cosmological
3. moral		7. anthropological
4. eschatological		
	8. epistemological	
	9. sectarian	
	10. psychological	

(v) Monotheism and its Modifications

We have already seen that an emphasis simply on the first two types of monotheism (creational and providential) could lead, and in the case of Josephus himself seems to have led, to what might appear a compromise with paganism. Equally, an emphasis on the third type (covenantal monotheism) could lead, and in the case of Qumran certainly did lead, to dualisms that went beyond the normal Jewish acceptance of the distinctions between (a) the creator and the world (type 2), (b) good and evil (type 3) and (c) the present age and the age to come (type 4). The socio-political pressure that caused *sectarian* duality (type 9) to flourish seems also to have created conditions for certain dualisms which were not otherwise present in first-century Judaism, and for the accentuation of dualities that were already there. Thus, within sectarian Judaism, we notice the following trends within the types of duality already listed:

1. There is a noticeable increase in speculation about heavenly beings other than the one god;[53]

2. The mainline Jewish distinction between the creator and the world is accentuated, with an abhorrence of the self and its cleaving to the dust of the earth;[54]

3. It naturally follows from this that the normal distinction between good and evil is highlighted and sharpened; more areas of life are subdivided and defined, so that 'grey areas' and ambiguities are progressively reduced. This characterizes both the Scrolls and the development of oral Torah among the Pharisees;

4. Eschatological duality was also accentuated. The only hope for the future was a radically new divine action which would break the power of the present regime and install the sect as the true heirs of Israel's promises. In so far as this could be combined with type 6 (cosmological duality), it is clear that this could lead to a hope for a non-earthly paradise. It is a measure of how little this route was taken that even at Qumran the hope seems to be, not for dis-

---

[53] cf. Chester 1991, 47–65.
[54] e.g. 1QS 11.9f., 21f., with antecedents such as Ps. 119.25.

embodied bliss, but for the renewal of Jewish society and the world in general;[55]

5. There is a tendency towards a sharp divide between the power of light and the power of darkness. Taken to its logical conclusion, this leads to forms of Jewish Gnosticism that appear in subsequent history;[56]

6. This creates a context within which moves towards the normal Hellenistic dualism of material/spiritual become likely, linking the mainline Jewish duality of good and evil with the mainline Greek dualism of physical and non-physical: this is exemplified in the practice of extreme asceticism;[57]

7, 10. Within this, it becomes easier to embrace the corresponding anthropological dualism of body and spirit, as happens in Philo. The dualities of 'two spirits' in the Community Rule and the 'two inclinations' in the rabbis (type 10) are 'softer' versions of this;[58]

8. A vital part of sectarian life is the belief in special revelation, whether through dreams, visions, or prophecies, or through new interpretations of scripture (whether legal or prophetic). The sect needs to sustain and legitimate its position by appeal to sources of knowledge not available to the parent group. Here, too, belongs the mysticism which, already in evidence in the first century, became an important component of some later forms of Jewish piety;[59]

(9. Sectarian duality is the presupposition for this sequence of thought, mentioned here again in case of confusion.)

I hope it is clear that many Jews could go quite a way down some or all of these roads without regarding themselves, or being regarded by others, as having given up their basic commitment to monotheism. As long as they were worshipping only the one god of Israel, such speculations could not be faulted by an appeal to monotheism alone. The point at which they would be open to criticism would be the point at which any of the dualisms properly so called (nos. 5, 6 and 7) began to take over, and to cast doubt on the *creational* or *providential* character of the monotheism. Hence the tension between creation and providence on the one hand and covenant on the other. Emphasizing the first two at the expense of the third could eventually lead to a diminution of all ten dualities, including, ultimately, those between god and the world (2), good and evil (3), and the present and the future (4): that is the route to pantheism, paganism or Gnosticism. Conversely, emphasizing the covenant at the expense of creation and providence can lead to a highlighting of all the serious dualisms.

---

[55] See Sanders 1992, 368; and chs. 7, 10 of the present work.

[56] On the problems of Gnostic tendencies in some early rabbinic thought see Segal 1977; Rowland 1982, ch. 12.; Pearson 1980; 1984.

[57] On asceticism among the Essenes and Therapeutae see e.g. Schürer 2.593f.

[58] cf. 1QS 3.18—4.26. Initially this passage seems to be suggesting that the elect are those who have the spirit of truth, and the wicked those who have the spirit of falsehood; but in 4.15ff. it is clear that each person partakes of both, and must choose to follow the one or the other. For the two inclinations see above, n. 44.

[59] See Gruenwald 1980; Rowland 1982, Part Four.

It perhaps needs emphasizing that this schema, which I offer here phenomenologically for the sake of clarifying issues that are often confused, should not be taken to mean that all Jews regularly thought in these neat categories or in such an abstract fashion. The different positions are not necessarily incompatible; most humans are quite good at holding together things which can be shown to be mutually contradictory. Nevertheless, underlying almost all these variations is the belief, which I suggest is central to Judaism in this period, that evil is not an *essential* part of creation, but is the result of a distortion within a basically good created order. As a result of this distortion, humans have lost the glory of the creator, that is, the wise stewardship of creation. Israel's vocation is to be the agent of the creator god in restoring to the world that which it has lost.

The main theological task, seen with the advantage of hindsight, was directly cognate with the main socio-political task: the question of how to maintain Israel's identity and vocation within the pagan world became, in theological terms, the question of how to retain one's hold on creational, providential and covenantal monotheism without denying the presence and radical nature of evil within the creation. When the form that evil took was very concrete—when evil marched through Palestine in army boots, exacted heavy taxes, and crucified young hotheads who tried to resist—then the evil angels who corrupted the good world were very easily identified as the angels who controlled the pagan nations, and the pagans themselves could be safely labelled as children of darkness. If, instead, one was sitting in Rome on a comfortable pension, with leisure and assistance to study and write, it was easy to underemphasize the covenant, and treat it as one more interesting set of local customs such as any ethnographer might collect. Between these two extremes, tending either towards dualism or towards assimilation, most Jews lived out their theological, as well as their day-to-day, lives.

One final note about the nature and variety of Jewish monotheism in this period. I have argued that the first type of duality (theological/ontological: the postulation of supernatural beings other than the one god) has nothing to do with a declining away from 'pure' monotheism—or, if it does, we must say that we have very few examples of 'pure' monotheism anywhere, including in the Hebrew Bible. Language about supernatural agencies other than the one god has to do, rather, with the theological problem of how to hold together providence (with covenant as a special case of providence) and a belief in a transcendent god. Unless this god is to collapse back into being a mere absentee landlord, in which case providence and covenant go by the board, or unless he ceases to be in any meaningful sense transcendent, moving instead towards pantheism or paganism, one is bound to develop, and second-temple Jews did develop, ways of speaking about the divine action in the world which attempt to do justice to these different poles of belief. Thus it is that language about angels, about the Shekinah or 'presence' of Israel's god, about Torah, about Wisdom, about the Logos—all of these make their appearances, not as mere fantasy or speculative metaphysics, but as varied (and not always equally successful) attempts to perform a necessary theological task. At one level this task was purely linguistic: speaking of the divine 'presence' or 'word' enabled one to speak of the one god active in his world without committing the solecism of suggesting that this god was somehow contained within this action, or indeed within the world.

In this context it is vital for our purposes that we stress one fact. Within the most fiercely monotheistic of Jewish circles throughout our period—from the Maccabaean revolt to Bar-Kochba—there is no suggestion that 'monotheism', or praying the *Shema*, had anything to do with the numerical analysis of the inner being of Israel's god himself. It had everything to do with the two-pronged fight against paganism and dualism. Indeed, we find strong evidence during this period of Jewish groups and individuals who, speculating on the meaning of some difficult passages in scripture (Daniel 7, for example, or Genesis 1), suggested that the divine being might encompass a plurality.[60] Philo could speculate about the Logos as, effectively, a second divine being;[61] the Similitudes of Enoch might portray the Son of Man/Messiah as an eternal divine being;[62] but none of these show any awareness that they are transgressing normal Jewish monotheism. Nor are they. The oneness of Israel's god, the creator, was never an analysis of this god's inner existence, but always a polemical doctrine over against paganism and dualism. It was only with the rise of Christianity, and arguably under the influence both of polemical constraint and Hellenizing philosophy, that Jews in the second and subsequent centuries reinterpreted 'monotheism' as 'the numerical oneness of the divine being'. The inner constraints of the earlier doctrine, and the outer constraints of socio-political conflict, ensured that in the first century the main emphases of monotheism were as we have described them. There is one god, the creator, who continues to govern his world and is active within it. And he has called from his world a unique people, Israel, through whom he is at work, and will be at work, to establish his rightful rule on earth, as it is in heaven. All of which brings us, not before time, to a consideration of the covenant itself.

3. Election and Covenant

(i) Introduction

Israel's belief in one god, as we have seen, was held in close conjunction with her belief that she was, in a unique sense, the people of this god. We have seen, further, that any attempt to state a monotheistic doctrine of whatever sort carries certain implications about the analysis of evil within the world. I shall now attempt to show the way in which covenant theology, especially in the second-temple period, functions as the answer which was offered to the problem of evil in its various forms. I shall argue the following threefold case.

---

[60] Segal 1977. Cf. too Lapide, in Lapide and Moltmann 1981, 34ff.
[61] *deuteros theos* (*de Som.* 1.229). See the accounts in Schürer 3.881–5; Borgen 1984, 273f.
[62] *1 En.* 48.2f.; cf. 61.8; 69.29.

(1) At the large-scale level, Jewish covenant theology claims that the creator has not been thwarted irrevocably by the rebellion of his creation, but has called into being a people through whom he will work to restore his creation. Without this, the creator would otherwise be a weak god, unable to handle evil, and monotheism would lapse towards a theological/moral duality (type 5 above).

(2) At a smaller-scale level, Israel's own sufferings, which create problems within covenant theology itself ('If our god is sovereign, why are we suffering?'), are answered from within the same covenantal doctrine: we are suffering because of our infidelity to the covenant, but our god will remain faithful and will restore us.

(3) At the individual level, which can only be isolated from the other two at the cost of potential distortion, the sufferings and sins of individual Jews may be seen in the light of the continual provision of forgiveness and restoration, as a kind of often-repeated small-scale version of the great restoration which was expected. Here the sacrificial system gains its full significance.

All of these are thus part of the second major doctrine of Judaism, which stands alongside monotheism and gives it more precise definition. The technical term for this doctrine is *election*. The creator god has found a way of restoring his world: he has chosen a people through whom he will act. Monotheism and election, together with the eschatology which they entail, form the fundamental structure of Jewish 'basic belief', the theological side of the worldview we studied in the previous chapter. They are a vital part of the grid through which all experience of the world is perceived, mediated and brought into coherence.

(ii) Covenant

The idea of covenant was central to Judaism in this period. This has sometimes been questioned on the basis of the relative infrequency of the regular Hebrew word for 'covenant' (*berith*) in many of the key texts. But, as Sanders has shown quite conclusively—so conclusively that one wonders how any other view could ever have been taken—covenantal ideas were totally common and regular at this time.[63] The basis of the covenant was of course the set of promises to the patriarchs (set out particularly in Genesis 12, 15, 17, 22, etc.), chief among which was 'blessing', whose overtones concerned especially the Land and its prosperity. The compilers of the Pentateuch saw the initial fulfillment

---

[63] Sanders 1977, 420f.: 'It has frequently been urged as evidence against the primacy of the covenantal conception in "late Judaism" that the word "covenant" does not often appear . . . Word studies are not always deceptive, but they can be, and this one is . . . I would venture to say that it is the *fundamental nature of the covenant conception which largely accounts for the relative scarcity of appearances of the term "covenant" in Rabbinic literature*' (emphasis original). He reiterates the point in 1990a, 330; 1992, 263–7. See also Segal 1986, 4; Vermes 1977, 169–88 on the covenantal theme which, despite its verbal infrequency, was central to the outlook of the community at Qumran. Cf. also the brief summary in Dunn 1991, 21–3. On recent developments in the study of earlier Jewish covenant theology see Miller 1985, 222f.; cf. too Longenecker 1991.

of the covenant in the events of the exodus (Exodus 2.24f.), and thus understood the Torah as the covenant document which, grounded upon the faithfulness of Israel's god, provided for his people the way of life by which they should express their answering fidelity to him. The book of Deuteronomy is the major work of covenant theology which stands at the head of a long line of subsequent writings on this theme (the Deuteronomic history, Jeremiah, etc.). The emphases throughout are on the promises made to Abraham, blessing as the consequence of covenant fidelity, the land as the gift of Israel's god to his people, and Israel as holding the place of honour among the nations. Thus, for instance:

> Look down from your holy habitation, from heaven, and bless your people Israel and the ground that you have given us, as you swore to our ancestors—a land flowing with milk and honey . . .
> Today you have obtained YHWH's agreement: to be your God; and for you to walk in his ways, to keep his statutes, his commandments, and his ordinances, and to obey him. Today YHWH has obtained your agreement: to be his treasured people, as he promised you, and to keep his commandments; for him to set you high above all nations that he has made, in praise and in fame and in honour; and for you to be a people holy to YHWH your God, as he promised.[64]

Deuteronomy then closes with two dramatic sections: the establishing of the covenant (chapters 27–30) and the farewell words of Moses (chapters 31–4). The first of these enumerates in detail the blessings and curses which attend the covenant—the blessings which will follow obedience and the curses which will follow disobedience. Significantly, these chapters envisage the curse not just as a possibility but as a certainty. Moses, within this text, knows that Israel is going to turn away from YHWH (28.15–68; 29.16–28; 31.16–21, 27, 29), and provides for this contingency: the ultimate curse will be exile (quite logically, since the promised land is the place of blessing), but *after* exile will come covenant renewal, the circumcision of the heart, the return to the Land, the perfect keeping of Torah (30.1–10).[65] Although we are not well informed about how widely read such passages were in the first century, we can say with confidence that the collocation of ideas, sometimes no doubt mediated through other writings both canonical (e.g. Jeremiah) and non-canonical (the Scrolls) were in wide currency.[66]

Covenantal ideas were therefore fundamental to the different movements and currents of thought within second-temple Judaism. The Maccabaean crisis was all about the covenant.[67] The setting up of Essene communities took place in the belief that Israel's god had renewed his covenant at last (but secretly, with them alone).[68] The book of *Jubilees* celebrated the special status of Israel

---

[64] Dt. 26.15, 17–19.

[65] A similar Deuteronomic summary of the curse of exile and the promise of restoration occurs in Dt. 4.25–40, which was read in the liturgy on one of the main fast-days already observed in the first century: Millgram 1971, 279f.

[66] I am indebted to Prof. James M. Scott of Trinity Western University, British Columbia, for letting me see his forthcoming article on 'Paul's Use of Deuteronomy', in which he discusses this 'Deuteronomic View of Israel's History', and its first-century appropriation, in some detail.

[67] Cf. 1 Macc.1.15; 2.20, 49–68 (esp. 50f.); 4.8–11; 2 Macc. 1.2–6; 7.36; 8.14–18.

[68] e.g. CD 6.19; see ch. 7 above.

in virtue of the covenant.[69] The later wisdom literature, for all its borrowings of ideas and idioms from Israel's neighbours, stressed the Jewish covenant if anything more strongly than the biblical wisdom tradition had done.[70] The apocalyptic writings looked in eager expectation for their god to fulfill his covenant, and thus to vindicate Israel.[71] The later rabbis examined ever more carefully the obligations through which Israel was to act out her part in the divine covenant.[72] It was the covenant which meant that Israel's oppression was seen as a theological as well as a practical problem, and which determined the shape which solutions to that problem would have to take. It was the covenant that drove some to 'zeal' for Torah, others to military action, others to monastic-style piety. The covenant raised, and helped to answer, the question as to who really belonged to Israel. Covenant theology was the air breathed by the Judaism of this period.

This complex of covenantal ideas gave Israel a particular understanding of who precisely she was as a people within the purposes of the creator God. This idea is not usually explored in the way that I think it should be, and we must now examine it more closely.

(iii) Israel, Adam and the World

I now wish to show that Israel's covenantal vocation caused her to think of herself as the creator's true humanity. If Abraham and his family are understood as the creator's means of dealing with the sin of Adam, and hence with the evil in the world, Israel herself becomes the true Adamic humanity. This belief can be made concrete and specific by taking soundings in documents representing various different styles or strands of Judaism. It must be stressed that we are attempting here to see things from a first-century perspective, not necessarily suggesting that all the original authors, redactors or editors of the different strands of material would have agreed with this reading.

(a) Pentateuch

Abraham emerges within the structure of Genesis as the answer to the plight of all humankind. The line of disaster and of the 'curse', from Adam, through Cain, through the Flood to Babel, begins to be reversed when God calls Abraham and says 'in you shall all the families of the earth be blessed'.[73] This

---

[69] e.g. *Jub.* 14.19f.; 15.1–34, esp. 30–2, 34; 22.15–19, 23.

[70] e.g. Wisd. 18.22, symptomatic of the whole book, which stresses the work of divine wisdom precisely in the history of *Israel*; Sir. 17.17; 24.8–23; 28.7; and the great hymnic recounting of Israel's history, from its beginnings to the writer's day, in 44–50.

[71] e.g. 4 Ezra 5.21–30 and frequently; *T. Mos.* 4.5, etc.

[72] Sanders 1977, 84–107.

[73] Gen. 12.3. The translation of this clause is a matter of dispute; but it is beyond question that the passage speaks of a blessing upon Abraham which involves the nations in some way or other.

point about the structure of the book of Genesis is reinforced by a consideration of the many passages in which the commands issued to Adam in Genesis 1
reappear in a different setting. Thus, for instance, we find the following
sequence:

> 1.28: And God blessed them, and God said to them, 'Be fruitful and multiply, and fill the
> earth and subdue it; and have dominion over the fish of the sea and over the birds of the air
> and over every living thing that moves upon the earth.'

> 12.2f.: I will make of you a great nation, and I will bless you, and make your name great, so
> that you will be a blessing. I will bless those who bless you . . .

> 17.2, 6, 8: I will make my covenant between me and you, and will multiply you exceedingly
> . . . I will make you exceedingly fruitful, . . . and I will give you, and to your seed after you, all
> the land of Canaan . . .

> 22.16ff.: Because you have done this . . . I will indeed bless you, and I will multiply your
> descendants as the stars of heaven and as the sand which is on the seashore . . . and by you
> shall all the nations of the earth bless themselves, because you have obeyed my voice.[74]

Thus, at major turning-points in the story[75]—Abraham's call, his circumcision,
the offering of Isaac, the transition from Abraham to Isaac and from Isaac to
Jacob, and in the sojourn in Egypt—the narrative quietly insists that Abraham
and his progeny inherit the role of Adam and Eve. There are, interestingly,
two differences which emerge in the shape of this role. The command ('be
fruitful . . .') has turned into a promise ('I will make you fruitful . . .'),[76] and
possession of the land of Canaan, together with supremacy over enemies, has
taken the place of Adam's dominion over nature.

This theme continues to sound at various points in the Pentateuch, especially as it would be read in the first century. The children of Abraham go to
Egypt and there, apparently, begin to fulfill the promise (Exodus 1.7). When
they are threatened with divine retribution because of the making of the
Golden Calf, Moses reminds God of these same promises (32.13). The promise of the Land is reaffirmed in these terms to the wandering people (Leviticus
26.9); and when the people are getting ready to enter the Land Moses reminds
them that they are what they are because God has been true to his word
(Deuteronomy 1.10f.). As a result, they must themselves remember the promises when they come to live in the land (7.13f.; 8.1), so that God will indeed
bless them if they keep their part of the covenant (28.63; 30.5, 16).[77] And, looking wider than simply Israel's own role, we find a preliminary statement of
another theme: Israel is to be the nation of priests (Exodus 19), the people
through whom the creator will bless his creation once more.

---

[74] The list could be continued: e.g. the promises to Isaac and Jacob in 26.3f.; 26.24; 28.3;
35.11f.; 47.27; 48.3f. On this see also Wright 1991a, 21–6.

[75] cf. too 9.1, 7; 16.10.

[76] An exception to this is 35.11f., echoed in 48.3f.

[77] We may observe also the 'subjugation' of the land (e.g. Num. 32.22), recalling in some
respects at least the subjugation of the world to Adam in Gen. 1.28.

(b) Prophets

Not only does this theme run through the Pentateuch; it emerges also in the prophets. As we will see in more detail later, the prophets call Israel to be the people through whom YHWH will act in relation to the whole world. The point of this, in terms (for the moment) of Israel's own role, is that she is taking the place—under God and over the world—which according to the Genesis picture was the place of Adam.

This emerges in a variety of themes. Isaiah and Micah speak of Zion as the place to which the nations would come, and of Israel's task as being their light.[78] The prophets who look ahead to the restoration of Jerusalem and the rebuilding of the temple see in this event the refounding of the Garden of Eden; Ezekiel envisages rivers flowing out to water and heal the rest of the world,[79] Zephaniah imagines the nations looking on in admiration as YHWH restores the fortunes of his people,[80] and Zechariah (who imitates Ezekiel's idea of the rivers) sees the restoration of Jerusalem as the signal for YHWH to become king over all the world, so that the nations will come to Jerusalem to keep the Jewish festivals.[81] Thus, in the literature which urged the exiled people to look forward to the coming age when all would be restored, the future glory of the land is described in terms borrowed from paradise-imagery; Israel after restoration will be like a new creation, with the people once again being fruitful and multiplying in her own land.[82] The picture is the same: Israel is to be the true people of the one God, whose fortunes are the key to those of the whole world.

(c) Wisdom Literature

One key expression of the vocation to be the genuine humanity is found in the so-called wisdom literature. Tracing their literary and theological ancestry back to the book of Proverbs and no doubt beyond, these books speak of Israel's calling and destiny in language borrowed from the traditions about the creation of the world and of humankind.[83] YHWH's 'wisdom' was the means by which he created the world. This may well be correctly read as the simple assertion that, when YHWH created the world, he did so wisely. In addition, the fact that such a figure of speech can be used in this way may be a signal of just how large a claim is being made in speaking of the creator as active within his world. But if 'wisdom' is thus the means by which YHWH acts, and if human

---

[78] Isa. 2.2–5; 42.6; 49.6; 51.4; Mic. 4.1–5, etc.

[79] Ezek. 40–7, esp. 47.7–12.

[80] Zeph. 3.20.

[81] Zech. 14.8–19. Similar imagery is used in Sir. 24.23–34 of Wisdom/Torah/Shekinah (see the equation of these in 24.8–10, 23).

[82] Isa. 11.1ff.; 45.8; Jer. 3.16; 23.3; Ezek. 36.11; Zech. 10.8, etc.

[83] Proverbs, and some other 'wisdom' writings, are of course based upon non-Jewish (e.g. Egyptian) traditions: see Crenshaw 1985, 369–71. My concern here is with how these books would be read by Jews in our period.

beings are then to become the means through which he acts, it is clear that wisdom is also precisely that which (like Solomon) they need to be his agents, acting wisely under obedience to the creator and in authority over the world. And, in obtaining wisdom, they will thereby become truly human. Now comes the crucial move: in the intertestamental period *'Wisdom' was identified with Torah*. Those who possessed and tried to keep Torah were therefore the true humanity: it was they who would be exalted to the place where humanity belonged, under the creator and over the creation.[84] In one particular tradition, that of Ben-Sirach, this theme was focused on the high priest and the Temple cult in particular. The high priest ruling over Israel is like Adam ruling over all creation; even his vestments were, according to one version of the tradition, the self-same garments which the creator had made for Adam.[85] From quite a different point of view, then, we reach the same conclusion. Israel, and her senior representative in particular, is called to be the true Adam, the truly human people of the creator god.

(d) Qumran

The same belief is visible in the writings found at Qumran:

> God has chosen them for an everlasting Covenant, and all the glory of Adam shall be theirs.

> Those who hold fast to [the sure house in Israel] are destined to live for ever and all the glory of Adam shall be theirs.

> Thou wilt keep thine oath and wilt pardon their transgressions; thou wilt cast away all their sins. Thou wilt cause them to inherit all the glory of Adam and abundance of days.

> . . . to the penitents of the desert who, saved, shall live for a thousand generations and to whom all the glory of Adam shall belong, as also to their seed for ever.[86]

In one passage 'the seed of man' (*zera' ha-adam*) is placed in parallel with the community of the renewed covenant:

> But the seed of man did not understand all that Thou caused [*sic*] them to inherit; they did not discern Thee in all Thy words and wickedly turned aside from every one. They heeded not Thy great power and therefore Thou didst reject them. For wickedness pleases Thee not, and the ungodly shall not be established before Thee. But in the time of Thy goodwill Thou didst choose for Thyself a people. Thou didst remember Thy covenant and [granted] that they should be set apart for Thyself from among all the peoples as a holy thing . . .[87]

All the glory of Adam, in other words, will be inherited by those who belong to the right group on the last day. They will be given 'glory' not simply in the

---

[84] For the identification of Wisdom and Torah in e.g. Ben-Sirach see the discussions of Nickelsburg 1981, 59–62; Skehan and Di Lella 1987, 336f.; Hayward 1991. The roots of this identification, of course, go back a long way in Jewish tradition.

[85] cf. Hayward 1991, 27f., citing (for the last point) Numbers Rabbah 4.8.

[86] 1QS 4.22f.; CD 3.19f.; 1QH 17.14f.; 4QpPs37 3.1f. Translations from Vermes 1987 [1962] ad loc.

[87] 1QLitPr 2.3–6 (Vermes 1987 [1962], 231)

sense of becoming human light bulbs, but in the sense of being set in authority over the world. This emphasis on Israel as the truly human people may have contributed towards the Qumran purity regulations. If the true Israel is to be the genuine humanity, anyone who has physical blemishes, indicating that his humanity is less than perfect, cannot be enrolled as a member of the inner circle.[88]

(e) Other Second-Temple Literature

We know from Josephus that the book of Daniel was a favourite with Jews of the first century AD.[89] One of the climactic moments in this book, arguably, is the scene in which the true Israel, seen in apocalyptic terms as a human figure, is exalted to a position of glory and authority over the mythical beasts who have been oppressing God's people. Whatever referents may have been in the mind of the original authors, there should be no doubt that in the first century many would read such imagery as referring to Israel and the nations, and would hear in the background the overtones of Genesis 2. Divine order will be restored to the creator's garden, through a genuine Adam—i.e., Israel—who will renounce idolatry and so, in obedience to the creator, rule wisely over the creation.[90]

The same conclusion may be reached from a slightly different starting-point by considering the doctrine of resurrection held by many in the first century. When and why this belief first arose is not our present concern. What matters is that in our period many Jews believed that they, or at least the true Israelites among whom they hoped to be numbered, would on the last day be reaffirmed as God's people by being raised from the dead. The point here is that this event would also be a reaffirmation of their *humanity*. They would become the fully human ones, recipients of a restored human life.[91] It may well be that the references to Adam's glory, as seen above in the Qumran passages, also refer to this doctrine.

Finally, we may simply note the comment on Genesis quoted earlier from the rabbinic midrash: Abraham is to restore what Adam has done.[92] Just as the theme of 'covenant' is everywhere present though not always stated, so the Israel-Adam link, which simply focuses the meaning of the covenant, seems to have been woven so thoroughly into Jewish thought and writing that it emerges in one form or another practically everywhere we look. But this raises a further question: if Israel is the true humanity, what about the fate of the other nations?

---

[88] e.g. 1QSa 2.3–10. This may be a result of the community's, regarding itself as the true priesthood. A priest has to be without blemish, and the Essenes, like the Pharisees, were effecting a democratization of the whole priestly system. See further ch. 7 above.

[89] See e.g. Jos. *Ant.* 10.266–8; Vermes 1991; and ch. 10 below.

[90] Dan. 7.11, 14, 17–18, 23–7; Gen. 1.26–8; 2.19–20a.

[91] e.g. 2 Macc. 7.9–11. See the full survey in Schürer 2.494–5, 539–47. On Wisd. 3 see ch. 10 below.

[92] See above, p. 251.

(f) Israel and the Nations

The natural corollary of Israel's being the true Adam is that the nations are seen as the animals over whom Adam rules. But this belief, however expressed, is then capable of bifurcating. Is Adam's rule to be beneficial, bringing order and blessing to the world, or is it to be one of judgment, consigning the threatening beasts to perdition? Evidence of both attitudes can be found in our period.

On the one hand, there is a train of thought which goes back at least to Isaiah, according to which Israel was to be the light of the nations. When Zion becomes what her god intends her to become, the Gentiles will come in and hear the word of YHWH. Though in some passages there is room for doubt as to whether the light will actually save the nations, or merely rescue Israel from among them, in other passages the universal scope of salvation is clear:

> It is too light a thing that you should be my servant to raise up the tribes of Jacob and to restore the survivors of Israel; I will give you as a light to the nations, that my salvation may reach to the end of the earth.[93]

Within the Jewish worldview itself, Israel's vocation is not compromised but is in a sense fulfilled when Gentiles come to join the people of God (like Ruth the ancestress of David), listen to his wisdom (like the Queen of Sheba), or otherwise share the life of his people.[94] This theme is continued into the second-temple period, as can be seen in a book like *Joseph and Aseneth*, which we discussed in the previous chapter.[95]

It is clear, however, that in many Jewish writings from this period a very different tone of voice prevailed. It is scarcely surprising, at a time when the Jews were frequently oppressed and overrun by foreign enemies, that the idea of their becoming the true Adam had more to do with the destroying of the evil hordes ranged against the true god and his people than with their welcome and blessing. In the visions of Daniel, particularly in chs. 2 and 7, the kingdoms of the earth will be destroyed by the setting up of the kingdom of the true god—which is of course closely aligned with the vindication of Israel.[96] Psalm 2 had spoken of the coming king ruling the nations with a rod of iron, and dashing them in pieces like a potter's vessel, and the idea clearly appealed to the first-century writer of the *Psalms of Solomon*:

> See, Lord, and raise up for them their king, the Son of David, to rule over your servant Israel ... Undergird him with the strength to destroy the unrighteous rulers, to purge Jerusalem from gentiles who trample her to destruction; in wisdom and in righteousness to drive out the sinners from the inheritance; to smash the arrogance of sinners like a potter's jar; to shatter all their substance with an iron rod; to destroy the unlawful nations with the word of his mouth ...[97]

[93] Isa. 49.6. See too Isa. 2.2–4; 11.9–10; 42.1, 6; Mic. 4.1–4.
[94] Ruth *passim*; 1 Kgs. 10.
[95] See above, p. 219f. Cf. also e.g. Tob. 13.11; 14.6; *Sib. Or.* 3.710–95.
[96] See below, ch. 10, p. 302–7, where Josephus' omission of ch. 7 is discussed.
[97] *Ps. Sol.* 17.21–4. Compare *Sib. Or.* 3.663–97 (though it should be noted that this is closely joined with passages predicting blessing for the Gentiles). A survey of similar material can be found in Schürer 2.526–9. In 1QM 2.10–14 the war is explicitly designed as the conquest of the whole world.

Israel will, it seems, bring the divine order to bear upon the recalcitrant nations.

The later rabbinic discussions of the place of the Gentiles within the divine purpose shows that there was continuing uncertainty, not to say disquiet, on this matter.[98] But that the fate of the nations was inexorably and irreversibly bound up with that of Israel there was no doubt whatsoever. This point is of the utmost importance for the understanding both of first-century Judaism and of emerging Christianity. What happens to the Gentiles is conditional upon, and conditioned by, what happens to Israel. In terms of the first level of covenant purpose, the call of Israel has as its fundamental objective the rescue and restoration of the entire creation. Not to see this connection is to fail to understand the meaning of Israel's fundamental doctrines of monotheism and election.[99] If the Gentiles, and the ultimate divine purpose for them, are ignored, then Israel's claim to be the one people of the one creator god is itself called into question.

4. Covenant and Eschatology

This belief in Israel's election, expressed in the covenantal theology we have just examined, was itself part of the cause of a second-order problem, which loomed large in the period between the Maccabees and Bar-Kochba. If the creator had entered into covenant with this particular nation, then why were they not ruling the world as his chosen people should? If the world had been made for Israel's sake, why was she still suffering?[100] What was the creator and covenant god now up to? And, within this, a further question: what should Israel be doing in the present to hasten the time when he would act on her behalf? How should one, how could one, be a faithful Jew in the time of present distress, in the time of puzzling delay? As we shall see, these questions gave characteristic form to the articulation both of Israel's hope and of the requirements of the covenant. This problem gives rise to the second level of covenant purpose. If the first level has to do with the divine intention to remake and restore the whole world, through Israel, this level deals with his intention to remake and restore Israel herself.

The need for this restoration is seen in the common second-temple perception of its own period of history. Most Jews of this period, it seems, would have answered the question 'where are we?' in language which, reduced to its simplest form, meant: we are still in exile. They believed that, in all the senses

---

[98] See Sanders 1977, 206–12; 1992, 265–70.

[99] I stress this point not least because it is, I discover, controversial and sometimes overlooked. My view is that this need not be the case. The literature is so full of it that there should be no argument. From the Bible to the Mishnah and Targumim; from apocalyptic to Wisdom; from Philo to Josephus—the line of thought I have sketched is everywhere both presupposed and repeatedly stated in one form or another.

[100] 4 Ezra 4.23ff., etc.

which mattered, Israel's exile was still in progress. Although she had come back from Babylon, the glorious message of the prophets remained unfulfilled. Israel still remained in thrall to foreigners; worse, Israel's god had not returned to Zion. Nowhere in the so-called post-exilic literature is there any passage corresponding to 1 Kings 8.10f., according to which, when Solomon's temple had been finished, 'a cloud filled the house of YHWH, so that the priests could not stand to minister because of the cloud; for the glory of YHWH filled the house of YHWH'. Instead, Israel clung to the promises that one day the Shekinah, the glorious presence of her god, would return at last:

> Listen! Your sentinels lift up their voices,
>   together they sing for joy;
> for in plain sight they see
>   the return of YHWH to Zion.[101]

> Then he brought me to the gate, the gate facing east. And there, the glory of the God of Israel was coming from the east; the sound was like the sound of mighty waters; and the earth shone with his glory . . . As the glory of YHWH entered the temple by the gate facing east, the spirit lifted me up, and brought me into the inner court; and the glory of YHWH filled the temple . . . He said to me: Mortal, this is the place of my throne and the place for the soles of my feet, where I will reside among the people of Israel forever.[102]

Nowhere in second-temple literature is it asserted that this has happened: therefore it still remains in the future. The exile is not yet really over. This perception of Israel's present condition was shared by writers across the board in second-temple Judaism. We may cite the following as typical:

> Here we are, slaves to this day—slaves in the land that you gave to our ancestors to enjoy its fruits and its good gifts. Its rich yield goes to the kings whom you have set over us because of our sins; they have power also over our bodies and over our livestock at their pleasure, and we are in great distress.[103]

This could not be. clearer: Israel has returned to the land, but is still in the 'exile' of slavery, under the oppression of foreign overlords. Similarly, the Damascus Document speaks of an exile continuing until the establishment of the sect:

> For when they were unfaithful and forsook Him, He hid His face from Israel and His Sanctuary and delivered them up to the sword. But remembering the Covenant of the forefathers, He left a remnant to Israel and did not deliver it up to be destroyed. And in the age of wrath, three hundred and ninety years after He had given them into the hand of king Nebuchadnezzar of Babylon, He visited them, and He caused a plant root to spring from Israel and Aaron to inherit His Land and to prosper on the good things of His earth . . . And God observed their deeds, that they sought Him with a whole heart, and He raised for them a Teacher of Righteousness to guide them in the way of his heart . . .[104]

---

[101] Isa. 52.8. This is closely bound up with the coming of the reign of Israel's god (52.7), and with his bringing of salvation (52.10).

[102] Ezek. 43.1–2, 4–5, 7. Cp. the ending of the book (48.35): 'the name of the city from that time on shall be, YHWH is there'.

[103] Neh. 9.36f.

[104] CD 1.3–11 (tr. from Vermes 1987 [1962], 83).

The exile, then, has continued long after the 'return', long after the work of Ezra and Nehemiah; it is finally being undone through the community that tells its story in this Scroll. Similarly, the book of Tobit (probably third century BC) speaks of a real post-exilic restoration of which the previous one was simply a foretaste:

> But God will again have mercy on them, and God will bring them back into the land of Israel; and they will rebuild the temple of God, but not like the first one until the period when the times of fulfilment shall come. After this they all will return from their exile and will rebuild Jerusalem in splendour; and in it the temple of God will be rebuilt, just as the prophets of Israel have said concerning it. Then the nations in the whole world will all be converted and worship God in truth . . . All the Israelites who are saved in those days and are truly mindful of God will be gathered together; they will go to Jerusalem and live in safety forever in the land of Abraham, and it will be given over to them. Those who sincerely love God will rejoice, but those who commit sin and injustice will vanish from all the earth.[105]

None of these wonderful things had come to pass in the first century; even the rebuilding of the Temple by Herod would hardly count (though Herod had hoped that it would), since the other signs of the real return had not yet taken place. The so-called first book of Baruch, probably composed around the same period, clearly reflects the same perspective:

> For you are the Lord our God, and it is you, O Lord, whom we will praise. For you have put the fear of you in our hearts so that we would call upon your name; and we will praise you in our exile, for we have put away from our hearts all the iniquity of our ancestors who sinned against you. See, we are today in our exile where you have scattered us, to be reproached and cursed and punished for all the iniquities of our ancestors, who forsook the Lord our God.[106]

A final example may be taken from 2 Maccabees, describing the prayer of Jonathan:

> Gather together our scattered people, set free those who are slaves among the Gentiles, look on those who are rejected and despised, and let the Gentiles know that you are our God. Punish those who oppress and are insolent with pride. Plant your people in your holy place, as Moses promised.[107]

The present age is still part of the 'age of wrath'; until the Gentiles are put in their place and Israel, and the Temple, fully restored, the exile is not really over, and the blessings promised by the prophets are still to take place.[108]

No faithful Jew could believe that Israel's god would allow her to languish for ever under pagan oppressors. If he did, the taunts of the nations would

---

[105] Tob. 14.5–7. Fragments of Tobit have been found at Qumran; clearly the hope expressed would be congenial to the sectarians. Cf. Schürer 3.222–32.

[106] Bar. 3.6–8. This forms the conclusion of the first, and perhaps the older, section of the book; see Schürer 3.733–8.

[107] 2 Macc. 1.27–9.

[108] See further Knibb 1976, referring to Dan. 9; *1 En.* 85–90, esp. 90; and other writings; Knibb 1987, 21, on CD 1.7–10, and comparing *1 En.* 93.9–10; Goldstein 1987, 70, 74. On the Scrolls cf. Talmon 1987, 116f.: the writers of the Scrolls 'intended to obliterate it [i.e. the return from exile as normally conceived] entirely from their conception of Israel's history, and to claim for themselves the distinction of being the first returnees after the destruction'. Other discussions of the same point, for which I am indebted to Prof. James M. Scott, include Scott 1992b; Steck 1967, 1968, 1980; Gowan 1977; Davies 1985; Goldingay 1989, 251; Collins 1990; Knibb 1983. Other primary sources, also quoted by Scott, include mYad. 4.7; Tg. Isa. 6.9–13.

after all be correct: he was only a tribal god, in competition with other tribal gods, and moreover losing the battle. As a result, Israel was able now to see the issue of good and evil in quite stark terms: evil became increasingly reckoned in terms of 'that which threatened the covenant people', and the judgment of the creator god on evil in his world in general would coincide with the judgment that would fall on the pagans (meted out, perhaps, by his chosen people). The little beleaguered nation looked out at the military might of Rome and the cultural power of Greece, felt both of them making painful and lasting inroads into her national life, and longed for the day when her covenant god would act to reverse the present state of affairs and come, himself, to deliver her and dwell again in her midst. Outside the walls of Israel there was evil, and her god would defeat it. Inside, sheltered behind the religious boundary-markers that (as we saw earlier) played so important a part in the whole story, Israel waited in faith and hope, in puzzlement and longing.

This problem is often seen in the later biblical and second-temple literature in terms of the covenant faithfulness (*tsedaqah*, 'righteousness') of Israel's god—a topic which becomes exceedingly important in the study of Pauline theology. The question of the righteousness of god, as expressed by Jews in this period, can be stated as follows: when and how would Israel's god act to fulfil his covenant promises?[109] The solutions on offer fell into a fairly regular pattern within the 'apocalyptic' writings. They can be set out as follows:

a. Israel's god was indeed going to fulfil the covenant. The hope is never abandoned.[110]

b. This will result in re-establishing the divinely intended order in all the world.[111]

c. Israel's present plight is to be explained, *within* the terms of the divine covenant faithfulness, as his punishment for her sin.[112]

d. The explanation for the apparent inactivity of the covenant god at the present moment is that he is delaying in order to give time for more people to repent; if he were to act now, not only the sons of darkness but a good number of the sons of light would be destroyed in the process. As a result of this process of delay, those who do not repent will be 'hardened' so that, when the time comes, their punishment will be seen to be just.[113]

[109] cf. e.g. Ezra 9.6–15; Neh. 9.6–38, esp. vv. 8, 17, 26f., 32f.; Dan. 9.3–19, esp. vv. 4, 7, 11, 16, 18; Tob. 3.2; and the whole thrust of Isa. 40–55, not least 54, and the (largely derivative) Bar. 3.9—5.9.

[110] As in Dan. 9.16; Neh. 9.8; Joel 2.15–32; *Ps. Sol.* 9; Bar. 5.9; *T. Jud.* 22.2; *1 En.* 63.3; *Jub.* 31.20, 25; *T. Mos.* 4.5; *T. Job* 4.11; *Sib. Or.* 3.704.

[111] e.g. Isa. 40–55; Dan. 7; Tob. 13–14, etc.

[112] Dan. 9.7, 8, 9 (LXX), 14 (the entire passage is significant). Cf. too Lam. 1.18; Ezek. 9.15; Neh. 9.33; and Dt. 27–32, *passim*; 2 Macc. 7.38; 12.6; Wisd. 5.18 (the whole passage is relevant); 12.9ff.; Sir. 16.22; 18.2; 45.26; *Ps. Sol.* 2.10–15; 8.7f., 23ff.; 9.2–4; Bar. 1.15; 2.9; 5.2, 4, 9; Song of Three (27) (=4); *Jub.* 1.6; 5.11–16; 21.4; *T. Job.* 37.5; 43.13; cf. Jos. *War* 3.351–4, and many other passages explaining the catastrophe of AD 70 as the result of Jewish sin.

[113] cf. e.g. 2 Macc. 16.12ff.; Wisd. 12.9ff., 15 *passim*; Sir. 5.4; *T. Mos.* 10.7; *2 Bar.* 21.19ff., 48.29ff.; 4 Ezra 7.17–25; 9.11; 14.32; *T. Abr.* 10. Cp. also CD 2.4f. The whole discussion in bSanh. 97 is very relevant; see Strobel 1961, 19–78; Bauckham 1980; 1983, 310–14.

e. The obligation on the covenant people was therefore to be patient and faithful, to keep the covenant with all their might, trusting him to act soon to vindicate them at last.[114]

It should be clear from this that the idea of 'god's righteousness' was inextricably bound up with the idea of the covenant.[115] These beliefs, which grew naturally out of the combination of monotheism and election, led to the characteristic shape of second-temple Jewish eschatology.

Monotheism and election thus result in what has been appropriately called 'restoration eschatology'.[116] Not until YHWH acted decisively to change things and restore the fortunes of his people would the exile be at an end. At the present time, the covenant people themselves were riddled with corruption, still undeserving of redemption. One major result was that Judaism always contained a tradition of fierce criticism-from-within, which stretched back to Moses and the early prophets. Such criticisms were a regular and classic feature of Judaism, and their appropriation by John the Baptist and Jesus (and, arguably, the early church) is paradoxically a sign, not of rejection of Judaism and all that it stood for, but of fidelity to one of Judaism's central traditions.

We will discuss second-temple eschatology more fully in the next chapter. For the moment, within the present argument, we may sum up what we have described as the second level of covenantal purpose. If Israel was called to be the means of the creator's undoing evil within his world, now that Israel has herself fallen victim to evil she herself needs restoration. The god of creation and covenant must act to redeem Israel herself from her continuing exile. But how could this come about?

5. Covenant, Redemption and Forgiveness

If Israel's god was to deliver his people from exile, it could only be because he had somehow dealt with the problem which had caused her to go there in the first place, namely her sin. The question of how this was to be done looms so large in various aspects of her life, culture and ritual that it is easy to think of the method of dealing with sin (centred, what is more, on the individual), as

---

[114] For this whole scheme of thought see particularly *2 Bar.* (e.g. 44.4; 78.5, and the 'letter' of 78–86) and 4 Ezra (e.g. 7.17–25; 8.36; 10.16; 14.32), on which cf. Thompson 1977, 320; Stone 1990, ad loc.; Longenecker 1991.

[115] Attempts to prise these two apart in the interests of a particular way of reading Paul (e.g. Käsemann 1969 [1965], 168–82; Stuhlmacher 1966; arguing for a non-covenantal technical sense of the phrase 'God's righteousness' on the basis of passages like 1QS 10.25f., 11.12–15, CD 20.20, and *T. Dan* 6.10, apparently without realizing that both are emphatically covenantal) have now proved unsuccessful, as we shall see in volume 3. In addition, the more recent editions of the Testaments show that *T. Dan* 6.10 reads 'the righteousness of the Law of God', and is thus not a proper part of the discussion. Käsemann and his followers are clearly correct to associate the divine righteousness with the intention to restore justice to the whole world, but crucially wrong in missing out the covenantal stage and theme.

[116] The phrase is that of Sanders 1985, 77ff.; the reality is ubiquitous.

the major focus of Judaism. But it is important for understanding the structure
of the Jewish worldview as a whole that we see it in perspective, which means
approaching the question from the larger issues of covenant theology set out
above.

That Israel's god will deal with her predicament is of course affirmed
strongly in the best-known prophecies of return from exile:

> Comfort, O comfort my people, says your God.
> Speak tenderly to Jerusalem, and cry to her
> that she has served her term, that her penalty is paid,
> that she has received from YHWH's hand
> double for all her sins.[117]

> The days are surely coming, says YHWH, when I will make a new covenant with the house
> of Israel and the house of Judah . . . they shall all know me, from the least of them to the
> greatest, says YHWH; for I will forgive their iniquity, and remember their sin no more . . .
> the days are surely coming, says YHWH, when the city shall be rebuilt for YHWH from the
> tower of Hananel to the Corner Gate . . . it shall never again be uprooted or overthrown.[118]

> I will take you from the nations, and gather you from all the countries, and bring you into
> your own land. I will sprinkle clean water upon you, and you shall be clean from all your
> uncleannesses, and from all your idols I will cleanse you . . . then you shall live in the land
> that I gave to your ancestors; and you shall be my people, and I will be your God.[119]

Throughout both major and minor prophets there runs the twin theme: Israel's
exile is the result of her own sin, idolatry and apostasy, and the problem will be
solved by YHWH's dealing with the sin and thus restoring his people to their
inheritance. Exile will be undone when sin is forgiven. Restoration and forgiveness were celebrated together annually at Passover and on the Day of
Atonement; belief in this possibility and hope formed an essential part of
Jewish belief in the faithfulness of her god. If her sin has caused her exile, her
forgiveness will mean her national re-establishment. This needs to be
emphasized in the strongest possible terms: the most natural meaning of the
phrase 'the forgiveness of sins' to a first-century Jew is not in the first instance
the remission of *individual* sins, but the putting away of the whole nation's sins.
And, since the exile was the punishment for those sins, the only sure sign that
the sins had been forgiven would be the clear and certain liberation from exile.
This is the major, national, context within which all individual dealing-with-sin
must be understood.

An attempt was made in some circles within second-temple Judaism to
ground this dealing-with-sin in the very earliest days of Israel's history. The
story of Abraham's would-be sacrifice of Isaac (Genesis 22) was appealed to as
the ultimate reason for Israel's redemption, standing behind the events of Passover, the redemption from Egypt and the redemption that was still to come.
The origin of this belief has been a matter of some debate in recent years; the
suggestion that the Akedah (= 'Binding', sc. of Isaac) tradition predated and

---

[117] Isa. 40.1–2.
[118] Jer. 31.31, 34, 38, 40.
[119] Ezek. 36.24–5, 28.

influenced Christianity has now been considerably undermined.[120] Its significance for us lies in the way in which some Jews thought in this period: if Israel needs redemption and forgiveness, this can only be achieved by an act of YHWH in response to a sacrifice greater and more powerful than anything within subsequent Jewish history and cult. When questions of dealing with sin and enslavement were raised it was to the notion of sacrifice that Jews naturally turned.

This is not surprising, considering the large place that the sacrificial system occupied within the social and religious life of Jews at this time.[121] At this point we are faced with something of a puzzle. We know beyond any doubt that the great majority of Jews took part in the sacrificial system, but we do not know why—or rather, we do not know what they would have said if asked why they went through these rituals. Doubtless there would be talk of Israel and her god, of forgiveness, cleansing, atonement, celebration, worship.[122] Doubtless, too, there would be mention of the Torah's having commanded that sacrifices be offered, and of the importance of performing them as one aspect of obeying Torah. But was there an inner rationale? And how would we know if and when we had found it?[123] Even Sanders, in his sensitive and detailed treatment of the sacrificial system, seems to deal with everything *except* the question which I for one would like to press: according to what inner rationale was the killing of animals or birds thought to *effect* the atonement and forgiveness which those who did it clearly believed it did effect? It cannot be thought that it effected purification, since purification was a necessary preliminary to the offering of sacrifice. And if it is the case that sacrifices are simply a convenient occasion for the really effective act of atonement, which is repentance and confession, that still does not explain why sacrifices themselves have any meaning at all.[124] In the nature of the case, this is not necessarily something that would be explicitly articulated by those taking part; it is more something to be discerned by the wise sociologist or philosopher of religion from the study of the overall pattern of observances. It seems, to put the matter in general terms, as though the sacrificial system functioned as a regular pointer back to the great acts of redemption such as the exodus, and equally as a pointer forward to the great redemption still to come. Since it spoke of

---

[120] See Vermes 1973b [1961]; Daly 1977; Davies and Chilton 1978, Chilton 1980; Segal 1984. The main relevant texts are *Jub.* 17.15—18.19; Jos. *Ant.* 1.222–36; *Ps-Philo* 32.1–4; 40.2–3, etc.; 4 Macc. 13.12, etc. On the rabbinic and targumic passages see Davies and Chilton 533–45.

[121] On the sacrifices see Schürer 3.292–308; Safrai 1976b; and particularly Sanders 1992, 103–18, 251–7.

[122] See Sanders 1992, 252–6.

[123] In Schürer 2.292–308, the only mention of the significance attached to the whole cultus comes in the remark: 'the Israelites regarded the accurate performance of this liturgy as an essential means of assuring divine mercy for themselves'. Similarly Safrai 1976b, 906.

[124] Sanders 1992, 252f. Sanders says that the idea of atonement through the shedding of blood was 'widespread' and 'common'. That is no doubt true, but it still does not explain what connection anyone in the ancient world saw between the one and the other. The old idea of sin being transferred to the sacrificial animal seems not to work either: sacrificial animals had to be pure, and the one time that sins are clearly placed on an animal's head the animal in question (the second goat on the Day of Atonement) is not sacrificed, but driven off into the wilderness.

Israel's reconciliation with her god, it could thus function as a cyclical reminder of a historical or historical/eschatological phenomenon. Since, beyond this remark, I have no new hypothesis to offer, we must here be content with some broad general comments, which may nevertheless be of some help in understanding the sacrificial system within the overall Jewish worldview of the time.[125]

There were of course considerable differences between one sort of sacrifice and another. At one end of the scale there were the sacrifices at the heart of the great national festivals: the Passover lamb signified the past act and the future hope of redemption for the nation. At the other end were the individual sin-offerings whereby an Israelite, conscious of an accidental breach of Torah, or of something done in ignorance of its being forbidden, would have his or her membership in the people of God reaffirmed despite the lapse. (Sinning 'with a high hand', i.e. deliberately, meant in theory that the sinner was cut off from Israel; there was no sacrifice for such offences. [126]) Somewhere logically in between those two was the Day of Atonement, a time of both individual and corporate offering of sacrifice, in which the nation as a whole, and the individual within the nation, recognized that at every level Israel had sinned against her god, deserved his judgment, but instead could receive his forgiveness and reaffirmation through offering sacrifice. Thus, although no clear theory may have been consciously formulated as to *how* and *why* the killing of certain animals under certain circumstances effected this result, the large-scale participation in festivals, and the regular use of the individual sacrifices, indicates clearly that the average Israelite believed firmly *that* the practice was effective.

In other words, the sacrificial system functioned as a way of enacting and institutionalizing one aspect of the worldview which we have already studied: the belief that Israel's covenant god would restore the fortunes of his people, creating them as his true redeemed humanity; and that what he would thus do for the nation as a whole he would also do for individuals within the nation. Of course, as so many writers have pointed out recently, this was not effected automatically.[127] It was held to depend, at least in part, on the attitude of the individual: one had to repent. But it is important here to see how the combination of repentance and sacrifice functioned within the worldview. There is no suggestion that either of them was seen, by Jews, as the means of entry into the covenant people. That was effected by birth and (for males) circumcision. Rather, repentance and sacrifice were part of the means by which Jews maintained their status as the covenant people, enabling Jews to stay within the boundaries when they might in theory have been excluded.[128]

---

[125] For current reflections on this topic at various levels, see Gunton 1988, ch. 5; Sykes (ed.) 1991, esp. the essay by Hayward (22–34), arguing that for Ben-Sirach at least the sacrificial cult is 'to some extent an earthly reflection of that divine order which permeates the universe and on which the creation stands' (29f.).

[126] cf. e.g. Num. 15.30f.; cp. mKer. 1.2; 2.6; 3.2; mShab. 7.1; 11.6; mSanh. 7.8; mHor. 2.1–6.

[127] e.g. Sanders 1977, 5ff., etc.; 1990a, 42f.; 1992, 251–78.

[128] This is obviously to sharpen up the categories 'getting in' and 'staying in' made popular by Sanders 1977. In this I follow Harper 1988, who proposes 'getting back in' and 'staying in after nearly being thrown out' as sharper categories.

One clue to the sub- or semi-conscious meaning accorded to sacrifice in this period may be its partial integration with the history of Israel as a whole. If the exile itself was seen as a 'death', and therefore return from exile as a 'resurrection', it is not a long step to see the death of Israel as in some sense sacrificial, so that the exile becomes not simply a time when she languishes in Babylon, serving a forlorn sentence in a foreign land, but actually a time through which the sin she has committed is expiated. The exile, it seems, was to be seen both as a punishment for the nation in its wickedness, and as in some sense a vocation to a righteous bearing of sin and evil. This step was taken explicitly in the fourth of the Servant Songs in Isaiah 40–55 (52.13—53.12). The Servant, acting out the tribulation and future restoration of Zion (see the context in 52.7–10), dies and rises again as a sin-offering:

> Yet it was the will of YHWH to crush him with pain.
> When you make his life an offering for sin,
>   he shall see his offspring, and shall prolong his days;
> through him the will of YHWH shall prosper.[129]

Exile itself is to be understood as a sacrifice. This understanding of Israel's own sufferings, or those of a representative or group, as somehow redemptive, effective to deliver the rest of the nation from the time of the divine wrath, is picked up most clearly in the language attributed to the Maccabaean martyrs:

> For we are suffering because of our own sins. And if our living Lord is angry for a little while, to rebuke and discipline us, he will again be reconciled with his own servants . . . I, like my brothers, give up body and life for the laws of our ancestors, appealing to God to show mercy soon to our nation and by trials and plagues to make you [i.e. Antiochus Epiphanes] confess that he alone is God, and through me and my brothers to bring to an end the wrath of the Almighty that has justly fallen on our whole nation.[130]

The parallels in 4 Maccabees make this theme even more explicit:

> You know, O God, that though I might have saved myself, I am dying in burning torments for the sake of the law. Be merciful to your people, and let our punishment suffice for them. Make my blood their purification, and take my life in exchange for theirs.[131]

> These, then, who have been consecrated for the sake of God, are honoured, not only with this honour, but also by the fact that because of them our enemies did not rule over our nation, the tyrant was punished, and the homeland purified—they having become, as it were, a ransom for the sin of our nation. And through the blood of those devout ones and their death as an atoning sacrifice, divine Providence preserved Israel that previously had been mistreated.[132]

[129] Isa. 53.10. On the interpretation of Isa. 53 in subsequent Jewish thought, see Schürer 2.547–9.

[130] 2 Macc. 7.32–3, 37–8; cf. 6.12–16, etc. Some have seen the story of Taxo in *T. Mos.* 9 as referring to the same incident (see Charlesworth 1983, 920; Schürer 3.282). Whether this is so or not, its present position, immediately followed by the poem in ch. 10 celebrating the vindication of Israel over the nations, shows the same overall collocation of ideas. The idea of an individual calming the wrath of god is associated with Phinehas and Elijah in Sir. 45.23; 48.10.

[131] 6.27–9: the last phrase reads *katharsion auton poieson to emon haima kai antipsychon auton labe ten emen psychen.*

[132] 17.20–2; cf. too 1.11. The 'ransom' phrase reads: *hosper antipsychon gegonotas tes tou ethnous hamartias,* which, with 6.29, gives the only LXX occurrence of *antipsychon.* The Greek for 'their death as an atoning sacrifice' is *kai tou hilasteriou tou thanatou auton.* 4 Macc. is of con-

This theme of sacrifice goes much deeper than the individual's remedy for a troubled conscience. The annual pilgrimages were not simply times when a multitude of individual Jews restored their individual relationships with their god; they were occasions of national celebration, and reaffirmation of national (i.e. political and social, as well as 'religious') hope.[133] And in this whole complex of ideas the sacrifices played an important part. Partly, no doubt, they were seen as simply the appointed worship of the one true god, whom to celebrate (in thank-offerings, peace-offerings, etc.) was in itself to reaffirm Israel's monotheism and election and hence her national identity and hope. Partly, though, there was most likely a sense that the sacrificial ritual itself dramatically enacted the movement of judgment and salvation, exile and restoration, death and resurrection for which Israel longed. The maintenance, and evident popularity, of the cult thus demonstrated not just the strength of individual piety but the fervour of national expectation.

One feature of Jewish thought in this period reflects the same overall theme in a more lurid and violent way. Some writers spoke of a coming period of intense suffering in terms of the birth-pangs of the new age, the so-called 'messianic woes'. As C. H. Cave remarks: 'reference to the last things [in Jewish writings of this period] is almost always accompanied by the notion, recurring in various forms, that a period of special distress and affliction must precede the dawn of salvation'.[134] This idea may be traced through such passages as follows:

> Ephraim's iniquity is bound up;
>   his sin is kept in store.
> The pangs of childbirth come for him,
>   but he is an unwise son;
> for at the proper time he does not present himself
>   at the mouth of the womb.[135]

> On the day when the Kittim fall, there shall be battle and terrible carnage before the God of Israel, for that shall be the day appointed from ancient times for the battle of destruction of the sons of darkness . . . And it shall be a time of great tribulation for the people which God shall redeem; of all its afflictions none shall be as this, from its sudden beginning until its end in eternal redemption.[136]

---

siderable interest not so much for attitudes taken in the second century BC, but for beliefs held at the time of its composition, i.e. quite possibly in the mid-first century of the Christian era: see Farmer 1956, *passim*; Schürer 3.591. (Some would argue for an earlier dating, but the point is that the book was known and popular in the first century.) For the appearance of similar ideas in the Qumran literature, see e.g. 1QpHab 8.1–3, etc.

[133] See ch. 8 above, on festivals.

[134] In Schürer 2.514. Cf. too Schweitzer 1925 [1901], 265ff.; Allison 1985, esp. 115f.; and the discussion in Rowland 1982, 28, 43, 156–60, esp. 159.

[135] Hos. 13.13; cf. also e.g. Isa. 42.13–16.

[136] 1QM 1.9–12. See also, from Qumran, the fourth of the *Hodayoth* (1QH 3.6–18), esp. lines 8–10: 'For the children have come to the throes of Death, and she labours in her pains who bears a Man. For amid the throes of Death she shall bring forth a man-child, and amid the pains of Hell there shall spring from her child-bearing crucible a Marvellous Mighty Counsellor; and a man shall be delivered from out of the throes' (tr. Vermes 1987 [1962], 173f.). Cp. also 1QpHab and 1QM, *passim*.

And there will be a great plague upon the deeds of that generation from the Lord and he will give them to the sword and to judgment and to captivity and pillage and destruction. And he will rouse up against them the sinners of the nations . . . In those days, they will cry out and call and pray to be saved from the hand of the sinners, the gentiles, but there will be none who will be saved . . . [the passage presently continues with the description of Israel's turning to Torah and so being saved][137]

Behold, the days are coming, and it shall be that when I draw near to visit the inhabitants of the earth, and when I require from the doers of iniquity the penalty of their iniquity, and when the humiliation of Zion is complete, and when the seal is placed upon the age which is about to pass away, then I will show these signs . . . [there follows a catalogue of signs and portents] . . . At that time friends shall make war on friends like enemies, and the earth and those who inhabit it shall be terrified, and the springs of the fountains shall stand still, so that for three hours they shall not flow. It shall be that whoever remains after all that I have foretold to you shall be saved and shall see my salvation and the end of the world.[138]

This then will be the sign: When horror seizes the inhabitants of earth, and they fall into many tribulations and further, they fall into great torments. And it will happen that they will say in their thoughts because of their great tribulations, 'The Mighty One does not anymore remember the earth'; it will happen when they lose hope, that the time will awake.[139]

Israel will pass through intense and climactic suffering; after this she will be forgiven, and then and thus the world will be healed.[140] How widespread this belief may have been in our period, in one or other of its varied forms, it is impossible to say. What is certain is that 'collective suffering as payment for national sin was a traditional preoccupation, and still alive in the first century';[141] it played an important role in Jewish national self-understanding amid the chaos and confusion of our period, and the early Christians (and probably Jesus himself) accepted and reinterpreted it.

We can see then that within the Jewish self-understanding there were various ways of dealing with the fact that Israel was herself, despite her election, a nation of sinners. Whether through the regular sacrifices and festivals, through the suffering of the martyrs, or through the coming great tribulation out of which the age to come would be born, the creator would bring his people through sin and death to his promised glorious future. It is important not to lose sight of the corporate nature of all these ideas. In so far as individual Jews reflected on their own state before God, it was as members of the larger group, whether the nation or some particular sect. Sacrifice and suffering were the strange, but divinely appointed, means through which the chosen people were to maintain their status as such, and through which eventually they would arrive at redemption. In this way the wider hope would likewise come to birth:

[137] *Jub.* 23.22–4.

[138] 4 Ezra 6.17–25; cf. 5.1–9; 7.33ff.; 9.1–12; 13.29–31.

[139] *2 Bar.* 25.2–4. Cf., in the same vein, *2 Bar.* 27.2–13; 48.31–41; 70.2–10; 72; 73; *1 En.* 90.13–19; 91.12.

[140] In the OT this is also reflected in e.g. Ezek. 38.20; Hos. 4.3; Zeph. 1.3; Dan. 12.1, and arguably some of the 'servant' passages in Isa. 40–55. In the NT, cf. e.g. Mk. 13 and parallels; Rom. 8.17–27; 1 Cor. 7.26; Rev. 16.8, etc.; in the rabbinic literature, mSot. 9.15. The idea of portents appearing immediately before the final moment is reflected in e.g. *Sib. Or.* 3.795–807; Jos. *War* 6.289, 299. See other texts listed in Schürer and Rowland, locc. cit. I am not sure that the passage in *War* 6.364 fits with the 'messianic woes' theme, as Goodman 1987, 217 suggests.

[141] Rajak 1983, 97; the whole discussion is significant.

the whole world would be brought back into its divinely intended order and harmony.

6. Beliefs: Conclusion

We have now briefly examined the network of belief that informed and sustained the Jewish hope in this period. We have seen, further, the way in which these beliefs gave rise to that hope which undergirded the various movements of thought and action among Jews of this period. In terms of the model sketched in Part II above, we may sum up the situation as follows.

We have already set out the basic worldview of second-temple Judaism (chapter 8 above). We have now found that the set of *basic beliefs*, which explicate the entire worldview theologically, may be summarized quite simply as monotheism, election and eschatology. There is one creator god, who has chosen Israel to be his people, giving her his Torah and establishing her in his holy land. He will act for her and through her to re-establish his judgment and justice, his wisdom and his *shalom*, throughout the world. The *consequent beliefs*, which in turn bring these basic beliefs to street-level expression, and in relation to which disagreement between different Jewish groups starts to become apparent, have to do with the details of what monotheism actually means. They concern the details of how the covenant is to be maintained, and Torah fulfilled, in the present; they focus on the details of what Israel's god can be expected to do in the immediate and longer-term future, and particularly on the question of what Israel should be doing, if anything, to help that future on its way. Detailed questions of ontology, ethics, eschatology and politics thus grow naturally out of the basic beliefs, and we can observe these questions puzzling and dividing Jews in our period. As we saw, this is often the case with consequent beliefs: those who suppose that they share a common worldview find that they nevertheless disagree about how that worldview comes to detailed expression. Put the other way round, when theological disagreement becomes sharp, it is probably because both sides perceive in the other a threat to the worldview which they cherish, which they see as necessarily entailing the basic and/or the consequent beliefs which are being questioned.

These, then, were the beliefs that gave shape not merely to a religious worldview but to the various different movements, political, social and particularly revolutionary, that characterized the period from 167 BC to AD 70. The basis of the eager expectation that fomented discontent and fuelled revolution was not merely frustration with the inequalities of the Roman imperial system, but the fact that this frustration was set within the context of Jewish monotheism, election and eschatology. The covenant god would act once more, bringing to birth the 'coming age', *ha'olam ha-ba'*, which would replace the 'present age', *ha'olam ha-zeh*, the age of misery, bondage, sorrow and exile. To this hope we now turn our attention.

Chapter Ten

THE HOPE OF ISRAEL

We have seen that the fundamental second-temple Jewish worldview, and the basic beliefs which characterized those who held it, necessarily included some sort of eschatology. There may have been some Jews, perhaps those wielding obvious power, who were happy to play down the possibility of radical change: but most were hoping, some fervently, for a new turn in Israel's fortunes. If there is one creator god, and Israel is his people, then this god must act sooner or later to restore her fortunes. Israel is still in a state of 'exile', and this must be put right. The symbols of covenantal life will be restored, because the covenant will be renewed: the Temple will be rebuilt, the Land cleansed, the Torah kept perfectly by a new-covenant people with renewed hearts. We must now look directly at this hope. To begin with, we must examine one of the characteristic language-systems used to express it.

1. 'Apocalyptic'

(i) Introduction

Like all aspects of second-temple Judaism, 'apocalyptic' has received a good deal of attention in recent years, and I cannot now even enter the debates, but must simply set out the view to which I have come over a period of time. In line with some recent writers, I draw back from offering a *definition* of 'apocalyptic', and proceed by the safer route of offering a *description*, which must itself involve several crucial distinctions; and once we make them we can drop the inverted commas, and treat the different meanings of 'apocalyptic' in their own right.[1]

(ii) A Literary Form and a Linguistic Convention

We meet apocalyptic writing all over the place in the second-temple period, not only in Judaism but in other ancient Mediterranean and Near Eastern reli-

---

[1] I here follow (more or less) Collins 1979, 1987. The latter, together with Rowland 1982, forms a good recent introduction to the whole subject.

gions, including Christianity.[2] When applied to literature, the word usually denotes a particular *form*, that of the reported vision and (sometimes) its interpretation. Claims are made for these visions: they are divine revelations, disclosing (hence 'apocalyptic', from the Greek for 'revelation' or 'disclosure') states of affairs not ordinarily made known to humans.[3] Sometimes these visions concern the progress of history, more specifically, the history of Israel; sometimes they focus on otherworldly journeys; sometimes they combine both. I give two examples, chosen more or less at random, beginning with a description of a vision put into the mouth of the patriarch Abraham:

> We came to God's mountain, glorious Horeb. And I said to the angel, 'Singer of the Eternal One, behold I have no sacrifice with me, nor do I know a place for an altar on the mountain, so how shall I make the sacrifice?' And he said, 'Look behind you.' And I looked behind me. And behold all the prescribed sacrifices were following us. . . and he said to me, 'Slaughter all these. . . the turtledove and the pigeon you will give to me, for I will ascend on the wings of the birds to show you [what] is in the heavens, on the earth and in the sea, in the abyss, and in the lower depths, in the garden of Eden and in its rivers, in the fullness of the universe. And you will see its circles in all.'[4]

'To show you what is in the heavens, on the earth . . . [and] in the fullness of the universe.' There is the essence of apocalyptic: to Abraham are revealed secrets of all sorts. As a result, he learns new ways of worshipping the true god, and finally glimpses (chapter 31) the future deliverance of Israel.

A second example is ascribed to Baruch, the secretary of Jeremiah:

> And when I had said this, I fell asleep at that place and saw a vision in the night. And behold there was a forest with trees that was planted on the plain and surrounded by high mountains and rugged rocks. And the forest occupied much space. And behold, over against it a vine arose, and from under it a fountain ran peacefully . . . And that fountain came to the forest and changed into great waves, and those waves submerged the forest and suddenly uprooted the entire forest and overthrew all the mountains which surrounded it. And the height of the forest became low, and that top of the mountains became low. And that fountain became so strong that it left nothing of the great forest except one cedar. When it had also cast that one down, it destroyed the entire forest and uprooted it so that nothing was left of it, and its place was not even known anymore. Then that vine arrived with the fountain in peace and in great tranquillity and arrived at a place which was not far away from the cedar, and they brought to him that cedar which had been cast down . . . and after these things I saw that the cedar was burning and the vine growing, while it and all around it became a valley full of unfading flowers. And I awoke and arose.[5]

Baruch then prays for understanding, and is given an interpretation: a wicked kingdom (the forest, of which one cedar is left) will be judged, and replaced by the messianic kingdom ('the dominion of my Anointed One which is like the fountain and the vine', 39.7), which 'will last for ever until the world of corruption has ended and until the times which have been mentioned before have been fulfilled' (40.3).

---

[2] See Hellholm 1983; Aune 1987, ch. 7.

[3] cf. the full definition given by Collins 1987, 4: 'a genre of revelatory literature with a narrative framework, in which a revelation is mediated by an other-worldly being to a human recipient, disclosing a transcendent reality which is both temporal, in so far as it envisages eschatological salvation, and spatial in so far as it involves another, supernatural world'.

[4] *Apoc. Abr.* 12.3–10.

[5] *2 Bar.* 36.1—37.1.

These two examples are reasonably typical of the literary form. In the first case, the seer is invited by the angel to view a wide range of things normally hidden, including secrets of the heavens and the earth, the beginning and the end of things. This will lead him to a full understanding and worship of the one god. It also points forward to the deliverance which Abraham's family, Israel, can expect at the last. In the second case, the vision is more specific, relating to a particular historical setting. It assures the faithful that the kingdom which is presently oppressing them will be overthrown, and Israel restored. These two extracts are reasonably typical of the regular content, as well as the form, of the apocalyptic genre.

How then, at the level of literary sensitivity, should such works be read?[6] Clearly, with an eye to the symbolic and many-layered texture of the language used. Baruch's vision of the coming fountain and vine owes a great deal to biblical imagery, and already awakens echoes of previous visions and prayers about the plight of Israel and her coming redemption.[7] The rich imagery of the prophets is revived in a somewhat more stylized form but with very similar intent. The writer of *2 Baruch* was clearly not writing, in the last analysis, about forestry and viticulture: living after the disaster of AD 70, he intended to say something about Israel, her oppression and her future hope. But the forests and plants are not irrelevant. They enable him to do (at least) two things over and above straight socio-religious discourse: to awaken the echoes of earlier biblical prophecy for hearers whose minds were attuned to such things, and to cast his message of patient hope into a form which lent it divine authority. Earlier prophets might say 'thus saith YHWH'; *2 Baruch* describes a god-given vision and interpretation, putting it in the mouth of a hero of several centuries before. The intended effect is much the same. The different layers of meaning in vision-literature of this type thus demand to be heard in their full polyphony, not flattened out into a single level of meaning. If this had been noted a century ago, biblical scholarship could have been spared many false trails. Apocalyptic language uses complex and highly coloured metaphors in order to describe one event in terms of another, thus bringing out the perceived 'meaning' of the first.[8]

We do this all the time ourselves. I have often pointed out to students that to describe the fall of the Berlin Wall, as one well might, as an 'earth-shattering event' might perhaps lead some future historian, writing in the *Martian Journal of Early European Studies*, to hypothesize that an earthquake had caused the collapse of the Wall, leading to both sides realizing they could live together after all. A good many readings of apocalyptic literature in our own century operate on about that level of misunderstanding.

Or take another example. Five people are describing the same event. One says 'I was aware of a blur of colour and a sudden loud noise.' The next says 'I saw and heard a vehicle driving noisily down the road.' The next says 'I saw an ambulance on its way to hospital.' The fourth says 'I have just witnessed a trag-

---

[6] cf. ch. 3 above.

[7] Fountain: Zech. 13.1; cf. Jer. 2.13. Vine, cedar: Ps. 80.8–19; Isa. 5.1–7; Ezek. 17.1–24.

[8] See Part II, chs. 3, 5 above. I here follow Caird 1980, ch. 14.

edy.' The fifth says 'This is the end of the world for me.' The same event gives rise to five true statements, with each successive one having more 'meaning' than the one before. A biblical example of a similar phenomenon occurs in 2 Samuel 18.29–33. David is waiting for news of his troops in the battle against his rebel son Absalom. The first messenger says 'I saw a great tumult, but I do not know what it was'. The second says 'May the enemies of my lord the king, and all who rise up to do you harm, be like that young man.' Both have described the same event; the second has invested it with its meaning. Not only, however, has he said what it was that David needed to hear, that Absalom is dead: he has also invested *that* news with the further comment, that he himself is a loyal subject of the king. Perhaps he knew David's penchant for anger against those who brought good but upsetting news (2 Samuel 1.11–16), and chose to give his message obliquely, couching it as an expression of loyalty. David, in turn, makes his own statement about the same event: 'O my son Absalom, my son, my son Absalom! Would I had died instead of you, O Absalom, my son, my son!' Each of the speakers is referring to the same event. The different modes of speech *invest* the reality referred to with increasing layers of meaning.

Statements about events are regularly invested in this way with all kinds of nuances and overtones, designed to bring out the significance and meaning of the events, to help people see them from the inside as well as the outside. In a culture where events concerning Israel were believed to concern the creator god as well, language had to be found which could *both* refer to events within Israel's history *and* invest them with the full significance which, within that worldview, they possessed. One such language, in our period, was apocalyptic.

More specifically, different manners of speaking were available to those who wished to write or talk of the coming day when the covenant god would act to rescue his people. Metaphors from the exodus would come readily to mind; and, since the exodus had long been associated with the act of creation itself,[9] metaphors from creation would likewise be appropriate. The sun would be turned to darkness, the moon to blood.[10] This is to say: when the covenant god acts, it will be an event (however 'this-worldly' by post-enlightenment standards, and however describable by secular historians) of cosmic significance. Once more, we can only understand this if we bear in mind what we discussed in the previous chapter: Israel believed that the god who had chosen to dwell on the hill called Zion was none other than the creator of the universe, and that the holy land was intended to be the new Eden. Within the context of creational and covenantal monotheism, apocalyptic language makes excellent sense. Indeed, it is not easy to see what better language-system could have been chosen to articulate Israel's hope and invest it with its full perceived significance.

We must not imagine that all 'apocalyptic' writings necessarily carried the same or even parallel layers of meaning. Quite the opposite is the case. In my

[9] e.g. Isa. 51.9–11.
[10] *T. Mos.* 10.5: see below. Jeremiah used 'cosmic' language about the unmaking of creation to refer to the events of the exile: Jer. 4.23–8 (see below).

earlier example, from the Apocalypse of Abraham, a great many of the things that Abraham is to be shown in his vision are (what we would call) supernatural or transcendent realities, whose only obvious link to the space-time world is that in some cases they concern the fate of those now long dead. Some of the visions are taken up with the glory of the heavenly realm itself. So far as we can tell, much of this is intended to be taken 'literally', that is, as straightforward description of heavenly reality.[11] So, too, it is possible and even likely that a book such as 4 Ezra, written like *2 Baruch* after the destruction of the Temple in AD 70, contains actual visions seen during actual mystical experience, and *at the same time* regularly intends to speak of actual Israel, her present suffering and her future hope.[12] The metaphorical language of apocalyptic invests history with theological meaning; sometimes, this metaphor may be intended by its authors to pierce the veil between heaven and earth and speak directly of the further side itself.

It is vital for our entire perception of the worldview of first-century Jews, including particularly the early Christians, that we see what follows from all this. When they used what we might call cosmic imagery to describe the coming new age, such language cannot be read in a crassly literalistic way without doing it great violence. The restoration which would be brought about was, of course, painted in glowing and highly metaphorical colours. Writers borrowed all the appropriate imagery they could to show the immense significance with which the coming historical events would be charged. How else could they give voice to the full meaning of what was to take place? If even a pragmatic British Prime Minister could admit to thinking of his political mission in terms of Moses leading the children of Israel to freedom,[13] it is no wonder if the historical children of Israel should use exodus- and creation-imagery to express their hope for a freedom that would be in somewhat more obvious continuity with such historical memories.

The cash-value of such language is, admittedly, often hard to determine precisely, and this indeed has been a matter of great debate this century.[14] Of great influence here has been the view of Albert Schweitzer, that Jews of the first century expected the physical world to be brought to an end.[15] Schweitzer envisaged this event as being a common Jewish expectation, involving the arrival on earth of a divine messianic figure. This has been commonly referred to, in language borrowed from a few early Christian sources, as the 'parousia', though the word does not belong in this sense in the early Jewish writings upon which Schweitzer based his theories. This hypothetical event was, so Schweitzer and his followers thought, regularly denoted by language about the coming kingdom of god.

---

[11] cf. *Apoc. Abr.* 19, 20, describing similar visions (as do many such texts) to the chariot-vision in Ezek. 1. On this whole theme see Gruenwald 1980.

[12] See now particularly Stone 1990.

[13] James Callaghan, on taking office in March 1976.

[14] See Caird 1980, ch. 14; Rowland 1982; Koch 1972; Hellholm 1983; Collins 1987; Stone 1984; etc.

[15] See Schweitzer 1954 [1910], 1968b [1931].

I have come to the view that the critique of Schweitzer launched by Caird, Glasson, Borg and others is on target.[16] Sometimes, no doubt, extraordinary natural phenomena were both expected, witnessed and interpreted within a grid of belief which enabled some to see them as signs and portents. No doubt eclipses, earthquakes, meteorites and other natural phenomena were regarded as part of the way in which strange socio-political events announced themselves. The universe was, after all, regarded as an interconnected whole (which is not the same thing as a closed continuum). But the events, including the ones that were expected to come as the climax of YHWH's restoration of Israel, remained within (what we think of as) the this-worldly ambit. The 'kingdom of god' has nothing to do with the world itself coming to an end. That makes no sense either of the basic Jewish worldview or of the texts in which the Jewish hope is expressed. It was after all the Stoics, not the first-century Jews, who characteristically believed that the world would be dissolved in fire. (This has the amusing corollary that scholars have thought of such an expectation as a Jewish oddity which the church grew out of as it left Judaism behind, whereas in fact it seems to be a pagan oddity that the church grew into as it left Judaism behind—and which, perhaps, some Jews moved towards as they despaired of the old national hope and turned towards inner or mystical hope instead.[17]) Far more important to the first-century Jew than questions of space, time and literal cosmology were the key issues of Temple, Land, and Torah, of race, economy and justice. When Israel's god acted, Jews would be restored to their ancestral rights and would practice their ancestral religion, with the rest of the world looking on in awe, and/or making pilgrimages to Zion, and/or being ground to powder under Jewish feet.

The 'literalist' reading of such language has of course had a profound effect on the study of the New Testament in the present century. If we imagine the majority of first-century Jews, and early Christians, as people who were confidently expecting the space-time universe to come to a full stop, and who were disappointed, we at once create a distance between them and ourselves far greater than that of mere chronology. We know that they were crucially wrong about something they put at the centre of their worldview, and must therefore either abandon any attempt to take them seriously or must construct a hermeneutic which will somehow enable us to salvage something from the wreckage. This was the programme to which Schweitzer and Bultmann—and Käsemann as in some ways the successor of both—gave such energetic attention. In addition, the thought of the space-time world coming to an end belongs closely with the radical dualism which brings together, in a quite unJewish way, three of the dualities discussed in the previous chapter: the distinction between the creator and the world, the distinction between the physical and the non-physical, and the distinction between good and evil. The result is a dualistic belief in the unredeemableness of the present physical world. This meant that 'apocalyptic' could be seen as far closer to Gnosticism than was really warranted by the evidence (see below); that it could be uprooted

---

[16] Caird, loc. cit.; see Glasson 1977; Borg 1987. Cf. too Cranfield 1982.
[17] I am grateful to Prof. R. D. Williams for pointing this out to me.

from its context as part of Israel's national expectation; and that it could thus function as a history-of-religions explanation for (say) Pauline theology, in a way which allowed quite a bit of the previous theory, that of derivation from Gnosticism, to remain in place.[18] That is why, no doubt, an insistence on the 'imminent expectation' of the end of the space-time world plays a vital and non-negotiable part in some such readings of the New Testament.[19]

There is, I suggest, no good evidence to suggest anything so extraordinary as the view which Schweitzer and his followers espoused. As good creational monotheists, mainline Jews were not hoping to escape from the present universe into some Platonic realm of eternal bliss enjoyed by disembodied souls after the end of the space-time universe. If they died in the fight for the restoration of Israel, they hoped not to 'go to heaven', or at least not permanently, but to be raised to new bodies when the kingdom came, since they would of course need new bodies to enjoy the very much this-worldly *shalom*, peace and prosperity that was in store.[20]

Within the literary form of standard apocalyptic writings, then, we have found a linguistic convention, which traces its roots without difficulty back to classical prophecy: complex, many-layered and often biblical imagery is used and re-used to invest the space-time events of Israel's past, present and future with their full theological significance. We shall continue to explore this in the rest of the present chapter.

(iii) The Contexts of Apocalyptic

There are three particular points that grow out of this consideration of the literary and linguistic phenomena we have just observed: the personal, social and historical contexts within which such writing came to birth and flourished.

First, the *personal*. One of the hardest questions about apocalyptic is whether any given writer actually experienced the visions he records, or whether he is simply employing a literary genre as a vivid and dramatic form of writing. Here there is most likely something of a continuum. Faced with the whole Jewish mystical tradition, which includes a well-worn path of meditation on the divine throne-chariot as described in Ezekiel 1, it would be extremely rash to suggest that no Jews of the second-temple period practised mystical meditation, and extremely arrogant to suggest that if they did they never experienced anything worth writing down. On the contrary, nothing is more probable than that many wise and godly Jews earnestly struggled to come close to Israel's god in prayer and meditation. If at the same time they used, as is again highly likely, techniques such as fasting; and if (as is again highly probable)

---

[18] On all this, see vol. 3 in the present series.

[19] 'Apokalyptic ist bei mir stets als Naherwartung verstanden' ('for me, apocalyptic always means imminent-expectation'), in a letter from Ernst Käsemann to the present author, dated 18 January 1983. See Käsemann 1969, chs. 4–5.

[20] On the idea of resurrection, and its place within this structure of thought, see section 5 below. A good example of a firmly this-worldly eschatology, though still invested with glorious overtones, can be found in *Sib. Or.* 3.500–800.

they had already stocked their minds to overflowing with meditation on Torah, prophets and wisdom writings; then there is every reason to suppose that some of them would have had experiences that they would unhesitatingly have regarded as divinely given visions. Some of them very likely wrote them down; some of these writings are most probably among the early Jewish apocalypses available in recent editions. The only problem is: which ones are they? Which apocalypses reflect this sort of experience, and which ones are 'purely literary' works?

There is no obvious criterion for deciding this question. It must remain a matter of judgment and, as often as not, guesswork. But if, as I have suggested, at least some vision literature originated in actual mystical experiences, it seems very likely also that others, who had not had the same mystical experiences, would employ the genre as a pious fiction, like Bunyan writing *Pilgrim's Progress*:

> As I walked through the wilderness of this world, I lighted on a certain place where was a den, and laid me down in that place to sleep; and as I slept, I dreamed a dream . . .

> Thus I set pen to paper with delight,
> And quickly had my thoughts in black and white.
> For having now my method by the end,
> Still as I pulled, it came . . .[21]

As Bunyan, so no doubt many writers of ancient apocalypses. 'I had a dream', they said; but what they had was a method. And none the worse for that: many a good argument has been advanced under a figure of speech, for the same reason as the Greeks advanced their crack troops inside a wooden horse. The oblique method may work where direct assault has failed.

We may therefore postulate, with some hope of being on target historically, a continuum of experience that gave rise to the writing of apocalypses. At one end of the scale are the full-blown mystics. At the other are those who write about socio-political events in colourful metaphor. In between, there were most likely pious Jews who, without dramatic visionary experiences, nevertheless wrote from a full and devout belief and longing, in words highly charged with religious emotion. Even Josephus (it would be difficult to imagine somebody in our period with less 'apocalyptic' about him) seems to have believed that Israel's god was active in the historical events he witnessed. One did not have to be a wild-eyed sectarian, or to have embraced all possible varieties of dualism, to write an apocalypse. Josephus himself could have done so, had he chosen, abandoning his normal style but not his worldview. But it was more likely that the apocalyptic style and genre would be chosen by those who found themselves on the wrong side of history. To understand this, we must move from the personal to the social.

The continuum of possible personal contexts is reflected in the variety of possible *social* contexts. It has often enough, and plausibly enough, been suggested that apocalyptic reflects a context of social deprivation. It is the litera-

---

[21] John Bunyan, *Pilgrim's Progress*. The first quotation is the opening sentence of the book, the second is taken from 'The author's apology for his book' which forms a preface.

ture of the powerless (Bunyan wrote his 'dream' in prison). To the extent that the writers may have been recording actual dreams and visions, it is quite possible (though not necessary) to understand their work as reflecting an essentially escapist worldview: things are so bad that the only hope is to leave the present world behind and find one's true home elsewhere. That way lies Gnosticism. Equally, though, those who used apocalyptic language to write about the past, present and future of Israel, whether or not their 'dreams' were real dreams or simply well-honed methods, are best understood in terms of the Trojan Horse. They are appealing to ancient authority, usually by means of pseudonymous authorship (Abraham, Baruch, etc.). They are claiming to have insight into the divine plan that is normally hidden from view; this enables a discontented or rebellious group to steal a march on their opponents, and to fortify themselves in the struggle. They are writing cryptically, using secret codes that may get past the censor ('let the reader understand'). They speak confidently of the great reversal which is to come, reflecting an eschatological though by no means necessarily a cosmological duality, just as politicians through the centuries have spoken of the great change that will take place when they come to power. And, as important as all of these, apocalyptic writers use imagery which makes an appeal on a different level from that of the conscious mind. The closest modern equivalent would be the cunning advertisement, using imagery borrowed from one sphere (e.g. romance) to sell products in another (e.g. clothes). On all counts, apocalyptic can function, and we may suppose was intended to function, as the subversive literature of oppressed groups—whether or not it was inspired by out-and-out mysticism, or by good literary technique.

Moving one stage further outwards, we may therefore suggest a broad *historical* continuum as the widest context of apocalyptic. We may expect to find it where intense longing for a reversal of current ill-fortune merges with intense devotion to the god who revealed secrets to his servants in former times and might be expected to do so again. Apocalyptic, in other words, might be expected to flourish in Israel in the Hasmonean and Roman periods, which is of course where we find a good deal of it. This is not simply a circular argument: we have shown why what we have is what we should expect to have. Equally important, we have shown that apocalyptic does *not* belong simply to a private 'movement', separated off from other groups or movements within second-temple Judaism. Its particular method owes a good deal to the use of imagery in the classical prophets: Amos' plumb-line and Jeremiah's smoking pot are proper (though briefer) antecedents for Baruch's cedar and vine, and Ezekiel's various trees are closer still.[22]

This discussion of the different contexts of apocalyptic raises a further important issue. We happen to possess good modern editions of quite a number of Jewish apocalyptic and other writings from this period. Two thousand years ago, the majority of Jews would not even have heard of half the writings, contemporary with them, with which scholars are now familiar; or, if they had

---

[22] Amos 7.7–9; Jer. 1.13; Ezek. 17.1–24. The question of whether some of these are 'natural', and some 'supernatural', visions is beside the point here.

heard of them, they might well have disapproved. Precisely because apocalyptic writing ventured into two dubious areas, mystical speculation and political subversion, many ordinary Jews would have regarded it with suspicion or distaste. As with the Qumran Scrolls, we cannot assume that because we possess a first-century text everyone in the first century possessed it too. The apocalyptic writings do not automatically reveal 'what all Jews thought'; they provide evidence for possible directions that Jewish thought *could* take, under certain specific circumstances.

A further complication occurs when, despite this proviso, a particular writing was taken up and read by a group different from the one where it was produced. It is quite likely that new readings would result, bearing no doubt a family likeness to the original intention but by no means reproducing it faithfully. When, in addition, such subsequent readings became rewritings, through interpolation, omission, or rearrangement, we find ourselves looking at a canvas on which many artists, and perhaps some heavy-handed restorers, have been at work.[23] Attempting to plot where the writing belongs within a historical framework, then, becomes harder, not easier, as more becomes known about it. These remarks do not indicate that apocalyptic writings are useless in helping us to understand how first-century Jewish minds worked, but they suggest caution in drawing conclusions from them.

(iv) On 'Representation'

One of the obvious features of apocalyptic language is the use of symbols and images to represent nations and races. Daniel 7.1–8 speaks of four great beasts that come up out of the sea: nobody imagines the writer to be suggesting that actual fabulous animals would be dragging themselves out of the Mediterranean and climbing up the escarpment, all wet and monstrous, to attack Jerusalem. The sea *represents* evil or chaos, and the beasts *represent* kingdoms and/or kings, as is explained in verse 17. Josephus' interpretation of the parallel vision in chapter 2 suggests that he understood the first beast, the lion, as representing the Babylonian empire.[24] The fourth beast (verses 7–8) clearly represents not simply an individual king, but a whole kingdom, out of which emerge ten 'horns' which represent individual kings (verses 19–26). This sense of 'representation' is common and well known. It is a standard feature of the genre. Jeremiah's smoking pot 'represents' the wrath which will be poured out on Israel. Nathan's 'ewe lamb' *represents* Bathsheba.[25] This is *literary* or *rhetorical* representation: a writer or speaker uses a figure, within a complex metaphor or allegory, to represent a person, a nation, or indeed anything else. In *Pilgrim's Progress*, people in the story *represent* qualities, virtues, temptations, and so forth, in real life.

---

[23] This is particularly clear in the case of *T. 12 Patr.*: see Nickelsburg 1981, 231–41; Schürer 3.767–81; Collins 1984, 342f.

[24] Jos. *Ant.* 10.208, interpreting Dan. 2.36–8. In 4QpNah. 1.6–9 the 'lion' clearly stands for an individual, normally taken to be Alexander Jannaeus.

[25] 2 Sam. 12.1–15.

There is, however, a second sense of 'representation', namely the *sociological* representation whereby a person or group is deemed to represent, to stand in for, to carry the fate or fortunes of, another person or group (the former does not necessarily have to be numerically smaller than the latter, though it usually is: one can imagine a group of people saying 'We have come to represent the Queen'). This has nothing necessarily to do with literary forms or conventions, and everything to do with social and political customs and beliefs. In particular, it has often been pointed out that in the ancient world, as sometimes in the modern, the leaders or rulers of nations 'represent' their people: a good example is the subversively royal act of David, fighting Goliath on behalf of all Israel, after his anointing by Samuel but long before the death of the reigning king, Saul.[26]

There is a third sense of 'representation', which will cause yet more confusion unless it is unearthed and clarified. In the mainline Jewish worldview, according to which the heavenly and the earthly realms are distinct but closely intertwined (instead of either being held apart, as in Epicureanism, or fused into one, as in pantheism), the belief emerges that heavenly beings, often angels, are the counterparts or 'representatives' of earthly beings, often nations or individuals. This *metaphysical* representation is clear in, for instance, Daniel 10.12–21, where the angel Michael is the 'prince' of Israel, fighting against the angelic 'princes' of Persia and Greece. This battle is not to be thought of as essentially different from the one taking place on earth. The language of metaphysical representation is a way of ensuring that the earthly events (puzzling and worrying though they may seem) are in fact bound up with the heavenly dimension, and thus invested both with a significance which may not appear on the surface and with a clear hope for a future that goes beyond what could be predicted from socio-political observation.

Confusion arises here, understandably, because it is perfectly possible to envisage these three quite different senses of 'representation' being used at the same time. Indeed, we have already seen that in the case of Daniel's first three beasts it is not clear whether, at the *literary* level, they represent individual kings or whole kingdoms, whereas with the fourth beast we are left in no doubt (the beast is the kingdom, its horns are the kings). The reason for this unclarity about the first three beasts occurs precisely because a king represents (in the *sociological* sense) the nation over which he rules. Similarly, it would be possible to argue that in Daniel 10 the 'princes' are simply literary devices, 'representatives' in a literary, and not a metaphysical, sense, on the grounds that in chapter 11 there is what seems to be an interpretation of chapter 10, in which the 'princes' are nowhere to be seen, and instead we have simply warring kingdoms. This, I think, would be wrong. There is sufficient evidence of belief in the actual existence of angels, some of whom were entrusted with special responsibility for particular nations, to warrant us in saying that first-century readers would believe in the actual existence of these 'princes' while not believing in the actual existence of the monsters of Daniel 7.2–8. Rather, the language of Daniel 10–11 is to be put on the same level as the language of

[26] 1 Sam. 17.

2 Kings 6.15–17:[27] what one can normally see is only one part of the total picture.

This examination of 'representation' within apocalyptic literature helps to explain, I think, why the genre is what it is. Because the heavenly and the earthly realm belong closely with one another—which is a way of asserting the presence of the creator god within his creation and in the midst of his people—it makes theological sense to think of penetrating the mysteries of the heavenly realm and emerging with information that would relate to the earthly realm. Granted this *metaphysical* belief, and granted the prophetic penchant for visionary images of various kinds, it is easy to see how a *literary* form could spring up which would sometimes make use of the metaphysical correspondence between the earthly and the heavenly, and sometimes not (the monsters of Daniel 7 were not, I think, supposed to be actual creatures in the supernatural, any more than in the natural, realm). Nor did this equation leave *sociological* representation out of consideration entirely. A king, appointed by the creator god to rule over (and 'represent', sociologically) his covenant people, might come to be regarded as a special locus of heavenly blessing and protection, a special channel or vehicle of the divine provision for the nation's needs.[28]

It is necessary to keep in mind this sometimes bewildering set of possibilities, because otherwise confusion very easily arises. But the main point should be clear. It is normal practice, within the genre of dream- and vision-literature, that a nation, a group, a collective entity should be represented, in the literary sense, by a single figure, be it lion, bear, leopard, city, forest, vine—or even a human figure. In none of these instances is it necessary to suggest that either sociological or metaphysical representation is present. For those, further evidence needs to be forthcoming. Unless it is, the demands of the genre are satisfied by highlighting literary representation alone.

(v) Daniel 7 and the Son of Man

'Even a human figure': that, of course, is where one of the largest problems lies, and I hope that, by approaching it from this angle, light may be shed on the vexed question of Daniel 7.13–14.[29] Reading the chapter as far as verse 12, there is no problem. The monsters 'represent' (in the literary sense) nations that war against Israel. Why then have critics read the 'son of man' figure, whom the beasts attack but who is finally vindicated, as a reference either to an individual human, or possibly divine, being, or to an angel? Part of the answer is the confusion between the different senses of representation. What we have in this chapter, I suggest, is *literary* representation, whereby a figure in the

---

[27] '. . . So YHWH opened the eyes of the servant, and he saw; the mountain was full of horses and chariots of fire all around Elisha.'

[28] e.g. Ps. 84.9.

[29] It is impossible to enter into detailed debate about this complex passage. For recent discussions, with extensive bibliography, see Goldingay 1989, 137–93; Casey 1991.

story—a human figure, surrounded by monsters—functions as a symbol for Israel, just as the monsters function as literary representations of pagan nations. This symbol is obviously pregnant with the meaning of Genesis 2, evoking the idea of the people of God as the true humanity and the pagan nations as the animals.[30] This strongly implies, with all the force of the imagery, that Israel, though beleaguered and battered, is about to be vindicated. To say, off the surface of the text, that either the writer or others reading his work would have thought the text was speaking of a 'son of man' who was a historical individual, and who, as such, 'represented' Israel as a nation in the second, *sociological*, sense, would be simply to confuse categories. Once again this can be seen by analogy with the monsters: nobody imagines that the author of Daniel, or any of his second-temple readers, thought that there would appear on earth actual monsters who would 'represent' the pagan nations much as an MP 'represents' a constituency. If anyone, within the first-century Jewish worldview, were to take the step of treating 'the son of man' as a *sociological* representative as well as a *literary* one—to suggest that the symbol might after all become reality—such a bold move could only be felt as radical and innovatory, new wine bursting old wineskins.[31] And if such a move were made, so that an individual figure within history were held to be in some sense the fulfilment of Daniel 7.13f., any attempt to make the *literary* imagery associated with this 'son of man' into literal *historical* truth—to imagine, for instance, that he should be attacked by monsters from the sea—would be an extreme clash of categories.

Equally, it would be wrong to jump from the *literary* 'representation', whereby the 'son of man' represents Israel within the logic of the vision-genre, to a *metaphysical* representation whereby the 'son of man' becomes a transcendent heavenly being existing in another realm. Any such suggestion (for instance, on the basis that the 'saints of the most high' in verses 18, 25, 27 must refer to angels rather than Israel) must be resisted again on the grounds that it is a confusion of categories. If, once more, anyone were to attempt to combine the metaphysical and literary senses at this point, I suggest that such an idea would be perceived in the world of the first century as a dramatic innovation.

With these distinctions in mind, we may now go further, and suggest a contextual reading of Daniel 7 which shows, I think, the extreme probability that those who read this (very popular) chapter in the first century would have seen its meaning first and foremost in terms of the vindication of Israel after her suffering at the hands of the pagans.[32] It is clearly important to establish, not

---

[30] So Hooker 1967, 71ff.

[31] See section 4 below; and vol. 2 in the present series.

[32] The point at which Josephus omits to mention Dan. 7 (*Ant.* 10.267f.) in his otherwise near-complete account of the book is also the point at which (cf. Moule 1977, 14, 16) he stresses how highly his Jewish contemporaries regarded Daniel as a prophet for their time. The reuse of ideas from Dan. 7 in e.g. *1 En.* 37–71; *4 Ezra* 11–13; *2 Bar.* 39 (on all of which, see below), shows that he was correct in this. This point, amplified in much of the argument to come, tells heavily against the insistence of Casey 1991 on subjecting all question of a reference to Dan. 7 to primarily *linguistic* tests; what counts even more than linguistic usage is the way the entire chapter, which forms the vital context of the crucial v.13, was read and understood at the time.

so much what Daniel 7 might have meant in some previous existence (e.g. to an original visionary or an earlier redactor), but what it will have meant to a first-century Jew. We have noted the cryptic evidence of Josephus, to which we shall return later. We must now look at chapter 7 in its context, in other words, as the logical conclusion of the first half of the book of Daniel.

Daniel 7 has long suffered from being read in isolation from chapters 1–6. True, the book seems in some senses to divide at the end of chapter 6, with the previous material consisting largely of stories about Daniel and his friends, and the following chapters offering increasingly complex eschatological visions. Even this simple division, however, is misleading. Daniel 2 and 4 have a good deal in common with the later visions, and indeed the early chapters continually stress Daniel's skill in knowing and making known hidden mysteries. Chapter 9, though it culminates in an eschatological revelation, consists mainly of a prayer which fits comfortably within the picture of a Jew in exile already drawn in chapters 1–6. In addition, the strange fact that 2.4b—7.28 is in Aramaic suggests that chapter 7 is not to be divorced from chapters 1–6, and indeed hints particularly at a possible link between chapters 2 and 7.[33]

The first six chapters of the book have, indeed, two common themes. First, Jews are invited or incited to compromise their ancestral religion, and refuse to do so. They are tested in some way, proved to be in the right, and exalted. Second, various visions and revelations are granted to the pagan king, and are then interpreted by Daniel. Thus, in chapter 1, we have a mild opening statement of the first theme: the four youths refuse the king's rich (and presumably idolatrous) food, but become healthier than ever, and are given a position of pre-eminence in the royal court. The second theme is introduced in chapter 2, where Daniel's superior wisdom is demonstrated: only he can reveal, and interpret, the king's dream. The dream itself is of a statue made of four different parts, and of a stone which breaks it in pieces and becomes a great mountain. When interpreted, this refers to four kingdoms, which will be ousted by the everlasting kingdom of Israel's god. The content of the vision (the second theme) is the same as the first theme itself. And this content is one with which we are by now very familiar. It is the main story of second-temple Judaism, told and retold in multiple forms throughout our period.[34] These two opening chapters thus serve not merely as an introduction to chapters 1–6 but as a setting of themes for the whole book.

In the third chapter, Daniel's three companions refuse to worship the king's golden image (possibly intended to link with the 'head of gold', representing Nebuchadnezzar, in 2.38), and are thrown into the fiery furnace, whence they are miraculously rescued and given promotion and honour. The same theme is found in inverted form in chapter 4: Nebuchadnezzar has a vision, interpreted

---

[33] See Goldingay 1989, 157f.: ch. 7 rounds off a chiasm that began with ch. 2. Professor Moule suggests to me in a letter a cautionary note: it is possible that 'the Aramaic bits in both books [i.e. Daniel and Ezra] are fortuitous, and probably due to the copyist's having a defective exemplar, and, faute de mieux, filling in the lacunae from an Aramaic Targum'.

[34] See ch. 8 above.

by Daniel, in which he is humbled after his great pride, and recognizes the eternal sovereignty of the one god of heaven, whom the reader of course identifies as the god of Daniel. This mutation is then combined with the first theme in chapter 5, when Belshazzar celebrates a pagan feast with the vessels from the Temple in Jerusalem. Daniel interprets the writing on the wall: the one true god is sitting in judgment on the pagan king who has vaunted himself against him. Israel's god is vindicated, and in his vindication Daniel, the Jew called in to explain the writing (5.13f.), is himself vindicated and exalted (5.16, 29).

This sets the scene for chapter 6, in which Daniel, under pressure himself to compromise his monotheism by praying to the king, refuses, and is cast into the den of lions. When the king comes in the morning and discovers Daniel alive, he has him taken up out of the den (6.23), causes his accusers to be killed in his place, and issues a decree, in language obviously reminiscent of 2.44, 4.3, and 4.34, extolling the god of Daniel:

> for he is the living God,
>   enduring for ever.
> His kingdom shall never be destroyed,
>   and his dominion has no end. (6.26)

There should be no doubt about how material such as Daniel 1–6 would be read and understood in second-temple Judaism, particularly in the Syrian and Roman periods. Pagan pressure for Jews to compromise their ancestral religion must be resisted: the kingdoms of the world will finally give way to the everlasting kingdom of the one true god, and when that happens Jews who had held firm will themselves be vindicated. We may cite 2 Maccabees 7 as a close parallel.[35]

This complex of beliefs and expectations, I suggest, provides the natural and obvious context in which chapter 7 is to be understood.[36] Within the second half of the book as a whole, the two themes from the first half are modified but not abandoned. The individual fortunes of Daniel and his companions become the national fortunes of Israel; and it is Daniel, now, who has the visions, which are interpreted by an angel. Putting chapter 7 in this setting, and reading it as a whole, instead of dismantling it in search of earlier meanings for its hypothetical earlier parts, a consistent picture emerges. The four beasts who come out of the sea (verses 2–8) culminate in the little horn of the fourth beast (verse 8), who makes war with 'the saints' (verse 21). But when the 'most high', the 'Ancient of Days', takes his seat, judgment is given in favour of 'the saints'/'one like a son of man' (verses 13, 18, 22, 27): they are vindicated and exalted, with their enemies being destroyed, and in their vindication their god himself is vindicated:

---

[35] Nor is there any necessary idea here of this vindication including the end of the space-time order. The doctrine of resurrection, developing as it was at the same time and under the same pressures, indicates that the present world would continue, with the righteous people of the covenant god now in control under his sole sovereignty, and the righteous dead returning to share in the triumph. See below.

[36] See Cohen 1987, 197.

His dominion is an everlasting dominion,
    that shall not pass away,
and his kingship is one
    that shall never be destroyed. (7.14)

We shall come to the details presently. For the moment we must note the more than striking parallel between this sequence of events and the whole preceding train of thought, particularly as it finds expression in chapter 6. Here, as there, the human figure is surrounded by threatening 'beasts'; as we saw, the first beast in 7.4 is like a lion, making the connection with the previous chapter about as explicit as it could be. Here, as there, the king comes in his authority: Darius in chapter 6 acts the part that will be taken by the Ancient of Days in chapter 7. In both, the human figure (Daniel in chapter 6; the 'son of man' in chapter 7) is vindicated and exalted, lifted up out of the reach of the beasts. In both, the one true god is glorified, and the enemies of his people subjugated. Both end with a celebration of the kingdom/kingship of the one true god. Dramatically, poetically, the sequence is identical. Granted the strong prevalence of exactly this story-line in so much other second-temple literature, it seems to me morally certain that a Jew of the period would have read Daniel 7 in just this way.

There are obvious points of dissimilarity between chapters 6 and 7: Darius is not himself divine; the lions of chapter 6 are not destroyed, but become the destroyers of the actual enemies of Daniel. But these make no difference to the close parallelism. One might almost suggest, in line with our earlier cautious suggestions about the personal and mystical origins of some apocalyptic literature at least, that chapter 7 is exactly the sort of dream—or nightmare—that someone might have if they had been through the harrowing experience of chapter 6, and had reflected on it theologically. No doubt a writer of sufficient subtlety to construct a book like that of Daniel could have made the same connection. Certainly I find it impossible to believe that whoever put Daniel into its final form was innocent of the parallelism.

But is it really legitimate to read chapter 7 in this way? It has become customary to separate out various different elements in it, obscuring the overall effect just sketched. In particular, (a) the 'one like a son of man' has been interpreted as a reference to a transcendent being, or to an angelic figure (or figures), and (b) the various stages of the narrative, particularly the moment of vindication, have been separated out and played off against one another (verses 13f., 18, 22, 27, speaking of 'one like a son of man', then 'saints of the most high', and then 'people of the saints of the most high').[37] Both moves, it seems to me, are in danger of misreading the apocalyptic genre.

(a) Collins is surely right to say that, if the reference is to an angel, that still does not nullify the meaning that the faithful Israelites will be vindicated, since the angel is their heavenly counterpart.[38] But this move, I think, is simply not necessary. Though it is true that in chapter 10 and elsewhere Michael, the 'prince' of Israel, fights against the 'princes' of the pagan nations, this need not

[37] See the detailed account of research in Goldingay 1989, 169–72.
[38] Collins 1987, 81–3. Cf. Goldingay 1989, 171f.

stand as a model for the interpretation of chapter 7; nor is the reference to
'the saints' necessarily to be taken to denote angels, despite the possible parallels in Qumran. We have here the confusion outlined above, between
apocalyptic metaphor, i.e. *literary* representation, and speculative ontology, i.e.
metaphysical representation. In the former, a 'vision' is a way of referring to
earthly realities while investing them with their theological significance. In the
latter, such a vision becomes a literal window on actual 'heavenly' events,
important no doubt because they will have their inevitable earthly counterpart,
but also attracting attention in and of themselves. There is, to be sure, a short
route between these two possible sets of meaning; but the parallels we have
seen between chapter 7 and chapters 1–6 encourage me to assert that in chapter 7 at least, whatever may be the case later on, the natural way of reading the
vision is to see the 'one like the son of man' as 'representing' (in the literary,
not the sociological or metaphysical, sense) the 'people of the saints of the
most high'. That is to say, the vision is *about* the suffering of Israel at the hands
of the pagans—more especially, of one pagan monarch in particular,
presumably Antiochus Epiphanes—and her coming vindication when the one
god reveals himself to be her god and destroys her enemies. Otherwise, we
would have expected the 'beasts' to be themselves 'princes' of the nations,
whereas they too 'represent' the nations in the literary, not the sociological or
metaphysical, sense. When Israel's god acts to vindicate his name, his people
will be revealed as his true humanity, as a 'human figure' in contrast to the
'beasts'.[39]

(b) It belongs to the apocalyptic genre that the meaning of the vision
should be unfolded step by step (if necessary), not that the meaning should
actually change from one unfolding to the next. It is thus perfectly proper to
allow the fullest, final statement (v. 27) to be determinative for the earlier
ones; and the addition of 'people' to 'saints of the most high' at this point can
therefore safely be taken as an indication that this was the reference always
intended.[40]

It therefore seems to me perfectly justifiable (though of course the above
account remains tendentious, since space forbids the full discussion that would
in principle be desirable) to read Daniel 7 in the light of the first half of the
book, and to suggest that a Jew of the second-temple period would have read
it like that too. Faced with pagan persecution, such a Jew would be encouraged to remain faithful while awaiting the great day of victory and vindication,
when Israel would be exalted and her enemies defeated, when the covenant
god would show himself to be god of all the earth, and would set up the kingdom which would never be destroyed. The later visions in Daniel 8—12, in my
opinion, are to be read as developments from this basic position, rather than
as themselves determining the meaning of the earlier portions of the book.
And if this is so, it is this overall context of meaning, rather than isolated

---

[39] cf. ch. 9 above, pp. 262–8.
[40] Following e.g. Moule 1977, 13. That this reference at least must include human beings is
acknowledged by Collins 1987, 83.

speculation about the figure who appears in 7.13–14, that must form the basis for understanding the multiple reuse of similar language in the first century.

Putting together the argument of the chapter so far, we may observe the irony of one of the standard features of twentieth-century gospel study. Many have read apocalyptic metaphor (the 'coming of the son of man with a cloud') as literal prediction (a human being floating on a real cloud), despite the fact that the rest of Daniel 7 has never been read in this way; and they have then read potentially literal statement (stories about Jesus in the gospels) as metaphor (allegorical or mythical expressions of the church's faith). This, as we will see on another occasion, is simply to misunderstand the genres involved.

(vi) Apocalyptic, History and 'Dualities'

As we saw in the last chapter, it is often asserted that apocalyptic literature is in some sense dualistic. We must now tease out the senses in which this is true, and the senses in which it is not. To begin with, it is clear that many apocalyptic writings hold an *eschatological duality* between the present age and the age to come. They are not alone in this: rabbinic writings do so, too, and so indeed do many of the biblical prophets ('It shall come to pass in the latter days . . .'). Equally, apocalyptic writings assume the vital distinction between the creator and the creation (*theological/cosmological duality*) and a firm *moral duality* between good and evil. These, too, they share with all mainline Judaism. Some, as we have seen, exemplify a strong *sectarian duality*, and all of necessity partake of an *epistemological duality*. These, too, have their parallels and origins in the Hebrew scriptures as a whole. Finally, many apocalyptic writings have a lot to say about heavenly beings other than the one creator god: that is, they, like some parts of the Hebrew Bible, express a *theological/ontological duality*.

But when apocalyptic writings are called 'dualistic', what is normally being asserted is that they have combined these dualities, which are common to much of Judaism, with one or more of the remaining three sorts. In particular, it is imagined that they envisage a *cosmological dualism* in which the present space-time universe is inherently evil, and so must be destroyed in order that a different and better world may take its place. Sometimes apocalyptic expressions of piety have led scholars to think that an *anthropological dualism* is present, in which the writer or the group regard their physicality as irrelevant and their spirituality as all-important. And sometimes they are supposed to have held a *theological/moral dualism*, regarding themselves as the people of the good god, and the world, or their opponents, as the creation of an equal and opposite bad god.

These distinctions between different types of dualities and dualisms enable us to see that affirming the presence of the first six types in a particular book in no way commits us to affirming the presence of the last three. The first six, being common to a good deal else in Judaism besides apocalyptic, are not therefore among its crucial defining characteristics. The literary form in and of itself has no necessary connection with the last three.

In particular, it is vital to grasp one basic point. The worldview to which many apocalyptic writings give voice is the worldview shared by many other Jewish writings of the period. In so far as they attempt to understand what the creator god, Israel's god, is doing within space-time history, the writers of apocalypses share that quest with Ben-Sirach and Josephus. The difference between (say) 4 Ezra and Josephus is not that the former believed in a god who acts in history and the latter does not, but (a) that the former believed that the destruction of Jerusalem was a great tragedy which only a major reversal could justify, while the latter took it as a sign that Israel's god had gone over to the Romans, and (b) that the two writers chose different literary forms, commensurate with their different standpoints, to express these beliefs.

So, too, in so far as the apocalyptic writings attempt to go further, and to speak of a great new act which this god will perform on the historical stage, they are in line with (for instance) Isaiah and Ezekiel. If they try to work out in great detail exactly when this will take place, that may mark them out (along with Daniel) as more given to speculation, but does not mean that they believed in a dualistic or deterministic world while Isaiah and Ezekiel believed in free will. To analyse these writings in such a way is to capitulate to a Josephus-like Hellenization of categories. The more oppressed a group perceives itself to be, the more it will want to calculate when liberation will dawn. But that there is a divine plan, which, though often opaque, is working its way out in history and will one day demonstrate the justice of all its workings—this is believed by the biblical writers, the wisdom literature, the Maccabaean martyrs, the writers of the Scrolls, Josephus, and almost everyone else one can think of in the period. It is not a sign that apocalyptic literature has gone out on a limb; merely, that it sometimes has a different way of expressing itself, a way which can be seen to arise not least from its particular socio-cultural situation.

The real problem is that much modern reading of these texts has taken place within a tacitly Deist framework, in which one either believes (a) in an absent god and a closed space-time continuum or (b) in a normally absent god who occasionally intervenes and acts in discontinuity with that space-time continuum. First-century Jews certainly believed that their god, being the creator of the world, could and did act in ways for which there was no other obvious explanation. But that he was normally absent, allowing his world and his people to get on with things under their own steam—if there were Jewish writers who believed this, I am unaware of them. The puzzle that faced some writers, namely, why their god was not acting as they wished him to, was solved, as we have seen, in quite other ways, not least through wrestling with the concept of the divine covenant-faithfulness.[41]

It follows from all this that there is no justification for seeing 'apocalyptic' as necessarily speaking of the 'end of the world' in a literally cosmic sense. This modern idea has regularly been fuelled by the belief that 'apocalyptic' is

---

[41] cf. ch. 9 above, pp. 268–72.

'dualistic', in a way which we have now seen to be unfounded. The great bulk of apocalyptic writing does not suggest that the space-time universe is evil, and does not look for it to come to an end. An end to the *present world order*, yes: only such language, as Jeremiah found, could do justice to the terrible events of his day.[42] The end of the space-time world, no. The implicit argument that has dominated scholarship over this last century has claimed that (a) the hugely figurative language about cosmic catastrophe must be interpreted literally, and (b) the clear dualities inherent in apocalyptic indicate a radical dualism which sought the destruction of the present world altogether.[43] Instead of this, we must insist on a reading which does justice to the literary nature of the works in question; which sets them firmly in their historical context, in which Jews of most shades of opinion looked for their god to act within continuing history; and which grasps the fundamental Jewish worldview and theology, seeing the present world as the normal and regular sphere of divine actions, whether hidden or revealed. Literature, history and theology combine to suggest strongly that we must read most apocalyptic literature, both Jewish and Christian, as a complex metaphor-system which invests space-time reality with its full, that is, its theological, significance. The results of this remain to be explored below.

2. The End of Exile, the Age to Come and the New Covenant

As I have suggested above, the fundamental Jewish hope was for liberation from oppression, for the restoration of the Land, and for the proper rebuilding of the Temple. This complex of expectations was the direct result of believing on the one hand that Israel's god was the king of the world while facing on the other hand the fact of Israel's present desolation. In the later parts of the Hebrew Bible, and in the post-biblical Jewish literature, we regularly find the same combination of themes, which summon up the key symbols of Israel's entire worldview. To speak of Temple or Land is to evoke the image of exile and restoration, and so to cling on to the hope of restoration.[44]

One of the central ways of expressing this hope was the division of time into two eras: the present age and the age to come.[45] The present age was a time when the creator god seemed to be hiding his face; the age to come would see the renewal of the created world. The present age was the time of Israel's misery; in the age to come she would be restored. In the present age wicked men seemed to be flourishing; in the age to come they would receive their just

---

[42] Jer. 4.23–8, speaking of the coming destruction of Judah and her Temple, and investing that space-time reality with a theological interpretation: this is like the unmaking of creation itself.

[43] This has then been transferred to some readings of early Christian literature: see Mack 1988 for a sustained polemic against the supposed radical dualism of Mark's gospel.

[44] On the different ways in which this hope might be expressed by different groups of Jews, see below, and also ch. 7 above. On the Jewish hope see now Sanders 1992, ch.14, and his summaries on e.g. 298.

[45] *ha-'olam hazeh* and *ha-'olam haba'*. On the two ages see e.g. Schürer 2.495.

reward. In the present age even Israel was not really keeping Torah perfectly, was not really being YHWH's true humanity; in the age to come all Israel would keep Torah from the heart. Although the 'age to come' is sometimes described as 'the messianic age',[46] it would be misleading to think that all such aspirations centred upon a messianic figure. As we shall see, in the comparatively rare places where Messianism is made explicit, it features as one aspect of the much wider and far more frequent expectation of a great reversal within the space-time world, in which Israel would be vindicated and the world at last set back to rights under its true king, Israel's covenant god. As we saw, the nations would flock to Zion, either to learn about the true god and how to worship him[47]—or to be dashed in pieces like a potter's vessel.[48]

A word is necessary at this point about the meaning of the term 'salvation' in the context of the Jewish expectation. It ought to be clear by now that within the worldview we have described there can be little thought of the rescue of Israel consisting of the end of the space-time universe, and/or of Israel's future enjoyment of a non-physical, 'spiritual' bliss. That would simply contradict creational monotheism, implying that the created order was residually evil, and to be simply destroyed. Even in the wisdom literature, which speaks of the righteous possessing immortal souls (e.g. Wisdom 3.1–4), there is continual concern with the actions of Israel's god *within* history (e.g. 10–19); and the immortal souls of Wisdom 3 are assured, not of a non-physical bliss, but of new responsibilities in a renewed creation: 'In the time of their visitation they will shine forth, and will run like sparks through the stubble. They will govern nations and rule over peoples, and YHWH will reign over them forever' (3.7–8).

Rather, the 'salvation' spoken of in the Jewish sources of this period has to do with rescue from the national enemies, restoration of the national symbols, and a state of *shalom* in which every man will sit under his vine or fig-tree.[49] 'Salvation' encapsulates the entire future hope. If there are Christian redefinitions of the word later on, that is another question. For first-century Jews it could only mean the inauguration of the age to come, liberation from Rome, the restoration of the Temple, and the free enjoyment of their own Land.[50]

As we saw in the last chapter, if this was to happen Israel's god had to deal with her sins. The end of exile, in fact, would be seen as the great sign that this had been accomplished. The promise of forgiveness and that of national restoration were thus linked causally, not by mere coincidence:

> Sing aloud, O daughter Zion;
> shout, O Israel!

---

[46] e.g. in Schürer 2, 488–554, where 'Messianism' really means 'the future hope (which sometimes contains messianic expectation)'.

[47] Isa. 2.2–4; Mic. 4.1–3; Zech. 8.20–3.

[48] Ps. 2.8–9; *Ps. Sol.* 17–18.

[49] cf. 1 Macc. 14.12, with its echoes of 1 Kgs. 4.25; Mic. 4.4, etc. On 'salvation' in Judaism cf. esp. Loewe 1981. At this point many recent interpreters have not, I think, gone far enough in rethinking the Jewish material; even Sanders continues to refer to 'salvation' as though it were an easy and univocal term (e.g. 1992, 350, 441).

[50] See Sanders 1992, 278: 'national survival looms much larger than does individual life after death'; cp. also 298.

Rejoice and exult with all your heart,
O daughter Jerusalem!
YHWH has taken away the judgments against you,
he has turned away your enemies.
The king of Israel, YHWH, is in your midst;
you shall fear disaster no more . . .
I will deal with all your oppressors
at that time.
And I will save the lame
and gather the outcast,
and I will change their shame into praise
and renown in all the earth.
At that time I will bring you home,
at the time when I gather you;
for I will make you renowned and praised
among all the people of the earth,
when I restore your fortunes
before your eyes, says YHWH.[51]

The means by which this was to be accomplished were variously conceived. In differing ways, sacrifice, suffering, and the experience of exile itself were held to carry redemptive significance.[52]

The age to come, the end of Israel's exile, was therefore seen as the inauguration of a new covenant between Israel and her god. Building on the earlier promises of restoration articulated by Isaiah, Jeremiah, and Ezekiel, the post-exilic and then the post-biblical writings gave varied expression to the belief that their god would soon renew his covenant—or, in the case of the Essenes, that he had done so already. This covenant renewal would not of course be an event different to the one we have been talking about. The *idea* of 'covenant renewal' focused attention on these same events seen *in a particular light*. When Israel finally 'returned from exile', and the Temple was (properly) rebuilt, and reinhabited by its proper occupant—this would be seen as comparable with the making of the covenant on Sinai. It would be the re-betrothal of YHWH and Israel, after their apparent divorce.[53] It would be the real forgiveness of sins; Israel's god would pour out his holy spirit, so that she would be able to keep the Torah properly, from the heart.[54] It would be the 'circumcision of the heart' of which Deuteronomy and Jeremiah had spoken.[55] And, in a phrase pregnant with meaning for both Jews and Christians, it would above all be the 'kingdom of god'. Israel's god would become in reality what he was already believed to be. He would be King of the whole world.

---

[51] Zeph. 3.14–20.
[52] See ch. 9 above.
[53] Isa. 54.4-8; cf. Hos., *passim*.
[54] Jer. 31.31ff.; Ezek. 11.19f.; 36.22–32; cf. 39.29; Joel 2.28, and also Isa. 32.15; Zech. 12.10. In the Scrolls, cf. 1QS 1.16—2.25; 1QH 5.11f.; 7.6f.; 9.32; 12.12; 14.13; 16.7, 12; 17.26; 1Q34bis 2.5–7; 4QDibHam 5. Cf. Cross 1958, 164 n.40.
[55] Dt. 10.16; 29.6; 30.6; Jer. 4.4; 31.33; 32.39, 40; Ezek. 11.19; 36.26–7; 44.7. The charge of 'spiritual uncircumcision' makes the same point negatively: cf. Lev. 26.41; Jer. 9.23ff.; Ezek. 44.7; Ex. 6.12, 30 (lips); Jer. 6.10 (ear). This theme, too, reappears in the Scrolls: 1QS 5.5; 1QpHab 11.13 (for the negative side see Leaney 1966, 167) and in early Christian literature (Ac. 7.51; Rom. 2.26-9; *Barn.* 9, *passim*; 10.12). See SB 3.126; *TDNT* 6.76ff. (R. Meyer).

3. No King but God

One slogan stands out from the revolutionary dreams of this period. The Fourth Philosophy, Josephus tells us, were 'zealous' in their attempts to get rid of Rome because they believed that there should be 'no King (*hegemon, despotes*) but God'.[56] Nor was this view confined to a fringe group. Those who rebelled against the census did so on these grounds;[57] the teachers who urged the young men to pull down the eagle held the same view;[58] the revolutionaries of 66–70 were fired by the same thought.[59] 'The kingdom of god', historically and theologically considered, is a slogan whose basic meaning is the hope that Israel's god is going to rule Israel (and the whole world), and that Caesar, or Herod, or anyone else of their ilk, is not. It means that Torah will be fulfilled at last, that the Temple will be rebuilt and the Land cleansed. It does not necessarily mean a holy anarchy (though there may have been some who wanted that).[60] Rather, it means that Israel's god will rule her in the way he intends, through properly appointed persons and means. This will certainly mean (from the point of view of the Pharisees, Essenes, and anyone loosely described as Zealots) a change in the high priesthood.[61] In some writings it also means a Messiah, though one of the striking features of the period is how comparatively infrequent, and completely unsystematized, expectations of a royal figure seem to be.[62] But however the slogan is interpreted in detail, it clearly implies a new order in which Israel is vindicated, and then ruled over, by her god—and, by implication, in which the rest of the world is ruled in some way or other, whether for blessing or judgment, through Israel.

How was the new age, the new covenant, to come about? I have discussed in chapter 6 the extent to which political or military revolution was in the air during the first half of the first century. My own view is to a large extent that of Goodman: 'anti-gentile attitudes which originated long before AD 6, perhaps in Maccabaean times, inspired many different groups, permeating the whole Jewish population and varying only in their intensity'.[63] The whole context of

[56] Jos. *Ant.* 18.23, pointing out that the only difference between the 'Zealots' and the Pharisees is the degree of passion with which their desire for liberty is held. That the view was held over a long period of time is affirmed in *War* 7.323. See the discussions in Goodman 1987, 93f.; Hengel 1989 [1961], 71–3, 86f., and esp. 90–110; Sanders 1992, 282f.

[57] Jos. *Ant.* 18.3-5; submitting to the census, they argued, 'carried with it a status amounting to downright slavery'.

[58] *Ant.* 17.149–63.

[59] *Ant.* 18.24; *War* 7.323ff.

[60] See Sanders 1992, 282; and see again *Ant.* 18.23: 'they think little of submitting to death . . . if only they may avoid calling any man master'. Cf. *War* 2.433, 443: Menahem, said by Josephus to be the descendant of Judas the Galilean, and to share his doctrine of 'no King but God', is himself killed by a group that takes this so literally as not to want Menahem himself as a ruler.

[61] See Jos. *War* 4.151-61 on the Zealot's appointment of a new high priest; *Ant.* 13.288-92 on Pharisaic opposition to Hyrcanus' holding of the high priesthood. On the attitude of the Essenes see e.g. Schürer 2.582 (for texts see e.g. 1QM 2, which lays plans for the installation of a true high priesthood while the holy war is in progress). See now Rofé 1988 for suggestions that this polemic considerably antedates the second century.

[62] See Part IV below.

[63] Goodman 1987, 108.

the times in general, of the biblical backdrop, of the Maccabaean example, of the uprisings under Herod, of the sporadic anti-Roman violence under the procurators, and of the two subsequent wars which were mounted by (among others) strict and 'zealous' Jews, all indicate that violent revolution against Rome was a very live option at this time, and that it would be supported not only by those out for their own 'non-religious' ends[64] but also by a solid and well-established religious tradition.[65] If Israel's god was going to become King, there were many who were eager to be the kingmakers, by whatever means might prove necessary.

The phrase 'kingdom of god', therefore, which occurs only sporadically in texts of this period, functions, when it occurs, as a crucial shorthand expression for a concept which could be spoken of in a variety of other ways, such as the impossibility of having rulers other than Israel's god, or the divine necessity of reversing the present political situation and re-establishing Israel, Temple, Land and Torah. This complex concept picks up and joins together the whole social, political, cultural and economic aspiration of the Jews of this period, and invests it with the religious and theological dimension which, of course, it always possessed in mainline Jewish thinking.

The idea of Israel's god becoming King is to be seen within the context of the whole historical expectation of Israel, dependent (in a people fiercely conscious of the importance of their own traditions) on Old Testament expressions of hope for the universal divine rule. Thus, for example:

All your works shall give thanks to you, O YHWH,
    and all your faithful shall bless you.
They shall speak of the glory of your kingdom,
    and tell of your power,
to make known to all people your mighty deeds,
    and the glorious splendour of your kingdom.
Your kingdom is an everlasting kingdom,
    and your dominion endures throughout all ages.[66]

For YHWH is our judge, YHWH is our ruler,
    YHWH is our king; he will save us.[67]

How beautiful upon the mountains
    are the feet of the messenger who announces peace,
who brings good news,
    who announces salvation,
    who says to Zion, 'Your God reigns.'[68]

---

[64] As Goodman 1987 argues in the case of the puppet Jewish aristocracy.

[65] There is clear evidence of the religious devotion of the revolutionaries on e.g. Masada: see chs. 6–7 above.

[66] Ps. 145.10-13; cf. Pss. 93, 96, 97, etc.

[67] Isa. 33.22.

[68] Isa. 52.7. The whole passage is instructive, seeing the end of exile, the return of YHWH to Zion, as the answer to the oppression of Israel and the inauguration of the universal reign of Israel's god. The setting of this passage immediately before the fourth servant song (52.13—53.12) provides further food for thought. Cp. Zeph. 3.14-20, with the kingship motif in v. 15.

These passages, of course, reflect not only the ideas cherished by certain thinkers and writers, but also the liturgy in which the hope was enacted over and over again.

One of the central biblical books which emphasized this theme was of course Daniel—which, significantly, was a favourite of revolutionary-minded Jews in the first century, since they reinterpreted it so that it spoke of a kingdom to be set up against the present Roman oppression.[69] Josephus is a little coy about this precise interpretation, no doubt because of his own Roman patronage, but there can be little doubt how his contemporaries read the book. In *Antiquities* 10.203-10 he describes the dream of Daniel 2.1-45, in which the idolatrous statue is destroyed by the 'stone', but he alters it to avoid making it explicit that the Roman empire is symbolized by the mixture of iron and clay (2.33, 41-3) or suggesting that Rome was to be destroyed by the 'stone'. The obvious inference is drawn by Josephus' modern editor, Ralph Marcus:[70] in first-century interpretation the stone was taken as a prophecy of the messianic kingdom which would destroy the Roman empire.[71] Of particular significance is the passage in *War* 6.312-15, which describes 'an ambiguous oracle' from the Jewish scriptures which 'more than all else incited [the Jews] to the war', proclaiming that 'one from their country would become ruler of the world'. Josephus, of course, interprets this to mean the Emperor Vespasian, who was first proclaimed as such on Jewish soil; but he notes that many 'wise men' believed that it referred to someone of Jewish race, 'until the ruin of their country and their own destruction convicted them of their folly'. Word of this oracle also reached the Roman historians Tacitus and Suetonius, probably independently.[72] Despite Josephus' own reinterpretation, the common first-century view shines through: from the Jews would arise a leader, a great king, who would rule over the whole world, destroying all rival empires.

The point can be made graphically with the help of two texts which we know to have been current in the first century. To begin with, the 'Testament of Moses' puts into the mouth of its hero a 'prophecy' about the corruption and wickedness of the second-temple period, and foretells the coming kingdom in which the pagans will be defeated and Israel vindicated. These very much this-worldly events are to be interpreted as the victory of Israel's god:

Then his kingdom will appear throughout his whole creation.
Then the devil will have an end.
Yea, sorrow will be led away with him.

[69] See chs. 7-8 above.

[70] Loeb edn., 6.275; cf. Sanders 1992, 289, who says, in dramatic if imprecise confirmation of our present point, that 'even the present-day reader of Daniel can see that the stone that breaks all other kingdoms is *the Kingdom of God, Israel*' (my italics).

[71] For Josephus' view of Daniel as a prophet of great significance see above, p. 266, and esp. *Ant.* 10.266–8; for his application of Dan. 8.21 to Alexander the Great, *Ant.* 11.337; of 11.31 and 7.25 to the Maccabaean period, 12.322; of Dan. 11–12 to the rise of Rome and the fall of Jerusalem, 10.276–7. Instead of exploring these last any further, Josephus turns aside instead to a general comment about the folly of the Epicureans in denying the doctrine of providence.

[72] Tac. *Hist.* 5.13; Suet. *Vesp.* 4. Josephus claims that he himself prophesied to Vespasian that he would become emperor: *War* 3.399-408. See further below, pp. 312f.

Then will be filled the hands of the messenger,
    who is in the highest place appointed.
Yea, he will at once avenge them of their enemies.

For the Heavenly One will arise from his kingly throne.
Yea, he will go forth from his holy habitation
    with indignation and wrath on behalf of his sons.
And the earth will tremble, even to its ends shall it be shaken.
And the high mountains will be made low.
Yea, they will be shaken, as enclosed valleys they will fall.

The sun will not give light.
And in darkness the horns of the moon will flee.
Yea, they will be broken in pieces.

It will be turned wholly into blood.
Yea, even the circle of the stars will be thrown into disarray.

And the sea all the way to the abyss will retire,
    to the sources of waters which fail.
Yea, the rivers will vanish away.

For God the Most High will surge forth,
    the Eternal One alone.
In full view will he come to work vengeance on the nations.
Yea, all their idols will he destroy.

Then will you be happy, O Israel!
And you will mount up above the necks and wings of an eagle.
Yea, all things will be fulfilled.

And God will raise you to the heights.
Yea, he will fix you firmly in the heaven of the stars,
    in the place of their habitations.

And you will behold from on high.
Yea, you will see your enemies on the earth.

And, recognizing them, you will rejoice.
And you will give thanks.
Yea, you will confess your creator.[73]

It should be clear from the context of this poem that its meaning is not to be found by taking the cosmic imagery 'literally'. Sun, moon and stars function within a poem like this as deliberate symbols for the great powers of the world: to speak of them being shaken or dimmed is the kind of language a first-century writer might use quite naturally to express the awesome significance of great political events, such as the terrifying year (AD 68–9) in which four Roman emperors met violent deaths, and a fifth marched from Palestine to claim the throne. And the vindication of Israel, which is the correlative of Israel's god becoming king, should not be thought of as her translation into a transcendent sphere, removed from the space-time universe: the hope is in

---

[73] *T. Mos.* 10.1–10, in the translation by J. Priest, in Charlesworth 1983, 931f. On the date and provenance of the book see ibid., 920–2.

direct continuity with the events which precede it, but because it is still (from the writer's point of view) in the future it cannot be described in the same way. The language and imagery of the poem is designed to *denote* future socio-political events, and to *invest* those events with their full 'theological' significance. Israel is to defeat her foes, under the leadership of an appointed 'messenger', perhaps a priest;[74] and *that means* that Israel's god is to become King.

The same point emerges from the vivid passage in the War Scroll which speaks in the same breath of detailed military preparations and plans and of Israel's god becoming king:

> Then two divisions of foot-soldiers shall advance and shall station themselves between the two formations. The first division shall be armed with a spear and a shield, and the second with a shield and a sword, to bring down the slain by the judgment of God, and to bend the enemy formation by the power of God, to pay the reward of their wickedness to all the nations of vanity. And sovereignty [*meluchah*, kingship] shall be to the God of Israel, and He shall accomplish mighty deeds by the saints of his people.[75]

It is clear from this that the detailed military plans are intended to put into effect the coming kingdom: that is, the writer of the Scroll believes that Israel's god will become king by means of the military action he is describing in advance. When Israel wins the victory, *that is to be seen as* the coming of the kingdom of YHWH. The deeds of his 'saints' are not something other than the operation of his mighty deeds; the two are identified. The modern distinction between socio-political events and the 'transcendent' dimension can only be related to the first-century Jewish worldview if we realize that the various different sets of language which were available at the time were used *to denote the same events*.[76]

An example from a very different context shows how widespread this 'kingdom'-language was. In the *Wisdom of Solomon*, hardly a book one would associate with strident revolutionary polemic, the vindication of the righteous ones will be the means of the divine kingship:

> In the time of their visitation they will shine forth,
>   and will run like sparks through the stubble.
> They will govern nations and rule over peoples,
>   and the Lord will reign over them forever.[77]

These instances show clearly enough the use of 'kingdom'-language in our period. It was a regular means of expressing the national hope, invoking in its support the belief that Israel's god was the only god—in other words, using Jewish monotheism and covenant theology in the service of eschatology. Israel's god would bring to pass the restoration from exile, the renewal of the covenant. Because he was also the creator god, this event could not adequately be described without the use of cosmic imagery. Israel's victory over the

---

[74] 'Then will be filled the hands' in the second stanza of the poem uses a technical term from priestly ordination: see Priest ad loc.

[75] 1QM 6.4–6 (tr. Vermes 1987 [1962], 111).

[76] cf. too 1QM 12.7 in its context.

[77] Wisd. 3.7f.

nations, the rebuilding of the Temple, the cleansing of the Land: all these together amounted to nothing short of a new creation, a new Genesis.

To speak of the kingdom of this god does not, therefore, mean that one is slipping into a dualistic mode of thought, or imagining that the event which is to come would be related only marginally or tangentially to space-time events. This kingdom was not a timeless truth, nor an abstract ethical ideal, nor the coming end of the space-time universe. Nor did the phrase itself *denote* a community, though it would *connote* the birth of a new covenant community. It would denote, rather, the action of the covenant god, within Israel's history, to restore her fortunes, to bring to an end the bitter period of exile, and to defeat, through her, the evil that ruled the whole world. This restoration of Israel, celebrated in the regular liturgy, is part of the meaning of her god's becoming king. Israel herself is the people through whom the king will rule.

One false trail must be marked off at this point. There is not much evidence for a direct connection between the symbol 'kingdom of god' and the coming of a Messiah.[78] Those texts that speak of a Messiah can of course be integrated into those that speak of the divine kingdom. The Messiah will fight the battles which will bring in this kingdom. But the apparent tension of YHWH as King and the Messiah as King does not really arise, mainly because the two are not usually spoken of in the same texts. In any case, as we saw, YHWH's being King does not mean that Israel will have no rulers at all, but that she will have the *right* rulers. Neither the Hasmoneans, nor Herod and his family, nor Caiaphas and his relations, nor Caesar himself, will rule Israel and the world. Rather, there will be a line of true priests who will minister before YHWH properly, and teach the people the true Torah; and (perhaps) a King who will be the true Son of David, who will dash the nations in pieces like a potter's vessel, and execute true justice within Israel. These hopes, which we may broadly call 'messianic', remained fragmentary. Where they occurred, this is how they fitted, without difficulty, into the wider and far more important overall expectation of YHWH's coming kingdom. To support this contention we must now look in a little more detail at the hope of a coming Messiah.

4. The King that would Come

Modern scholarship has made one thing quite clear: there was no single, monolithic and uniform 'messianic expectation' among first-century Jews.[79] Most of the Jewish literature we possess from the period has no reference to a Messiah; a good deal of prominent and powerful writing ignores the theme altogether. Such evidence as there is is scattered and diverse, spread across very different writings with a hint here, a dark saying there, and only occasionally a clear statement about a coming Son of David who would execute YHWH's wrath on the Gentiles, or rebuild the Temple, or otherwise

---

[78] As is suggested by e.g. Beasley-Murray 1986.

[79] On messianic expectations see particularly Neusner ed. 1987; Horsley and Hanson 1985, ch. 3; Sanders 1992, 295–8; Schürer 2.488–554, not least the bibliography on 488–92.

fulfil Israel's hopes. Nor can we easily appeal to the rabbis for help here, any more than elsewhere in second-temple Judaism. Their conceptions of a coming Messiah were so coloured by their awareness of the failure of the two great wars that we cannot expect much early historical material to have survived unscathed.[80] So, despite the confident pronouncements of many generations, both Christian and Jewish, we must conclude initially that we cannot say what, if anything, the average Jew-in-the-market-place believed about a coming Messiah. In the surviving literature, 'when an individual Messiah is envisaged, his role and character remain vague and undefined'.[81]

This apparently unpromising start invites an explanation, and three obvious possibilities emerge. First, the idea of a Messiah may have been comparatively unimportant in the period. Second, the literature we happen to have may not be very representative. Third, messianic expectations may have been suppressed in literature composed after the failure of one or other of the would-be messianic movements, or after the rise of Christianity. There may be some truth in all of these suggestions. But at the same time the very diversity and unstandardized nature of the evidence suggests that the idea of a Messiah was at least latent in several varieties of Judaism; that it could be called to consciousness if circumstances demanded; and that there were at least *some* more or less constant factors within the diversity. We must now examine the evidence and see what can be made of it.

We may begin with four fairly solid historical points. First, Josephus informs us of various messianic movements up to and during the war of 66–70, and we know a good deal about the subsequent one under bar-Kochba. We have already told the story of these movements in chapters 6 and 7 above. What matters here is the fact that they existed at all: that, under certain circumstances, reasonably large numbers of Jews would choose a previously unknown man (or, in the case of the Sicarii, a member of a would-be dynasty) and put him forward as a king, giving him a regal diadem and expecting him to lead them in a populist movement towards some kind of revolution. No doubt there are distinctions to be made between these various movements. But all of them bear witness to a reasonably widespread Jewish hope, cherished no doubt among some classes more than others, that there would come a king through whom Israel's god would liberate his people. In at least one case, the movement seems to have taken an explicitly 'Davidic' form.[82] If we knew nothing more than this, we would already know a lot.[83]

Second, we may note the significance of the aspirations apparently cherished by Herod the Great. According to Josephus, Herod undertook the massive project of rebuilding the Temple in a deliberate attempt to imitate,

[80] On Messianism in the later period see Landman 1979. Despite its title, this book contains valuable older scholarship on the early period as well.

[81] Harvey 1982, 77, referring also to Scholem 1971.

[82] See Horsley and Hanson 1985, 120ff. on Simon bar Giora.

[83] It is going too far to say (Horsley and Hanson 1985, 114) that Josephus 'studiously avoids such terms as "branch" or "son of David" and "messiah" '. It is true that he passes rapidly over two key biblical passages, Dan. 2.44f. and Dan. 7 (*Ant.* 10.210, and probably *War* 6.312f.: see above). But none of these technical terms occurs in either of the biblical passages in question.

and perhaps outdo, David's son Solomon.[84] As we saw in looking at Temple-ideology in chapter 8, he who builds the Temple legitimates himself as king, just as the Maccabaean triumph was able to launch a century-long dynasty not least because Judas Maccabaeus had successfully cleansed the Temple from its pagan pollution. Herod, perhaps realizing that the Jews would never come to accept him as the fulfillment of their hopes, married Mariamne, a Hasmonean princess, probably hoping that, if he had a son by her, that the son would not only complete the rebuilding of the Temple, but would also perpetuate the royal claim of the predecessors whom Herod himself had supplanted. Once again, what matters for our purposes is not that this plan failed, since the Temple was not finally completed until Herod's line had been reduced to insignificance, and since Mariamne and her two elder sons were suspected of treachery and murdered while Herod was still alive; nor that many Jews did not accept the Hasmonean claim, and many more did not accept Herod's either. What matters is that such claims could even be advanced. We may assume that Herod had some idea of how his contemporaries' minds worked. If he was hoping to play on a popular idea of a coming messianic king, then we must assume that such an idea at least existed, even if he was quite able, because of its vagueness, to remould it in his own way.

Third, we may note the significance of the bar-Kochba rebellion. It was clearly a messianic movement, as the solid rabbinic tradition attests, citing Akiba, one of the Mishnah's heroes, as having hailed the unfortunate rebel leader as 'Son of the Star' and Son of David.[85] Again, the details are not important. What matters is that we have here further evidence that throughout the second-temple period messianic ideas *could*, under certain circumstances, be evoked; that ordinary people would know what was being talked about; and that many Jews would instinctively rally to a sufficiently credible messianic claimant.

Fourth, we may note the importance of the New Testament itself within this historical sketch. It has been customary in many scholarly circles to assert that the early church quite soon abandoned Jewish messianic ideas, and referred to Jesus in quite different terms. In the light of the comparative scarcity of such ideas in Judaism itself, however, it is all the more remarkable that not only the title *Christos* but also several clearly messianic themes—Davidic descent, key texts from the Jewish Bible, key themes such as the link with the Temple—still remain even in the gospels, which are commonly thought to date from about a generation after Jesus, and quite likely after the war. My own view is that the scholars here are wrong, misled by a generation that sought to strip Christianity of all things Jewish, and that the early Christians retained the messianic idea in a modified but still quite recognizable form.[86] After all, even Justin Martyr, in the middle of the second century, regarded it as important

---

[84] *Ant.* 15.380–7, esp. 385.

[85] See chs. 6–7 above. Another saying attributed to Akiba, interpreting Daniel 7.9 to refer to two thrones, one for the Ancient of Days and one for David, i.e. the Messiah, may be significant here: see Horbury 1985, 36–8, 45f., discussing bHag. 14a; bSanh. 38b.

[86] See Part IV below. On Messiahship in Paul see Wright 1991a, chs. 2–3.

that Jesus should have been the true Jewish Messiah. But even if these scholars were right—indeed, especially if they were right, and if Christianity did officially give up Messianism as such—then the persistence of messianic themes throughout most of the New Testament is all the more powerful a witness to the fact that, whether or not we have a large amount of first-century Jewish evidence, and whether or not we can recreate a single unified picture of Jewish expectation, such expectation certainly existed. The early Christians seem to have done, in this sense, what Herod had done: they took a vague general idea of the Messiah, and redrew it around a new fixed point, in this case Jesus, thereby giving it precision and direction. It is especially striking that the *Davidic* Messiahship of Jesus should be given such prominence.[87]

These solid historical starting-points give us a more viable framework to begin from than we would have if we simply started with odd references in apocalyptic and other writings. They indicate, moreover, a further solid and undisputable fact. If we know anything about the formation of Jewish belief and expectation in this period we know that it had a good deal to do with the reading of scripture. And the Hebrew Bible, and the Septuagint in which many Jews were accustomed to hear it read, has a good deal to say about a coming king. The promises made to David, and often repeated, come across loud and clear.[88] They are celebrated in the Psalms.[89] Some of the most wonderfully poetic passages in the whole Bible include passages where the idea of a coming deliverer is prominent: we might cite, obviously, Isaiah 9 and 11, 42, and 61. True, it is important not to assume that if we discover a potentially 'messianic' passage in the Hebrew Bible we can deduce that first-century Jews regarded it thus; but it is even more important not to ignore the regular reading and singing of scripture as a major force in forming the total Jewish worldview, messianic expectations included.

This point is highlighted when we look at four types of second-temple sources which speak unambiguously of a Messiah. In each case, the view taken is based foursquare on scripture. We may begin with the Scrolls, and take first the remarkable fragment recovered from Cave IV at Qumran, dated most likely late in the first century BC, which collects key biblical texts and makes them speak with one voice about the coming king. After a detailed exegesis of 2 Samuel 7.10–11, showing that the writer interpreted the sectarian community in terms of the Temple, the text continues (with biblical quotations here in italics):

> The Lord declares to you that He will build you a House. I will raise up your seed after you. I will establish the throne of his kingdom [for ever]. I *[will be] his father and he shall be my son.* He is the Branch of David who shall arise with the Interpreter of the Law [to rule] in Zion [at the end] of time. As it is written, *I will raise up the tent of David that is fallen.* That is to say, the fallen *tent of David* is he who shall arise to save Israel . . .
> *Why do the nations [rage] and the people meditate [vanity, the kings of the earth] rise up, [and the] princes take counsel together against the Lord and against [His Messiah]?* Inter-

---

[87] So Sanders 1992, 526 n.17.
[88] e.g. 2 Sam. 7.4–29; cf. 1 Kgs. 3.6; 8.23–6, etc.
[89] e.g. Pss. 2, 89, etc.

preted, this saying concerns [the kings of the nations] who shall [rage against] the elect of Israel in the last days . . .[90]

Here we see what some Jews at any rate were thinking around the time of the death of Herod and the birth of Jesus of Nazareth. The Scrolls, as is well known, envisage not only a royal Messiah but also another figure, either a teacher (as here, 'the Interpreter of the Law') or a priest as in the 'Messianic Rule'.[91] But the biblical basis of this picture of the royal Messiah is clear, and it is further filled out in a passage like the following, from the 'Blessings' Scroll:

> May the Lord raise you up to everlasting heights, and as a fortified tower upon a high wall!
> [May you smite the peoples] with the might of your hand and ravage the earth with your sceptre; may you bring death to the ungodly with the breath of your lips!
> [May he shed upon you the spirit of counsel] and everlasting might, the spirit of knowledge and of the fear of God; may righteousness be the girdle [of your loins] and may your reins be girdled [with faithfulness]!
> May he make your horns of iron and your hooves of bronze; may you toss like a young bull [and trample the peoples] like the mire of the streets!
> For God has established you as the sceptre. The rulers . . . [and all the kings of the] nations shall serve you. He shall strengthen you with His holy Name and you shall be as a [lion; and you shall not lie down until you have devoured the] prey which nought shall deliver . . .[92]

Here again the biblical basis is clear: allusions to the Psalms (61.2f.), and particularly quotations from Isaiah (11.1–5) and Micah (4.13), are the foundation. This, we may be confident, was how some Jews at least understood some quite prominent passages in their Bible.

Moving on from Qumran, we find a similar picture in a second source, the well-known passage in the Psalms of Solomon:

> See, Lord, and raise up for them their king,
> the son of David, to rule over your servant Israel
> in the time known to you, O God.
> Undergird him with the strength to destroy the unrighteous rulers,
> to purge Jerusalem from gentiles
> who trample her to destruction;

[90] 4Q174 (= 4QFlor) 1.10–13, 18f. (tr. Vermes 1987 [1962], 294). The biblical quotations are from 2 Sam. 7.11, 12, 13 and 14; Amos 9.11; Ps. 2.1. For the date see Vermes 1987 [1962], 293. On this text see above all Brooke 1985.

[91] 1QSa 2.11–21, etc. On the 'two Messiahs' in Qumran see Vermes 1977, 184ff., and esp. Talmon 1987; the idea presumably goes back to such passages as Zech. 6.11; Jer. 33.14–18.

[92] 1QSb 5.23–9 (tr. Vermes 1987 [1962], 237). Horsley and Hanson (1985, 130) make an extraordinary claim about this passage: because the future king will destroy the nations with 'the word of his mouth', the passage has an 'unreal, transcendent' tone, and we should think of the warfare as taking place on an idealized, ethereal level rather than in serious military engagement. The rest of the passage gives the lie to this theory, whose real origin is in the authors' embarrassment at the existence of messianic expectations among classes other than their heroes, the peasants. I do not find 'the might of his hand', the 'hooves of iron and bronze', and the image of a young bull tossing and trampling, to be either unreal, transcendent or ethereal, and in any case 'the word of his mouth' and 'the breath of his lips' are of course quotations from Isa. 11.4, the main source of imagery for the entire passage. Horsley and Hanson's summary of Qumran's Messiahs as 'genteel, spiritual figures' is (not least in view of the realism of 1QM 1.9ff. and similar passages) a remarkable triumph of ideology over historiography.

in wisdom and in righteousness to drive out
the sinners from the inheritance;
to smash the arrogance of sinners
like a potter's jar;
To shatter all their substance with an iron rod;
to destroy the unlawful nations with the word of his mouth;
At his warning the nations will flee from his presence,
and he will condemn sinners by the thoughts of their hearts.

He will gather a holy people
whom he will lead in righteousness . . .
There will be no unrighteousness among them in his days,
for all shall be holy,
and their king shall be the Lord Messiah.[93]

Once again the biblical echoes stand out clearly: Psalms 2, 18, 104 and 101 are all audible, as are Isaiah 42 and other passages. We must be quite clear: here we have evidence that some Jews of the Roman period were reading their Bible with a definite view of a messianic figure, prophesied therein, who would come and deliver them from the Gentiles. If the Psalms of Solomon are Pharisaic, as used to be thought and is still not disproved, this becomes all the more interesting for the complete picture.[94]

We must now consider, as a third source, a passage we have already noted in another connection. In his account of the build-up to the war in 66, Josephus describes various portents and prophecies which presaged the coming devastation. Why, then, he asks, did the Jews carry on down the road to ruin, even despite 'oracles' in the Bible which warned of their ruin? Because of another passage in the Bible:

But what more than all else incited them to the war was an ambiguous oracle, likewise found in their sacred scriptures, to the effect that at that time one from their country would become ruler of the world. This they understood to mean someone of their own race, and many of their wise men went astray in their interpretation of it. The oracle, however, in reality signified the sovereignty of Vespasian, who was proclaimed Emperor on Jewish soil. For all that, it is impossible for men to escape their fate, even though they foresee it. Some of these portents, then, the Jews interpreted to please themselves, others they treated with contempt, until the ruin of their country and their own destruction convicted them of their folly.[95]

If there is one thing I wish Josephus had added to his entire corpus, it is the footnote to this text which would have told us for sure which biblical passage

---

[93] *Ps. Sol.* 17.21–32 (tr. R.B. Wright in Charlesworth 1985, 667). The rest of the psalm continues to describe the coming warrior king, as does *Ps. Sol.* 18.5–9. Once again, Horsley and Hanson attempt (1985, 105f., 119, 130f.) to suggest that this passage concerns not a military leader but a 'teacher-king' (106), and that this Messianism therefore has nothing to do with serious peasant-based expectations. Their frequent reference to 'the word of his mouth' needs to be set in the context of the smashed potter's jar and the iron rod.

[94] See Schürer 3.194f.; Nickelsburg 1981, 203; and the note of caution sounded by Charlesworth 1985, 642.

[95] *War* 6.312–15. Thackeray, citing the similar remarks in Tac. *Hist.* 5.13 and Suet. *Vesp.* 4, says it is unlikely that Tacitus had read Josephus, and postulates a common source. I doubt if Josephus needed to get this information from a source: he of all people might be expected to know what 'the wise' were saying in Jerusalem in the mid-60s. And I think it quite likely that Tacitus had read Josephus, not least because of such passages as *War* 6.299f. and Tac. *Hist.* 5.13; so Rajak 1983, 193.

he had in mind. There are, however, significant clues. The passage, clearly, was one which 'the wise men' interpreted this way; and it had to do with chronol ogy ('at that time').[96] The most obvious candidate is the book of Daniel: if we know anything about first-century chronological calculations, we know that Daniel was combed fairly thoroughly for information about eschatological time-sequences, particularly by 'wise' groups of scholars (compare Daniel 12.3). But which bit of Daniel? The most obvious passage in terms of chronological speculation is chapters 8–9, which provide arcane timetables for calculating the restoration of Jerusalem; these reappear in various works of the period. It has been cogently argued that, according to one way of comput-ing the figures involved, the 'seventy weeks of years' mentioned in Daniel 9.24–7 as being the time between the exile, on the one hand, and the rebuild-ing of Jerusalem and the coming of 'an anointed prince', on the other, would be entering upon their last 'week' in the mid-60s AD. This would help to explain why those who adopted such a chronology, which is basically Pharisaic, would be inclined to support moves towards revolution in that period.[97] But if Daniel 9.24–7 gives the chronological scheme, where does the idea of a 'world ruler'[98] come from? The obvious passage is Daniel 2.35, 44–5: after the four great kingdoms, represented by the statue made of four metals,[99] 'a stone was cut out, not by human hands, and it struck the statue' and broke it in pieces; 'but the stone that struck the statue became a great mountain and filled the whole earth'. When interpreted, this vision indicates that 'in the days of those kings the god of heaven will set up a kingdom that shall never be destroyed, nor shall this kingdom be left to another people. It shall crush all these king-doms and bring them to an end, and it shall stand forever.'[100] Josephus' retell-ing of this story in *Antiquities* 10 is interesting for a number of reasons. Not only does he omit to explain what precisely the stone is doing: he changes the text of Daniel 2.29 from 'to you . . . came thoughts of what would be hereafter' to 'when you were anxious about who should *rule the whole world* after you'.[101] Though in one sense this refers to all the kingdoms that are to come, it partic-ularly refers to the last one, that of the stone. It looks as though we have located Josephus' missing footnote: Daniel, the book which not only foretells things but gives a chronology, was being read in the 60s as a prophecy of

[96] Gk. *kata ton kairon ekeinon*, which has a quite specific and not merely general force.

[97] See the very full discussion in Beckwith 1981. Beckwith argues (532) against the rival candidate, Num. 24.17–19 (supported e.g. by the important discussion in Hengel 1989 [1961], 237–40) on the reasonable grounds that Numbers does not offer a chronological scheme, which is what Josephus specifically says Daniel does (*Ant.* 10.267). It should be noted that my present argument is not in favour of Dan. 7 itself as the *primary* reference, which is what Hengel rightly rejects, but of Dan. 9 and 2, with ch. 7 implied by association: see below. Rajak 1983, 192 says it is fruitless to speculate about which passage Josephus had in mind. This would be so only if there were no obvious candidates.

[98] Gk. *tis arxei tes oikoumenes*.

[99] It should be noted that, according to 2.40–3, the feet of the statue, made of a mixture of iron and clay, does not denote a fifth kingdom but a division within the fourth one. Certainly this was how Josephus understood it (*Ant.* 10.206–9).

[100] Dan. 2.34f., 44.

[101] Gk. *tis arxei tou kosmou*, closely echoing the *War* passage.

imminent messianic deliverance, through a combination of its second and ninth chapters.

But if this is so—and it seems to me easily the best explanation on offer of a tricky passage in Josephus—it is hard to believe that the very similar passage in Daniel 7 was not part of the equation also. Two bits of evidence point this way. First, we have already observed the very close parallel between Daniel 2 and Daniel 7: the sequence of four kingdoms, followed by Israel's god setting up a new kingdom which will last for ever, is identical in both. Second, as we shall see presently, it was Daniel 7 that provided the source-material for several other, quite different, first-century messianic speculations. It looks as though some first-century exegetes, combining Daniel 9 (which is explicitly messianic) with Daniel 2 (which can be made so via the figure of the 'stone', which is a messianic term elsewhere),[102] had achieved what we described earlier as a radical new possibility: a messianic, i.e. individualized, reading of Daniel 7.13f.

So, then, unless we are to conclude that some groups (those referred to by Josephus) only called on Daniel 2 and 9, and others (represented by such writings as 4 Ezra and 2 Baruch) only made use of Daniel 7, in their messianic speculations—which seems absurd—it is better to reach the following conclusion: that Josephus' cryptic mention of a widely believed messianic oracle refers to the book of Daniel in general, and to chapters 2, 7 and 9 in particular. These happen to be the three parts of the book about which, despite his full recounting of many other parts, Josephus remains silent.[103] Arguments from silence are notoriously unreliable; here the silence is eloquent indeed.

From Josephus to the apocalyptic writings of 4 Ezra, 2 Baruch and 1 Enoch seems a long jump, but these books too, as our fourth section of evidence, demonstrate a biblically based messianic expectation during the first century. In the case of 4 Ezra and 2 Baruch at least, this expectation had survived the ravages of AD 70, and was looking for a deliverance still to come.[104]

We may begin by noting that for most of 4 Ezra the question of Israel's future can be discussed without any detailed mention of a Messiah.[105] Then, in the 'eagle-vision' of chapters 11–12, we discover not only a Messiah, but a Messiah who clearly belongs within a rereading of Daniel 7. 'Ezra' sees a vision of a many-headed and many-winged eagle, whose wings and heads clearly 'represent' (in the literary sense) various kings within dynasties. Then a new creature appears:

---

[102] e.g. Isa. 28.16; Ps. 118.22f.; and the citations in Mt. 21.42f. and pars.; Ac. 4.11; Rom. 9.33; 1 Pet. 2.6.

[103] *Ant.* 10.186–281 covers most of the book, with the omission of ch. 7 occurring after 10.263. 10.276, suggesting that Daniel also prophesied the Roman destruction of Jerusalem, is an addition to the other MSS, based on a reading in Chrysostom.

[104] On the whole area see Charlesworth 1979.

[105] The exception being 7.28f.: 'for my son the Messiah shall be revealed with those who are with him, and those who remain shall rejoice four hundred years. And after these years my son the Messiah shall die, and all who draw human breath . . .', after which will come the resurrection and the judgment. On the Messianism of 4 Ezra see Stone 1987; 1990, 207–13, and other literature there.

> And I looked, and behold, a creature like a lion was aroused out of the forest, roaring; and I heard how he uttered a man's voice to the eagle, and spoke, saying, 'Listen and I will speak to you. The Most High says to you, "Are you not the one that remains of the four beasts which I had made to reign in my world, so that the end of my times might come through them? You, the fourth that has come, have conquered all the beasts that have gone before; and you have held sway over the world with much terror, and over all the earth with grievous oppression . . . And so your insolence has come up before the Most High, and your pride to the Mighty One. And the Most High has looked upon his times, and behold, they are ended, and his ages are completed! Therefore you will surely disappear, you eagle, and your terrifying wings, and your most evil little wings, and your malicious heads, and your most evil talons, and your whole worthless body, so that the whole earth, freed from your violence, may be refreshed and relieved, and may hope for the judgment and mercy of him who made it." '[106]

As usual in the genre, 'Ezra' finds this perplexing, and prays for an interpretation. When it comes, the link with Daniel is made explicit:

> He said to me, 'This is the interpretation of this vision which you have seen: The eagle which you saw coming up from the sea is the fourth kingdom which appeared in a vision to your brother Daniel. But it was not explained to him as I now explain or have explained it to you. Behold, the days are coming when a kingdom shall arise on earth, and it shall be more terrifying than all the kingdoms that have been before it . . . [there follows a long interpretation of the eagle with its various wings and heads]. And as for the lion that you saw rousing up out of the forest and roaring and speaking to the eagle and reproving him for his unrighteousness, and as for all his words that you have heard, this is the Messiah [literally, 'anointed one'] whom the Most High has kept until the end of days, who will arise from the posterity of David, and will come and speak to them; he will denounce them for their ungodliness and for their wickedness, and will cast up before them their contemptuous dealings . . . But he will deliver in mercy the remnant of my people, those who have been saved throughout my borders, and he will make them joyful until the end comes, the day of judgment, of which I spoke to you at the beginning. This is the dream that you saw, and this is its interpretation.'[107]

This passage is remarkable on many counts. First, it exploits the fact that Daniel's fourth beast is unspecified (the first three are a lion, a bear and a leopard), and makes it an eagle, which obviously represents (in the literary sense) the Roman empire, and is facilitated in doing so because actual images of eagles were used to represent the Roman empire in the socio-cultural symbolic sense. Second, it is explicit about offering a new interpretation of Daniel 7. Third, at the point in the vision where Daniel introduces 'one like a son of man', this vision introduces 'a lion, [who] uttered a man's voice'. The best explanation of this seems to be that the 'man's voice' ties the lion to the 'son of man' in Daniel 7, while the fact of his being a lion, which would be thoroughly confusing within Daniel 7 itself, is an echo of Davidic Messianism.[108] Finally, the dénouement of the scene is, on the one hand, judgment on the eagle (as the dénouement of Daniel 7 is judgment on the fourth beast) and, on the

---

[106] 4 Ezra 11.36–46.
[107] 4 Ezra 12.10–35 (tr. B. M. Metzger in Charlesworth 1983, 549f.). On the 'end' of the messianic kingdom (12.34) see 7.29; 1 Cor. 15.24–8.
[108] On the strength of Gen. 49.9, picked up in Rev. 5.5, etc. See Stone 1990, 209, citing also 1QSb 5.29 (see above) and other passages.

other, rescue and relief for 'the remnant of my people'.[109] The 'saints of the most high' of Daniel 7.18, 27, which in its original context, as we saw, is the interpretation of 'the one like a son of man' in 7.13, have come into their own. Treating our passage as a rereading of Daniel 7 as a whole, we must say that for 4 Ezra the 'one like a son of man' represents, in the literary sense, the Messiah, who in turn represents, in the sociological sense, the remnant of Israel. And in this rereading it is quite clear what is going on in real-life terms: 'the chief activity that the Messiah performs in both this and the next vision is the destruction of the Roman Empire'.[110] This explicit reuse not only of Daniel 7 but more explicitly of verses 13–14 shows that it ought to be out of the question to discuss the 'son of man' problem on the basis of occurrences of the phrase alone, or without consulting the root meaning of the imagery in Daniel 7 itself.[111]

The final passage in 4 Ezra concerns a 'man who came up from the sea'[112] and who 'flew with the clouds of heaven' (13.3):

> After this I looked, and behold, an innumerable multitude of men were gathered together from the four winds of heaven to make war against the man who came up out of the sea. And I looked, and behold, he carved out for himself a great mountain, and flew up upon it ... [the multitude approached the man, whereupon] he neither lifted his hand nor held a spear or any weapon of war, but I saw only how he sent forth from his mouth as it were a stream of fire, and from his lips a flaming breath, and from his tongue he shot forth a storm of sparks ... [which destroyed the multitude]. After this I saw the same man come down from the mountain and call to him another multitude which was peaceable. Then many people came to him, some of whom were joyful and some sorrowful ...[113]

Once again this vision disturbs 'Ezra', and he asks for the interpretation. The man from the sea, he is told, has been kept by the most high for the appointed time, when he will go forth to execute judgment. Then,

> when these things come to pass and the signs occur which I showed you before, then my son will be revealed, whom you saw as a man coming up from the sea. And when all nations hear his voice ... an innumerable multitude shall be gathered together, as you saw, desiring to come and conquer him. But he will stand on the top of Mount Zion. And Zion will come and be made manifest to all people, prepared and built, as you saw the mountain carved out without hands. And he, my Son, will reprove the assembled nations ...[114]

Once again there are links with Daniel, though this time there is less emphasis on chapter 7 and more on chapter 2, with the difference that whereas in

---

[109] Stone 1987, 211f., notes that the idea of legal judgment is imported, not from Daniel, into the sequence of thought. Nevertheless, it seems to me that the Danielic scene, too, is forensic at least in outline; and that Stone goes too far in suggesting (1987, 219f.) that the messianic rule in 4 Ezra is 'judgmental *rather than* military' (my italics).

[110] Stone 1987, 212.

[111] A recent example: Hare 1990, 9–21; as the index shows, Hare concentrates on 4 Ezra 13, with only a couple of passing mentions of ch. 12, never pointing out its strongly and explicitly Danielic content.

[112] This is confusing, since in Daniel, and in 4 Ezra 11, the sea is the origin of the *evil* beasts. An explanation is offered in 13.51f.; just as no one knows what is in the sea, so no one can see the Son except when he is revealed.

[113] 4 Ezra 13.8–13 (Metzger 551f.).

[114] 4 Ezra 13.32–7 (Metzger 552).

Daniel the stone is carved out and turns into a mountain, here the mountain is carved out and then turns into Zion. The link with Daniel 7 is made largely through the initial mention of the man 'flying with the clouds of heaven', in other words, through one image alone, and not, as in the previous section, through the whole sequence of thought.

Two things need to be said about this passage for our present argument. First, by the end of the first century AD, when this book was written, it was clearly possible to use and reuse the imagery of Daniel in a variety of ways, focused on the coming deliverance for Israel, and representing the coming Deliverer in a variety of literary images. But that Daniel 2 and 7 were used in this way there can be no doubt. Second, as with Daniel itself, so with the writings that reuse it: it is simply a misreading of the apocalyptic genre to imagine that Jews of the period would take the vivid and often surrealistic imagery of such passage as literal predictions of physical events. Anyone who still doubts this should reread the eagle vision of 4 Ezra 11. The question is, what do these literary images represent in the world of space, time and history?

Both of these points relate equally to the apocalypse which is closely parallel to 4 Ezra, i.e. 2 Baruch. In chapters 39–40, as we saw earlier, the Danielic image of four kingdoms is set out, after which the Anointed One will be revealed, and will convict the last of the wicked rulers on Mount Zion, whereupon 'his dominion will last forever until the world of corruption has ended and until the times which have been mentioned before have been fulfilled'.[115] Whether or not this is dependent on 4 Ezra, and hence does not count as a fully independent witness, it is still evidence for yet another way in which Daniel 7 was being read messianically, and combined with other biblical themes clearly taken as messianic prophecies, around the end of the first century AD.

Moving from 4 Ezra and 2 Baruch to *1 Enoch*, not least to the Similitudes (chapters 37–71), means exchanging comparative clarity for comparative puzzlement. This judgment is, of course, highly subjective, but it is important to stress that, despite the long history of scholarly wrestling with the 'son of man' figure in *1 Enoch*, if we are looking for clear reuse of the material in Daniel 7 we will find it much more easily in the passages we have just examined. For our present purposes it is not important to examine the rambling and convoluted details of *1 Enoch*; we need simply note the different use of imagery.[116]

In particular, the second 'Similitude' (chapters 45–57), though clearly based on Daniel 7, does not attempt to retell the story of that chapter as do 4 Ezra and 2 Baruch. Instead, it begins more or less where Daniel 7 leaves off: with the son of man already on the throne before the Ancient of Days, and now turning attention to the details of the judgment and the righteous rule which

---

[115] *2 Bar.* 40.3 (tr. A. F. J. Klijn in Charlesworth 1983, 633). The interpretation of the forest-vision in terms of the Danielic four kingdoms is in 39.2–8.

[116] On the vexed question of the date of the Similitudes, see the discussion in Schürer 3.256–9, and the summary by Isaac in Charlesworth 1983, 7. The majority of scholars now favour a non-Christian origin and a date some time in the first century AD.

are the concluding point of Daniel's vision and interpretation.[117] The two figures of the Ancient of Days and the son of man (or the 'Elect One', as in 45.3 and many other passages; or the Messiah, as in e.g. 52.4) are simply the starting-points for the detailed judgment scene which unfolds; they are taken for granted, and do not themselves have a developing role. We must discuss in a subsequent volume the relationship between these passages and the early Christian writings which make use of similar imagery. For our present purposes it is enough to note that *1 Enoch* does not introduce and explain the 'son of man' figure, but simply assumes it.[118] This implies that at whatever stage the Similitudes were written, the picture we have seen in more detail in Daniel 7, 4 Ezra and 2 Baruch was well enough known to be taken for granted. The four kingdoms, the great reversal, and the vindication of the elect, could be assumed. One could then move on to something else, namely the intricacies of judgment.

This remains the case in the third Similitude (chapters 58–69). In chapters 62–3 there takes place the judgment scene that is the climax of the whole section of the book.[119] Once again the Elect One (62.1), the son of man (62.5–9), is simply revealed. He does not appear after a sequence of four kingdoms, nor is he exalted after suffering as in Daniel 7.21-2. He is simply demonstrated before the whole world as the chosen one of the 'Lord of the Spirits', and the result of the judgment is joy in his presence for some (62.14) and shame for others (63.11).[120]

What we have in *1 Enoch*, then, is a substantial development from the picture of Daniel 7. We should not imagine this development as taking place on a unilinear chronological scale: there is no reason at all why different groups and individuals should not have made their own variations on a theme, returned to the original for fresh inspiration, or harked back to earlier interpretations behind current ones.[121] Nor is there any need to postulate dependence, whether literary or otherwise, between *1 Enoch* on the one hand and 4 Ezra, 2 Baruch and the gospels on the other. Rather, what we have here is one more strand in the richly variegated tapestry of first-century Jewish messianic belief and rereading of scripture. What is more, it is a strand which indicates that the authors expect the ideas to be well known. A single piece of literature may thus open up a window on a larger world of potential discourse.

[117] *1 En.* 46.2–8; 48.1–10. 48.10 also echoes Ps. 2.2.

[118] This is the point made by Moule (1977, 14–17, and elsewhere), suggesting that the anarthrous form 'a son of man' in Dan. 7 has become '*that* son of man' in *1 En.*: i.e. 'the "son of man" of whom you know from Daniel'. I think the dependence of *1 En.* on Dan. here is clear from the wider context; the philological point may give it further support (though cf. Casey 1991, 40f.).

[119] So Nickelsburg 1981, 219.

[120] Substantially the same picture is presented in summary form in 69.27–9. As is well known, the conclusion of the Similitudes offers an unexpected twist: Enoch himself is the son of man (71.14). (The translation of Isaac in Charlesworth 1983, here as elsewhere, needs checking in the light of Sparks 1984, here at 256.)

[121] For this reason I find the argument of Nickelsburg 1981, 222 unconvincing (just as he oversystematizes when he suggests a crucial difference between Daniel, where the judgment comes before the exaltation of the son of man, and *1 En.* and the gospels, where it comes afterwards). This is a very flat and unliterary way to read a text like Daniel 7.

What have we learned from this survey of four very different types of evidence—Qumran, the *Psalms of Solomon*, Josephus and some apocalyptic writings?[122] We have reinforced the commonly accepted view, that there was no one fixed view of a Messiah in the period. But we have also seen that generalized and loosely formed messianic themes and ideas were current and well known; that they characteristically drew on and reused well-known biblical passages and motifs; and that, though the language in which they are sometimes couched is heavily symbolic, the referent in many cases is the very this-worldly idea of a ruler or judge who would arise within Israel and who would enact the divine judgment and vengeance on Israel's oppressors.[123] In particular, we have seen that one recurring biblical text was Daniel 7. The controversies about this passage are too varied and complex to be settled here. But if the interpretation of apocalyptic in general and Messianism in particular which I have offered here is anything like on target, then I am led to concur with the judgment of Horbury, in one of the fullest recent articles on the subject:

> At the beginning of the Christian era, the Davidic hope already constituted a relatively fixed core of messianic expectation, both in Palestine and in the Diaspora. Exegetical interconnections attest that 'the son of man' is likely to have acquired, within its wide range of meaning, definite associations with this hope.[124]

We may emerge from this discussion with some cautious conclusions about messianic expectations in the first century. These may be stated in a series of theses.

1. Expectation was focused primarily on the nation, not on any particular individual. The hope we explored earlier in this chapter remains fundamental, occurring far more widely than expressions of hope for a Messiah or similar figure. Sometimes, indeed, texts which might be thought to speak of a Messiah are referred to the whole community, a process which is already visible within the Hebrew Bible itself.[125]

2. This expectation could, under certain circumstances, become focused upon a particular individual, either expected imminently or actually present. The circumstances under which this was possible seem to have been threefold: the appearance of an opportunity (such as at the death of Herod); the particular pressure of anti-Jewish action by pagans (such as under Hadrian); and the crescendo of speculation connected with the attempt to work out messianic chronology.

3. When this happened, the generalized expectation of a coming figure can be redrawn in a wide variety of ways to fit the situation or person concerned. Davidic descent can clearly be waived. The idea of two Messiahs is not a contradiction in terms. The particular felt needs of the time can influence the pre-

---

[122] A totally different genre, that of tragedy, also bears witness to a similar pattern of thought: see Horbury 1985, 42f., discussing *Ezekiel the Tragedian* 68–89 (now to be found in Charlesworth 1985, 811f.).

[123] This picture is drawn on in many passages not so far mentioned, e.g. *Apoc. Abr.* 31.1–8.

[124] Horbury 1985, 52f.

[125] e.g. the reading of Amos 9.11 in CD 7.16f. Cp. Isa. 55.3.

sentation: Herod could hope for his son to be the true king; the Sicarii could put forward Menahem, or the peasants Simon bar Giora.

4. The main task of the Messiah, over and over again, is the liberation of Israel, and her reinstatement as the true people of the creator god. This will often involve military action, which can be seen in terms of judgment as in a lawcourt. It will also involve action in relation to the Jerusalem Temple, which must be cleansed and/or restored and/or rebuilt.

5. It is clear that whenever the Messiah appears, and whoever he turns out to be, he will be the agent of Israel's god. This must be clearly distinguished from any suggestion that he is in himself a transcendent figure, existing in some supernatural mode before making his appearance in space and time. Generations of scholars have discussed Jewish messianic expectation as though this were the main issue. We have now made a survey of many of the key texts without discovering the theme at all. The only place where it appears for certain is *1 Enoch*, and there (in my judgment) the question presses as to which parts of the writing are lurid *literary* representation and which are to be 'taken literally'—whatever that overworked phrase might mean in this case. Certainly there is no reason to hypothesize any widespread belief that the coming Messiah would be anything other than an ordinary human being called by Israel's god to an extraordinary task.

6. Nor is it the case that the Messiah was expected to suffer. The one or two passages which speak of the death of the Messiah (e.g. 4 Ezra 7.29) seem to envisage simply that the messianic kingdom, being a human institution, to be inaugurated within present world history, will come to an end, to be followed by a yet further 'final age to come'. The traditions we studied earlier which speak of redemptive suffering undergone by some Jews in the course of the struggle (e.g. 2 Maccabees 7) are not applied to the Messiah.[126]

The coming of the King, where it was looked for, would thus be the focal point of the great deliverance. But what would this deliverance actually consist of? Would it be political, or spiritual, or in some sense both?

5. The Renewal of the World, of Israel, and of Humans

We have learned in these last few chapters that a good many things often held apart need to be put together again if we are to understand second-temple Judaism. This is nowhere more true than in the study of the Jewish hope. It is no doubt right, if we are to avoid fuzzy thinking, that we should study different aspects and themes as though they were the only ones in the world. But it is then appropriate, if we are to avoid spurious atomism, that we put the newly polished elements back in their proper relation to one another. Jews of the period were hoping for the 'real' return from exile. They were also hoping for a full 'forgiveness of sins'. Those are not two separate things, but two ways of looking at the same thing. They were looking for the covenant god to fulfil his promises, to display his 'righteousness'. That too is simply a different reading

---

[126] See the discussion and bibliography in Schürer 2.547–9.

of the same basic phenomena. Some were looking for a coming Messiah who would be the agent appointed by their god to accomplish redemption; but the redemption was the same. They were looking for a restored Temple, and for their god to come and dwell within it; that is the largest dimension of all, but it is still a dimension of the same thing. We cannot split any of these off from one another.

If all these beliefs and hopes are to be integrated closely with one another, they must also be integrated with the basic first-century Jewish worldview which we have studied. And the purpose of such worldview study is to help us to understand history: to enable us to see behind the events to the meaning, in the sense explored in Part II above.

Before we can finally draw these threads together, we must face a question which arises not least from the apocalyptic literature we have studied in the present chapter. How did this expectation, the longing for a national restoration, fit in, if it did, with the hope for a non-spatio-temporal life after death? How did personal hope fit in with national hope? How did 'spiritual' aspiration cohere with 'political'? And, in the middle of all this, what about the idea of resurrection?

It is clear that some first-century Jews at least had already adopted what may be seen as a Hellenized future expectation, that is, a hope for a non-physical (or 'spiritual') world to which the righteous and blessed would be summoned after death, and a non-physical place of damnation where the wicked would be tormented. There are some texts which use language of this sort. They can by no means be dismissed as simply the projection on to a non-historical screen of expectations that can be reduced to purely historical terms. Nothing is more probable than that, in the confusion of non-standardized second-temple Judaism, all sorts of groups and individuals held all sorts of views about life after death, including some that, from our perspective, seem closer to a Hellenistic idea of a shadowy afterlife than to any thought of resurrection, or indeed of the renewal of the space-time world of creation and history.

Nevertheless, I believe it would be a great mistake to regard a Hellenized expectation as basic, and to place the socio-political hope in a secondary position. We have seen throughout this Part of the book that much second-temple Judaism made a serious attempt to integrate what post-Enlightenment thought holds apart, the sacred and the secular. We have also seen that it is easy to mistake literary representation (the use of vivid imagery to denote space-time reality and connote its theological significance) for metaphysical representation (whereby a 'spiritual' or 'transcendent' being is the heavenly counterpart of an earthly reality); and that in this confusion it is all too easy to imagine that language which, in a culture other than our own, would be recognized as highly figurative, is flatly literal. Further, we have seen in our study of Josephus that, precisely when he is discussing the beliefs of Jewish groups, he has a penchant for 'translating' out of the hard political meaning of his Jewish contemporaries into a less threatening meaning, more easily assimilable by his cultured pagan readers.

The problem here seems to be that the language can be read as metaphorical *in either direction*. On the one hand, we shall see that Josephus and some of the apocalyptic works *refer* to physical resurrection while using the *language* of immortality, i.e. a non-physical life after death. On the other hand, it can also be suggested that a writer *refers* to immortality while using the *language* of physical resurrection, in order to make the hope more vivid.[127] How can we gain a foothold in an area of which even the large-scale revision of Schürer declares that 'there are so many opinions in Jewish religious thought that it is not feasible to enter into them all at the present time'?[128] The best course seems to be simply to outline the spectrum of ancient opinion (rather than the spectrum of modern opinion about it, which would be tedious indeed), and point up the various options.[129]

We may begin once more on solid ground, and again in the book of Daniel:

> There shall be a time of anguish, such as has never occurred since nations first came into existence. But at that time your people shall be delivered, everyone who is found written in the book. *Many of those who sleep in the dust of the earth shall awake, some to everlasting life, and some to shame and contempt.* Those who are wise shall shine like the brightness of the sky, and those who lead many to righteousness, like the stars forever and ever.[130]

The italicized sentence of this extract unquestionably refers to physical resurrection, which in this case is of just and unjust alike. We should note, however, that this is flanked by two other statements. First, the opening sentence refers to a time of great national anguish, followed by the great national deliverance. The hope for resurrection is part and parcel of the hope for national restoration after the 'messianic woes'. Second, the last sentence refers to the luminosity of the blessed, the 'wise': they will shine like the sky, or like the stars.[131] By itself, this sentence could easily have been taken to refer to a non-physical 'heavenly' existence; in its present context, it demands to be read as a metaphor for the glory which will be enjoyed by those who are raised to everlasting life (which in Hebrew and Greek is 'the life of the age', i.e. the 'age to come', not simply 'unending life'). It is not clear whether the earlier statements of similar views in such passages as Isaiah 26.19, Ezekiel 37.1–14, and Hosea 5.15—6.3 were understood in this literal sense in the pre-Maccabaean period; there, their natural literary meaning is that they invest the future restoration of Israel with its theological significance. But we can be sure that those who read Daniel 12 in the full sense just described would have reread such earlier passages and found in them confirmation of the view to which they had come. After all, as we have seen throughout this Part, the antithesis which many have imagined between the national and the individual hope, between the political and the 'spiritual', is an anachronism.[132]

---

[127] See the discussion in Vermes 1987 [1962], 55f.

[128] Schürer 2.539.

[129] Out of the vast bibliography on the subject, we may note particularly Nickelsburg 1972; Perkins 1984; and the survey in Schürer 2.539–47.

[130] Dan. 12.1b–3 (italics of course added); see Nickelsburg 1972, 11–31.

[131] Nickelsburg 1972, 24f. argues that this verse contains several signs of derivation from Isaiah 52–3.

[132] See, rightly, Nickelsburg 1972, 23; taking the opposite view, C. H. Cave in Schürer 2.546f.

A second firm starting-point is found in 2 Maccabees. In one of the most grisly passages in the whole of our literature, seven brothers are being tortured in the vain attempt to make them submit to the edict of Antiochus Epiphanes. In refusing, many of them explicitly refer to the coming resurrection in which they will be vindicated and given back the bodies that are now being torn apart:

> And when he was at his last breath, he said, 'You accursed wretch, you dismiss us from this present life, but the King of the universe will raise us up to an everlasting renewal of life, because we have died for his laws.'
>
> When he was near death, [another] said, 'One cannot but choose to die at the hands of mortals and to cherish the hope God gives of being raised again by him. But for you there will be no resurrection to life!'
>
> [The mother] . . . said to them, 'I do not know how you came into being in my womb. It was not I who gave you life and breath, nor I who set in order the elements within each of you. Therefore the Creator of the world, who shaped the beginning of humankind and devised the origin of all things, will in his mercy give life and breath back to you again, since you now forget yourselves for the sake of his laws . . . accept death, so that in God's mercy I may get you back again along with your brothers.'
>
> [The young man said]. . . 'If our living Lord is angry for a little while, to rebuke and discipline us, he will again be reconciled with his own servants . . . for our brothers after enduring a brief suffering have drunk of everflowing life, under God's covenant; but you, by the judgment of God, will receive just punishment for your arrogance. I, like my brothers, give up body and life for the laws of our ancestors, appealing to God to show mercy soon to our nation and by trials and plagues to make you confess that he alone is God, and through me and my brothers to bring to an end the wrath of the Almighty that has justly fallen on our whole nation.'[133]

This remarkable passage not only demonstrates again the extremely physical nature of the anticipated resurrection. It also shows the close link between this belief and four others. First, those who were assured of resurrection were those who had died for the ancestral laws. Second, the future bodily life will be a gift of the creator of the universe, an act of new creation, not a mere continuation of an immortal soul. Third, the hope could be phrased in more general terms ('they have drunk of everflowing life'), which by itself might have been interpreted in a Hellenistic direction, without detracting from the emphatically physical view expressed throughout the chapter. Fourth, the hope for resurrection is placed fair and square within the national, covenantal expectation, conjoined with the belief that the significance of the martyr's sufferings has to do with their efficacy in bearing the wrath of Israel's god against his sinful people. Here, in a book which we know to have been in circulation in the first century, is a powerful statement of one regular form of the Jewish worldview.

One other comment on 2 Maccabees 7 is in order at this stage. The first-century AD work known as 4 Maccabees was based more or less entirely on 2 Maccabees, and a good deal of 4 Maccabees (chapters 8–17) is taken up with

---

[133] 2 Macc. 7.9, 14, 21–3, 29, 33, 36–8. See also 12.43–5; 14.45f.: a certain Razis, escaping torture by falling on his sword, then ran through the crowd, and 'with his blood now completely drained from him, he tore out his entrails, took them in both hands and hurled them at the crowd, calling upon the Lord of life and spirit to give them back to him again'. On ch. 7 see Nickelsburg 1972, 93–111, and esp. Kellerman 1979.

the retelling and expansion of the chapter we have just studied. Yet, in keeping with the aim of the later book, which is the glorification of Reason by historical examples of those who were prepared to suffer rather than abandon this virtuous faculty, the mention of bodily resurrection has been toned down almost completely, in favour of a much more Hellenistic approach. 'For we,' say the young men in 4 Maccabees, 'through this severe suffering and endurance, shall have the prize of virtue and shall be with God, on whose account we suffer' (9.8). 'I', said one, 'lighten my pains by the joys that come from virtue' (9.31); 'See, here is my tongue,' said another; 'cut it off, for in spite of this you will not make our reason speechless' (10.19); and so on.[134] This is an excellent example of what we will find in Josephus: a firmly physical account of resurrection can easily, under the right rhetorical constraints, be 'translated' into a Hellenistic doctrine of the immortal memory of the virtuous dead.[135]

We find exactly this when we put Josephus' own statements side by side. Take, first, the speech which he puts into his own mouth when defending his right not to commit suicide after the fall of Jotapata. Those who lay violent hands on themselves, he declares, go into the darker regions of the nether world, while he himself believes

> that they who depart this life in accordance with the law of nature and repay the loan which they received from God, when He who lent is pleased to reclaim it, win eternal renown; that their houses and families are secure; that their souls, remaining spotless and obedient, are allotted the most holy place in heaven, whence, in the revolution of the ages, they return to find in chaste bodies a new habitation.[136]

This is as clear a statement of one mainline Jewish view as we could wish for. The righteous dead are presently in 'heaven', the domain of the creator god; but there is coming a new age, *ha-'olam ha-ba'*, in which the creation will be (not abolished, but) renewed; and the righteous dead will be given new bodies, precisely in order that they may inhabit the renewed earth. 'The revolution of the ages' is not the Stoic doctrine of the fiery consumption and remaking of a phoenix-like world, but the Jewish distinction between the present age and the age to come. We are left in no doubt that the age to come would be a renewed physical, space-time world, and that the righteous dead, at present resting in 'heaven', would return to share its physical life.

Armed with this passage, which Josephus has claimed as his own view, we may note the slight toning-down which has already taken place in the exposition of Jewish belief in the book *Against Apion*. No mere financial or other

---

[134] cp. 13.16f.; 15.2f.; 16.18f. (arguing that since God is the creator, one ought to be prepared to suffer for him, unlike 2 Macc. 7.23, 28, which assert that because God is the creator he will give new life the other side of death); 16.23; 17.5, 18. See Nickelsburg 1972, 110; Schürer 2.542 n.99.

[135] A similar process is evident in Tacitus' account of Jewish belief in *Hist.* 5.5. See Hengel 1989 [1961], 270, showing also that Tacitus connects this Jewish belief with the idea of martyrdom. At the same time, one should note the phrase 'live to God' in 4 Macc. 7.19, which hints at the resurrection of the patriarchs; cp. Lk. 20.38; Rom. 6.10; 14.8f.; Gal. 2.19, where resurrection (in some sense) seems to be in view. I owe this point to S. A. Cummins.

[136] *War* 3.374.

prize, Josephus claims with pride, awaits those who follow our ancestral laws: rather,

> each individual . . . is firmly persuaded that to those who observe the laws and, if they must needs die for them, willingly meet death, God has granted a renewed existence and in the revolution of the ages the gift of a better life.[137]

By itself, this passage might have been thought potentially Stoic, or at least capable of a general Hellenized interpretation. In the light of the earlier passage, there can be no doubt that here, too, we have the same belief as in 2 Maccabees.

It is when we turn to Josephus' statements about the beliefs of the different parties that we would have difficulty, were it not for these clearer statements. The Pharisees, he says, hold a doctrine of conditional resurrection, while the Sadducees reject it:

> Every soul, they [the Pharisees] maintain, is imperishable, but the soul of the good alone passes into another body, while the souls of the wicked suffer eternal punishment . . . As for the persistence of the soul after death, penalties in the underworld, and rewards, they [the Sadducees] will have none of them.[138]

Once again, if these passages were all we had, we would still think of the imperishability of the soul as the main Pharisaic doctrine, rather than the resurrection of the body. Even though the idea of the soul's 'passing into another body' makes it clear that this is not pure Platonism (the soul escaping its bodily prison and inheriting disembodied bliss), the phrase by itself could be interpreted as meaning transmigration (the soul passing at death into another physical being), as indeed some modern interpreters have suggested.[139] In the considerably later parallel passage in the *Antiquities*, this highlighting of the immortal soul has been taken a large step further:

> They [the Pharisees] believe that souls have power to survive death and that there are rewards and punishments under the earth for those who have led lives of virtue or vice: eternal imprisonment is the lot of evil souls, while the good souls receive an easy passage to a new life. Because of these views they are, as a matter of fact, extremely influential among the townsfolk . . . The Sadducees hold that the soul perishes along with the body.[140]

Again, if this passage were all we had to go on, we might conclude that Josephus had gone the whole way into a Hellenistic doctrine of the immortality of the soul. The souls go 'under the ground' where they receive rewards or punishments; the mention of an 'easy passage to a new life' could by itself be interpreted simply as the blessed disembodied life of the successful *post mortem* Platonist. But in the context of the earlier extracts we must con-

---

[137] *Apion* 2.218.
[138] *War* 2.163, 165. It is misleading, in the light of the passage from *War* 3 noted above, to describe this Pharisaic view as 'the reincarnation of the soul' (Thackeray in the Loeb edn., ad loc.). See Feldman's critique of Thackeray's view in the Loeb vol. 9 (*Ant.* 18–20), 13.
[139] See the discussion in Schürer 2.543 n.103 and the previous note above.
[140] *Ant.* 18.14, 16. Feldman points out in his note, ad loc., that the word he translates 'to a new life' is *anabioun*, cognate with *anabiosis* in 2 Macc. 7.9, where bodily resurrection is clearly meant.

clude that the 'passage to a new life' is a hint, here all but obscured by the language about the immortal soul, of the position which is clear elsewhere: upon death, the souls of the righteous go to heaven, or to be with their god, or under the earth—but this is only temporary. A new, embodied life awaits them in the fullness of time.

Josephus clearly knows all about the Hellenistic views of immortal souls shut up in the prison-house of the body, because that is the view he ascribes to the Essenes, labelling it specifically 'the belief of the sons of Greece'.[141] According to the Essenes, he says, righteous souls go to a place of blessedness beyond the ocean, corresponding to the Greek 'isles of the blessed'. How far this was actually true of the Essenes it is hard to say, and it may be that Josephus' account has been considerably distorted here by his desire to present the different groups as Hellenistic philosophical schools.[142] It is interesting, though, that despite the way his descriptions of the Pharisees' doctrines change in the direction of a softening of the hard resurrection belief, he does not ascribe to them the fully-blown Hellenistic view which he is happy to postulate of the Essenes.

The most strikingly Hellenized account of life after death in Josephus is put on the lips of Eleazar, the leader of the Sicarii on Masada. Advocating mass suicide, Eleazar urges his followers to embrace death as that which gives liberation to the soul:

> Life, not death, is man's misfortune. For it is death which gives liberty to the soul and permits it to depart to its own pure abode, there to be free from all calamity; but so long as it is imprisoned in a mortal body and tainted with all its miseries, it is, in sober truth, dead, for association with what is mortal ill befits that which is divine. True, the soul possesses great capacity, even while incarcerated in the body . . . But it is not until, freed from the weight that drags it down to earth and clings about it, the soul is restored to its proper sphere, that it enjoys a blessed energy and a power untrammelled on every side, remaining, like God himself, invisible to human eyes . . . For whatever the soul has touched lives and flourishes, whatever it abandons withers and dies; so abundant is her wealth of immortality.[143]

No Stoic rhetorician could have put it better. That is probably the point. Josephus is almost certainly putting into the mouth of this rebel leader a speech which would endear itself to a respectable Roman audience, to whom the arguments (and the poetic allusions, e.g. to Sophocles)[144] would be quite familiar. It is remarkable that in the following passage Eleazar goes on to speak of sleep as an analogy to death, and instead of drawing the point that those who sleep will wake again (cp. 1 Corinthians 15.20; 1 Thessalonians 4.13–15, etc.), he employs the thoroughly pagan idea that during sleep humans

---

[141] *War* 2.154–8, at 155; there is a summary statement of the same position in *Ant.* 18.18. This Essene doctrine seems clearly stated in *Jub.* 23.31.

[142] Some have held that e.g. 1QH 6.34 refers to resurrection; most, however, read the passage as metaphorical. See Vermes 1987 [1962], 55f. I am inclined to agree with Vermes that at least some Essenes embraced the doctrine of resurrection, not least when members of the sect died without their hope having been fulfilled.

[143] *War* 7.343–8.

[144] Soph. *Trach.* 235, alluded to in the last sentence; see Thackeray's note in the Loeb ed. of Josephus, ad loc.

become independent beings, conversing with the deity, ranging the universe, and foretelling the future.[145]

If Josephus describes the Sicarii chieftain Eleazar, almost certainly quite wrongly, as having used language appropriate to paganism and particularly Stoicism, it is interesting, finally, that when he creates another speech about facing death, this time on the lips of those he knows to be Pharisees, he draws back from such an extreme position. The learned doctors who incited the young men to pull down the eagle on the Temple, he says, urged that even if the action should prove hazardous,

> it was a noble deed to die for the law of one's country; for the souls of those who came to such an end attained immortality and an eternally abiding sense of felicity.[146]

Immortality here is a gift to the virtuous, not an innate property of the soul; it is still immortality, not (apparently) resurrection, but there is no talk of the soul being weighed down by the body. The later account of the same incident puts the point thus: that

> to those about to die for the preservation and safeguarding of their fathers' way of life the virtue acquired by them in death would seem far more advantageous than the pleasure of living. For by winning eternal fame and glory for themselves they would be praised by those now living and would leave the ever-memorable [example of their] lives to future generations. Moreover, they said, even those who live without danger cannot escape the misfortune [of death], so that those who strive for virtue do well to accept their fate with praise and honour when they depart this life.[147]

From this passage we would not glean any hint of resurrection, but nor would we have inferred the presence of the Stoic view, that one should simply be prepared to die for the cause of virtue. Because we know on other grounds that the teachers were Pharisees, we are able to see behind the smokescreen of Josephus' apologetic stance. Josephus is trying to tell his Roman audience that the teachers were urging their followers to die in a noble cause, much as a good Roman might have done. What they were actually saying, we may be sure, was this: Die for the law, and you will receive resurrection when our god vindicates his people! They might have been reading 2 Maccabees.

Josephus, then, is valuable in this discussion in two ways. First, on occasion he clearly states a doctrine of bodily resurrection. Second, he demonstrates equally clearly that such a doctrine could quite easily be described, for rhetorical reasons, in language which by itself could easily be taken to refer to the immortality of the soul. We thus see, in the work of one writer, what we observed above in the transition from 2 Maccabees to 4 Maccabees.

Where on this scale should we put the Psalms of Solomon?

> The destruction of the sinner is for ever,
>   and God will not remember him when he visits the righteous.

---

[145] *War* 7.349f. Cp. Lane Fox 1986, 149–67, including a passage from the fourth-century philosopher and alchemist Synesius (PG 66.1317, quoted by Lane Fox, 149f.) which is very close to Eleazar's speech at this point. Clearly the idea was widespread in both time and space.

[146] *War* 1.650, repeated substantially by the culprits themselves in 1.653.

[147] *Ant.* 17.152f.

This is the portion of sinners for ever;
But they that fear the Lord shall rise to life eternal,
And their life shall be in the light of the Lord, and shall come to an end no more.[148]

R. B. Wright, commenting on this passage, says that it is unclear whether it refers to the resurrection of the body (rising from the grave) or the immortality of the spirit (rising to god), or if indeed the author necessarily distinguished the two.[149] The same question faces the reader of the Solomonic Psalms 14.10 and 15.13, and indeed the older belief that these propounded a doctrine of resurrection may have been based on the belief that they were Pharisaic, rather than the other way round. It is, however, perhaps asking too much to expect doctrinal precision from this sort of poetry. The Psalms are quite compatible with the resurrection belief of 2 Maccabees and the explicit passage in Josephus, but by themselves they cannot be forced to yield a clear statement.

Whatever we think about the Psalms of Solomon, it is clear from Josephus, the New Testament, and the later rabbinic evidence that the resurrection was one of the principal distinguishing marks of the Pharisees. Or perhaps it would be more accurate to say that it was the *denial* of the resurrection that became one of the chief distinguishing marks of the Sadducees, the arch-opponents of the Pharisees.[150] As we saw earlier, this dispute between Pharisees and Sadducees is not an isolated point of disagreement, but is exactly cognate with their major bone of contention: the Pharisees looked for a great renewal in which the present state of things would be radically altered, while the Sadducees were content with the status quo. To that extent, it is not surprising that Acts depicts the early Christians as being opposed by Sadducees precisely because they were 'announcing the resurrection of the dead by means of Jesus'.[151] This has the stamp of early tradition upon it: in later periods, the name of Jesus would have been the problem, but in the early days of Christianity those in power were more worried about an excited announcement of resurrection, with all the socio-political connotations that might have. This also helps to explain John's story about the chief priests wanting to kill Lazarus after Jesus had raised him from the dead.[152] The early Christian writings bear witness to the same spread of belief in resurrection: speculation that Jesus was John the Baptist raised from the dead is something that the early church is unlikely to have made up, and it could only have arisen in circles where the idea of resurrection was held as a distinct (though not clearly defined) possibility.[153] It seems, in fact, that Sanders' view here is correct: the great majority of Jews of the period believed in some sense or other in the

---

[148] *Ps. Sol.* 3.11f. (14f.) (tr. S. P. Brock in Sparks 1984, 659). On resurrection in *Ps. Sol.* see Nickelsburg 1972, 131–4.

[149] R. B. Wright, in Charlesworth 1985, 655. See also Sanders 1977, 388.

[150] Mt. 22.23, 34 and pars.; Ac. 23.6–9, cf. 4.1f.; mAb. 4.22; mSanh. 10.1 (on which see Urbach 1987 [1975, 1979], 652, and the notes (991f.) on mBer. 5.2; mSot. 9.15). The second of the Eighteen Benedictions praises the creator for making the dead alive.

[151] Ac. 4.1f.

[152] Jn. 12.10f.

[153] See e.g. Lk. 9.7, 19.

resurrection.[154] Only those who had gone some way towards assimilation, and who therefore adopted a belief in the immortality of the non-physical soul, or those who for socio-political reasons were committed to denying any speculation about a future life, held back.[155]

This widespread belief in resurrection can be seen in a range of apocalyptic texts from roughly the first century BC/AD. The *Life of Adam and Eve*[156] states clearly that the creator god promised to Adam that he would raise him on the last day, in the general resurrection, with every man of his seed, and envisages the archangel Michael saying to Adam's son Seth that all dead humans are to be buried 'until the day of resurrection', and that the sabbath day is 'a sign of the resurrection'.[157] *1 Enoch* speaks of Sheol and hell giving back their dead, with great rejoicing on the part of the whole of creation;[158] *4 Ezra*, of the earth giving up those who 'are asleep in it';[159] the Testament of Judah, of the patriarchs being raised to life, at a time when

> those who died in sorrow shall be raised in joy;
> and those who died in poverty for the Lord's sake shall be made rich;
> those who died on account of the Lord shall be wakened to life.
> And the deer of Jacob shall run with gladness;
> the eagles of Jacob shall fly with joy;
> the impious shall mourn and sinners shall weep,
> but all peoples shall glorify the Lord forever.[160]

In all of these texts, which can scarcely be thought to come from one single sect alone, we see a well-shaped belief. The righteous will rise to life in the age to come, so that they can receive their proper reward. This belief functions within the context of suffering and martyrdom for Israel's god and his law, and hence as an incentive to a more serious keeping of that law and a more zealous maintenance of all that Judaism was and stood for.[161] Thus, as we shall see presently, belief in resurrection, though often thinking particularly of individual human beings and their future life, was not divorced from, but was rather a quintessential part of, the overall belief, hope, and worldview of a major segment of second-temple Judaism.

It is common to suggest that the Wisdom of Solomon speaks of a blessed, but not physical, future. This is usually illustrated by the following passage:

> But the souls of the righteous are in the hand of God,
> and no torment will ever touch them.
> In the eyes of the foolish they seemed to have died,

---

[154] Sanders 1985, 237; more cautiously, 1992, 303.
[155] These two groups would, of course, be likely to overlap quite heavily; i.e. political and philosophical assimilation would go together, both causing the assimilators to tone down the mainline Jewish expectation.
[156] Sometimes misleadingly called the *Apocalypse of Moses*: see Schürer 3.757.
[157] *Adam and Eve* 41.3; 43.2f.; 51.2.
[158] *1 En.* 51.1–5; cf. 90.33; 91.10. On the personal eschatology of *1 En.* see Schürer 2.541f.
[159] *4 Ezra* 7.32; cf. 7.97; *2 Bar.* 30.1; 50.1–4. 4 Ezra also speaks of the period of waiting between death and resurrection, which is clear evidence of a hope other than simply the immortality of the soul: 4.35; 7.95, 101; cp. *2 Bar.* 30.2.
[160] *T. Jud.* 25.1–5 (the quote is from 4–5). Cp. *T. Benj.* 10.2–9.
[161] See Nickelsburg 1972, *passim*.

and their departure was thought to be a disaster,
and their going from us to be their destruction;
but they are at peace.
For though in the sight of others they were punished,
their hope is full of immortality . . .[162]

I suggest, however, that this quite clearly refers, not to the permanent state of
the righteous dead, but to their temporary home. The passage, which we
quoted earlier in another connection, continues:

Like gold in the furnace he tried them
and like a sacrificial burnt offering he accepted them.
In the time of their visitation they will shine forth,
and will run like sparks through the stubble.
they will govern nations and rule over peoples,
and the Lord will reign over them forever . . .
The righteous who have died will condemn the ungodly who are living . . .
For [the ungodly] will see the end of the wise,
and will not understand what the Lord purposed for them,
and for what he kept them safe.

[The ungodly] will come with dread when their sins are reckoned up,
and their lawless deeds will convict them to their face.
Then the righteous will stand with great confidence
in the presence of those who have oppressed them
and those who make light of their labours.
When the unrighteous see them,
they will be shaken with dreadful fear,
and they will be amazed at the unexpected salvation of the righteous . . .

But the righteous live forever,
and their reward is with the Lord;
the Most High takes care of them.
therefore they will receive a glorious crown
and a beautiful diadem from the hand of the Lord,
because with his right hand he will cover them
and with his arm he will shield them.[163]

These passages, it seems to me, demonstrate beyond reasonable doubt that
the 'immortality' spoken of in the first passage is the same as the temporary
rest in 'heaven' of which Josephus spoke as preceding the resurrection itself.
There is a clear time-sequence: first, the righteous die, and the unrighteous
celebrate; then, a further event at which the unrighteous will discover their
mistake when confronted with the righteous as their judges. No doubt some
Hellenistic readers of the Wisdom of Solomon might have missed the point in
a casual reading. But against the full Jewish background the book seems to
represent the majority position rather than a Hellenization.[164]

---

[162] Wisd. 3.1–4; cf. 4.7; 5.15f.; 6.17–20. In the last passage there is a sequence: desire for
instruction leads to love of wisdom, thence to keeping of her laws, and thence to 'assurance of
immortality', which in turn 'brings one near to God': 'so the desire for wisdom leads to a kingdom'. Cf. too Tob. 3.6, 10.

[163] Wisd. 3.6–8; 4.16f.; 4.20—5.2; 5.15f.

[164] Wisd. 5.1 used the verb *stesetai*, cognate with *anastasis*, 'resurrection'; cf. too the LXX of
2 Sam. 7.12, *kai anasteso to sperma sou meta se*, 'and I will raise up your seed after you . . .'

If we want to find the latter, we turn, not surprisingly, to Philo:

> When Abraham left this mortal life, 'he is added to the people of God' [quoting Genesis 25.8], in that he inherited incorruption and became equal to the angels.[165]

> [Moses] represents the good man as not dying but departing . . . He would have the nature of the fully purified soul shewn as unquenchable and immortal, destined to journey from hence to heaven, not to meet with dissolution and corruption, which death appears to bring.[166]

When people die, much of the personality is laid in the grave with them;

> but if anywhere . . . there grows up a virtue-loving tendency, it is saved from extinction by memories, which are a means of keeping alive the flame of noble qualities.[167]

This perspective was not confined to Hellenistic, or Alexandrian, speculative philosophers. It also emerges, for instance, in an apocalyptic work: in the Testament of Abraham, the angels are instructed to take Abraham into Paradise,

> where there are the tents of my righteous ones and [where] the mansions of my holy ones, Isaac and Jacob, are in his bosom, where there is no toil, no grief, no moaning, but peace and exultation and endless life.[168]

There appear, then, to be three basic positions taken by Jews in our period, with, no doubt, minor modifications within each. The Sadducees stand out as unusual in that they will have nothing to do with a future life, neither with immortality nor with resurrection. No doubt a substantial and perhaps growing minority of Jews, including those who have quite clearly drunk deeply from the Platonic and general Hellenistic well, could write of the immortality of the soul. But the majority speak of the bodily resurrection of the dead, and frequently address the problem of an intermediate state; this last point is itself strong evidence for belief in bodily resurrection, since only on this premise is there a problem to be addressed. Sometimes, in describing this latter state, they borrow Hellenistic language which in its own context denotes a *permanent* disembodied state; but they still make it clear that bodily resurrection is the end they have in sight.

Why did the belief in resurrection arise, and how did it fit in with the broader Jewish worldview and belief-system which we have sketched in the preceding chapters? Again and again we have seen that this belief is bound up with the struggle to maintain obedience to Israel's ancestral laws in the face of persecution. Resurrection is the divine reward for martyrs; it is what will happen after the great tribulation. But it is not simply a special reward for those who have undergone special sufferings. Rather, the eschatological expectation

---

[165] Philo, *Sac.* 5. Is there an echo of this belief in Lk. 20.36?

[166] Philo, *Heir* 276.

[167] Philo, *Migr.* 16.

[168] *T. Abr.* [recension A] 20.14 (tr. E. P. Sanders in Charlesworth 1983, 895). Sanders points out, in his note ad loc., the illogicality of Isaac and Jacob preceding Abraham into Paradise, and of Abraham's bosom somehow being there in advance as well. On Paradise as originally a temporary staging-post in a longer journey, which gradually became identified in later Jewish works with the goal of the journey itself, see Schürer 2.541f.

of most Jews of this period was for a renewal, not an abandonment, of the present space-time order as a whole, and themselves within it. Since this was based on the justice and mercy of the creator god, the god of Israel, it was inconceivable that those who had died in the struggle to bring the new world into being should be left out of the blessing when it eventually broke upon the nation and thence on the world.[169]

The old metaphor of corpses coming to life had, ever since Ezekiel at least, been one of the most vivid ways of *de*noting the return from exile and *con*noting the renewal of the covenant and of all creation. Within the context of persecution and struggle for Torah in the Syrian and Roman periods, this metaphor itself acquired a new life. If Israel's god would 'raise' his people (metaphorically) by bringing them back from their continuing exile, he would also, within that context, 'raise' those people (literally) who had died in the hope of that national and covenantal vindication. 'Resurrection', while focusing attention on the new embodiment of the individuals involved, retained its original sense of the restoration of Israel by her covenant god. As such, 'resurrection' was not simply a pious hope about new life for dead people. It carried with it all that was associated with the return from exile itself: forgiveness of sins, the re-establishment of Israel as the true humanity of the covenant god, and the renewal of all creation.[170] Indeed, resurrection and the renewal of creation go hand in hand. If the space-time world were to disappear, resurrection would not make sense. Alternatively, if there was to be no resurrection, who would people the renewed cosmos?

Thus the Jews who believed in resurrection did so as one part of a larger belief in the renewal of the whole created order. Resurrection would be, in one and the same moment, the reaffirmation of the covenant and the reaffirmation of creation. Israel would be restored within a restored cosmos: the world would see, at last, who had all along been the true people of the creator god.[171] This is where the twin Jewish 'basic beliefs' finally come together. Monotheism and election, taken together, demand eschatology. Creational/covenantal monotheism, taken together with the tension between election and exile, demands resurrection and a new world. That is why some of the prophets used gorgeous mythical language to describe what would happen: lions and lambs lying down together, trees bearing fruit every month, Jerusalem becoming like a new Eden. This, too, was simply the outworking, in poetic symbol, of the basic belief that the creator of the universe was Israel's god, and vice versa. When he acted, there would be a great celebration. All creation, in principle, would join in.

To write this seems almost uncontroversial as a historical summary of Jewish belief. Dozens of texts of the period point this way; we are on absolutely firm historical ground. Sanders, summarizing the Jewish hope in this period, writes:

---

[169] This goes back, *mutatis mutandis*, at least as far as Ps. 49.15; 73.24.

[170] Sanders 1992, 303, sets the Jewish belief in an afterlife side by side with the belief in a new world order, but makes no attempt to trace the connection between them. C. H. Cave, in Schürer 2.546f., provides a classic example of holding apart things that should be kept together.

[171] We may compare again the graphic scene in Wisd. 3–5.

Many Jews looked forward to a new and better age . . . The hopes centred on the restoration of the people, the building or purification of the temple and Jerusalem, the defeat or conversion of the Gentiles, and the establishment of purity and righteousness . . . The hope that God would fundamentally change things was a perfectly reasonable hope for people to hold who read the Bible and who believed that God had created the world and had sometimes intervened dramatically to save his people.[172]

What Sanders never does, however, is to draw out the highly polemical nature of this claim in the context of the twentieth-century reading of first-century Jewish texts, including the texts of those first-century Jews who called themselves Christians.[173] But the point must surely be drawn out. Within the mainline Jewish writings of this period, covering a wide range of styles, genres, political persuasions and theological perspectives, *there is virtually no evidence that Jews were expecting the end of the space-time universe.* There is abundant evidence that they, like Jeremiah and others before them, knew a good metaphor when they saw one, and used cosmic imagery to bring out the full theological significance of cataclysmic socio-political events. There is almost nothing to suggest that they followed the Stoics into the belief that the world itself would come to an end; and there is almost everything—their stories, their symbols, their praxis, not least their tendency to revolution, and their entire theology—to suggest that they did not.

What, then, did they believe was going to happen? They believed that *the present world order* would come to an end—the world order in which pagans held power, and Jews, the covenant people of the creator god, did not.[174] Sects like the Essenes believed that the present order, in which the wrong Jews held power, would come to an end, and a new world order would be inaugurated in which the right Jews, i.e. themselves, attained power instead. We cannot, of course, rule out the possibility that some Jews believed that the physical world would come to an end, just as we cannot rule out the possibility that some Jews thought there were five gods, or that the Egyptians were the one chosen people of the creator god. But such views are marginal not only to the literature of all sorts that we possess from the period, but to the worldview of the great majority of (non-writing) first-century Jews, which we can reconstruct from their symbols, their stories and above all their praxis. Jews simply did not believe that the space-time order was shortly to disappear.

At a seminar at the Society of Biblical Literature Annual Meeting in November 1989, I listened to Professor John Collins expound a view of Jewish eschatology not dissimilar to that which I have just outlined. At the end I suggested that if Albert Schweitzer had heard that paper a hundred years ago, the entire course of New Testament studies in the twentieth century would have

---

[172] Sanders 1992, 298, 303; cp. 456f.

[173] The closest he comes, I think, is at 1992, 368, where he says that the dramatic change in the future, to which the Qumran sect looked forward, should not be called 'the eschaton', 'the last [event]', as modern scholars often do call it, 'since like other Jews the Essenes did not think that the world would end'.

[174] Sanders 1985 uses phrases like 'the present world order' in a somewhat different sense, keeping the option open of a less spatio-temporal future hope. He seems now (1992) to have come down more firmly on the line that I have taken.

been different. Collins, with due modesty, agreed that that might well be the case.[175] Schweitzer was right, I believe, when at the beginning of the twentieth century he drew attention to apocalyptic as the matrix of early Christianity. It is now high time, as the century draws towards its close, to state, against Schweitzer, what that apocalyptic matrix actually was and meant.

It should be noted most emphatically that, although 'resurrection' is naturally something that individuals can hope for, for themselves or for those they love, the belief we have studied is always focused on a *general* resurrection at the end of the present age and the start of the age to come. This will be a raising to life in which all Israel (with suitable exceptions, depending on one's point of view) will share. Seen from one angle, it will constitute Israel's *salvation*: after the long years of oppression and desolation, she will be rescued at last. From another angle, it will constitute Israel's *vindication* (or 'justification'): having claimed throughout her history to be the people of the creator god, the resurrection will at last make the claim good. Creational and covenantal monotheism, and the eschatology to which they give birth, thus form a context within which what is sometimes called 'Jewish soteriology', the beliefs that Jews held about salvation, may be situated accurately and fruitfully. It is important that we spell this out a little further.

6. Salvation and Justification

The word 'salvation' would denote, to a first-century Jew, the hope which we have studied throughout this chapter, seen particularly in terms of Israel's rescue, by her god, from pagan oppression. This would be the gift of Israel's god to his whole people, all at once. Individual Jews would find their own 'salvation' through their membership within Israel, that is, within the covenant; covenant membership in the present was the guarantee (more or less) of 'salvation' in the future.

We have already seen how first-century Jews understood covenant membership. The whole Jewish worldview, with its stories, its symbols, and its praxis, gives a clear answer. The covenant was entered through Jewish birth or proselyte initiation; it was sealed, for males, in the fact of circumcision; it was maintained through fidelity to the covenant document, Torah. This is most significant: as Sanders has argued extensively, membership in the covenant is *demonstrated*, rather than *earned*, by possession of Torah and the attempt to keep it. When the age to come dawns, those who have remained faithful to the covenant will be vindicated; this does not mean 'those who have kept Torah completely', since the sacrificial system existed precisely to enable Israelites who knew themselves to be sinful to maintain their membership none the less. And the attempt to keep Torah, whether more or less successful, was normally and regularly understood as response, not as human initiative. This is Sanders'

---

[175] It is only fair to say that I think Collins would still disagree with several of the details of this Part of the present book.

thesis, and, despite some criticisms that have been launched, it seems to me thus far completely correct as a description of first-century Judaism.[176]

It is within this context that there arose, within our period, debates as to who precisely would be vindicated when the covenant god finally acted to liberate Israel. 'All Israel has a share in the age to come'; but not Sadducees, not those who deny Torah, not Epicureans.[177] The sectaries who wrote the Scrolls would have agreed with the sentiment, but with a different list of exclusions: they and they alone were 'Israel', and the Pharisees ('the speakers of smooth things') and the official Temple hierarchy were definitely to share the lot of the Sons of Darkness. We can be fairly sure that the different factions in the war threw similar anathemas at one another.

The first-century question of soteriology then becomes: what are the badges of membership that mark one out in the group that is to be saved, vindicated, raised to life (in the case of members already dead) or exalted to power (in the case of those still alive)? For the Pharisees, there was a programme of intensification of Torah. For the Essenes, there was a (varying) set of communal rules, and an appeal to loyalty to a Teacher. For many rebel groups, there were subtly differing agendas, probably including, in the case of the Sicarii, loyalty to a would-be dynasty, and, in the case of the Zealots in the narrow sense, loyalty to a particular agenda and, at one stage at least, to a particular leader (Simon bar Giora). For Josephus, it was quite different: rescue, in the very practical sense, came by acknowledging that Israel's god had gone over to the Romans, and by following suit.

In all of these cases we are witnessing different interpretations of the fundamental Jewish soteriology. The sequence of thought is precisely that of the many stories we examined earlier as representative of the basic Jewish worldview, and may be set out logically as follows:

a. The creator god calls Israel to be his people;
b. Israel, currently in 'exile', is to be redeemed, precisely because she is the covenant people of this god;
c. Present loyalty to the covenant is the sign of future redemption;
d. Loyalty to this covenant is being tested at this moment of crisis;
e. At this moment, what counts as loyalty, and hence what marks out those who will be saved/vindicated/raised to life, is . . . [with the different groups filling in the blank according to their own agendas].

We have already seen that a great deal of Jewish literature of the period tells this story in some shape or form.

What matters, then, is not simply (in Sanders' categories) 'getting in' (how one becomes a member of the covenant) and 'staying in' (how one remains a member of the covenant). What matters, when Israel's symbols are under

---

[176] See Sanders 1977, 1983, and now 1992, 262–78. I shall discuss the criticisms elsewhere.

[177] mSanh. 10.1. The fact that Akiba is then quoted as making an addition to the list (to include a ban on those who read the heretical books, or who attempt magical cures) indicates that the basic saying is earlier, at the latest in the second half of the first century AD.

threat—when the question of what it means to be a Jew is everywhere raised and nowhere settled—is staying in *at this time of crisis*; or, to put it another way, staying in when there was a risk of finding oneself suddenly outside, or, perhaps, getting back in after finding oneself suddenly excluded.[178] That is the situation that sects exploit. It is exactly the situation that we find in first-century Palestine.

What counts above all at a time like that is adherence to the right symbols: not simply the mainline symbols of Temple, Torah and Land, because the rival groups claim them as well, but the symbols which show that one is a member of the correct sub-group. Those who die a martyr's death rather than break Torah will receive their bodies again (said the Maccabaean martyrs).[179] Those who 'have faith in' the Teacher of Righteousness will be delivered (said some of the Essenes).[180] Those who pull down the eagle from the Temple gate can look forward to a glorious resurrection (said the teachers who were egging them on).[181] Those who follow Menahem will be vindicated when the war is won (said his Sicarii followers).[182] Those who follow our strict interpretation of Torah, according to the tradition of the fathers, will be vindicated as true Israelites (said the rabbis, and some of their putative Pharisaic predecessors).[183] This is soteriology in practice, first-century style. It has little or nothing to do with moralizing or the quiet practice of abstract virtue. It has to do with life after death only to the extent that, if one dies before the great day dawns (especially if one dies as a martyr in the struggle), one needs to be assured that one will not be left out when salvation arrives, complete with restored Temple, cleansed Land, and Israel exalted at last over her enemies.

This is the point when a vital theological move can be made. When the age to come finally arrives, those who are the true covenant members will be vindicated; but, if one already knows the signs and symbols which mark out those true covenant members, this vindication, this 'justification', *can be seen already in the present time*. Covenant faithfulness in the present is the sign of covenantal vindication in the future; the badges of that present covenant faithfulness may vary from group to group, but those who wear the appropriate ones are assured that the true god will remain faithful to them and bring them safely into the new world that will soon be ushered in. We may again take the Essenes as an example. To suffer with the elect, to cling to the Teacher of Righteousness, and to abide by his teaching—this would be the sign *in the present* that one belonged to the group which, though marginal for the moment, would be vindicated as the true Israel in the future. The covenant god had renewed his covenant with this group, and they could therefore trust his covenant faithfulness (*tsedaqah*, 'righteousness'), that he would vindicate them,

---

[178] cf. Harper 1988.
[179] 2 Macc. 7, etc.
[180] 1QpHab 8.1–3, interpreting a text (Hab. 2.4) well known to readers of the NT (Rom. 1.17; Gal. 3.11).
[181] *War* 1.648–50.
[182] cf. *War* 2.433–48.
[183] mSanh. 10.1.

giving them favourable judgment (*mishpat*, 'justification') as his new-covenant people, when his action, at present secret, at last became public:

As for me,
    my justification is with God.
In His hand are the perfection of my way
    and the uprightness of my heart.
He will wipe out my transgression
    through his righteousness.

From the source of His righteousness
    is my justification
and from His marvellous mysteries
    is the light in my heart.

As for me,
    if I stumble, the mercies of God
    shall be my eternal salvation.
If I stagger because of the sin of flesh,
    my justification shall be
    by the righteousness of God which endures for ever.[184]

Justification is *both* future (the vindication, the 'judgment', when Israel's god finally acts) *and* present. Both depend on the divine covenant faithfulness; both will occur despite the continuing sinfulness of the worshipper. The present justification is secret, and depends simply on maintaining valid membership in the sect. The justification to come will be public, and will consist of the victory of the sect, and the establishment of its members as the true rulers of Israel and hence of the world.

How then does one become a member of the group that will inherit this glorious destiny, and who may perhaps believe that the future vindication can be anticipated, albeit secretly, in the present? Clearly, in the case of a sect, it is a matter of choice. To the extent that the Essenes were celibate, one could not join by birth. But the Scrolls teach quite clearly that this choice reflects an antecedent divine choice. This is simply the natural extension of regular biblical teaching. Deuteronomy made it quite clear that Israel was the people of the creator god, not because Israel was special, but because this god simply loved her.[185] The Essenes were, they believed, the true Israel; therefore, what was true of Israel was true of them. They were the elect ones, chosen to bear the destiny of Israel into the age to come.[186] There is no reason to suppose that any Jewish group or sect would have thought any differently.

Salvation, then, was a matter of a new world, the renewal of creation. Within this, Israel's god would call some from within the nation to be a new Israel, the spearhead of the divine purpose. Within this again, this renewed people were to be the holy, pure, renewed human beings, living in a covenant fidelity which would answer to the covenant faithfulness of the creator god, and which would end in the renewal, i.e. resurrection, of human bodies them-

---

[184] 1QS 11.2–3, 5, 11–12.
[185] Dt. 7.7f., etc.
[186] On election in the Scrolls see e.g. Vermes 1987 [1962], 41–6.

selves. When this god acted, those who belonged, by his grace alone, to this group, would be rescued, and thereby vindicated as the true people of god that they had claimed to be all along. Those who had died in advance of that day would be raised in order to share it. It is thus, within the context of the entire future hope of Israel, and in particular within the context of the promise of resurrection, that we can understand the essentially simple lines of second-temple Jewish soteriology. The doctrines of justification and salvation belong within the story we have seen all along to characterize the fundamental Jewish worldview.

7. Conclusion: First-Century Judaism

I have argued in this chapter for a particular way of understanding the hope which, in its varied forms, was embraced by Jews in the two centuries on either side of the turn of the eras. This completes our survey, in this Part of the book, of the second-temple Jewish history, worldview and belief-system. For the most part this has not been intentionally controversial, though no doubt some will want to challenge this or that aspect of my case. Any resulting controversy, actually, is quite likely to arise not in relation to Judaism in itself but from the effect of this reconstruction upon readings of early Christianity.

I have tried to show above all that, despite the wide variety of emphasis, praxis and literature for which we have ample evidence, which indeed justify us in speaking of 'Judaisms' in relation to this period, we can trace the outlines of a worldview, and a belief-system, which can properly be thought of as 'mainline', and which were shared by a large number of Jews at the time. Having begun with the history, we moved on to the stories which were told by the Jews who lived out that history, the symbols which were common to those who told those stories, and the praxis that went with those symbols. From this, and from the literature we possess, we have now examined the basic belief-system of first-century Jews, and have looked in particular at the hope which they cherished, a hope which drew together symbol, story and belief and turned it into worship, prayer and action. The explanatory circle is complete. It was within this history that we discovered this hope; it was because of this hope that this history turned out as it did.

It was to a people cherishing this hope, and living in this (often muddled) state of tension and aspiration, that there came a prophet in the Jordan wilderness, calling the people to repent and to undergo a baptism for 'the forgiveness of sins', and warning them that Israel was about to pass through a fiery judgment out of which a new people of Abraham would be forged. It was to this same people that another prophet came, announcing in the villages of Galilee that now at last Israel's god was becoming king. We should not be surprised at what happened next.

Part Four

The First Christian Century

Chapter Eleven

THE QUEST FOR THE KERYGMATIC CHURCH

1. Introduction

We know far less about the history of the church from AD 30–135 than we do about second-temple Judaism. This stark fact is not, I think, faced as often as it should be. There is no equivalent of Josephus for the early church. There are very few archaeological finds which come to our aid. The sources we do have are tiny in comparison with the Jewish material: the Greek New Testament is dwarfed on a shelf beside the Apocrypha, Pseudepigrapha, Mishnah and Scrolls, and even when we add the so-called Apostolic Fathers the bulk is not that much greater. Even if we were to assign the highest historical value to Acts, the bright light it would shed on a few areas would only emphasize the total darkness elsewhere. Eusebius, who wrote the best-known early history of the church in the early 300s, stands to the first generation much as the Talmud stands to pre-70 Judaism, full of interest, full of problems.[1]

Yet it was in the first generation or so that the crucial moves were made which determined the direction that Christianity would take from then on. This, obviously, is why so many have laboured so long to produce what the vagaries of time have denied us, namely, a history of the development of the Christian movement between Jesus and Justin Martyr, or between Paul and Polycarp. Much of this attempt, unlike the attempts to write the history of Judaism, is sheer if unacknowledged speculation. It is remythologization, the invention of stories about the past which will sustain a certain view of the present. There is, in fact, a great need in our generation for a full-length book that will do for the Quest for the Kerygmatic Church what Albert Schweitzer did for the nineteenth-century Quest for the Historical Jesus, describing what has been written, exposing its character as fantasy, and setting out a provocative new thesis. The project would have a direct analogy to Schweitzer's: just as the 'study' of Jesus was one of the most distinctive features of New Testament scholarship in the nineteenth century, so the 'study' of the early church has been one of its most distinctive features in the twentieth.

---

[1] On the problems of writing the history of early Christianity see e.g. Hengel 1979, ch.1. Eusebius incorporates some writing from earlier sources, notably Hegesippus (middle to late second century; cf. Quasten 1950, 284–7).

The reason for this concentration on what is largely thin air can itself be traced back to Schweitzer. Once he had thrown out the old liberal portraits of Jesus, and hung up instead his strange (Nietzschean?) sketch of an apocalyptic hero, where could one turn if one wished to read the New Testament as in any way normative for contemporary Christianity? Only, it seemed, to the earliest church. So Bultmann focused his attention on the primitive kerygmatic community, seeking there the vibrant faith that would serve as model and inspiration for modern Christians. The great majority of subsequent scholarship, one way or another, has followed his agenda, though not always his results. This is ironic; as we shall see, it is actually possible to know a good deal more about Jesus than about most of the early church.

If it is hard to be committed to the study of next to nothing, it is easier if those who are engaged in it can agree on some conventions, some 'fixed' points around which research can concentrate, like moons circling a wandering planet. The first, and best-known, of these fixed and yet unfixed points was found in the struggle between Judaism and Hellenism. This was projected on to the early church, producing what have been called 'Jewish Christianity' and 'Hellenistic Christianity'.[2] Not much thought was given to the facts that the distinction between the two cultural blocks was difficult to press in the first century anyway; that Judaism and Hellenism, in so far as one can separate them, were themselves sufficiently pluriform to make the labels fairly useless; that almost all first-generation Christianity was in some sense 'Jewish'; and that the one Christian writer whom we know beyond any doubt to have been active within twenty years of the crucifixion of Jesus was given to saying things like 'there is neither Jew nor Greek . . . for you are all one in Christ Jesus'.[3] A basic categorization that ignores such warning signs is unlikely to provide continuing possibilities for fruitful research. The planet will turn out to have been a black hole all along.

A similar problem is encountered (though one would not necessarily have guessed it from the confident tone of some scholars) if we try to acquire a second fixed point by studying early Christian *expectation*. A good deal has been made, this century, of the idea that the earliest and most Jewish Christians confidently expected the imminent end of the space-time universe, and that the development of Christianity was marked by the fading of this expectation.[4] Another version of the same modern story is that some branches of early Christianity were not interested in this expectation, and that the gospel of Mark, or perhaps some other document, reintroduced the idea of an imminent end to the world into a tradition that had either not known it or at least not made it central.[5] But in either case, and also with the many possible variations on this theme, there are two large problems to be addressed. First, the great bulk of the evidence used in making such reconstructions of the hypothetical

---

[2] The pioneer of this line was F. C. Baur in the mid-nineteenth century. See Baur 1878–9 [1860], and the discussions in Kümmel 1972, ch. 4; Neill and Wright 1988, 20–31.
[3] Gal. 3.28.
[4] Good examples are Käsemann 1969 [1965], chs. 4–5; Conzelmann 1973, 15, 18, etc.
[5] cf. ch. 14 below.

entity 'apocalyptic Christianity' consists, as we shall see, of reworkings of passages such as Daniel 7, and depends for its supposed force on a reading of that text, and others like it, which we have shown in Part III to be false. Second, it is quite clear that the expectation of a coming great reversal, with Jesus returning as judge, continued unabated in the second century and beyond, with no apparent embarrassment or signs of hasty rewriting of predictions. All sorts of charges were being rebutted by apologists, but there is no sense that Christianity had changed its character, or been put in jeopardy, by the failure of Jesus to return within a generation of Easter. A full reappraisal of the nature and place of eschatology within early Christianity seems called for.

A third attempt at finding a fixed point has been made by those who argue for an early date for the Gnostic traditions contained in the Nag Hammadi finds.[6] Like everything else in early Christianity, this thesis is indeed possible, and if true would give a definite shape to our perception of the whole. But, as with all *possible* historical theses, the crucial question is: is it *likely* or even *probable*? We shall see, in chapter 14, good reason to question whether Gnosticism in any form existed as a major segment of Christianity until at least the early second century.

For those interested in such things, we may at this stage draw up a small map of the scholars who have taken various different approaches. To begin with, we have the line begun by F. C. Baur. His distinction between Jewish Christianity and Hellenistic Christianity, and his (Hegelian) suggestion that the tension between the two was resolved in 'early catholicism', has been maintained, in different ways, by Adolf Harnack, Albert Schweitzer, Rudolf Bultmann, Ernst Käsemann, Hans Conzelmann, and, most recently, Helmut Koester.[7] Within this, the idea that Christianity's move away from Judaism to Hellenism (including the incorporation of Gnosticism) was a positive and necessary move, made already by Paul and to be recovered by those who would claim his support, is inherent in the entire programme of Bultmann, followed with variations by Conzelmann, Käsemann (who managed to incorporate a fair bit of Schweitzer into his synthesis as well), and Koester (who proposes a fascinating but highly tendentious geographical scheme), and drawn on recently by Mack and Crossan. These writers, taken broadly together, see the essence of early Christianity as only marginally or tangentially Jewish. The main lines run, rather, through the Hellenistic world, the world of Cynic teaching, of early Gnosticism, of the wisdom-traditions shared by many peoples. The Jewish expectation of the kingdom has provided some of the language of early Christianity, but its substance is of a different order altogether.

[6] See below, pp. 435ff. This thesis, which reflects the position of Bultmann (e.g. 1956), is advanced today by e.g. Koester 1982b, 1990; Mack 1988; Crossan 1991. The hermeneutic design of this stance is clear from the rare moments when Koester lets slip his normally impassive mask: his real heroes, it seems, are Valentinus, Marcion and, in some ways, Ignatius (1982b, 233, 328–34, 279–87).
[7] Baur 1878-9 [1860]; Harnack 1957 [1900]; Schweitzer 1925 [1901], 1968a; Bultmann 1956; Käsemann 1964, 1969; Conzelmann 1973; Koester 1982b (the last work, significantly, is dedicated to the memory of Bultmann).

This whole scheme of thought, with its neat ethnic divisions and its tidy chronology, has a pleasing simplicity. It has recently become apparent, however, that these are achieved at the cost of the data. It cannot accommodate phenomena which are increasingly making themselves felt, such as Jewish Gnosticism, Gentile apocalypticism, or signs of 'early catholicism' (such as an insistence on the passing on of tradition) which occur in the very earliest stratum.[8] It is for that reason that Schweitzer protested against the whole thesis at the turn of the century, a protest that was partially heard by Käsemann (who, however, incorporated Schweitzer's insistence upon the Jewish apocalyptic background into his own essentially post-Baur-and-Bultmann scheme), and that eventually bore fruit in the sea-change of history-of-religion study that took place in the 1940s.[9]

This change takes us to the other end of the spectrum, to writers who understand early Christianity as simply a Jewish sect, not too unlike the many other Jewish sects of the period. This new point of view owes something to the discovery of the Scrolls in 1947/8, but more to the change in general attitudes towards Judaism in the period following the Second World War.[10] Suddenly Jewish material was good, pure, early, 'biblical', and Hellenistic material was corrupt, distorted, later and non-'biblical'. These evaluative sub-texts precipitated a widespread new reading of the period. Phenomena that had been confidently labelled 'Hellenistic' were, quite suddenly, relabelled 'rabbinic'. The Apocrypha and Pseudepigrapha were re-edited and reread, and were discovered to contain thousands of previously unnoticed clues to the real nature of early Christianity. Adolf Schlatter in the pre-war period, W. D. Davies and J. Jeremias in the post-war period, and more recently scholars like M. Hengel and C. Rowland, have made out a strong case for seeing early Christianity as a Jewish messianic sect, going out into the world with the news that the god of Abraham, Isaac and Jacob had now revealed himself savingly for all the world in the Jewish Messiah, Jesus.[11] This movement of thought has dominated a good deal of research in the last forty years. Until the recent American work of Koester, Crossan and others it could have been said that the balance had shifted decisively in its favour, and away from the Hellenistic, Cynic and/or Gnostic theories. Now, however, the field looks more open again, and the time is ripe for a reappraisal. Many scholars are now of the opinion that the main problem in describing the origin of Christianity is to account fully *both* for the thorough Jewishness of the new movement *and* for the break with Judaism that had come about at least by the middle of the second century.[12]

---

[8] For the latter point, see e.g. Rom. 6.17, which Bultmann (1967, 283) deleted as a later gloss, having his eye on simplicity rather than doing justice to the data.

[9] Another writer who stood out against the Baur scheme was J. Munck, notably in his book on Paul (1959 [1954]).

[10] See Neill and Wright 1988, 369f.; above, p. 16f.

[11] See Schlatter 1955 [1926]; Davies 1980 [1948], 1964; Jeremias 1971; Hengel 1976, 1979, 1983; Rowland 1985; Meyer 1986.

[12] See recently Dunn 1991.

In between the two extreme positions, some scholars have remained content to plot the sociological and cultural location of various groups. The works of W. A. Meeks, G. Theissen and A. J. Malherbe on the early Pauline churches, and of Theissen on the early Jesus-movement, have produced sharper and more nuanced readings than can arise from broad generalizations; so have the works of M. Hengel, B. F. Meyer and C. C. Hill on the early Jerusalem community.[13] But it remains the case that the revolutions which have taken place recently in the study of Judaism, of Jesus and of Paul have not yet completely filtered through to the study of the early Christian movements which stood in a complex relation to Judaism, which told the story of Jesus, and which seem to have had a love–hate relationship with Paul. There is therefore every reason to suppose that a new study of the evidence, using the methods articulated in Part II, and bearing in mind the reading of Judaism in Part III, may shed fresh light on the whole area.

2. Tasks and Methods

The reconstruction of the history of early Christianity must attempt to make sense of certain data within a coherent framework. It must put together the historical jigsaw of Judaism within its Greco-Roman world, of John the Baptist and Jesus as closely related to that complex world, and of the early church as starting within that world and quickly moving into the non-Jewish world of late antiquity. It must create a context within which not only Paul and the other New Testament writers, but also figures such as Ignatius, Justin and Polycarp may believably be situated. It must also draw attention to the blanks in the jigsaw, and not attempt to fill them in with material which distorts the pieces we actually possess.

As with any historical task, then, we must do justice to the sources. This means, basically, the New Testament, the literature of the early patristic period (both 'orthodox' and otherwise), and the pagan and Jewish references to early Christianity. Very few of these can be tied down tightly to a definite date, so that it is still possible to find serious works of scholarship dating the entire New Testament before AD 70 and equally serious works dating several of the Gnostic traditions to that (early) period and much of the New Testament considerably later.[14] As so often in ancient history, therefore, what we need first is an imaginative (not imaginary) hypothesis which will do justice to the data, which will attain an appropriate simplicity and clarity of line, and which will shed light beyond its own borders. As with all serious history, we are aiming not at bare chronicle but at the 'inside' of the events; the aims, intentions and ultimately worldviews of the actors concerned.[15] There is at the pre-

---

[13] Meeks 1983; Theissen 1978, 1982, 1991; Malherbe 1983 [1977]; Hengel 1979, 1983; Meyer 1986; Hill 1992.

[14] For the former, see Robinson 1976, and cp. Wenham 1991; for the latter, Koester 1982b; Crossan 1991, esp. 427–34.

[15] See ch. 4 above; and cp. Meyer 1986, 23–35.

sent time no shortage of competing hypotheses, which is why the subject of New Testament studies is in such a state of interesting confusion. What is required in addition, therefore, is wise judgment between hypotheses.

One of the main things that such hypotheses must do is to plot the definition and development of different groups within early Christianity. Our earliest sources indicate quite clearly that there were sharply divergent groups within the new movement. These are an important indication of historicity, since it is unlikely that the fact of division would be invented out of nothing—though of course a later writer recording an earlier division may well project backwards an anachronistic understanding *of* that division. At the same time, these sources provide a way in to a serious reading of the social and cultural setting of early Christianity, since divisions in a religious movement, even if articulated in 'purely' theological terms, regularly reflect questions at other levels. This, obviously, is the reason for the 'discovery' within the early church of 'Jewish Christianity', 'Gentile Christianity', 'apocalyptic Christianity', and 'early catholicism'.[16]

In this task of historical reconstruction, it ought to be a first priority to establish the parameters of wider history within which the subject-matter is to be located. It is strange, therefore, that those who have given themselves to this task in the last two hundred years have often paid little attention to the Jewish history of the period. Even the fall of Jerusalem, which must have been a far more significant event for early Christianity as a whole than (say) the persecution in Rome under Nero, has of course been taken for granted, but has only seldom been brought into the actual discussion. A bright spotlight has recently been shone on the rabbis at Jamnia, and on the possibility that they promulgated an anti-Christian prayer in order to exclude Jewish Christians from the synagogue; but as we saw in chapter 6 this has a less secure base in actual history than is often thought.[17] Since we know relatively little about events in the non-Jewish world that touch on early Christianity in the relevant period, this failure to situate the task within Jewish history has meant that, as Austin Farrer observed about the dating of New Testament documents, the range of possible hypotheses, like a line of tipsy revellers with linked arms, can lurch this way and that, each piece kept in place by its neighbours, without encountering any solid object.[18] What we need to do before we go any further, therefore, is to place at least some solid objects in their path.

3. Fixed Points: History and Geography

Where, then, are the fixed points around which we must work? And, granted them, how can we best go about charting and understanding the course of early Christianity?

---

[16] See e.g. Dunn 1977, chs. 11–14.
[17] See above, pp. 161–5.
[18] Farrer 1964, 37 (quoted in Robinson 1976, 343).

The outer chronological limits for this investigation may be set by two events which form an interesting counterpoint. At the beginning there is of course the crucifixion of Jesus, which is probably to be dated in AD 30.[19] At the end, about 125 years later, there is the burning of a bishop in the beautiful seaport of Smyrna, in Asia Minor.

The crucifixion sets not only the chronological and (in the full sense) historical starting-point for the movement: it also actually sets the tone for most of the major fixed points. But the earliest years of the resultant movement, as we have seen, present notorious problems for anyone trying to find solid historical ground. We will therefore do well to leave them on one side for the moment, and work backwards towards them cautiously, beginning at the end. There are nine pieces of evidence to be considered, not counting Jesus' crucifixion itself.

Somewhat after the end of the first hundred years of Christianity, there took place an event so striking that it is worth quoting the earliest account of it:

> There was a great uproar of those who heard that Polycarp had been arrested. Therefore when he was brought forward the Pro-Consul asked him if he were Polycarp, and when he admitted it he tried to persuade him to deny [his Christian faith], saying: 'Respect your age,' and so forth, as they are accustomed to say: 'Swear by the genius of Caesar, repent, say: "Away with the Atheists" '; but Polycarp, with a stern countenance looked on all the crowd of lawless heathen in the arena, and waving his hand at them, he groaned and looked up to heaven and said: 'Away with the Atheists.' But when the Pro-Consul pressed him and said: 'Take the oath and I let you go, revile Christ,' Polycarp said: 'For eighty and six years have I been his servant, and he has done me no wrong, and how can I blaspheme my King who saved me?'[20]

The martyrdom of Polycarp, bishop of Smyrna (modern Izmir), took place in about AD 155/6.[21] Several points of interest for us stand out from this account of it, which, even though no doubt reflecting a somewhat later hagiographical piety, clearly witnesses to certain key features of early Christianity.

First, it is clear that the trial and execution of Christians has already become a matter of regular form. There are certain established procedures, certain standard things that Christians could do to escape the punishment, and certain fixed assumptions about what Christianity was. We can trace the earlier stages in this process in the letter of Pliny to Trajan (see below); by the middle of the second century these things had become the norm. In particular, it is assumed that Christians are members of a subversive sect. They do not believe in the normal pagan gods, and so have incurred the charge of atheism that was sometimes levelled at the Jews.[22] In particular, they do not owe

---

[19] cf. e.g. Bruce 1969, 188.

[20] *Mart. Pol.* 9.1–3.

[21] Schoedel 1989, 467, following Lightfoot and others. Koester 1982b, 281, 306 prefers a date after 161 on the grounds that Eusebius places the event in 167, in the reign of Marcus Aurelius (161–80). On Polycarp see now Tugwell 1989, ch. 7.

[22] See ch. 6 above. Justin discusses this charge in detail in *1 Apol.* 5f. Cf. too Tertullian *Apol.* 10–17; Lucian *Alexander* 25 (a reference I owe to Moule 1982 [1962], 45).

allegiance to Caesar, and refuse to swear by his 'genius'.[23] Christ is seen as a rival monarch, a king to whom is due an allegiance which allows no room for the dictatorship of the emperor. Already it is clear that the Christianity to which Polycarp (and/or his biographer) had given allegiance was rooted in Judaism. The idea of Christ as a supreme king, which defines Christianity conclusively over against paganism, would scarcely have begun, in the face of inevitable hostility, unless it were based on some kind of messianic belief. Equally, Christianity is defined over against Judaism itself by the allegiance to this particular king, as is clear from the sequel, in which the Jews of Smyrna join the pagans in calling for Polycarp's death.[24] His confession of Christ, and his refusal either to deny him, or to take an oath of loyalty to Caesar, or to offer the token sacrifice which would imply that he was prepared to fit his Christianity in to the dominant belief-system[25]—all these things show that the major cultural symbols and praxis of paganism on the one hand, and of Judaism on the other, have been exchanged for a new set.

What is more, Polycarp refers, in his most famous phrase, to his eighty-six years of allegiance to Christ. Assuming with most commentators that this is accurate, and that it means he was born into a Christian family and baptized as an infant, this puts the date of his birth, into an already Christian family in Asia Minor, at AD 69/70. We must therefore hypothesize that there was an established, though probably small, Christian church, holding allegiance to the royal figure of Jesus, and denying the pagan gods, in Smyrna within forty years of the crucifixion. This is not particularly controversial. But it provides us with a remarkably solid fixed point. The Gentile mission of the church, seen as the summoning of non-Jews to a risky allegiance to a Jewish-style Messiah, was apparently already established in Asia Minor before the fall of Jerusalem; was recognized by the authorities as a dangerous and subversive superstition by the time Pliny was governor in Bithynia (around 110); and was dealt with as a matter of routine by the middle of the second century. Whatever other trajectories may be drawn through the first hundred years of Christianity, this one must be regarded as settled.

The mention of Pliny must now be filled in, to provide us with a second highly valuable fixed point at the start of the second century. Pliny the Younger (whose uncle, the naturalist Pliny the Elder, had died while observing the eruption of Vesuvius in AD 79[26]) was governor of Bithynia, in northern Asia Minor, for some years between about 106 and 114. He found himself faced with a problem. Various people were brought before him charged with being Christians, and he did not know how to deal with them. He recounts to Trajan, the then emperor, the action he was taking:[27]

---

[23] The word is *tyche*, which most likely stands for the Latin *fortuna*, i.e. 'good luck', as a personified deity. Christian refusal at this point is defended by Tertullian *ad Nationes* 1.17.

[24] *Mart. Pol.* 12.2; 13.1.

[25] *Mart. Pol.* 8.2.

[26] See Pliny *Letters* 6.16.

[27] The following quotations are from Pliny *Letters* 10.96 (tr. Radice).

> I considered that I should dismiss any who denied that they were or ever had been Christians when they had repeated after me a formula of invocation to the gods and had made offerings of wine and incense to your statue . . . and furthermore had reviled the name of Christ.

The Christians examined by Pliny reveal their characteristic practice as follows:

> They had met regularly before dawn on a fixed day to chant verses alternately amongst themselves in honour of Christ as if to a god, and also to bind themselves by oath, not for any criminal purpose, but to abstain from theft, robbery, and adultery, to commit no breach of trust and not to deny a deposit when called upon to restore it. After this ceremony it had been their custom to disperse and reassemble later to take food of an ordinary, harmless kind; but they had in fact given up this practice since my edict, issued on your [i.e. Trajan's] instructions, which banned all political societies. This made me decide that it was all the more necessary to extract the truth by torture from two slave-women, whom they call deaconesses. I found nothing but a degenerate sort of cult carried to extravagant lengths.

This cult was, however, spreading rapidly:

> A great many individuals of every age and class, both men and women, are being brought to trial, and this is likely to continue. It is not only the towns, but villages and rural districts too which are infected through contact with this wretched cult.

As a result, according to Pliny, pagan practice, too, has taken on a new lease of life; he seems to suggest that this is the result of people being awakened to religious possibilities through Christianity, and then reverting to a hitherto dormant paganism, but it might equally be that latent paganism was stirred to life in opposition to a Christianity that was rejecting its tenets:

> There is no doubt that people have begun to throng the temples which had been almost entirely deserted for a long time; the sacred rites which had been allowed to lapse are being performed again, and flesh of sacrificial victims is on sale everywhere, though up till recently scarcely anyone could be found to buy it.

Almost every phrase of this remarkable letter, and indeed of Trajan's reply to it,[28] sheds such light on early Christianity and on pagan perceptions of it that it is tempting to spend longer examining it than is here possible. For our present purposes we note the following. First, it is clear that Christianity was already widespread in Asia Minor, beyond the area evangelized by Paul in the early days,[29] and that, although Pliny can assume that serious Christians must be punished, probably with death, there was no established procedure, no civil servants' rule of thumb, for how to go about it. This indicates that previous persecutions by Roman authorities had probably been sporadic and occasional rather than systematic. Pliny, with his filing-cabinet mind, would have been embarrassed to write to Trajan about something he should have learned before leaving Rome for his new post. He was forced, rather, to investigate a

---

[28] Pliny *Letters* 10.97. Trajan affirms the practice Pliny has adopted, but warns against allowing anonymous pamphlets to be used in evidence against people. These, he says, 'are quite out of keeping with the spirit of our age'. It is interesting to observe this 'enlightened' attitude of Trajan, probably contrasting his reign with that of the gloomy and ill-liked Domitian; the new 'spirit of the age' still permitted capital punishment for Christians, but not the socially degrading practice of informing against them. The irony of this is fully exploited by Tertullian *Apol.* 2.6–9.

[29] Ac. 16.7.

new possibility, and to take more official notice of the new cult, because, it seems, the local residents were themselves bringing charges.

Second, the litmus test for conviction as a Christian was, as in Polycarp's case, ritual actions and declarations which, small in themselves, carried enormous socio-cultural significance. These only make sense on the assumption that Christians of all sorts in the area, who would mostly not have been trained theologians, regarded it as fundamental that their allegiance to Christ cut across any allegiance to Caesar.

Third, they were therefore classified as a *political* society,[30] and as such came under a ban on corporate ritual meals. That is, they were seen not just as a religious grouping, but one whose religion made them a subversive presence within the wider Roman society. Though probably suspected of cannibalism or the like (note Pliny's surprised stress on their 'ordinary, harmless' kind of food), they were self-consciously law-abiding and upright citizens, except for their supreme devotion to Christ.

At this point we may recall Josephus. He was after all a near-contemporary of Pliny, living in Rome when Pliny was there before being posted to Bithynia, and was writing not many years before this letter. Anyone reading Pliny's narrative with half an ear open for echoes of Josephus may hear at least a faint resonance:

> They ... met ... to bind themselves by oath ... to abstain from theft, robbery, and adultery ... I found nothing but a degenerate sort of cult carried to extravagant lengths.

> This school agrees in all other respects with the opinions of the Pharisees, except that they have a passion for liberty that is almost unconquerable, since they are convinced that God alone is their leader and master.[31]

Devoted pursuit of personal holiness, and the extravagant refusal to recognize any other master: these were the hallmarks of the Jewish resistance movement. There have, of course, been certain vital changes. But from a Roman point of view it would be the similarities between Judaism and Christianity that would stand out. The Christians in Bithynia in 110, and in Smyrna in 155, shared some salient characteristics with the Jews of the pre-70 era. In particular, their worldview looks suspiciously as though it included a Jewish-style adherence to the kingship of god.

The third fixed point, though he has not always been regarded as such, is Ignatius of Antioch. It is historically certain that Ignatius travelled from Antioch to Rome to face martyrdom in the latter years of the reign of Trajan, and that the seven letters now normally ascribed to him were written during this journey.[32] Ignatius offers a wealth of material about the Christianity of his day, which we shall examine in more detail elsewhere. For our present purposes what matters is the event and (as Ignatius himself saw) its significance:

---

[30] The word is rare: *hetaeria*.

[31] Pliny, loc. cit.; Jos. *Ant*. 18.23.

[32] The letters may be found in the LCL edn. of the Apostolic Fathers, ed. Lake (1965), and in the Penguin Classics edn., ed. Louth (1968). See the recent discussions in Bammel 1982; Koester 1982b, 279–87; Tugwell 1989, ch. 6; Hall 1991, 33f.

the bishop of the greatest city in Roman Syria going to Rome to be torn apart by wild beasts. He exhorts the Roman church not to plead on his behalf, since if his martyrdom proceeds uninterrupted it will have great power as an announcement of the gospel:

> For neither shall I ever have such an opportunity of attaining to God, nor can you, if you be but silent [i.e. and do not speak up on my behalf], have any better deed ascribed to you. For if you are silent concerning me, I am a word [or perhaps the word] of God; but if you love my flesh [i.e. if you act to prevent my martyrdom], I shall again be only a cry. Grant me nothing more than that I be poured out to God, while an altar is still ready, that forming yourselves into a chorus of love, you may sing to the Father in Christ Jesus, that God has vouchsafed that the bishop of Syria shall be found at the setting of the sun, having fetched him from the sun's rising. It is good to set the world towards God, that I may rise to him.[33]

Apart from his concerns about his own martyrdom, Ignatius was anxious chiefly for the unity of each local church within itself, which, he believed, was to be attained through the churches uniting around their bishops. It is clear that he saw the church, not least the one he had left in Antioch, suffering from potential and actual schism, caused partly by those who were mixing Christianity up with Judaism and partly by those who were preaching docetism, the idea that Jesus had only seemed to be, without really being, truly human.[34] This fight on two fronts locates him accurately and credibly as a theologian deeply aware that Christianity is born of Judaism, and hence cannot become a variety of paganism, but also that, being born through the death of the Jewish Messiah, it cannot collapse back into being merely a variety of Judaism itself. The extent to which Ignatius represents a thoroughly Hellenized Christianity can be debated. Some have suggested, for instance, that there are to be found in his letters traces of Gnostic ideas, though it is far more likely that he is actually combating Gnosticism.[35]

Another fixed point, working back from Polycarp, Pliny and Ignatius, is the incident recounted by the second-century church historian Hegesippus, preserved in Eusebius' *History*.[36] This incident took place under the emperor Domitian, who succeeded Titus, and reigned from 81 to 96. Certain men were brought before Domitian accused of being blood-relatives of Jesus himself, being descended from the Judas who was 'said to have been [Jesus'] brother according to the flesh'. They were clearly under the suspicion of being members of a royal house, a potentially subversive dynasty. When, however, they demonstrated that they were merely poor labourers, Domitian questioned them 'about the Messiah and his kingdom, its nature, origin and time of appearance'. This, we may be sure, was not an abstract theological debate. Like Herod in Matthew 2.1–18 (Hegesippus makes this parallel), Domitian was clearly worried about potential threats to his own position. The answer, though, was clear: the men explained that this kingdom was 'neither of the

[33] Ign. *Rom.* 2. See the discussion in Tugwell 1989, 121, 128.
[34] Ign. *Philad.* 6.1; *Mag.* 10.3; *Smym.* 1–4; *Trall.* 9–10.
[35] See the discussion on Ignatius' advocacy of the silence of bishops (e.g. Ign. *Eph.* 6.1) in Tugwell 1989, 118f., and other refs. there.
[36] Euseb. *HE* 3.19–20. See the full discussion, with reference to other relevant texts, in Bauckham 1990, 94–106.

world nor earthly, but heavenly and angelic, and it would be at the end of the age', when Christ would return as judge.[37] Domitian thereupon ceased his persecution of the church, though the men in question were held in honour in the Christian community.

This story, for all that it may well contain legendary features,[38] coheres well with the picture of the early church we are developing. A movement with all the overtones of Jewish Messianism on the one hand, but without the nationalist and military overtones on the other; a movement looking back to Jesus as Messiah in a sense which could easily be misunderstood in a human dynastic sense; a movement which flouted the Roman emperor's claim to be the ultimate object of allegiance. However we draw the main lines of early Christian development, they must include these in some central way. The four pieces of evidence we have examined so far (Polycarp, Pliny, Ignatius and Hegesippus) cohere in a remarkable way. Even long after the destruction of Jerusalem, Christianity seems to have retained, in some manifestations at least, a recognizably Jewish form, with redefinitions which pulled it, not in the direction of paganism or syncretism, but in a new direction of its own. We will not discover a satisfactory hypothesis about the early church until we have found an explanation for this basic phenomenon.

Continuing to work backwards, and ignoring evidence that might at this stage lead into endless discussion, we may note the fall of Jerusalem in 70 as a major event not only for Judaism but also for early Christianity. We shall explore this more fully later on. But it is clear from many passages, not least in the synoptic gospels and Acts, that the early Christians *both* cherished a strong critique of the Jerusalem Temple (Mark 13; Acts 7) *and* continued to worship there (Luke 24; Acts 1, 3). This means that they would be bound to see its destruction as simultaneously a vindication of their critique and a major sociopolitical tragedy. The first of these is expressed most clearly in the Letter of Barnabas (16.1–5); the second is evident from the account in Eusebius of the flight of Christians from Jerusalem to Pella, across the Jordan, in obedience (he says) to an oracle.[39]

We next meet the famous, or rather infamous, passage in Tacitus, in which Nero attempts to shift on to the Christians in Rome the blame for the great fire of AD 64:

---

[37] The Greek for 'at the end of the age' is *epi sunteleia tou aionos*, clearly reflecting Mt. 28.20. On the distinction between the kingdom looked for by Christians and ordinary worldly kingdoms, see e.g. Jn. 18.36; Justin *1 Apol.* 11. The distinction does not seem to me to imply that the kingdom of Christ is itself to be non-physical, only that it is not a direct competitor, on all fours with the present worldly kingdoms.

[38] cf. Bauckham 1990, 99–106.

[39] The date of *Barn.* cannot be established more precisely than that it must be after 70 (because it refers to the fall of Jerusalem) and considerably before 200 AD (because Clement of Alexandria, writing then, regarded it as the authentic work of the Barnabas who was Paul's companion). For the flight to Pella, cf. Euseb. *HE* 3.5.3. The specific mention of a place shows that this cannot be *simply* a 'deduction' from (e.g.) Mk. 13.14–20; and in any case fleeing from Jerusalem across the Jordan is hardly 'fleeing to the mountains'. This non-derivation from Mark does not, of course, prove the historicity of the account, but it demonstrates at least a later Christian awareness that the events of 66–70 left their mark on the Christian, and not just the Jewish, community of Judaea. See further Moule 1982 [1962], 172–6.

To suppress this rumour [of arson], Nero fabricated scapegoats—and punished with every refinement the notoriously depraved Christians (as they were popularly called). Their originator, Christ, had been executed in Tiberius' reign by the governor of Judaea, Pontius Pilatus. But in spite of this temporary setback the deadly superstition had broken out afresh, not only in Judaea (where the mischief had started) but even in Rome. All degraded and shameful practices collect and flourish in the capital.

First, Nero had self-acknowledged Christians arrested. Then, on their information, large numbers of others were condemned—not so much for incendiarism as for their anti-social tendencies [*odio humani generis,* because of their hatred of the human race]. Their deaths were made farcical. Dressed in wild animals' skins, they were torn to pieces by dogs, or crucified, or made into torches to be ignited after dark as substitutes for daylight ... Despite their guilt as Christians, and the ruthless punishment it deserved, the victims were pitied. For it was felt that they were being sacrificed to one man's brutality rather than to the national interest.[40]

This, once more, is a remarkably interesting passage, not least for what Tacitus tells us by the way. It is clear *both* that he, and presumably others, held the lowest possible opinion of the Christians (perhaps the charge of cannibalism or clandestine vice had already been laid against them because of their secret meetings), *and* that no systematic pagan persecution of Christians had been envisaged before this point.[41] The Christians may have been regarded as anti-social; refusal to take part in regular cultic activities, and the giving of personal loyalty to the movement and its leader rather than to old ties of kin and friendship, would have been quite enough to gain them that reputation. But Nero's attack on them was not, according to Tacitus, part of a sustained or orchestrated campaign. We see here the roots of the second-century attitude, but not yet its full fruit.

This brings us back to the first of the Jewish sources which provides a fixed point in early Christianity. In AD 62 the procurator Festus died in office, and Nero appointed Luccius Albinus to succeed him. During the interregnum, the newly appointed high priest Ananus seized his opportunity to do away with one of the early Christian leaders. Josephus tells the story like this:

Ananus thought that he had a favourable opportunity because Festus was dead and Albinus was still on the way. And so he convened the judges of the Sanhedrin and brought before them a man named James, the brother of Jesus who was called the Christ, and certain others. He accused them of having transgressed the law and delivered them up to be stoned. Those of the inhabitants of the city who were considered the most fair-minded and who were strict in observance of the law were offended at this. They therefore secretly sent to King Agrippa urging him, for Ananus had not even been correct in his first step [i.e. convening the Sanhedrin], to order him to desist from any further such actions. Certain of them even went to meet Albinus, who was on his way from Alexandria, and informed him that Ananus had no authority to convene the Sanhedrin without his consent. Convinced by these words, Albinus angrily wrote to Ananus threatening to take vengeance upon him. King Agrippa, because of Ananus' action, deposed him from the high priesthood which he had held for three months and replaced him with Jesus the son of Damnaeus.[42]

This story is quoted by Eusebius, following his retelling of Hegesippus' longer

---

[40] Tac. *Ann.* 15.44. This seems to be the basis for Suetonius' remark in his *Nero* 16.2.
[41] cf. Moule 1982 [1962], 153f.
[42] *Ant.* 20.200–3. On this cf. Schürer 1.430–2.

account, which, though confused, clearly refers to the same incident.[43] Among the many fascinating aspects of the Josephus passage is the clear implication that the Pharisees were incensed at a blatant Sadducean action against one so devout as James 'the Just', i.e. 'the *tzaddik*', the Righteous One. Equally, important, however, is the clear implication that Josephus knows of Jesus, and of his being referred to as 'the Christ'; if Tacitus and Suetonius knew of this title, there is every reason to suppose that Josephus would have as well. The passage shows no signs of being a Christian interpolation, as is often suggested about the more famous one describing Jesus himself.[44] It is clear evidence of a well-known Christian community, with an even more well-known leader, still in Jerusalem as war drew closer; and of hostility to this community and its leader on the part of some Jews, but not all. James' staunch Jewish piety seems to have enabled him to avoid the kind of Jewish persecution which Paul encountered.

Still working back, we must here include something about Paul. Though attempts to date the details of his career are notoriously complex, it is agreed more or less on all sides that he was active, not least in Ephesus and Corinth, in the first half of the 50s. It is usually reckoned that he arrived in Corinth for the first time in 49, about eighteen months before Gallio's arrival as proconsul of Achaia, an event usually dated (because of a famous inscription) to 51.[45] Paul appeared before Gallio, who acquitted him of charges brought by the local Jewish community.[46] There is a good deal more to be said than this, but Paul provides at this stage another fixed point which must be taken very seriously.[47]

We come finally to the evidence of Suetonius, who was born around 69 and wrote in the time of Hadrian (117–38). Racy and unreliable though he often is, the following extracts are normally regarded as referring to actual events. In

---

[43] Euseb. *HE* 2.23.1–25 (cf. *HE* 3.5.2, and Origen *Contra Celsum* 1.47; *Comm. Matt.* 10.17); the Hegesippus passage is in *HE* 2.23.4–18, and includes the well-known description of James' deep piety, with his knees growing hard like a camel's because of his constant praying for his people. Hegesippus, followed by Eusebius, makes this incident the reason, under divine providence, for the start of hostilities by Vespasian against Jerusalem; Eusebius quotes a passage from Josephus, not now extant in any of Josephus' works, to similar effect.

[44] *Ant.* 18.63–4. I suspect that more of the latter passage is original to Josephus than is sometimes allowed. In particular the crucial sentence, *houtos en ho Christos*, normally rendered 'he was the Christ', and therefore regarded as clear evidence of Christian interpolation, should be translated the other way round. The definite article (*ho*) indicates the subject, not the complement: ' "The Christ" [of whom Josephus' readers will, he presumes, have heard] was this man.' See further Schürer 1.428–41. (Professor Moule raises a query with me at this point: does the rule about subject and complement still hold if the noun in question is a title or proper name? I suspect it does; cf. Jn. 20.31, with Carson 1987.)

[45] See Barrett 1987 [1956], 51f.; for a dissenting voice, cf. Slingerland 1991. This dating of Claudius' expulsion of the Jews from Rome agrees with the fifth-century historian Orosius (*Hist.* 7.6.15f.) against Dio Cass. 60.6.6f. (the incidents may be different: Dio states explicitly that Claudius did not expel the Jews, he merely banned public meetings; for Dio, it was Tiberius who expelled the Jews, cf. 57.18.5a). Cf. Hengel 1983, 49, 167; Hemer 1989, 167f.

[46] Ac. 18.12–17. On Paul in Ephesus, facing a riot (which Luke is unlikely to have invented) for undermining local paganism, cf. Ac. 19.23–40.

[47] cf. Hengel 1983, 49 ('at this point we are still treading on firm ground'). For various positions on Pauline chronology see e.g. Jewett 1979; Lüdemann 1980; Hemer 1989, chs. 6–7.

his *Life of Claudius* (25.4) he describes Claudius' policies towards foreign nationals in Rome. When he comes to the Jews he has this to say:

> Because the Jews at Rome caused continuous disturbances at the instigation of Chrestus [*impulsore Chresto*], he expelled them from the City.

It has often been pointed out that the difference in pronunciation between *Chrestus* and *Christus* would be minimal in this period,[48] and there is no good reason to doubt that what we have here is a garbled report of disturbances within the large Jewish community in Rome, brought about by the presence within that community of some who claimed that Jesus of Nazareth was the Messiah. This expulsion from Rome is also mentioned in the New Testament, in Acts 18.2.[49] The reference in Acts suggests (though this is controversial) that the episode took place in about 49 AD, since some of those expelled found their way to Corinth in time to meet Paul when he arrived there around that time (see above).

We now have an initial series of fixed historical points, largely owed to non-Christian report, all involving non-Christian action:

30	Jesus' crucifixion
49	Claudius' expulsion of Jews from Rome because of Christian disturbances
49–51	Paul in Corinth; some time later, in Ephesus
62	Killing of James in Jerusalem
64	Nero's persecution after the fire of Rome
70	Fall of Jerusalem
c.90	Domitian's investigation of Jesus' relatives
c.110–14	Pliny's persecutions in Bithynia
c.110–17	Ignatius' letters and martyrdom
155/6	Martyrdom of Polycarp

These events form a chain stretching across a century in which, time after time, the Roman authorities found the Christians (as they found the Jews) a social and political threat or nuisance, and took action against them. The Christians, meanwhile, do not seem to have taken refuge in the defence that they were merely a private club for the advancement of personal piety. They continued to proclaim their allegiance to a Christ who was a 'king' in a sense which precluded allegiance to Caesar, even if his kingdom was not to be conceived on the model of Caesar's. This strange belief, so Jewish and yet so non-Jewish (since it led the Christians to defend no city, adhere to no Mosaic code, circumcise no male children) was, as we shall see, a central characteristic of the whole movement, and as such a vital key to its character.

It is frequently assumed that there ought to be another fixed point in such a list, namely, a serious persecution of Christians by Domitian. This is often cited as the natural home for early Christian literature which seems to reflect a period of persecution (e.g. 1 Peter). In fact there is very little evidence for such a thing. Suetonius' descriptions of Domitian's cruelty are clear enough, but

---

[48] The close similarity allows Justin (*1 Apol.* 4) to make a pun between 'Christian' and 'Chrestian' (= 'excellent').

[49] It is quite possibly alluded to, or at least presupposed, in Rom. as well: see several articles in Donfried 1991 [1977], and Wright 1992a.

that cruelty was directed against all sorts of people, not only Christians. Eusebius' account of persecution under Domitian is generalized (except for the story of John on Patmos).[50] His account of Domitian's investigation of the supposed Christian 'royal family' does not suggest a large-scale, sustained or fierce putting down of the movement; and in any case, had such occurred, Pliny might not have needed to ask Trajan what to do about this strange cult.[51] Though it may well be the case that Christians died for their faith under Domitian, we have only the slenderest evidence for saying so, and nothing very sure can be built on this foundation.

Turning from history to geography, we have already said enough to show what sort of geographical spread took place within the first century of Christian activity. Jerusalem and surrounding Judaea; Samaria; Antioch, Damascus and surrounding Syria; Asia Minor (Smyrna and Bithynia); the cities of Greece; Rome; all these are clearly indicated in the texts we have examined, and in the New Testament, as major centres of Christianity. This much is uncontroversial. Beyond this, however, it is very difficult to go with any certainty. Paul's letters give us a very clear impression of the churches in Asia Minor and Greece in the 50s; Ignatius', of the same churches in the early years of the second century. Of Rome we gain more knowledge from the second-century writings of Justin and others; of Jerusalem, we glean tantalizing hints in the pages of Acts, and in Josephus' reference to the martyrdom of James the Just. It appears that for some at least of the very early Christians Jerusalem held a place of high theological honour, though once the city had fallen we do not find Christians bemoaning its loss in the same way as their Jewish contemporaries were to do.[52] Of Syria (Antioch excepted) and Egypt it is impossible to say anything for sure; but something must be said, because of the evident presence and power of Christianity in both places by the later second century. It is, frankly, simply not possible to sustain the sweeping claims of Koester, that Syria was 'the country of origin of Christian Gnosticism', or that a good many of the Gnostic writings found at Nag Hammadi in Egypt are of very early origin.[53] The documents upon which such claims are based simply do not admit of such geographical or chronological precision, and must join other early writings in the queue of candidates waiting for admission into the more

[50] Euseb. *HE* 3.17–18.

[51] Dio's description (67.13f.) of the execution of the ex-consuls Glabrio and Flavius Clemens, and the banishment of Flavia Domitilla, is seen by Eusebius 'as testimony to Christ' (*HE* 3.18), presumably on the grounds that Dio gives the charge as 'atheism', which could mean either Jewish or Christian practices or beliefs. The account in Suetonius (*Domitian* 15) does not mention such a charge, and Graves ad loc. (in the Penguin Classics translation) suggests that they were converts not to Christianity, but to Judaism. In any case, Domitian, like other emperors, executed and banished people for all sorts of reasons, no doubt sometimes on vague and trumped-up charges. Even if all three (Glabrio, Flavius Clemens and Flavia Domitilla) were Christians, this does not suggest a major persecution, but rather the opposite: they are mentioned as special cases. On the whole subject see, with further bibliography, Robinson 1976, 231–3.

[52] See above. On the symbolic significance of Jerusalem for the earliest church, see Meyer 1986, ch. 4.

[53] Koester 1982b, 207–33.

solidly established historical framework. Clearly Syria and Egypt were among the important early centres of Christianity, but it is extremely difficult to say about them, any more than about most other places, exactly what their brand of Christianity was like. Of Antioch itself too much, perhaps, has been made of its possible link with the gospel of Matthew. It is perfectly possible that Matthew was written there, but this remains speculative. To regard the link as sufficiently definite to enable us to reconstruct the nature of early Antiochene Christianity by reading between the lines of Matthew's gospel is a prime example of scholarship going further than the evidence will allow.[54]

4. Filling in the Gaps: Literature in Search of Setting

It is vital to be clear about the task that now lies before the would-be historian of early Christianity. About the fixed points listed above there is no doubt, except for the odd date that may be pulled a little this way or that. About almost everything else there is room for a very great deal of doubt. Anyone who imagines that (say) one of the gospels, or one of the so-called 'catholic' epistles, can be dropped into a vacant slot in the framework without more ado is indulging in wishful thinking.[55]

In terms of literature, there should be no question that the two great letter-writers, Paul and Ignatius, are the easiest to fit into the sequence that we have to date. No serious scholar now doubts the substantial authenticity of at least six or seven of the Pauline letters and seven of Ignatius's. Virtually everyone will date the former between the late 40s and the late 50s AD, and the latter somewhere late in the reign of Trajan, who died in 117. The contents of these letters thus form an initial layer of historical reference-points to be added to the fixed points already set out. This conclusion, however, though thoroughly warranted, could lead us into a false optimism. Paul and Ignatius are by no means necessarily to be imagined as representatives of a 'main stream' of early Christianity, whatever that might be. Both were conscious of struggling against opposition from within the church as well as against persecution from outside.

Two other writers may safely be placed into the middle of the second century, possibly earlier. Aristides, whose *Apology* was until the last century known only through references in other writers, may have addressed it to the

---

[54] A danger not entirely escaped by Brown and Meier 1983; cf. Balch 1991. Cp. Malherbe 1983 [1977], 13: it is possible 'that some documents were rescued from obscurity, not because they represented the viewpoints of communities, but precisely because they challenged them'. On the wider social context of early Christianity see now the helpful short work of Stambaugh and Balch 1986.

[55] A particularly striking example of this is Koester's support (1982b, 297–308) for the idea that the pastoral epistles were written by Polycarp in the middle of the second century. The fact that we happen to know about Polycarp does not mean that he was the best-known leader of the church at that time, nor that he was therefore the likely author of these letters; nor do the letters presuppose a long period of peace; nor does the fact that we know very little about the church in 120–60 mean that it enjoyed such peace (all against Koester 305). Putting Pliny and Polycarp together suggests that a policy of repression and persecution began to set in early in the century and continued at least sporadically.

emperor Antoninus Pius (138–61), though Eusebius says it was directed at Hadrian and hence, most likely, written in the 120s or 130s.[56] Justin Martyr, a Greek born in Samaria who studied philosophy and came to see Christianity as its fulfilment, wrote two *Apologies* to explain it to his pagan contemporaries, and his *Dialogue with Trypho* to demonstrate its claim to be the fulfilment also of Judaism.[57] Both may be used with caution as evidence for some forms of Christianity not only in their own time but also in some preceding decades.

We are still, however, not much further forward when it comes to the other early Christian writings, and to the groups and movements to which, directly or obliquely, they bear witness. Somewhere we must fit in the gospels (canonical and otherwise) and acts (canonical and otherwise); the *Didache*; the other letters in the New Testament and the Apostolic Fathers; and both the canonical Apocalypse and several non-canonical ones, including the *Shepherd of Hermas*. Somewhere we must fit in the clearly Jewish elements, and emphases, in early Christianity; the clearly Gentile elements, and emphases; the continuing use of apocalyptic language; the beginnings of Gnosticism, and its interlinking with Christianity; the fact of persecution, both by Jews and pagans; the rise, spread and continuing appeal of the church's mission; the reuse, sometimes with additions, of Jewish traditions and books. Somewhere in the middle of all of this, as a matter of the greatest importance, we must locate the seemingly ineradicable early Christian habit, far more widespread than the writing of gospels, of telling stories about Jesus.

These complex tasks are usually approached, in works of 'New Testament Introduction' and the like, head on. We take a particular writing, and see what can be said about it. The answer, if we are looking for solid history, is usually 'not much'. If we attempt without more ado to integrate the fixed historical points, the geographical spread of the early church, and the writings which we know came from the first Christian century, we find ourselves going round in unproductive circles of imaginative hypotheses. I suggest that we proceed by a different route, similar to that which we took in examining Judaism: we must look first at the elements of the early Christian worldview. Even from the scanty evidence we have, these can be seen reasonably clearly. In the next chapter we shall examine the praxis and symbols, and the questions and answers, which marked out early Christianity. We shall then look in some detail at the characteristic stories which the early Christians told and wrote. From this we will be able to form quite a clear impression of the whole movement, and be able to draw some preliminary conclusions. We shall not be able to fill in all the gaps. But we will have a clear framework within which we can set the two main characters who dominate the landscape: Jesus and Paul.

---

[56] Euseb. *HE* 4.3.3, linking it with a work, still undiscovered, by Quadratus. Aristides' *Apology* can be found in ANF 9.261–79.

[57] On Justin cf. von Campenhausen 1963 [1955], ch. 1; Chadwick 1966, ch. 1; Hall 1991, ch. 5.

Chapter Twelve

PRAXIS, SYMBOL AND QUESTIONS: INSIDE EARLY CHRISTIAN WORLDVIEWS

1. Introduction

If we are to have any hope of understanding what the early Christians were doing, and why, we must at least begin the task of assembling the elements of their worldview, and plotting significant variations within it. The stories they told will need separate treatment; here we shall concentrate on their praxis and symbols. As with the Judaisms of the first century, we cannot assume that all or even most early Christians knew, or even knew of, the writings that we can casually pull off a shelf today and treat as 'typical' of first- or second-century Christianity. (Also as with Judaisms, we cannot assume that there is no diversity within Christianity; we shall come to this in due course.) With praxis and symbol we are on surer ground. Even those who wrote nothing, and read little, took certain styles of behaviour for granted, and gave allegiance to certain central symbols. We can study these, and from them certain conclusions can be drawn. In this light, we can reread some of the stories they told, in the hope of rediscovering the ways in which these stories reinforced their worldview, and attempted to subvert those of Jews, pagans, and (sometimes) other sorts of Christians.

2. Praxis

The single most striking thing about early Christianity is its speed of growth. In AD 25 there is no such thing as Christianity: merely a young hermit in the Judaean wilderness, and his somewhat younger cousin who dreams dreams and sees visions. By AD 125 the Roman emperor has established an official policy in relation to the punishment of Christians; Polycarp has already been a Christian in Smyrna for half a century; Aristides (if we accept the earlier date) is confronting the emperor Hadrian with the news that there are four races in the world, Barbarians, Greeks, Jews and Christians; and a young pagan called Justin is beginning the philosophical quest which will take him through the greatest of the pagan thinkers and lead him, still unsatisfied, to Christ.[1]

---

[1] See Aristides, *Apol.* 2 (in the Syriac recension; the Greek has assimilated his 'four races' to the more normal three: pagans, Jews and Christians); Justin *Dial.* 2–8.

Christianity did not spread by magic. It is sometimes suggested that the world was, so to speak, ready for Christianity: Stoicism was too lofty and dry, popular paganism metaphysically incredible and morally bankrupt, mystery-religions dark and forbidding, Judaism law-bound and introverted, and Christianity burst on the scene as the great answer to the questions everyone was asking.[2] There is a grain of truth in this picture, but it hardly does justice to historical reality. Christianity summoned proud pagans to face torture and death out of loyalty to a Jewish villager who had been executed by Rome. Christianity advocated a love which cut across racial boundaries. It sternly forbade sexual immorality, the exposure of children, and a great many other things which the pagan world took for granted. Choosing to become a Christian was not an easy or natural thing for the average pagan. A Jew who converted might well be regarded as a national traitor. Even slaves, who might be supposed to have less to lose than others, and hence to appreciate an elevation of status through conversion, might face a cost: as we saw, Pliny thought it normal to interrogate, with torture, slave-girls who happened to be part of the early Christian movement. We have no reason to suppose that interrogation under torture was any easier for a young woman in the second century than it is in the twentieth.

Why then did early Christianity spread? Because early Christians believed that what they had found to be true was true for the whole world. The impetus to mission sprang from the very heart of early Christian conviction. If we know anything about early Christian praxis, at a non- or sub-literary level, it is that the early Christians engaged in mission, both to Jews and to Gentiles. 'The irresistible expansion of Christian faith in the Mediterranean world during the first 150 years is the scarlet thread running through any history of primitive Christianity.'[3] This missionary activity was not an addendum to a faith that was basically 'about' something else (e.g. a new existential self-awareness). 'Christianity was never more *itself* than in the launching of the world mission.'[4]

This is clear throughout the sources we have already mentioned. Justin tells of his meeting with an old man who talked to him about Jesus. Pliny speaks of the poison of Christianity spreading into villages and countryside. Ignatius finds churches wherever he goes throughout Asia Minor. Tacitus, in the tone of voice of one who has come across a dead rat in his water-tank, comments that all the worst features of world culture find their way to Rome sooner or later.[5] And if we look for a moment at the canonical writings, we find them full

---

[2] cf. e.g. Caird 1955, 17. For a cautious sociological version of the same idea, cf. Meeks 1983, 174f., with the comments of Meyer 1986, 32f.

[3] Hengel 1983, 48.

[4] Meyer 1986, 18 (italics original). Professor Christopher Rowland has suggested to me that this is going beyond the evidence, since Christianity could well have spread simply by pagans seeing the evidence of a new community and opting to join it. I can only say that the evidence seems to me to point emphatically in the direction taken by Hengel and Meyer. Cf. also Schäfer-diek 1991.

[5] See above. The charge is frequently repeated in other Latin writers, e.g. Sallust *Cat.* 37.5; Juvenal *Sat.* 3.62.

of mission: Matthew's Jesus instructs the disciples to make disciples and baptize in all the world, Luke's Jesus commissions his followers to go to Jerusalem, Judaea, Samaria and the ends of the earth, and John's Jesus says 'as the Father sent me, so I send you'.[6] The story of Acts *is* the story, or rather a story, of early Christian mission. And whatever we may think about the portrait of Paul in Acts, the letters confirm that not only he but a good many other Christians, in some cases holding significantly different views, believed it their business to travel around the known world telling people that there was 'another king, this Jesus'.[7]

World mission is thus the first and most obvious feature of early Christian praxis. We shall discuss its underlying rationale when more aspects of the worldview have been examined.

What did the Christians get up to behind closed doors?[8] It is clear that this question was asked, and answered with sneering accusations, by many non-Christians in the late first and early second century, and we have no reason to suppose that things were different in the earliest period. It was assumed that they were immoral, practising secret orgies. Other cults that met in secret were like that; why should Christians be any different?[9] Instead, the characteristic praxis of the early Christian meetings is stressed again and again by the early apologists. Christians administer baptism to converts and their families, and they celebrate the eucharist. They 'sing hymns in honour of Christ as to a god', as Pliny discovered. They do not keep the Jewish or the pagan festivals; traces of the former remain, and analogues of the latter are found, but Justin (for instance) is clear that baptism and the eucharist are quite distinct from either of these.[10] For our present purpose the point is that already by the middle of the second century baptism and eucharist, as significantly new forms of religious praxis, had become so much second nature to the Christian church that new questions and theories could be advanced about them. They were not strange actions which some Christians might on odd occasions perform, but ritual acts which were taken for granted, part of that praxis which constituted the early Christian worldview. Whenever we date the *Didache* (and it is presumably no later than the time of Hadrian, i.e. in the 130s at the latest), the same point emerges: the writer assumes that baptism and eucharist take place, and offers suggestions as to forms of words.[11] This itself is interesting; it implies, as indeed do the variant accounts in the synoptic tradition and Paul, that, though the praxis of eucharist was invariable, the words that were used were not.[12]

---

[6] Mt. 28.19; Lk.24.47; Ac. 1.8; Jn. 20.21.

[7] Ac. 17.7.

[8] On all this, cf. Meeks 1983, ch. 5, including his distinction between 'minor rituals' and the major celebrations of baptism and eucharist.

[9] cf. Aristides *Apol.* 15, 17; Justin *1 Apol.* 29, 65–7; *Mart. Pol.* 3.2; Tac. *Ann.* 15.44; Tertullian *Apol.* 4.11, 7.1—8.9, etc.

[10] Justin *1 Apol.* 61f., 65f.

[11] *Did.* 7–10.

[12] cf. ch. 14 below.

It is clear, remarkably, that these two basic forms of Christian praxis were equally taken for granted as early as the 50s of the first century. Paul can write of baptism as a given, from which theological conclusions can be drawn (Romans 6.3–11). He can describe, or allude to, the eucharist in similar fashion (1 Corinthians 10.15–22), taking it as read that the Corinthian church regularly meets to partake of the Lord's Meal together, and moving on to argue on this basis about what is and is not appropriate in their behaviour within a pagan city. The retelling in the synoptic tradition of the original Lord's Meal, and the command to baptize, cannot therefore be seen as an attempt, by the evangelists, to institute something not previously known.

Mission and sacrament both came into focus at the very centre of the church's life, that is, its worship. The early Christians were quite emphatic from the first that they were monotheists in the same sense that Jews were. But at point after point, not least in what are probably the very earliest strata of the New Testament, we find that when the Christians are worshipping this one true god, the creator, they are doing so *with reference also to Jesus.* This, of course, brought about all sorts of headaches for the later Fathers, who struggled to provide a rationalization for the practice; but the practice itself, rather than the (sometimes tortuous) theological explanations, shows every sign of being a central feature of Christianity from the beginning. Paul writes, or perhaps quotes, passages in which specifically and indeed fiercely monotheistic texts from the Hebrew Bible are used, in explicit confutation of paganism; and there, in the middle of them, is Jesus. In place of

Hear, O Israel:
The lord our god, the lord is one.[13]

we have

For us there is one god
(the father, from whom are all things and we to him)
and one lord
(Jesus Christ, through whom are all things and we through him).[14]

The same phenomenon is visible across virtually all early Christianity for which we have evidence.[15]

Along with mission, sacrament and above all worship there went (what we would call) a strong and clear ethical code. We can trace this from Paul's appeals to his converts, through the *Didache*'s description of the true way of life, to Justin's invitation to Antoninus Pius that he make impartial investigation of the Christians and discover for himself just how upright their behaviour was.[16] This suggests, remarkably enough, that the appeals of the first generation or two had been sufficiently successful for subsequent generations to say: see how differently we behave from you pagans! The Christians, as we saw, did

[13] Dt. 6.4.

[14] 1 Cor. 8.6. On this cf. Wright 1991a, ch. 6. For other examples, cf. Phil. 2.6–11; Col. 1.15–20 (discussed in ibid., chs. 4–5).

[15] cf. Bauckham 1980–1; France 1982; Moule 1982 [1962], 26–32.

[16] e.g. 1 Cor. 6; Rom. 12; *Did.* 1–6; Justin *1 Apol.* 1–5.

not expose their children, nor did they indulge in sexual immorality. What is more, they did not attempt to overthrow governments; did not commit suicide; and in particular—astonishing in a world where trust and affection were normally confined to family and friends—they cared for one another across the barriers formed by normal culture:

> Their oppressors they appease and make them their friends; they do good to their enemies . . . they love one another, and from widows they do not turn away their esteem; and they deliver the orphan from him who treats him harshly. And he, who has, gives to him who has not, without boasting. And when they see a stranger, they take him in to their homes and rejoice over him as a very brother; for they do not call them brethren after the flesh, but brethren after the spirit and in God. And whenever one of their poor passes from the world, each one of them according to his ability gives heed to him and carefully sees to his burial . . .[17]

We should not, of course, read these claims uncritically. The church, we may be sure, was never as totally pure and worthy as this, nor were its enemies as totally depraved as the apologists made out.[18] But that there was a striking difference in general praxis as between pagans and Christians there can be no doubt. That there was even a viable *expectation* of a striking difference is remarkable in itself; even when a Christian teacher is bemoaning the fact that his congregation is not pulling its weight morally, there is a sense of a norm, an accepted praxis, to which the people are being disobedient. And it is this *assumed* praxis that matters for our present purposes. Early Christians took it for granted that in the details of their behaviour they should be significantly different, in clearly defined ways, from their pagan neighbours.

Among the striking features of early Christian praxis must be reckoned one thing that early Christians did *not* do. Unlike every other religion known in the world up to that point, the Christians offered no animal sacrifices. Some early Jewish Christians may, of course, have continued to participate in the sacrificial cult in Jerusalem, and it is not impossible that the letter to the Hebrews was written to warn them off.[19] Some pagan Christians undoubtedly participated in the sacrificial cult of pagan deities, and it is likely that 1 Corinthians was written partly in order to tell them to stop. But no Christians offered animal sacrifice *qua Christians*. Nobody ever thought that the worship of the god now made known in Jesus of Nazareth required the blood of calves or lambs. At this point the evidence is clear and unambiguous, and its significance is enormous. Although sacrificial *language* was used often enough—it could hardly be avoided, since it was the regular language of both pagan and Jewish devotion—it is clear from our earliest records that the usage, in relation to Christian devotion and ethics, is completely metaphorical.[20] The dis-

[17] Aristides *Apol.* 15.

[18] See Lane Fox 1986, 549–60.

[19] On Christian attitudes to sacrifice cf. Meyer 1986, 56 n.6. Neusner 1989, 290 suggests that, from the time of Jesus himself, Christianity saw the eucharist as an alternative sacrificial system to that of the Temple. If there is a grain of truth here, it is in my view hidden within a sheaf of misunderstanding.

[20] The exception that proves the rule is the use of sacrificial language referring to Jesus' actual death; though there, perhaps, a different level of metaphor is operating.

tinction not only between the pagan gods and the one true god, but also between the sort of worship appropriate for each, was taken for granted from the first; so, too, was the difference (within a close similarity) between Jewish and Christian worship. This negative praxis is striking enough in retrospect. At the time it must have stood out a mile to any observer.

Another striking feature of praxis was the regular Christian attitude to suffering and death. Paganism knew of martyrs. It often advocated noble suicide, holding up such examples as Cato and Socrates.[21] Judaism, of course, had its martyrs, and gained more under the same Hadrian to whom Aristides addressed his *Apology*.[22] The retelling of their stories, and the exhortation to imitate them if need arose, functioned at a level deeper than the mere imitation of heroes. They were signs that in Judaism the living god was at work and would defeat the pagan gods. The early Christians soon had their equivalent of both these pagan and Jewish models, but they were equivalents which radically redefined both. Here we see the same development as in ethics: the leaders of the first generation exhorted their followers to be ready to suffer, and the leaders of subsequent generations pointed proudly to the fact that their people did in fact suffer and die gladly rather than deny Christ.[23] Again, the record is of course not without blemish. Pliny knows of some who have recanted. But many Christians, from at least the days of Nero onwards, went through torture and death for the sake of their faith; and many in earlier days, if Paul himself is to be believed, underwent suffering at the hands of Jews, both in Judaea and elsewhere, rather than abandon the Christian way.[24] That this attitude is totally different from the suicide of the Stoic is argued by Justin.[25] Ignatius, who has somewhat more to say than most when it comes to martyrdom, can be accused of courting death in a way which subsequent generations came to find unhealthy, but at no point is his rhetoric anything like that of, say, Epictetus, with the latter's oft-repeated invitation to suicide: 'the door stands open'.[26] The Christian martyrs quickly acquired symbolic value, so that apologists could appeal to the fact of martyrdom, not merely to the heroic example of those involved, as powerful evidence for the truth of the Christian claim. To this extent it is appropriate to list readiness to suffer, and willingness to die rather than recant, among the features of early Christian praxis which were, or which soon came to be, taken for granted in the early church, and which marked it out from its pagan neighbours. The Stoic was fairly cynical about life anyway.

[21] On Cato's suicide after the battle of Thapsus in 47 BC see Cary 1954 [1935], 406: 'Cato's suicide, which obtained undeserved notoriety and almost set a fashion, was a tribute to the Stoic philosophy to which he had become an addict.' Even though Socrates had been condemned to death by a court, the fact that he clearly could have saved himself had he wished, and that he ended up administering to himself the fatal poison, was easily enough to guarantee him a symbolic, not just a heroic, place within the worldview of first-century paganism: see e.g. Epict. *Disc.* 1.29.29.

[22] Josephus refers glowingly to the readiness of his countrymen to face death rather than see their laws defiled: e.g. *Apion* 2.232–5.

[23] e.g. Justin *2 Apol.* 11f.

[24] e.g. 1 Thess. 2.13–16; Gal. 1.13; 4.29; 6.12; etc. Cf. too Ac. 13.50; 14.19; etc.

[25] *2 Apol.* 4.

[26] See e.g. Ign. *Rom.* 4–8; Epict. *Disc.* 1.25.18; 2.6.22; 2.15.6, etc.

The Christians affirmed its goodness, but were ready to leave it in obedience to an even greater good.[27] In the same way, martyrdom for Christ redefined Jewish martyrdom for Torah; the same loyalty to the one true god lay at its heart, but it carried no national or racial overtones.

We must wait until later to draw conclusions from this brief description of characteristic early Christian praxis. But already one point stands out a long way. The characteristic actions and activities of Christians marked them out from the very beginning as a new sort of grouping in the ancient world. In many ways they were not like a 'religion'; they had no sacred sites, no animal sacrifices. They were not like a political group, since they looked for a kingdom not of this world. They were like Jews, not pagans, in that they gave allegiance to the one creator god, and they reused standard Jewish polemic against paganism. But they insisted, too, upon using the language of divinity for Jesus, and upon a completely non-racial fellowship, both of which put them decidedly outside the range of mainstream Judaism. What sort of movement was this? From our brief study of early Christian praxis we can only say that Aristides got it about right. It was a new sort of movement, that could only properly be described by creating a new category alongside Greeks, barbarians and Jews. It was a new way of construing what it meant to be human.[28]

3. Symbols

We have seen in earlier chapters how the symbols of Judaism functioned in close harmony with the praxis and stories that also contributed to the Jewish worldview and its variants. These symbols—Temple, Torah, Land and ethnic identity—marked the Jews out from their pagan neighbours, whose symbols included the many trappings of pagan worship, such as reverence for oracles, offering of incense to the 'genius of Caesar', and such like; the statues of gods, heroes and emperors; the coins which proclaimed a triumphant message about a particular country or state; the glorification of military might and achievements; and the entertainments (gladiatorial shows and the like) which attracted large crowds and provided a focal point of popular identity. In what way did the early Christian symbols differ from these?

The short answer is, in every way. The early Christians did not consult oracles. They refused to burn incense to Caesar. They did not make statues of their god. Not being a state, they did not produce their own coinage, or organize themselves into a military force. If Christians attended gladiatorial displays, it was not usually in the capacity of spectators.[29]

Nor did they adhere to the symbols of the Jewish worldview. Their initially ambiguous attitude to the Temple, which we mentioned earlier, gave birth to a

---

[27] I thus find myself taking a very different line from that of Droge and Tabor 1992. Their reading of the evidence is too selective: e.g. they ignore Justin *2 Apol.* 4, which argues specifically against the point they try to prove (139) from the same work.

[28] Here I go some way beyond Moule 1982 [1962], ch. 3.

[29] cf. Tertullian *de Spect.*

use of Temple-language as a rich source of metaphor through which they lent depth to their beliefs both about Jesus and about the church itself. Similar metaphorical transformation took place in the language of worship and sacrifice.

Likewise, the Torah was reinterpreted in such a way that it no longer functioned as a code marking out Israel as a separate nation. All had been fulfilled in Christ, even if (as in the *Epistle of Barnabas*) it sometimes took a good deal of exegetical ingenuity to demonstrate the point. What mattered was that the *symbolic* function of Torah, as the ancestral code of the people of the one god, had gone entirely, and in its place there arose a new *apologetic* function: careful reading of Torah, and Prophets and Psalms as well, would show that the true god had prepared the way for the coming of Christ through the whole story of Israel, which had reached its intended climax with his death and resurrection. The early Christian rereading of Jewish scripture is one of the most characteristic symbolic actions for which we have clear evidence.[30]

So, too, the Land no longer functioned as the key symbol of the geographical identity of the people of god, and that for an obvious reason: if the new community consisted of Jew, Greek, barbarian alike, there was no sense in which one piece of territory could possess more significance than another. At no point in this early period do we find Christians eager to define or defend a 'holy land'.[31]

In particular, the Jewish sense of the ethnic identity of the people of god had gone. The attempt in so-called 'Jewish Christianity', as evidenced in the (quite late) Pseudo-Clementines, to restore into Christianity an emphasis on Torah and Jewish nationhood, is clearly a secondary development without visible continuity with the first two generations.[32] On the other side, it is clear from some writings in the early Christian canon (e.g. Paul's letter to the Romans), and in a different way from the work of the second-century leader Marcion, that some in the early church actually hoped to turn Christianity into a non-Jewish movement altogether, but this was firmly resisted. The gospel was for all humans, Jew and Gentile alike.[33]

The early Christians, then, gave allegiance to none of the regular symbols of either Judaism or paganism. What did they put in their place? In part this question must wait until much later; only in the light of a fuller study can we say in detail which symbol 'replaced' which, and in what sense. But a start can be made. Already by the time of Justin Martyr one symbol had become so associated with the early Christian movement that Justin could mount a polemically tendentious argument about it, suggesting that all people give it tacit allegiance. The symbol in question is the cross:

[30] Which raises, of course, a host of problems: cf. Moule 1982 [1962], ch. 4 and e.g. Hays 1989. On Christian retellings of the Jewish story cf. chs. 13–14 below.

[31] At this point Meyer 1986, 176 (following Davies 1974) is imprecise: it is not that the symbol of Jesus himself simply took over from Temple, Place and Land. Jesus and the church together are the new Temple; the world, I suggest, is the new Land.

[32] cf. Hennecke 1965, 532–70; Koester 1982b, 205–7.

[33] For Paul's rebuttal of incipient Marcionism see e.g. Rom. 11.11ff. On Marcion, who was opposed by (among others) Irenaeus and Tertullian, the standard work is still that of Harnack 1924; see the sympathetic account in Koester 1982b, 328–34.

> This [the cross] is the greatest symbol of His [Christ's] power and rule; as is proved by the things which fall under our observation. For consider all the things in the world, whether without this form they could be administered or have any community. For the sea is not traversed except that trophy which is called a sail abide safe in the ship; and the earth is not ploughed without it: diggers and mechanics do not their work, except with tools which have this shape. And the human form differs from that of the irrational animals in nothing else than in its being erect and having the hands extended. . .[34]

The fact that Justin is obviously stretching a point further than it can go demonstrates precisely the place that the symbol of the cross came to have in nascent Christianity. If we, with twenty 'Christian' centuries behind us, find this somewhat natural or obvious, we may need reminding that crucifixion, though common in the Roman world, was so utterly horrible that it was not mentioned in polite society: 'the Roman world was largely unanimous that crucifixion was a horrific, disgusting business'.[35] Justin himself knows that to worship a crucified man is at once to incur the charge of madness.[36] It is not only Paul who sees the message of the cross as 'foolishness' (1 Corinthians 1.18): generations of Christians faced repeated accusations to this effect. Yet, with significant exceptions,[37] they made no effort to tone down the story. Instead, they grasped it to themselves as the paradoxical truth by which the world was saved. Within a short time the cross became the central Christian symbol, easy to draw, hard to forget, pregnant both in its reference to Jesus himself and in its multiple significance for his followers.

Alongside this central symbol there emerged others, less striking but no less powerful. The early Christian mission itself was not merely a key aspect of praxis; it had a high symbolic value, since it only made sense on the premise that Jesus was enthroned as the true Lord of the world, claiming allegiance from all. As such, mission to the whole world seems to have taken the place held, within the Jewish symbolic universe, by the Land. The church itself, in its various local and trans-local manifestations, became not just a convenient collocation of the like-minded, but a powerful symbol. To be part of this family was to be part of the new human family, called into being by the creator god, transcending all race and nationhood. As such, the church, precisely in its cutting across the traditional lines of race, class and gender, seems to have taken the place occupied, in Israel's symbolic world, by (Jewish) ethnic identity. So, too, the codes of personal behaviour, which occur in a variety of forms both in the New Testament and in writings such as the *Didache* and the Apostolic Fathers, take part at least of the symbolic place of Torah. Instead of a behaviour-code which demarcated a certain race and nation, the early Christians articulated in various ways a behaviour-code appropriate for truly human beings of every nation.

---

[34] Justin, *1 Apol.*, 55. Cf. Minucius Felix, *Octavius*, 29.6–8. The fact that Minucius Felix in this passage, and Tertullian in *Apol.* 16.6–8, need to defend Christians against the charge of *worshipping* the cross shows that it was already becoming known as a major symbol.

[35] Hengel 1977, 37; the whole book is necessary reading on the subject.

[36] *1 Apol.* 13. Cf. Ign. *Eph.* 18.1.

[37] It is often suggested that 'Q', like the *Gospel of Thomas*, had no place for the cross in its theology. See ch. 14 below.

Finally, instead of the Temple, the geographical and theological centre of Judaism, the early Christians spoke of Jesus as the one who had embodied the living presence of the creator god, and of his own spirit as the one who continued to make that god present in the lives and assemblies of the early church. They realized, soon enough, that this transfer of symbolism was forcing them to articulate the meaning of the word 'god' itself in a new way. This drove them, in due course, from the early credal formulae such as 1 Corinthians 8.4–6 and 15.1–8 to the fully-blown formulae which speak of the creator and redeemer god in terms of a story, indeed the Jewish story: creation and redemption accomplished in Jesus and applied through the divine spirit. It is in this context that we can readily understand the wholesale transfer to Jesus, and the church, of Jewish Temple-imagery.[38]

In this context, too, it is no accident that the Latin name for a creed is precisely *symbolum*. The early creeds, and the baptismal confessions which partly underlay them, were not little pieces of abstract theologizing to satisfy the curious intellect, but symbols which functioned as such, badges which marked out this community from others in terms of the god in whom they believed.[39] From the start, Christian creeds were not so much a matter of 'faith seeking understanding' as 'community seeking definition'—and finding it in *that which was believed about the true god*. Statements of belief in a god now known through Jesus and the divine spirit thus took the place, within the early Christian symbolic world, that had been occupied within Judaism by the badges of Torah—circumcision, kosher laws, sabbath. We can see this process going right back to the earliest documents of Christianity that we possess.[40]

Christian 'theology', then, was born and nurtured in the context of faith, worship, baptism and eucharist, and came to expression through the need to mark out the community which worshipped this god from communities that worshipped others. If everybody agrees about the gods, or about their particular god, there is no need for theology. The nearest we come to it in pre-Christian Judaism is, perhaps, in the anti-pagan polemic of the wisdom writers. But when the question of god is forced into the centre of the agenda, as it was at once in early Christianity, then theology, as an activity associated more with mission than with metaphysics, more with suffering than with speculation, is the inevitable result. The place and status of theology within developing Christianity, not as abstract philosophy or whimsical scholarship, but as part of the inner life of the church, was assured from the first.[41]

---

[38] e.g. 1 Cor. 3.16f.; 6.19; cf. Rom. 8.9; Ign. *Eph.* 9.2; 15.3; *Magn.* 7.2.

[39] See Kelly 1971 [1950], 52–61, following in part the explanation offered by the fourth-century scholar Rufinus.

[40] e.g. 1 Cor. 8.6, which marks Christians off from pagans and Jews alike: see Meeks 1983, 165–70; Wright 1991a, ch. 6. On the resultant theology of justification see ch. 15 below.

[41] This may suggest an answer to Petersen's pertinent question, as to whether Paul was after all the first 'theologian'—since, as he says, 'in his time there was no recognizable social role called "theologian" ' (Petersen 1985, 201, with n.4). Whether or not Paul was in fact the first, it seems that the sort of 'theology' that quickly came to characterize Christianity, and the place that it took within the movement, grew from the inner logic of the early Christian symbolic universe, as the work of apologists like Justin and Tertullian makes clear.

To this list of symbols we must add one more feature. As we saw, from its very early days Christianity had its martyrs. They were not merely venerated as heroes. Their very existence quickly acquired symbolic value, being interpreted in terms of the central symbol of the cross. This was a movement which, like the Judaism of the Maccabees, saw itself as witness to a life stronger than death.

4. Questions

This brief survey of early Christian symbols could of course be filled in a great deal more, not least by considering early Christian art. But it is enough to show the thoroughly new contours of the worldview. We can see this more clearly, in conclusion, if we cash out praxis and symbols together in terms of the implicit worldview-questions, to which they generate certain quite clear answers. People who take for granted that they will act within the world in these sorts of ways, and who see the world through the lens of these symbols, clearly believe certain things about themselves and the world which suggest particular answers to the key questions.[42]

Who are we? We are a new group, a new movement, and yet not new, because we claim to be the true people of the god of Abraham, Isaac and Jacob, the creator of the world. We are the people for whom the creator god was preparing the way through his dealings with Israel. To that extent, we are like Israel; we are emphatically monotheists, not pagan polytheists, marked out from the pagan world by our adherence to the traditions of Israel, and yet distinguished from the Jewish world in virtue of the crucified Jesus and the divine spirit, and by our fellowship in which the traditional Jewish and pagan boundary-markers are transcended.

Where are we? We are living in the world that was made by the god we worship, the world that does not yet acknowledge this true and only god. We are thus surrounded by neighbours who worship idols that are, at best, parodies of the truth, and who thus catch glimpses of reality but continually distort it. Humans in general remain in bondage to their own gods, who drag them into a variety of degrading and dehumanizing behaviour-patterns. As a result, we are persecuted, because we remind the present power-structures of what they dimly know, that there is a different way to be human, and that in the message of the true god concerning his son, Jesus, notice has been served on them that their own claim to absolute power is called into question.

What is wrong? The powers of paganism still rule the world, and from time to time even find their way into the church.[43] Persecutions arise from outside, heresies and schisms from within. These evils can sometimes be attributed to supernatural agency, whether 'Satan' or various demons. Even within the indi-

---

[42] See ch. 5 above, esp. p.122–6.
[43] It should perhaps be noted here that the major early Christian answer to 'what is wrong' would have nothing to say about Judaism, except in so far as Jews were persecuting the church.

vidual Christian there remain forces at work that need to be subdued, lusts which need to be put to death, party-spirit which needs to learn humility.

What is the solution? Israel's hope has been realized; the true god has acted decisively to defeat the pagan gods, and to create a new people, through whom he is to rescue the world from evil. This he has done through the true King, Jesus, the Jewish Messiah, in particular through his death and resurrection. The process of implementing this victory, by means of the same god continuing to act through his own spirit in his people, is not yet complete. One day the King will return to judge the world, and to set up a kingdom which is on a different level to the kingdoms of the present world order. When this happens those who have died as Christians will be raised to a new physical life. The present powers will be forced to acknowledge Jesus as Lord, and justice and peace will triumph at last.[44]

We must now pause and take stock. We have set out certain fixed points which all historians must take seriously as landmarks in the reconstruction of the first century or so of the Christian church. We have seen that alongside these fixed points there are certain writings which reflect definite periods within the time-frame: the work of Paul in the 50s, of Ignatius in roughly 110–20, of Aristides and Justin between 120 and 160. Relying more or less entirely on these works, and refusing as yet to import other literature, whether canonical or otherwise, into the picture, we have already built up a substantial sketch of (at least one form of) the early Christian worldview, as seen in its praxis, its symbols and the implicit answers it offers to the key worldview questions. It is now time to move to the fourth corner of the worldview diamond. What stories did the early Christians tell? How did they bring the worldview into articulation? What other stories did they attempt to subvert as they did so?

---

[44] This belief in the future judgment and salvation was held by writers throughout the first Christian centuries, without any noticeable sense that it had been called into question by failing to happen at the end of a generation. See ch. 15.

Chapter Thirteen

STORIES IN EARLY CHRISTIANITY (1)

1. Introduction

Praxis and symbols tell us a good deal about a worldview, but stories are the most revealing of all. What sort of stories did the early Christians tell, and how do those stories dovetail into the worldview that we have sketched so far? This is an enormous topic, big enough for several books in itself, and we must devote two chapters to it. In the present one, we will examine some of the larger stories that meet us on the surface of the New Testament; in the next, we will probe beneath, and uncover the smaller stories of which these larger ones are mostly composed. It is tempting to reverse this order, and begin with material that may be chronologically earlier. But this temptation is to be resisted. It is greatly preferable to begin with the known and move towards the less known. We possess Luke and Acts, Matthew, Mark, and John, and for that matter other books, such as the letters of Paul, which can be shown to possess clear narrative substructures. We can read them in their own right. We do not have Q as such; still less, the original forms of the stories that comprise most of the gospel tradition.

This chapter and the next one play a doubly vital role in the overall argument of this book and of the larger project of which it forms the opening volume. First, they are crucial within the task of the present section, in which we attempt to get inside the worldview of the early Christians. The fact that within the first hundred years books like these emerged within the movement tells us an enormous amount about that worldview, if we have eyes to see. Second, these stories, large and small alike, are almost the only sources we have for the life of Jesus himself. It is therefore vital, as part of the function of the present volume in preparing for the following one in particular, that we understand the nature of these stories not only as revealing the worldview of those who told, retold, transmitted and eventually transcribed them, but also as providing the critical historian with essential information about Jesus himself. The way to the latter task is through the former. That is why it is vital that, after looking in this chapter at some of the larger stories which offer themselves within the New Testament as it stands, we should, in the next, study some of the material, both extant and hypothetical, that has sometimes been supposed to form an equally important set of strata for such historical reconstruction.

In the previous two chapters we set out certain fixed points about early Christianity. These two chapters draw attention to another which deserves to be put alongside them. The early Christians were *story-tellers*. There were plenty of philosophies on offer in the ancient world whose commitment to stories was less obvious than theirs (though no doubt equally capable of being teased out by a persistent modern narratologist). The writings of the Stoics, for example, consist far more of maxims and isolated *obiter dicta*, with only the occasional short story, either anecdote or parable, thrown in by way of illustration.[1] With the early Christians, I shall argue throughout this and the next chapter, stories were visibly and obviously an essential part of what they were and did. Though there may be some early material which bears some comparison with the pagan collections of maxims, the overwhelming impression is that of narrative.

The present chapter, dealing with the longer stories that take up whole books, can only be a tendentious account. The secondary literature in each case is vast and unwieldy, full of conflicting agendas and massive arguments that often merely cross paths, like huge ships in a thick fog, with only a dim awareness of each other, let alone of cargo and destination. We here face the problem of the necessary circle of all historical knowing.[2] We need to study the early Christian stories in themselves in order to find out about Jesus; but only when we presuppose something about Jesus can we study those stories in their full depth.[3] At the moment, then, all we can offer is a preliminary reading. We shall hope to return to a fuller treatment later in the project.

Where to begin? The most obvious place, in terms of early Christian literature, is the work of Luke.[4] Luke's gospel and Acts together, agreed virtually on all sides to come from the same hand, occupy about two-fifths of the entire New Testament, appreciably more than the whole Pauline corpus. Within early Christian literature only Hermas comes near to Luke for sheer bulk, and it would be a bold move indeed to put that collection of musings and visions alongside Luke's gospel and Acts. In addition, since we are considering stories, it makes sense to begin with a writer who explicitly set out to tell one, or possibly two, stories in particular.

We have spent a good deal of time in this book in the company of Josephus. Luke and Josephus were near-contemporaries; both may well have been writing in Rome, around the same time. Underneath their obvious differences, they had similar tales to tell. It will be instructive, before we even consider such abstract issues as genre, to stand the two of them side by side and see what we learn from the juxtaposition.

---

[1] Epictetus is an obvious example.

[2] cf. chs. 2, 4 above.

[3] If this should be doubted, let the reader turn up pages at random in Bultmann 1968 [1921]. In passage after passage an assumption about what did or did not happen in Jesus' ministry is the basis for moving towards a hypothesis about the early church.

[4] Throughout this volume I make no assumptions about the actual identity of the evangelists, and use the traditional names for simplicity only. I shall discuss this matter further elsewhere.

2. Luke and his Stories

(i) A Strange Comparison?

Luke has often been compared with Josephus.[5] This exercise has focused almost entirely on points of language and detailed content, which are interesting in themselves but do not take account of the larger picture. Taking their works as wholes, there are at least four reasons why the comparison should be made:[6]

a. Josephus, in his two larger works, tells the story of Israel reaching its crucial moment. In the *Jewish War* he skims over the early history, focuses quickly on the build-up to the war, and then describes the war itself in lavish and horrendous detail. He writes, so to speak, a passion narrative (the war itself) with an extended introduction. If anyone had asked him why he had done so, there would have been obvious answers, not least his desire to present the Jews, despite the war, as a peaceable, not a rebellious, people. If anyone were to wonder whether Josephus was concerned about the earlier parts of Israel's history, they could be sent on to his later work, the *Antiquities*. There, though the treatment of Israel's history from earliest times is of course far fuller, the eventual focus of interest still lies on what led up to the great war. Previous disasters prepared the way for this one. This event, it seems, is what Israel's history was really all about.

Luke's gospel is parallel to the *War*, not to the *Antiquities*. It takes care to hook the story in to the long history of Israel: the first two chapters can only be understood by someone with that history firmly in mind, preferably known in one of the current Greek versions. Time and again in the narrative itself we are reminded of the longer story of which this is the climactic moment. Though the phrase is overworked and not entirely accurate, Luke, like Mark as well as Josephus, writes a long passion narrative with an extended introduction, in the light of which the reader can make sense of the climactic event itself.[7] Luke did not write an equivalent of the *Antiquities*. But he makes it quite clear that he could have done so had he wished: the events that have just taken place, he says, are the end towards which Israel's whole story has been leading all along.[8]

Though Luke's story thus focuses on Jesus' death as Josephus' does on the fall of Jerusalem, and hence forms a close parallel, Luke too is aware of Jerusalem's fall (whether as prophecy, or as past event, we cannot here discuss). 'Unless you repent, you will all likewise perish'; the words are those of

---

[5] e.g. Hubbard 1979; Schreckenberg 1980 (with full bibliography); Downing 1980a, 1980b, 1982; and see discussion in Hemer 1989, 63–100, 371–3. The basic studies are Krenkel 1894; Schlatter 1960 [1931], 562–658. I am grateful to Mrs Barbara Shellard for helpful discussion of this topic.

[6] Downing 1980a, 1980b instructively compares Josephus and Luke as wholes, but with an eye mainly to their redactional methods. My suggestions run somewhat in parallel.

[7] See now the discussion of the proportional space given to different material in the gospels in Burridge 1992, 201f.

[8] cf. esp. Lk. 24.26f., 44.

Luke's Jesus (13.3, 5), but they could easily have been those of Josephus, urging the rebels to lay down their arms and trust him for a different model of loyalty to the ancestral traditions.[9] Luke's narrative has, in this sense, a double climax to Josephus' single one, and that (I think) is part of the point: the fall of the Temple, seen as future from within Luke's narrative world, is set in close parallel with the death of Jesus. The distinction between Luke and Josephus at this point is a powerful clue to the theological point that Luke is making.

b. Josephus claims that Israel's history has had a strange, dark and unlooked-for ending: Israel's god has gone over to the Romans.[10] The providence that has watched over Israel throughout her history has finally abandoned her, because of her sin, leaving the Temple desolate. This god, the creator, has instead elevated Rome to the position of world sovereignty. Militant Jews read in their scriptures prophecies which spoke of a world ruler coming forth from Judaea:[11] according to Josephus, these prophecies referred to Vespasian, who was in Judaea when he was hailed by his troops as emperor, and who went from there to Rome to claim the kingdom under which Josephus himself subsequently enjoyed patronage.[12]

Luke knows all about Daniel's prophecies, and makes his own use of them. I think it very probable that the story of the ascension of Jesus in Acts 1 owes a good deal to Daniel 7: Jesus is exalted on a cloud, presumably to the right hand of the Ancient of Days. As a result, he has received the kingdom, the world rulership, which is that for which Israel longed, but which is now seen in a different guise. The disciples' question and Jesus' answer in Acts 1.6–9 effect a transformed reading of prophecy not unlike that of Josephus. First there is the question, reflecting normal Jewish expectations:

> So when they had come together, they asked him, 'Lord, is this the time when you will restore the kingdom to Israel?'

Jesus reaffirms the expectation, but alters the interpretation:

> He replied, 'It is not for you to know the times or periods that the Father has set by his own authority. But you will receive power when the Holy Spirit has come upon you; and you will be my witnesses in Jerusalem, in all Judea and Samaria, and to the ends of the earth.'

This is at once linked to the kingdom promised in Daniel 7, since in the next verse Jesus is described in language proper to the vindicated, kingdom-receiving son of man:

> When he had said this, as they were watching, he was lifted up, and a cloud took him out of their sight.

Jesus is exalted as Lord in Judaea, in order then to be proclaimed as such in Rome. Luke's narrative proceeds to tell how the proclamation, not of Vespasian, but of 'another king' (Acts 17.7), finds its way through hardship,

---

[9] *Life* 110, etc.

[10] *War* 2.390; 5.362–74, 376–8, 412, etc.

[11] As we argued in chapter 10, Josephus is most likely referring to Dan. 2, 7 and 9 (above, pp. 312ff.).

[12] cf. e.g. *War* 3.399–408.

struggle, dispute and disaster until it, like Vespasian (only actually earlier), arrives in the capital:

> [Paul] lived there [i.e. in Rome] two whole years at his own expense and welcomed all who came to him, proclaiming the kingdom of God and teaching about the Lord Jesus Christ with all boldness and without hindrance.[13]

Every word counts in this brief closing statement. Paul is in Rome as a free man (more or less),[14] propagating the gospel freely. And the gospel is the news of the kingdom of Israel's god, that is, the message that there is no king but this god. More specifically, it is this Jewish message now crystallized as the news about Jesus, the Messiah, whom Paul announced as *kyrios*, Lord. And this subversive message could be proclaimed boldly and without hindrance. It looks as though, for Luke, Christianity has taken on the traditional role of Judaism: it is the divine answer to paganism. Here at last is a Jew living in Rome itself (i.e. not just hiding in the hills of Galilee), and declaring that, in and through Jesus, Israel's god is the sole king of the world. This is Luke's full answer to the question the disciples asked of Jesus in Acts 1.6. Israel's god has restored his kingdom for his people.

The shape of the narrative in the closing chapters of Acts is also most instructive. A quick comparison with Luke's gospel reveals a close parallel: Paul, like Jesus, goes on a long journey, ending up being tried before both Jews and Romans. The equivalent of the crucifixion, however, is not Paul's own death. Luke has no intention of making Paul a second redeemer, dying for the sins of the world. The crucifixion narrative in the gospel is echoed by the storm and the shipwreck in Acts; the resurrection, by the safe arrival of Paul and his party in Rome, leading to the open and unhindered proclamation of the kingdom of Israel's god, the god now revealed in the risen Lord Jesus.[15] The gospel of Jesus advances by the same means as Jesus himself had done; the cross and resurrection are stamped upon the life of the church that bears witness to them. But the work of the church *derives from* that of Jesus, and is not merely parallel to it.

Luke's framework for Acts provides an analogue to that of Josephus. In both cases, the writer claims that this is the true reading of scriptural prophecy.[16] In both cases, the new story radically subverts the old one: neither Josephus nor Luke suggests that there will be a fulfilment along the lines expected by militant Jews.[17] In both cases, Israel's god is responsible for a royal progress from Jerusalem to Rome. Vespasian, and Jesus, are proclaimed king, first in Judaea, then in Rome. In each case, Jerusalem is left in ruins, the rebellious counter-kingdom.

---

[13] Ac. 28.30–1.

[14] cp. Ac. 28.16 with 28.30f.

[15] cf. the close links between Lk. 24 and Ac. 28, e.g. Lk. 24.26, 44 with Ac. 28.23; Lk. 24.47 with Ac. 28.28.

[16] cf. Ac. 28.23–8; *War* 6.312–15.

[17] Some have seen hints of a further, more characteristically Jewish, fulfilment, in Lk. 21.24 and Ac. 1.7, and in what Josephus does *not* say in (for instance) *Ant.* 10.206–9, 263f. See above, pp. 304, 312ff.

c. Josephus consistently paints Rome, especially its highest officials, in a favourable light. True, the procurators who governed Judaea before the war draw from him some choice remarks, but these were easy to make: the men concerned, even if still alive, carried no weight in Rome under Vespasian or Titus.[18] Of these latter two, however, Josephus had nothing but good to say. Vespasian, he declared, was the one prophesied by Daniel. Titus, his son and heir, is to be exonerated from vice or malice. He simply did what was forced upon him by the folly of the Jewish rebels. In particular, he was not responsible for setting fire to the Temple.[19] These details are, of course, simply the tip of the iceberg. Josephus wrote the *War* intending to present it to Vespasian and Titus;[20] the whole work was designed to show the Jewish race in a favourable light in the eyes of the Flavian dynasty, and to explain the great catastrophe as the work of foolish rebels rather than as the effect of large-scale long-held national aspirations. At the same time, it is not implausible to suggest that Josephus intended to portray the Romans to the Jews, in Rome and elsewhere, in a good light. The Jews, he believed, would have to come to terms with Roman government; aristocrats like Josephus had learned to do that long ago, and it was time for the rest of the Jews to learn it too.

Luke's motives for writing his double work are complex, to be sure, but it seems highly likely that they include a similar measure of apologetic, perhaps in both directions.[21] It is quite true that if one started off simply wanting to address an apologia for early Christianity to Roman authorities, one would not necessarily produce a work like Luke-Acts. There is far too much material which seems extraneous; comparison with the work of Aristides, Justin and the other second-century apologists reveals enormous differences.[22] Equally, one cannot provide a complete explanation for Luke-Acts by the hypothesis that Luke was trying to persuade his Christian readers that they could rely on the Roman authorities. But if we take a step back from these two somewhat narrow conceptions of 'apologetic', a larger picture may emerge in which both are held together.

Whatever date we assign to the gospel, Luke was writing in a context where Judaism had for a long time been put in a special category by the Romans. As far as the Romans were concerned, the Jews were anti-social atheists. But they were not persecuted by Rome simply for being Jews; they had been granted the status of a permitted religion.[23] Luke's massive two-volume work can be read as claiming, among many other things, that this status ought now to belong to the Christians. They are the ones who have inherited the Jewish promises of salvation; they are the ones to whom accrues the status proper to a

---

[18] cf. e.g. his description of Gessius Florus, *Ant.* 20.252–8.

[19] *War* 5.97 (disclaiming flattery!); 5.319, 360f.; 6.236–66; cf. 6.324.

[20] *Apion* 1.51.

[21] See the discussions in e.g. Maddox 1982; Walasky 1983; Houlden 1984; Evans 1990, 104–11, with other refs.

[22] This is the strong point behind Barrett's often-quoted remark (1970 [1961], 63) to the effect that no Roman official would have waded through so much (to him) irrelevant material to reach so small an apologia. But this objection misses the point to be made below.

[23] cf. above, p. 154.

religion of great antiquity.[24] They, time and again, are shown to be in the right, to be innocent, even when magistrates have pronounced them guilty: from Jesus on the cross, to the apostles before the Sanhedrin, to Paul (in Philippi, before Agrippa and Festus, or on the boat), the Christians are declared to be innocent of the charges of sedition or subversion that are laid against them.[25] The Romans, meanwhile, are shown in as good a light as possible, with the exception of Pilate; as in Josephus, there is no need to whitewash a procurator long dead and discredited.[26] The Jewish revolutionaries, in both works, will reap their own reward. Josephus and Luke both speak up on behalf of what they regard as the true continuation of the true Israel: Josephus, arguably, on behalf of the Jamnia rabbis who were trying to reconstruct a new sort of Judaism; Luke, on behalf of the followers of Jesus.[27]

d. The fourth point is more controversial, but it seems to me to follow clearly from what has been said so far. Josephus did not just intend to write propaganda. Taking Thucydides as one of his models, he desired and attempted to describe events that had actually happened in the past.[28] As a well-taught Jew, that was how he perceived the world: the god of Israel had committed himself to acting within history, and even when events seemed to have disproved the hypothesis there was always some drastic proposal that could be made which would keep it afloat after all. At no point does Josephus lapse into an ahistorical worldview, into any idea that history is meaningless and that one might as well pursue a private spirituality or philosophy. The reason for his work is precisely that history matters, and that recent historical events appear to falsify the Jewish worldview. His task is to argue that in fact they do not, not that history is irrelevant. History is what matters; that is why he writes about it.

In the same way, Luke clearly intends to write about actual events that have taken place in the actual past. Whether or not he thus distorts Mark or the pre-Markan tradition is another question (depending of course not least on source-critical assumptions), to which we shall return. But Luke, of all the evangelists, is most clear in stating what he is about:

> Since many have undertaken to set down an orderly account of the events that have been fulfilled among us, just as they were handed on to us by those who from the beginning were eyewitnesses and servants of the word, I too decided, after investigating everything carefully from the very first, to write an orderly account to you, most excellent Theophilus, so that you may know the truth concerning the things about which you have been instructed . . .
> In the fifteenth year of the reign of Emperor Tiberius, when Pontius Pilate was governor of Judea, and Herod was ruler of Galilee, and his brother Philip ruler of the region of Iturea

[24] cf. Aune 1987, 136–8.

[25] Lk. 23.47; Ac. 5.33–9; 16.35–9; 26.32; 27.3, 43.

[26] cf. Lk. 13.1–3. This needs to be set alongside any sense that Luke is exonerating Pilate, based perhaps on 23.4, 14f.

[27] It is sometimes asserted that Luke reflects a time when the church was at peace in its social world, hence perhaps in the second century (e.g. Koester 1982b, 308–23); but the motive just described presupposes that some sort of appeal for permission to exist is still necessary. In any case, our lack of information about much of the second century gives us no cause to suppose that things were any easier for the Christian church then than earlier; if anything, as more people in authority came to hear of the new movement, it was more likely to be persecuted.

[28] cf. chs. 3–4 above, esp. pp.67f., 83f.

and Trachonitis, during the high priesthood of Annas and Caiaphas, the word of God came to John son of Zechariah in the wilderness . . .[29]

Anyone who wrote like that was intending to describe historical events. We have seen that this does not mean that Luke was 'objective' or 'neutral', any more than any other historian, ancient or modern. Luke was precisely a *historian*, not too unlike Josephus. Josephus sometimes tells a story in one way in one book and in another way in another book. This does not mean that the basic event did not happen, only that he is presenting it from a different angle. So, too, Luke is at liberty to tell two different versions of the same event: the classic example is the ascension, which seems to take place on Easter day in the gospel (24.51) and forty days later in Acts (1.3). This does not mean that he is making the whole thing up. For Luke, as for Josephus, history was the sphere of divine operation. Both writers held to recognizable variations within the Jewish worldview we have already sketched. The story of Israel is the subject-matter; how that story reaches its climax is the key question. There can be no suggestion, for either writer, that history had ceased to matter.

What, then, shall we say about the relationship between Luke and Josephus? One could, no doubt, mount an argument for dependence, and if this were to be done it seems far more likely that Luke would have had access to Josephus (supposing Luke to be writing late enough for that) than vice versa. But nothing hinges on such a relationship, which seems to me at best a remote possibility. Luke and Josephus are literary cousins, not child and parent or even uncle and nephew. The importance of their relationship, for our present purposes, lies in what we can now say about the nature of Luke's story.

(ii) The Form of Luke's Story

When John begins his work with the words 'In the beginning . . .', we know he is imitating the start of Genesis. When Matthew opens with 'The book of the generation . . .', we know he is evoking a regular link-phrase, again from Genesis.[30] But what is Luke up to? His formal and rounded prologue (1.1–4) evokes the literary openings of several works of the Hellenistic period, including, interestingly, two of Josephus' books.[31] He is intending this book to be placed, not in the first instance within the Jewish, biblical world (it will include that, but is not contained by it) but within the general world of serious Hellenistic writing, not least history-writing.[32]

As soon as this intention is announced, however, Luke leads us off to a small corner of the Hellenistic world, and introduces us, like Shakespeare

---

[29] Lk. 1.1–4; 3.1–2. On the Lukan prologue and its significance, see the commentaries of Nolland 1989, 4–12; Evans 1990, 115–36; and also Alexander 1986; Hemer 1989, 321–8; and Alexander 1993 (forthcoming).

[30] e.g. Gen. 2.4; 5.1; 10.1; 25.12, 19, etc.

[31] *War* 1.17; *Apion* 1.1–18: see the literature cited above, n.27.

[32] cf. Aune 1987, 139f. Mealand 1991 points out the close lexical similarity between Acts and Hellenistic historians such as Polybius.

beginning a play with a pair of minor characters, to Elizabeth and Zechariah, who are to become the parents of John the Baptist. No Roman emperors, no state occasions, no flourish of Hellenistic trumpets; just a pious elderly Jewish couple, in the latter days of Herod, longing for a child. For those with ears to hear, however, Luke is after all doing much the same as John and Matthew. This time, though, the allusion is not to Genesis, the creation of the world, but to 1 Samuel, the creation of Israel's monarchy. The innocent beginning to this great Hellenistic-style history masks the long-term subversive purpose.

The story of Elizabeth and Zechariah in Luke 1.5–25, 39–45, 57–80 is without a doubt intended to take the reader's mind back to the story of Hannah and Elkanah in 1 Samuel 1.1—2.11. This time it is the father (Zechariah), not the mother (Hannah), who is in the Temple, and he is himself a priest, not merely appearing before one as Hannah does before Eli. But the story has not only the same shape (the couple whose longing for a child is taken up within the divine purpose) but also the same triumphant conclusion (Hannah's song is picked up by both Mary's and Zechariah's). And in both there is a longer purpose waiting to be uncovered, a purpose which encompasses the message of judgment and salvation for Israel.

It is, first, a message of judgment. Samuel, Hannah's son, will announce to Eli that his days, and his son's days, are numbered, and that the ark of Israel's god will be taken away. John, Elizabeth's son, will declare divine judgment on Israel, a message which will be picked up by John's associate and successor, Jesus, in ever more explicit warnings against Jerusalem and the Temple. The story of David, which grows out of that of Samuel, is from the beginning a story of warning for the house of Saul; it is because Israel's god has decided to reject Saul that David is anointed in the first place. David's story progresses through his life as an outcast, leading a motley crew of followers in the Judaean wilderness, and reaches its initial climax at the moment when Saul and Jonathan are slain and he, David, is anointed king over Israel. And one of his first acts is to go to Jerusalem to take the city as his capital.[33] Jesus' story progresses through his wandering with his motley followers in Galilee and elsewhere, and reaches its initial climax when he comes to Jerusalem amid expectations that now at last Israel's god was to become king. This is a message of judgment for the existing regime.[34]

It is also a message of salvation. The highest moment in the story of Samuel is not his denunciation of Israel, but his anointing of the young David. On that occasion, according to 1 Samuel 16.13, 'the spirit of YHWH came mightily upon David from that day forward'. This was the David of whose son Israel's god said, later in the narrative, that he would establish his kingdom for ever, and moreover that 'I will be a father to him, and he shall be a son to me' (2 Samuel 7.14). The highest moment in the story of John is not his prophetic warning of wrath to come, but his baptism of Jesus, the occasion when, according to Luke 3.22, 'the Holy Spirit descended upon [Jesus] in bodily form like a dove', and when a voice from heaven announced to him, in words full of Davidic over-

[33] 2 Sam. 1.1ff.; 5.1–5; 5.6–10.
[34] Lk. 19.11, 28–48.

tones, 'You are my son, the beloved; with you I am well pleased.' Within the often-remarked artistry which enables Luke to draw a complete picture with a few strokes of his pen, he has said as clearly as he can that John the Baptist is playing Samuel to Jesus' David. And, with that, the Hellenistic and Roman kingdoms of the world, the world to which Luke's prologue so nobly addresses itself, receive notice that there is a new kingdom, a kingdom of Israel's god, and that the young man now anointed by his cousin in the Jordan is the king through whom it is to be set up.

The story of salvation continues in parallel. David's anointing is followed, in the narrative of 1 Samuel, by his taking on Goliath single-handed, as the representative of Israel. Jesus' anointing is followed at once by his battle with Satan.[35] David returns from his encounter to a rapturous popular welcome and the jealousy of Saul; Jesus returns from his encounter to make what is in effect a messianic proclamation in Nazareth, as a result of which he is rejected by his fellow-townsmen, though welcomed enthusiastically by others.[36] David eventually leaves the court to wander as a hunted fugitive with his band of followers; Jesus spends much of Luke's gospel travelling with his band of followers, sometimes being warned about plots against his life.[37]

None of this is to imply that the parallel with 1 Samuel is the only, or even necessarily the main, key to Luke's gospel. But the close similarity so far suggests strongly (against classical form-criticism) that Luke is not simply collecting bits of tradition and stringing them together at random; and it suggests, too (against the main forms of redaction-criticism) that the arrangement which Luke is adopting is not simply in pursuit of a home-made scheme of theology invented against a background of events at the start of the second Christian generation, but that he is telling his story in a particular way in order that it may say, as much by its shape and outline as by its detailed content: this story is the climax towards which Israel's history has been building all along.

When we turn to the end of the gospel, and to the start of Acts, the Davidic parallel is still clear. It is made explicit in, for instance, Luke 20.41–4 (the question about David's Lord and David's son); in the messianic material in the crucifixion scene (23.35–43); and in the note of fulfilment, particularly of royal hopes, in 24.26, 44–9. Luke is insisting that Jesus dying on the cross, and Jesus risen from the dead, is to be understood in Davidic categories. He has become king in the paradoxical way demanded as the true fulfilment of the Jewish scriptures. The start of Acts picks up exactly where Luke left off: now that the Davidic king has been exalted, the message of salvation is to go out to the world.[38] It is as though Luke were to say: after the death of David came his son Solomon, to whom the world came to hear wisdom, and to whom the nations were subject.[39] Now, after the death and resurrection of David's true son Jesus, the true Davidic kingdom has been established, and the nations will become

---

[35] 1 Sam. 17; Lk. 4.1–13.
[36] 1 Sam. 18.6–16; Lk. 4.14–44.
[37] 1 Sam. 19–30; Lk. 9.51—19.28, with e.g. 13.31–3.
[38] cf. the prominent Davidic theme in Ac. 2.25–36; 4.24–30.
[39] cf. 1 Kgs. 4.21–34; 10.1–29; cp. Pss. 72; 89.19–37, etc.

subject to it. The end of Acts, as we remarked earlier, completes this picture, with the kingdom of Israel's god announced in Rome openly and unhindered.

It is important to stress that this is not simply 'typology'. Typology takes an event from the past and sets it in close relation to a parallel event in the present time. Luke's Davidic theme is indeed typological—Jesus really is seen as the 'true David'—but this is neither random nor arbitrary: it is held firmly *within a historical scheme*. Jesus' life, death and resurrection, and the sending of the divine spirit, are the end-product of the long story that began with David and the divine promises made to him. The similarities, the parallels, are there because of the overall story, not vice versa. Luke is telling the story of Jesus *as* the fulfilment, the completion, of the story of David and his kingdom.

From this perspective, we can see that a complete account of the nature of Luke's story must include two elements which are normally thought of as quite distinct. On the one hand, we have the Davidic story as just outlined, and with it the sense that Luke is conscious of telling, in a manner similar to Josephus, how it was that Israel's long story reached its paradoxical fulfilment. On the other hand, we must take full account of the recent arguments that the gospels, and perhaps Luke in particular, belong within the broad genre of Hellenistic biography. This possibility, long ignored because of the dogmas of form-criticism, is now supported in several studies too detailed for discussion here.[40]

How do these genres—the Jewish story reaching its climax, and the Hellenistic *bios*, the life-story of a human individual within the Greco-Roman world—fit together? The answer, I suggest, lies in Luke's grasp of a central theological point, which enables him to tell the story of Jesus in the way that he does. Like so many Jews (and presumably well-taught proselytes) of the period, Luke believed that, prior to Jesus, Israel's story had yet to reach its climax. The exile was not over; redemption had yet to appear.[41] It was appropriate, within that context, that he should tell the story of the one life in which, he believed, the exile became most truly exilic, sin was finally dealt with, and redemption at last secured. But at the same time Luke clearly grasped the equally important Jewish belief that when Israel was redeemed the whole world would be blessed. Israel's salvation was not to be a private affair only: it was to be for the benefit of all. The good news of the established kingdom would have to impinge on the Gentile world. Since, therefore, he believed that this good news had taken the form of the life, and particularly the death and resurrection, of one human being, and since this was a *Jewish* message for the *Gentile* world, Luke blended together two apparently incompatible genres with consummate skill. He told the story of Jesus *as* a Jewish story, indeed as *the* Jewish story, much as Josephus told the story of the fall of Jerusalem as the climax of Israel's long and tragic history. But he told it in such a way as to say to his non-Jewish Greco-Roman audience: here, in the life of this one man, is the Jewish message of salvation that you pagans need.[42]

---

[40] cf. e.g. Stanton 1974; Talbert 1977; Moule 1982 [1962] 9–13, with other references; Dihle 1983; Berger 1984, 352ff.; Aune 1987, chs. 1–4; Hemer 1989, 91–4; Lemcio 1991; and esp. Burridge 1992.

[41] cf. chs. 9–10 above.

[42] This is, I think, in line with Dihle 1983, though with a more developed sense of the Jewish story.

As such, Luke's story subverts the mainline stories of both the worlds that he is drawing on and addressing. First, he has told the story of Israel without allowing it to lapse into the closed, ahistorical world of the ghetto, or into the violent revolutionary world of Josephus' Fourth Philosophy. He has shown, rather, that the kingdom of Israel's god, which is inaugurated in public history, powerfully subverts the pagan world and its kingdoms without using armed force. To put it another way, Luke sees the eschaton, expected by many first-century Jews, as having already occurred but as being still to occur. The End has happened in Calvary, Easter and Pentecost; one need no longer fight for it, since it has already happened. At the same time, the End is yet to come, with the return of Jesus (Acts 1.11); history, including the history of Jesus' people as the renewed people of Israel's god, must continue, with all its ambiguities and puzzles. If this double End enables Luke to avoid the false antithesis of the ghetto and the sword, it also enables him to avoid the bland triumphalism of Eusebius, who in turn subverts Luke's story by combining the story of the kingdom of Israel's god with the story of the kingdom of Constantine.[43]

Luke, then, has retold the story of Israel in such a way as to subvert other first-century tellings of it. Or, more precisely, he has told a story which he intends to be the *true climax* of the story of Israel. He presupposes the story from Adam, through Abraham, through David, to the exile and beyond, highlighting especially the promises of salvation through David's heir. Just as 1 Maccabees told the story of the revolt against Antiochus Epiphanes in such a way as to legitimate the Hasmoneans as the true priest-kings of Israel,[44] Luke has told the story of Jesus in such a way as to legitimate him as the true Davidic king. Luke's gospel is intended to be the final scene in the story of the creator god and his covenant people, and hence the penultimate scene (hence the need for Acts) in a larger drama still, that of the creator and the world.[45] Only if we read it in this light can we understand the significance of the narrative. In Griemasian terms, Luke presents his gospel as the vital Topical Sequence of a larger drama, and Acts as inaugurating the Final Sequence. He presupposes, as the Initial Sequence, the story of the world and Israel to date:

---

[43] The irony is that the church has often read Luke as if he were simply an earlier edition of Eusebius, thus misunderstanding him just as radically as Paul is misunderstood if he is seen as an earlier edition of Luther.

[44] cf. esp. 1 Macc. 14.4–15, telling the story of Jonathan's reign (in the 140s BC) as the fulfilment of glorious prophecies.

[45] Tannehill 1985b is right to argue that, in terms of the story of Israel, Luke's narrative is essentially tragic (rather than anti-Semitic). Cf. above, pp.74ff.

This story has reached an impasse: Israel is herself unredeemed, and cannot bring the divinely planned salvation to the world. Luke then tells the story of Jesus as the Topical Sequence:

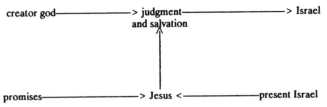

The result is that he can at last set out, in Acts, the story of how the Final Sequence achieves what the Initial Sequence could not:

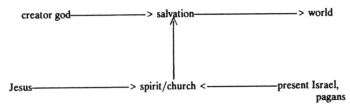

The narrative analysis of Luke's whole work, therefore, demonstrates that he, like Josephus in the *War*, intends his complex story to be seen as the completion of a larger one. The story of Israel has reached its basic fulfilment in the story of Jesus, in order that its long-term further goal may be attained through the mission of Jesus' spirit in the church. Luke's story, being a recognizable form of the basic Jewish story, intends to subvert the ways of telling that story which were available in his own day. His writing of a second volume does not represent, as has so often been imagined, a declining away from a fully Jewish and indeed apocalyptic worldview. The history that has come to a close with the death and resurrection of Jesus is not the history of the world as a whole, but the history of one vital phase in the purposes of the creator god. Precisely because that phase has been successfully concluded, world history now becomes the theatre of the final act in the drama.

If Luke has subverted Israel's story, he has also, second, subverted the pagan one, by telling (part of) the story of the pagan world without losing his grip on Jewish theology. This theology, with its firm base of monotheism, election and eschatology, claims that there is a way of understanding and responding to the world which is better than the way offered in paganism, just as there is 'another king, this Jesus'. There is a true creator god, of whom the pagan idols are but parodies. This true god, made known in the history of Israel and now supremely in Jesus and the divine spirit, claims the world as his own. Luke has written a *bios* which subverts the normal thrust and context of pagan *bioi*.

The story Luke tells, therefore, only means anything if it takes place within public, world history. At the same time, his story only means anything if it has to do with theology. Recent studies are right to emphasize that Luke is a historian *and* a theologian: the split between those two always was a projection of post-Enlightenment dualism on to an unwilling first-century text. We can now see, within that double truth, a further doubling on each side. Luke, as a historian, inhabited the worlds of both Judaism and Hellenism. As a theologian, he remained firmly Jewish while claiming to address the world of paganism. Like all well-taught Jews, he believed that one could understand paganism from the perspective of creational monotheism, as one who knows what a sphere is can understand what a circle is; and that, if one was called by the creator god to a task *vis-à-vis* the pagan world, one could accomplish that task by subverting the world's story with the true Jewish one. That, I suggest, is precisely what Luke has done.

3. The Scribe and the Plot: Matthew's Story

'Every scribe who has been trained for the kingdom of heaven is like the master of a household who brings out of his treasure what is new and what is old.' These words, concluding the collection of parables that falls midway through Matthew's gospel, have been seen often enough as a kind of signature, a hint that in this book we have exactly that: things new and things old, a treasure-house of scribal lore.[46] But how is this treasure laid out? What sort of a book has 'Matthew' written? What sort of story does he tell? What is its narrative structure, its plot?[47]

We have already seen that the synoptic gospels are to be classified, at one level at least, as Hellenistic-style 'lives' or biographies. But we have also seen that Luke, while emphatically belonging in this category, also situates himself within the world of the Jewish story, and particularly the story of how the god of Israel 'has looked favourably on his people and redeemed them' by raising up 'a mighty saviour for us in the house of David his servant' (Luke 1.68f.). Now if there is one thing commonly recognized about the gospel of Matthew, it is that the book has a thoroughly Jewish flavour. It is often treated as a representative of that hard-to-define entity, 'Jewish Christianity', though it is sometimes pointed out that Matthew's gospel, for all that it affirms the abiding validity of the law (5.17–20), agrees with Mark in the abolition of the kosher laws (15.10–20), and contains some of the harshest words against the Jewish leaders anywhere in the New Testament (23.1–39).[48] The situation is clearly not straightforward. How are we to get at the heart of Matthew's carefully crafted work?

A strong case has recently been made out by Mark Powell for seeing an overall plot for Matthew's gospel in terms of the programmatic statement in

[46] Mt. 13.52; cf. e.g. Strecker 1983 [1966], 77.

[47] For a stimulating attempt to read Matthew through the lens of narrative theology, see Thiemann 1989 [1985]; for a recent discussion of Matthew's structure, highlighting his concern with the disciples, see Doyle 1988.

[48] Matthew as 'Jewish Christian': e.g. Dunn 1977, 246ff. Against: e.g. Pettem 1989. For judicious assessments of the current debating-points, cf. Stanton 1992, chs. 5–7. On the debate about the meaning of 'Jewish Christianity' see ch. 15 below.

1.21, where the angel tells Joseph: 'You are to name him Jesus, for he will save his people from their sins.' The gospel can be understood as the story of how this is accomplished, through the paradoxical sub-plots whereby Jesus is successfully opposed by the Jewish leaders on the one hand, and unsuccessfully supported by the disciples on the other.[49] This is a kind of comedy-through-tragedy: the sub-plots look as though they will prevent the hero from accomplishing his mission, but in fact they precipitate him into the real—and ultimately successful—battle, which was all along not against the Jewish leaders but against Satan. Powell points out that this story, as far as Matthew is concerned, is part of a larger story: the gospel ends with a beginning, as the disciples are sent out to preach to the whole world.[50] But this is not all. The very sentence which is found to be thematic for the main plot—the prediction that Jesus 'will save his people from their sins'—presupposes a previous story as well. It assumes that the plot of the gospel comes towards the end of a larger and longer plot, in which 'his people' fall victim to 'their sins'. And it does not take much imagination, much reading in Matthew, or much knowledge of the Jewish background, to see what story that is. It is the story of Israel, more specifically the story of exile.

Matthew's first chapter has long been a puzzle to modern Western readers. The genealogy (1.1–17) appears to be about as unexciting an opening as it could be. But to those with eyes to see (itself a Matthean theme, as in 13.16), it tells the story that must be grasped if the plot of the whole gospel is to be understood. We begin with Genesis, literally and metaphorically: Matthew's opening words, *Biblos Geneseos*, mean literally 'the book of Genesis', or, as in Genesis itself (2.4; 5.1), 'the book of the generation . . .' Matthew starts off by deliberately hooking his own plot into the larger plot, the story of the people of Abraham, Isaac and Jacob.[51]

The structure of the genealogy shows where he will lay the stress. Other Jewish books of the period structured Israel's history into significant periods;[52] Matthew is following a standard tradition, though adapting it to his own ends. His three periods of fourteen generations may well be intended to hint at *six* periods of *seven* generations, so that Jesus starts the seventh seven, the climactic moment of the series.[53] Abraham is the start: this is not the story of the world as a whole, as in Luke (whose genealogy goes back to Adam), though Matthew has not forgotten the world outside Israel, as we shall see. It is the story of Israel. The next focal point is David: Matthew's story, like Luke's though with a different emphasis, focuses on Jesus as the true David, the Messiah. The third focal point is unexpected: the exile. This is not so regular a

---

[49] Powell 1992, drawing together the insights of Edwards 1985, Matera 1987, and Kingsbury 1988.

[50] Powell 1992, 203f.

[51] On 1.1 cf. Davies and Allison 1988, 149–55.

[52] e.g. *1 En.* 93.1–10; 91.12–17; *2 Bar.* 53–74.

[53] Davies and Allison 1988, 162 object that if Matthew had meant this he should have said so; but there was nothing special about the seventh, the twenty-first, or the thirty-fifth generation for him to focus on them. I doubt if educated first-century Jews would have had difficulty in making the mathematical connection.

marker within Jewish schemes, but for Matthew it is crucial. As we saw, most Jews of the second-temple period regarded themselves as still in exile, still suffering the results of Israel's age-old sin. Until the great day of redemption dawned, Israel was still 'in her sins', still in need of rescue. The genealogy then says to Matthew's careful reader that the long story of Abraham's people will come to its fulfilment, its seventh seven, with a new David, who will rescue his people from their exile, that is, 'save his people from their sins'. When Matthew says precisely this in 1.18–21 we should not be surprised.

But as soon as we think of Israel's god delivering his people from their sins, through the agency of a human being, our minds are drawn back to a different figure. The story which is not mentioned explicitly in the first chapter, but which looms up behind the introduction like a great mountain, is the story of Moses and the exodus, of Sinai and the covenant, of the journey to the promised land. This is how the story of Abraham's people is to find resolution.[54] When the new David comes to save his people from their present exile, it will be like a new exodus, a new covenant.

These are the themes that enable us to make sense of the extremely intricate story that Matthew has told. Much has been made, in Matthaean scholarship, of the various 'markers' which Matthew has put into his text, indicating (so it is often thought) major divisions of material. Perhaps the best known is the marker at the end of the five large blocks of teaching:

> And it came to pass, when Jesus finished these words . . .
> And it came to pass, when Jesus finished instructing his twelve disciples . . .
> And it came to pass, when Jesus finished these parables . . .
> And it came to pass, when Jesus finished these words . . .
> And it came to pass, when Jesus finished all these words . . .[55]

Much ink has been spilled on the precise significance of these 'markers'.[56] Too much, in my view, has sometimes been claimed for them. The attempt to make each block of teaching, and perhaps the narrative material that goes with it, correspond to one of the books of the Pentateuch produces strained and distorted readings. Yet so obvious a refrain, in a book so clearly crafted and sculpted, and, moreover, one which proclaims on page after page that it chronicles the way in which the scriptures were fulfilled, cannot be ignored. Is there a way of understanding this structure which does justice to the text itself?

I suggest that the first and last of the blocks of teaching provide a clue.[57] The passages in question are chapters 5–7 and 23–5, two blocks of three chapters each. These, as it appears more particularly from the number of verses involved (111 in chapters 5–7, 136 in 23–5) are significantly longer than the three blocks of teaching in the middle (10.1–42; 13.1–52; 18.1–35).[58] The great

---

[54] cf. Ex. 2.23–5; 6.2–8; etc.

[55] Mt. 7.28; 11.1; 13.53; 19.1; 26.1.

[56] The major 'Pentateuchal' reading of these sections was that of Bacon 1930; see the discussions in Davies 1964, 14–25, and Davies and Allison 1988, 58–72, acknowledging the importance of the fivefold structure but not drawing any great significance from it.

[57] Unlike some scholars, I take the last 'block' of teaching to include ch. 23.

[58] The last of these looks somewhat artificial, since it includes a certain amount of dialogue, and one long parable, suggesting that Matthew was constructing a fourth 'discourse', in preparation for his fifth and climactic one, but with less of a tight thematic centre.

discourses of 5–7 and 23–5 each focus initially on a repeated phrase: 5.3–11 gives the celebrated nine 'beatitudes', and 23.13–33 the contrasting seven 'woes':

Blessed are the poor in spirit
Blessed are those who mourn
Blessed are the meek
Blessed are those who hunger and thirst for righteousness
Blessed are the merciful
Blessed are the pure in heart
Blessed are the peacemakers
Blessed are those who are persecuted for righteousness' sake
Blessed are you when people revile you . . . for my sake

Woe to you, scribes and Pharisees, hypocrites, because you shut up the kingdom of heaven
Woe to you, scribes and Pharisees, hypocrites, because you . . . make the proselyte twice as much a child of hell as yourselves
Woe to you, blind guides, who say 'whoever swears by the temple, it is nothing'
Woe to you, scribes and Pharisees, hypocrites, because you tithe herbs and abandon the more serious matters of the law
Woe to you, scribes and Pharisees, hypocrites, because you cleanse the outside of the cup
Woe to you, scribes and Pharisees, hypocrites, because you are like whitewashed tombs
Woe to you, scribes and Pharisees, hypocrites, because you build the tombs of the prophets

This arrangement seems to me deliberately stylized. If Matthew has indeed marked off the five discourses deliberately, it is easy to see that he might well have arranged them in a roughly chiastic structure, with the first and the last, at any rate, corresponding to one other.[59] But what is the effect of setting these 'blessings' and 'woes' in parallel with each other?

The Pentateuch is indeed the clue, but not, I suggest, the Pentateuch seen as a sequence of five books, nor simply in a scheme of slavish repetition. Rather, I propose the Pentateuch seen as *covenant*, and summarized as such in Deuteronomy 27–30, part of the great concluding speech of Moses to Israel as the people gather on the east of the Jordan before going in to possess the land.[60] There, the covenant between YHWH and his people is set out in terms of a list of *curses* and a list of *blessings*. The curses, sixteen of them in all, are elaborated in Deuteronomy 27.15–26 and 28.16–19 and amplified in 28.20–68, ending with the threat of certain exile if the people do not keep the covenant. The blessings, four of them, are set out in 28.3–6, and amplified in 28.1–2, 7–14. These are then summarized again in Deuteronomy 29, in which Moses reminds the children of Israel of the events by which they have come to this point, and in chapter 30, in which he promises that, even if the curse comes upon them because of their sin, they will be rescued and the covenant renewed. He stresses that the commandment which they have been given is

---

[59] Another indication of this may be found in the parable of the houses on rock and sand (7.24–7), which foreshadows the judgment parables of 25.1–12, 14–30 and 31–46 (cf. too 7.21–3 with 25.11f., 44f.), and which also, in speaking of the great house which is to fall, looks ahead to ch. 24 as a whole.

[60] cf. above, pp. 260–2.

not too hard, nor too far away: it is 'very near to you; it is in your mouth and in your heart for you to observe' (30.14). The speech ends (30.15–20) with the great choice that faces the people:

> See, I have set before you today life and prosperity, death and adversity. If you obey the commandments of YHWH your God that I am commanding you today, by loving YHWH your God, walking in his ways, and observing his commandments, decrees, and ordinances, then you shall live and become numerous, and YHWH your God will bless you in the land that you are entering to possess. But if your heart turns away and you do not hear, but are led astray to bow down to other gods and serve them, I declare to you today that you shall perish; you shall not live long in the land that you are crossing the Jordan to enter and possess. I call heaven and earth to witness against you today that I have set before you life and death, blessings and curses. Choose life so that you and your descendants may live, loving YHWH your God, obeying him, and holding fast to him; for that means life to you and length of days, so that you may live in the land that YHWH swore to give to your ancestors, to Abraham to Isaac, and to Jacob.

The concluding chapters of Deuteronomy (31–4) contain Moses' final blessing, his going up the mountain to see the land which the people would possess, and his eventual death.

Matthew, I suggest, had the entire scene in mind as he arranged his material into its eventual form. The theme of the whole passage in Deuteronomy is thoroughly germane to the complex theme of his first chapter: Israel has indeed fallen into the curse of exile because of her sins, and now the story of Abraham's people is to be brought back on course by a new exodus, by the renewal of the covenant. As a result, Israel is again faced with a choice. Life or death, curse or blessing; the house on the rock or the sand; the wise or the foolish maidens; the sheep or the goats. Jesus, like Moses, goes to his death with the promises and warnings still ringing in his people's ears. After his resurrection, Jesus, like Moses, goes up the mountain and departs from his people, leaving them with a commission to go in and possess the land, that is, the entire world (28.16–20). And, if my suggestion is correct, Matthew has woven this covenantal choice into the very structure of his gospel, portraying it as the choice set before his contemporaries by Jesus, and thereby himself setting the same choice before the church of his own day. There is a way by which Israel can be rescued from her exile, can receive the promised forgiveness of sins rather than the ultimate curse. It is the way of following Jesus. Those who come by this way are not a *new* Israel, as though created suddenly from nothing. They are the true descendants of Abraham, Isaac and Jacob.

Matthew's story, I suggest, is structured so as to bring out this entire theme. The motifs of plot noted by Powell and others are on target, but need to be set within this wider framework. Matthew presupposes a telling of the Jewish story according to which Israel has failed, has ended in exile, and needs a new exodus; and he undertakes to show that this new exodus was accomplished in the life, death and resurrection of Jesus. He does this at a multiplicity of levels: the often-remarked 'fulfilment' passages ('All this took place to fulfill what had been spoken by the Lord through the prophet . . .')[61] are simply the tip of a very large iceberg. Matthew's plot and structure presuppose the entire Jewish

---

[61] Mt. 1.22; 2.5f., 15, 17f., 23, etc.

story-line to date. They claim to be bringing about that of which Moses spoke in Deuteronomy 30. They are not simply a collection of types, historical precedents arbitrarily repeated. They claim to be the continuation and proper completion of the whole history itself. Jesus, for Matthew, is both the new David and the new Moses, but also something more. Moses had promised that

> YHWH your God himself will cross over before you. He will destroy these nations before you, and you shall dispossess them. Joshua also will cross over before you, as YHWH promised ... Be strong and bold; have no fear or dread of them, because it is YHWH your God who goes with you; he will not fail you or forsake you.[62]

For Matthew, Jesus (the name is of course the Greek translation of 'Joshua') is the fulfilment of both parts of this prophecy. He is Emmanuel, Israel's god in person, coming to be with his people as they emerge from their long exile, remaining with them still as they go on to possess the land (1.23; 28.20). And the land they now possess is the whole world; as the wise men from the east came to pay homage to Jesus, as the centurion demonstrated a faith which Jesus 'had not found in Israel', and as the Canaanite woman had 'great faith',[63] so the ministry of Jesus, which at the time was only to the 'lost sheep of the house of Israel',[64] will result in a salvation for 'all nations'. In a manner very similar to Luke, Matthew clearly understands the plot of his story as a Topical Sequence which presupposes an Initial Sequence and issues in a Final Sequence. There is a slight difference: the opening scene is already set up in terms of Israel's need of rescue. We move straight to the Topical Sequence:

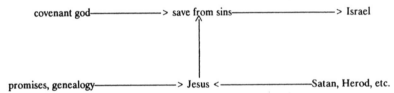

This, however, only makes sense *as a plot* if it is part of a larger whole. In that larger whole, which forms an assumed Initial Sequence, Israel is a means of blessing to the world:

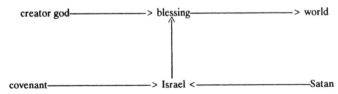

This Initial Sequence has been thwarted because of the story implicit in the genealogy: Abraham's family have sinned, and have gone into exile. Jesus, by rescuing his people from this plight, enables the Final Sequence to come about at last:

[62] Dt. 31.3–6.
[63] 2.1–12; 8.5–13; 15.21–8.
[64] 15.24; cf. 10.5f.

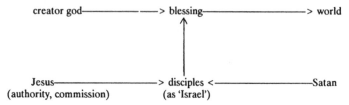

It is therefore vital that we recognize Matthew's blend of genres, as we recognized Luke's earlier. There is, once more, no doubt that Matthew has written the story of Jesus as a Hellenistic-style *bios*, a biography.[65] But at the same time he has told it as the continuation and climax of the story of Israel, with the implicit understanding that this story is the clue to the story of the whole world. And if this is so, there can be no doubt, either, that he intends it to be read *both* as instruction for the church of his day *and* as history. He has located himself firmly within the basic Jewish worldview, in which, as we saw, the idea of a non-historical understanding of the divine dealings with Israel was a contradiction in terms. Once we understand both the plot and the structure of Matthew's gospel, we are forced to reject the false antithesis which has for so long dominated the world of *Redaktionsgeschichte*. Of course Matthew arranged and ordered his material in such a way as to address the church of his day. But the story which he tells only means anything if it has to do with things that actually happened.[66] And if these things actually happened, then Matthew's story subverts the Jewish worldview of his time, whenever that time may have been.

4. 'Let the Reader Understand': The Story of Mark

Mark, at first blush the easiest of the synoptics, retreats from the advancing interpreter like a rainbow's end. A simple outline, it seems; eight chapters to explain who Jesus is, eight to explain that he is going to die. An abrupt beginning and a mysterious end, granted; but a straightforward account in between. But we reckon thus without the literary critics. The abruptness of the opening, and the darkness of the ending, permeate the whole. Mark is a book of secrets, of veils, of mysteries.[67]

What is required, therefore, is understanding. Mark says as much:

---

[65] See above; esp. Burridge 1992, 191–219.

[66] This point is made by Strecker 1983 [1966], 72: Matthew sees the ministry of Jesus 'as a unique event, temporally and geographically distant from his own situation'. Strecker, perhaps predictably, thinks this an artificial 'historicizing' of an originally non-historical message.

[67] See esp. Kermode 1968, 1979. I am among the minority who think that the opening and closing of the original are lost, and therefore unavailable for us as evidence of Mark's intention. On 1.1 (and possibly 1.2a?) as redactional see such diverse writers as Moule 1982 [1962], 131 n.1; Koester 1989, 370; and 1990, 13, citing also Schmithals, and arguing that the use of the word 'gospel' for a written account of Jesus' life belongs to the second century at the earliest. I drafted this brief account of Mark before I saw Fowler 1991, who had the same idea for a title, and before I had come to grips with Myers 1990, who has similar ideas about Mark and apocalyptic.

To you has been given the secret of the kingdom of God, but for those outside, everything comes in parables, in order that they may indeed look, but not perceive . . .
They were utterly astounded, for they did not understand about the loaves, but their hearts were hardened.
Then do you also fail to understand?
Do you still not perceive or understand? Are your hearts hardened? Do you have eyes, and fail to see? Do you have ears, and fail to hear? Do you not remember? . . . Do you not yet understand?
Let the reader understand.[68]

These warnings, even on the surface, resonate at three levels. Jesus' disciples are those who have grasped the secret, and then they are those who have not grasped it. Mark's readers, too, have a secret to grasp, which is, to be sure, cognate with the others, but presumably not identical. Much effort has gone into hypotheses purporting to explain what was 'really' going on in all of this: Mark's 'disciples', it is suggested, are thinly veiled portraits of leaders in his own church, and he is setting out to correct their theology.[69] Behind these theories lie others more hoary. Mark, some suggest, is constructing out of thin air a narrative version of a theory which explained the basic problem of early Christianity, as follows. (i) Jesus did not think he was Messiah, or divine; (ii) the early church thought he was both; therefore (iii) something appeared very wrong with the whole business; therefore (iv) somebody, after the early period but before Mark, had the bright idea that Jesus *had* thought these things after all, but had kept them secret; then (v) Mark used this theory as the basis for his narrative.[70] The theory falls at its first supposition, since Wrede, its proponent, lumped 'Messiah', 'Son of Man', 'Son of David' and 'Son of God' together, assuming quite wrongly that Mark intended them all to refer, undifferentiatedly, to Jesus as the divine figure of the later creeds;[71] at its second and third, since precisely what the earliest Christians thought is very difficult to assess; and at its fourth, since there is no evidence whatsoever of such a pre-Markan theory; at its fifth, since if Mark intended to portray a consistent secret he made a poor job of it. Such theories have, however, glimpsed something that remains to be explained. Mark is indeed a book of mystery, which invites the reader to grasp a secret lying beneath the surface. How are we to explain its narrative force? What sort of a story is it?[72]

Once again, we may begin by noting that, though Mark's book is clearly more than a typical Hellenistic biography, it is certainly not less.[73] Whatever he thinks he is doing, he has done it by telling the story of Jesus in a manner recognizable in its Hellenistic environment. But, as with Matthew and Luke, there are reasons for thinking that he was also writing within a Jewish framework of thought. And I suggest that the model which best describes what he

[68] Mk. 4.11f.; 6.51f.; 7.19; 8.17–21; 13.14.
[69] e.g. Weeden 1985 [1968]; Tannehill 1985a [1977]; see the balanced assessments in Best 1986; Hooker 1991, 12f.
[70] This theory was invented by William Wrede 1971 [1901]. It is fully discussed in Tuckett 1983a; Räisänen 1990b [1976].
[71] cf. Moule 1975; 1982 [1962], 110, 131.
[72] On Mark as story see Rhoads and Michie 1982; Best 1983; van Iersel 1989 [1986].
[73] Burridge 1982, ch. 8; cf. already e.g. Schulz 1985 [1964], 164.

was doing is the much-misunderstood category of apocalyptic. That is where mysteries are propounded and revealed, where secrets unavailable elsewhere find their paradoxical elaboration.

This at once needs a caveat in terms of recent scholarship. Some have argued that Mark was 'deeply anti-apocalyptic';[74] others, that he was writing precisely that: an apocalypse.[75] I agree with neither assessment, because both are, to my mind, based on a misreading of what 'apocalyptic' actually is, either as a literary genre or as a way of viewing the world. Both the judgments quoted assume that 'apocalyptic' is deeply dualistic, coming to terms with a failure of expectation in the present world and so looking for a totally new world to break in and destroy the old one. Mark, on this view, either rejected a Jewish dualism in favour of a Christian stress on history (Schulz) or embraced this dualism once the early church's expectation had been disappointed (Mack).[76] Since most modern theologians disapprove of dualism, this key interpretative question has the result of making Mark either a hero or a villain.[77]

I argued in chapter 10 that this reading of 'apocalyptic' is fundamentally misleading. As a literary genre, 'apocalyptic' is a way of investing space-time events with their theological significance; it is actually a way of affirming, not denying, the vital importance of the present continuing space-time order, by denying that evil has the last word in it. It is only when such literature is read without a fully historical understanding that it is in danger of being mistaken for the Stoic philosophy, which, unlike early Judaism, really did envisage the space-time universe being dissolved at some future date. A measure of this possibility of misreading, in the first century as in the twentieth, is provided when Luke takes steps to avoid it. Mark writes one of his most cryptic sentences, and adds 'let the reader understand'; Luke, knowing presumably that his readers will *not* understand, translates the code into plain statement.[78] When, therefore, I speak of Mark as 'apocalyptic', I do so in the sense for which I have argued earlier, not in the sense in which the debate has normally been carried on.

The strength of the suggestion has already been noted: Mark, supremely among the gospels, highlights the notion of a secret to be penetrated, of a mystery to be explored and grasped. From this point of view, Mack is quite right: the whole book, not only chapter 13, is 'apocalyptic'.[79] But a classic

---

[74] Schulz 1985 [1964], 166.

[75] e.g. Perrin and Duling 1982 [1974], 89, 233–61; Kee 1977, 64–76; Mack 1988, 325–31, cf. 330: 'Mark's Gospel did not just happen to contain an apocalyptic speech, it forced an apocalyptic view of the reader's history and times.'

[76] Schulz (1985 [1964], 165) has a revealing comment: 'Vv. 1–23 [of Mk. 13] are completely de-apocalypticized by Mark and related to history.' This shows the huge distance between the normal conception of 'apocalyptic', which Schulz espouses, and that for which I argued at length in ch. 10 above—and indeed from the surface of the text. Mk. 13.1–23 is all about false teachers, wars, earthquakes, synagogues, persecutions, and fleeing to the mountains—in other words, thoroughly this-worldly, historical events. Any suggestion that the text had a previous life in which it referred to non-spatio-temporal matters is a figment of the critical imagination.

[77] Mark the Villain is a major theme in Mack 1988: cf. e.g. 14, 368–76.

[78] Mk. 13.14; Lk. 21.20.

[79] Mack 1988, 330.

apocalypse, as we saw earlier, was not a book about the end of history, of the space-time universe.[80] It was a book which, in a complex blend of myth and metaphor, told the story of Israel's history, brought it into the present, and pointed forward to the moment when the forces of (this-worldly) evil would be routed and the (this-worldly) liberation of Israel would finally take place. It offered the clue to the *interpretation of* history, not the escape from it. Like Elisha at Dothan, Mark intends to draw back the veil for a moment, allowing the heavenly reality to be seen in the midst of the earthly.[81] Mark has told the story of Jesus in such a way as to say: the glorious expectation of Israel, as expressed in just these Jewish writings and traditions, has been fulfilled, paradoxically, in the death and resurrection of Jesus, and is to be further fulfilled (or, perhaps, has recently been further fulfilled) in the destruction of Jerusalem.[82] The gospel subverts the normal Jewish apocalyptic tellings of Israel's story, not by renouncing the ideas and literary modes of apocalyptic, but by redirecting its central thrust. Jerusalem is the great city that has opposed the true people of Israel's god; like Babylon, this city will fall as the sign of the liberation of that true people. The suffering righteous ones who hold on to their god-given calling and are vindicated in the great reversal are not those who rely on the intensification of Torah, but are quite simply Jesus and his people.

Mark's new-style apocalypse functions, therefore, on at least two levels. Clearly, chapter 13 dominates the scene as a recognizable piece of apocalyptic writing in the full Jewish style, replete with dark allusions to scripture, and, like 4 Ezra, reaching its climax in a rereading of Daniel 7. But it was always a mistake to think of Mark 13 as a 'little apocalypse', as though the chapter would come away clean from its context, leaving a non-apocalyptic Mark, and perhaps a non-apocalyptic Jesus, cleared of complicity with a dark non-Christian Jewish genre.[83] Mark has been leading the eye up to this point for several chapters, certainly since 8.34—9.1 and arguably much longer; and it is only in the light of chapter 13 that the sense Mark wishes his readers to obtain from the court scene in chapter 14, and from the crucifixion scene in chapter 15, can be grasped. Mark 13 is not simply about something *other than* the life, trial and death of Jesus; it is the lens through which those earth-shattering events (let the reader understand) must be viewed. To put it the other way round, it invests those earthly events with their heavenly significance.

But Mark 13 is not the only obvious 'apocalypse' in the gospel. Were it not the case that the parables had been read for so long as 'earthly stories with heavenly meanings', and then for so long as stories making only one point, without any suspicion of 'allegory', the parallel between Mark 4.1–20 and the

---

[80] For possible exceptions, see ch. 10 above.

[81] 2 Kgs. 6.15–19.

[82] The question of the gospel's date is, for the moment, secondary.

[83] On this cf. e.g. Lane 1974, 444–50, with older literature; Hooker 1991, 297–303. On Mk. 13 in general see now the fascinating discussion of Theissen 1991, ch. 3, arguing that a version of the chapter existed in written form around AD 40. This makes the similar proposal of Wenham 1984 (arguing for a date before 50) look comparatively mild.

fairly standard 'apocalyptic' style would surely have been obvious long ago.[84]
First, we have a story about a sower and some seed; it might have been about
an eagle and its wings, or perhaps about four beasts coming up out of the sea,
but the point is the same. Then we have a short dialogue in which the hearers
proclaim themselves unable to understand what is being said, and the story-
teller declares that a great mystery is hereby revealed to certain hearers and to
them alone. The story-teller then takes the strange narrative piece by piece,
bringing out its hidden meaning, which turns out to apply directly to the current situation of the people of god. Finally, as we look back over the story, we
realize what its shape has been: three phases of tragedy, one of vindication. It
might have been four beasts and a figure like a son of man; it might have been
numerous wings on an eagle, and then a figure that looked like a lion. It was,
in fact, three sowings of seed which bore no fruit, and one sowing which bore a
great deal. The point is the same. Mark 4.1–20 is, ironically, one of the most
obvious, and at the same time most neglected, examples of 'apocalyptic' writing anywhere in the New Testament.

With this difference: that the speaker is not an angel, but Jesus; that the
listeners are not great seers of old, but disciples who are to spend much of the
rest of the story being told off for incomprehension, and who will eventually
run away and leave Jesus alone. Mark's apocalypse has come to life in a way as
startling in the first century as it is incomprehensible to modern critics. Instead
of telling the story of Israel as a whole by means of apocalyptic imagery, he has
told *the story of Jesus telling the story of Israel* by such means. To this extent the
book is, as it were, a meta-apocalypse.

But the deepest level at which Mark is to be considered an apocalypse is the
level for which these two passages, Mark 4 and 13, are simply signs and symp-
toms. It is often observed that Mark, like some novelists and film-makers
today, structures his gospel not least around certain climactic moments, which
demand to be set in parallel and treated as mutually interpretative. Thus:

> And immediately, as he was going up out of the water, he saw the heavens opened, and the
> spirit descending like a dove upon him; and there came a voice out of the heavens: You
> are my son, the beloved one, in you I am well pleased.
> Peter answered and said to him: You are the Messiah.
> And there came a cloud overshadowing them, and there came a voice out of the cloud: This
> is my son, the beloved one; listen to him.
> Again the high priest asked him and said to him: You are the Messiah, the son of the
> blessed?
> When the centurion who was standing by saw that he thus breathed his last, he said: Truly,
> this man was the son of god.[85]

Two of these passages are themselves 'apocalyptic' in flavour. The 'opening
of the heavens' (in the first) is a regular way of speaking of the disclosure of

---

[84] I shall discuss parables more fully in a subsequent volume.

[85] Mk. 1.10f.; 8.29; 9.7; 14.61; 15.39. In 14.61 I follow the Greek exactly: it is only the question
mark which differentiates Caiaphas' first clause from Peter's statement in 8.29. This point is
often made; I first had it brought to my notice about twenty years ago, in a lecture by
M. D. Hooker. The centurion's statement in 15.39 is sometimes read as '*a* son of god'; but this is
a confusion. In Greek the complement does not take the definite article.

truth normally hidden, and the cloud (in the third) is an obvious sign of the divine presence. The other three passages are full of ambiguity. We should resist the idea that Peter's confession of Jesus' Messiahship was regarded by Mark (or for that matter by Jesus) as a blundering mistake (or, for that matter, as a confession of *divinity*), but it is also clear from the sequel that neither Peter nor the other disciples had grasped what Mark at least believed was the true nature of Jesus' Messiahship: that it would subvert Israel's national hope and lead to Jesus' crucifixion. Equally, the high priest asks his question with heavy irony. He does not believe that Jesus is the Messiah, and Jesus' affirmative answer does nothing to change his mind. The centurion is more ambiguous still. Mark may well intend his reader to hear the echoes of later Christian faith: here, he is saying, is the first man to look on the dying Jesus and confess him son of god. But as it stands the passage demands to be read, like Caiaphas' question, on at least two levels. Neither Mark nor his readers could seriously imagine that a centurion, himself involved with the business of executing Jesus, would make a fully comprehending, or comprehensive, Christian confession of faith.

The five passages, taken together (one at the start, two in the middle, three at the end of the gospel), stand out not least because for most of the rest of the time the theme of Jesus' Messiahship, his divine sonship, is conspicuous by its absence. (I take it as read that 'son of god' in these passages means first and foremost 'Messiah', whatever other connotations may have been later added to the phrase.[86]) Mark tells the story of Jesus as the story of a Galilean prophet, announcing the kingdom of Israel's god, summoning Israel to change her direction, that is, to repent.[87] The baptism, the transfiguration, and the words of Peter, Caiaphas and the centurion are moments when the veil is lifted, the eyes are opened, and, like Elisha's servant, the reader sees the horses and chariots of fire round about the prophet. *Mark's whole telling of the story of Jesus is designed to function as an apocalypse.* The reader is constantly invited by the gospel as a whole to do what the disciples are invited to do in the parable-chapter, that is, to come closer and discover the inner secret behind the strange outer story. The story-line is common enough, against the background of Josephus: a Jewish prophet, a would-be Messiah, is abandoned by his (already tiny) group of followers, arrested, tried and executed by the occupying forces. Mark's telling of this story is totally subversive: this was actually the coming of the kingdom of Israel's god, the event of which prophets had spoken in golden terms, that for which Israel had longed, revolutionaries had fought, martyrs had died. The truth (from Mark's point of view) is so staggering, not least because of what is implied all through, and eventually is stated plainly enough in chapter 13. The coming of the kingdom does not mean the great vindication of Jerusalem, the glorification of the Temple, the real return from exile envisaged by the prophets and their faithful readers. It means, rather, the desolation of Jerusalem, the destruction of the Temple, and the vindication of Jesus and his people. Jerusalem and its hierarchy have now

---

[86] On the meaning of 'son of god' see e.g. Hengel 1976; Moule 1977, 22–31.
[87] Jesus as prophet: 6.4; his proclamation of the kingdom, and summons to repent: 1.15.

taken on the roles of Babylon, Edom and Antiochus Epiphanes in this stark retelling of their story. They are the city whose fall spells the vindication of the true people of Israel's god. The prophecies of rescue from the tyrant have come true in and for Jesus and in his people. When this city falls they must get out and run; this is their moment of rescue, salvation, vindication.[88]

It is tempting to go on to suggest, on this basis, a possible date and location for the writing of Mark. But that is a task for another day, another book. For the moment, our purpose is simply to enquire: what sort of story is being told here? The answer is surely clear. Mark has written a Christian apocalypse, in which the events of Jesus' life—so clearly events of Jesus' life that the work shares the characteristics of a Hellenistic *bios*—form the vital theatre in which Israel's history reaches its moment of 'apocalyptic' crisis. From then on, true, that history is to be re-evaluated. But once again, as with Luke and Matthew, it is clear that Mark's story only makes sense if we presuppose as its backdrop this whole history of Israel, apocalyptically conceived. Mark's opening sequence already shows this. Luke at least takes time and trouble to locate his readers on a map of world events, and to introduce his main theme with a series of human scenes full of intrinsic interest. Matthew opens with a genealogy that is as fascinating to a first-century reader as it is opaque to many today. But Mark opens with a stark sequence of events: within twenty verses we are introduced to John, witness Jesus' baptism, hear the kingdom announced, and watch the call of the first disciples. We are expected to work out where we are in the middle of all this activity; the drama makes sense against a particular background. The only background which will do is the turbulent, 'apocalyptic' story of Israel. Mark, like Matthew and Luke, has written a story which presupposes a larger story of which it will provide the strange but crucial final chapter. In that larger story, and hence in Mark's own, the world, and history, are neither condemned nor abolished, but redeemed. Let the reader understand.

5. Synoptic Gospels: Conclusion

All three synoptic gospels, we have seen, share a common pattern behind their wide divergences. All tell the story of Jesus, and especially that of his cross, not as an oddity, a one-off biography of strange doings, or a sudden irruption of divine power into history, but as the end of a much longer story, the story of Israel, which in turn is the focal point of the story of the creator and the world. What is more, they are telling this complex story, not simply for antiquarian or theological interest, but in such a way as to make it the foundation-story, the historical 'founding myth', for their communities, communities whose very existence depended on their being called by the same god to carry on the same story in its new phase. Their theological, practical and pastoral concerns came together in this: that they should announce, and integrate congregations into,

---

[88] cf. Jer. 51.26 with Mk. 13.2; Isa. 13.10 and 34.4 with Mk. 13.24; Isa. 52.11f. and Jer. 51.6, 45 with Mk. 13.14–17; Jer. 51.46 with Mk. 13.7f.; Zech. 2.6 (in context) with Mk. 13.27; and of course Dan. 7.13f. with Mk. 13.26.

the events which had taken place in recent memory concerning Jesus of Nazareth. We must now, drawing the threads together, spell this out a little further.

First, the story the evangelists tell is not 'about' something else. It *is* the thing 'about' which everything else revolves. This, they are saying, is the centre of world history. It is not an example of an abstract doctrine (the love of god, for instance), as though that were the 'real' thing. Like the writers of the Old Testament, the evangelists are thinking as good creational monotheists. What goes on in the creator's world, and, within that, in Israel, is what matters. To this extent, the Reformers were in tune with the gospel writers in their insistence on the unique and unrepeatable nature of the events, even though, ironically, they could not sustain this emphasis as far as the ministry of Jesus, which they made merely exemplary.[89]

Second, therefore, the fact that the evangelists believed themselves to be bringing the story of Israel to its great climax, the turning-point from which at last the long history of the world would change course, means inescapably that they believed themselves to be writing (what we call) history, the history of Jesus. This was not something they might conceivably have been doing as it were on the side, while doing something else as their 'real' concern. History was where Israel's god must act to redeem his people. The whole Jewish creational monotheistic tradition revolts against the idea that when the decisive event happens it should be a non-event, or that the 'significance' should consist not in events in the external world but in 'principles' or other timeless things that can be deduced from them. Jewish monotheism has been used in recent years, illegitimately in my view, as an argument against an early high christology. What it really cuts against at this point is the dualism that separates Israel's god from his world as though he were not its creator and redeemer. If we are to think Jewishly, and to see the evangelists as doing so too, we cannot but conclude that they intended to refer to Jesus and his historical ministry. Whether or not they were successful in this is a question to be addressed elsewhere.

We should note carefully what would result from saying anything else. It is perfectly conceivable, and it certainly happened in the case of some intertestamental novelettes such as Judith and Tobit, that stories with the regular Jewish form and basic content could be told and written without having an actual or necessary historical referent. They would have the function, however, of sustaining and keeping alive the Jewish hope, which itself remained historical: that Israel's god would act within history at last, as he had done at the exodus, to deliver his historical people from historical bondage.[90] But if *all* Jewish stories were fictions, and known to be fictions (in the normal, popular sense of 'fictions'), the whole worldview would collapse upon itself. If someone in, say, AD 75 were to tell a Jew a fiction (in the same sense) and to claim that in this very story the long hope of Israel had finally been fulfilled, the response would have been not just that he was a liar, but that he had not understood

---

[89] cf. ch. 1 above.
[90] See chs. 8, 10 above.

what the Jewish worldview was all about. Even Josephus, with his radical redrawing of the fulfilment of Israel's hope, kept that fulfilment *within history*; that is one of the reasons why his reinterpretation is so scandalous. If, then, the gospels are deliberately telling how the story of Israel reached its climax in the story of Jesus, they are either intending to refer to historical events, or they are saying that creational monotheism was wrong after all, and that the Platonist world of abstract ideas, divorced from space and time—which epitomized the paganism against which the Jews had struggled—had been the true world all along.

Third, the evangelists, most noticeably Luke and Matthew, regard the time of the ministry of Jesus as a special time, unlike the time before or since.[91] This, as we shall see later, results in the fact that they do not attempt to project back into Jesus' lifetime the major controversies of the early church, and that on the contrary they preserve material vital for understanding what was going on in the ministry—but only relevant for the church in so far as it was vital for the church to know precisely what happened *in* that ministry. Faced with this evidence, we can say one of two things. We can either suggest that the evangelists invented this distinction between Jesus' time and their own, it not having been perceived thus before they wrote. Or—and the fact that they all seem to have come to the same conclusion and expressed it in different ways tells strongly in this direction—we can claim that the ministry of Jesus *always* appeared to the early church as a special time, unlike that before and after, and that the evangelists are simply reflecting, and reflecting upon, this fact.[92] This latter solution seems to me far the more likely. The evangelists believed themselves to be living in the last Act of the divine drama, and were conscious that, living there, they were writing about the Act which had immediately *preceded* theirs, and upon which their own Act totally depended.

Narrative analysis of the synoptic gospels as wholes thus makes it clear that, so far from their telling the Jesus-story as a retrojection of their own Christian experience, that very experience included, as a vital point, the sense of dependence upon unique and unrepeatable events which had taken place earlier. The evangelists were not—of course they were not!—trying to narrate 'bare facts' without interpretation. As we saw in chapter 4, that positivist dream, nowhere realized because in fact totally unrealizable, must give way to the more sensitive account: their intention was to tell stories about events which really took place, and to invest those stories with the significance which, within their total worldview, they irreducibly possessed.

Fourth, we have now uncovered a solid reason for the evangelists' wanting to give their readers actual information about an actual historical person. This goes beyond the argument advanced by Stanton, Moule and others: Christians who had not known Jesus personally would be bound to want to know *about* him, what exactly happened, and so forth.[93] This is undoubtedly true, but it

[91] cf. Perrin and Duling 1982, 289, 303f.; Strecker 1983 [1966]; Conzelmann 1960 [1953]; Moule 1967, 56–76, 110f.; etc.

[92] On the pre-gospel traditions cf. ch. 14 below.

[93] Moule 1982 [1962], 4, 10f., 122f., and the summary on 133; Stanton 1974.

appears somewhat *ad hoc* as an explanation, and does not fully meet the theological proposals of those who doubt the evangelists' (or the tradition's) intention to speak of Jesus rather than to speak in non-historical myths. If they were telling the story of Jesus *as* the climax of Israel's story, there is every reason, over and above biographical curiosity, why they would have intended that their stories should have a clear historical referent.

Fifth, a strong argument may be mounted on the basis of the significance that was attached by the early Christians to the resurrection.[94] We saw in chapter 10 what it was that first-century Jews were expecting: the raising to life of all the righteous dead, as part of the dramatic moment, within history, at which Israel's god would return to Zion and restore the fortunes of his people. Now it must be said clearly that at first sight the coming to life of a single dead body, within the midst of a history which in other respects was proceeding as though nothing had changed, would be, though of course exceedingly striking, quite insufficient to make Jews of the time declare that the longed-for redemption, the eventual release from exile, had in fact occurred.[95] Nor, it should be added, would such an event have at once the significance that so many modern scholars have imagined. In the ancient Jewish world, as in the modern Western one, for someone who had been certifiably dead to become visibly alive again would mean that the world was indeed a stranger place than one had imagined; it would not at all justify a claim that the person to whom this odd event had happened was therefore the saviour of the world, the 'son of god', or anything else in particular. If, coming closer to the topic, one of the two *lestai* crucified along with Jesus had been raised to life a few days later, we may suppose it very unlikely that he would have been hailed in any such way, or that anyone would deduce from the event that Israel's fortunes had now been restored, that the kingdom of Israel's god was indeed inaugurated, and so forth. This forces us to ask: could the belief that someone had been raised from the dead, whatever precisely was understood by that, have produced the results it did—*unless certain things were known, and continued to be known, about the one who had thus been raised after having been crucified?*

We could press this point another way. Suppose that Jesus had been known to have been a person of bad character. If, for example, he had been a known drunkard or philanderer, or if he had had the reputation of preaching for personal financial reward, then the whole idea that his death on a Roman cross had somehow, through his coming to life again, achieved significance of whatever sort for the lives of others, let alone the crowning significance attached to those events in the New Testament, would simply be laughable. If, again, he had simply been a teacher of great timeless moral platitudes, it may be doubtful whether he would have been crucified in the first place; but even if we get over that hurdle, we may be sure that his death, even if followed by a strange resurrection, would not have been understood as his life's greatest achievement, but rather its sad curtailment. Any resurrection that might be claimed for such a figure would hardly carry the meaning that Israel and the

---

[94] This argument has some analogies with that of Moule 1967, chs. 1, 3–4.
[95] cf. Mt. 27.52.

world were now renewed. It might at best be the occasion for yet more teaching, perhaps now including stories about a life 'beyond' (noticeably absent from the teaching ascribed to the risen Jesus in the gospels and Acts). But let us suppose that (within a context of first-century Jewish belief that the covenant god was to intervene within the course of history to deliver his people from their oppression and exile) Jesus had done and said certain things which led people, in however muddled a fashion, to believe that somehow their god was achieving this purpose in and through his work. In such a case, the beginnings of post-resurrection belief in the saving significance of his death, articulated first as the rescue of Israel from exile, is far more credible. The cross and resurrection, in short, are clearly central to virtually all known forms of early Christianity. But the rise of that early Christian understanding is only comprehensible on the basis that certain things continued to be known, as history, about the one who (among so many others) was crucified outside Jerusalem and who (unlike any others before or since—a fact of some significance) was declared by his followers to be alive shortly afterwards. The resurrection thus vindicates *what Jesus was already believed to be*; it cannot be the sole cause of that belief which sprang up around it.

More particularly, if the resurrection was believed to be part of that complex of events through which the covenant god would restore the fortunes of his people, any telling of a 'resurrection' story about Jesus could only make sense in a context of *telling Israel's story in the form of Jesus' story*. It would not do simply to announce that there was a man who had died, even who had died a particularly brutal death, and who had then been found to be alive. That is not the point. The gospel of the early church, of Paul, of the evangelists, is that the promises of the Jewish scriptures had come true in the resurrection. That is why Paul and others keep insisting that Jesus' death and resurrection happened 'according to the scriptures', or in fulfilment of them.[96] People often write of such phrases (sometimes to commend them, sometimes to condemn) as if they meant that the early church could find proof-texts to show that Israel's god had predicted the resurrection long before. Either one then searches for texts and comes up with small bits and pieces like Hosea 6.2 and (perhaps) Job 19.25; or, giving that up as a bad job, one writes that the early church did not have any particular texts in mind, but held the general belief that Israel's god had been at work in Jesus, so of course it must be 'according to the scriptures', even if one could not say precisely which scriptures were in mind. As we saw in chapter 8, however, the point of such ideas is that Israel's scriptures *as a whole* tell of the covenant; of the exile as the result of Israel's god punishing his people for their sins; and of the great 'return' that will happen when that dark period is finally over and done. What the early church is saying, when telling the story of Jesus' resurrection and announcing it to the world as the summons to obedient faith, is that the history of, and promises to, Israel had come true in Jesus, that in his death he had taken the exile as far as it could go, and that in his resurrection he had inaugurated the real return from that real exile. Once again, therefore, we are driven to the conclusion: to

[96] e.g. 1 Cor. 15.3–4, etc.

announce the resurrection, and to do so (in shorthand) 'according to the scriptures', is *to tell Israel's story in the form of Jesus' story*. Underlying the church's proclamation to the world is Israel's unshakeable belief that her history, just like her geography, was at the centre of the created universe. Her god was the creator of the world.

It is therefore to be expected that the very earliest church would tell stories about Jesus in such a way as to express the belief that in him Israel's history had reached its climax. That was their *raison d'être*. When we find early formulae which say precisely that—1 Corinthians 15.3f. is the best example—we should not be surprised. The early church told stories about Jesus because that was the only way to bring out the significance they perceived within the events of his life, death and resurrection. They told *Israel*-stories about him, stories whose form and style, as well as whose detailed content, shouted that this was the dramatic climax of Israel's whole history. In doing this the early Christians were of course legitimating the sort of movement they perceived themselves to be part of. They were also, of course, undergirding their own personal religious experience. But in so doing they were also, necessarily, telling *stories about Jesus of Nazareth*. In order, then, to articulate 'resurrection faith', with the meaning which it had—the only meaning it could have had, granted the worldview out of which all the early Christians came—it was necessary that they should tell stories about Jesus, stories which represented events that actually happened, stories which by their form and content explained that Israel's history had been brought, in this way and no other, to its god-intended climax.[97]

Sixth, the evangelists, in telling the story of Jesus as the climax of Israel's story, are thereby implicitly saying that this story is not the absolute end. It cannot be. It is, rather, that which enables the final end now to come into sight. It is the end of the central section of the story, which brings it into its home straight, though not yet to the finishing-line itself. There is now a further task, that of bringing the world into subjection to its creator, through the redeemed Israel; and this further task is as yet unrealized. The evangelists were not, then, expecting the imminent end of the space-time order. That is a simple misreading of their use of Jewish apocalyptic language, whose real referent is the end of the present *world order*.[98] As a family is a different entity after the death of the grandfather, or the marriage of the eldest child, so, only much more, the world is a different place (so the evangelists are saying) because its creator has acted decisively to bring to a climax his plan for rescuing it from its corruption. This is only what one would expect, if the Jewish story is indeed the focal point of the world's story. This, as we have argued, can be seen in terms of the narrative analysis of the gospel stories themselves.

What must therefore be said about the literary genre of the gospels, which is after all a principal key to how they are to be read?[99] As we have seen, they tell the story of Jesus in such a way as to convey the belief that this story is the

[97] See further ch. 14 below.
[98] cf. ch. 10 above.
[99] cf. Moule 1976, 100–14; Lemcio 1991; Baird 1991; etc.

climax of Israel's story. They therefore have the *form* of the story of Israel, now reworked in terms of a single human life. Since, then, Israel's story has been embodied in one man, the gospels have also the form of what we must call quasi-biography. Modern study of ancient secular biography has shown, as we saw, that the gospels are *at least* biographies. But they are more than that. They are, in fact, Jewish-style biographies, designed to show the quintessence of Israel's story played out in a single life. Their nearest analogue at that level is the martyr-literature, where the focus of attention is not on the date of someone's birth or the colour of their hair, but on their fidelity to YHWH, their consequent suffering, and their hope of vindication.

What Jesus has done, the evangelists are saying, is to bring to its climax not simply the chain of the stories of individual faithful Jews but the whole history of Israel. The gospels are therefore the story of Jesus *told as the history of Israel in miniature*: the 'typology' which is observed here and there by critics is simply a function of this larger purpose of the evangelists. Matthew gives us, in his first five chapters, a Genesis (1.1), an Exodus (2.15), and a Deuteronomy (5–7); he then gives us a royal and prophetic ministry, and finally an exile (the cross) and restoration (the resurrection). What more could we want? In the gospels we witness the history of Israel with her god, the story which, Israel believed, was the real though secret history of the creator and the world. We witness this story *told as* the story of the creator, Jesus and Israel. It is not surprising that scholars have had difficulty putting this whirlwind into the bottle of post-Enlightenment categories. The wind must be allowed to blow where it wills.

But if this is so, it means that the gospels are not simply Hellenistic-style biographies, modified slightly in a Jewish direction. They are Jewish stories; indeed, they claim to be The Jewish Story. Because that story has now to do with an individual human being, and because the story of this human being must now be announced to the Gentile world, as part of the fulfilment of the story itself, it must be told precisely *as a biography*, albeit a biography with a difference. Had the story, and the underlying worldview, been of a different order, the gospels could have been written more like *Pirke Aboth* or the *Gospel of Thomas*. They could have been collections of sayings. They were not. They are the Israel-story told as biography, modified in the direction of the secular genre (Luke especially shows evidence of this) but without using the secular genre as either the base or the goal. That is the grain of truth in the old critical contention that the gospels were not biographies. This explains, better than any other solution, both the similarities and the remaining differences between the gospels and their secular analogues.[100]

The gospels, then, were written to invite readers to enter a worldview. In this worldview, there is one god, the creator of the world, who is at work in his

---

[100] This is not far, perhaps surprisingly, from the view of Käsemann (1969 [1965], 97): the 'incomparable literary form of the Gospels' is that they 'present us in a highly unique fashion with something like the life of a man, from an eschatological perspective and according to an eschatological interpretation'. Of course, Käsemann understands by 'eschatology' something rather different from what I have set out above.

world through his chosen people, Israel. Israel's purpose, say the evangelists, is now complete, and her own long bondage ended, in Jesus. The gospels' major focus on the death and resurrection of Jesus is *not* to be explained as the reading back of 'later Christian theology' into a story whose 'biographical' intent should have kept such reference to a minimum. The evangelists were not downplaying the significance of the life and mission, the aims and achievements, of the one who was thus crucified and raised, but were emphasizing these latter events as the proper and necessary climax of precisely the type of story that was being told. The evangelists' theological and pastoral programme has in no way diminished their intent to write about Jesus of Nazareth. It actually demands that they do just that. If they do not, they deceive, promising the reader a worldview which they do not in fact deliver. If modern or post-modern readers want to rule the evangelists' worldview out of court as a possible one for us today, that is a quite different matter, to be debated on other grounds. Even postmodernism cannot be made an excuse for committing historical anachronisms.

The question remains, however: is this way of telling the story an innovation, sprung on Christianity at the start of the second generation? Has Mark, no less than Matthew or Luke, 'historicized' a message that originally had little or nothing to do with history, let alone the history and expectations of Israel? That was the major argument of Bultmann and his school. This movement seemed to run out of steam in the post-war period, with the 'New Quest', and then the 'Third Quest', increasingly emphasizing the essential Jewishness of Jesus' own message and of the early Christians' theology and mission.[101] But Bultmann's views have had a sustained revival in recent years. Scholars like Mack, Crossan and Cameron have argued for a Gnostic or Cynic early Christianity, into which the synoptics came as tidiers up, as historicizers, who put the clock back to a Jewish way of thinking which had been alien to the first Christian generation.[102] In order to assess this thesis, for the moment simply at the level of the early Christian story, we must move initially into waters every bit as turbulent as those of synoptic study. We have only one fixed point in the literature of very early Christianity, and that is Paul.

6. Paul: From Adam to Christ

Paul has not often been studied in terms of the stories he tells. But there is every reason to suppose that his letters will yield a good deal to such investigation: 'letters have stories, and it is from these stories that we construct the narrative worlds of both the letters and their stories'.[103] As Norman Petersen has shown in his ground-breaking book *Rediscovering Paul*, a flood of light can be thrown on any letter, be it a brief papyrus note or a polished gem like Paul's letter to Philemon, if we consider it in terms of two levels. First, there is the

---

[101] See Neill and Wright 1988, 379–403.
[102] cf. Mack 1988; Crossan 1973, 1983, 1991; Cameron 1982; Koester 1990.
[103] Petersen 1985, 43.

poetic sequence, the order of things as they appear in the text itself. Second, there is a *referential sequence*, the assumed and/or reconstructed order of events within the total narrative world of the letter.[104] This analysis can take place at a comparatively trivial and easy level. Philemon (it is normally thought) had a runaway slave, Onesimus, who became Paul's convert; Paul sent him back with a subtle letter urging Philemon to accept him as a brother in Christ. As readers, we presuppose Onesimus' arrival and its consequences. This is the close-up narrative world of the letter.[105] These events do not occur in this order in the letter itself, but are related tangentially to the 'poetic' sequence of the text.

At this level, Petersen has in one sense simply provided a clear methodological label for something that most historical critics have tried to do anyway. The difference is that the second level of analysis is not to be labelled 'history' without more ado, but rather, at least in the first instance, 'story'. We are concerned at this stage with the *narrative world of the text*, not, unless we make a further move, with the narrative world of public history. The study of this narrative world enables Petersen then to mount a sociological analysis of the complex implied relationships between Paul, Onesimus and Philemon. The letter to Philemon is obviously the easiest Pauline letter to use in such methods. One could in principle apply them, however, to the other letters: say, to the Corinthian correspondence, which would involve a good deal more labour, and might not, I suspect, offer hope of getting much further than commentators using more traditional descriptions of their task. The narrative world of the Corinthian correspondence—the implied sequence of events from Paul's first visit to the projected final one—has been the subject of intense research and speculation for some time.[106] But the possibility of reading Paul's letters in search of narrative worlds is inviting when we come to ask about the kind of story which formed his *larger* narrative world—that is, when we come to put Paul on the map of the large early Christian stories that we have been reconstructing throughout this chapter. What were the stories which gave narrative depth to Paul's worldview, which formed an irreducible part of his symbolic universe?

It would be possible to construct from the Pauline corpus a narrative world of Paul's own life and experience. Such a referential sequence would move from his upbringing as a Pharisee, through his call/conversion, to his missionary and pastoral work, with its attendant suffering; and it would constantly presuppose a future closure, in terms either of transformation at the return of the Lord, or of death and subsequent resurrection. That, we may safely say, was the narrative world upon which Paul drew to make sense of his day-to-day experience. At that level, his personal narrative world should be seen as a

---

[104] cf. Petersen 1985, 47–9.

[105] cf. Petersen 1985, 65–78, 287–302, arguing among other things for the necessity of supplying at least a hypothetical 'closure', an ending to the implicit narrative. The general points are valid even if a different reconstruction of the narrative world of Philemon is accepted, e.g. that of Knox 1935; Houlden 1970, 225f.; or Winter 1984, 1987; see Wright 1986a, 164–70; Nordling 1991.

[106] Among recent literature cf. Georgi 1986 [1964]; Fee 1987, 4–15; Wright 1991a, ch. 6.

deliberate and subversive variant on the Jewish story of the devout Pharisee: Paul tells it as such in, for instance, Philippians 3.1–11. This, he says, is how he has found true covenant membership, true justification, true membership in the people of Israel's god.[107] The significance of this may be grasped if we realize what sort of stories Paul is *not* telling. Though he behaved like a wandering Cynic or Stoic preacher or philosopher, to the extent that he was travelling round the Mediterranean world telling people about a way of life that challenged their present comfortable one, the story he told about himself, had a totally different shape from that of the narrative world we can discover behind, say, the *Discourses* of Epictetus. The analogies between Paul and the Stoics remain essentially superficial. As soon as we reach implicit narrative, and with it the level of worldview, we must see that Paul's story is essentially the Jewish story, albeit *manqué*—or, as he would have said, straightened out.

The basis on which he would have made such a claim is not difficult to elucidate. Within all his letters, though particularly in Romans and Galatians, we discover a larger implicit narrative, which stands out clearly as the true referential sequence behind the poetic sequence demanded by the different rhetorical needs of the various letters. Like his own story, this larger narrative is the Jewish story, but with a subversive twist at almost every point. Paul presupposes this story even when he does not expound it directly, and it is arguable that we can only understand the more limited narrative worlds of the different letters if we locate them at their appropriate points within this overall story-world, and indeed within the symbolic universe that accompanies it.[108]

The story begins with the creation of the world by the one god, a good and wise god. So far, so Jewish, though Paul does not say, as 4 Ezra would later, that the world was made *for the sake of Israel*.[109] It continues, equally Jewishly, with the creation and fall of Adam and Eve, as the eponymous parents of all humankind. Skipping over Noah, Paul's story highlights Abraham, whom he sees, in company with Jewish tradition,[110] as the beginning of the divine answer to the problem of Adam. Unlike Jewish tradition, however, Paul insists that the covenant promises to Abraham held out to him not just the land of Israel but the entire *kosmos*, the world.[111] Abraham's child and grandchild, Isaac and Jacob, become the carriers of the promise, while Ishmael and Esau are left behind; again Paul subverts the normal Jewish telling of the story, since he insists that this process of narrowing down the promise-bearing family continues on *beyond* Jacob.[112] Israel's god then calls his people out of Egypt under the leadership of Moses, giving them the Torah. For an orthodox Jew, then as now, Torah was the great gift which signalled Israel's special status and vocation. For Paul this remains true, but with a dark twist: the special status and

---

107 On Phil. 3.2–11 cf. Wright 1991a, 88. Cf. too Gal. 2.15–21, with its deliberate paradoxes ('I through the law died to the law . . .' etc.).

108 For much of what follows, see Hays 1983, 1989; Wright 1991a, *passim*, and 1992b. I intend to substantiate these remarks fully in volume 3 of the present series.

109 4 Ezra 6.55–9; 7.11; cf. *2 Bar.* 14.19; 15.7; 21.24; *T. Mos.* 1.12f.

110 cf. pp. 262ff. above.

111 Rom. 4.13.

112 Rom. 9.14ff.; contrast e.g. *Jubilees*.

vocation is that Torah should *convict Israel of sin*, so that Israel should be cast away in order that the world might be redeemed.[113] All that Torah does within Israel, even to the best of its adherents, is to convict them of their sharing in Adam's sin, so that the highest they can attain to is the level—the irony is heavy at this point—of the best of the pagan philosophers.[114]

Torah holds out to Israel life and death, prosperity and exile, and then (in Deuteronomy 30) speaks of new life the other side of that exile/death. Israel chooses exile/death; the prophets warned that this would happen, and happen it did. Again, Paul is on common ground with his kinsmen according to the flesh. But again he subverts the Jewish story from within. The end of this exile, and the real 'return', are not now future events to be experienced in terms of a cleansed Land, a rebuilt Temple, an intensified Torah. The exile came to its cataclysmic end when Jesus, Israel's representative Messiah, died outside the walls of Jerusalem, bearing the curse, which consisted of exile at the hands of the pagans, to its utmost limit.[115] The return from exile began when Jesus, again as the representative Messiah, emerged from the tomb three days later. As a result, the whole complex of Jewish expectations as to what would happen when the exile finished had come tumbling out in a rush. Israel's god had poured out his own spirit on all flesh; his word was going out to the nations; he had called into being a new people composed of all races and classes, and both sexes, without distinction. These major features of Paul's theology only make sense within a large-scale retelling of the essentially Jewish story, seen now from the point of view of one who believes that the climactic moment has already arrived, and that the time to implement that great achievement is already present. Paul fitted his own personal narrative world into this larger framework. His own vocation, to be the apostle to the Gentiles, makes sense within a narrative world according to which Israel's hopes have already come true.

Clearly, there remained a fulfilment yet to come. Paul, like Luke, believed both that the End had come and that the End was yet to come. 1 Corinthians 15 is the fullest version we have of his retelling of the still-future part of the Jewish story. It is a redrawn apocalypse, which again only makes sense in terms of the story of Israel, the story we studied in chapter 8, now seen in a new light. The same could be said of the 'apocalyptic' passage in Romans (8.18–27).[116] The narrative needs an ending, and Paul hints at it in these and other passages: the creation as a whole will be set free from its bondage to decay. The

---

[113] Rom. 9.14–29; see Wright 1991a, 152, 198f., 210–13, 239–48.

[114] Rom. 7.7–21: see Wright 1991a, 196–200, 217–19, 226–30. To these arguments should be added the following point. Rom. 7.15–20 ('the good I want, I do not . . .') clearly reflects a *topos*, a line of thought that was widely current in the pagan world of Paul's day: cf. e.g. Ovid *Metamorph.* 7.19ff.; Epictetus *Disc.* 2.26.1–5 (cp. too 3.7.18; 4.1.147); Plautus *Trin.* 657; other refs. in Hommel 1961–2. These passages may well all look back to Arist. *Nic. Eth.* book 7. Paul in Rom. 7 has so analysed the effect of Torah on Israel as to show that Israel, striving after the law of her god, attains simply to the level of the wise but puzzled pagan. Cp. also Gal. 5.17f.

[115] cf. Wright 1991a, ch. 7.

[116] On which see, as a preliminary statement, Wright 1992a, ch. 10. When Moule describes this passage as 'non-apocalyptic' (1982 [1962], 142, 267) he means, I take it, 'not referring to the parousia'.

exodus of Israel was a model for the death and resurrection of Jesus, and both of these events point forward to a greater exodus to come, when the whole cosmos will be liberated from its Egypt, its present state of futility.[117]

Because this story is the story of Israel *understood as* the story through which the creator god is restoring the creation, and with it the race of Adam and Eve, it addresses, confronts, and attempts to subvert the pagan world and its stories. We therefore often see Paul, as he says himself, 'taking every thought captive to obey Christ', meeting pagan ideas coming towards him and, like Jehu, bidding them turn around and ride in his train. Some readers, starting at least with Marcion in the second century, have seen this as evidence that he abandoned the Jewish story altogether, embracing a quite different symbolic universe, a different narrative world. But Paul's fundamental narrative world gives no deep echo to that of paganism in any of its first-century or other forms. It continues to resonate with the story of Israel. Because Israel's story speaks of a creator god who claims all people, all lands, as his own, Paul is able to reach out from within that story and address Jew and Gentile alike. He thus claims that the story of Jesus fulfills the purpose for which the creator god called Abraham in the first place. Although his telling of the story subverted the narrative world of his Jewish contemporaries, his claim was that it actually reinstated the true sense of the covenant promises.[118]

What had made the difference, clearly, was Jesus; or, more fully, Jesus and the divine spirit. Paul's theology can, I suggest, be plotted most accurately and fully on the basis that it represents his rethinking, in the light of Jesus and the divine spirit, of the fundamental Jewish beliefs: monotheism (of the creational and covenantal sort), election, and eschatology. This theology was integrated with the rethought narrative world at every point.

In the light of this, we can see how Paul's brief, often clipped, references to Jesus function within the letters as mini-stories, small indices of the rudder by which the great Jewish narrative world had been turned in a new direction. Richard Hays studied some of these passages with the help of Griemas' analytic method, and reached the conclusion that, even in small formulations such as Galatians 3.13–14 and 4.3–6, we find 'the presence and shape of a gospel story to which Paul alludes and appeals'.[119] The list of such passages could be extended almost indefinitely: simply within Romans, obvious passages include 3.24–6; 4.24–5; 5.6–10; 6.9–10; 7.4; 8.3–4; 10.3–4; 15.3, and 15.7–9. Even taken individually, these passages all show that *the story of Jesus*, interpreted precisely within the wider Jewish narrative world, was the hinge upon which Paul's rereading of that larger story turned. Taken together, they are all the more powerful.

How does Paul normally evoke this whole world of thought, this storied worldview? Among many other ways, I suggest that he does so with his use of the very word *Christ*. This is not simply, for Paul, a proper name. It is a title which means 'Messiah'. 'Messiah' implies 'Israel'; to call this Jesus 'Messiah'

---

[117] I am grateful to Sylvia Keesmaat for several stimulating discussions on this topic.
[118] cf. esp. Rom. 4; Gal. 3.1—4.7; and particularly Rom. 10.1–4.
[119] Hays 1983, 125.

means to claim that Israel's destiny has reached its fulfilment in him. Any attempt to split off 'Messiahship' from Paul's conception of Jesus is doomed to failure, as I have argued elsewhere.[120] But this means that in passage after passage the entire train of thought is latent, so that when it appears in full dress, as it does in the passages above, it does not intrude, but takes its proper and natural place.

What about the celebrated passage in 2 Corinthians in which Paul is supposed to have disclaimed all interest in the human Jesus?

> So, then, from now on we know no-one according to the flesh; even if we once knew the Messiah according to the flesh, we know him now no longer. So if anyone is in Christ—new creation! The old has passed away; see, it has become new.[121]

Bultmann argued, influentially, that in this passage Paul not only disclaimed knowledge of the human Jesus but also declared such knowledge irrelevant.[122] This has been firmly resisted by other commentators,[123] but the impression remains in some quarters that Paul still sat loose to Jesus himself. In fact, the passage as a whole, and the verse in detail, militate against Bultmann's conclusion. The entire argument (2.14—6.13) deals with the new-covenant ministry which Paul exercises, and one of its major focal points is the exposition, in 4.7–15, of what it means to see 'the light of the knowledge of the glory of God in the face of Jesus Christ' (4.6). Here the heart of the matter is that the apostles are 'always bearing about in our body the death of Jesus, so that the life of Jesus also may be manifest in our body' (4.10). In this and the subsequent verses, 'Jesus' refers unambiguously, as elsewhere in Paul, to the human Jesus, specifically in his being put to death. The word 'Christ' is not mentioned in the whole paragraph (4.7–15); Paul's point is precisely that the pattern of the ministry of Jesus, which led to his death, is now being reproduced in the apostles, and that this is the sign of their authenticity.

What Paul then rejects in 5.16 is not knowledge of the historical Jesus, or the usefulness of such knowledge for theology, but a particular mode of knowing the Messiah. 'According to the flesh' (*kata sarka*) is a regular Pauline phrase denoting, among other things, the status, attitudes and theology of Jews and/or some Jewish Christians.[124] The sort of Messiah they had wanted would be one who would affirm and underwrite their national aspirations. Instead, the true Messiah, Jesus, had been obedient to a different messianic vocation, in which the 'flesh' dies in order to rise again. The reason Paul knows this is precisely that he knows about Jesus, and claims that he, and none other, is the true Messiah. 2 Corinthians 5.16 thus not only does not deny or reject the possibility or usefulness of knowledge about Jesus, but actually depends on such knowledge for the theological point it is making.

This can be reinforced further by a consideration of Romans 15.1–9. Here it is notable that Paul draws explicitly on what was known of the ministry of

[120] Wright 1991a, chs. 2–3.
[121] 2 Cor. 5.16–17 (my translation).
[122] Bultmann 1951–5, 1.237–9; 1985 [1976], 155; cp. also Käsemann 1969 [1965], 121 n.16.
[123] e.g. Moule 1970; Barrett 1973, 171; Furnish 1984, 330–3. Cf. too Meyer 1979, 73–5.
[124] e.g. Rom. 4.1; 1 Cor. 10.18; Gal. 4.23, etc.

Jesus—not even, here, focusing on his death—as the ground and basis of the appeal he is making, which in fact plays a larger role within the purpose of Romans than is usually recognized: the different backgrounds of the various Christians in Rome should not prevent them from uniting in common worship. 15.3 and 15.7–9 speak of the ministry which the true Messiah undertook, recognizing his proclamation to Jews as a distinct stage in the outworking of god's universal purposes. At precisely this point in his argument it would have been totally inappropriate for Paul to refer to the historical Jesus—*if* he had taken the position attributed to him by Bultmann and his followers, that concentration on Jesus was a feature of Jewish Christianity that he ought to leave behind. Paul, then, knows the outline of the story of Jesus, and can use it as it stands, or, more frequently, as a substructure for theological argument.[125]

This survey of Paul is, of course, woefully incomplete. There is much which is here left for another occasion. But I hope it is sufficient to demonstrate at least a strong case for saying that, at one fixed point in the early years of Christianity, the story which was being told has substantially the same shape as the story which we observed in Luke, Matthew and Mark. It is the Israel-story, fulfilled, subverted and transformed by the Jesus-story, and now subverting the world's stories. In its new form, it generates and sustains a symbolic universe, in which the writers of epistles and gospels alike understand themselves and their readers as living: the world in which this fulfilled Israel-drama is now moving towards its closure, its still unreached ending.

7. The Narrative World of the Letter to the Hebrews

Entering the world of the letter to the Hebrews after a close study of Paul is a bit like listening to Monteverdi after listening to Bach. We are clearly in the same world, but the texture is different, the allusions are different, the whole flavour is changed. There is neither space nor need to enter at this point into a full discussion of Hebrews;[126] I simply want at this point to draw out one aspect of its narrative world that is not often noted, namely, the parallel between the climax of the letter and the equally climactic final main section of Ben-Sirach.

We glanced earlier at the narrative function of Sirach 44.1—50.21.[127] There we saw that the list of heroes brings the history of the world, and of Israel, to a climax with the worship of YHWH in the Jerusalem Temple, especially the spectacular ministry of the high priest, Simon ben Onias:

> How glorious he was, surrounded by the people,
>   as he came out of the house of the curtain.
> Like the morning star among the clouds,
>   like the full moon at the festal season;
> Like the sun shining on the temple of the Most High,

---

[125] I leave aside for the present the vexed question of Paul's supposed appeals to Jesus' teaching, as in e.g. 1 Cor. 7.10–12. My main point is established without reference to this issue.

[126] For full recent treatments of Hebrews in general cf. Lindars 1989; Attridge 1989; Hurst 1990; Lane 1991.

[127] Above, p. 217.

like the rainbow gleaming in splendid clouds; . . .
When he put on his glorious robe
 and clothed himself in perfect splendor,
When he went up to the holy altar,
 he made the court of the sanctuary glorious.[128]

This is where Israel's history has been leading: a great high priest, magnificently robed, splendid in his liturgical operations, coming out of the sanctuary after the worship to bless the people. It is clear that this provides a close echo of a theme that characterizes Hebrews all through: Jesus is the 'great high priest who has passed through the heavens', who is 'holy, blameless, separated from sinners, and exalted above the heavens', who is 'seated at the right hand of the throne of the Majesty in the heavens', and who, having finished his own performance of ritual duties (offering his own blood in the heavenly sanctuary) 'will appear a second time . . . to save those who are eagerly waiting for him'.[129] What is not so often seen is that the list of 'heroes of faith' in Hebrews 11 *is designed to make the same point*, by means of its clear subversion of the story in Ben-Sirach 44–50. Instead of the present high priest in the Temple being the point towards which all Israel's history was tending, it is Jesus, the true High Priest: Hebrews 12.1–3 stands to 11.4–40 as Sirach 50.1–21 does to 44.1—49.16.[130] Though speaking at the surface level of Jesus as the supreme example of enduring faith, at the strongly implicit level 12.1–3 powerfully reinforces the point made in 8.1—10.28. Once again the distinction between poetic sequence and referential sequence, coupled with a careful listening for intertextual echoes, draws out of the text a rich vein of meaning.

Underneath the poetic sequence of Hebrews, then, lies a clear implicit narrative sequence. The story of the world, and of Israel, has led up to a point, namely, the establishment of the true worship of the true god.[131] This has now been achieved, not through the Jerusalem Temple and its high priesthood, but through Jesus. Hebrews focuses on the Temple cult rather than on more general theological or practical issues, but the underlying story corresponds to what we found in the synoptics and Paul. Jesus has brought Israel's story to its paradoxical climax.[132]

8. The Story of John

Everyone knows that John is a very different sort of book to Luke, Matthew and Mark. But it is not as different as all that. If we put the four canonical gospels into a scale alongside a reconstructed 'Q' source, and with such non-

---

[128] Sir. 50.5–7, 11.

[129] Heb. 4.14; 7.26; 8.1; 9.28.

[130] Frost 1987, 169 sees the parallel between Simon ben Onias and Jesus, but does not draw from it the point that I am making.

[131] Against e.g. Bultmann 1956, 187, who roundly declares that, for the Christians who read Hebrews 11, 'the history of Israel is no longer their own history'.

[132] This means that we must reject the characterization of Heb. as 'apocalyptic gnosis', suggested by Koester 1982b, 272–6.

canonical material as the *Gospel of Thomas,* the *Gospel of Peter,* and the more fragmentary sources, then John comes out at least as much like the synoptics as it is unlike. There is no question here of attempting a detailed study of the Fourth Gospel.[133] All we can do, in pursuance of our question about the large stories that characterized early Christianity, is to conduct a brief exploration of the implicit narrative world of the gospel as we have it.[134]

John's story sends us back to the beginning of all things, indeed to before the beginning of all things:

In the beginning was the word
 and the word was with God
 and the word was God.
He was in the beginning with God:
 all things were made through him,
 and without him nothing was made.
In him was life,
 and the life was the light of humans;
 and the light shines in the darkness,
 and the darkness did not overcome it.[135]

John confronts his readers with a strange new Genesis. Whatever else his story is about, it is to be interpreted in the light of a total narrative world that stretches back to the beginning of all creation. What is more, it is focused quite explicitly on the Jewish story, not only in Genesis itself, but in the subsequent writings:

the Law was given through Moses;
grace and truth came through Jesus Christ.[136]

These hints in the prologue are fully substantiated in the body of the gospel. The figures of Abraham and Moses are not simply heroes from the past, wheeled in to give depth and colour; they are part of a long story that is now reaching its crucial phase. The long debate about Abraham and his true children in chapter 8 is crucial to the whole story: part of the question at issue in the book is precisely whether Jesus or the Judaeans of his day are the true children of Abraham.[137] The question was of course fundamental to all intra-Jewish debate, and was always to be understood in terms of the story of Israel as a whole: who, in this or that context, represented the true succession? Likewise, the varied references to Moses presuppose a telling of the story which includes the giving of the Torah, the wilderness wanderings, and the abiding validity of Moses' writings as the constitutive code of Judaism.[138]

---

[133] For recent work on John see Kysar 1985; Beutler 1985; Ashton 1986, 1991; Hengel 1989b; Koester 1990, ch. 3; Lemcio 1991, ch. 5; Burridge 1992, ch. 9. On the period between 1965 and 1985 see Neill and Wright 1988, 430–9 (including a discussion of Robinson 1985).

[134] Not, in other words, of the reconstructed sources, which remain extremely hypothetical. On narrative criticism as applied to John see now, above all, Stibbe 1992.

[135] Jn. 1.1–5.

[136] Jn. 1.17.

[137] Jn. 8.31–59.

[138] cf. Jn. 1.45; 3.14; 5.45f.; 6.32; 7.19, 22, 23; 9.28f.

These in turn, however, point to a feature of the gospel which runs deeper than occasional references to Israel's past. It has often been pointed out that the narrative highlights a succession of Jewish feasts: Passover three times, and Tabernacles, Hannukah, and another unnamed festival once each.[139] John, that is, locates the ministry of Jesus in terms of Jewish sacred time, with each festival not only having a specific reference-point in past history but also giving a specific shape to the future expectation of the people. Jesus, it seems, is bringing Israel's history towards its intended goal. Again, at numerous points in the narrative John is deliberately evoking scenes from Israel's past in order to say: all this is now reaching its appointed fulfilment. Jesus, like Moses only more so, feeds the people in the wilderness with bread from heaven; Jesus is the true shepherd who, as in Ezekiel 34, is to be distinguished from the false shepherds; he is the true Passover lamb.[140]

All of this goes towards the making of a narrative which is, more obviously than the synoptic gospels, a story about Jesus and the Jewish people of his day—or, more precisely, Jesus and the (geographically defined) *Judaean* people of his day.[141] But just when the narrative seems to concentrate on a small focal point, it contains the seeds of the larger picture which makes John the book it is. The prologue, and hints at various points all through, indicate how this story of Jesus-and-the-Judaeans is to be read. It is the microcosm, the focal point, of the story of the creator god and the world. With great subtlety, John has so told the story of Jesus, at one level a Hellenistic-style *bios* just like the synoptic gospels,[142] that it encapsulates one of the most fundamental points of the Jewish narrative world. What the covenant god does in and with Israel is what the creator god is doing in and with the world as a whole.[143] This emerges from the start, in the parallelism within the prologue:

> He was in the world, and the world came into being through him;
>   yet the world did not know him.
> He came to what was his own,
>   and his own people did not accept him.[144]

The question of the creator and the *kosmos*, the world, becomes the question of Jesus and Israel. And when that question is resolved, with the full paradox and irony of the crucifixion of the King of the Jews, then at once the world can become the beneficiary:

> Now among those who went up to worship at the festival were some Greeks. They came to Philip . . . and said to him, 'Sir, we wish to see Jesus.' Philip went and told Andrew; then Andrew and Philip went and told Jesus. Jesus answered them, 'The hour has come for the son of man to be glorified. Very truly, I tell you, unless a grain of wheat falls into the earth

---

[139] Passover: Jn. 2.13–25; 6.4; 11.55—19.42; Tabernacles: 7.2ff.; Hannukah: 10.22; 'a festival' (possibly Passover, more likely Tabernacles, cf. Robinson 1985, 138 n.48): 5.1.
[140] 6.25–71; 10.11–18; 1.29, 36; 19.31–6. See further Dahl 1986 [1962], 128–32.
[141] On the debate about the meaning of *hoi Ioudaioi* in John see e.g. Dahl 1986 [1962], 126ff.; Lowe 1976; Ashton 1985.
[142] Burridge 1992, ch. 9.
[143] cf. Dahl 1986 [1962], 131f.
[144] Jn. 1.10f.

and dies, it remains just a single grain; but if it dies, it bears much fruit . . . And I, when I am lifted up from the earth, will draw all people to myself.

As you have sent me into the world, so I have sent them into the world . . . As you, Father, are in me and I am in you, may they also be in us, so that the world may believe that you have sent me . . . I in them and you in me, that they may become completely one, so that the world may know that you have sent me.

Jesus said to them again, 'Peace be with you. As the Father has sent me, so I send you.'[145]

The implicit narrative world of the gospel as a whole, then, must take in at least four movements. There is the initial creation, accomplished through the *logos*. There is the call and history of Israel, which results in ambiguity; the world has rebelled against its creator, and Israel has shared in that rebellion. Then there is the ministry of Jesus, in which the *logos*, now identified with the human being Jesus of Nazareth, confronts the world, now identified with his Jewish contemporaries. Various points in the poetic sequence of the narrative strongly imply a future closure to the referential sequence within the overall narrative world: Jesus' disciples will go out from the microcosmic world of Israel to the larger world of the Gentiles, to announce to the non-Jewish world that its creator god, the god of Israel, has redeemed it. This focus, not only on the story of Jesus but on the vital significance, for the creation as a whole, of the story of Israel, shows that John's gospel shares the same large story-world which characterizes, as we saw, the synoptics and Paul.

This impression is strongly confirmed if we focus, in conclusion, on the prologue itself. The opening words indicate, as we have already suggested, that John is intending his hearers to pick up the echoes of Genesis 1. But there is another passage in Jewish literature, closer to John in time, which is also strongly echoed, and which, it may be suggested, John is intending to subvert with a different retelling of the story:[146]

Wisdom praises herself, and tells of her glory in the midst of her people.
In the assembly of the Most High she opens her mouth,
    and in the presence of his hosts *she tells of her glory*:
'I came forth *from the mouth of the Most High*,
    and covered the earth like a mist.
I dwelt in the highest heavens,
    and my throne was in a pillar of cloud.
Alone I compassed the vault of heaven
    and traversed the depths of the abyss.
Over waves of the sea, over all the earth,
    and over every people and nation I have held sway.
Among all these I sought a resting place;
    in whose territory should I abide?
Then the Creator of all things gave me a command,
    and my Creator chose *the place for my tent*.
He said, "Make your dwelling in Jacob,
    and in Israel receive your inheritance."
Before the ages, *in the beginning*, he created me,
    and for all the ages I shall not cease to be.

---

[145] Jn. 12.20–4, 32; 17.18–23; 20.21.
[146] On this cf. esp. Ashton 1986a.

In the holy tent I ministered before him,
    and so I was established in Zion.
Thus in the beloved city he gave me a resting place,
    and in Jerusalem was my domain.
I took root in an honoured people,
    in the portion of the Lord, his heritage . . .
Like *the vine* I bud forth delights,
    and my blossoms become glorious and abundant fruit.
Come to me, you who desire me,
    and eat your fill of my fruits . . .
Whoever obeys me will not be put to shame,
    and those who work with me will not sin.
All this is the book of the covenant of the Most High God,
    the law that Moses commanded us
    as an inheritance for the congregations of Jacob.
It overflows, like the Pishon, with wisdom,
    and like the Tigris at the time of the first fruits.
It runs over, like the Euphrates, with understanding,
    and like the Jordan at harvest time.
It pours forth instruction like the Nile,
    like the Gihon at the time of vintage.
The first man did not know wisdom fully,
    nor will the last one fathom her . . .[147]

The echoes of Genesis 1–2 are clear throughout this wonderful poem. So is the central emphasis. 'Wisdom', the personified breath and word of YHWH, the one created 'in the beginning' before all else, and the one through whom, in other closely related passages, all creation was made[148]—this Wisdom is now to be identified with two other personifications, namely the Shekinah and the Torah. Shekinah is the 'tabernacling' presence of YHWH in the Temple of Jerusalem. Torah, of course, is the law given to Moses. When we come back to the Johannine prologue with this passage in mind, the echoes run all through. There is a *logos*, a 'word', present with the creator from the beginning as his self-expression. This *logos* comes to *make its tabernacle with us*: the phrase 'and dwelt among us' in John 1.14 is in Greek *kai eskenosen en hemin*, which echoes the language of Sirach 24.8, 10, with *skene* being both the Greek for 'tent' or 'tabernacle' and also, interestingly, an apparent cognate of the Hebrew *Shekinah* itself. The result is that 'we have beheld his glory', the glory of the truly human being, who, like Wisdom in another Jewish book, is the 'unique' one, *monogenes*.[149] Moreover, this *logos* quietly takes the place not only of Shekinah but also of Torah: the law was given through Moses, while grace and truth came through Jesus Christ. It is important not to add the word 'but' to the second clause, as though John were anticipating Marcion and treating Moses as the antithesis of the *logos*. Equally, it is clear that he is saying: that which Judaism had thought to find in Torah is truly found in Jesus. Other echoes of Sirach 24 continue throughout John: Jesus is the true vine, the giver of living water.[150]

---

[147] Sir. 24.1–28, my italics.
[148] Prov. 8.22–31; Wisd. 8.4; 9.9.
[149] Wisd. 7.22.
[150] Jn. 15.1–8; 4.13–15; 7.37–9.

What is the significance of this background for the Johannine prologue? Bultmann, classically, thought that by demonstrating this close relation to Sirach he had demonstrated John's dependence on early Gnostic thought.[151] But, however unfashionable the point may be, we must insist on a large difference between the worlds of Jewish wisdom and early Gnosticism. In Sirach, the figure of Wisdom comes to live, permanently, among humans, more specifically in the Temple at Jerusalem. In Gnosticism, the redeemer-figure comes down to the world of humans, but only in order to return from that wicked sphere to his own true home. The background to the Johannine prologue in wisdom thought is evidence, not of its leaning in the direction of early Gnosticism, but of its emphatically Jewish and world-affirming orientation.

This is not to say that the Johannine prologue is simply an affirmation, with minor modifications, of the worldview of Sirach. Rather, it must be seen, at least in part, as a subversive retelling of the story of Wisdom. There were other, different, subversive retellings of this story within the broad Jewish tradition. The most striking is *1 Enoch* 42, which provides perhaps the starkest cosmic dualism anywhere in Jewish apocalyptic:

> Wisdom could not find a place in which she could dwell;
>   but a place was found for her in the heavens.
> Then Wisdom went out to dwell with the children of the people,
>   but she found no dwelling place.
> So Wisdom returned to her place
>   and she settled permanently among the angels.
> Then Iniquity went out of her rooms,
>   and found whom she did not expect.
> And she dwelt with them,
>   like rain in a desert,
>   like dew on a thirsty land.

This terrifying parody of Sirach's beautiful poem is a clear example of the way in which Jewish apocalyptic could transform itself in a Gnostic direction. The world has become irredeemable. Worse: Wisdom, in this retelling, does not (as in Gnosticism) snatch up a few holy souls to rescue them from the ruin. Wisdom is not, here, a redeemer-figure, but a brief lone visitor. This stanza is a flat denial of Sirach's claim: Wisdom tried to find somewhere to live, but, finding none, went back home. Instead, Iniquity has gone out and found somewhere to dwell, somewhere surprising, somewhere where she is able to irrigate the land thoroughly, like the rivers in Genesis 2 and Sirach 24. The place which should have been Wisdom's home has become the den of Iniquity. There is no hope for the world, or Israel, or individual humans, within *1 Enoch* 42.

John's subversion of the Wisdom poem in Ben-Sirach is of a different order altogether. He agrees with Sirach that the divine Wisdom does indeed find a home. He recognizes, and takes on board, the tragedy which lies behind *1 Enoch* 42: the world did not know the *logos*, its creator, and even 'his own people did not receive him'. But this did not make him return home having

---

[151] e.g. Bultmann 1986 [1923], followed by e.g. Koester 1982b, 208.

abandoned the world to 'iniquity'. The light shines in the darkness, and the darkness did not overcome it. The *logos* has come, as mainstream Judaism would expect, not to judge the world but to redeem it.[152] But instead of Shekinah and Torah, the Jerusalem Temple and the covenant code, as the places where Wisdom/*logos* dwells and reveals the divine glory, John says that the *logos* became flesh, became a human being, became Jesus of Nazareth. Sirach's positive worldview is reaffirmed, but now deals with the problem that *1 Enoch* saw and that Sirach, with its optimism, did not address. 'We beheld his glory': for John, the supreme revelation of this glory was on the cross, where the *logos* died as the good shepherd giving his life for the sheep, as the Passover lamb liberating the people from their slavery.[153]

In particular, it is vital to the whole thrust of John's theology that the *logos* becomes a *human being*. Sirach, somewhat loftily, could not envisage a human being ever fully fathoming Wisdom. John sees this Wisdom becoming, fully, a human being. In doing so he is still conscious of writing a new version of Genesis. The climax of the first chapter of Genesis is the creation of the human being in the image of the creator (Genesis 1.26–8). The climax of John's prologue is the coming to full humanness of the *logos*, who, in taking on so many of the characteristics of Wisdom, may be assumed also to be the divine image-bearer.[154] When Pilate declares to the crowds, 'Here is the man', John intends his readers to hear echoes that have been present since the very beginning. Jesus, as the *logos* having become flesh, is the truly human being.[155]

Two results, one small, one large, both very important, follow from this (all too brief) analysis of John and particularly of the prologue. First, the story which the prologue tells is clearly modelled on, and intended as a gentle but firm subversion of, the Jewish wisdom-tradition which, like John, was retelling Genesis and focusing it on a particular point. Sirach was claiming that Jerusalem and the Torah were the focal points of the entire cosmos, the place where the creator's own Wisdom had come, uniquely, to dwell. John claims exactly this for Jesus. The resonance of Sirach 24 and, behind that but also independently, of Genesis 1, makes it highly likely that, in terms of the composition of the Johannine prologue, verses 14–18, the present climax, were envisaged from the start. There is no justification for postulating a non-incarnational early edition, or a pre-Johannine Gnostic poem about a non-human *logos* descending and reascending. Whoever wrote the first verses of the prologue intended them to reach their natural climax, echoing both Genesis and Sirach, in verse 14, and to develop the point to the end now found in verses 15–18.[156]

Second, the story which the prologue thus tells is, most importantly, the story of the gospel as a whole in miniature. This is the story of Jesus *told as* the true, and redeeming, story of Israel, *told as* the true, and redeeming, story of

[152] Jn. 3.17, etc.
[153] cf. Jn. 10.11, 15, 17f.; 11.49–52.
[154] cf. Wisd. 7.26.
[155] Jn. 19.5; cf. Johnston 1987.
[156] cf. the discussions in Bultmann 1986 [1923], 31f.; Käsemann 1969 [1965], ch. 6; Dunn 1980, 239–45.

the creator and the cosmos. John's gospel, through and through, tells the recognizably Jewish story of Israel and the world, but, like Paul and the synoptics in their very different ways, draws the eye on to Jesus as the fulfilment, and hence the subversion, of that story. The original ending of the book (chapter 20) picks up the prologue at point after point: the light overcomes the darkness of the early morning, the light which is the true life of human beings. To those who receive him, Jesus gives the right to share his status: 'I am ascending to my Father *and your Father*, to my God *and your God*.'[157] Thomas finally puts into words what the whole book has been sketching out, ever since the prologue spoke of the incarnate *logos* as 'the only-begotten god': 'My Lord, and my God.'[158] The close fit between 1.1–18 and chapter 20 is, indeed, further reason for suggesting that they were composed with each other in mind, rather than the prologue coming from a different source and being attached to the book at a late stage.[159]

John, then, shares in outline the same story-line, the same narrative world, as Paul, Hebrews and the synoptics. As we survey the ground we have covered in this chapter, we may conclude that these writings provide, *prima facie*, the earliest of the large-scale tellings of the Christian story. The great bulk of the canonical writings, now studied in brief, witness to a perception of the world, its creator, and its redemption which takes the form of a retelling of the basic Jewish story focused now on Jesus. This is a major and important conclusion, tying in tightly to our study, in the previous chapter, of the praxis and symbols of early Christianity.

But do these books accurately reflect *all* the early Christian stories, including the smaller ones that were taken up within the larger works? And what about those that did not find their way into the orthodox canon, which was after all ratified at a later stage? This must be the subject of a separate chapter.

---

[157] Jn. 20.17; cf. 1.12.
[158] 1.18 (there are of course variant readings for this striking phrase); 20.28.
[159] Against Robinson 1984, 71–6.

Chapter Fourteen

STORIES IN EARLY CHRISTIANITY (2)

1. Introduction: Form-Criticism

Biographies usually contain anecdotes; but biographies and anecdotes are not the same thing. Jewish histories and folk-tales contain vignettes of kings, prophets, holy men, pious women; but Jewish histories and personal vignettes are not the same thing. The canonical gospels, which I have argued are a unique combination of Hellenistic biography and Jewish history, contain anecdotes and vignettes, almost all about Jesus. We cannot presume that these are the same sort of thing as the gospels themselves. Having examined (some of) the large stories in early Christianity, we must turn our attention to the smaller, and in many cases earlier, ones, to see whether they reflect the same patterns and concerns.

The study of these smaller and earlier stories is therefore clearly demanded by the logic of the argument within the present Part of the book. It is also highly desirable in view of one aspect at least of the larger project of which this book forms a part. Without a serious consideration of the forms taken by Jesus-stories prior to their inclusion within the gospels, we are at least open to the charge of ignoring crucial parts of the evidence when it comes to thinking about Jesus himself, as we intend to do in the next volume. Rather than take space, in a book about Jesus, to write about the context and content of the stories which circulated about him during the subsequent generation, it is far more natural to discuss these stories at this point, where they really belong. Form-criticism, despite often being treated simply as a tool for discovering about Jesus, is designed primarily to shed light on the early church. Since that is our present topic, it is appropriate to address these issues here.

Study of the early history of stories in the gospels has traditionally gone under two names: tradition-criticism (or tradition-history) and form-criticism. The two are sometimes used interchangeably; properly speaking, 'tradition-criticism' is the wider term, dealing with all early traditions, while 'form-criticism' is the more focused, concentrating on those traditions that have specific and recognizable 'forms'. The principle behind all such activity is sometimes obscured in a maze of technicality, and it may be worth spelling it out at this stage.

Traditions do not lie around unshaped. As we saw in Part II, all history involves interpretation. In order for something to be told, it has to be put into some kind of form. There are few things more frustrating than having to listen—as one sometimes does with a child, or a drunk—to a story that remains unshaped and unsorted, with the salient facts that might have made the tale worth telling being hidden behind the fog of irrelevant information and comment. But there are different sorts of shaping. When my wife and I tell our children the story of their births, as we sometimes do on their birthdays, we naturally minimize the medical details, and highlight the sense of parental excitement, the delight at discovering a new member of the family, that accompanied the event. The story often concludes by retelling a remark made by one of us at the time, or by a nurse in the hospital, epitomizing the feelings of those present. If, however, we tell the same story to a doctor, especially if there is concern about the present health of the child, we select different information, highlight different things. Our feelings at the time are of little significance; whether the child began to breathe at the appropriate moment is far more important. It would thus be possible in principle to deduce, from the *form* of the story (its emphases, highlights, and perhaps concluding quotations), the context and purpose in and for which it was being told.

The basic insight of the form-critics was to apply this fairly obvious point to small units (*pericopae* or paragraphs) of material in the gospels.[1] Here is a story about Jesus. He performs a healing, enters into controversy, utters a memorable saying. The entire episode, if acted out using the gospel narrative as script, would take less than a minute. We may assume without more ado that it has been compressed, as all stories are, in the telling; that the story will not contain details of every single thing that happened, or that was said. We may assume, further, that it was told in a variety of forms, now lost, by the people involved, to highlight a multiplicity of things—their own feelings and emotions, what some other bystander said, and so on. Anecdotes are told for a variety of reasons, and the reasons dictate the form. What we have in the gospels are stories in which the telling and retelling has been made to focus on a particular point, one of many that could in principle have been made. This can tell us, again at least in principle, what sort of situation the teller was addressing, or was involved in. It is not 'neutral information': there is, as we have seen, no such thing. It is directed at particular needs, and makes a particular point.

So far, we have simply followed the implications of common sense. Serious study of forms begins, however, when we discover that some stories regularly fall into a more or less clearly defined pattern, suggesting that we might be able to construct a grid to determine, from the form of the story, the kind of setting it may have had. This is the sort of analysis of the stories in the gospels offered by the classic form-critics earlier this century. As the work progressed, 'tradition-criticism' set it on a broader canvas, attempting the second-order activity of studying the way in which particular traditions, particular tellings of one or more stories, developed over time and through different phases of the life of the early church.

[1] See the classic works of Schmidt 1919; Dibelius 1934 [1919]; Bultmann 1968 [1921]; Taylor 1933. Among recent works cf. Moule 1982 [1962], *passim*, esp. ch. 5; Berger 1984. The clearest recent survey in English is Sanders and Davies 1989, Part III.

The task of form-criticism is both important and difficult. Important, because the small stories came before the larger ones that we now possess, and with them we move back into the period about which we know virtually nothing except through Paul and Acts. Difficult, not least because of the intrinsic difficulties, which should not be minimized, in reading between the lines of a later document to find traces of earlier non-documentary story-telling. I suspect that even the most confident form-critic would become anxious if asked for proveable hypotheses about the pre-literary life of anecdotes which now form part of the biography of some twentieth-century figure. To attempt to reconstruct the equivalent phenomenon with first-century documents seems even more presumptuous. Difficult too, however, precisely because confident critics, undeterred by this problem, have left a tangled web of theories, hypotheses, misunderstandings, unproven speculations and downright bad guesses strewn around the subject, so that anyone wanting to come to it fresh finds a prickly hedge barring the way.[2]

Among the misunderstandings, we may here mention three. First, when form-criticism burst upon the scene in the years after the First World War, it was not designed primarily as a tool to find out about Jesus. In the hands of Rudolf Bultmann in particular, it was a tool to find out about the early church. Bultmann assumed that we could know certain things about Jesus—not very much, but enough to know that most of the gospel stories could not have taken place as narrated. He therefore looked for possible situations within the early church within which stories like these could have been told *to express some aspect of the church's faith and life.* For Bultmann, as we saw earlier, Jesus within his historical context was not the focus of Christianity. Far more important was the faith of the early Christians. Once this is realized, a good deal of the reaction to form-criticism, not least in England, is shown to be off the point. The tool was not originally designed as a means of finding Jesus; that it proved unsuccessful in this task is not a telling criticism.

A second misunderstanding, once that one is out of the way, is the assumption that the discipline of form-criticism necessarily belongs with one particular hypothesis about the origin and development of the early church. Since the major practitioners of the discipline had a fairly clear idea of how Christianity grew and changed, it was comparatively easy for them to assign gospel anecdotes, or fragments of them, to different periods or stages. As Bultmann assumed that he knew a certain amount about Jesus, so he assumed that he knew a certain amount about the early church: that it began as a kind of variant on Gnosticism, though using some Jewish language; that it developed in two strands at least, one of which carried on the Gnostic or 'wisdom' tradition, while another interpreted Jesus within a more Jewish-style development; that these two were combined in the writing of the first canonical gospel; that Christianity quickly spread beyond its original base, which merely happened to have been Jewish, and that it translated the language of its earliest expression into Hellenistic thought-forms as it did so, which was all the easier to do since

---

[2] Well-known problems with form-criticism are noted by e.g. Hooker 1972; Stanton 1975; Güttgemanns 1979 [1971]; Schmithals 1980; Sanders and Davies 1989, 127–37.

the Jewish thought-forms had in any case been mere accidental features of a message that was more akin to Hellenism.[3] The Bultmannian paradigm, showing just how much it remained rooted in that of F. C. Baur, thus envisaged Jewish Christianity and Hellenistic Christianity existing more or less independently, side by side, until they were combined, some time in the second generation, to form the beginnings of early catholicism.

These were the assumptions of the pioneers of form-criticism. Their analysis of forms, and their hypothetical history of traditions, is heavily dependent on this picture. In consequence, it is often assumed that to practise form-criticism is to accept this view of Christian origins. But by itself the idea of examining the form of individual *pericopae*, and searching for their probable setting in the life of the early church, need not be committed to accepting one view of early Christian history rather than another.

A third misunderstanding concerns the belief of many early form-critics that the stories in the early tradition reflected the life of the early church *rather than* the life of Jesus, in that the early church invented (perhaps under the guidance of 'the spirit of Jesus') sayings of Jesus to address problems in their own day. The main problem with this assumption is that the one fixed point in the history of the early church, i.e. Paul, provides a string of good counter-examples, which work in two directions.[4]

On the one hand, as is often pointed out, Paul regularly addresses questions of some difficulty, in which he does not even quote words of Jesus, in the synoptic tradition, which could have been helpful to him. Still less does he appear to attribute sayings to Jesus which were not his.[5] Why was he so reticent, if 'words of Jesus' were regularly invented by Christian prophets, of whom Paul was assuredly one, to address problems in the early church?

On the other hand, as is not so often noted, Paul provides evidence of all sorts of disputes which rocked the early church but left not a trace in the synoptic tradition. From Paul, we know that the early church was torn in two over the question of circumcision. There is no mention of circumcision in the whole synoptic tradition.[6] From Paul, we know that some parts at least of the early church had problems in relation to speaking in tongues. There is no mention of this in the main stream of synoptic tradition.[7] From Paul, it is clear that the doctrine of justification was a vital issue which the early church had to hammer out in relation to the admission of Gentiles to the church. The only mentions of the admission of Gentiles in the synoptic tradition do not speak of justification, and the only mention of justification has nothing to do with

---

[3] cf. Bultmann 1951–5, 63–183; 1956, 175ff.

[4] For other difficulties cf. e.g. Hill 1979, ch. 7; Aune 1983, 1991b, esp. 222ff.; Meyer 1979, 74; Lemcio 1991.

[5] cf. Sanders and Davies 1989, 138–41. They accept too uncritically, though, the possibility that prophets in the early church were inspired to utter words of the Lord which were then regarded as sayings of Jesus: see the previous note.

[6] Apart, of course, from Jesus' own circumcision (Lk. 2.21). That sayings about circumcision could easily be invented is clear from *Gos. Thom.* 53.

[7] The longer ending of Mark is the exception that proves the rule: Mk. 16.17.

Gentiles.[8] In Paul it is clear that questions have been raised about apostleship, his own and that of others. Apostleship is of course mentioned in the synoptic tradition, but so far is the tradition from addressing post-Easter issues here that it does not discuss the question of subsequent apostolic authority except for one passage—and in that passage it still envisages Judas sharing the glorious rule of the twelve.[9] In Paul we meet the question of geographical priority: does the church in Jerusalem have a primacy over those working elsewhere? In the synoptic tradition the criticisms of Jerusalem have to do with its past and present failures, and with its wicked hierarchy, not with the place of its church leaders within a wider emerging Christianity. So we could go on: slavery, idol-meat, womens' headgear, work, widows; and, perhaps above all, the detailed doctrines of Christ and the divine spirit. The synoptic tradition shows a steadfast refusal to import 'dominical' answers to or comments on these issues into the retelling of stories about Jesus. This should put us firmly on our guard against the idea that the stories we do find in the synoptic tradition were invented to address current needs in the 40s, 50s, 60s or even later in the first century.

Conversely, it has been shown often enough that the synoptic tradition has preserved material which is not so relevant to, or so obviously taken up by, the first-generation church. Well-known examples include the concentration on Israel;[10] Jesus' attitude to women;[11] and many other features. As Moule concludes, 'Aspects of Jesus' attitude and ministry have survived in the traditions, despite the fact that the early Christians do not seem to have paid particular attention to them or recognized their christological significance.'[12]

Recognizing these points does not, however, mean that we must abandon the discipline of form-criticism. On the contrary. There is every reason to study the early stories and their forms. A good case can be made out for saying that oral history within the early church was likely to have been strong and formative.[13] Three basic moves need to be made here: one about Jesus, one about his first followers, and one about the meaning of 'oral history'.

First, unless we are to operate with a highly unlikely understanding of Jesus and his ministry, we must assume some such picture as we find in Gerd Theissen's brilliant work, *The Shadow of the Galilean*. Jesus was constantly moving from place to place, working without the benefit of mass media. It is not just likely, it is in the highest degree probable, that he told the same stories again and again in slightly different words, that he ran into similar questions and problems and said similar things about them, that he came up with a slightly different set of beatitudes every few villages, that he not only told but retold and adapted parables and similar sayings in different settings, and that he

[8] Gentiles (but not justification): e.g. Mt. 8.5–13. Justification (but not Gentiles): Lk. 18.9–14.

[9] Mt. 19.28, par. Lk. 22.30.

[10] cf. Caird 1965.

[11] Moule 1967, 63–6.

[12] Moule 1967, 76.

[13] See particularly Gerhardsson 1961, 1964, 1979, 1986; Riesenfeld 1970; Davids 1980; Riesner 1981; Kelber 1983; and the collection of important essays in Wansbrough 1991.

repeated aphorisms with different emphases in different contexts.[14] Scholars of an older conservative stamp used to try to explain varieties in the synoptic tradition by saying cautiously that 'maybe Jesus said it twice'. This always sounded like special pleading. Today, once a politician has made a major speech, he or she does not usually repeat it. But the analogy is thoroughly misleading. If we come to the ministry of Jesus as first-century historians, and forget our twentieth-century assumptions about mass media, the overwhelming probability is that most of what Jesus said, he said not twice but two hundred times, with (of course) a myriad of local variations.[15]

Second, those who heard Jesus even on a few of these occasions would soon find that they remembered what was said. We do not even have to postulate a special sort of oral culture to make this highly likely; even in modern Western society those who hear a teacher or preacher say the same thing a few times can repeat much of it without difficulty, often imitating tones of voice, dramatic pauses, and facial and physical mannerisms. Moreover, when there is an urgent or exciting reason for wanting to tell someone else what the teacher has said and done, a hearer will often be able to do so, in summary form, after only one hearing; then, once the story has been *told* two or three times, the effect will be just as strong if not stronger as if it had been *heard* that often. This is a common-sense point, which would not need spelling out, were it not so often ignored. When we add to this the high probability that Palestinian culture was, to put it at its weakest, more used to hearing and repeating teachings than we are today, and the observation that much of Jesus' teaching is intrinsically highly memorable, I submit that the only thing standing in the way of a strong case for Jesus' teaching being passed on effectively in dozens of streams of oral tradition is prejudice.[16] The surprise, then, is not that we have on occasion so many (two, three, or even four) slightly different versions of the same saying. The surprise is that we have so few. It seems to me that the evangelists may well have faced, as a major task, the problem not so much of how to cobble together enough tradition to make a worthwhile book, but of how to work out what to include from the welter of available material.[17] The old idea that the evangelists must have included everything that they had to hand was always, at best, a large anachronism.[18]

The material available would, then, have been 'oral history', that is, the often-repeated tales of what Jesus had said and done. This is to be distinguished from 'oral tradition' proper, according to which a great teacher will take pains to have his disciples commit to memory the exact words in which

[14] cf. Theissen 1987.
[15] Hence the validity, and importance, of Aune's comment (1991b, 240): the study of Jesus' aphorisms leads to the conclusion that 'the interplay between oral and written transmission of the Jesus tradition was an extraordinarily complex phenomenon which will probably never be satisfactorily unraveled'.
[16] e.g., in an extreme form, Schmithals 1980. Güttgemanns (1979 [1971]) has argued that oral and written tradition are very different things, and that one cannot easily pass from one to the other. This may well be so, but that does not undercut the virtual certainty of a strong and early oral tradition which was eventually transformed into a written one.
[17] This is of course implied in Lk. 1.1–4; Jn. 20.30; 21.25.
[18] cf. the critique in Hooker 1975, 29.

the teaching is given.[19] If that had been Jesus' intention, and the disciples' practice, one might have supposed that at least the Lord's Prayer, and the institution narrative of the eucharist, would have come out identical in the various versions (in Paul as well, in the latter case) that we now possess.[20] Jesus, it seems, did not act as a rabbi, saying exactly the same thing over and over until his disciples had learned it by rote. He acted more as a prophet, saying similar things in a variety of contexts; not only his disciples, but most likely many of his wider circle of followers, would have talked about them, in their own words, for years to come. And it is morally certain that they would, without even thinking about it, have cast this material into a variety of forms, which we can now observe in their eventual literary contexts.

There remains, therefore, a valid and indeed vital task for form-criticism to perform, once it has shed unnecessary assumptions. The critics of form-criticism have not, to my knowledge, offered a serious alternative model of how the early church told its stories.[21] Here there has been a hiatus in gospel study. The heyday of form-criticism coincided with the heyday of a Hellenistic history-of-religions 'explanation' for the New Testament. When the latter gave way, after the Second World War, to a Jewish history-of-religions hypothesis, enthusiasm for form-criticism was on the wane in any case. Neither the redaction-criticism of the 1950s and 1960s, nor the serious study of Jesus of the 1970s and 1980s, needed it; indeed, it has sometimes been pointed out that if the redaction-critics were right, that is, if the evangelists really took as much liberty with their material as they seem to have done, the chances of finding pre-literary forms in their 'pure' state is fairly limited.[22] The revival of interest in form-criticism in recent years has taken place, perhaps not surprisingly, within the revived Bultmann school, offering updated versions of the Hellenistic hypothesis.[23] Without wishing to prejudge the issue, it seems to me that a prima facie case could be made out for a different approach.

One final preliminary issue must be faced in relation to form-criticism. It has often been supposed that the best word to describe what the early tradition produced was 'myth'. The reason for this is clear: communities, as we have often remarked, tell stories, often about remote antiquity, as a characteristic way of articulating their worldview and maintaining it in good repair. Subversive groups and individuals within societies tell variants on these myths as a way of advancing their modification of the worldview or, more radically, their replacement for it. It is quite clear that the stories about Jesus which circulated in the early church functioned in some such ways *vis-à-vis* the early Christian communities and the Jewish communities from which, initially, they sprang.

[19] cf. Sanders and Davies 1989, 141–3.

[20] Mt. 6.9–13; Lk. 11.2–4; Mt. 26.26–9; Mk. 14.22–5; Lk. 22.15–20; 1 Cor. 11.23–6; cf. too *Did.* 9.1–5; Justin *I Apol.* 1.66.3. Cf. ch. 12 above.

[21] At one level, a notable exception is Moule 1982 [1962], esp. 3f., 107–38. But Moule does not develop a detailed study of the synoptic tradition on the basis of his reconstructions.

[22] cf. Kermode 1979, 68. For work on Jesus one need only cite, e.g., Harvey 1982 and Sanders 1985, neither of whom makes significant use of form-criticism in writing about Jesus.

[23] Crossan 1973, 1983; Berger 1984; Mack 1988.

Therefore, if that is what we mean by 'myth', that is indeed what these stories, quite manifestly, are.

Unfortunately, things are not so straightforward. As is now often pointed out, Bultmann confused this sense of 'myth' (legitimating quasi-historical stories) with several others, notably the 'myth' that primitive people use to explain 'natural' phenomena (e.g. 'Thor is hammering' in reference to thunder). He also added the notion of 'myth' as the projection of an individual human consciousness on to reality.[24] The first of these additional senses he was able to relativize as 'primitive'; the second (projection), as claiming a spurious objectivity. But this does no justice to the reality. First, many societies, modern as well as ancient, have held worldviews in which, however distasteful to Enlightenment thought-forms this may be, the idea of divine activity and that of space-time events are somehow held together. Describing the language-systems of such worldviews as 'mythological' may help to alert us to the way the systems work; it cannot function of itself as a critique. Second, we spent some time in Part II demonstrating that the empiricist critique of the possibility of knowledge of extra-mental, and extra-linguistic, worlds cannot carry the day. Humans do 'project' on to reality, but not everything that they say, not even when they are articulating worldviews, can be reduced to terms of that projection.

There is, in fact, an essential irony to Bultmann's analysis of the material in the gospels. He was right to see apocalyptic language as essentially 'mythological', in that it borrows imagery from ancient near eastern mythology to clothe its hopes and assertions, its warnings and fears, in the robes of ultimacy, seeing the action of the creator and redeemer god at work in 'ordinary' events. But he was wrong to imagine that Jesus and his contemporaries took such language literally, as referring to the actual end of the space-time universe, and that it is only we who can see through it and discover its 'real' meaning. This is the mirror-image of the mistaken idea that the stories about Jesus, which are prima facie 'about' Jesus himself, were really, in the sense described above, 'foundation myths' and nothing more. Bultmann and his followers have read metaphorical language as literal and literal language as metaphorical. We must note once more that almost all language, and especially that dealing with those things in which human beings are most involved at a deep personal level, is metaphorical, or at least laden with metaphors. That last clause is itself a metaphor, suggesting that the abstract entity 'language' is like a cart, piled high with another abstract entity, 'metaphors'. Specifically, the language of myth, and eschatological myths in particular (the sea, the fabulous monsters, etc.), are used in the biblical literature as complex metaphor systems to denote historical events and to invest them with their theological significance (see chapter 10 above). The language functions as a lens through which historical events can be seen as bearing the full meaning that the community believed them to possess. However foreign to post-Enlightenment thought it may be to see meaning within history, such language grows naturally out of Israel's basic

---

[24] Bultmann 1961, with the other essays in that volume. Cf. the full discussions in Thiselton 1980, ch. 10; Caird 1980, ch. 13, distinguishing no fewer than nine different senses of 'myth'.

monotheistic and covenantal theology. To fail to see this—to imagine, for instance, that the New Testament writers were the prisoners of a primitive, literalistically circumscribed supernaturalist worldview—is simply a gross distortion.[25]

A further point about myths also tells quite heavily against the theory that much of the gospel tradition consists of them. Myths of the basic kind Bultmann envisaged (quasi-folk tales, articulating the worldview of a people) characteristically take a long time to develop, at least in a complex and intricate form. But the first generation of Christianity is simply too short to allow for such a process. This point has been made often enough, but it is still necessary to repeat it. The hypothesis about the early church necessary to support the idea that the first Christians told 'foundation myths' to legitimate their faith and life is far too complex to be credible. On Bultmann's view of Mark, two strands of thought were developing independently. On the one hand there was the early Christian experience, orientated away from the past—including the past of Jesus—and towards the present and the future. This was quickly translated into Hellenistic categories, becoming the Hellenistic kerygma so famous in the twentieth century and so unknown (perhaps) in the first.[26] Within this kerygma, 'Jesus-stories' were invented or possibly adapted for the needs of the community. Meanwhile, there were a few real 'Jesus-stories' still floating loose in the memory of some early Christians. What Mark has done is to produce a combination of these, expressing the Hellenistic kerygma in terms of Jesus-stories, i.e. using material which might conceivably be historical but without actually intending to refer to Jesus himself. (For Bultmann, this was a brilliant move on Mark's part: for Mack in our own day, a disaster.) Such a scheme is incredibly complex, and looks very much like a reconstruction designed to save the phenomena of the gospels without damaging a hypothesis (that Jesus was a certain type of person and that the early church was uninterested in him) which is threatened by the actual evidence. When it is suggested that these developments took place within forty years at the outside, it becomes not just incredibly complex but simply incredible.

The gospels, then, *are* 'myth' in the sense that they are foundational stories for the early Christian worldview. They *contain* 'mythological' language which we can learn, as historians, to decode in the light of other 'apocalyptic' writings of the time. But they have these features because of their underlying, and basically Jewish, worldview. Monotheism of the creational and covenantal variety demands that actual history be the sphere in which Israel's god makes himself known. But this means that the only language in which Israel can appropriately describe her history is language which, while it does indeed intend to refer to actual events in the space-time universe, simultaneously invests those events with (what we might call) trans-historical significance. Such language is called 'mythological', if it is, not because it describes events which did not happen, but *because it shows that actual events are not separated from ultimate sig-*

[25] cf. Caird 1980, 219–21: the idea of history as a 'closed continuum' is itself a fallible presupposition of modern study.
[26] cf. Bultmann 1951–5, 1.63–183.

nificance by an ugly ditch, as the whole movement of Deist and Enlightenment thought would suggest, but on the contrary carry their significance within them.

2. Towards a Revised Form-Criticism

(i) Introduction

All theories about the history of tradition are parasitic upon assumptions about Jesus and the early church, and we must say something about each in order to establish some ground rules. To begin again with Jesus: Jesus was born, lived, worked and died within a Jewish environment. This world was, as we saw, permeated with Hellenistic influence, but that is not a reason to marginalize the deep and rich Jewishness of his context. Further, a good deal of Jesus' teaching, on almost anybody's showing, had to do with the coming kingdom of Israel's god. I shall argue in the next volume that this Jewish context makes sense—more sense than the currently fashionable Cynic alternatives—of Jesus' agenda and of the reasons for his death; until very recently, all the main work on Jesus simply assumed this. Second, we have seen that the major books written about Jesus later on in the first century all took the shape of the Jewish story for granted, and interpreted Jesus within that framework. So did Paul. Significantly, even when Christians of a somewhat later date (Ignatius, Justin, Polycarp) were facing their own world, that of paganism, they held tenaciously to a form of Christianity which remained recognizably Jewish. It is true that, at least by the mid-second century, quite different strains had appeared. We shall look at some of them presently. But the case needs to be spelled out for seeing the whole of the first generation of Christianity as essentially Jewish in form, however subversive of actual Judaism it was in content.[27] If Jesus was Jewish, and thought and acted within a world of Jewish expectations and understandings of history; if Paul did the same; if the synoptic evangelists and even John retold the Jewish story so as to bring it to its climax with Jesus; and if even in the second century, even out in the pagan world, Christianity still bore the same stamp—then it seems highly likely a priori that the early tellings of stories about Jesus would also carry the same form. What we need, and have never had in the history of the discipline, is a hypothesis that would show at least the possibility of a *Jewish* form-criticism of the synoptic tradition, a reading of the stories which did justice to the high probability that their earliest form was Jewish, and that Hellenistic features may be signs of later development.

The question may be sharpened up as follows. Did the evangelists 'Judaize' a tradition which, until Mark (or whoever) got hold of it, did not have the Jewish story-line as a basic component? This has been the hypothesis of the Bultmann school all along, supported in our own generation by a good many

---

[27] cf. the admission by Koester 1982b, 198: 'One could with justification designate the whole first generation of Christians as "Jewish Christian".'

studies which first strip off the 'Jewish' elements from a passage and then purport to show its 'original' Hellenistic, perhaps Cynic, meaning.[28] I suggest that this makes no sense historically. The sayings do not for the most part exist in that simple form, except sometimes in the *Gospel of Thomas*, which ought to be *sub judice* at this point.[29] To put it crudely, if Christianity had started off as a not-very-Jewish movement, it is extremely implausible to suggest that it suddenly developed a penchant for rereading Jesus within a Jewish framework, just when, because of AD 70, that Jewish framework must have seemed singularly unattractive to Christians who had up till then had little time for Jewish tradition anyway. I suggest, on the contrary, that the high historical probability is the other way about, namely that (i) Christianity began within a firmly Jewish context; (ii) its earliest tellings of stories about Jesus naturally fell into recognizably Jewish forms; (iii) it was only when the stories began to be told in other contexts, where recognition of or familiarity with Jewish storytelling modes was not so likely, that they began to take on more obviously non-Jewish forms. That such a development is intrinsically likely is clear from the parallel with Josephus, who, as we saw, transforms Jewish traditions and ideas at many points into apparently Hellenistic ones. This hypothesis of development, like most others, is obviously too simplistic. There was certainly movement and change in all sorts of directions. But if we may hypothesize a *general* drift, it is far more likely to be from Jewish to Greek, not vice versa.

Classical form-criticism began with forms taken from the world of Hellenistic literature: 'apophthegms', wonder-working miracle stories, and so forth. (An 'apophthegm' is a short story leading up to a pithy saying; another, perhaps better, word for it is '*chreia*'.[30]) There are parallels to these in some Jewish writings, for instance in the rabbinic sources, but these are generally much later. To these, the classic form-critics added 'parable', of course, and other less well-defined categories such as 'legend' and the now notorious 'myth'. There was, and still is, much debate as to whether the 'pure' form of a story was likely to be original, and a more complex form a later development (as Bultmann thought), or whether to the contrary the 'pure' form represented a smoothing off, over time, of an originally rough-hewn tradition (as Taylor

---

[28] e.g. Downing 1988a, *passim*.

[29] See below, pp. 435ff.

[30] See the discussion of technical terms in Sanders and Davies 1989, 146–8. Examples of *chreiai* abound in writers such as Epictetus: e.g. *Disc.* 1.9.1: 'If what is said by the philosophers regarding the kinship of God and men be true, what other course remains for men but that which Socrates took when asked to what country he belonged, never to say "I am an Athenian", or "I am a Corinthian", but "I am a citizen of the universe"?'; 3.6.10: 'And so also [Musonius] Rufus for the most part tried to dissuade men [from the pursuit of philosophy], using such efforts to dissuade as a means of discriminating between those who were gifted and those who were not. For he used to say, "Just as a stone, even if you throw it upwards, will fall downwards to earth by virtue of its very constitution, so is also the gifted man; the more one beats him back, the more he inclines toward his natural object" '; *Frag.* 11: 'When Archelaus [king of Macedon] sent for Socrates with the intention of making him rich, the latter bade the messenger take back the following answer: "At Athens four quarts of barley-meal can be bought for an obol, and there are running springs of water".' On *chreiai* see also e.g. Buchanan 1984, ch.2; Mack 1988, 179–92. It should be noted that the word *chreia* itself continues, of course, to carry its regular non-technical meaning of 'need' in the great majority of its occurrences.

suggested). There is a lot to be said for reckoning with the possibility that traditions *both* expand *and* contract, and for refusing to accept simplistic developmental theories either way.[31]

From our earlier study of stories within the Jewish world of the first century, a case can be made out that we know what sort of stories Jesus' contemporaries regularly told and retold, forming a grid through which they perceived the whole of reality.[32] They told stories of Israel's suffering and vindication; of exile and restoration; of Passover, exodus, wandering and settlement. They told stories about Israel's god coming to redeem his people; about prophets and kings whose mighty acts were signs of this divine liberation; of the biblical stories coming true, whether secretly or openly. These are, of course, descriptions of *content*, not of *form*; yet in this case content powerfully suggests form. An excellent example of this occurs in 1 Maccabees' account of the state of things under the rule of Simon (140–34 BC). Instead of saying 'Israel lived in peace and prosperity', the writer chooses to tell the story in words which awaken all sorts of prophetic echoes:

> They tilled their land in peace;
>> the ground gave its increase,
>> and the trees of the plains their fruit.
> Old men sat in the streets;
>> they all talked together of good things,
>> and the youths put on splendid military attire.
> He supplied the towns with food,
>> and furnished them with the means of defense,
>> until his renown spread to the ends of the earth.
> He established peace in the land,
>> and Israel rejoiced with great joy.
> All the people sat under their own vines and fig trees,
>> and there was none to make them afraid . . .
> He made the sanctuary glorious,
>> and added to the vessels of the sanctuary.[33]

Thus, in typical Jewish manner, the story was invested with its full significance.

Moving back to the gospel traditions, our earlier remarks about oral history suggest that the place to start a form-critical investigation ought to be with the questions: how did Jesus' contemporaries perceive him?; how would people of that background tell stories about someone whom they perceived in that way?; and, what forms would such stories naturally take? If we proceed by this route—which has an excellent prima facie claim to be taken seriously from a historical point of view—the answers are striking.

(ii) Prophetic Acts

Jesus was perceived as a prophet. Some thought him more than that, none less; some thought him a false prophet, but this still presupposes that 'prophet'

---

[31] See above all on this point Sanders 1969.
[32] cf. ch. 8 above.
[33] 1 Macc. 14.8–15; cf. 1 Kgs. 4.25; Isa. 17.2; 36.16; Mic. 4.4; Zech. 3.10.

was the category within which he should be perceived. There were other prophet-figures in first-century Judaism: they promised their followers signs and liberation. It is highly likely that Jesus was seen in much the same way.[34] This means that from the start a good many of those who witnessed him at work in the Galilean villages would be inclined to tell stories about him which fitted their perceptions of how a prophet ought to behave. When, therefore, Jesus was perceived to be accomplishing strange deeds that reminded people of the tales of prophets of old, it was natural that retellings of them would quickly be cast into a mould which reflected, and perhaps echoed, biblical precedent.[35]

This, of course, stands normal assumptions on their head.[36] It is usually supposed that a 'biblicization' of stories took place at a fairly late, and theologically reflective, stage. I fail to see why this should be so. Granted the setting in first-century Judaism that we have set out in Part III, it is every bit as likely that Palestinian Jews in the 20s and 30s AD would tell stories about a strange healing prophet which had overtones of stories about Elijah and Elisha as it is likely that stories which originally had no such overtones would acquire them a generation later. Stories of healings are more likely to have *begun* as prophet-stories than to have developed into them with the passage of time. If, later, the same stories were retold in a context or setting where these overtones would not so readily be heard, it is at that stage, not the earlier one, that we should look for parallels in the stories of wonder-workers, 'divine men', and the like, in the Hellenistic world.

There is of course a common pattern in the 'form' of healing stories. The ailment is described; Jesus' help is sought; Jesus says and/or does something to the sufferer; a cure is effected; the cured person and/or the bystanders express astonishment and joy. I cannot regard this as striking evidence of anything in particular. It is really quite difficult to see how the story of a healing could take any other form. Certainly the formal parallels with non-biblical healing stories prove almost nothing except that one healing looks quite like another.

One of the greatest prophets was, of course, Moses; Moses had led the children of Israel through the Red Sea, and had been the divine agent in causing them to be fed in the wilderness. It is clear that some of the strange things[37] which Jesus did—the stilling of storms, the multiplication of loaves—were regarded as echoing these themes. Once again, as with the healings, it is far more likely that the stories were originally told in a Jewish framework which allowed overtones of exodus, and of psalms which spoke of YHWH's victory over the mighty waters, to be clearly heard, than that they started as Hel-

---

[34] See Horsley and Hanson 1985, ch. 4; Crossan 1991, ch. 8.
[35] cf. Moule 1982 [1962], 109f. Cp. e.g. Mk. 10.46–52 with Isa. 35.5f.; Lk. 7.11–17 with 1 Kgs. 17.17–24; 2 Kgs. 4.32–7; cf. Lk. 9.8, 19; 13.32f.
[36] cf. e.g. Mack 1988, ch. 8.
[37] We should hesitate to call them 'miracles', since that word imports all sorts of anachronistic eighteenth-century ideas into the discussion. Luke calls them 'paradoxes' (5.26). See further e.g. Craig 1986 and the discussion in the next volume of the present series.

lenistic 'proofs' of Jesus' mighty power and only developed scriptural associations at a later stage.[38]

(iii) Controversies

If Jesus was perceived as a prophet, he was also perceived as the focal point of some sort of new group, movement or perhaps sect within Judaism. From our earlier study of sects and groups it is clear that such bodies would tell and retell the biblical stories in which a righteous Jewish remnant stands up for Israel's god against pagan (or even Jewish) authorities, and is vindicated.[39] A group that had already begun to regard itself like this, and which was fortifying itself with such retellings, would naturally interpret opposition to itself or its leader in terms of biblical stories that provided a precedent. One way of doing this is clearly visible in the Scrolls: the book of Habakkuk is mined for secret clues about the battle between the Teacher of Righteousness and the Wicked Priest on the one hand, and between the community and the Kittim (i.e. the Romans) on the other.[40] This gives a parallel in content, though not in form, to the synoptic stories; the form of the Habakkuk commentary reflects a quasi-academic exercise arising out of an incident, rather than, as with the synoptic material, a retelling of the incident itself.

I suggest that the controversy stories in the synoptic gospels may well have started life in a similar setting—not the academic exercise, but the sense of a small group perceiving opposition to itself in the light of biblical precedent. It is highly likely that Jesus met with opposition during his work; this cannot be substantiated in detail here, but will be spelled out in the next volume. It is also extremely probable that such opposition, when it occurred, did not take the form of a single question or challenge, answered by a single remark from Jesus—which is of course the form of most controversy stories in the gospels. Debate is likely to have raged to and fro, more like the protracted and frankly rambling discussion in John 6 than like any of the well-known stories in Mark 2 and 3. It is, further, highly probable that a group like that around Jesus, regarding itself as the nucleus of a divinely called remnant, as some sort of spearhead of renewal, would instantly 'read' any opposition in terms of the battle, with clear scriptural precedent, that all such groups would expect to fight. It is therefore to be expected that, as they told and retold the story of this or that brush with opposition, whether official or self-appointed, they would naturally both shrink the scene to its bare essentials *and choose as those bare essentials the elements which highlighted the group's identity as the beleaguered renewal movement awaiting vindication.* If a group has fuelled its hopes on biblical tales in which the true Israelites are called to account by the authorities, and subsequently vindicated, and if this group then perceives itself to be in an

---

[38] cf. Mt. 14.13–27, etc.; and e.g. Ps. 66.5f.; 93.1–5.
[39] cf. ch. 8 above, discussing e.g. Daniel and Susannah.
[40] On the Wicked Priest: 1QpHab 1.12f.; 2.1–10; 5.9–12; 8.3—10.5; 11.3—12.10; on the Kittim: 2.11—5.8.

analogous situation, it will 'see' the events in question through this grid of expectation, and will be highly likely to tell the story of the events in a way which reflects the same form.[41]

I suggest, therefore, that the 'apophthegms', 'paradigms', 'pronouncement stories', '*chreiai*', or whatever we like to call them, should have their form-critical history reassessed, and that the normal (i.e. Bultmannian) way of reading them should be stood on its head.[42] These stories are of course normally regarded as having started out life as detached individual sayings, which gradually acquired a story-line in order to provide a more fitting showcase for the telling rejoinder of Jesus to his opponents. The early church is supposed to have remembered (or created) isolated sayings for isolated needs, and only gradually thought of giving them a narrative framework.[43] I suggest that, within the original contexts, the most natural Jewish way for supporters of Jesus to tell stories about his controversial actions and words was to tell them in the form of Jewish controversy-stories, such as we find (for instance) in the book of Daniel. These contexts can be explored one by one. At one level, there is the context of Jesus' ministry itself. Stories would be told quickly, excitedly, when Jesus was still in the same village. At another level, there are memories of events concerning him which were retold during his lifetime when he had moved on elsewhere. At another level again, there are the memories of him which were cherished after Easter. In each case, the pattern of the story would be the same, and would carry the same echoes of Jewish tradition. The true Israelites act boldly; they are challenged by real or self-appointed authorities; they stick to their guns, often with a well-chosen phrase; and they are vindicated. In the greatest Danielic controversy-and-vindication story of all, it is 'one like a son of man' who is vindicated. The gospel stories have exactly this form, and as often as not end with a reference to Jesus as the 'son of man'.[44]

If the earliest form of the controversy-stories is therefore likely to have been that of the Jewish stories of the struggles and vindication of the little remnant or renewal movement, it is not difficult to see how these stories could have become smoothed down over time into something more like Hellenistic *chreiai*, especially as the news of Jesus passed beyond the area where Jewish-style controversy-and-vindication stories would be an expected form. This, I suggest, is the most likely explanation for works like the *Gospel of Thomas*. So far from isolated sayings becoming short *chreiai*, and then longer stories, the opposite process seems to me historically far more probable. The greater number of such isolated sayings in Luke may well serve as initial confirmation of this suggestion.[45]

---

[41] Nickelsburg 1980 has argued this out in relation to the passion narrative. I suggest it holds good for the smaller-scale controversy stories as well.

[42] For a fresh statement of the traditional view see Mack 1988, ch. 7, e.g. 199: the later tradition turned Jesus the 'Cynic sage' into 'an imperious judge and sovereign' who 'rules by fiat'.

[43] A good recent example of this is Koester's argument (1990, 85–113) that many of the sayings in *Gos. Thom.* are more original than their equivalents in the synoptic tradition, since they lack a narrative framework and such features as apocalyptic judgment.

[44] e.g. Mk. 2.1–12, 15–17, 18–22, 23–8; 3.1–6; 14.53–64; all with pars. in Mt. and/or Lk.

[45] e.g. Lk. 17.20–1, which has exactly the form, and the detachment, of *chreiai* in regular Hellenistic works.

(iv) Parables

We have already discussed the best-known parable in the synoptics, and have suggested that Mark 4.1–20 is to be seen as a whole, within its Jewish context, and as approximating at the level of form to an apocalyptic revelation.[46] The normal form-critical reading of parables, again, runs the other way. Parables originally had a simple form, made a single point, and were close to real life. As the tradition developed, moving out towards Hellenism, they became more fanciful, odd details were added, and above all they became (the dreaded conclusion) allegory.[47]

Such a conclusion could only be seriously advanced, I submit, in a world that had failed completely to understand the Jewish background to the New Testament. Granted the absurdity of the allegorical fancies of some of the later church Fathers, it remains the case that parabolic stories are to be found throughout Jewish writings, reaching one particular high point in the often bizarre visions of apocalyptic. These should not be isolated as though they did not belong with the wider prophetic tradition, in which Isaiah could sing a song of a vineyard; in which Hosea could take an entire book to explore the strange relationship between his own marriage and that of YHWH with Israel; and in which Nathan could tell David a thoroughly subversive story about a rich man, a poor man, and a little ewe lamb. Jesus, again as a prophet, drew on this rich tradition in order to tell stories which were designed, one way and another, to break open his contemporaries' worldview every bit as subversively as Nathan did David's; to announce that the wedding feast of YHWH and his people was now being spread, but that many who assumed that they would enjoy it would not; and to speak of the vineyard and its present tenants, and of the owner's son who would be rejected when he came to get the fruit. When Jesus' hearers retold these and other parables, the high historical probability is that they would tell them precisely as prophetic, and sometimes as apocalyptic, stories.

The form of Mark 4.1–20 reflects this, as was shown in the previous chapter. So does the (split) form of the parable of the wheat and the weeds in Matthew 13.24–30, 36–43, where the apocalyptic imagery ceases to be mere overtone and becomes the main theme:

> . . . so will it be at the close of the age: the Son of Man will send out his angels, and gather into his kingdom all causes of stumbling and those who create lawlessness, and throw them into the furnace of fire, where there shall be weeping and gnashing of teeth. Then the righteous will shine like the sun in the kingdom of their father.[48]

That might have come straight out of *1 Enoch* or 4 Ezra. It seems to me far more likely that such traditions were cherished and retold, and put into some-

---

[46] Above, p. 394.

[47] The well-known line of scholarship from Jülicher 1910 [1899], through Dodd 1978 [1935], to Jeremias 1963 [1947]. For the contrary view see e.g. Boucher 1977; Caird 1980, 160–7; Moule 1982 [1962], 111–18; Drury 1985.

[48] Mt. 13.40–3. Prof. C. F. D. Moule suggests to me that 'the weeping and gnashing of teeth' may be a reference to Ps. 112.10, turning that verse (originally aimed at 'the wicked') into a stern warning to renegade *Israel*.

thing approaching their present form, within the context of an eager Jewish hope that believed itself fulfilled through the work of Jesus, rather than that they began life as simple one-dimensional stories, and gradually acquired their apocalyptic (or other) interpretations at a later date.[49] To suggest that the form, as well as the content, of these parables speaks of a rejection and opposition which is unthinkable in the ministry of Jesus, but is credible when set in the 50s and later, is, I submit, to misunderstand both the literary form and the ministry of Jesus.[50] Equally, to suggest that parables become more allegorical as they become more Hellenistic is to ignore the *Gospel of Thomas*. There, in perhaps the most overtly Hellenistic moment in the synoptic tradition, we find a complete absence of any 'interpretations' attached to the parables. The development seems, if anything, to have run in exactly the opposite direction to that normally imagined.[51] The fuller explanations, drawing out the thrust of the stories in terms of apocalyptic Jewish ideas, are likely to have come very early. In some cases at least it seems as though the more clipped and cryptic forms were the later developments.

(v) Longer Units

A similar case could also be made out for an early, and very Jewish, development of some of the longer units in the synoptic tradition. I have already indicated that I do not think Mark 13 a 'foreign body' within that gospel;[52] but this does not mean that a discourse something like that chapter did not attain an oral form quite early on, perhaps within ten or twenty years of the crucifixion. That has recently been argued, indeed, from two very different points of view.[53] It is impossible to discuss these proposals here; it is enough to note that they can be made very seriously. Similarly, the story of Jesus' trial and death—the so-called 'passion narrative'—has been examined from this point of view, and suggestions have been made both that it embodies a well-known Jewish form and that it reflects, in its earliest reconstructible version, events that are very early in the life of the church.[54] It is not just possible, but very likely, that the first post-Easter followers of Jesus would tell the story of his death, as 1 Maccabees 14 told the story of Simon's rule, in such a way as to awaken biblical and traditional echoes.[55] Though it is again impossible to discuss this further here, the fact that such proposals can be made indicates that form-criticism by itself, so far from predisposing us to imagine an early non-

[49] As to the parable's present positioning: it seems to me highly likely that the evangelist found, or knew, Mt. 13.24–30, 36–43 as a single unit, and that he has deliberately split it up in order to create a frame for the two shorter parables (13.31–2, 33) and the summary (13.34–5).

[50] Against Mack 1988, ch. 6.

[51] e.g. *Gos. Thom.* 65 (the 'Wicked Tenants'). Cf. Kermode 1979, 43: 'the parable [of the Wicked Tenants] is an allegory, and has no point except as an allegory'.

[52] Above, p. 393.

[53] Wenham 1984; Theissen 1991, ch. 3.

[54] Nickelsburg 1980; Theissen 1991, ch. 4. For an entirely different attempt to understand the passion narrative, cf. Crossan 1988.

[55] cf. too Moule 1982 [1962], 137f.

narrative Christianity and a later 'historicized' one, may well eventually tell in the opposite direction.

(vi) Conclusion

It therefore seems clear to me—though lack of space means that this argument is bare to the point of indecency—that a case can at least be made out for a form-critical analysis of the major types of material in the synoptic gospels, as follows. The initial forms of the stories correspond to forms which are known to have been available to Jesus' first followers, and to forms characteristic of stories that were used within first-century Judaism, particularly among those who were longing for their god to act in calling a great renewal movement around a prophetic, or indeed messianic, figure. It is also likely that these early forms will have been subject to change, and particularly to modification in the direction of Hellenistic stories, or detached *chreiai*. To suggest, as is regularly done, that the development can only have been in the opposite direction, with short *chreiai* first and fully-grown stories last, is to exploit our comparative ignorance of early Christianity beyond acceptable limits. Such a view, finding apocalyptic distasteful, has produced a new myth of innocence, in which the early church, and indeed Jesus himself, were uncorrupted by any of the wicked notions that Mark and the rest were to foist on to the tradition a generation later. But this is a strange Hellenistic innocence, which bears little relation to anything we actually know about Jesus, the early church, or indeed the church of the second generation. It is indeed, ironically, a 'myth' in a more developed Bultmannian sense: created out of nothing, it seems to be invoked to sustain certain twentieth-century worldviews. The only viewpoint to which it corresponds in the first two hundred years of Christianity is the strange, unstoried world apparently represented by the *Gospel of Thomas* and the (extremely hypothetical) early Q. There is every reason to suppose *both* that the great majority of the Jesus-stories that circulated within very early Christianity were vitally shaped by the theology and agenda of the early Christians, *and* that they remain, irreducibly, stories about Jesus.[56]

3. Stories but no Story? Q and *Thomas*

For fifty years, covering the middle of the present century, more or less all New Testament scholars believed that the main sources of Matthew and Luke were Mark and a lost document which may for convenience be called Q.[57] The

---

[56] An irreverent analogy may be permitted at this point. A well-known brand of malt whisky makes advertising capital of the fact that it is stored in casks formerly used for sherry. This gives the product its characteristic bouquet and flavour. But it remains whisky. The early Christian casks in which the Jesus-stories were stored for a generation have flavoured them in all sorts of ways. But they remain Jesus-stories.

[57] For the reasons for, and history of, the hypothesis, cf. e.g. Bellinzoni 1985; Neill and Wright 1988, 128–36; for recent discussion, Lührmann 1989; Piper 1989; Koester 1990, 128–71. The classic text is Streeter 1930 [1924].

hypothesis has declined in popularity over the last twenty years or so, but despite strong attacks is still equally strongly defended.[58] But its role in scholarship has undergone, for the most part, a radical and fascinating change.

At the same time, it has long been the received wisdom among students of early Christianity that the so-called *Gospel of Thomas*, a collection of sayings of Jesus which was found among a collection of Coptic codices at Nag Hammadi in Upper Egypt in 1945, belongs to a comparatively late stage in the development of the Christianity.[59] It is first mentioned by Hippolytus and Origen in the early years of the third century. It is a random collection of short sayings, almost all introduced simply with the phrase 'Jesus said . . .', and without any attempt at a connecting narrative, even at the beginning or the end. Like Q, its role in New Testament scholarship has changed dramatically within the last few years.

The original proposers of the Q hypothesis came to it by a detached, almost mathematical argument. Matthew and Luke overlap in a good many places where there is nothing in Mark. It makes sense to suggest that in these passages they were following a common document, now lost. 'Q' was a way of producing a simple hypothesis which appeared to fit the evidence. Q clearly pre-dated Matthew and Luke, and so was early. The Oxford scholars whose work on the synoptic problem was eventually crystallized in Streeter's major work *The Synoptic Gospels* were for the most part interested in Q as a means of gaining access to the historical—by which they would have meant the 'real'—Jesus. Mark, they thought, gives us an outline of the ministry and the main events; Q, a solid collection of Jesus' sayings. Both can be accepted confidently as going back, more or less, to Jesus himself. The additions in Matthew and Luke are less certain, but not so much hinges on them if the agenda of the moment is (as it was for Streeter and his colleagues) the defence of something like traditional Christianity against the ravages of David Friedrich Strauss and his successors.[60]

The Q hypothesis held sway, virtually unchallenged, for half a century. Solid doubts were expressed from outside the mainstream guild, and small pinpricks were aimed at it from within;[61] however, the consensus was not disturbed. Farmer's book (1964) was the first to shake the foundations, and they are still regarded as shaky in many quarters today.[62] But, just when debate on the synoptic problem looked like becoming simply an irrelevant crossword-puzzle,

---

[58] For the attacks: e.g. Farmer 1964; Stoldt 1980 [1977]. For the defence: e.g. Neirynck 1974; Styler in Moule 1982 [1962], 285–316, esp. 298–304; Tuckett 1983b. For recent representative articles on relevant topics see Boismard et al (eds.) 1990.

[59] The Coptic text was subsequently identified as a translation of a Greek original, known in some fragmentary mss. For a full discussion, cf. Koester 1990, 75–128; for a detailed comparison of *Gos. Thom.* with the Greek papyri, Bartsch 1960; Fitzmyer 1971, ch.15; for the history of research on *Thomas* see Fallon and Cameron 1988. Koester 1990, 43f. speaks of 'the prevailing prejudice' against *Thomas* and other 'apocryphal' gospels.

[60] On this agenda in Germany as well as in Britain cf. Lührmann 1989, 51–3.

[61] e.g. Jeremias 1966 [1930], 90–2; Chapman 1937; Farrer 1955.

[62] e.g. Sanders and Davies 1989, 112–19; O'Neill 1991. O'Neill suggests (483) that 'the scholarly community of New Testament experts has cut itself very badly with Occam's Razor'.

a new motive has emerged for the study of Q, strong enough to give fresh impetus to what had seemed almost a dying cottage-industry.[63]

Q, it is believed in some quarters today, not only existed as a document, but *developed* in a way which can be plotted with some accuracy. Moreover, its original existence does indeed take us quite close to Jesus, but it is a Jesus quite unlike the Jesus that Streeter and his colleagues thought they would find by this route. In its original form, Q reflects a very early Christian community for whom the Jewish stories, both in form and in content, were not particularly important. The focus, instead, was on a different style and content of teaching: the Hellenistic philosophy known as Cynicism, on the one hand, and, on the other, a tradition of teaching which offered a secret wisdom, a secret Gnosis. It was, in fact, a community that would have been just about as happy with the *Gospel of Thomas*. Jesus was a teacher of aphoristic, quasi-Gnostic, quasi-Cynic wisdom; his first followers collected his sayings in the way that one would expect with that sort of teacher—as, for example, Arrian did with Epictetus. Q is one result of this process. Its later use by Matthew and Luke represents an attempt, which may have already begun in the later strands of Q, to blend these non-historical, aphoristic and potentially Gnostic teachings with a Jewish-style telling of the Jesus-stories, and the Jesus-Story, that offers a fundamental change of direction and emphasis to that embodied in at least the early strands of Q itself.[64] It should be stressed that by no means all contemporary supporters of the Q hypothesis would take this line. Some continue to insist that the document(s) must be seen as prophetic and Jewish-Christian, rather than within a Cynic, Stoic or Gnostic matrix.[65] But the majority of recent Q scholarship is firmly within the tradition I have just described.

This Q-and-*Thomas* hypothesis belongs closely with, and both reinforces and is reinforced by, a way of telling the story of early Christianity which runs as follows.[66] The earliest stage, dated within ten to thirty years of the death of Jesus, is represented by the first version of Q. This is basically a 'sapiential' document, offering its readers the choice of two ways, the way of wisdom and the way of folly. At this stage, Q knows nothing of an apocalyptic future expectation, and is silent about the 'coming of the son of man': the End, in the only sense that matters, has already come with the teaching of Jesus, specifically with the purveying of a special and hidden wisdom which sets his hearers apart from the rest of the world. This is, as it were, a 'vertical', rather than a 'horizontal', eschatology. The 'End' has nothing to do with the events for which Israel was waiting, but rather with a fresh, secret divine revelation. No connection is made with Jewish expectations: there is no controversy between the followers of Jesus and those of John the Baptist.

---

[63] Not all modern study of Q has taken this new line; cf. e.g. Theissen 1991, ch. 5, and others in n.65 below.

[64] cf. e.g. Kloppenborg 1987; Downing 1988; Mack 1988; Crossan 1991. Cf. too the many detailed studies in recent periodical literature, e.g. Seeley 1992.

[65] cf. e.g. Tuckett 1989; Theissen 1991, ch. 5; Catchpole 1992.

[66] cf. e.g. Kloppenborg 1987; Koester 1990, 128–71.

This (hypothetical) first stage of Q is therefore very close in substance, as well as quite close in form, to the *Gospel of Thomas*. *Thomas* knows nothing of an apocalyptic future: the hidden wisdom in the present is what matters—a 'realized eschatology' that actually has nothing to do with Jewish 'eschatology' per se, and everything to do with a secret or hidden revelation that Jesus imparts to his followers in the present. So close are *Thomas* and Q that a saying which occurs in only one of either Matthew or Luke can be confirmed by a parallel in *Thomas* as a Q saying, omitted by the other evangelist, rather than special material of Matthew or Luke.[67]

Q then undergoes a redaction. At this stage the motifs previously absent are introduced: 'the most obvious signs of a secondary redaction of Q can be found in the apocalyptic announcement of judgment and of the coming of the Son of man which conflicts with the emphasis upon the presence of the kingdom in wisdom sayings and prophetic announcements'.[68] This leaves some traces at the level of *form*: a collection of sapiential speeches becomes a wisdom-plus-apocalyptic book. But, despite the protests of its proponents, it is clear that the basic difference is *theological*. The original Q had a realized eschatology, i.e. a 'kingdom of god' in the here and now. The redacted Q has a future-orientated, much more Jewish, eschatology.[69]

At about this stage, some little while after AD 70, Luke makes use of Q. It has long been believed by those who support the Q hypothesis that Luke is closer to the supposed 'original Q' than Matthew: where these two canonical gospels overlap with 'Q material', Luke's version is regularly supposed to be the earlier and less developed.[70] But this does not mean that the 'developments' evidenced in Matthew are simply the work of the evangelist himself. A further version of Q seems to have been produced between Luke's use of it and Matthew's: at this stage the (second) Q redactor, reflecting perhaps a decision by his community, comes down in favour of Christians continuing to observe the Jewish Torah, something that was not envisaged in the early period. Finally, Matthew makes use of this doubly-redacted Q, weaving it into new patterns of his own devising.[71]

What is to be said about this detailed and intricate hypothesis? Some might find it easy to pour scorn on it. 'Q' is no more, after all, than a figment of scholarly imagination (i.e. a hypothesis). Not one scrap of manuscript evidence has turned up which can plausibly be thought of as part of this document, in any of its recensions. The three supposed stages by which it came into its final form, visible in Matthew, reflect suspiciously closely the theological and history-of-religions predilections of one strand within modern New Testament studies, rather than any hard evidence within the first century. The neat 'coincidence' whereby the *earliest* form of Q happens to have so much in com-

---

[67] e.g. Lk. 17.20f., par. *Gos. Thom.* 113; cf. Koester 1990, 89.

[68] Koester 1990, 135, citing Lührmann 1969; Kloppenborg 1987.

[69] cf. Koester 1990, 149f. The echoes of this scheme are, of course, Bultmannian: cf. Bultmann 1956, 186f.

[70] My suggestion above, that short *chreiai* may well in certain cases be the more 'developed' form, and Jewish-style narratives the more primitive, might compel a reopening of this question.

[71] cf. Koester 1990, 162–71; on developments in Q between Lk. and Mt., 167–70.

mon with the *Gospel of Thomas* could conceivably be due to (a) the theory's having made a brilliant guess at how to strip off redactional layers and (b) a very early date for *Thomas*. Almost anything is possible in history, and one cannot rule out this solution from the start. But equally—some would say, far more likely—it may be due to (a) a desire on the part of some modern readers to imagine early Christianity as very similar to the religion of *Thomas* and (b) the consequent critical activity of pulling apart what is already a purely hypothetical document, Q, in order to reveal an 'early version' which just happens to fit the history-of-religions theory. Frankly, some of the arguments advanced along the way within the suggested model look suspiciously naïve; others, manifestly and damagingly circular.[72]

These general problems about the Q-plus-*Thomas* hypothesis lead to some more particular ones, to do with the categories involved. First, by what stretch of the imagination can we insist, in relation to a hypothetical document whose origin is supposedly found in otherwise unknown Jewish-Christian groups in first-century Palestine, that a firm distinction could be made between 'sapiential' and 'prophetic' traditions? Koester wisely attempts to hold them together;[73] yet elsewhere in recent discussion they are firmly set over against one another.[74] But once we admit 'prophetic' material in Q, it becomes extremely difficult, given the high profile of apocalyptic language and imagery in first-century Palestine, to keep 'apocalyptic' out as well.[75] Q looks more and more like a combination of wisdom-tradition *and* prophetic discourse; and there is every reason, within the actual known history of first-century Palestinian religion, as opposed to the mythical model constructed by some scholars, why such a combination should be perfectly natural.

Likewise, there is every reason not to split apart 'realized' and 'future' eschatology. To drive a wedge between the two in the interests of an Early Q that looks to the present and a Late Q that looks to the future is totally unwarranted. At this point we may refer to a well-known Jewish book never mentioned by Koester in his recent and full discussion of Q. The *Community*

---

[72] The acceptance at face value of *Thomas'* testimony about its origin (saying 12) by Crossan 1991, 427, and the citing of traditions about Matthew from *Gos. Thom.* and *Dial. Sav.* in Koester 1990, 166f., are the sort of arguments that would be laughed off the stage if they were advanced in respect of a canonical work. Examples of risky circularity occur in Kloppenborg 1987, 262 (the temptation story came into Q late, since it signifies Q's movement towards 'a narrative or biographical cast': contrast Theissen 1991, 206–20!); Koester 1990, 137 (sayings are given a place in Early Q because of their parallel with *Thomas*, when the only reason for thinking *Thomas* and Early Q to be parallel is the similarity between *Thomas* and Early-Q-as-thus-defined); 146 (the parable of the faithful and unfaithful servant cannot be Early Q, *because* it is 'an allegorizing admonition which is wholly dominated by the expectation of the coming of the Son of man', when elsewhere we are told that son of man sayings cannot be in Early Q *because* that document only contained sapiential and realized-eschatology sayings); and elsewhere.

[73] Koester 1990, 156f.

[74] Supporting 'sapiential': Kloppenborg 1987. In favour of 'prophetic': Sato 1988 (though cf. Downing's review in *Biblica* 72, 1991, 127–32) and Catchpole 1992. On the split, cf. Crossan 1991, 227–30 and elsewhere.

[75] See Catchpole 1992, 220f. On the nature of 'apocalyptic' see ch. 10 above; if the argument there is anywhere near correct, the entire reading of 'apocalyptic' within the recent discussions of Q and *Thomas* ought to be rethought.

Rule from Qumran is, like the hypothetical Q, a book which sets out the 'two ways' that one may follow, the way of wisdom and the way of folly (3.13—4.26). The same book makes it quite clear that the community is already living in the time of salvation: 'realized eschatology' is evident in every column, since the basis of the community's very existence is its belief that Israel's god has re-established his covenant with precisely this group. There is even some reason to understand this 'realized eschatology' in a vertical as well as a horizontal sense, since the wonderful hymns with which the book ends contain several passages which, if detached from their contexts, would look perfectly at home in the *Gospel of Thomas*.[76] The same book, equally, sees a future still before the community: the Messiahs of Israel and of Aaron are yet to come (9.11), and the Day of Revenge is still awaited (9.23). Here we have, I submit, a document' which is far closer to Q 'as we have it' (i.e. at its most obvious reconstruction out of the non-Marcan portions of Matthew and Luke) than is the *Gospel of Thomas*. Moreover, it is manifestly a piece of Jewish sectarian literature, as Q must have been if it existed; it is the manifesto, the community rule, of its group, enshrining the teachings of its founder on the one hand and the present ordering, experience and hope of the community on the other: again, Q, if it existed, must have been this sort of book. The Qumran *Community Rule* offers excellent evidence that the divisions made in the Q material by Kloppenborg and others have no real basis in the actual history of first-century religion, but belong rather to the world of contemporary mythologizing, projecting unwarranted distinctions on to the screen of speculative history.

One of the most telling weaknesses in the whole Q-and-*Thomas* hypothesis, it seems to me, is the presence within *Thomas* of sayings about the 'kingdom of god', or, as the book regularly calls it, the kingdom of the Father.[77] From our earlier study of the Jewish evidence, it is unthinkable that this motif should be introduced into a community from scratch with the meaning that it comes to have in *Thomas*, i.e. the present secret religious knowledge of a heavenly world. It is overwhelmingly likely that the use of this emphatically Jewish kingdom-language originated with an overtly Jewish movement which used it in a sense close to its mainline one, i.e. which spoke of the end of exile, the restoration of Israel, the rebuilding of the Temple, the return of YHWH to Zion, and so forth, however much these ideas were transformed within the ministry of Jesus and the lives of his first followers. If there has been a shift in the usage one way or the other, it is far more likely to have been *from* this Jewish home base into a quasi-Gnostic sense, rather than from a Gnostic sense, for which there is no known, or imaginable, precedent, to a re-Judaized

---

[76] e.g. 1QS 11.5–7: 'From His marvellous mysteries/ is the light in my heart. My eyes have gazed/ on that which is eternal,/ on wisdom concealed from men,/ on knowledge and wise design/ [hidden] from the sons of men;/ on a fountain of righteousness/ and on a storehouse of power,/ on a spring of glory/ [hidden] from the assembly of flesh.' A similarity between 1QS and Gnostic writings is seen by e.g. Rudolph 1983 [1977], 280. The same writer (277f.) stresses that, though Gnosticism has some links with Jewish apocalyptic, the latter retains a 'horizontal' eschatology as opposed to Gnosticism's 'vertical' one.

[77] See esp. *Gos. Thom.* 3, 22, 46, 49, 97, 113, 114.

one—a shift which, on the hypothesis, must have taken place somewhere between an early *Thomas* and a later Mark.

If this Q-and-*Thomas* hypothesis creates so many difficulties, does this mean that we should abandon the Q hypothesis altogether? By no means. There are clearly other ways of stating the hypothesis, which are not open to any of the objections just raised, and which focus simply on the attempt to solve the synoptic problem in its own terms. There are also completely different traditio-historical possibilities on offer in relation to Q in current scholarship; one need only cite again the work of Theissen.[78] There is no reason why some form of this hypothesis should not continue to be fruitful, though I suspect it will be more a matter of 'Q material', floating traditions to which Matthew and Luke both had access, than of a solid and reconstructible document. But it does seem to me that the more speculation there is about Q the less plausible the hypothesis appears overall.

This may be unfair: bad coin is perhaps driving out good. But some of the coin is bad indeed. So many unproveable and mutually contradictory things are said about Q that the non-specialist may well feel the whole discussion is a waste of time. In particular, as soon as the argument turns to the potential relationship between *Mark* and Q, the sceptic must protest: those who first hypothesized Q, after all, saw it simply and solely as consisting of those passages in Matthew and Luke *which do not overlap with Mark*. Of course, if Q existed, and if it extended beyond those overlaps, as most proponents of Q are now inclined to suggest, it may well have contained all sorts of things for which there is now no evidence. It may, in particular, have contained birth narratives, passion narratives, Peter's confession, and all sorts of interesting christological, apocalyptic and other material. We simply do not know. Once we admit that any of the evangelists, or any transmitters of written tradition, chose to omit any scrap of evidence available to them, there is no means whatever of being certain about the extent of earlier hypothetical documents.[79] Supporters of Q should beware; if first-century editors were allowed to omit as well as to add material, the case for saying that Luke simply used Matthew looks more and more plausible.[80] It would therefore be as well to keep on a tight rein any theories which depend on the significance of, for instance, Q's *not* having a passion narrative. Proceeding down that sort of road is like walking blindly into a maze without a map.

Finally in relation to Q: if some sort of Q existed, and if it contained roughly the material it was originally imagined to have contained, is there a more plausible life-setting for it than those sketched above? Here we rely again, as all searches for life-settings do, on assumptions about Jesus and about the subsequent church. These assumptions, to avoid the wrong sort of circularity, must stand up to being tested in the light of material other than simply that which is to be explained. In this process, we cannot ignore the evidence of Paul, or assume that Q belonged to a totally different branch of

---

[78] Theissen 1991.
[79] For this problem in Pauline studies, cf. Wright 1991a, 100.
[80] cf. Goulder 1974, and the discussion in Sanders and Davies 1989, 112–15.

Christianity to that which he represents. Q belongs, if anywhere, within the early missionary community of Jesus' followers, but how do we conceive of that group? The early Palestinian Christians, still with a strong awareness of Jesus as a prophet announcing the kingdom, and with a clear sense that this kingdom would subvert the existing Jewish structures, almost certainly announced to their contemporaries that the kingdom for which they had longed had indeed arrived in and through Jesus, even though it was not as they imagined it. However, the all-important difference between expectation and reality was *not* that the kingdom was Gnostic or Platonic rather than essentially Jewish and historical, but that it was based upon Jesus rather than upon a restoration of Jewish national and ethnic primacy, and that the former actually subverted the latter. This was a message which could naturally draw upon traditions containing 'apocalyptic' sayings as well as 'wisdom' sayings, embracing between those two many 'prophetic' aspects as well. The document, if it existed, may have been more a collection of preachers' materials than any attempt at a total narrative. Yet if Catchpole and others are right, and Q began with the story of John the Baptist, it may be the case that some sense of the total story of Jesus, rather than simply an abstracted collection of sayings, was present from the beginning. If so, the story in question belongs clearly on the map we have already sketched of both the large and the small stories which characterized the early Christian movement. It will not have been primarily a Cynic-style document. It will have been a Jewish-style story capable of taking on the Hellenistic world. It will have seen Jesus as *both* the focal point of the Jewish sapiential, prophetic and apocalyptic traditions *and* the one who had inaugurated the worldwide kingdom of Israel's god, the creator of the world.[81]

Finally in relation to *Thomas*: it seems to me equally clear that some of the sayings in *Thomas* are derived from the synoptic tradition and that some, which may well go back a very long way, are independent.[82] But hardly any of them (except for the parables) contain stories in themselves, and the work as a whole has, at the level of poetic sequence, no plot whatsoever. This in itself is strong evidence of a matrix outside the entire context that we have been considering in the last three chapters.[83] If, granted this absence of narrative or plot

---

[81] On the debate as to whether Q reflects a Cynic background, cf. Downing 1988 (in favour); Tuckett 1989 (against).

[82] Tuckett (1988) has argued strongly that some sayings in *Gos. Thom.* reflect elements in the synoptics which are arguably redactional, thus showing dependence on the synoptics themselves rather than on pre-synoptic material. For the debate as a whole see Fallon and Cameron 1988, 4213–24.

[83] Against Koester 1990, 124. It also shows, despite the protestations of Koester 1990, 80, that *Thomas* is fundamentally *un*like *Sirach* or the *Wisdom of Solomon*. Both of those books have sequence and, to a considerable extent, plot; so, even, do some parts of Proverbs (e.g. chs. 1–9). James and the *Didache*, also cited by Koester as parallels to *Thomas*, have far more sequential thought, and are certainly different in form from a collection of sayings almost all beginning with 'Jesus said . . .' (though on James cf. Schenke 1983, esp. 225–7). Even *Pirke Aboth*, another work which should perhaps be brought into the discussion, has more movement of thought than *Thomas*. The only real parallel to *Thomas* in the first century turns out to be Q—more specifically, the 'early' version of Q, painstakingly 'reconstructed' by those committed to finding early parallels for *Thomas*.

at the level of poetic structure, we approach *Thomas* with the insistent question as to its implied narrative world, the reply we get is most instructive. It presupposes a story in which the traditional concerns of Judaism play no part at all. Its implicit story has to do with a figure who imparts a secret, hidden wisdom to those close to him, so that they can perceive a new truth and be saved by it. 'The Thomas Christians are told the truth about their divine origins, and given the secret passwords that will prove effective in the return journey to their heavenly home.'[84] This is, obviously, the non-historical story of Gnosticism. As we conclude our discussion of stories in early Christianity it has to be said that *Thomas* stands out from everything else we have examined. It is simply the case that, on good historical grounds, it is far more likely that the book represents a radical translation, and indeed subversion, of first-century Christianity into a quite different sort of religion, than that it represents the original of which the longer gospels are distortions. Some of the technical terms, and recognizable versions of many sayings, are there, but the essential substance is altered.[85] *Thomas* reflects a symbolic universe, and a worldview, which are radically different to those of the early Judaism and Christianity which we have studied. In particular, it marks itself out as different from the longer gospels and Paul; different also from the shorter units of which the longer gospels are mostly composed; and even (if indeed it ever really existed) different from Q.

---

[84] Koester 1990, 125, cf. 124–8. Compare Fallon and Cameron 1988, 4230–6.
[85] This is therefore not prejudice, as Koester alleges, but historical judgment.

Chapter Fifteen

THE EARLY CHRISTIANS: A PRELIMINARY SKETCH

1. Introduction

It remains to draw together the threads of this Part of the book. Who were the early Christians? What were their aims and objectives? What did they believe? What did they hope for? This can only be a rough statement, as much agenda as conclusion. Without a full treatment of Jesus and Paul, and without a far more detailed study of the gospels and their traditions than has been possible in this volume, we cannot go nearly as far as we might like (and as we hope to do in succeeding volumes). But some preliminary points can be made. As with all historical reconstruction, we hereby take risks: 'Anyone who is not prepared to enter on risky experiments deserves our respect for his solid principles. But, conversely, perhaps he will concede to us that historical work cannot live without reconstructions . . .'[1]

2. Aims[2]

Jerusalem witnessed Jesus' death; within, at the most, twenty-five years, Athens and Rome had heard of it too. This sums up two fundamental things about early Christianity. It spread like wildfire: as religions and philosophies go, it was exceedingly quick off the starting-line. And it soon made inroads into cultures quite different from that of its birth: the Greco-Roman world was forced to come to terms with what was originally a Jewish message.

I have argued in the previous chapters that the spread of Christianity had a good deal to do with the nature of the stories it characteristically told. It is often claimed, in one way or another, that Christianity spread into the Gentile world because some of the Jews who embraced it had a none-too-solid attachment to their ancestral traditions, so that they were ready to modify or abandon them if it would gain them a hearing in the wider world. Clearly there is a superficial point here: a missionary religion that demands circumcision is likely to have less of an immediate appeal than one which does not. But that only touches the surface of the issue. For a pagan of whatever background,

---

[1] Käsemann 1969 [1965], 83.
[2] cf. Meyer 1986, 15ff.

Christianity demanded, and was known from quite early on to demand, an allegiance that might very well involve not only a previously unimagined self-denial, but also social ostracism, imprisonment, torture and death. Early Christianity certainly does not look as if it spread because demands were being trimmed to the hearers' expectations or wishes. We must look further for the motive of both missionary and convert. We must move towards the 'inside' of the historical drama.[3]

The motivating force behind the early Christian mission, as revealed in the stories that fan out across the spectrum of first-generation Christianity, is found in the central belief and hope of Judaism interpreted in the light of Jesus. The stories we have examined, and the praxis and symbol that went so closely with them, only make sense if the story-tellers believed that the great Jewish story had reached its long-awaited fulfilment, and that now world history had entered a new phase, the final phase in the drama of which the Jewish story itself was only one part. Israel believed, sometimes, that when she was redeemed, the Gentiles would share in the blessing. The widespread early Christian impetus towards what was often a risky and costly mission can only be explained in terms of the belief that Israel *had* now been redeemed, and that the time for the Gentiles had therefore come. As I have argued elsewhere and shall set out at more length in Volume 3, this is one of the basic presuppositions for Pauline theology.[4] But it is presupposed everywhere in the early Christian mission. In Paul's case, the stories that fuelled and legitimated the Gentile mission had a very personal emphasis, focused on the cross of Jesus on the one hand and his own encounter with the risen Lord on the other.[5] But even where these were lacking, or where parallel experience was expressed in other terms, we find the same structure of motivation. Where we fail to find the same enthusiasm for this mission (where, for example, there are signs of opposition to the free entry of Gentiles into the community of Jesus' people, as in Acts 15.1 or Galatians 2.11–15) the most likely explanation is that the Christians in question were holding to a different retelling of the Jewish story. Many Jews, not least in the first century, believed that when Israel's god acted to deliver her, the Gentiles would not be blessed, but would be brought to book. In that context, any Gentile who wanted to be rescued would have to show his or her submission to Israel's god, which meant of course submission to Israel's Torah. The humiliating conversion of Aseneth would serve as a model for any ingathering of Gentiles that might take place.[6]

This all indicates that the history of early Christian religion did not proceed by systematically translating out its Jewish emphases into Hellenistic ones, so that they might address a wider audience.[7] Christianity did, of course, take on the language of its ports of call. But, as we saw clearly enough in chapter 11,

---

[3] cf. ch. 3 above; and Meyer 1986, 31f.

[4] Wright 1991a.

[5] Gal. 2.19–21; 1 Cor. 15.9f.; 2 Cor. 4.1–15; etc.

[6] On *Jos. & As.* see ch. 8 above.

[7] This is the fundamental position of Bultmann, e.g. 1956, 175–9.

the structure of thought, right across the fixed points in the first Christian century, remains recognizably Jewish.[8]

When the early Christians spoke of their motivation, they regularly did so in terms of the divine spirit. This could be seen simply as a logical deduction from their belief that in the events of Jesus' death and resurrection Israel's god had finally vindicated his people. There were plenty of prophecies which spoke of the age of vindication being the time when YHWH would pour out his spirit upon his people in a new way. After all, those who wrote the Qumran Scrolls believed that these promises had come true for them. But early Christian language about the divine spirit seldom if ever sounds like a mere logical, or even a theological, deduction from fixed premises and ancient texts. Indeed, so clearly does the spirit-language sound like the language of *experience* that one could hazard a guess at an opposite deduction: the overwhelming sense of being sustained and driven on by a new kind of inner motivation, which they could only attribute to the outpouring of the divine spirit, compelled the early Christians to the conclusion that the strange events concerning Jesus that they had witnessed really did constitute the fulfilment of Israel's covenant expectations, really were the end of exile and the beginning of the 'age to come' for which Israel had longed.[9]

A new belief; a new experience. Important though these two lines of derivation are, I suspect that both of them are too clinical, and that both must be allowed to contribute to a larger whole. 'Theology' developed slowly into the vital and mainstream Christian activity that we know it to be by the late second century. This is not to say that Jews, and early Christians, could not and did not think and speak about Israel's god, and could not tell wise and foolish speech, coherent and incoherent, from one another. But by the time we meet even the earliest clearly articulated theology, that of Paul, the Christian mission has already been in full swing for nearly twenty years. Equally, in the ancient world as in the modern, religious experience of all shapes and varieties was on offer. The early Christians were not the only ones to speak with strange new tongues. Exorcisms and healings were well known in many cultures. A sense of union with a divine being was common in the mystery-religions. The belief in a special divine vocation, to which one must be obedient, would not have marked out an early Christian particularly from some of the Stoics. The call to leave home and family and pursue the life of a wandering evangelist has several analogies with the Cynics. Believing that the spirit of Israel's god had been poured out upon oneself and one's community was something the early Christians shared with the Essenes. A new form of 'religious experience', by itself, does not account historically for the development of early Christianity through the fixed points enumerated earlier.

What, then, is this larger whole, beyond simply 'theology' and 'experience'? The most obvious candidate is the early community itself, within which theology and religious experience took their places. There were other religious communities. There were other Jewish sects. But there was nothing quite like

---

[8] cf. too Dix 1953.
[9] cf. Dunn 1975.

this. From our earliest evidence, the Christians regarded themselves as a new family, directly descended from the family of Israel, but now transformed.

3. Community and Definition

The community, the *ekklesia*, had from the beginning a central symbolic, practical and theological role. Everything about it spoke both of the fulfilment of Israel's hopes and of a new role *vis-à-vis* the world.[10] The sacramental act of baptism linked the early Christians directly with the beginnings of their movement in John's baptism, and thus with the imagery of a Jewish sect (including exodus-typology and so forth). But we trace, very early, a sense that, though baptism was indeed the mode of entry into the eschatological people of Israel's god, it was this *because* it had to do with Jesus, who had himself brought Israel's history to its appointed destiny, and who as Messiah summed up Israel in himself. Our earliest evidence for Christian baptism involves the *name* of Jesus (and sometimes a larger formula) and the *death and resurrection* of Jesus.[11] The specificity of Jesus as a historical individual, in whom the promises of Israel's god had come true, and the particular events with which his own career had reached its climax, were built in to the Christian understanding of baptism from the beginning. Equally, baptism was for all, Jew and Gentile, Jewish priest and layperson, slave and free, male and female. At the height of the controversy over whether Gentile converts should be circumcised, there was never any question that it had been right to administer baptism to them. More particularly, baptism could be seen within the Gentile world as the entry into a particular community, just as initiation of various sorts admitted one into this or that cult. Attempts to show a *derivation* of Christian baptism from pagan cults have been tried and found wanting;[12] but it is not controversial to postulate a clearly visible, if theologically superficial, parallel. Baptism is thus a direct link to the history of Israel, particularly to the symbol of the exodus and to the use of that symbol in the claims of a new sect; and a gateway into this quasi-sect through which all alike might enter; and a symbolic and verbal way of tying those two together with specific historical reference to Jesus himself, and to his death and resurrection.

The eucharist made, effectively, the same points. The fact that Paul can chide his congregation in Corinth for their misbehaviour at the eucharist shows that this celebratory meal was so inbuilt into the structure of early Christianity that even within a very early congregation it could be taken for granted and abused. Paul's appeal to the Corinthians, taken in conjunction with the synoptic institution narratives and the references to the eucharist in the *Didache* and Ignatius, make it clear that this sacramental act was, like baptism, associated directly with the Jewish background of Passover, exodus and

---

[10] cf. Meyer 1986, chs. 2–4.
[11] e.g. Mt. 28.19; Ac. 2.38; 8.16; 10.48; 19.5; Rom. 6.2–11.
[12] cf. esp. Wedderburn 1987.

(Davidic) kingdom.[13] It occupied a place similar to that of Passover in the Jewish community, except that it was celebrated not just once a year, but at least every week, reflecting the regular celebration of Jesus' resurrection on the first day of the week. It thus tied the life of early Christianity very firmly to the historical life of Israel. At the same time, Paul is not afraid to use, in relation to the eucharist, language which goes daringly close to that of pagan celebration.[14] Equally, we know of no early eucharist that did not recite the events of Jesus' death, much as the Passover liturgy recited the events of the exodus. Eucharist, like baptism, tied together continuity with Jewish history, an implicit claim *vis-à-vis* the pagan world, and Jesus.

Baptism and eucharist thus both draw the eye up to the most striking feature of the life of the early community: the worship of Jesus. We have discussed this already;[15] such worship was not, certainly within the first Christian century, a sign that the community was moving away from creational or covenantal monotheism, but rather a sign of a radical reinterpretation within that monotheism. Within seventy years of the crucifixion, Clement, the bishop of Rome, can write such incipiently trinitarian sentences as these:

Have we not one God, and one Christ, and one Spirit of grace poured out upon us?

. . . for as God lives and as the Lord Jesus Christ lives and the Holy Spirit . . .[16]

Yet even these are, arguably, anticipated a full generation earlier.[17] The placing of Jesus, and indeed the divine spirit, within a monotheistic framework, without any sign as yet of a developed theological rationale (certainly no mention of persons, natures, substances and so forth) is a clear indication of the centrality of Jesus-worship within early Christianity.

The common life of the church, centred upon (though not of course limited to) this symbolic praxis and focus on Jesus, seems to have functioned from the first in terms of an alternative family. The impetus to pool resources speaks of a community organization which resembles in some quite striking ways the discipline of the Essenes.[18] The problems which arose in relation to the care of the needy, particularly widows, are most readily comprehensible if we envisage the church, not as a part-time voluntary organization of the like-minded which left normal social and familial attachments unaffected, but as a group with definite boundaries.[19] If one belonged to it, one did not belong any more, certainly not in the same way, to one's previous unit, whether familial or racial. The fact that contact with one's original family, race and culture would most likely continue was taken for granted, but the way it was addressed proves the point: it was seen in terms of the way one copes with the anomalies thereby

---

[13] 1 Cor. 10.1–22; 11.17–34; *Did.* 9.1–5; Ign. *Eph.* 20.2.
[14] cf. Wright 1991c.
[15] cf. ch. 12 above.
[16] *1 Clem.* 46.6; 58.2.
[17] e.g. Gal. 4.1–6; 1 Cor. 12.4–6.
[18] cf. Ac. 2.44–7; 4.32–7; 5.1–11; cf. Capper 1985.
[19] cf. Ac. 6.1; 1 Tim. 5.3–16. That the new obligations could be abused is clear from e.g. 2 Thess. 3.6–13.

aroused, rather than in terms of a retreat to a less clear-cut demarcation. From baptism onwards, one's basic family consisted of one's fellow-Christians.[20]

This called for a new socio-political orientation. On the one hand, there was 'another King', and this King required allegiance and worship of a sort that radically subverted the allegiance and worship demanded by Caesar, and other lesser lords. On the other hand, the subversion in question was not that of the ordinary political revolutionary, and in the normal run of things Christians must submit to legitimate authority.[21] This meant, as well, that Jewish Christians, including and indeed especially those living in Jerusalem, must not align themselves with preparations for, or acts of, war against the Romans. Their sort of Jewish sectarianism was so subversive that, like Josephus, though for a very different reason, they must recognize Jerusalem's devastation by Rome as the direct result of its refusing the will of Israel's god.[22] The early church was thus marked out from the first as a familial community, loyalty to which overrode all other considerations.[23]

The result was that this family could not be entirely at ease within either Jewish or pagan society. Of course, there is plenty of evidence that the unease was moderated by what rigorists like Paul regarded as compromise, either with the Jewish world (Galatians) or the pagan (1 Corinthians). But there is also plenty of evidence that the community was persecuted both by Jews and by pagans in the first decades of its existence. We have already seen something of the pagan persecution.[24] That Jews persecuted the young movement from its very early days is also clear, even if there remains a good deal of debate about precisely who persecuted which Christians, and why.[25] Paul is hardly likely to have invented his own persecuting activity (Galatians 1.13); nor is he likely to have invented, in a letter to a church that knew him well, details of his own suffering at the hands of fellow-Jews (2 Corinthians 11.24).

But why *was* the early church persecuted? Why is any group persecuted? We have already looked at the pagan persecutions, and the answer at first sight is various: because Nero wanted a scapegoat; because the Christians were suspected of secret vice; because they were atheists; because they would not do the required homage to the emperor. All of these make sense, and are clearly part of the sufficient condition for persecution in each instance; but they do not quite explain the regularity of the persecution, nor the apparent frequency of people, not themselves in authority, *informing against* Christians.[26] Lots of cults in the empire practised vice, whether secretly or openly; plenty of people had eccentric theological views; some, like Cynic philosophers, made

---

[20] cf. e.g. Rom. 9.1–5; 10.1–2; 1 Cor. 5.9–13. We cannot here go further into the question of the social description of early Christian groups, important though that study is: cf. Judge 1960; Theissen 1978, 1982; Meeks 1983; Malherbe 1983 [1977]; Stambaugh and Balch 1986; etc.

[21] Rom. 13.1–7; 1 Pet. 2.13–17; cp. 1 Cor. 10.32f. Cf. too the response made to Domitian by Jesus' relatives (above, p. 351f.).

[22] cf. Lk. 13.1–5; 19.41–4; 21.10–19 and pars.

[23] Mt. 10.34–9 and pars.; Mk. 3.31–5 and pars.; 8.34–8 and pars.; etc.

[24] Chapter 11 above.

[25] cf. Moule 1982 [1962], 154–64; Hengel 1991, ch. 5; Hill 1992, ch. 2.

[26] cf. Pliny *Letters* 10.97.

light of their obligations to the authorities. The Christians came into all of those categories in the popular mind, but none of them is big enough to do justice to the evidence.

What we seem to be faced with is the existence of a community which was perceived to be subverting the normal social and cultural life of the empire precisely by its quasi-familial, quasi-ethnic life *as* a community. Evidence of similar phenomena abounds in our own time. A member of a tight-knit Roman Catholic community in rural Quebec becomes a Baptist; his house is burned down, he has to flee the village, and the police do nothing. A Protestant pastor in Northern Ireland makes a gesture of reconciliation, on Christmas Day, towards the Roman Catholic priest on the other side of the square; he receives death threats, at the communion rail, from senior members of his own congregation. A Muslim boy in the occupied West Bank, cared for in a Christian hospital, converts, and is unable to return to his family because they will kill him. A Jewish woman is told that if she becomes a Christian her right to live in Israel will be called into question. When communities react like this, it can only be because they feel that their very foundations are being shaken. Mere belief—acceptance of certain propositional statements—is not enough to elicit such violence. People believe all sorts of odd things and are tolerated. When, however, belief is regarded as an index of subversion, everything changes. The fact of widespread persecution, regarded by both pagans and Christians as the normal state of affairs within a century of the beginnings of Christianity, is powerful evidence of the sort of thing that Christianity was, and was perceived to be. It was a new family, a 'third race', neither Jew nor Gentile but 'in Christ'. Its very existence threatened the foundational assumptions of pagan society. In Crossan's happy phrase, apropos Matthew's story that Pilate's wife had troubled dreams on the night of Jesus' trial,

> That never happened, of course, but it was true nonetheless. It was a most propitious time for the Roman Empire to start having nightmares.[27]

But why did Jews persecute Christians? Were they not both in the same boat—branded as atheists, regarded as the scum of the earth, scorned when doing badly and resented when doing well? The answer here clearly lies in the ferocity of polemic between different pressure-groups, parties and/or sects within the same parent body. Sibling rivalry is fiercest when the siblings have an inheritance to share, or when one feels that another is ruining the chances of any of them inheriting it at all. Reading between Paul's lines, that seems to have been what was going on in his case at least. The Pharisees' programme of Torah-intensification was radically questioned by the Christian movement, not because they threw open their doors to Gentiles (lots of Jews ate with Gentiles; there was, as we saw in chapter 8, something of a regular sliding scale of assimilation, and so far as we know the Pharisees did not use violence to curb it), but because they claimed that *precisely in doing so* they were celebrating the fulfilment of Israel's long-cherished hopes. This has a direct analogue in Paul's surely deliberate irony in 1 Corinthians 7.19: neither cir-

---

[27] Crossan 1991, 394.

cumcision nor uncircumcision counts for anything, since what matters is *keeping the god-given commandments*, of which of course circumcision is one. There are some things that can only be expressed through such irony and apparent contradiction, and I suspect that the early Christian claim is one of them: the claim, that is, to be acting in accordance with the whole divine purpose for Israel, precisely in dismantling those aspects of traditional praxis, and in disregarding those traditional symbols, by which for centuries Jews had ordered their lives.

Here we reach the heart of it. What evokes persecution is precisely that which challenges a worldview, that which up-ends a symbolic universe. It is somewhat threatening to other first-century Jews to regard your community as the true Temple, and perhaps it is just as well to keep such ideas within the walls of an enclosed community in the desert; but since the belief, as held in Qumran, involves an intensification of Torah, the vicarious purification of the Land, the fierce defence of the race, and the dream of an eventually rebuilt and purified physical Temple in Jerusalem itself, one can imagine Pharisees debating it vigorously but not seeking authority from the chief priests to exterminate it. It embodied, after all, too many of the central worldview-features. The equivalent belief as held within Christianity seems to have had no such redeeming features. No new Temple would replace Herod's, since the real and final replacement was Jesus and his people. No intensified Torah would define this community, since its sole definition was its Jesus-belief.[28] No Land claimed its allegiance, and no Holy City could function for it as Jerusalem did for mainline Jews; Land had now been transposed into World, and the Holy City was the new Jerusalem, which, as some Jewish apocalyptic writers had envisaged, would appear, like the horses and chariots of fire around Elisha, becoming true on earth as it was in heaven.[29] Racial identity was irrelevant; the story of this new community was traced back to Adam, not just to Abraham, and a memory was preserved of Jesus' forerunner declaring that Israel's god could raise up children for Abraham from the very stones.[30] Once we understand how worldviews function, we can see that the Jewish neighbours of early Christians must have regarded them, not as a lover of Monet regards a lover of Picasso, but as a lover of painting regards one who deliberately sets fire to art galleries—and who claims to do so in the service of Art.[31]

I therefore suggest that the beginning of the break between mainline Judaism and nascent Christianity came not with AD 70, not with some shakily reconstructed decree promulgated by the historically dubious 'Council of Jan-

---

[28] See below. For Matthew as a possible exception to this, see vol. 4 of the present project.

[29] 2 Kgs. 6.15–17. Cf. Gal. 4.26; Heb. 12.22; Rev. 21.2, 10–27; cf. Isa. 28.16; 54.11–14; Ezek. 40.1—48.35; Tob. 13.7–18; 4 Ezra 10.27, 50–5; 2 Bar. 4.1–6. The interpretation of these passages is of course intriguing, since there is no clear dividing line between expectations for the restoration of the present earthly Jerusalem and visions of the glory of the future, 'heavenly' one. Cf. Davies 1974; Lincoln 1981.

[30] Mt. 3.9, par. Lk. 3.8.

[31] On Jewish persecution of Christians cf. Moule 1982 [1962], 154–76, and other refs. there.

nia',[32] but with the very early days in which a young Pharisee named Saul believed it his divine calling to obtain authority to attack and harry the little sect. Analogies within the Jewish world suggest that this pattern is correct. The deep divisions between the Essenes and the Hasmoneans on the one hand, and the Pharisees on the other, emerge bit by bit in the Essene writings, and yet the actual splits which produced them clearly occurred at specific times which considerably antedate those writings. So, too, the even deeper division between those who claimed to be the heirs of the scriptural promises on the basis of Temple, Land, Torah and race, and those who claimed the same thing on the basis of Jesus and his spirit, goes back behind any writings or decrees which we possess or can guess at, to the moment when some hitherto frightened and puzzled Jews came to the conclusion that Israel's hope, the resurrection from the dead, the return from exile, the forgiveness of sins, had all come true in a rush in Jesus, who had been crucified. This, it should be noted carefully within present debate, does not make Christianity anti-Jewish, any more than the Essenes, the Pharisees, or any other sect or group, were anti-Jewish.[33]

The church, then, lived under pressure from the very first. It is perhaps this, as much as anything else, which kept it united when so many other pressures might have driven it towards division.

4. Development and Variety[34]

It is not surprising that Christianity developed in a multiplicity of ways. The 'myth of Christian origins', or in more vulgar language the 'big bang' theory of church origins, has been shown up as a later Christian fiction. A 'pure' period, when everyone believed exactly the same thing, lived in a community without problems or quarrels, and hammered out True Doctrine for the coming Great Church, never existed.[35] It is, perhaps, important to point out that the author of Acts would be happy to say: I told you so. Though Acts is often regarded as an attempt to whitewash the early Christians, it must be judged singularly unsuccessful. The sin of Ananias and Sapphira, the dispute between Hebrews and Hellenists, the vacillating of Peter, the major division over circumcision, the fierce quarrel between Paul and Barnabas—even the heroes of Acts are shown emphatically to have feet of clay.[36] The idea of early uniformity and stability owes more to Eusebius and his successors than to any first-century writing; the reality was too close to be covered up.

At the same time, we must also resist the more subtle myths that crowd in once we reject the facile one. If the early church was not a pure community, and to be imitated as such, no more can we assume that it was an early version of the ecumenical movement, and to be imitated as such.[37] Whether or not

---

[32] See above, pp. 161ff.
[33] On the whole discussion cf. recently Segal 1986; Dunn 1991.
[34] On this cf. Dunn 1977; Moule 1982 [1962], ch. 7.
[35] cf. Wilken 1971.
[36] Ac. 5.1–11; 6.1 (cf. Hill 1992); 10.1—11.18; 15.1f.; 15.36–40.
[37] This is a tendency, in part, of Dunn 1977, and of some other writers.

Burton Mack is right, and Mark has perpetrated a 'Myth of Innocence', portraying Jesus and his first followers in glowing and unhistorical terms, Mack may be equally in danger of setting up a new, merely different, myth of Christian beginnings, in which his own heroes, a Cynic-style Jesus and his Cynic-style early followers, take centre stage instead.[38] In neither of these cases is the nettle really grasped: why should we assume that 'primitive' Christianity is automatically 'normative'?[39]

It is important at this stage to insist on residual untidiness. This comes hard to most New Testament scholars, whose long training schools them in habits of collecting, arranging, labelling and pigeon-holing. This tendency is helped both by the tendency for the discipline to avoid (for theological reasons) the rigours of historical work, and by the fact, remarked upon earlier, that we do not know very much and, failing major new discoveries, can never know very much about the first Christian century. It is desperately easy to cover over this ignorance with theory, to make hypothesis do where history will not.[40] Thus we have the prevalent view, sustained at every level of the discipline for well over a century: the early church split down racial lines, which determined theological groupings; there were Jewish Christians, who held firmly to Torah, and Gentile Christians, who rejected it; this split goes back to the division between Hebrews and Hellenists in Acts 6.1; it explains Paul, and pits Peter against him; it enables us to carve up the early Christian writings into neat groups, which is of course useful for the purposes of teaching. This theory has everything in its favour, except for one thing: it bears no real relation to history.[41]

For a start, all early Christianity was Jewish Christianity.[42] All early missionary work among Gentiles was undertaken by Jewish Christians. The decision not to require circumcision of Gentile converts has as much right to be labelled 'Jewish Christian' as does the position of those who bitterly opposed it. Every single document in the New Testament is in some sense 'Jewish Christian'; the fact that Matthew, for instance, acquiesces in the abolition of the Jewish dietary regulations does not make his work any the less 'Jewish'.[43] Paul's theology, in which the Jewish worldview he had embraced as a Pharisee is systematically rethought and remade, only makes sense if it is still seen nevertheless as Jewish theology. It is emphatically not a variant on paganism.

---

[38] Mack 1988. Cf. F. Gerald Downing's review of Smith 1990, in *JTS* 42, 1991, 705.

[39] cf. ch. 1 above.

[40] cf. Hengel 1979, 130: 'In the realm of ancient history the fortuitousness and fragmentariness of surviving sources and the distance between ancient consciousness and our own can very easily lead to a simplified representation of past reality.' This, I suspect, is a deliberate (almost English!) understatement.

[41] cf. again esp. Hill 1992; for a precursor on one key point, largely ignored in subsequent debate, cf. Moule 1958–9. Cp. too Moule 1982 [1962], 201f.; Hengel 1983, 1–11, 54–8; Meyer 1986, 68. On the significance of Stephen, cf. Bruce 1979, ch. 2; Stanton 1980; Hengel 1983, 18–25; Meyer 1986, 68f.; Hill 1992, ch. 3.

[42] cf. Koester 1982b, 198; Conzelmann 1973, 37f. Conzelmann, however, restricts this to the first few years only; after that, the connection of Christianity with Judaism is merely superficial, something that 'an observant contemporary' might notice (79).

[43] Pettem 1989 operates with a limited definition of 'Jewish Christian', from which point of view Matthew is (artificially, in my view) excluded from the category.

The only way the historian can handle this basic fact is to set up large and diverse spectrums of possible, and perhaps actual, 'Jewish Christian' viewpoints, and admit that there was almost certainly room for people to move this way and that within these spectrums. Plotting of this has been attempted by various writers, with a measure of plausibility; 'success' is too much to ask for, since (again, we must insist) we simply do not know precisely what went on.[44] It is highly likely that there were at least *some* Christians at every point on just about every possible spectrum of Jewish-Christian opinion.

One spectrum could be defined in terms of attitudes towards resistance against Rome. Are Christians bound to be loyal Jews, when the worst comes to the worst, or are they committed to remaining uninvolved in revolutionary activity? Another spectrum could be defined in terms of one's own practice of the purity codes. Some would see no reason to break the dietary habits of a lifetime; others, every reason to show that Jesus meant what Mark 7.14–23 says he said. Another spectrum would involve attitudes to the Jerusalem Temple: should Christians continue to offer sacrifice there, or not? Yet another spectrum would address the well-known issue of Gentile circumcision; another, ethical behaviour; another, the nature of the new eschatological expectation; another, the choice of Hebrew, Aramaic or Greek for worship and/or the reading and/or the study of scripture; another, theological questions about Jesus. So we could go on. *There is no reason to assume that these different spectrums would correspond to each other.* Someone who was a rigorist on one issue might well seem 'compromised' on another. Judaism, as we have seen often enough, was thoroughly pluriform in the first century. Its central symbols, stories and praxis allowed for a multiplicity of divergent variations on central themes. There is no reason to doubt, and every reason to assume, that Christianity started off with exactly the same pluriformity, and that it provided a powerful impetus towards yet more. If that means that some early Jewish Christians may have looked, with hindsight, like Marcionites, others like Ebionites, others like proto-Gnostics, others simply like rabbis who happened to believe that the Messiah had come, and others like surprised and somewhat muddled people trying to make sense of it all and not always succeeding, that is precisely what we should expect.

If this is true when it comes to Jewish Christianity, it is surely *a fortiori* true when it comes to Gentile Christianity—though we must remind ourselves again that 'Gentile Christianity' is in one sense *part of* 'Jewish Christianity', since it derived its origin, its scriptures, its form of church organization, its sacraments, even the god in whom it believed, from Jewish Christianity. What is surprising is not how many new forms Christianity took during its first century, but how remarkably well it held together, given its rapid geographical and cross-cultural expansion. Too little real historical work has as yet been done on the varieties of emerging Gentile Christianity, but once we move away from stereotypes there will be plenty to do.[45]

[44] cf. Brown 1983; Riegel 1978; Hill 1992, esp. 193–7.
[45] The fact that Theissen (1982) and Meeks (1983, 1986) still seem like pioneers is sufficient evidence of this.

The Jew–Gentile spectrum, and the variations within both Jewish and Gentile Christianity, are in fact only one way of plotting the enormous differences which are visible in the sources. Others that come to mind may be listed as follows. Some Christians seem to have emphasized a salvation-history in which continuity with Israel was extremely important; others, an ahistorical faith with a 'vertical' eschatology. Some Christians seem to have regarded forms of ministry with what Clement and Ignatius, at least, felt was extreme flexibility; others, including those two bishops, advocated the recognition of fixed forms as being certainly of the *bene esse*, and quite possibly of the *esse*, of the church. Some Christians (though, as I shall argue, fewer than normally imagined) evidently expected a great cosmic catastrophe; others knew that divine and human time worked on different scales. Some may well have seen Jesus simply as a unique human being; others certainly placed him within the god-dimension of Jewish monotheism.[46] Some may well have placed little emphasis on the salvific effect of his cross; others, by no means only in the Pauline tradition, emphasized it as central to the divine plan of salvation. Some were undoubtedly 'enthusiasts'; others, 'early catholics'; according to one analysis, Luke at least was both.[47] Once again it must be stressed: it is residually likely that these spectrums coexisted without a single, easily describable pattern. Attempts to force them all into the 'Jew/Gentile?' category fail: it is sometimes suggested that the pure, early, Jewish gospel was corrupted when Hellenistic categories drove it into fixed forms and rigid dogmas—and it is also suggested that this latter activity represents a re-Judaizing of a 'pure', early, Hellenistic kerygma! Equally, attempts to arrange the different spectrums on a chronological scale come to grief: good counter-examples in one key area are the early book Galatians, in which the future hope is not mentioned, and the late book Romans, in which it is. At another point, the earliest evidence we have for New Testament christology, in the possibly pre-Pauline fragments such as Philippians 2.6–11, indicate a very high christology indeed;[48] for an unambiguous and well-developed 'low' christology we have to go to the third-century Pseudo-Clementines.[49] In all of these matters we do well to suppose that early Christianity was far more pluriform, far less logical and tidy, than we might like to suppose.

With all this variety, is there anything at all that held early Christianity together?[50] This question has been addressed in various ways recently, and there is always a danger of producing lowest-common-denominator answers that do not really advance understanding. I suggest that if we examine the question from the angle of the analysis of worldview and theology set out in Part II, and already applied to first-century Judaism in Part III, there are

[46] cf. Hengel 1983, 30–47; Marshall 1972–3.
[47] Dunn 1977, 352–8.
[48] cf. Wright 1991a, ch. 4; cp. Caird 1968.
[49] cf. Hennecke 1975, 532–70.
[50] cf. Meyer 1986, 16f., warning of the danger that, by adopting 'nominalist and positivist premises', scholarship is always likely to manufacture, wrongly, a picture of the early church as syncretistic.

certain constants which stand out clearly, and which emerge all the stronger for their being at the heart of such rich and widespread diversity.[51]

The worldview of the earliest Christians, as we saw in chapters 12–14, focused on their praxis as a community, their symbols as the replacement of the Jewish symbols, and their stories as multiple, and multiform, retellings of the Jewish story. Before we even arrive at the key worldview questions, and the theology which cashes them out into particular belief-systems, it should be quite clear that what united early Christians, deeper than all diversity, was *that they told, and lived, a form of Israel's story which reached its climax in Jesus and which then issued in their spirit-given new life and task.* Their diversities were diverse ways of construing that basic point; their disputes were carried on not so much by appeal to fixed principles, or to Jewish scripture conceived as a rag-bag of proof-texts, but precisely by fresh retellings of the story which highlighted the points at issue. Their strong centre, strong enough to be recognizable in works as diverse as those of Jude and Ignatius, James and Justin Martyr, was not a theory or a new ethic, not an abstract dogma or rote-learned teaching, but a particular story told and lived. Even works like the *Gospel of Thomas* bear witness, in their frequent Jewish allusions, to the root from which the plant has grown, even if now transplanted into different soil and watered from a different spring. Right across the spectrum of fixed points within the first Christian century, the early church lived and breathed within a symbolic universe which was, first, emphatically Jewish rather than pagan, and then, second, emphatically Christian rather than Jewish in the sense of an ethnic and Torah-based identity. The lens through which the Christians viewed the whole of reality was a recognizable variation on the Jewish worldview. The symbols had been radically transformed, but the story remained, offering in its newly developed retellings reasons for the radical transformation of the symbols.

5. Theology

We saw at the end of chapter 12 that the symbols and praxis of the early Christians generated a preliminary set of answers to the worldview-questions. When we trace these through to actual theology, in the light of the present discussion, certain things again emerge with clarity. The focus of this theology cannot be the particular issues of later Christian debate, which, when projected back to the first century, produce shallow anachronisms, but the issues which were manifestly live ones at the time. The following sketch must of course be brief and hence highly tendentious, but I hope it will serve to make the point and to state, if not fully to argue, the case.[52]

[51] So, rightly, Moule 1982 [1962], 214; cf. Hengel 1983, xi: 'For all the multiplicity brought about by the work of the Spirit, I would still see earliest Christianity as an intrinsically connected and in essentials quite amazingly coherent movement . . . Anyone who wants to reduce earliest Christianity to often quite different and indeed unconnected "lines of development" can no longer explain why the church in the second century remained a unity despite all the deviations . . . In their view the church should have fallen apart into countless groups.'

[52] For the terms and categories used in this section, cf. chs. 5 and 9 above.

Early Christianity was monotheistic in the sense in which Judaism was monotheistic and paganism was not; that is, the early Christians embraced *creational*, *covenantal* and hence *eschatological* monotheism. They were not polytheists, pantheists, or Epicurean proto-Deists. Their monotheism necessarily included, and was not compromised by, the two central dualities which characterized mainline Judaism, i.e. the dualities of the creator and the creation on the one hand, and good and evil on the other. Likewise, their creational and covenantal monotheism necessarily addressed, and was not compromised by addressing, the issues of how the creator acted in relation to the creation, and of how the good creator had acted and would act to deal with evil within creation. In Judaism, these issues were dealt with in a variety of ways which we studied in chapter 9. The early Christians faced the same issues, and dealt with them in ways which are recognizably drawn from the same Jewish sources. But they reorganized those themes, again and again, around two fixed points: Jesus and the divine spirit. Paul is one of the greatest of the theologians who thrashed this out, but the same fundamental scheme is everywhere apparent.

The basic Jewish answer to the question, How is the creator active within the creation? was, as we saw, to develop varieties of language that spoke of Wisdom, Torah, Spirit, and Shekinah. At their most fundamental level, these were ways of asserting most strongly the presence, power, grace and providence of the one creator god within the world; or, to put this another way, they were ways of asserting that the divine power at work in creation, and within Israel, was not to be thought of as independent from, or over against, the one creator god. At another level, they became ways of asserting the unique claim of Judaism: that this creator god, everywhere active and powerful, had acted specifically within the history of Israel. The early Christians developed exactly the same ideas, transposing them again and again into language about Jesus and the divine spirit. They thus maintained the Jewish insistence on monotheism over against paganism and dualism, while bringing the unique and striking claim of Judaism to a new focal point: this creator god had acted specifically and climactically in Jesus, and was now acting through his own spirit in a new, Jesus-related, way.

The basic Jewish answer to the question, How is the creator dealing with evil within his creation? was of course that he had called Israel. This, as we saw, created second-order difficulties, since Israel became, so to speak, part of the problem as well as the means of the solution. The early Christians, on the basis of everything we know of them from both within and outside the canonical 'New Testament', accepted this answer, recognized this second-order difficulty, and asserted that Israel's god had dealt with the difficulty in and through Jesus and had thereby affirmed the basic answer. Israel's purpose had come to its head in Jesus' work, which itself had led up to its appropriate, though highly paradoxical, culmination in his death and resurrection. Those who now belonged to Jesus' people were not identical with ethnic Israel, since Israel's history had reached its intended fulfilment; they claimed to be the *continuation of Israel in a new situation*, able to draw freely on Israel-images to express their self-identity, able to read Israel's scriptures (through the lens of Messiah and spirit) and apply them to their own life. They were thrust out by that claim, and that reading, to fulfil Israel's vocation on behalf of the world.

This entire scheme of thought is as clear in Matthew as it is in Paul, as well worked out in Luke as it is in Hebrews, as much presuppositional for Revelation as it is for Romans. What is more, it is also the presupposition of the *defeated* party in Acts 15; of the theology of Paul's *opponents* in some at least of the letters; of the fissiparous churches that Ignatius and Clement struggled to bring into unity. The inner-Christian polemics of at least the first eighty or a hundred years are, as far as we can see, conducted from *within* this worldview, by people who all accepted this basic theology. Only with works like the *Gospel of Thomas* do we find a clash with other groups that use apparently Christian language to clothe a radically different worldview.

Putting the two basic questions together, we arrive at the following framework of early Christian theology. The fundamental theological position is a view of creator and creation, of evil within creation and the rescue of creation from that evil, of hope fulfilled and hope to come, of a people who are both rescued and rescuers. Christology, pneumatology, and ecclesiology grow naturally and Jewishly from this basis.

In particular, the Jewish doctrines of salvation and justification are reflected across early Christianity, even where those terms are not necessarily used. The church appropriated for itself the Jewish belief that the creator god would rescue his people at the last, and interpreted that rescue in terms of a great law-court scene. This is the doctrine of the 'righteousness of God', the *dikaiosune theou*, which is best seen in terms of the divine covenant faithfulness, and which comes to major expression in Paul's letter to Rome. The major underlying difference between the Christian and the Jewish views at this point was that the early Christians believed that *the verdict had already been announced* in the death and resurrection of Jesus. Israel's god had at last acted decisively, to demonstrate his covenant faithfulness, to deliver his people from their sins, and to usher in the inaugurated new covenant. As a result, the question of present justification could be, as it were, worked at from both ends. To the Jewish formulation ('how can we tell, in the present, who will be justified in the future?') the Christians added a second question: how can we tell, in the present, who is implicitly included in the death and resurrection of Jesus? This gave a different form to the Jewish question, which set the context for a different answer: those whom the covenant god will rescue at the last, who are deemed to be included within the event of Jesus' death and resurrection, are circumscribed not by race, geography or ancestral code, but by Jesus, and hence by faith. The doctrine of present justification (the language is largely Pauline, but the reality is everywhere in early Christianity) was hammered out between those two poles, future and past, as a matter of the self-definition of the church.[53]

---

[53] See further vol. 3 in the present series.

6. Hope

What did the early Christians hope for, on the basis of this worldview and theology? Here, again, there has been a radical redrawing. It is basic to early Christianity that *the Jewish hope has already been fulfilled*. 'All the god-given promises find their "yes" in Christ', said Paul.[54] A good deal of New Testament scholarship has been obsessed with a purely imaginary hypothesis, that first-century Jews expected something called 'the parousia', which would involve the end of the space-time world and the arrival of a (super?)human figure travelling on a cloud—and that the early Christians took over this hope lock, stock and barrel, applying it to Jesus, who may or may not have had something to say on the matter. In the light of our rereading of apocalyptic in general and Daniel 7 in particular (in chapter 10 above), we may state categorically that what Jews in general were expecting and longing for was the release of Israel from exile and the return of YHWH to Zion. Among the great images that were used to express this hope was that of the human figure exalted over the animals, and given rule and dominion under the sovereignty of Israel's god. Another great metaphor used to express the significance of the literal, historical hope was that of resurrection. In some Jewish circles, notably in times of persecution, this metaphor had itself begun to be used literally. It was precisely because the early Christians believed that Jesus of Nazareth, whom they had regarded as Messiah, had himself been raised from the dead, that they were able to reverse the linguistic process, taking resurrection as the fixed literal point and treating the return from exile as the great metaphor which explained its significance.

But the very shape of this belief demanded that there be another hope, a hope yet to come. Precisely because Jesus' resurrection was the raising of one human being in the middle of the history of exile and misery, not the raising of all righteous human beings to bring the history of exile and misery to an end, there must be a further end yet in sight. Four elements began to be worked out within early Christianity, all of them innovations, but all based foursquare on the rereading of Jewish hopes in the light of Jesus and the divine spirit.

First, there was vindication. Jesus had set his face, prophetically, against Jerusalem. He had staked his prophetic reputation upon the claim that the Temple would be destroyed. (Even if Jesus said none of the things attributed to him on this subject by the synoptic gospels, it is clear that he was widely believed to have said something like this.) In the light of this, those who claimed to be his followers were bound to see the continuing existence of Herod's Temple, and the city which housed it, as a paradox. Jesus would not be vindicated as a true prophet until it was destroyed by enemy action. (We may remind ourselves that the Essenes seem to have hoped for something like this, too, and that Josephus likewise saw the hand of Israel's god in the Temple's destruction.) But it was not only Jesus who would be vindicated when the Temple fell. The Temple represented the heart of the system from which flowed one source at least of the persecution suffered by the early church. Its destruction would be their salvation. Mark 13 said as much.[55] It seems to me highly likely that one of the main early Christian meanings of the word 'salvation' had to do with historical liberation from the great city that had been persecuting those who transferred its claim, to be the place of YHWH's dwelling, on to their crucified Messiah-figure and thence on to themselves. Granted the presence in all three synoptic gospels of the powerful discourse of Mark 13 and parallels,[56] most people within the earliest Christian groups seem to have believed that their movement was somehow bound up with Jerusalem's coming destruction. When Paul, or an early imitator, speaks of a coming day of the Lord (2 Thessalonians 2.2), the passage cannot be referring to the end of the space-time universe. It envisages the possibility that the Thessalonians might hear of the great event *by letter*. This is a key index of the this-worldly referent of 'apocalyptic' language within early Christianity, as within Judaism.[57]

Second, the kingdom of Israel's god is to spread into all the world. Here the lines run out towards the second century without a clear ultimate agenda, but with a clear sense of direction. 'Thy will be done, on earth as it is in heaven': the Jewish roots of this prayer leave no room for any idea of a purely abstract kingdom, a semi-Gnostic escape to another world. Even Luke's tradition, which did not use this phrase, retained the explosive 'Thy kingdom come'.[58] Luke, too, at the conclusion of his story, has Paul announcing the kingship of Israel's god in Rome; Paul, for his own part, declares that he takes every thought captive to obey Christ, and that all the principalities and powers of world rulership exist at Christ's behest, were defeated on his cross, and are now under his authority.[59] Matthew's Jesus declares that all authority in heaven and on earth has been given to him, and on that basis sends the disciples out to make more disciples in all the world; John's, having defeated the world in his own defeat, now embraces it with his own love.[60] It is clear that the success of this vocation is not measured, at least not by any of these writers, in terms either of large numbers or of socio-political influence; but it is clear, too, that they all envisage, as does the possibly pre-Pauline poem of Philippians 2, that every knee will bow before Jesus, and every tongue acknowledge him as *Kyrios*—a title to which Caesar was the normal claimant.

The point at which this hope remains unfocused is the point at which we meet the third aspect of early Christian expectation. Like the Pharisees, and probably most other Jews, the Christians believed that Israel's god, being the creator, would physically recreate those who were his own, at some time and in some space the other side of death. Unlike the Pharisees, they believed that this still-future hope had begun to happen already, in Jesus' resurrection, and that this event served as the prototype for that of others. Paul is again one of the clearest spokesmen for this view, but it is emphasized all over, in John,

---

[55] cf. p. 395f. above.
[56] Which may go back to a very early original; cf. ch. 14 above.
[57] cf. Moule 1982 [1962], 169–71.
[58] Mt. 6.9–13; Lk. 11.2–4; *Did.* 8.2.
[59] Ac. 28.31; 2 Cor. 10.4–5; Rom. 8.38f.; 1 Cor. 3.22f.; Col. 1.15–20; 2.15.
[60] Mt. 28.20; Jn. 16.33; 3.16; 10.11–18; 12.31f.

1 Peter, Revelation, and elsewhere.[61] The details of this hope remain, in the nature of the case, almost as imprecise as they do in the relevant Jewish texts;[62] but that there would be a new, bodily, life the other side of the grave, which could not be reduced to terms simply of a generalized Hellenistic-style immortality, was everywhere taken for granted in the early period. The fact that the early Christians clung to this hope, in a line from Paul through to Polycarp and beyond, when so many groups in the pagan world were insisting that what mattered was the personal immortality of the mystery-religions or the non-physical bliss of some Gnostic systems, demonstrates the tenacity with which the church clung to its essentially Jewish roots. Acts 23.6 has Paul declare before a Jewish court that he is on trial for maintaining the national hope, i.e. 'resurrection from the dead'. This rings true both to Paul's setting and to that of later writers.

To Paul and Revelation, also, goes the credit for articulating in three passages a hope which goes beyond the individual, or even the merely ecclesial, and embraces the whole of creation. Romans 8.18–27 speaks of the whole creation experiencing a great exodus of which the biblical exodus will be simply a foretaste.[63] 1 Corinthians 15.20–8 speaks of the messianic kingdom of Jesus which, already inaugurated, will finally be consummated with the abolition of death itself, and the subjection of everything that exists to Jesus, and finally to the true god. Revelation 21 and 22 speak in even more highly coloured language of a renewed world order, with heaven and earth united in a single embrace; of a city without need of a Temple, a world without need of sun or moon, because of the presence of the living creator god, and of Jesus. All these passages, rich rewritings of Jewish apocalyptic in the light of Jesus, express a wider hope which forms the setting for the specific belief in a future resurrection. New, bodily human beings will require a new world in which to live. In this transformed world order, the veil will be lifted for all time. The realities of the heavenly world will be visibly united with the realities of the earthly.

The fourth and final aspect of the Christian hope is the expectation of the return of Jesus. It is vital to stress *both* that most of the texts normally drawn on in this connection have nothing to do with the case, *and* that there are several others which still bear on it directly. Following our exposition in chapter 10, it should be clear that texts which speak of the 'coming of the son of man on a cloud' have as their obvious first-century meaning the prediction of vindication for the true Israel. Furthermore, from the use of these texts in the synoptic gospels it should be clear that the early Christians believed that Jesus was taking the place of that true Israel. He it was who would suffer, and now had suffered, at the hands of the pagans, then to be vindicated. The most likely meaning for these particular 'apocalyptic' texts within early Christianity, then, is not the expectation of the *return* of Jesus, but the proclamation that he had already been vindicated, in his resurrection and exaltation, and that he would

---

[61] 1 Cor. 15.12–28; Jn. 11.25; 1 Pet. 1.3–5; Rev. 2.10; etc.
[62] cf above, pp. 320–32.
[63] cf. Wright 1992a, ch. 8.

be further vindicated when the city which had opposed him, and over which he had pronounced his sternest warnings, would in turn be destroyed. Just as Jewish writers looked at Pompey's eventual downfall and interpreted it in terms of the divine wrath, coming on him at long last after his earlier desecration of the Temple, so the early church awaited the destruction of Jerusalem, and then reflected on it as a past event, interpreting it all the while in terms of the divine wrath coming upon the city at last, a generation after its rejection of the one who announced to it the way of peace.[64] As a foretaste of that vindication, Luke speaks of the cessation of Jesus' resurrection appearances in terms which strongly echo Daniel 7: 'he was lifted up, and a cloud took him out of their sight' (Acts 1.9). Just as 'resurrection' ceases to be a metaphor for the return from exile, and becomes the historical point around which other themes now cluster as explanatory images, so 'coming (to Israel's god) on a cloud' ceases, in this passage, to be a metaphor for the vindication of Israel, and becomes, for Luke, the historical point around which other images (enthronement, lordship) will now organize themselves.

It is here, for the first time in Luke's story, that mention is made of the *return* of Jesus:

> While he was going and they were gazing up toward heaven, suddenly two men in white robes stood by them. They said, 'Men of Galilee, why do you stand looking up toward heaven? This Jesus, who has been taken up from you into heaven, will come in the same way as you saw him go into heaven.'[65]

This is the real novelty. Judaism knows nothing of a human being appearing from heaven in this manner. But it is not an *arbitrary* innovation. Like Paul's explanation of the two-stage resurrection (first Jesus, then his people at a later date), this innovation is occasioned directly by the redrawing of Israel's hope around the actual events of Jesus' life, death and resurrection. As he has taken Israel's destiny upon himself, being now exalted to the position of power and authority for which Daniel 1–6, as well as Daniel 7, provided some of the models, so it is inconceivable from within the early Christian worldview that the ultimate future of the world should have no place for him. And, since that ultimate future is not a disembodied bliss but a renewal of the whole created order, in which evil will be judged and defeated, that renewal, that judgment, and his return will belong closely with one another.[66]

This means, of course, that the old scholarly warhorse of the 'delay of the parousia' has had its day at last, and can be put out to grass once and for all. This is becoming increasingly recognized in some circles at least: Hengel speaks of the idea as a 'tired cliché'.[67] The word 'parousia' is itself misleading,

---

[64] On Pompey cf. *Ps. Sol.* 2.25–31; see above, p. 160.

[65] Ac. 1.10f.

[66] This is one possible context in which Mt. 25.31 may make sense. Here we have a reference to Zech. 14.5, which 'attracts' the idea of the 'coming of the son of man' from Dan. 7.13, and places it in a different context from that of e.g. Mt. 24.30. Alternatively, the passage can still be seen as another reference to the great judgment which is involved in the vindication of Jesus himself.

[67] Hengel 1983, 184 n.55. See too Bauckham 1980.

anyway, since it merely means 'presence'; Paul can use it of his being present with a church, and nobody supposes that he imagined he would make his appearance flying downwards on a cloud.[68] The motif of delay ('how long, O Lord, how long?'[69]) was already well established in Judaism, and is hardly a Christian innovation, as is often imagined. The usual scholarly construct, in which the early church waited for Jesus' return, lived only for that future and without thought for anything past (such as memories of Jesus himself), only to be grievously disappointed and to take up history-writing as a displacement activity, a failure of nerve—this picture is without historical basis.[70] The church expected certain events to happen within a generation, and happen they did, though there must have been moments between AD 30 and 70 when some wondered if they would, and in consequence took up the Jewish language of delay. Jerusalem fell; the good news of Jesus, and the kingdom of Israel's god, was announced in Rome, as well as in Jerusalem and Athens. But there is no sign of dismay, in any of the literature that has come down to us from the period after AD 70, at the fact that Jesus himself had still not returned. Clement looks forward to the return of Jesus without any comment on its timing.[71] Ignatius is worried about many things, but not that. Justin Martyr, in the middle of the second century, is as emphatic as anyone that the event will happen. He does not know when; but then, the key passages in the New Testament always said that it would be a surprise.[72] Tertullian, at the end of the second century, looks forward to Jesus' return as the greatest show on earth, outstripping anything one might see at the stadium or theatre.[73] As far as the early Christians were concerned, the most important event—the resurrection of Jesus—had already happened. One did not need to worry about the timing of that which was still to come. Back in the first generation, Paul could quite easily see the whole complex of events, including the Lord's return, as being likely to happen at any time: 1 Thessalonians 4 and 5 bear witness to that. But there is no suggestion that the Lord's return itself must happen within a generation, or that its failure to do so would precipitate any sort of crisis, or that it was only after such a crisis that the church would start to look to its historical

---

[68] 2 Cor. 10.10; Phil. 1.26; 2.12; cf. 1 Cor. 16.17; 2 Cor. 7.6f.

[69] cf. Rev. 6.10.

[70] Moule 1982 [1962], 139f., 143f.: 'It is the more impressive that hope deferred so seldom made the heart sick.' 2 Pet. 3.1–13 is the exception, not the rule, perhaps dealing with a non-Jewish misunderstanding of Jewish apocalyptic language.

[71] *1 Clem.* 23.4f., quoting Isa. 13.22 and Mal. 3.1.

[72] Justin *1 Apol.* 51, quoting Mt. 25.31 (which as we saw combines Dan. 7.13 and Zech. 14.5) and ascribing the text to Jeremiah. This imprecision makes it unsurprising that he does not appear to read Dan. 7 in the way that a first-century Jew would have done (cf. ch. 10 above). The final chapter (16) of the *Didache* is heavily dependent on Mt. 24 and pars., and could either be read as I have suggested that that passage should be, i.e. as a prediction of the fall of Jerusalem (in which case, of course, we would have to date it very early), or, like Justin, as the beginning of a rereading of Jewish apocalyptic in an unJewish way. Its inclusion of resurrection in the 'timetable' of events (16.6), and the difficulties with an early date, suggest the latter; in which case we have another piece of evidence for a second-generation expectation of Jesus' return which contains no anxiety about its having been 'delayed'. On the unknown timing of Jesus' return, cp. 1 Thess. 5.1–11, on which see Caird 1980, ch. 14.

[73] *De Spect.* 30.

basis in the actual life of Jesus, instead of simply to the future coming of the Lord.

The myth of 'apocalyptic' Christianity, then, needs radical revision. To be sure, the early Christians continued to use 'apocalyptic' language. But all the evidence suggests that they used it very much as first-century Jews did, i.e. to invest space-time reality with theological significance. Problems about 'taking it literally' only arise, in modern and perhaps ancient readings, when the Jewish background is ignored or misunderstood.[74]

7. Conclusion

The test of any worldview-analysis is whether it enables us to make sense of what people do and say. I submit that this brief account of the early Christians meets this test. Virtually every point I have made is of course controversial. Yet it seems to me to follow, at least as a summary hypothesis, from the study of early Christian praxis, symbol and story which has occupied us in the three previous chapters. And it certainly provides an overarching context of belief and hope within which we can understand, from at least one angle, why it was that the early Christians lived and worked together in the way that they did, why they engaged in mission, faced persecution, wrote letters, debated with learned Jews, argued their case before emperors. All good hypotheses, as we have often remarked, must get in the data, do so with simplicity, and shed light beyond their own borders. The appropriate sort of simplicity, i.e. that which belongs to history as a form of critical knowledge, is I think provided by the account I have given. I have suggested some of the ways in which the complex and pluriform data involved can begin to settle down within this framework, and I intend to examine a good deal more in successive volumes. In addition, from this perspective it is not difficult to understand why Christianity developed as it did, and why other movements with some claim to be Christian, but with a completely different worldview, grew out of it. That too, however, is another story for another day.

---

[74] This requires radical revision of certain well-known theories, e.g. that 'apocalyptic' is 'the mother of all Christian theology' (Käsemann 1969 [1965], chs. 4 and 5). I agree with Käsemann (and Schweitzer) on the role of 'apocalyptic', but, as should now be clear, I disagree radically over what 'apocalyptic' *means*. Käsemann's own warning ('One does not conquer apocalyptic and escape scot-free', ibid. 115, n.8) remains potent: but who, in modern scholarship, is the real conqueror of apocalyptic?

Part Five

Conclusion

Chapter Sixteen

THE NEW TESTAMENT AND THE QUESTION OF GOD

1. Introduction

The wind blows where it wishes; we hear the sound, but cannot tell where it comes from or where it is going. The history of first-century religious developments has something of this feel to it. We are listening to the sound, sometimes to the echo, of great and turbulent movements of at least the human spirit, and perhaps the divine; but to trace their origins is extremely difficult. We know something of their eventual destination, since we can observe the same movements in subsequent centuries; but we cannot be sure that Judaism and Christianity developed as their early adherents expected or intended.

We have been engaged in the study of the literature, history and theology of Judaism and Christianity at one of their most traumatic moments: the birth of the latter, and the death and rebirth of the former. In our retelling of the stories of these first-century movements, we have hoped to move in the direction of a realist, albeit a thoroughly critical, understanding of their history. In particular, we have examined the stories that these movements themselves told, in order to arrive at an understanding of their own self-awareness. At the end of the day, we are confronted with a striking fact: towards the end of the first century there were two recognizably distinct communities, *each making more or less the same claim*. Within fifty years of the death of Jesus, by the time that Ignatius and Akiba were young men, those who saw themselves as Jesus' followers were claiming that they were the true heirs of the promises made by the creator god to Abraham, Isaac and Jacob, and that the Jewish scriptures were to be read in terms of a new fulfilment. At the same time, as Judaism reconstructed itself in the aftermath of AD 70, the ground upon which it stood was the same: the creator god would somehow, despite all appearances, remain faithful to the covenant with Abraham, Isaac and Jacob, and he would make his will known in the scriptures, read now as Torah.

We have seen that, as was inevitable unless such communities were totally isolated from each other, the two clashed in various ways. Christianity's claim to be the true tenants of the vineyard was, naturally, resented, just as the Pharisees, Sadducees and Essenes had long resented each other's competing claims. So, far from being mutually isolated, Christianity and Judaism were, for the first generation at least, intertwined in ways that must at the time have seemed quite inextricable. The community of Jews knew that the Way of Jesus had been born and nurtured in their midst; the early Christians knew it too. Nor was it even clear to many first-generation followers of Jesus that there were in fact two communities. In the very early days, when, according to Acts, Jews were sometimes converted in large numbers, some people undoubtedly thought that the ethnic people of the creator god, and the new community created in and around Jesus, would end up coterminous.

Two communities; two different readings of scripture; two ways of self-understanding; one common root. The questions that face any student of this phenomenon must then be: why did it happen in this way? What does it 'mean'? Can we test the claims, and if so what do we find? The three focal points that emerge as we engage with these issues are the questions of Jesus, of the New Testament, and, finally, the question of god.

2. Jesus

The historian of the first century, faced with the evidence we have studied in this book, cannot shrink from the question of Jesus. We may feel that the evidence may be insufficient to say very much; that the results of such a quest may be theologically dubious; or that there will not be very much that is new to say. But the existence of the double community, these two 'peoples of god', Jewish and Christian, forces the historian to look at origins, whether or not this is congenial or difficult, tortuous or risky. We must ask: why did this Jewish sect, out of all the other groups and movements within the first century, develop in this way, so strikingly different from all others? And, whenever we approach the early Christian writings with this question, we have a strong sense that it was not simply a matter of the sect's early corporate decisions, enthusiasm, shrewd planning or anything else. It was something to do with Jesus.[1]

This points us inexorably towards the task which awaits us in the next volume, for which the present one is in many ways preparatory. Who was Jesus? What were his aims? Why, historically speaking, did he die? And why, granted all this, did early Christianity turn out as it did? What exactly happened at Easter, to cause this new movement to come to birth in *this* form, making *these* claims? Jesus stands between the two communities, living and working within that first-century Judaism which we mapped out in Part III, and being claimed as the starting-point of the community we mapped out in Part IV. The community of his followers remained recognizably Jewish, and yet redrew its belief and life in significantly new ways. The only means by which we can finish off this historical jigsaw lies in attempting to answer these basic questions about Jesus himself. We have seen in earlier chapters that the stories, large and small, in the New Testament, and in a good many of the other early Christian writings, do indeed purport to speak of Jesus, despite

---

[1] cf. the pertinent remarks of Hengel 1991, 82: 'Scholars sometimes argue about the earliest church as if Jesus had never lived or as if he had been rapidly forgotten.'

suggestions to the contrary within twentieth-century scholarship. On this basis, we can and must move cautiously forward, to engage seriously with the enormously difficult task of reconstructing the history that lies between the work of John the Baptist and the emergence of the Christian church.

3. The New Testament

The historian faces the question of Jesus; the theologian, the question of god. The literary critic—and at this point historians and theologians are compelled to be literary critics as well—faces the question of the New Testament. What is to be done with it?

I argued in Parts I and II of this book for a holistic reading of the New Testament that would retell its stories faithfully, that would allow its overtones as well as its fundamentals to be attended to. The outworking of that task is, from one point of view, a matter for the commentator and the preacher as much as for the historian and theologian. But these latter must insist that one can only understand the New Testament by seeing its component parts as straddling the two worlds from which Christianity was born. It is a Jewish book, telling Jewish-style stories, yet telling them for the world. It is a book of the world, retelling the story of the world as the story of Israel, and the story of Israel as the story of Jesus, in order to subvert the world's stories, and to lay before the world the claim of Jesus to be its sovereign. It is a Christian book, pouring new wine into the old bottles of Judaism, and new Jewish wine into the old bottles of the world, intending that this double exercise should have its inevitable and explosive double effect.

Thus it is that (what we now call) the New Testament can only properly be understood if we recognize that it is a collection of writings from precisely this community, the subversive community of a new would-be 'people of god'. These writings, moreover, were not written in order to provide merely an account of first-century Christianity, as though by a detached observer. Nor were they merely a commentary on it, as though first-century Christianity were a thing in itself, and the writings in question were a discussion or theological analysis of it conducted from behind an invisible glass screen. They were part of that complex entity, first-century Christianity, itself. Though we must of course use the New Testament as our main evidence for our own description and analysis of first-century Christianity, since there is no better evidence available, we must do so in the knowledge and recognition that it was not designed primarily for this use. The writing of the books that now form the New Testament arose naturally from within the daily life of the early church. The task of writing was interwoven with preaching and praying, with mission, sacrament and reflection. If the New Testament is to find an appropriate reading, it will be one which takes all this fully into account.[2]

---

[2] Even if there were other sources, for instance an outsider's account of early Christianity, on the analogy of Josephus' account of the Essenes, or for that matter Herodotus' (bk. 2) of the Egyptians, we would of course have to take fully into account the fact that it came precisely *from* an outsider, and as such came under suspicion of misunderstanding and distortion.

The question as to what one should do with the New Testament, however, is hereby restated, not solved. It is hard to see what kind of an obligation one might be under to treat *any* book exactly as its author wished. There may, nevertheless, be some kind of sliding scale of potential treatments. If we may revert to an illustration from chapter 1: to use Shakespeare's plays as the basis for a study of Elizabethan society or language does not reflect the intention of the author, but it may be quite a worthy task, and one of which the author would not in principle have disapproved, unless it got to the point at which readers seemed to be forgetting that these were plays, meant to be *staged*. To use the same book to prop up a broken table-leg, however, might well be thought outside the bounds of appropriateness. In the same way, there may be a sliding scale of appropriateness for the use of the New Testament. It may quite properly be used to reconstruct the life, language, religion and beliefs of the early Christians, provided we remember that it was not written for that purpose, but rather as something more like a play to be staged, that is, as a charter for a community, a set of books designed (in their very different ways) to fuel worship and witness. To use these books, as they have often been used, to prop up the broken leg of this or that theological, political or pietist scheme looks like falling off the end of the scale of appropriateness. The New Testament must, ultimately, be treated in a way that allows it to remain itself. Just as the Talmud is not appropriately used if it is quarried to provide spurious validation for distorted would-be 'Christian' readings of Judaism, so the New Testament cannot be used in ways which violate its basic identity and integrity. Or, if it is so used, any impression that such use carries some kind of authority must be firmly rejected.

We thus return, by a circuitous route, to the question which occupied us in chapters 1 and 5. What sort of authority does the New Testament possess? If the answer is, as it has often been, that the New Testament is the closest historical witness to the origin and rise of Christianity, some will object. Q, if we possessed it, would be earlier; if someone dug it up in the sands of Egypt, would we bind it up in Bibles along with Matthew, Mark and Luke? The *Gospel of Thomas*, some say, is earlier; if this were really so, ought it to be regarded as more authoritative than the canon as it now stands? The impression often given by the supporters of an early date for *Thomas* is that we should. Yet this idea is based on the belief that *early* Christianity is automatically *normative*; and this belief is self-contradictory, since nobody in early Christianity itself seems to have believed that earliness implied normativity.

The question looks as if it might begin, once more, to lurch to and fro along the epistemological scale. At one end we have Wrede's positivism: the Christian canon is irrelevant, the task is mere description of facts, and nothing in the past can be regarded as normative for the present. At the other, we have the ghetto of subjectivism: Christians regard the New Testament as 'their' book, a private text, which means something to them, and which cannot be expected to mean the same thing, or indeed necessarily anything much, to anyone else. As a third option, the critical realism we suggested earlier might support a model of authority linked to narrative. The New Testament offers itself, both explicitly and implicitly, as a set of stories, and a single Story, which, like all stories, lays claim to attention. It does this even when treated simply as myth: someone innocent of history, but at home in the world of fairy stories, or indeed of Tolkien's Middle Earth, could well find the New Testament powerful and evocative. This mythological power is in no way lost, but in fact enhanced, when historical study suggests that something very like this story actually happened. That, of course, is the point at which the relativist's account of the whole process is called into question, which is precisely why, in a relativistic age, the move from 'simply myth' to history-as-myth, or myth-as-history, is so often attacked. But that is the move that our whole study suggests and commends. If we read the New Testament as it stands, it claims on every page to be speaking of things which are true in the public domain. It is not simply, like so many books, a guide for private spiritual advancement. To read it like that is like reading Shakespeare simply to pass an examination. The New Testament claims to be the subversive story of the creator and the world, and demands to be read as such. Any authority it exercises in the process will be a dynamic, not a static, authority; the New Testament will not impose itself from a great height, and to attempt to use it in that fashion is at once to falsify it. Its claim is less brittle, and, if true, more powerful. It offers itself as the true story, the true myth, the true history of the whole world.

4. The Question of God

Cognate with the question of the New Testament, finally, is the question which will haunt this project all through. If the historian cannot escape the question of Jesus, nor the literary critic the question of the New Testament, the theologian cannot escape the question of god. Here, too, the historian and the literary critic, if they are true to their own subject-matter, will find that that subject-matter calls into question any specialization which excludes the question of god from consideration. Ultimately, as we saw in Part II, history, literature and theology belong together.

The question of god, though conspicuous by its absence from the great majority of books about the New Testament, is in fact the question which lies at the root of most if not all of the issues which are more frequently discussed. The question of Paul and the law is at bottom a question about god. The issues raised by the gospel of Matthew, or the book of Revelation, are at their heart questions about god. So we could go on. These questions look initially as though they presuppose agreement about the referent of the word 'god' itself, and simply enquire about what precisely this (known) god wants, has done, intends to do. But increasingly they begin to look as though they are probing to a deeper stage, so that literally nothing is assumed: they are enquiring after the meaning of the word 'god' itself. Who precisely is this god of whom the Jewish scriptures had spoken, the god who made himself known to Abraham, Moses, David and the prophets? Which community (of the two in question, at least) is speaking truly, or at least more truly, about this god? Increasingly, as early Christianity develops, there is a strong sense that new claims are being made at this fundamental level, not only in language but also in symbol and praxis, not least in the symbolic praxis of reading the Jewish scriptures in a new way:

> It is the contention of [the New Testament writers] that with the coming of Jesus the whole situation of mankind has so altered as to change the semantic content of the word 'God'.[3]

This fact about the New Testament, I suggest, provides one of the best clues to explain why, even when the question of god has not been explicitly raised, these writings have been felt to contain a power and appeal, an intrinsic authority. They are written, in their different ways, to articulate *and invite their hearers to share* a new worldview which carries at its heart a new view of 'god', and even a proposal for a way of saying 'God'.

Judaism and Christianity each claimed to be the 'people of god', and meant by that word 'god' the transcendent being who had created the world, who guided and directed its life and course, who had entered into covenant with Israel, and who, both communities believed, would one day act, precisely as the creator and covenant god, to put the entire world to rights and to rescue his true people from oppression. But if there were two such distinct communities, each making this claim, the historian's question, how this came to be so, will be matched by the theologian's questions: are these two claims equally coherent? Is there any way of telling whether one or other might have made more sense from the perspective of the first century? Which of them makes more sense *to us*? What might it mean for a community in a subsequent generation, whether in the second or the twentieth century, to claim continuity with one or other of these communities?

To this complex of questions some have sought to reply: the two systems are simply different. Each, no doubt, makes sense in its own world of discourse, but comparing them, within a first-, never mind a twentieth-century, perspective, makes no sense:

> Judaism and Christianity are completely different religions, not different versions of one religion ... The two faiths stand for different people talking about different things to different people.[4]

There is something to be said for this as an approach to mutual understanding and common dialogue in the twentieth century. Whatever tasks or obligations Judaism and Christianity conceive themselves as having towards each other in our own generation, those tasks cannot be advanced, nor those obligations discharged, by imagining ourselves simply as odd variants of each other, Christians as Jews *manqués* or vice versa. Yet, when we move in the world of the first century, the claim of utter differentiation seems to me quite obviously false—just as false, in fact, as the claim, which is also sometimes advanced, that the two religions are really just the same, so that one may elide the two movements into each other, downplaying differences, smoothing off rough

---

[3] Caird 1980, 51. Cf. too Morgan 1987, 200 n.14; Räisänen 1990a, 138.
[4] Neusner 1991, 1; cf. 28, 129.

corners and edges, and producing an inoffensive but historically incredible picture of both.[5]

Neusner is too good a historian to accept this latter proposal. Yet his thesis of complete difference is, in its way, equally relativistic. In seeking to do justice to, and even to honour, such (to him) remote religious features as Roman Catholic veneration of Mary, Neusner is in danger of making both Judaism and Christianity simply different distorting windows on the one divine reality. Ultimately, the two proposals (1. our religions are really the same; 2. our religions are completely different responses to the same god) lead to the same destination: if none of us is so very clear about the meaning of the word 'god', we can simply recognize our differences while admitting that they are not ultimately very important. And that suggestion, while attractive within both modernism and postmodernism, has little if anything in common with the world (or worlds) of Judaism and Christianity in the first century. The question of the meaning of the word 'god' therefore lies at the heart of the account we give of the first-century communities that we have been studying.

What claims, then, are advanced for the meaning of the word 'god'? As I said in the Preface, justifying my use of the lower case for the initial 'g', it can be highly misleading to think of 'God' as though the word were univocal. A prime example of this occurs in Neusner's attempt to hold Judaism and Christianity at arm's length from each other:

> What other understanding can we seek [in common with each other]? My answer derives from the commonplace fact that, after all, we really do worship one God, who is the same God, and who is the only God, we [i.e. Jews and Christians] and the Muslims with us. Within that common ground of being, a human task before us emerges. It is to seek in the religious experience of the other, the stranger and outsider, that with which we within our own world can identify.[6]

An 'Enlightenment' agenda and proposal, indeed. It is a 'commonplace' that those who use the word 'God' mean the same thing by it; all that this leaves us to do is to explore 'religious experience'. The trouble with this is that it projects an eighteenth-century way of doing theology back on to the first century, and, in so doing, distorts. In the first century, claims about any god could become controversial, even polemical. The claims made by pagans for their gods, over against Israel's god, were regularly polemical in the sense of accompanying actual military, social and economic oppression.[7] Israel's counter-claim was always polemical *vis-à-vis* the whole pagan world: her literature abounded with tales of pagans coming to acknowledge her god as the true one,[8] or of her god doing battle with the pagan gods and defeating them.[9] The whole point of the glad shout on Israel's watchtowers after the defeat of

---

[5] cf. Gager 1983; Gaston 1987; etc. The 'two-covenant' theory, in which Judaism is the intended religion for Jews, and Christianity for Gentiles, was pioneered by F. Rosenzweig, and is criticized as 'condescending' by Neusner 1991, 118f.

[6] Neusner 1991, 121; cf. 29

[7] cf. 1 Sam. 17.43; Isa. 36.18–20 (and cp. 36.10!); Dan. 3.12–29; 5.3–4, 23; Bel 4–5, 24–5; 1 Macc. 1.43; etc.

[8] 2 Kgs. 5.15–18; Zech. 8.22–3; Dan. 2.47; 3.29; 4.2–3, 34–7; 6.26–7; *Jos. & As.*; etc.

[9] 1 Sam. 5.1–5; 17.26, 36, 45–6; Isa. 37.23; 1 Macc. 4.30–3; etc.

Babylon is that that event will demonstrate Israel's god to be the true king, and Babylon's to be a mere idol:

> How beautiful upon the mountains are the feet of the messenger
>   who announces peace, who brings good news,
> Who announces salvation, who says to Zion, *'Your God* reigns.'
> YHWH has bared his holy arm before the eyes of all the nations;
>   and all the ends of the earth shall see the salvation of *our God*.[10]

Within later Judaism, the same polemic is applied over and over again to Christianity. Christians say that they worship a god who is both three and one, which Jews see as compromising monotheism; Christians say that Jesus is the full and complete revelation of this one god, which Jews regard as a paganization of the god in whom they believe, almost a contradiction in terms.[11] In a work which many date as early as the first century, but which certainly reflects attitudes at a period not much later, one rabbi declares that the Minim ('heretics', probably including Christians) 'know Him [i.e. Israel's god] and yet deny Him',[12] the reason being that they have introduced into the pure Jewish idea of god the belief that Jesus is, in an ontological and not merely a messianic sense, the 'son of god'. Christianity thus becomes in Jewish eyes a form of paganism, and is castigated to this day by some writers on exactly this ground.[13] (Several Christian writers, believing that Judaism was a degenerate form of religion, have been happy to go along with the historical judgment behind this assessment.)

This critique, however, does no justice to early Christianity, just as generations of 'Christian' critiques have done no justice to first-century Judaism. In the first century, as we saw in the previous chapter, the claim was regularly advanced that the god of Israel had now made himself known in and through, and even *as*, Jesus and the divine spirit. For the historian of first-century theologies, there can be no getting away from the choice which the two communities posed. Judaism claimed that Christianity, by putting Jesus in the middle of its doctrine of god, had irreparably damaged that doctrine. Christianity claimed that mainline Judaism, in clinging to the idea of national privilege and not recognizing the righteous saving act of her own god in the death and resurrection of Jesus, had stepped aside from the covenant. Both religions claimed that they were giving the true meaning to the word 'god', in line with prior scriptural revelation, and that the other was not.

For the first-century Jew, Torah was non-negotiable as divine revelation; the Christians seemed to be sitting loose to it; therefore, the Christians were wrong. The defence of Israel's Temple and Land against pagan pollution was, for many Jews, a non-negotiable part of the task laid upon Israel by her god; Christians ignored these tasks; therefore, the Christians were wrong, not just about a detail, but about Israel's god. Conversely, for the early Christians, the

---

[10] Isa. 52.7, 10 (italics, of course, added).

[11] e.g. Epstein 1959, 134: 'the "Trinity in Unity" of Christianity . . . remains a direct denial of the *only* God who, from the beginning, had chosen Israel in His service' (italics original).

[12] tShabb. 13.5; see Urbach 1987, 26.

[13] e.g. Maccoby 1986; 1991.

death and resurrection of Jesus were the full revelation in action of the one god, the great divine act for which Israel had been waiting; further, this meant that Israel's god, the world's creator, had made himself known uniquely *in* Jesus. Pagans and Jews alike refused to acknowledge this Jesus, *and hence to recognize this god* in what he had done. Even when common ground is sought, as in Romans 1, or the Areopagus speech, or Romans 9–11, the argument is precisely that though pagans and Jews are confronted by the true god, they have refused to submit to the reality of who he is.[14] Paul, John and the others steer a delicate course in order to avoid dualism (non-Christians know nothing whatever of the true god), paganism (we worship our god, you worship yours, and we go our separate ways), deism (the deity is distant, and we cannot know much about it), and relativism (we all follow different paths up the same misty mountain). The New Testament writers claim that, though there is only one god, all human beings of themselves cherish wrong ideas *about* this one god. In worshipping the god thus wrongly conceived, they worship an idol. Pagans worship gods of wood and stone, distorting the creator by worshipping the creature. Jews, Paul argues in parallel with this, have made an idol of their own national identity and security, and so have failed to see what the covenant faithfulness of their god, the god of Abraham, had always entailed.[15] Christians, as the addressees of the New Testament writings, are clearly not exempt from the possibility of idolatry, of using the words 'Jesus' and 'Christ' while in fact worshipping a different god.[16] Our study of the history of Judaism and Christianity in the first century leads us inexorably to the conclusion that both cannot be right in their claims about the true god.

Both might, of course, be wrong. The Stoics might be right: there is one god, since the whole world is divine, and we humans are part of it. The Epicureans, and their modern successors the Deists, might be right: there is a god, or possibly more than one, whom none of us knows very well and all of us distantly acknowledge, with ignorance and distortion. The pagans might be right: there are different 'divine' forces in the world, which need to be propitiated when angry, and harnessed to one's own advantage when not. The Gnostics might be right: there is a good, hidden god who will reveal himself to some of us, thereby rescuing us from this wicked world of matter and flesh, which are the creation of an evil god. Or the modern atheists or materialists might be right. There is no neutral ground here. We are at the level of worldview, and here ultimate choices are involved. The claim of first-century Judaism, and of subsequent Judaism, is that the creator of the world has revealed himself in Torah in ways which simply do not allow for the claims of Stoicism, Epicureanism, paganism, Gnosticism and the rest—or for those of Christianity. The claim of Christianity from its earliest days, and subsequently, is that the creator of the world, the god of Abraham, has revealed himself

[14] Rom. 1.18–23; Ac. 17.22–31; Rom. 10.2–3, 16–17. Cf. too Jn. 8.39–59.

[15] Rom. 2.17–29, which parallels and draws on 1.18–32. Rom. 2.17ff. is expanded further, in a crescendo of irony, in 7.7–25; 9.30–10.13.

[16] cf. e.g. 1 Cor. 12.1–3 (at once followed by the implicitly trinitarian 12.4–6); Gal. 4.8–11 (immediately preceded by the implicitly trinitarian 4.1–7); 1 Jn. 5.21.

through Jesus, and through his own spirit, in ways which disallow the various pagan claims—and also those of a Judaism that rejects Jesus. This conclusion is of course unpalatable in a world (our own) that has been dominated by neo-Epicureanism with its distant, unknowable divinities. It is all the more unpalatable in view of the ugly resurgence of violence between soi-disant 'religious' communities, however much it may be shown that the generating force of the violence has nothing to do with the religion in whose name it is perpetrated. But it represents the way things were seen in the first century, within the two communities that claimed to be the people of the one true god.

How might one decide between these competing claims? First-century Jews looked forward to a public event, a great act of liberation for Israel, in and through which their god would reveal to all the world that he was not just a local, tribal deity, but the creator and sovereign of all. YHWH would reveal his salvation for Israel in the eyes of all the nations; the ends of the earth would see that he had vindicated his people. The early Christians, not least in the writings that came to be called the New Testament, looked back to an event in and through which, they claimed, Israel's god had done exactly that. On this basis, the New Testament, emerging from within this strange would-be 'people of god', told the story of that people as a story rooted in Israel's past, and designed to continue into the world's future. It repeated the Jewish claim: this story concerns not just a god but God. It revised the Jewish evidence: the claim is made good, not in national liberation, but in the events concerning Jesus.

Appendix

CHRONOLOGICAL CHART OF SECOND-TEMPLE JEWISH HISTORY AND OF EARLY CHRISTIANITY

Dates are vital for historians, but for ancient historians always controversial. A good deal in what follows remains hypothetical; some particularly difficult issues are addressed in the relevant sections of the book. I have added in italics a selection of events and features which relate to various discussions, particularly those in Part III.

1. From Babylon to Rome

a. Babylonian Period

597	Jerusalem taken by Nebuchadnezzar II
587	Jerusalem destroyed . . . exile
539	Fall of Babylon; Cyrus' victories

b. Persian/Greek Period   538–320

538 on:	return of exiles; rebuilding of temple begun (completed 516)
450s/440s:	Ezra and Nehemiah in Jerusalem
336	Alexander the Great comes to power
332	Alexander conquers Palestine
323	Alexander dies: empire divided

c. Egyptian Period   320–c.200

Palestine under Ptolemies; local government of High Priests

d. Syrian Period   200–63

200	Antiochus III defeats Egyptians
175	Antiochus IV Epiphanes (= A. E.) enthroned
171	Menelaus High Priest: favours A. E.: Jews rise against Menelaus
167	(25 Dec.) A. E. desecrates temple: builds altar to Zeus Olympus
166	Judas Maccabaeus becomes leader after death of Mattathias
164	(25 Dec.) Judas cleanses temple
164–42	running battles with Syria
161–59	Alcimus High Priest
160	Death of Judas M.
160–52	Jonathan leader of nationalist forces

159–2?	Essene Teacher of Righteousness = High Priest?
152–43	Jonathan High Priest [= Wicked Priest of Scrolls??]
	first mention of Pharisees: Jos. Ant. 13.171
143	Jonathan captured by Trypho
142	semi-independence (tax exemption) attained under Simon
	(Hasmonean High Priests [= HP]/rulers in **bold type**)
140–34	**Simon:** HP and ethnarch
142	murder of Jonathan
	Qumran objection to Hasmonean rule: e.g. 1QpHab 3.4—6.12
140	legitimation of Simon's position by Jewish people
134–104	**John Hyrcanus:** HP and ethnarch
	War 1.67–9 says he provoked 'stasis'
	Eleazar asks Hyrcanus to give up being HP: Ant. 13.288–99
104–103	**Aristobulus I:** HP and King ['Philhellene']
103–76	**Alexander Jannaeus:** HP and King
	'stasis' at festival: War 1.88–98; Ant. 13.372–83; bSukk. 48ab
76–67	**Hyrcanus II:** HP only
	(Salome/Alexandra, Alexander Jannaeus's widow, as Queen)
	War 1.112: 'she ruled Israel, the Pharisees ruled her'
	Ant. 13.398–418: Pharisees in favour, as A. J. had advised her
67–63	**Aristobulus II:** HP and King (younger son of Alexandra)
	(defeated Hyrcanus in battle at Jericho)

2. Under Rome: 63–

a. Under Republic

63	Jerusalem taken by Pompey (cf. *Ps. Sol.* 17.8, 1QpHab 4–6??)
	HPs wield power under Roman protectorate
63–40	**Hyrcanus II:** HP (reinstated after intervention of Pompey)
	Antipater emerges as power behind Hyrcanus
48	Pompey murdered in Egypt (*Ps. Sol.* 2.30–2!)
43	Antipater assassinated
44	Death of Julius Caesar: civil wars in Roman world
40	Parthians invade Syria/Judaea, imprisoning Hyrcanus and putting in
40–37	**Antigonus:** HP and King (last son of Aristobulus)
40	Herod (son of Antipater) declared King of Judaea in Rome,
	with support of Antony/Octavian
	(Herod, not qualified to be HP, fills the office with nonentities)
40–38	Parthian invasion
37	Herod retakes Jerusalem for Rome after Parthian invasion
	(interrupts siege to marry Mariamne, granddaughter of Hyrcanus:
	Ant 14.465–7)
37–4	**Herod the Great**
31 (2 Sept)	Battle of Actium:
	Octavian defeats Antony, confirms Herod in office
	Herod spares Pollio the Pharisee and Samias
20?	*Pollio and Samias refuse to take oath to Herod (Ant. 15.370)*
19	Herod starts rebuilding temple (consecrated 9 BC)
10?	*6000+ Pharisees refuse oath to Caesar (Ant. 17.41–6)*
4 BC	Death of Herod: disturbances before and after
	Eagle Incident (Judas and Matthias) (Ant. 17.149–67, War 1.648–55)
	revolt of Judas son of Hezekiah (= J the Galilean?) (War 2.56 etc.)
	'messianic' movements of Simon (Ant. 17.273–7)
	and Athronges (Ant. 17.278–84)

4 BC	Kingdom divided:

Antipas Tetrarch of Galilee and Perea (until 38); Marries Herodias
Archelaus 'King' (= ethnarch) of Judaea, Samaria, Idumea; (deposed, AD 6)
Philip Tetrarch of N. E. Palestine (until 34)

6 AD	Archelaus deposed after protests
	Judaea a Roman Province, under 'Prefects'
	Census riots: Judas the Galilean, Saddok the Pharisee (Ant. 18.1–10)

b. Under Emperors and Prefects [Emperors in **bold type**; prefects underlined]

–14 AD	**Augustus**	
	6-9	Coponius
	9-12	Marcus Ambivius
	12-15	Annius Rufus
14-37	**Tiberius**	
	15-26	Valerius Gratus
	18	Caiaphas High Priest
	26-36	Pontius Pilate
	30	Crucifixion of Jesus
	31?	Conversion of Saul/Paul
	36	Nabatean King invades Perea, defeats Antipas
37-41	**Gaius**	
	37-41	Marullus
	40	Crisis over Gaius' statue
		Herod Agrippa, grandson of Herod the Great,
		becomes King of Philip's (37) and Antipas' (39) areas
		Antipas and Herodias banished
41-54	**Claudius**	
	41	Claudius makes Herod Agrippa King of Judaea too
		Agrippa executes James the brother of John, Passover (Ac. 12.2)
	44	death of Herod Agrippa (Ac. 12): Judaea reverts to Procurators
	44-46	Cuspius Fadus
	44	famine (Ac. 11.28)
	46-48	Tiberius Alexander
		Crucifixion of Jacob and Simon, sons of Judas the Galilean (Ant. 20.102)
		Late 40s—late 50s: Paul's missionary journeys
	48-52	Ventidius Cumanus
	49	Claudius expels Jews from Rome *impulsore Chresto* (Ac. 18.2 etc.)
		49–51 Paul in Corinth (Gallio, Ac 18.12)
		50 Agrippa II (son of Agrippa I) becomes King of various areas
	52-60	Antonius Felix (brother of Pallas, Nero's freedman)
		54 Jews return to Rome after Claudius' death
54-68	**Nero**	
	60-62	Porcius Festus
		62 James the Just executed during interregnum (Ant. 20.200)
	62-65	Lucceius Albinus
		63 Temple finally completed
		64 Fire of Rome: Persecution of Christians
	65-66	Gessius Florus

66-70 JEWISH WAR

	9 June 68: Nero commits suicide
68-69	**Galba**
	69 'Year of Four Emperors'
69	**Otho**
69	**Vitellius**
69-79	**Vespasian**
	70 Titus takes Jerusalem

c. After 70

		Establishment of Academy at Javneh under Johanan ben Zakkai
	74	Capture of Masada (last stronghold)
79-81	**Titus**	
81-96	**Domitian**	
		c. 90 Domitian's investigation of Jesus' relatives
		92/3 death of Agrippa II
96-98	**Nerva**	
98-117	**Trajan**	
	c.110	Pliny Governor of Bithynia
	c.110–115	Letters of Ignatius
	115-7	Jewish Revolts in Egypt, Cyrene, Cyprus
117-38	**Hadrian**	
	132	Hadrian's anti-semitic legislation: temple of Jupiter in Jerusalem
	133-5	Rebellion of Simeon Ben Kosiba (Bar-Kochba)
	135	*Martyrdom of Akiba*
138-61	**Antoninus Pius**	
	140s–160s	Justin Martyr active in Rome (martyred c. 165)
	155/6	Martyrdom of Polycarp, Bishop of Smyrna
161–80	**Marcus Aurelius**	
	c.130–200	Irenaeus: Bishop of Lyons in 180s/190s
	c.160–220	Tertullian
180–92	**Commodus**	
		c. 200 compilation of Mishnah

Bibliography

Abbreviations

ANF	Ante-Nicene Fathers
ANRW	*Aufstieg und Niedergang der Römischen Welt*, ed. H. Temporini and A. Haase. Berlin: de Gruyter.
Arist.	Aristotle
CAH	*Cambridge Ancient History*
cf.	confer
CHJ	*Cambridge History of Judaism*
Compendia	*Compendia Rerum Iudaicarum ad Novum Testamentum*. Section One: *The Jewish People in the First Century*, ed. S. Safrai and M. Stern. 2 vols. Section Two: *The Literature of the Jewish People in the Period of the Second Temple and the Talmud*, ed. M. J. Mulder, M. E. Stone and S. Safrai. 3 vols. Philadelphia: Fortress; Assen/Maastricht: Van Gorcum. 1976–87.
cp.	compare
Dio Cass.	Dio Cassius
Diod. Sic.	Diodorus Siculus
Epict.	Epictetus (*Disc.* = *Discourses*)
esp.	especially
Euseb.	Eusebius
Ign.	Ignatius
Jos.	Josephus
JTS	*Journal of Theological Studies*
LCL	Loeb Classical Library
LXX	Septuagint version of the Old Testament (see below)
NRSV	New Revised Standard Version (see below)
NT	New Testament
OT	Old Testament
par(s).	and parallel(s) [in the synoptic tradition]
PG	J. P. Migne, *Patrologia Graeca*. Paris, 1857–66.
SB	H. L. Strack and P. Billerbeck, *Kommentar zum Neuen Testament aus Talmud und Midrasch*. 6 vols. Munich: C. H. Beck, 1926–56.
Schürer	E. Schürer, *The History of the Jewish People in the Age of Jesus Christ (175 B.C.—A.D. 135)*. Rev. & ed. M. Black, G. Vermes, F. G. B. Millar. 4 vols. Edinburgh: T & T Clark, 1973–87.
Suet.	Suetonius
Tac.	Tacitus
TDNT	*Theological Dictionary of the New Testament*, ed. G. Kittel and G. Friedrich. 10 vols. Trans. & ed. G. W. Bromiley. Grand Rapids, Mich.: Eerdmans, 1964–76.

A

Primary Sources

1. Bible

Biblia Hebraica Stuttgartensia, ed. K. Elliger and W. Rudolph. Stuttgart: Württembergische Bibelanstalt Stuttgart, 1968–76.
Septuaginta: Id est Vetus Testamentum Graece iuxta LXX interpres, ed. A. Rahlfs. 8th edn. 2 vols. Stuttgart: Württembergische Bibelanstalt Stuttgart, 1965 [1935].
Novum Testamentum Graece, ed. K. Aland, M. Black, C. M. Martini, B. M. Metzger, and A. Wikgren. 26th edn. Stuttgart: Deutsche Bibelgesellschaft, 1979 [1898] [= 'Nestle-Aland'].
The Holy Bible, Containing the Old and New Testaments with the Apocryphal/Deuterocanonical Books: New Revised Standard Version. New York & Oxford: OUP, 1989.

2. Other Jewish Texts

The Mishnah, Translated from the Hebrew with Introduction and Brief Explanatory Notes by Herbert Danby. Oxford: OUP, 1933.
The Old Testament Pseudepigrapha, ed. James H. Charlesworth. 2 vols. Garden City, N.Y.: Doubleday, 1983–5.
The Apocryphal Old Testament, ed. H. F. D. Sparks. Oxford: Clarendon Press, 1984.
The Authorised Daily Prayer Book of the United Hebrew Congregations of the British Commonwealth of Nations, trans. S. Singer. New edn. London: Eyre & Spottiswood, 1962.
Josephus: *Works*, ed. H. St. J. Thackeray, R. Marcus, A. Wikgren and L. H. Feldman. 9 vols. LCL. Cambridge, Mass.: Harvard U. P.; London: Heinemann, 1926–65.
Philo: *Works*, ed. F. H. Colson, G. H. Whitaker, J. W. Earp and R. Marcus. 12 vols. LCL. Cambridge, Mass.: Harvard U. P. London: Heinemann, 1929–53.
Qumran: *Die Texte aus Qumran*, ed. E. Lohse. Darmstadt: Wissenschaftliche Buchgesellschaft, 1964.
——, trans.: *The Dead Sea Scrolls in English*, trans. & ed. G. Vermes. 3rd edn. London: Penguin Books, 1987 [1962].

3. Other Early Christian and Related Texts

Aristides: *The Apology of Aristides*, in ANF 9:257–279.
Apostolic Fathers: *The Apostolic Fathers*, ed. and trans. J. B. Lightfoot. 5 vols. London: Macmillan, 1889/90.
——: *The Apostolic Fathers*, ed. and trans. Kirsopp Lake. 2 vols. London: Heinemann; Cambridge, Mass.: Harvard U. P., 1965.
——, trans.: *Early Christian Writings*, translated by Maxwell Staniforth, introduced and edited by Andrew Louth. London: Penguin Books, 1968.
——, trans.: *The Apostolic Fathers*, 2nd edn. (of Lightfoot 1889/90). Ed. Michael W. Holmes. Grand Rapids: Baker, 1989.
E. Hennecke, *New Testament Apocrypha*, ed. W. Schneemelcher. English trans. ed. by R. McL. Wilson. 2 vols. London: SCM; Philadelphia: Westminster, 1963–5 [1959–64].

Eusebius, ed. and trans.: *Eusebius. The Ecclesiastical History*, ed. and trans. Kirsopp Lake, H. J. Lawlor and J. E. L. Oulton. 2 vols. London: Heinemann; Cambridge, Mass.: Harvard U. P., 1973–75.
———, trans.: *Eusebius. The History of the Church from Christ to Constantine*, 2nd edn., translated by G.A. Williamson, revised and edited with a new introduction by Andrew Louth. London: Penguin Books, 1989.
Justin Martyr: in ANF 1:157–306.
Minucius Felix: *Octavius*, trans. G. H. Rendall. LCL. Cambridge, Mass.: Harvard U. P.; London: Heinemann, 1984.
Nag Hammadi texts: *The Nag Hammadi Library in English*, ed. James M. Robinson. Leiden: Brill; San Francisco: Harper & Row, 1977.
Origen: *Contra Celsum*. In ANF vol. 4.
Orosius: *Historiae adversus Paganos*, ed. K. Zangemeister. Stuttgart: Teubner, 1889.
Synesius: *De Insomniis*. In PG 66.1281–1320.
Thomas: *The Gospel According to Thomas*, ed. A. Guillaumont et al. Leiden: Brill; London: Collins, 1959.
Tertullian: *Apology*; *De Spectaculis*, trans. T. R. Glover. LCL. Cambridge, Mass.: Harvard U. P.; London: Heinemann, 1984.

4. Pagan Texts

Aristotle: *Aristotle. The 'Art' of Rhetoric*. Ed. and trans. J. H. Freese. LCL. London: Heinemann; Cambridge, Mass.: Harvard U. P., 1947.
———, *Nicomachaean Ethics*: *The Ethics of Aristotle*. Trans. J. A. K. Thomson. London: Penguin Books, 1955 [1953]
Cicero: *De Natura Deorum*. In vol. 19 of *Cicero*. Ed. and trans. H. Rackham. LCL. London: Heinemann; New York: G. P. Putnam's Sons, 1933.
Dio Cassius: *Dio's Roman History*. Ed. and trans. E. Cary. LCL. 9 vols. London: Heinemann; Cambridge, Mass.: Harvard U. P., 1954–5.
Diodorus Siculus: *Diodorus Siculus*. Ed. and trans. C. H. Oldfather and others. LCL. 12 vols. London: Heinemann; New York, Putnam, 1933–67.
Dionysius of Halicarnassus: *The Roman Antiquities of Dionysius of Halicarnassus*. Ed. and trans. E. Cary. LCL. 7 vols. London: Heinemann; Cambridge, Mass.: Harvard U. P., 1937–50.
Epictetus: *The Discourses as reported by Arrian, the Manual, and Fragments*. Ed. and trans. W. A. Oldfather. LCL. 2 vols. London: Heinemann; Cambridge, Mass.: Harvard U. P., 1978–9.
Hecataeus: in *Fragmente der griechischen Historiker*, ed. F. Jacoby, 1923– , vol. 1.
Herodotus: *Herodoti Historiae*, ed. C. Hude. 3rd edn. 2 vols. Oxford: OUP 1926.
———, trans.: *Herodotus. The Histories*. Newly translated and with an Introduction by Aubrey de Sélincourt. London: Penguin Books, 1954.
Juvenal: *Juvenal: The Satires*. Ed. J. Ferguson. New York: St Martin's Press, 1979.
———, trans.: *Juvenal, the Sixteen Satires*. 2nd edn. Trans. P. Green. London: Penguin Books, 1974 [1967]
———, trans.: *Juvenal: The Satires*. Trans. N. Rudd; introd. and notes by W. Barr. Oxford: Clarendon Press, 1991.
Lucian: *Lucian*. Ed. and trans. A. M. Harmon et al. LCL. 8 vols. London: Heinemann; Cambridge, Mass.: Harvard U. P., 1913–67.
Ovid: *Ovid. Metamorphoses*, trans. F. J. Miller. LCL. 2 vols. Cambridge, Mass: Harvard U. P.; London: Heinemann, 1960.
Plautus: *T. Macci Plauti Comoediae*, ed. W. M. Lindsay. 2 vols. Oxford: Clarendon Press, 1905.
———, trans.: *Plautus: The Rope and Other Plays*, trans. E. F. Watling. London: Penguin Books, 1964.
Pliny the Elder: *Pliny the Elder*. Ed. and trans. H. Rackham et al. LCL. 10 vols. London: Heinemann; Cambridge, Mass.: Harvard U. P., 1949–62.
Pliny the Younger: *C. Plini Caecili Secundi Epistularum Libri Decem*, ed. R. A. B. Mynors. Oxford: OUP. 1963.
———, trans.: *The Letters of the Younger Pliny*, translated with an introduction by Betty Radice. London: Penguin Books, 1963.

Sallust: *Sallust*. Trans. J. C. Rolfe. LCL. London: Heinemann; Cambridge, Mass.: Harvard U. P., 1975.

Sophocles: *Sophocles: The Text of the Seven Plays*. Ed. R. C. Jebb. Cambridge: CUP, 1897.

——, trans.: R. C. Jebb, *The Tragedies of Sophocles Translated into English Prose*. Cambridge: CUP, 1904.

Suetonius: *C. Suetoni Tranquili Opera*, vol. 1. *De Vita Caesarum Libri VIII*. Ed. M. Ihm. Stuttgart: Teubner, 1978 [1908].

——, trans.: *Suetonius. The Twelve Caesars*, translated by Robert Graves. London: Penguin Books, 1957.

Tacitus, *Agricola*: *Cornelii Taciti de Vita Agricolae*, ed. H. Furneaux. 2nd edn. by J. G. C. Anderson. Oxford: Clarendon Press, 1922.

Tacitus, *Annals*: *Cornelii Taciti Annalium ab Excessu Divi Augusti Libri*, ed. C. D. Fisher. Oxford: Clarendon Press, 1906.

——, trans.: *Tacitus. The Annals of Imperial Rome*, translated with an introduction by Michael Grant. London: Penguin Books, 1956.

Tacitus, *Histories*: *Cornelii Taciti Historiarum Libri*, ed. C. D. Fisher. Oxford: Clarendon Press, n.d.

——, trans.: *Tacitus. The Histories*, translated by Kenneth Wellesley. London: Penguin Books, 1964.

Thucydides: *Thucydidis Historiae*, ed. H. S. Jones. 2 vols. Oxford: OUP, 1898.

——, trans.: *Thucydides: History of the Peloponnesian War*. Translated with an introduction by Rex Warner. London: Penguin Books, 1954.

B

Secondary Literature

Abbagnano, Nicola. 1967. 'Positivism.' In *The Encyclopedia of Philosophy*, ed. P. Edwards, vol. 6, 414–19. New York: Macmillan Co. & The Free Press; London: Collier-Macmillan Ltd.

Alexander, Loveday C. A. 1986. 'Luke's Preface in the Context of Greek Preface-Writing.' *Novum Testamentum* 28:48–74.

———. 1993. *The Preface to Luke's Gospel: Literary Convention and Social Context in Luke 1:1–4.* Society for New Testament Studies Monograph Series. Cambridge: CUP. [Forthcoming]

Alexander, Philip S. 1972. 'The Targumim and Early Exegesis of "Sons of God" in Genesis 6.' *Journal of Jewish Studies* 13:60–71.

Allison, Dale C. 1985. *The End of the Ages has Come: An Early Interpretation of the Passion and Resurrection of Jesus.* Philadelphia: Fortress.

Alon, Gedalyahu. 1977. *Jews, Judaism and the Classical World: Studies in Jewish History in the Times of the Second Temple.* Trans. I. Abrahams. Jerusalem: Magnes Press.

Alter, Robert. 1981. *The Art of Biblical Narrative.* New York: Basic Books.

Appignanesi, Lisa, and Hilary Lawson. 1989. *Dismantling Truth: Reality in the Post-Modern World.* London: Wiedenfeld & Nicolson.

Applebaum, S. 1976. 'Economic Life in Palestine.' In *Compendia* 1.2.631–700.

Ashton, John. 1985. 'The Identity and Function of the Ioudaioi in the Fourth Gospel.' *Novum Testamentum* 27:40–75.

———, ed. 1986a. *The Interpretation of John.* Issues in Religion and Theology, no. 9. Philadelphia: Fortress; London: SPCK.

———. 1986b. 'The Transformation of Wisdom. A Study of the Prologue of John's Gospel.' *New Testament Studies* 32:161–86.

———. 1991. *Understanding the Fourth Gospel.* Oxford: Clarendon Press.

Attridge, Harold W. 1984. 'Historiography.' In *Compendia* 2.2.157–84.

———. 1989. *The Epistle to the Hebrews.* Hermeneia. Philadelphia: Fortress.

Aune, David E. 1976. 'Orthodoxy in First-Century Judaism? A Response to N. J. McEleney.' *Journal for the Study of Judaism* 7:1–10.

———. 1983. *Prophecy in Early Christianity and the Ancient Mediterranean World.* Grand Rapids, Mich.: Eerdmans.

———. 1987. *The New Testament in Its Literary Environment.* In Library of Early Christianity, ed. Wayne A. Meeks. Philadelphia: Westminster.

———. 1991a. 'On the Origins of the "Council of Javneh" Myth.' *Journal of Biblical Literature* 110:491–3.

———. 1991b. 'Oral Tradition and the Aphorisms of Jesus.' In *Jesus and the Oral Gospel Tradition*, ed. H. Wansbrough, 211–65. Journal for the Study of the New Testament Supplement Series, vol. 64. Sheffield: Sheffield Academic Press.

Ayer, A. J. 1946 [1936]. *Language, Truth and Logic.* 2nd edn. London: Gollancz.

———. 1956. *The Problem of Knowledge.* London: Penguin Books.

Bacon, B. W. 1930. *Studies in Matthew.* London: Constable.

Baird, J. Arthur. 1991. *A Comparative Analysis of the Gospel Genre: The Synoptic Mode and its Uniqueness.* Lewiston/Queenston/Lampeter: Edwin Mellen Press.

Balch, David L., ed. 1991. *Social History of the Matthean Community: Cross-Disciplinary Approaches.* Minneapolis: Fortress.

Bammel, Caroline P. H. 1982. 'Ignatian Problems.' *Journal of Theological Studies* 33:62–97.

Banner, Michael C. 1990. *The Justification of Science and the Rationality of Religious Belief.* Oxford: Clarendon Press.

Baras, Zvi. 1987. 'The *Testimonium Flavianum* and the Martyrdom of James.' In *Josephus, Judaism and Christianity*, ed. L. H. Feldman and G. Hata, 338–48. Leiden: Brill.

Barbour, Ian G. 1966. *Issues in Science and Religion*. London: SCM.

———. 1974. *Myths, Models and Paradigms: A Comparative Study in Science and Religion*. New York: Harper & Row.

Barclay, John M. G. 1987. 'Mirror-Reading a Polemical Letter: Galatians as a Test Case.' *Journal for the Study of the New Testament* 31:73–93.

Barker, Margaret. 1991. *The Gate of Heaven: The History and Symbolism of the Temple in Jerusalem*. London: SPCK.

Barnett, P. W. 1975. ' "Under Tiberius all was Quiet".' *New Testament Studies* 21:564–71.

Barr, James. 1987. 'Words for Love in Biblical Greek.' In *The Glory of Christ in the New Testament: Studies in Christology in Memory of George Bradford Caird*, ed. L. D. Hurst and N. T. Wright, 3–18. Oxford: Clarendon Press.

Barraclough, Geoffrey. 1967 [1964]. *An Introduction to Contemporary History*. London: Penguin Books.

Barrett, C. K. 1970 [1961]. *Luke the Historian in Recent Study*. 2nd edn. Philadelphia: Fortress; London: SPCK.

———. 1973. *A Commentary on the Second Epistle to the Corinthians*. Black's New Testament Commentaries. London: A & C Black.

———., introd. & ed. 1987 [1956]. *The New Testament Background: Selected Documents*. Rev. edn. London: SPCK; New York: Harper & Row.

Barton, J. 1984. *Reading the Old Testament: Method in Biblical Study*. London: Darton, Longman & Todd.

———. 1986. *Oracles of God*. London: Darton, Longman & Todd.

Bartsch, Hans-Werner. 1960. 'Das Thomas-Evangelium und die synoptische Evangelien: zu G. Quispels Bemerkungen zum Thomas-Evangelium.' *New Testament Studies* 6:249–61.

Bauckham, Richard J. 1980. 'The Delay of the Parousia.' *Tyndale Bulletin* 31:3–36.

———. 1981. 'The Worship of Jesus in Apocalyptic Christianity.' *New Testament Studies* 27:322–41.

———. 1983. *Jude, 2 Peter*. Word Biblical Commentary, vol. 50. Waco, Tex.: Word Books.

———. 1990. *Jude and the Relatives of Jesus in the Early Church*. Edinburgh: T & T Clark.

Baumgarten, A. I. 1983. 'The Name of the Pharisees.' *Journal of Biblical Literature* 102:411–28.

———. 1991. 'Rivkin and Neusner on the Pharisees.' In *Law in Religious Communities in the Roman Period: The Debate Over Torah and Nomos in Post-Biblical Judaism and Early Christianity*, ed. Peter Richardson and Stephen Westerholm, 109–26. Studies in Christianity and Judaism, no. 4. Waterloo, Ontario: Wilfrid Laurier U. P.

Baur, Ferdinand Christian. 1878–9 [1860]. *History of the Church in the First Three Centuries*. Trans. Allan Menzies. 3rd edn. London: Williams & Norgate.

Beardslee, William A. 1969. *Literary Criticism of the New Testament*. Philadelphia: Fortress.

———. 1989. 'Recent Literary Criticism.' In *The New Testament and Its Modern Interpreters*, ed. Eldon J. Epp and George A. MacRae, 175–98. Atlanta, Ga.: Scholars Press; Philadelphia: Fortress.

Beasley-Murray, G. R. 1986. *Jesus and the Kingdom of God*. Grand Rapids, Mich.: Eerdmans.

Beckwith, Roger T. 1980. 'The Significance of the Calendar for Interpreting Essene Chronology and Eschatology.' *Révue de Qumran* 38:167–202.

———. 1981. 'Daniel 9 and the Date of Messiah's Coming in Essene, Hellenistic, Pharisaic, Zealot and Early Christian Computation.' *Révue de Qumran* 40:521–42.

Bellinzoni, Arthur J. 1985. *The Two-Source Hypothesis: A Critical Appraisal*. Macon, Ga.: Mercer U. P.

Berger, Klaus. 1984. *Formgeschichte Des Neuen Testaments*. Heidelberg: Quelle & Mayer.

———. 1988. 'Jesus als Pharisäer und Frühe Christen als Pharisäer.' *Novum Testamentum* 30:231–62.

Berger, Peter L. 1969. *The Sacred Canopy*. New York: Doubleday.

Berger, Peter L., and Thomas Luckmann. 1966. *The Social Construction of Reality: A Treatise in the Sociology of Knowledge*. Garden City, N.Y.: Doubleday.

Bergonzi, Bernard. 1990. *Exploding English: Criticism, Theory, Culture*. Oxford: Clarendon Press.

Berkhof, Louis. 1941 [1939]. *Systematic Theology*. London: Banner of Truth.

Bernstein, R. J. 1983. *Beyond Objectivism and Relativism: Science, Hermeneutics and Praxis*. Oxford: Blackwell.

Best, Ernest. 1983. *Mark: The Gospel as Story*. Studies of the New Testament and its World. Edinburgh: T & T Clark.

———. 1986. *Disciples and Discipleship: Studies in the Gospel According to Mark*. Edinburgh: T & T Clark.

Betz, Hans-Dieter. 1979. *Galatians: A Commentary on Paul's Letter to the Churches in Galatia*. Hermeneia. Philadelphia: Fortress.

Beutler, Johannes. 1985. 'Literarische Gattungen Im Johannesevangelium: Ein Forschungsbericht 1919–1980.' *ANRW* 2.25.3:2506–68.

Bilde, P. 1979. 'The Causes of the Jewish War According to Josephus.' *Journal for the Study of Judaism* 10(2):179–202.

———. 1988. *Flavius Josephus, between Jerusalem and Rome: His Life, his Works, and their importance*. Journal for the Study of the Pseudepigrapha Supplement Series, no. 2. Sheffield: JSOT Press.

Blenkinsopp, Joseph. 1981. 'Interpretation and the Tendency to Sectarianism: An aspect of Second-Temple History.' In *Aspects of Judaism in the Greco-Roman Period*, ed. E. P. Sanders, A. I. Baumgarten and Alan Mendelson. *Jewish and Christian Self-Definition*, vol. 2, 1–26. Philadelphia: Fortress.

Boismard, M.-E., William R. Farmer, F. Neirynck, and David L. Dungan, ed. 1990. *The Interrelations of the Gospels: A Symposium Led by M.-E. Boismard, W. R. Farmer, F. Neirynck, Jerusalem 1984*. Biblotheca Ephemeridium Theologicarum Lovaniensium, vol. 95. Leuven: Leuven U. P./ Peeters.

Bokser, B. M. 1982/3. 'The Wall Separating God and Israel.' *Jewish Quarterly Review* 73:349–74.

Borg, Marcus J. 1971. 'The Currency of the Term "Zealot" ' *Journal of Theological Studies* 22:504–12.

———. 1984. *Conflict, Holiness and Politics in the Teachings of Jesus*. Studies in the Bible and Early Christianity, vol. 5. New York & Toronto: Edwin Mellen Press.

———. 1987. 'An Orthodoxy Reconsidered: The "End-of-the-World Jesus" ' In *The Glory of Christ in the New Testament: Studies in Christology in Memory of George Bradford Caird*, ed. L. D. Hurst and N. T. Wright, 207–17. Oxford: OUP.

Borgen, Peder. 1984. 'Philo of Alexandria.' In *Compendia* 2.2.233–82.

Bornkamm, Günther. 1969. *Early Christian Experience*. Trans. P. L. Hammer. London: SCM.

Boucher, Madeleine. 1977. *The Mysterious Parable: A Literary Study*. Catholic Biblical Quarterly Monograph Series, no. 6. Washington: Catholic Biblical Association of America.

Brearley, Margaret. 1988. 'Hitler and Wagner: The Leader, the Master and the Jews.' *Patterns of Prejudice* 22:3–22.

Brooke, George J. 1985. *Exegesis at Qumran: 4QFlorilegium in Its Jewish Context*. Journal for the Study of the New Testament Supplement Series, vol. 29. Sheffield: JSOT Press.

Broshi, Magen. 1982. 'The Credibility of Josephus.' *Journal of Jewish Studies* 33:379–84.

———. 1987. 'The Role of the Temple in the Herodian Economy.' *Journal of Jewish Studies* 38:31–7.

Brown, Raymond E. 1983. 'Not Jewish Christianity and Gentile Christianity but Types of Jewish/Gentile Christianity.' *Catholic Biblical Quarterly* 45:74–9.

Brown, Raymond E., and John P. Meier. 1983. *Antioch and Rome: New Testament Cradles of Catholic Christianity*. New York: Paulist.

Bruce, F. F. 1972. *New Testament History*. Garden City, N.Y.: Doubleday, Anchor.

———. 1969. *New Testament History*. London: Thomas Nelson.

———. 1977. *Paul: Apostle of the Free Spirit* [in USA: *Paul: Apostle of the Heart Set Free*]. Exeter: Paternoster; Grand Rapids, Mich.: Eerdmans.

———. 1979. *Men and Movements in the Primitive Church* [in USA: *Peter, Stephen, James and John: Studies in Early Non-Pauline Christianity*]. Exeter: Paternoster; Grand Rapids, Mich.: Eerdmans.

Brueggemann, Walter. 1977. *The Land: Place as Gift, Promise and Challenge in Biblical Faith*. Overtures to Biblical Theology. Philadelphia: Fortress.

Buchanan, George W. 1984. *Jesus: The King and His Kingdom*. Macon, Ga.: Mercer.

Buckert, W. 1985. *Greek Religion*. Oxford: Blackwell.

Bultmann, Rudolf. 1910. *Der Stil der paulinischen Predigt und die kynisch-stoische Diatribe*. Göttingen: Vandenhoek und Ruprecht.

———. 1951–5. *Theology of the New Testament*. Trans. Kendrick Grobel. New York: Scribner's; London: SCM.

——. 1956. *Primitive Christianity in Its Contemporary Setting*. Trans. R. H. Fuller. New York: Meridian; London: Thames & Hudson.

——. 1958 [1934]. *Jesus and the Word*. Trans. L. P. Smith and E. H. Lantero. New York: Scribner's.

——. 1960. *Existence and Faith*. Ed. Schubert M. Ogden. Living Age Books. New York: World Publishing, Meridian.

——. 1967. *Exegetica*. Tübingen: Mohr.

——. 1968 [1921]. *The History of the Synoptic Tradition*. Trans. John Marsh. Oxford: Blackwell.

——. 1985 [1976]. *The Second Letter to the Corinthians*. Trans. Roy A. Harrisville. Minneapolis: Augsburg.

——. 1986 [1923]. 'The History of Religions Background of the Prologue to the Gospel of John.' Trans. John Ashton. In *The Interpretation of John*, ed. John Ashton. Issues in Religion and Theology, no. 9. Philadelphia: Fortress; London: SPCK.

Bultmann, Rudolf, with Ernst Lohmeyer, Julius Schniewind, Helmut Thielicke, and Austin Farrer. 1961. *Kerygma and Myth: A Theological Defense*. Rev. edn. Ed. Hans Werner Bartsch. Trans. Reginald H. Fuller. New York: Harper & Row, Harper Torchbooks/Cloister Library.

Burridge, Richard A. 1992. *What Are the Gospels? A Comparison with Graeco-Roman Biography*. Society for New Testament Studies Monograph Series, vol. 70. Cambridge: CUP.

Bury, J. B. 1951 [1909]. *A History of Greece to the Death of Alexander the Great*. 3rd edn. London: Macmillan.

Butterfield, H. 1969. *Man on His Past*. Cambridge: CUP.

Caird, George B. 1955. *The Apostolic Age*. London: Duckworth.

——. 1964. 'The Descent of Christ in Ephesians 4:7–11.' In *Studia Evangelica II = Texte und Untersuchungen* 87:535–45.

——. 1965. *Jesus and the Jewish Nation*. London: Athlone Press.

——. 1968. 'The Development of the Doctrine of Christ in the New Testament.' In *Christ for Us Today*, ed. N. Pittenger, 66–80. London: SCM.

——. 1980. *The Language and Imagery of the Bible*. London: Duckworth.

Calloway, Phillip R. 1988. *The History of the Qumran Community: An Investigation*. Journal for the Study of the Pseudepigrapha Supplement Series, vol. 3. Sheffield: JSOT Press.

Cameron, Ronald D. 1982. *The Other Gospels: Non-Canonical Gospel Texts*. Philadelphia: Westminster.

Campenhausen, Hans von. 1963 [1955]. *The Fathers of the Greek Church*. Trans. L. A. Garrard. London: A & C Black.

Capper, Brian J. 1985. *PANTA KOINA: A Study of Earliest Christian Community of Goods in Its Hellenistic and Jewish Context*. Unpublished Ph. D. Dissertation. Cambridge University.

Carnegy, Patrick. 1973. *Faust as Musician. A Study of Thomas Mann's 'Doctor Faustus'*. London: Chatto & Windus.

Carr, E. H. 1987 [1961]. *What is History?* Ed. R. W. Davies. 2nd edn. London: Penguin Books.

Carson, Donald A. 1987. 'The Purpose of the Fourth Gospel: John 20:31 Reconsidered.' *Journal of Biblical Literature* 106:639–51.

Cary, M. 1954 [1935]. *A History of Rome Down to the Reign of Constantine*. 2nd edn. London: Macmillan.

Casey, P. Maurice. 1991. 'Method in Our Madness, and Madness in Their Methods. Some Approaches to the Son of Man Problem in Recent Scholarship.' *Journal for the Study of the New Testament* 42:17–43.

Catchpole, David R. 1992. 'The Beginning of Q: A Proposal.' *New Testament Studies* 38:205–21.

Chabrol, Claude. 1976. 'An Analysis of the "Text" of the Passion.' In *The New Testament and Structuralism*, ed. Alfred M. Johnson, Jr., 145–86. Pittsburgh Theological Monograph Series, no. 11. Pittsburgh: The Pickwick Press.

Chadwick, Henry. 1966. *Early Christian Thought and the Classical Tradition: Studies in Justin, Clement, and Origen*. Oxford: OUP.

Chapman, John. 1937. *Matthew, Mark and Luke: A Study in the Order and Interrelation of the Synoptic Gospels*. London: Longmans, Green & Co.

Charlesworth, James H. 1969. 'A Critical Comparison of the Dualism in 1QS III, 13—IV,26 and the "Dualism" Contained in the Fourth Gospel.' *New Testament Studies* 15:389–418.

———. 1979. 'The Concept of the Messiah, in the Pseudepigrapha.' *ANRW* 19.2.188–218.
———. 1980. 'The Origin and Subsequent History of the Authors of the Dead Sea Scrolls: Four Transitional Phases Among the Qumran Essenes.' *Révue de Qumran* 10:213–33.
———, ed. 1983. *The Old Testament Pseudepigrapha*. Vol. 1. *Apocalyptic Literature and Testaments*. Garden City, N.Y.: Doubleday.
———, ed. 1985. *The Old Testament Pseudepigrapha*. Vol. 2. *Expansions of the 'Old Testament" and Legends, Wisdom and Philosophical Literature, Prayers, Psalms and Odes, Fragments of Lost Judaeo-Hellenistic Works*. Garden City, N.Y.: Doubleday.
Chester, Andrew. 1991. 'Jewish Messianic Expectations and Mediatorial Figures and Pauline Christology.' *Paulus und das antike Judentum*, ed. Martin Hengel and Ulrich Heckel, 17–89. Wissenschaftliche Untersuchungen zum Neuen Testament, 58. Tübingen: Mohr.
Chilton, Bruce D. 1980. 'Isaac and the Second Night: A Reconsideration.' *Biblica* 61:78–88.
———. 1983. *The Glory of Israel: The Theology and Provenience of the Isaiah Targum*. Journal for the Study of the Old Testament Supplement Series, vol. 23. Sheffield: JSOT Press.
———. 1984. *A Galilean Rabbi and His Bible*. Wilmington: Michael Glazier.
Cohen, Shaye J. D. 1979. *Josephus in Galilee and Rome: His Vita and Development as a Historian*. Columbia Studies in the Classical Tradition, vol. 8. Leiden: Brill.
———. 1980. Review of Rivkin, *A Hidden Revolution*. *Journal of Biblical Literature* 99:627–9.
———. 1984. 'The Significance of Yavneh: Pharisees, Rabbis, and the End of Jewish Sectarianism.' *Hebrew Union College Annual* 55:27–53.
———. 1987. *From the Maccabees to the Mishnah*. In *Library of Early Christianity*, ed. Wayne A. Meeks. Philadelphia: Westminster Press.
Collingwood, R. G. 1956 [1946]. *The Idea of History*. New York: OUP, Galaxy.
———. 1968. *Faith and Reason: Essays in the Philosophy of Religion*. Ed. Lionel Rubinoff. Chicago: Quadrangle.
Collins, John J., ed. 1979. *Apocalypse: The Morphology of a Genre*. Semeia, vol. 14. Missoula, Mont.: Scholars Press.
———. 1984. 'Testaments.' In *Compendia* 2.2.325–55.
———. 1987. *The Apocalyptic Imagination*. New York: Crossroad.
———. 1990. 'Was the Dead Sea Sect an Apocalyptic Movement?' In *Archaeology and History in the Dead Sea Scrolls: The New York University Conference in Memory of Yigael Yadin*, ed. Lawrence H. Schiffman, 25–51. Journal for the Study of the Pseudepigrapha Supplement Series, vol. 8. Sheffield: JSOT Press.
Conzelmann, Hans. 1960 [1953]. *The Theology of Luke*. Trans. Geoffrey Buswell. London: Faber & Faber; New York: Harper & Row.
———. 1969. *An Outline of the Theology of the New Testament*. Trans. John Bowden. New York: Harper & Row.
———. 1973. *History of Primitive Christianity*. Trans. John E. Steely. Nashville: Abingdon.
Cotterell, Peter, and Max Turner. 1989. *Linguistics and Biblical Interpretation*. London: SPCK.
Craig, William Lane. 1986. 'The Problem of Miracles: A Historical and Philosophical Perspective.' In *Gospel Perspectives*, ed. David Wenham and Craig L. Blomberg, vol. 6. *The Miracles of Jesus*, 9–48. Sheffield: JSOT Press.
Cranfield, Charles E. B. 1982. 'Thoughts on New Testament Eschatology.' *Scottish Journal of Theology* 35:497–512.
Crenshaw, James L. 1985. 'The Wisdom Literature.' In *The Hebrew Bible and Its Modern Interpreters*, ed. Douglas A. Knight and Gene M. Tucker, 369–407. Chico, Calif.: Scholars Press; Philadelphia: Fortress.
Crites, Stephen. 1989 [1971]. 'The Narrative Quality of Experience.' In *Why Narrative? Readings in Narrative Theology*, ed. Stanley Hauerwas and L. Gregory Jones, 65–88. Grand Rapids, Mich.: Eerdmans.
Cross, Frank M. 1958. *The Ancient Library of Qumran and Modern Biblical Studies*. Garden City, N.Y.: Doubleday.
Crossan, J. Dominic. 1973. *In Parables: The Challenge of the Historical Jesus*. New York: Harper & Row.
———. 1976. *Raid on the Articulate: Comic Eschatology in Jesus and Borges*. New York: Harper & Row.
———. 1980. *Cliffs of Fall: Paradox and Polyvalence in the Parables of Jesus*. New York: Seabury Press.

——. 1983. *In Fragments: The Aphorisms of Jesus.* San Francisco: Harper & Row.

——. 1988a. *The Cross That Spoke: The Origins of the Passion Narrative.* San Francisco: Harper & Row.

——. 1988b [1975]. *The Dark Interval: Towards a Theology of Story.* 2nd edn. Sonoma, Calif.: Polebridge Press.

——. 1991. *The Historical Jesus: The Life of a Mediterranean Jewish Peasant.* San Francisco: Harper; Edinburgh: T & T Clark.

Dahl, Nils A. 1986. 'The Johannine Church and History.' In *The Interpretation of John,* ed. John Ashton, 122–40. Issues in Religion and Theology, no. 9. Philadelphia: Fortress; London: SPCK.

Daly, R. J. 1977. 'The Soteriological Significance of the Sacrifice of Isaac.' *Catholic Biblical Quarterly* 39:45–75.

Davids, Peter H. 1980. 'The Gospels and Jewish Tradition: Twenty Years After Gerhardsson.' In *Gospel Perspectives: Studies of History and Tradition in the Four Gospels,* ed. R. T. France and David Wenham, vol. 1, 75–99. Sheffield: JSOT Press.

Davies, Philip R. 1977. 'Hasidim in the Maccabean Period.' *Journal of Jewish Studies* 28:127–40.

——. 1982. *The Damascus Covenant: An Interpretation of the 'Damascus Document'.* Journal for the Study of the Old Testament Supplement Series, vol. 25. Sheffield: JSOT Press.

——. 1985. 'Eschatology at Qumran.' *Journal of Biblical Literature* 104:39–55.

——. 1987. *Behind the Essenes: History and Ideology in the Dead Sea Scrolls.* Brown Judaic Studies, vol. 94. Atlanta, Ga.: Scholars Press.

——. 1990. 'The Birthplace of the Essenes: Where is "Damascus"?' *Révue de Qumran* 14:503–19.

Davies, Philip R., and Bruce D. Chilton. 1978. 'The Aqedah: A Revised Tradition History.' *Catholic Biblical Quarterly* 40:514–46.

Davies, W. D. 1964. *The Setting of the Sermon on the Mount.* Cambridge: CUP.

——. 1974. *The Gospel and the Land: Early Christianity and Jewish Territorial Doctrine.* Berkeley: U. of California Press.

——. 1980 [1948]. *Paul and Rabbinic Judaism.* 4th edn. Philadelphia: Fortress.

——. 1987. 'Canon and Christology.' In *The Glory of Christ in the New Testament: Studies in Christology in Memory of George Bradford Caird,* ed. L. D. Hurst and N. T. Wright, 19–36. Oxford: Clarendon Press.

Davies, W. D., and Dale C. Allison. 1988, 1991. *A Critical and Exegetical Commentary on the Gospel According to Saint Matthew.* 2 vols. to date. International Critical Commentary (new series). Edinburgh: T & T Clark.

de la Mare, Walter. 1938. *Stories, Essays and Poems.* London: J. M. Dent.

Derrett, J. D. M. 1975. 'Cursing Jesus (1 Cor. xii.3): The Jews as Religious "Persecutors"' *New Testament Studies* 21:544–54.

Dibelius, Martin. 1934 [1919]. *From Tradition to Gospel.* Trans. Bertram Lee Woolf and Martin Dibelius. New York: Scribner's.

Dihle, A. 1983. 'Die Evangelien und die griechische Biographie.' In *Das Evangelium und die Evangelien,* ed. P. Stuhlmacher, 383–411. Wissenschaftliche Untersuchungen zum Neuen Testament, vol. 28. Tübingen: Mohr.

Dillistone, F. W. 1977. *C. H. Dodd: Interpreter of the New Testament..* London: Hodder & Stoughton.

Dimant, D. 1984. 'Qumran Sectarian Literature.' In *Compendia* 2.2.483–550.

Dix, Gregory. 1953. *Jew and Greek: A Study in the Primitive Church.* London: A & C Black.

Dodd, C. H. 1978 [1935]. *The Parables of the Kingdom.* Rev. edn. London: Nisbet; New York: Scribner's.

Donaldson, T. L. 1990. 'Rural Banditry, City Mobs and the Zealots.' *Journal for the Study of Judaism* 21:19–40.

Donfried, Karl P., ed. 1991 [1977]. *The Romans Debate.* 2nd edn. Peabody, Mass.: Hendrikson.

Doran, R. 1990. *Theology and the Dialectics of History.* Toronto: U. of Toronto Press.

Downing, F. Gerald. 1980a. 'Redaction Criticism: Josephus' *Antiquities* and the Synoptic Gospels (I).' *Journal for the Study of the New Testament* 8:46–65.

——. 1980b. 'Redaction Criticism: Josephus' *Antiquities* and the Synoptic Gospels (II).' *Journal for the Study of the New Testament* 9:29–48.

——. 1982. 'Common Ground with Paganism in Luke and Josephus.' *New Testament Studies* 28:546–59.

———. 1988a. *Christ and the Cynics: Jesus and Other Radical Preachers in First-Century Tradition.* JSOT Manuals, no. 4. Sheffield: Sheffield Academic Press.

———. 1988b. 'Quite Like Q. A Genre for "Q": The "Lives" of Cynic Philosophers.' *Biblica* 69:196–225.

———. 1991. Review of Smith 1990. *Journal of Theological Studies* 42:703–5.

———. 1992. 'A Paradigm Perplex: Luke, Matthew and Mark.' *New Testament Studies* 38:15–36.

Doyle, B. R. 1988. 'Matthew's Intention as Discerned by His Structure.' *Révue Biblique* 95:386–403.

Droge, Arthur J., and James D. Tabor. 1992. *A Noble Death: Suicide and Martyrdom Among Christians and Jews in Antiquity.* San Francisco: HarperSanFrancisco.

Drury, John. 1985. *The Parables in the Gospels: History and Allegory.* London: SPCK.

Dunn, James D. G. 1975. *Jesus and the Spirit: A Study of the Religious and Charismatic Experience of Jesus and the First Christians as Reflected in the New Testament.* London: SCM; Philadelphia: Westminster.

———. 1977. *Unity and Diversity in the New Testament: An Inquiry Into the Character of Earliest Christianity.* London: SCM; Philadelphia: Westminster.

———. 1980. *Christology in the Making: A New Testament Inquiry Into the Origins of the Doctrine of the Incarnation.* London: SCM; Philadelphia: Westminster.

———. 1985. 'Works of the Law and the Curse of the Law (Galatians 3.10–14).' *New Testament Studies* 31:523–42.

———. 1988. 'Pharisees, Sinners and Jesus.' In *The Social World of Formative Christianity and Judaism: Essays in Tribute to Howard Clark Kee,* ed. Jacob Neusner, Ernest S. Frerichs, Peder Borgen, and Richard Horsley, 264–89. Philadelphia: Fortress.

———. 1990. *Jesus, Paul and the Law.* London: SPCK.

———. 1991. *The Partings of the Ways Between Christianity and Judaism and Their Significance for the Character of Christianity.* London: SCM; Philadelphia: Trinity Press International.

Dunn, James D. G., and James P. Mackey. 1987. *New Testament Theology in Dialogue.* Biblical Foundations in Theology. London: SPCK.

Eagleton, Terry. 1991. *Ideology: An Introduction.* London & New York: Verso.

Edwards, R. A. 1985. *Matthew's Story of Jesus.* Philadelphia: Fortress.

Eichrodt, Walther. 1961, 1967. *Theology of the Old Testament.* 2 vols. Trans. J. A. Baker. The Old Testament Library. Philadelphia: Westminster; London: SCM.

Elton, G. R. 1984 [1967]. *The Practice of History.* London: Flamingo.

Epp, Eldon J., and George W. MacRae, ed. 1989. *The New Testament and Its Modern Interpreters.* In *The Bible and Its Modern Interpreters,* ed. Douglas A. Knight. Atlanta, Ga.: Scholars Press; Philadelphia: Fortress.

Epstein, Isidore. 1959. *Judaism: A Historical Presentation.* London: Penguin Books.

Evans, Christopher F. 1990. *Saint Luke.* SCM/TPI New Testament Commentaries. London: SCM; Philadelphia: Trinity Press International.

Evans, Craig A. 1989a. 'Jesus' Action in the Temple and Evidence of Corruption in the First-Century Temple.' In *Society of Biblical Literature 1989 Seminar Papers,* ed. David J. Lull, 522–39. Atlanta, Ga.: Scholars Press.

———. 1989b. 'Jesus' Action in the Temple: Cleansing or Portent of Destruction?' *Catholic Biblical Quarterly* 51:237–70.

Falck, Colin. 1989. *Myth, Truth and Literature: Towards a True Post-Modernism.* Cambridge: CUP.

Fallon, Francis T., and Ron Cameron. 1988. 'The Gospel of Thomas: A *Forschungsbericht* and Analysis.' In *ANRW* 2.25.6:4195–251.

Farmer, William R. 1956. *Maccabees, Zealots, and Josephus: An Inquiry Into Jewish Nationalism in the Greco-Roman Period.* New York: Columbia U. P.

———. 1964. *The Synoptic Problem: A Critical Analysis.* London & New York: Macmillan.

Farrer, Austin M. 1955. 'On Dispensing with Q.' In *Studies in the Gospels: Essays in Memory of R. H. Lightfoot,* ed. Dennis E. Nineham, 55–86. Oxford: Blackwell.

———. 1964. *The Revelation of St John the Divine.* Oxford: OUP.

Fee, Gordon D. 1987. *The First Epistle to the Corinthians.* The New International Commentary on the New Testament. Grand Rapids, Mich.: Eerdmans.

Feldman, Louis H. 1984. *Josephus and Modern Scholarship.* Berlin & New York: de Gruyter.

Ferguson, Everett. 1987. *Backgrounds of Early Christianity.* Grand Rapids: Eerdmans.

Filson, Floyd V. 1965. *A New Testament History*. London: SCM.

Finkelstein, Louis. 1962 [1938]. *The Pharisees: The Sociological Background of Their Faith*. 3rd edn. Philadelphia: Jewish Publication Society of America.

Fishbane, Michael. 1985. *Biblical Interpretation in Ancient Israel*. Oxford: OUP.

Fitzmyer, Joseph A. 1971. *Essays on the Semitic Background of the New Testament*. London: Geoffrey Chapman.

Flannery, Austin, ed. 1975. *Vatican Council II: The Conciliar and Post Conciliar Documents*. Dublin: Dominican Publications.

Florovsky, G. 1974. *Christianity and Culture*. Collected Works, vol. 2. Belmont, Mass.: Nordland.

Flusser, David. 1976. 'Paganism in Palestine.' In *Compendia* 1.2.1065–1100.

Ford, David F. 1989. *The Modern Theologians: An Introduction to Christian Theology in the Twentieth Century*. 2 vols. Oxford: Basil Blackwell.

Fornara, C. W. 1983. *The Nature of History in Ancient Greece and Rome*. San Francisco: U. of California Press.

Fowl, Stephen E. 1990. *The Story of Christ in the Ethics of Paul: An Analysis of the Function of the Hymnic Material in the Pauline Corpus*. Journal for the Study of the New Testament Supplement Series, vol. 36. Sheffield: Sheffield Academic Press.

Fowler, Robert M. 1991. *Let the Reader Understand: Reader-Response Criticism and the Gospel of Mark*. Minneapolis: Fortress.

France, R. T. 1982. 'The Worship of Jesus: A Neglected Factor in Christological Debate?' In *Christ the Lord: Studies in Christology Presented to Donald Guthrie*, ed. H. H. Rowdon, 17–36. Leicester: IVP.

Freeman, Gordon M. 1986. *The Heavenly Kingdom: Aspects of Political Thought in Talmud and Midrash*. Lanham and Jerusalem, Philadelphia, Montreal: University Press of America; Jerusalem Centre for Public Affairs.

Frei, Hans W. 1974. *The Eclipse of Biblical Narrative: A Study in Eighteenth and Nineteenth Century Hermeneutics*. New Haven: Yale U. P.

Freyne, S. 1980. *Galilee from Alexander the Great to Hadrian. a Study of Second Temple Judaism*. Wilmington, Del.: Glazier/Notre Dame U. P.

——. 1988. *Galilee, Jesus and the Gospels: Literary Approaches and Historical Investigations*. Philadelphia: Fortress.

Frost, Stanley. 1987. 'Who Were the Heroes? An Exercise in Bi-Testamentary Exegesis, with Christological Implications.' In *The Glory of Christ in the New Testament: Studies in Christology in Memory of George Bradford Caird*, ed. L. D. Hurst and N. T. Wright, 165–72. Oxford: Clarendon Press.

Frye, Northrop. 1983. *The Great Code: The Bible and Literature*. San Diego: Harcourt Brace Jovanovich.

Fuller, Reginald H. 1989. 'New Testament Theology.' In *The New Testament and Its Modern Interpreters*, ed. Eldon J. Epp and George W. MacRae, 565–84. Atlanta, Ga.: Scholars Press; Philadelphia: Fortress.

Fuller, Russell. 1991. 'Text-Critical Problems in Malachi 2:10–16.' *Journal of Biblical Literature* 110:47–57.

Funk, Robert. 1988. *The Poetics of Biblical Narrative*. Sonoma, Calif.: Polebridge Press.

Furnish, Victor P. 1984. *II Corinthians*. Anchor Bible. New York: Doubleday.

Gafni, Isaiah M. 1984. 'The Historical Background [i.e. to Jewish Writings of the Second Temple Period].' In *Compendia* 2.2.1–31.

——. 1987. 'The Historical Background [i.e. to the Literature of the Sages].' In *Compendia* 2.3.1–34.

Gager, John G. 1983. *The Origins of Anti-Semitism*. Oxford: OUP.

Galland, Corina. 1976. 'An Introduction to the Method of A. J. Griemas.' In *The New Testament and Structuralism*, ed. & trans. Alfred M. Johnson Jr., 1–26. Pittsburgh Theological Monograph Series, vol. 11. Pittsburgh: The Pickwick Press.

Garcia-Martinez, F., and A. S. van der Woude. 1990. 'A "Groningen" Hypothesis of Qumran Origins and Early History.' *Révue de Qumran* 14:521–41.

Garnsey, Peter, and Richard Saller. 1982. *Greece and Rome: New Surveys in the Classics No. 15. The Early Principate: Augustus to Trajan*. Oxford: Clarendon Press.

Gärtner, Bertil. 1965. *The Temple and the Community in Qumran and the New Testament*. Society for New Testament Studies Monograph Series, vol. 1. Cambridge: CUP.

Gaston, Lloyd. 1987. *Paul and the Torah*. Vancouver: U. of British Columbia Press.

Geertz, Clifford. 1973. *The Interpretation of Cultures*. New York: Basic Books.

Georgi, Dieter. 1986 [1964]. *The Opponents of Paul in Second Corinthians*. Trans. H. Attridge and others. Studies of the New Testament and its World. Edinburgh: T & T Clark; Philadelphia: Fortress.

Gerhardsson, Birger. 1961. *Memory and Manuscript: Oral Tradition and Written Transmission in Rabbinic Judaism and Early Christianity*. Uppsala: Gleerup.

———. 1964. *Tradition and Transmission in Early Christianity*. Uppsala: Gleerup.

———. 1979. *The Origins of the Gospel Tradition*. London: SCM.

———. 1986. *The Gospel Tradition*. Lund: Gleerup.

Gerhart, Mary, and Allan Russell. 1984. *Metaphoric Process: The Creation of Scientific and Religious Understanding*. Fort Worth: Texas Christian U. P.

Gilkey, Langdon. 1976. *Reaping the Whirlwind: A Christian Interpretation of History*. New York: Seabury Press, Crossroads.

———. 1981. *Society and the Sacred: Toward a Theology of Culture in Decline*. New York: Seabury Press.

Ginzberg, L. 1928. *Students, Scholars, and Saints*. Philadelphia: Jewish Publication Society of America.

Glasson, T. F. 1977. 'Schweitzer's Influence— Blessing or Bane?' *Journal of Theological Studies* 28:289–302.

Golb, N. 1985. 'Who Hid the Dead Sea Scrolls?' *Biblical Archaeologist* 48:68–82.

———. 1989. 'The Dead Sea Scrolls.' *The American Scholar* 58:177–207.

Goldberg, Michael. 1982. *Theology and Narrative: A Critical Introduction*. Nashville: Abingdon.

Goldingay, John E. 1989. *Daniel*. Word Biblical Commentary, vol. 30. Dallas, Tex.: Word Books.

Goldstein, Jonathan A. 1981. 'Jewish Acceptance and Rejection of Hellenism.' In *Jewish and Christian Self-Definition*, vol. 2. *Aspects of Judaism in the Greco-Roman Period*, ed. E. P. Sanders, A. I. Baumgarten, and A. Mendelson, 64–87. Philadelphia: Fortress.

———. 1987. 'Biblical Promises and 1 and 2 Maccabees.' In *Judaisms and Their Messiahs at the Turn of the Christian Era*, ed. Jacob Neusner, William S. Green, and Ernest S. Frerichs, 69–96. Cambridge: CUP.

———. 1989. 'The Hasmonean Revolt and the Hasmonean Dynasty.' In *Cambridge History of Judaism*, vol. 2, 292–351. Cambridge: CUP.

Goodblatt, D. 1989. 'The Place of the Pharisees in First Century Judaism: The State of the Debate.' *Journal for the Study of Judaism* 20:12–29.

Goodman, Martin. 1987. *The Ruling Class of Judaea: The Origins of the Jewish Revolt Against Rome A.D. 66–70*. Cambridge: CUP.

Goppelt, Leonhard. 1981. *Theology of the New Testament*. Vol. 1. *The Ministry of Jesus in Its Theological Significance*.Trans. John E. Alsup. Ed. Jürgen Roloff. Grand Rapids, Mich.: Eerdmans.

———. 1982. *Theology of the New Testament*. Vol. 2. *The Variety and Unity of the Apostolic Witness to Christ*. Trans. John E. Alsup. Ed. Jürgen Roloff. Grand Rapids, Mich.: Eerdmans.

Goulder, Michael. 1974. *Midrash and Lection in Matthew*. London: SPCK.

Gowan, Donald E. 1977. 'The Exile in Jewish Apocalyptic.' In *Scripture in History and Theology: Essays in Honor of J. Coert Rylaarsdam*, ed. Arthur E. Merrill and Thomas W. Overholt, 205–23. Pittsburgh Theological Monograph Series, vol. 17. Pittsburgh: Pickwick.

Greene, John. 1981. *Science, Ideology and World View: Essays in the History of Evolutionary Ideas*. Berkeley: U. of California Press.

Griemas, A. J. 1966. *Sémantique structurale*. Paris: Seuil.

———. 1970. *Du Sens*. Paris: Seuil.

Gruenwald, Ithamar. 1980. *Apocalyptic and Merkavah Mysticism*. Arbeiten zur Geschichte des Antiken Judentums und des Urchristentums, vol. 14. Leiden: Brill.

Gunton, Colin E. 1985. *Enlightenment and Alienation: An Essay Towards a Trinitarian Theology*. Contemporary Christian Studies. Basingstoke: Marshall, Morgan & Scott.

———. 1988. *The Actuality of Atonement: A Study of Metaphor, Rationality and the Christian Tradition*. Edinburgh: T & T Clark.

Gutmann, Joseph, ed. 1981. *Ancient Synagogues: The State of Research*. Brown Judaic Studies, no. 22. Chico, Calif.: Scholars Press.

Güttgemanns, Erhardt. 1979 [1971]. *Candid Questions Concerning Gospel Form Criticism. A Methodological Sketch of the Fundamental Problematics of Form and Redaction Criticism.* Pittsburgh: Pickwick.

Hall, Stuart G. 1991. *Doctrine and Practice in the Early Church.* London: SPCK.

Hare, Douglas R. A. 1990. *The Son of Man Tradition.* Minneapolis: Fortress.

Hare, Richard M. 1963. *Freedom and Reason.* Oxford: Clarendon Press.

Harnack, Adolf. 1924 [1921]. *Marcion: Das Evangelium von fremden Gott.* 2nd edn. Texte und Untersuchungen, no. 45. Leipzig: Hinrichs.

———. 1957 [1900]. *What is Christianity?* Trans. Thomas Bailey Saunders. New York: Harper & Row, Harper Torchbooks/Cloister Library.

Harper, George. 1988. *Repentance in Pauline Theology.* Ph.D. Dissertation, McGill University, Montreal.

Harvey, Anthony E. 1982. *Jesus and the Constraints of History: The Bampton Lectures, 1980.* London: Duckworth.

Harvey, David. 1989. *The Condition of Postmodernity: An Enquiry Into the Origins of Cultural Change.* Oxford: Blackwell.

Hauerwas, Stanley, and L. Gregory Jones, ed. 1989. *Why Narrative? Readings in Narrative Theology.* Grand Rapids, Mich.: Eerdmans.

Hawking, Stephen W. 1988. *A Brief History of Time: From the Big Bang to Black Holes.* London: Transworld.

Hayman, Peter. 1991. 'Monotheism—A Misused Word in Jewish Studies?' *Journal of Jewish Studies* 42:1–15.

Hays, R. B. 1983. *The Faith of Jesus Christ: An Investigation of the Narrative Substructure of Galatians 3:1–4:11.* SBL Dissertation Series. Chico, Calif.: Scholars Press.

———. 1989. *Echoes of Scripture in the Letters of Paul.* New Haven: Yale U. P.

Hayward, C. T. R. 1991. 'Sacrifice and World Order: Some Observations on Ben Sira's Attitude to the Temple Service.' In *Sacrifice and Redemption: Durham Essays in Theology,* ed. Stephen W. Sykes, 22–34. Cambridge: CUP.

Hellholm, David. 1983. *Apocalypticism in the Mediterranean World and the Near East: Proceedings of the International Colloquium on Apocalypticism, Uppsala, August 12–17, 1979.* Tübingen: Mohr.

Hemer, Colin J. 1989. *The Book of Acts in the Setting of Hellenistic History.* Ed. Conrad J. Gempf. Tübingen: Mohr.

Hengel, M. 1974. *Judaism and Hellenism: Studies in Their Encounter in Palestine During the Early Hellenistic Period.* Trans. John Bowden. 2 vols. London: SCM; 1 vol. edn., Philadelphia: Fortress (1991).

———. 1976. *The Son of God: The Origin of Christology and the History of Jewish-Hellenistic Religion.* Trans. John Bowden. Philadelphia: Fortress.

———. 1977 [1976]. *Crucifixion in the Ancient World and the Folly of the Message of the Cross.* Trans. John Bowden. London: SCM; Philadelphia: Fortress.

———. 1979. *Acts and the History of Earliest Christianity.* Trans. John Bowden. Philadelphia: Fortress.

———. 1983. *Between Jesus and Paul: Studies in the Earliest History of Christianity.* Trans. J. Bowden. London: SCM.

———. 1989a. *The 'Hellenization' of Judaea in the First Century After Christ.* London: SCM; Philadelphia: Trinity Press International.

———. 1989b. *The Johannine Question.* Trans. John Bowden. London: SCM; Philadelphia: Trinity Press International.

———. 1989 [1961]. *The Zealots: Investigations Into the Jewish Freedom Movement in the Period from Herod I Until 70 A.D.* Trans. David Smith. Edinburgh: T & T Clark.

———. 1991. *The Pre-Christian Paul.* Trans. John Bowden with Roland Dienes. London: SCM; Philadelphia: Trinity Press International.

Hennecke, Edgar. 1963. *New Testament Apocrypha.* ed. Wilhelm Schneemelcher and R. McL. Wilson. Vol. 1. *Gospels and Related Writings.* Philadelphia: Westminster Press; London: SCM.

———. 1965. *New Testament Apocrypha.* ed. Wilhelm Schneemelcher and R. McL. Wilson. Vol. 2. *Writings Related to the Apostles: Apocalypses and Related Subjects.* Philadelphia: Westminster Press; London: SCM.

Hill, Craig C. 1992. *Hellenists and Hebrews: Reappraising Division Within the Earliest Church*. Minneapolis: Fortress.

Hill, David. 1979. *New Testament Prophecy*. London: Marshall, Morgan & Scott.

Hirst, R. J. 1967. 'Phenomenalism.' In *The Encyclopedia of Philosophy*, ed. P. Edwards, vol. 6, 130–5. New York: Macmillan Co. & The Free Press; London: Collier-Macmillan Ltd.

Holmes, Arthur F. 1983a. *All Truth is God's Truth*. Downer's Grove, Ill.: IVP.

———. 1983b. *Contours of a Worldview*. Grand Rapids, Mich.: Eerdmans.

Holz, Traugott. 1968. *Untersuchungen über die alttestamentlichen Zitate bei Lukas*. Texte und Untersuchungen, vol. 104. Berlin: Akademie.

Hommel, H. 1961/2. 'Das 7. Kapitel des Römerbriefes im Licht antiker Überlieferung.' *Theologia Viatorum* 8:90–116.

Hooker, Morna D. 1967. *The Son of Man in Mark*. London: SPCK.

———. 1972. 'On Using the Wrong Tool.' *Theology* 75:570–81.

———. 1975. 'In His Own Image?' In *What About the New Testament? Essays in Honour of Christopher Evans*, ed. Morna D. Hooker and Colin Hickling, 28–44. London: SCM.

———. 1991. *A Commentary on the Gospel According to St Mark*. Black's New Testament Commentaries. London: A & C Black.

Horbury, William. 1982. 'The Benediction of the *Minim* and Early Jewish-Christian Controversy.' *Journal of Theological Studies* 33:19–61.

———. 1984. 'The Temple Tax.' In *Jesus and the Politics of His Day*, ed. Ernst Bammel and Charles F. D. Moule, 265–86. Cambridge: CUP.

———. 1985. 'The Messianic Associations of "the Son of Man".' *Journal of Theological Studies* 36:34–55.

Horsley, Richard A. 1979a. 'Josephus and the Bandits.' *Journal for the Study of Judaism* 10(1):37–63.

———. 1979b. 'The Sicarii: Ancient Jewish "terrorists".' *Journal of Religion* 59:435–58.

———. 1981. 'Ancient Jewish Banditry and the Revolt Against Rome, A.D. 66.' *Catholic Biblical Quarterly* 43:409–32.

———. 1984. 'Popular Messianic Movements Around the Time of Jesus.' *Catholic Biblical Quarterly* 46:471–95.

———. 1986a. 'Popular Prophetic Movements at the Time of Jesus: Their Principal Features and Social Origins.' *Journal for the Study of the New Testament* 26:3–27.

———. 1986b. 'The Zealots: Their Origin, Relationships and Importance in the Jewish Revolt.' *Novum Testamentum* 28(2):159–92.

———. 1987. *Jesus and the Spiral of Violence: Popular Jewish Resistance in Roman Palestine*. San Francisco: Harper & Row (from 1992: Philadelphia: Fortress).

Horsley, Richard A., and John S. Hanson. 1985. *Bandits, Prophets and Messiahs: Popular Movements at the Time of Jesus*. Minneapolis: Winston Press; Edinburgh: T & T Clark.

Houlden, J. Leslie. 1970. *Paul's Letters from Prison*. London: Penguin Books.

———. 1984. 'The Purpose of Luke.' *Journal for the Study of the New Testament* 21:53–65.

House, John. 1977. *Monet*. Oxford: Phaidon Press; New York: E. P. Dutton.

Hubbard, Benjamin J. 1979. 'Luke, Josephus and Rome: A Comparative Approach to the Lukan *Sitz Im Leben*.' In *Society of Biblical Literature 1979 Seminar Papers*, ed. Paul J. Achtemeier, 59–68. Missoula, Mo.: Scholars Press.

Hultgren, Arland J. 1987. *Christ and His Benefits: Christology and Redemption in the New Testament*. Philadelphia: Fortress.

Hurst, Lincoln D. 1990. *The Epistle to the Hebrews: Its Background of Thought*. Society for New Testament Studies Monograph Series, vol. 65. Cambridge: CUP.

Iersel, Bas van. 1989 [1986]. *Reading Mark*. Trans. W. H. Bisscheroux. Edinburgh: T & T Clark.

Isaac, B., and A. Oppenheimer. 1985. 'The Revolt of Bar Kokhhba: Ideology and Modern Scholarship.' *Journal of Jewish Studies* 36:33–60.

Jacobson, D. M. 1988. 'King Herod's "Heroic" Public Image.' *Révue Biblique* 95:386–403.

Jeanrond, Werner G. 1990. 'Hermeneutics.' In *A Dictionary of Biblical Interpretation*, ed. R. J. Coggins and J. L. Houlden, 282–4. London: SCM; Philadelphia: Trinity Press International.

Jencks, Charles. 1989 [1986]. *What is Post-Modernism?* 3rd edn. London: Academy Editions.

Jeremias, Joachim. 1963 [1947]. *The Parables of Jesus*. Rev. edn. Trans. S. H. Hooke. London: SCM; New York: Scribner's.

——. 1966 [1930]. 'Zur Hypothese einer schriftlichen Logienquelle Q.' In *Abba: Studien Zur Neutestamentlichen Theologie und Zeitgeschichte*, 90–2. Göttingen: Vandenhoek und Ruprecht.

——. 1969a. *Jerusalem in the Time of Jesus: An Investigation Into Economic and Social Conditions During the New Testament Period.* Trans. F. H. Cave and C. H. Cave. Philadelphia: Fortress.

——. 1969b. 'Paulus als Hillelit.' In *Neotestamentica et Semitica: Studies in Honour of M. Black*, ed. E. E. Ellis and M. Wilcox, 88–94. Edinburgh: T & T Clark.

——. 1971. *New Testament Theology: The Proclamation of Jesus.* Trans. John Bowden. New York: Scribner's.

Jewett, Robert. 1979. *Dating Paul's Life.* London, Philadelphia: SCM, Fortress.

Johnson, Alfred M. Jr., ed. & trans. 1976. *The New Testament and Structuralism.* Pittsburgh Theological Monograph Series, no. 11. Pittsburgh: The Pickwick Press.

Johnston, George. 1987. 'Ecce Homo! Irony in the Christology of the Fourth Evangelist.' In *The Glory of Christ in the New Testament: Studies in Christology in Memory of George Bradford Caird*, ed. L. D. Hurst and N. T. Wright, 125–38. Oxford: Clarendon Press.

Jonas, Hans. 1963 [1958]. *The Gnostic Religion: The Message of the Alien God and the Beginnings of Christianity.* 2nd. edn. Boston: Beacon Press.

Jones, A. H. M. 1967 [1938]. *The Herods of Judaea.* Oxford: Clarendon Press.

Judge, Edwin A. 1960. *The Social Pattern of Christian Groups in the First Century.* London: Tyndale Press.

Juel, D. 1977. *Messiah and Temple. the Trial of Jesus in the Gospel of Mark.* Missoula: Scholars Press.

Jülicher, Adolf. 1910 [1899]. *Die Gleichnisreden Jesu.* 2nd edn. Tübingen: Mohr.

Kadushin, M. 1938. *Organic Thinking: A Study in Rabbinic Thought.* New York.

Kampen, John. 1988. *The Hasideans and the Origin of Pharisaism: A Study in 1 and 2 Maccabees.* SBL Septuagint and Cognate Studies Series, no. 24. Atlanta: Scholars Press.

Käsemann, Ernst. 1964 [1960]. *Essays on New Testament Themes.* Trans. W. J. Montague. Studies in Biblical Theology, vol. 41. London: SCM.

——. 1969 [1965]. *New Testament Questions of Today.* Trans. W. J. Montague. London: SCM.

——. 1970. *Das Neue Testament als Kanon.* Göttingen: Vandenhoek und Ruprecht.

——. 1971 [1969]. *Perspectives on Paul.* Trans. Margaret Kohl. London: SCM.

——. 1973. 'The Problem of a New Testament Theology.' *New Testament Studies* 19:235–45.

——. 1980. *Commentary on Romans.* Trans. & ed. Geoffrey W. Bromiley. Grand Rapids: Eerdmans.

Kasher, Aryeh. 1990. *Jews and Hellenistic Cities in Eretz-Israel: Relations of the Jews in Eretz-Israel with the Hellenistic Cities During the Second Temple Period (332 BCE–70 CE).* Texte und Studien zum Antiken Judentum, vol. 21. Tübingen: Mohr.

Katz, S. T. 1984. 'Issues in the Separation of Judaism and Christianity After 70 C. E.: A Reconsideration.' *Journal of Biblical Literature* 103:43–76.

Kee, Howard C. 1977. *Community of the New Age: Studies in Mark's Gospel.* London: SCM.

——. 1990. 'The Transformation of the Synagogue After 70 C.E.: Its Import for Early Christianity.' *New Testament Studies* 36:1–24.

Kelber, Werner. 1983. *The Oral and Written Gospel.* Philadelphia: Fortress.

Kellerman, Ulrich. 1979. *Auferstanden in den Himmel. 2 Makkabäer 7 und die Auferstehung der Märtyrer.* Stuttgarter Bibelstudien 95. Stuttgart: Verlag Katholisches Bibelwerk.

Kelly, J. N. D. 1972 [1950]. *Early Christian Creeds.* 3rd edn. London: Longman.

Kelsey, David H. 1989. 'Paul Tillich.' In *The Modern Theologians: An Introduction to Christian Theology in the Twentieth Century*, ed, David F. Ford, vol. 1, 134–51. Oxford: Basil Blackwell.

Kermode, Frank. 1968. *The Sense of an Ending: Studies in the Theory of Fiction.* Oxford: OUP.

——. 1979. *The Genesis of Secrecy: On the Interpretation of Narrative.* Cambridge, Mass: Harvard U. P.

Kerr, Fergus. 1989. 'Idealism and Realism: An Old Controversy Dissolved.' In *Christ, Ethics and Tragedy: Essays in Honour of Donald MacKinnon.* Ed. Kenneth Surin, 15–33. Cambridge: CUP.

Kimelman, Reuven. 1981. '*Birkat Ha-Minim* and the Lack of Evidence for an Anti-Christian Jewish Prayer in Late Antiquity.' In *Aspects of Judaism in the Greco-Roman Period.* In

Jewish and Christian Self-Definition, ed. E. P. Sanders with A. I. Baumgarten and Alan Mendelson, 226–44, 391–403. Philadelphia: Fortress.

Kingdon, H. Paul. 1972–3. 'The Origins of the Zealots.' *New Testament Studies* 19:74–81.

Kingsbury, Jack D. 1988 [1986]. *Matthew as Story*. 2nd edn. Philadelphia: Fortress.

Klinzing, Georg. 1971. *Die Umdeutung des Kultus in der Qumrangemeinde und im Neuen Testament*. Studien zur Umwelt des Neuen Testaments, vol. 7. Göttingen: Vandenhoek & Ruprecht.

Kloppenborg, J. S. 1987. *The Formation of Q: Trajectories in Ancient Wisdom Collectons*. Studies in Antiquity and Christianity. Philadelphia: Fortress.

Knibb, Michael A. 1976. 'The Exile in the Literature of the Intertestamental Period.' *Heythrop Journal*:253–79.

——. 1983. 'Exile in the Damascus Document.' *Journal for the Study of the Old Testament* 25:99–117.

——. 1987. *The Qumran Community*. Cambridge Commentaries on Writings of the Jewish and Christian World, 200 BC to AD 200. Cambridge: CUP.

Knox, John. 1935. *Philemon Among the Letters of Paul*. Chicago: Chicago U. P.

Koch, Klaus. 1969. *The Growth of the Biblical Tradition: The Form-Critical Method*. New York: Scribner's.

——. 1972 [1970]. *The Rediscovery of Apocalyptic: A Polemical Work On a Neglected Area of Biblical Studies and Its Damaging Effects on Theology and Philosophy*. Trans. Margaret Kohl. Studies in Biblical Theology, vol. 2.22. London: SCM.

Koester, Helmut. 1982a [1980]. *Introduction to the New Testament*. Vol. 1. *History, Culture and Religion of the Hellenistic Age*. Philadelphia: Fortress; Berlin & New York: de Gruyter.

——. 1982b. *Introduction to the New Testament*. Vol. 2. *History and Literature of Early Christianity*. Hermeneia: Foundations and Facets. Philadelphia: Fortress; Berlin & New York: de Gruyter.

——. 1989. 'From the Kerygma-Gospel to Written Gospels.' *New Testament Studies* 35:361–81.

——. 1990. *Ancient Christian Gospels: Their History and Development*. London: SCM; Philadelphia: Trinity Press International.

Kraft, Robert A., and George W. E. Nickelsburg, ed. 1986. *Early Judaism and Its Modern Interpreters*. In *The Bible and Its Modern Interpreters*, ed. Douglas A. Knight. Atlanta, Ga.: Scholars Press; Philadelphia: Fortress.

Krenkel, M. 1894. *Josephus und Lucas. Der schriftstellerische Einfluss des jüdischen Geschichtsschreibers auf der christlichen nachgewiesen*. Leipzig: Haessel.

Kuhn, Thomas S. 1970 [1962]. *The Structure of Scientific Revolutions*. 2nd edn. Chicago: Chicago U. P.

Kümmel, Werner G. 1972 [1970]. *The New Testament: The History of the Investigation of Its Problems*. Trans. S. M. Gilmour and H. C. Kee. Nashville: Abingdon; London: SCM.

——. 1973. *The Theology of the New Testament: According to Its Major Witnesses, Jesus—Paul—John*. Nashville: Abingdon.

Küng, Hans. 1964 [1957]. *Justification: The Doctrine of Karl Barth and a Catholic Reflection*. Trans. T. Collins, E. E. Tolk, and D. Grandskou. London: Burns & Oates.

——. 1967. *The Church*. Trans. Ray Ockenden and Rosaleen Ockendon. New York: Sheed & Ward.

Kysar, Robert. 1985. 'The Fourth Gospel: A Report on Recent Research.' In *ANRW* 2.25.3:2389–480.

Landman, Leo, ed. 1979. *Messianism in the Talmudic Era*. New York: Ktav.

Lane, William L. 1974. *The Gospel of Mark: The English Text with Introduction, Exposition and Notes*. New International Commentary on the New Testament. Grand Rapids, Mich.: Eerdmans.

——. 1991. *Hebrews 1–8, 9–13*. Word Biblical Commentary, vol. 47. Dallas, Tex.: Word Books.

Lane Fox, Robin. 1986. *Pagans and Christians*. New York: Alfred A. Knopf; London: Penguin Books.

Lang, Bernhard, ed. 1981. *Der einzige Gott: die Geburt des biblischen Monotheismus*. Munich: Kösel.

Lapide, P. E., and J. Moltmann. 1981 [1979]. *Jewish Monotheism and Christian Trinitarian Doctrine: A Dialogue*. Trans. Leonard Swidler. Philadelphia: Fortress.

Layton, Bentley, ed. 1980. *The Rediscovery of Gnosticism: Proceedings of the International Conference on Gnosticism at Yale, New Haven, Connecticut, March 28–31, 1978*. Vol. 1. *The*

School of Valentinus. Studies in the History of Religions (Supplements to *Numen*). Leiden: Brill.

———, ed. 1981. *The Rediscovery of Gnosticism: Proceedings of the International Conference on Gnosticism at Yale, New Haven, Connecticut, March 28–31, 1978*. Vol. 2. *Sethian Gnosticism*. Studies in the History of Religions (supplements to *Numen*). Leiden: Brill.

Leaney, A. T. C. 1966. *The Rule of Qumran and Its Meaning: Introduction, Translation and Commentary*. London: SCM.

Leavis, F. R. 1963 [1932]. *New Bearings in English Poetry: A Study of the Contemporary Situation*. London: Penguin Books.

Lemcio, Eugene E. 1991. *The Past of Jesus in the Gospels*. Society for New Testament Studies Monograph Series, vol. 68. Cambridge: CUP.

Levine, Lee I. 1978. 'On the Political Involvement of the Pharisees Under Herod and the Procurators.' *Cathedra* 8:12–28.

———., ed. 1987. *The Synagogue in Late Antiquity*. Philadelphia: American School of Oriental Research.

Lewis, C. S. 1943 [1933]. *The Pilgrim's Regress: An Allegorical Apology for Christianity, Reason and Romanticism*. 2nd edn. London: Bles.

———. 1961. *An Experiment in Criticism*. Cambridge: CUP.

Lewis, J. P. 1964. 'What Do We Mean by Jabneh?' *Journal of Bible and Religion* 32:125–32.

Lincoln, Andrew T. 1981. *Paradise Now and not Yet: Studies in the Role of the Heavenly Dimension in Paul's Thought with Special Reference to His Eschatology*. Society of New Tetament Studies Monograph Series, vol. 43. Cambridge: CUP.

———. 1990. *Ephesians*. Word Biblical Commentary, vol. 42. Waco, Tex.: Word Books.

Lindars, Barnabas. 1989. 'The Rhetorical Structure of Hebrews.' *New Testament Studies* 35:382–406.

Loewe, R. 1981. ' "Salvation" is not of the Jews.' *Journal of Theological Studies* 22:341–68.

Logan, A. H. B. and A. J. M. Wedderburn, ed. 1983. *The New Testament and Gnosis: Essays in Honour of Robert McL. Wilson*. Edinburgh: T & T Clark.

Longenecker, Bruce W. 1991. *Eschatology and the Covenant in 4 Ezra and Romans 1–11*. Journal for the Study of the New Testament Supplement Series, vol. 57. Sheffield: Sheffield Academic Press.

Lonergan, Bernard J. F. 1973. *Method in Theology*. 2nd edn. New York: Herder & Herder.

———. 1978. *Insight: A Study of Human Understanding*. New York: Harper & Row.

Louth, Andrew. 1983. *Discerning the Mystery: An Essay on the Nature of Theology*. Oxford: Clarendon Press.

Lowe, Malcolm. 1976. 'Who Were the 'Ιουδαῖοι?' *Novum Testamentum* 18:101–30.

Lucas, John R. 1976. *Freedom and Grace*. London: SPCK.

Lüdemann, Gerd. 1980. *Paulus, der Heidenapostel*. Vol. 1. *Studien zur Chronologie*. Forschungen zur Religion und Literatur des Alten und Neuen Testaments, vol. 123. Göttingen: Vandenhoek & Ruprecht. [ET 1984: *Paul, Apostle to the Gentiles: Studies in Chronology*. Philadelphia: Fortress.]

Lührmann, Dieter. 1969. *Die Redaktion der Logienquelle*. Wissenschaftliche Monographien zum Alten und Neuen Testament. Neukirchen-Vluyn: Neukirchener Verlag.

———. 1989. 'The Gospel of Mark and the Sayings Collection Q.' *Journal of Biblical Literature* 108:51–71.

Lundin, Roger, Clarence Walhout, and Anthony C. Thiselton. 1985. *The Responsibility of Hermeneutics*. Grand Rapids: Eerdmans; Exeter: Paternoster.

Lyotard, Jean-François. 1984 [1979]. *The Postmodern Condition: A Report on Knowledge*. Trans. Geoff Bennington and Brian Massumi. Theory and History of Literature, vol. 10. Manchester: Manchester U. P.

Lyttleton, Margaret, and Werner Forman. 1984. *The Romans: Their Gods and Beliefs*. London: Orbis.

———. 1991. *Paul and Hellenism*. London: SCM; Philadelphia: Trinity Press International.

McEleney, Neil J. 1973. 'Orthodoxy in Judaism of the First Christian Century.' *Journal for the Study of Judaism* 4:19–42.

McGrath, Alister E. 1986. *The Making of Modern German Christology: From the Enlightenment to Pannenberg*. Oxford: Blackwell.

MacIntyre, Alasdair. 1985 [1981]. *After Virtue: A Study in Moral Theory*. 2nd. ed. Notre Dame, Indiana: Notre Dame U. P.

McKelvey, R. J. 1969. *The New Temple: The Church in the New Testament*. London: OUP.

MacKinnon, Donald M. 1979. *Explorations in Theology*. London: SCM.

McLaren, James. 1991. *Power and Politics in Palestine: The Jews and the Governing of Their Land 100 BC—AD 70*. Journal for the Study of the New Testament Supplement Series, vol. 63. Sheffield: JSOT Press.

McManners, J. 1981. 'The Individual in the Church of England.' In *Believing in the Church: The Corporate Nature of Faith*, The Doctrine Commission of the Church of England, 209–36. London: SPCK.

MacMullen, Ramsey. 1967. *Enemies of the Roman Order*. Cambridge, Mass.: Harvard U. P.

———. 1974. *Roman Social Relations 50 B.C. to A.D. 284*. New Haven: Yale U. P.

———. 1981. *Paganism in the Roman Empire*. New Haven: Yale U. P.

Macquarrie, John. 1966. *Principles of Christian Theology*. London: SCM; New York: Scribner's.

———. 1990. *Jesus Christ in Modern Thought*. London: SCM; Philadelphia: Trinity Press International.

Maccoby, Hyam. 1986. *The Mythmaker: Paul and the Invention of Christianity*. London: Wiedenfeld & Nicolson.

Mack, Burton L. 1988. *A Myth of Innocence: Mark and Christian Origins*. Philadelphia: Fortress.

Maddox, R. 1982. *The Purpose of Luke-Acts*. Edinburgh: T & T Clark.

Malherbe, Abraham J. 1983 [1977]. *Social Aspects of Early Christianity*. 2nd edn. Philadelphia: Fortress.

———. 1987. *Paul and the Thessalonians: The Philosophic Tradition of Pastoral Care*. Philadelphia: Fortress.

Mann, Thomas. 1961. *The Genesis of a Novel*. Trans. Richard Winston and Clara Winston. London: Secker & Warburg.

———. 1968 [1947]. *Dr Faustus: The Life of the German Composer Adrian Leverkühn as Told by a Friend*. Trans. H. T. Lowe-Porter. London: Penguin Books.

Marin, Louis. 1976a. 'Jesus Before Pilate: A Structural Analysis Essay.' In *The New Testament and Structuralism*, ed. Alfred M. Johnson, Jr., 97–144. Pittsburgh Theological Monograph Series, no. 11. Pittsburgh: The Pickwick Press.

———. 1976b. 'The Women at the Tomb: A Structural Analysis Essay of a Gospel Text.' In *The New Testament and Structuralism*, ed. Alfred M. Johnson, Jr., 73–96. Pittsburgh Theological Monograph Series, no. 11. Pittsburgh: The Pickwick Press.

Marshall, I. Howard. 1972–3. 'Palestinian and Hellenistic Christianity: Some Critical Comments.' *New Testament Studies* 19:271–87.

Marshall, Paul A., Sander Griffioen, and Richard J. Mouw, ed. 1989. *Stained Glass: Worldviews and Social Science*. Lanham, N.Y.: University Press of America.

Martin, Luther H. 1987. *Hellenistic Religions: An Introduction*. New York & Oxford: OUP.

Mason, S. N. 1988. 'Priesthood in Josephus and the "Pharisaic Revolution".' *Journal of Biblical Literature* 107:657–61.

———. 1989. 'Was Josephus a Pharisee? A Re-Examination of *Life* 10–12.' *Journal of Jewish Studies* 40:31–45.

———. 1991. *Flavius Josephus on the Pharisees: A Composition-Critical Study*. Studia Post-Biblica, vol. 39. Leiden: Brill.

Matera, Frank J. 1987. 'The Plot of Matthew's Gospel.' *Catholic Biblical Quarterly* 49:233–53.

Mealand, David L. 1991. 'Hellenistic Histories and the Style of Acts.' *Zeitschrift für die neutestamentliche Wissenschaft* 82:42–66.

Meeks, Wayne A. 1983. *The First Urban Christians: The Social World of the Apostle Paul*. New Haven: Yale U. P.

———. 1986. *The Moral World of the First Christians*. Philadelphia: Westminster; London: SPCK.

Menuhin, Yehudi. 1977. *Unfinished Journey*. London: MacDonald and Jane's.

Meshorer, Yaakov. 'Jewish Numismatics.' In *Early Judaism and Its Modern Interpreters*, ed. Robert A. Kraft and George W. E. Nickelsburg. In *The Bible and Its Modern Interpreters*, ed. Douglas A. Knight, 211–20. Atlanta, Ga.: Scholars Press; Philadelphia: Fortress.

Meyer, Ben F. 1979. *The Aims of Jesus*. London: SCM.

———. 1986. *The Early Christians: Their World Mission and Self-Discovery*. Good News Studies, no. 16. Wilmington, Del.: Michael Glazier.

———. 1989. *Critical Realism and the New Testament*. Princeton Theological Monograph Series, vol. 17. Allison Park, Pennsylvania: Pickwick Publications.

———. 1990. 'A Tricky Business: Ascribing New Meaning to Old Texts.' *Gregorianum* 71(4):743–61.

———. 1991a. 'A Caricature of Joachim Jeremias and His Work.' *Journal of Biblical Literature* 110:451–62.

———. 1991b. 'The Philosophical Crusher.' *First Things: A Monthly Journal of Religion and Public Life* 12 (April):9–11.

Milbank, John. 1990. *Theology and Social Theory: Beyond Secular Reason.* Signposts in Theology. Oxford: Blackwell.

Millar, Fergus G. B. 1981 [1967]. *The Roman Empire and Its Neighbours.* 2nd edn. London: Duckworth.

———. 1990. 'Reflections on the Trial of Jesus', ed. P. R. Davies and R. T. White. In *A Tribute to Geza Vermes: Essays on Jewish and Christian Literature and History*, 355–81. Journal for the Study of the Old Testament Supplement series, vol. 100. Sheffield: JSOT Press.

Miller, Patrick D. 1985. 'Israelite Religion.' In *The Hebrew Bible and Its Modern Interpreters*, ed. Douglas A. Knight and Gene M. Tucker, 201–37. Chico, Calif.: Scholars Press; Philadelphia: Fortress.

Millgram, A. E. 1971. *Jewish Worship.* Philadelphia: Jewish Publication Society of America.

Moltmann, Jürgen. 1974. *The Crucified God: The Cross of Christ as the Foundation and Criticism of Christian Theology.* Trans. R. A. Wilson and John Bowden. New York: Harper & Row.

———. 1985. *God in Creation: A New Theology of Creation and the Spirit of God.* Trans. Margaret Kohl. San Francisco: Harper & Row.

———. 1990 [1989]. *The Way of Jesus Christ: Christology in Messianic Dimensions.* Trans. Margaret Kohl. London: SCM.

Momigliano, Arnaldo. 1984 [1981]. 'Greek Culture and the Jews.' In *The Legacy of Greece: A New Appraisal*, ed. M. I. Finley. 2nd edn., 325–46. Oxford: OUP.

Moore, George Foot. 1927–30. *Judaism in the First Centuries of the Christian Era: The Age of the Tannaim.* 3 vols. Cambridge, Mass.: Harvard U. P.

Moore, Stephen D. 1989. *Literary Criticism and the Gospels: The Theoretical Challenge.* New Haven, London: Yale U. P.

Morgan, Robert. 1973. *The Nature of New Testament Theology: The Contribution of William Wrede and Adolf Schlatter.* Studies in Biblical Theology (second series), no. 25. London: SCM.

———. 1977. 'A Straussian Question to "New Testament Theology" ' *New Testament Studies* 23:243–65.

———. 1987. 'The Historical Jesus and the Theology of the New Testament.' In *The Glory of Christ in the New Testament: Studies in Christology in Memory of George Bradford Caird*, ed. L. D. Hurst and N. T. Wright, 187–206. Oxford: Clarendon Press.

———. 1988. *Biblical Interpretation.* In collaboration with John Barton. Oxford Bible Series. Oxford: OUP.

Mørkholm, O. 1989. 'Antiochus IV.' In *Cambridge Ancient History*, ed. W. D. Davies and L. Finkelstein, vol. 2. *The Hellenistic Age*, 278–91.

Moule, Charles F. D. 1958/9. 'Once More, Who Were the Hellenists?' *Expository Times* 70:100–2.

———. 1967. *The Phenomenon of the New Testament: An Inquiry Into the Implications of Certain Features of the New Testament.* Studies in Biblical Theology 2nd series, vol. 1. London: SCM.

———. 1970. 'Jesus in New Testament Kerygma.' In *Verborum Veritas (für G. Stählin)*, ed. O. Böcher and K. Haaker, 15–26. Wuppertal: Brockhaus.

———. 1975. 'On Defining the Messianic Secret in Mark.' In *Jesus und Paulus: Festschrift Für Werner Georg Kümmel Zum 70. Geburtstag*, ed. E. Earle Ellis and Erich Grässer, 239–52. Göttingen: Vandenhoek & Ruprecht.

———. 1977. *The Origin of Christology.* Cambridge: CUP.

———. 1982 [1962]. *The Birth of the New Testament.* 3rd edn. London: A & C Black; San Francisco: Harper & Row.

Mulder, Michael Jan. 1987. *Mikra: Text, Translation, Reading and Interpretation of the Hebrew Bible in Ancient Judaism and Early Christianity. Compendia* 2.1.

Munck, Johannes. 1959 [1954]. *Paul and the Salvation of Mankind.* Trans. Frank Clarke. London: SCM; Richmond, Va.: John Knox.

Murphy, Frederick J. 1985. '2 *Baruch* and the Romans.' *Journal of Biblical Literature* 104:663–9.

Murphy-O'Connor, J. 1974. 'The Essenes and Their History.' *Révue Biblique* 81:215–44.

Myers, Ched. 1990. *Binding the Strong Man: A Political Reading of Mark's Story of Jesus*. Maryknoll, N.Y.: Orbis.

Neill, Stephen C. 1976. *Jesus Through Many Eyes: Introduction to the Theology of the New Testament*. Philadelphia: Fortress.

Neill, Stephen C., and N. Thomas Wright. 1988 [1964]. *The Interpretation of the New Testament, 1861–1986*. 2nd edn. Oxford: OUP.

Neirynck, Frans. 1974. *The Minor Agreements of Matthew and Luke Against Mark*. Bibliotheca Ephemeridum Theologicarum Lovaniensium, no. 37. Leuvain: Leuven U. P.

Neusner, Jacob. 1970. *A Life of Johanan Ben Zakkai*. Studia Post-Biblica, vol. 6. Leiden: Brill.

——. 1971. *The Rabbinic Traditions About the Pharisees Before 70*. Leiden: Brill.

——. 1973. *From Politics to Piety*. Englewood Cliffs: Prentice-Hall.

——. 1979. 'The Formation of Rabbinic Judaism: Yavneh (Jamnia) from A.D. 70 to 100.' In *ANRW* 2.19.2:3–42.

——. 1987. ed., with W. S. Green and E. Frerichs. *Judaisms and Their Messiahs at the Turn of the Christian Era*. Cambridge: CUP.

——. 1989. 'Money-Changers in the Temple: The Mishnah's Explanation.' *New Testament Studies* 35:287–90.

——. 1991. *Jews and Christians: The Myth of a Common Tradition*. London: SCM; Philadelphia: Trinity Press International.

Newbigin, Lesslie. *Foolishness to the Greeks: The Gospel and Western Culture*. Geneva: WCC.

——. 1989. *The Gospel in a Pluralist Society*. London: SPCK; Grand Rapids, Mich.: Eerdmans.

Newton-Smith, W. H. 1981. *The Rationality of Science*. London: Routledge.

Nickelsburg, George W. E. 1972. *Resurrection, Immortality and Eternal Life in Intertestamental Judaism*. Harvard Theological Studies, vol. 26. Cambridge, Mass.: Harvard U. P.

——. 1980. 'The Genre and Function of the Markan Passion Narrative.' *Harvard Theological Review* 73:153–84.

——. 1981. *Jewish Literature Between the Bible and the Mishnah*. Philadelphia: Fortress; London: SCM.

——. 1984. 'The Bible Rewritten and Expanded.' In *Compendia* 2.2.89–156.

Nineham, Dennis. 1976. *The Use and Abuse of the Bible: A Study of the Bible in an Age of Rapid Cultural Change*. Library of Philosophy and Religion. London: Macmillan.

Nolland, John. 1989. *Luke 1—9:20*. Word Biblical Commentary, vol. 35a. Dallas, Tex.: Word Books.

Nordling, John G. 1991. 'Onesimus Fugitivus: A Defense of the Runaway Slave Hypothesis in Philemon.' *Journal for the Study of the New Testament* 41:97–119.

O'Donovan, Oliver M. T. 1986. *Resurrection and Moral Order: An Outline for Evangelical Ethics*. Leicester: IVP; Grand Rapids, Mich.: Eerdmans.

O'Neill, John C. 1991. 'The Lost Written Records of Jesus' Words and Deeds Behind Our Records.' *Journal of Theological Studies* 42:483–504.

Oakman, Douglas E. 1986. *Jesus and the Economic Questions of His Day*. Studies in the Bible and Early Christianity, vol. 8. Lewiston, Queenston: Edwin Mellen Press.

Olthuis, James H. 1989 [1985]. 'On Worldviews.' In *Stained Glass: Worldviews and Social Science*, ed. Paul A. Marshall, Sander Griffioen, and Richard J. Mouw, 26–40. Lanham, N.Y.: University Press of America.

Oppenheimer, A. 1977. *The Am Ha-Aretz. a Study of the Social History of the Jewish People in the Hellenistic-Roman Period*. Leiden: Brill.

Pannenberg, Wolfhart. 1968 [1964]. *Jesus: God and Man*. Trans. Lewis L. Wilkins and Duane A. Priebe. Philadelphia: Westminster Press.

——. 1970 [1963]. *Basic Questions in Theology: Collected Essays*. Philadelphia: Westminster; London: SCM.

——. 1971 [1967]. *Basic Questions in Theology: Collected Essays*. Philadelphia: Westminster; London: SCM.

Passmore, John. 1967. 'Logical Positivism.' In *The Encyclopedia of Philosophy*, ed. P. Edwards, vol. 5, 52–7. New York: Macmillan Co. & the Free Press; London: Collier-Macmillan Ltd.

Patte, Daniel. 1976. *What is Structural Exegesis?* Philadelphia: Fortress.

——. 1983. *Paul's Faith and the Power of the Gospel: A Structural Introduction to the Pauline Letters*. Philadelphia: Fortress.

Patte, Daniel, and Aline Patte. 1978. *Structural Exegesis: From Theory to Practice*. Philadelphia: Fortress.

Pearson, Birger A. 1980. 'Jewish Elements in Gnosticism and the Development of Gnostic Self-Definition.' In *Jewish and Christian Self-Definition*, vol. 1. *The Shaping of Christianity in the Second and Third Centuries*, ed. E. P. Sanders, 151–60. Philadelphia: Fortress.

———. 1984. 'Jewish Sources in Gnostic Literature.' In *Compendia* 2.2.443–81.

Perkins, Pheme. 1984. *Resurrection: New Testament Witness and Contemporary Reflection*. London: Geoffrey Chapman.

Perrin, Norman. 1970. *What is Redaction Criticism?* London: SPCK.

———. 1983 [1974]. 'Apocalyptic Christianity.' In *Visionaries and Their Apocalypses*, ed. Paul D. Hanson, 121–45. Issues in Religion and theology, no. 2. Philadelphia: Fortress; London: SPCK.

Perrin, Norman, and Dennis C. Duling. 1982 [1974]. *The New Testament: An Introduction. Proclamation and Parenesis, Myth and History*. 2nd edn. New York: Harcourt Brace Jovanovich.

Petersen, Norman R. 1978. *Literary Criticism for New Testament Critics*. Philadelphia: Fortress.

———. 1985. *Rediscovering Paul: Philemon and the Sociology of Paul's Narrative World*. Philadelphia: Fortress.

Pettem, Michael. 1989. *Matthew: Jewish Christian or Gentile Christian?* Unpublished Doctoral Dissertation, McGill University, Montreal.

Piper, Ronald A. 1989. *Wisdom in the Q Tradition: The Aphoristic Teaching of Jesus*. Society for New Testament Studies Monograph Series, vol. 61. Cambridge: CUP.

Pixner, Bargil. 1976. 'An Essene Quarter on Mount Zion?' *Studia Hierosolymita* 1:245–84.

Polanyi, Michael. 1958. *Personal Knowledge: Towards a Post-Critical Philosophy*. London: Routledge & Kegan Paul.

———. 1966. *The Tacit Dimension*. Garden City, N.Y.: Doubleday.

Polzin, Robert M. 1977. *Biblical Structuralism: Method and Subjectivity in the Study of Ancient Texts*. Philadelphia: Fortress; Missoula: Scholars Press.

Porton, Gary G. 1986. 'Diversity in Postbiblical Judaism.' In *Early Judaism and Its Modern Interpreters*, ed. Robert A. Kraft and George W. E. Nickelsburg. In *The Bible and Its Modern Interpreters*, ed. Douglas A. Knight, 57–80. Atlanta, Ga.: Scholars Press; Philadelphia: Fortress.

Powell, Mark A. 1992. 'The Plot and Subplots of Matthew's Gospel.' *New Testament Studies* 38:187–204.

Poythress, Vern S. 1978–9. 'The Philosophical Roots of Phenomenological and Structuralist Literary Criticism.' *Westminster Theological Journal* 41:165–71.

Propp, Vladimir. 1968. *The Morphology of the Folktale*. Trans. L. Scott. 2nd edn. Austin, Tex.: U. of Texas Press.

Quasten, J. 1950. *Patrology*. Vol. 1. *The Beginnings of Patristic Literature*. Utrecht: Spectrum.

Rad, Gerhard von. 1962. *Old Testament Theology*. Trans. D. M. G. Stalker. Vol. 1. *The Theology of Israel's Historical Traditions*. New York: Harper & Row.

Räisänen, Heikki. 1990a. *Beyond New Testament Theology: A Story and a Programme*. London: SCM; Philadelphia: Trinity Press International.

———. 1990b [1976]. *The 'Messianic Secret' in Mark*. Trans. Christopher M. Tuckett. Edinburgh: T & T Clark.

Rajak, Tessa. 1983. *Josephus: The Historian and His Society*. London: Duckworth; Philadelphia: Fortress.

———. 1990. 'The Hasmoneans and the Uses of Hellenism.' In *A Tribute to Geza Vermes: Essays on Jewish and Christian Literature and History*, ed. Philip R. Davies and Richard T. White, 261–80. Journal for the Study of the Old Testament Supplement Series, vol. 100. Sheffield: Sheffield Academic Press.

Ramsey, Ian T. 1964a. *Models and Metaphors*. London: OUP.

———. 1964b. *Models and Mystery*. London: OUP.

Rapske, Brian M. 1991. 'The Prisoner Paul in the Eyes of Onesimus.' *New Testament Studies* 37:187–203.

Reinhartz, A. 1989. 'Rabbinic Perceptions of Simeon Bar Kosiba.' *Journal for the Study of Judaism* 20:171–94.

Rhoads, David M. 1976. *Israel in Revolution 6–74 C.E. A Political History Based on the Writings of Josephus*. Philadelphia: Fortress.

Rhoads, David M., and Donald Michie. 1982. *Mark as Story: An Introduction to the Narrative of a Gospel*. Philadelphia: Fortress.

Riches, John K. 1990. *The World of Jesus: First-Century Judaism in Crisis*. Understanding Jesus Today. Cambridge: CUP.

Ricoeur, Paul. 1977. *The Rule of Metaphor: Multi-Disciplinary Studies of the Creation of Meaning in Language*. Trans. Robert Czerny, Kathleen McLaughlin, and John Costello. Toronto: Toronto U. P.; London: Routledge & Kegan Paul.

———. 1984, 1985, 1988. *Time and Narrative*. Trans. Kathleen McLaughlin and David Pellauer. 3 vols. Chicago: Chicago U. P.

Riegel, Stanley K. 1978. 'Jewish Christianity: Definitions and Terminology.' *New Testament Studies* 24:410–15.

Riesenfeld, Harald. 1970. *The Gospel Tradition*. Philadelphia: Fortress.

Riesner, Rainer. 1981. *Jesus als Lehrer*. Tübingen: Mohr.

Rivkin, Ellis. 1969–70. 'Defining the Pharisees: The Tannaitic Sources.' *Hebrew Union College Annual* 40/41:205–49.

———. 1978. *A Hidden Revolution*. Nashville: Abingdon.

———. 1984. *What Crucified Jesus?* Nashville: Abingdon; London: SCM.

Robinson, John A. T. 1984. *Twelve More New Testament Studies*. London: SCM.

———. 1976. *Redating the New Testament*. London: SCM.

Rofé, Alexander. 1988. 'The Onset of Sects in Postexilic Judaism: Neglected Evidence from the Septuagint, Trito-Isaiah, Ben Sira, and Malachi.' In *The Social World of Formative Christianity and Judaism: Essays in Tribute to Howard Clark Kee*, ed. Jacob Neusner, Peder Borgen, Ernest S. Frerichs, and Richard Horsley, 39–49. Philadelphia: Fortress.

Roth, C. 1962. 'The Pharisees in the Jewish Revolution of 66–73.' *Journal of Semitic Studies* 7:63–80.

Rowe, William. 1989. 'Society After the Subject, Philosophy After the Worldview.' In *Stained Glass: Worldviews and Social Science*, ed. Paul A. Marshall, Sander Griffioen, and Richard J. Mouw, 156–83. Lanham, N.Y.: University Press of America.

Rowland, Christopher C. 1982. *The Open Heaven: A Study of Apocalyptic in Judaism and Early Christianity*. New York: Crossroad.

———. 1985. *Christian Origins: From Messianic Movement to Christian Religion*. London: SPCK; Minneapolis: Augsburg.

Rowley, H. H. 1946. *The Re-Discovery of the Old Testament*. Philadelphia: Westminster.

Rudolph, Kurt, ed. 1975. *Gnosis und Gnostizismus*. Wege der Forschung, vol. 162. Darmstadt: Wissenschaftliche Buchgesellschaft.

———. 1983 [1977]. *Gnosis: The Nature and History of an Ancient Religion*. Trans. & ed. R. McL. Wilson. Edinburgh: T & T Clark.

Runnals, D. R. 1983. 'The King as Temple Builder.' In *Spirit Within Structure. Essays in Honour of George Johnston on the Occasion of His Seventieth Birthday*, ed. E. Furcha, 15–37. Allison Park, Pennsylvania: The Pickwick Press.

Russell, Bertrand. 1961 [1946]. *History of Western Philosophy and Its Connection with Political and Social Circumstances from the Earliest Times to the Present Day*. 2nd edn. London: George Allen & Unwin.

———. 1967 [1957]. *Why I Am not a Christian and Other Essays on Religious and Related Subjects*. Ed. Paul Edwards. London: George Allen & Unwin.

Safrai, S. 1976a. 'Religion in Everyday Life.' In *Compendia* 1.2.793–833.

———. 1976b. 'The Temple.' In *Compendia* 1.2.865–907.

———. 1987. ed. *Compendia*. Section Two. Vol. 3. *The Literature of the Sages, First Part: Oral Torah, Halakha, Mishnah, Tosefta, Talmud, External Tractates*. Philadelphia: Fortress; Assen, Maastricht: Van Gorcum.

Safrai, S. and Stern, M., ed. 1974–6. *Compendia*. Section 1. *The Jewish People in the First Century: Historical Geography, Political History, Social, Cultural and Religious Life and Institutions*. 2 vols. Philadelphia: Fortress; Assen, Maastricht: Van Gorcum.

Saldarini, Anthony J. 1975. 'Johanan Ben Zakkai's Escape from Jerusalem: Origin and Development of a Rabbinic Story.' *Journal for the Study of Judaism* 6:189–204.

———. 1988. *Pharisees, Scribes and Sadducees in Palestinian Society*. Wilmington, Del.: Michael Glazier; Edinburgh: T & T Clark.

Salmon, Edward T. 1968 [1944]. *A History of the Roman World 30 B.C.—A.D. 138*. Methuen's History of the Greek and Roman World. London: Methuen.

Sanders, E. P. 1969. *The Tendencies of the Synoptic Tradition*. Society for New Testament Studies Monograph Series, no. 9. Cambridge: CUP.

———. 1977. *Paul and Palestinian Judaism: A Comparison of Patterns of Religion*. London: SCM; Philadelphia: Fortress.

———. 1983. *Paul, the Law, and the Jewish People*. Philadelphia: Fortress; London: SCM.

———. 1985. *Jesus and Judaism*. London: SCM; Philadelphia: Fortress.

———. 1990a. *Jewish Law from Jesus to the Mishnah: Five Studies*. London: SCM; Philadelphia: Trinity Press International.

———. 1990b. 'Jewish Association with Gentiles and Galatians 2:11–14.' In *The Conversation Continues: Studies in Paul and John in Honor of J. Louis Martyn*, ed. Robert T. Fortna and Beverly R. Gaventa, 170–88. Nashville: Abingdon.

———. 1991a. 'Defending the Indefensible.' *Journal of Biblical Literature* 110:463–77.

———. 1991b. *Paul*. Past Masters. Oxford: OUP.

———. 1992. *Judaism: Practice and Belief, 63 BCE—66 CE*. London: SCM; Philadelphia: Trinity Press International.

Sanders, E. P., and Margaret Davies. 1989. *Studying the Synoptic Gospels*. London: SCM; Philadelphia: Trinity Press International.

Sato, Migaku. 1988. *Q und Prophetie*. Wissenschaftliche Untersuchungen zum Neuen Testament. Tübingen: Mohr.

Schäfer, Peter. 1975. 'Die sogennante Synode von Jabne: Zur Trennung von Juden und Christen im ertsen/zweiten Jh. n. Chr.' *Judaica* 31:54–64, 116–24.

———. 1979. 'Die Flucht Johanan b. Zakkais aus Jerusalem und die Gründung des "Lehrhauses" in Jabne.' In *ANRW* 2.19.2:43–101.

———. 1990. 'Hadrian's Policy in Judaea and the Bar Kokhba Revolt: A Reassessment.' In *A Tribute to Geza Vermes: Essays on Jewish and Christian Literature and History*, ed. Philip R. Davies and Richard T. White, 281–303. Journal for the Study of the Old Testament Supplement Series, vol. 100. Sheffield: Sheffield Academic Press.

———. 1991. 'Der vorrabinische Pharisäismus.' In *Paulus und das antike Judentum*, ed. Martin Hengel and Ulrich Heckel, 125–72. Wissenschaftliche Untersuchungen zum Neuen Testament, vol. 58. Tübingen: Mohr.

Schäferdiek, Knut. 1991. 'Christian Mission and Expansion.' In *Early Christianity: Origins and Evolution to AD 600. In Honour of W. H. C. Frend*, ed. Ian Hazlett, 65–77. London: SPCK.

Schechter, S. 1961 [1909]. *Aspects of Rabbinic Theology: Major Concepts of the Talmud*. New Edn. New York: Schocken Books.

Schenke, Hans-Martin. 1983. 'The Book of Thomas (NHC II.7): A Revision of a Pseudepigraphical Epistle of Jacob the Contender.' In *The New Testament and Gnosis: Essays in Honour of Robert McLachlan Wilson*, ed. A. H. B. Logan and A. J. M. Wedderburn, 213–28. Edinburgh: T & T Clark.

Schiffman, Lawrence H. 1983. 'Legislation Concerning Relations with Non-Jews in the *Zadokite Fragments* and in Tannaitic Literature.' *Révue de Qumran* 11:378–89.

———, ed. 1989. *Archaeology and History in the Dead Sea Scrolls*. Journal for the Study of the Pseudepigrapha Supplement Series, vol. 8. Sheffield: JSOT Press.

Schlatter, Adolf. 1955 [1926]. *The Church in the New Testament Period*. Trans. Paul P. Levertoff. London: SPCK.

———. 1960 [1931]. *Das Evangelium des Lukas: aus seinem Quellen erklärt*. 2nd edn. Stuttgart: Calwer Verlag.

———. 1973 [1909]. 'The Theology of the New Testament and Dogmatics.' In *The Nature of New Testament Theology*, ed. & trans. Robert Morgan, 117–66. London: SCM.

Schmidt, F. 1982. 'Hésiode et l'Apocalyptique: acculturation et résistance juive à l'hellénisme.' *Quaderni Di Storia* 15.

Schmidt, Karl Ludwig. 1919. *Der Rahmen der Geschichte Jesu. Literarkritische Untersuchungen Zur Ältesten Jesus Überlieferung*. Berlin.

Schmithals, W. 1980. 'Kritik der Formkritik.' *Zeitschrift für Theologie und Kirche* 77:149–85.

Schoedel, William R. 1989. 'The Apostolic Fathers.' In *The New Testament and Its Modern Interpreters*, ed. Eldon J. Epp and George W. MacRae, 457–98. Atlanta, Ga.: Scholars Press.

Schoeps, H. -J. 1961 [1959]. *Paul: The Theology of the Apostle in the Light of Jewish Religious History*. Trans. H. Knight. London: Lutterworth.

Scholem, Gershom. 1971. *The Messianic Idea in Judaism, and Other Essays on Jewish Spirituality*. New York: Schocken.

Schrage, Wolfgang. 1979. 'Die Frage nach der Mitte und dem Kanon im Kanon des Neuen Testaments in der Neueren Diskussion.' In *Rechtfertigung. Festschrift für Emst Käsemann zum 70. Geburtstag*, ed. J. Friedrich, W. Pöhlmann, and P. Stuhlmacher, 415–42. Tübingen: Mohr; Göttingen: Vandenhoek & Ruprecht.

Schreckenberg, H. 1980. 'Flavius Josephus und die lukanischen Schriften.' In *Wort in der Zeit: Neutestamentliche Studien. Festgabe für Karl Heinrich Rengstorf zum 75. Geburtstag*, ed. Wilfrid Haubeck and Michael Bachmann, 179–209. Leiden: Brill.

Schulz, Siegfried. 1985 [1964]. 'Mark's Significance for the Theology of Early Christianity.' In *The Interpretation of Mark*, ed. William R. Telford. Issues in Religion and Theology, no. 7. Philadelphia: Fortress; London: SPCK.

Schürer, E. 1973–87. *The History of the Jewish People in the Age of Jesus Christ (175 B.C.—A.D. 135)*. Rev. & ed. G. Vermes, F. Millar, and M. Black. 3 vols. Edinburgh: T & T Clark.

Schwartz, D. R. 1983. 'Josephus and Nicolaus on the Pharisees.' *Journal for the Study of Judaism* 14:157–71.

———. 1992. *Studies in the Jewish Background of Christianity*. Wissenschaftliche Untersuchungen zum Neuen Testament, vol. 60. Tübingen: Mohr.

Schweitzer, Albert. 1925 [1901]. *The Mystery of the Kingdom of God*. Trans. W. Lowrie. London: A & C Black.

———. 1954 [1910]. *The Quest of the Historical Jesus: A Critical Study of Its Progress from Reimarus to Wrede*. Trans. W. B. D. Montgomery. 3rd edn. London: A & C Black.

———. 1968a [1967]. *The Kingdom of God and Primitive Christianity*. Ed. Ulrich Neuenschwander. Trans. L. A. Garrard. London: A & C Black.

———. 1968b [1931]. *The Mysticism of Paul the Apostle*. Trans. William Montgomery. New York: Seabury Press.

Scott, James M. 1992a. *Adoption as Sons of God. An Exegetical Investigation Into the Background of* ΥΙΟΘΕΣΙΑ *in the Pauline Corpus*. Wissenschaftliche Untersuchungen zum Neuen Testament, vol. 48. Tübingen: Mohr.

———. 1992b. ' "For as Many as Are of Works of the Law Are Under a Curse" (Galatians 3.10).' In *Paul and the Scriptures of Israel*, ed. James A. Sanders and Craig A. Evans. Journal for the Study of the New Testament Supplement Series. Sheffield: JSOT Press. [Forthcoming]

Seeley, D. 1992. 'Jesus' Death in Q.' *New Testament Studies* 38:222–34.

Segal, Alan F. 1977. *Two Powers in Heaven: Early Rabbinic Reports About Christianity and Gnosticism*. Leiden: Brill.

———. 1984. ' "He Who Did not Spare His Own Son . . . :" Jesus, Paul and the Akedah.' In *From Jesus to Paul: Studies in Honour of Francis Wright Beare*, 169–84. Waterloo, Ontario: Wilfrid Laurier U. P.

———. 1986. *Rebecca's Children: Judaism and Christianity in the Roman World*. Cambridge, Mass.: Harvard U. P.

Sevenster, J. N. 1975. *The Roots of Pagan Anti-Semitism in the Ancient World*. Supplements to Novum Testamentum, vol. 41. Leiden: Brill.

Shanks, Hershel. 1979. *Judaism in Stone: The Archaeology of Ancient Synagogues*. San Francisco: Harper & Row.

Sherwin-White, Adrian N. 1969 [1963]. *Roman Society and Roman Law in the New Testament*. 3rd edn. Oxford: OUP.

Skehan, Patrick W., and Alexander A. di Lella. 1987. *The Wisdom of Ben Sira: A New Translation with Notes*. The Anchor Bible, vol. 39. New York: Doubleday.

Slingerland, Dixon. 1991. 'Acts 18:1–18, the Gallio Inscription, and Absolute Pauline Chronology.' *Journal of Biblical Literature* 110:439–49.

Smith, Jonathan Z. 1990. *Drudgery Divine. On the Comparison of Early Christianity and the Religions of Later Antiquity*. London: School of Oriental and African Studies.

Smith, Morton. 1971. 'Zealots and Sicarii, Their Origins and Relation.' *Harvard Theological Review* 64 (January):1–19.

———. 1977 [1956]. 'Palestinian Judaism in the First Century.' In *Essays in Greco-Roman and Related Talmudic Literature*, ed. H. Fischel, 183–97. New York: Ktav.

———. 1978. *Jesus the Magician*. London: Gollancz.

Smith, Ralph L. 1984. *Micah—Malachi*. Word Biblical Commentary, vol. 32. Waco, Tex.: Word Books.

Sorri, Mari and Jerry H. Gill. 1989. *A Post-Modern Epistemology: Language, Truth and Body.* Lewiston, NY, and Lampeter: Edwin Mellen Press.

Soskice, Janet Martin. 1985. *Metaphor and Religious Language.* Oxford: Clarendon Press.

Sparks, H. F. D., ed. 1984. *The Apocryphal Old Testament.* Oxford: Clarendon Press.

Stambaugh, John, and David Balch. 1986. *The Social World of the First Christians.* Philadelphia: Westminster; London: SPCK.

Stanton, Graham N. 1974. *Jesus of Nazareth in New Testament Preaching.* Society for New Testament Studies Monograph Series. Cambridge: CUP.

———. 1975. 'Form Criticism Revisited.' In *What About the New Testament? Essays in Honour of Christopher Evans,* ed. Morna D. Hooker and Colin Hickling, 13–27. London: SCM.

———. 1980. 'Stephen in Lucan Perspective.' In *Studia Biblica 1978.* 3 vols. Journal for the Study of the New Testament Supplement Series, vol. 3, 345–60. Sheffield: JSOT Press.

Steck, Odil H. 1967. *Israel und das gewaltsame Geschick der Propheten. Untersuchungen zur Überlieferung des deuteronomistischen Geschichtsbildes im Alten Testament, Spätjudentum und Urchristentum.* Wissenschaftliche Monographien zum Alten und Neuen Testament, vol. 23. Neukirchen-Vluyn: Neukirchener Verlag.

———. 1968. 'Das Problem theologischer Strömungen in nachexilischer Zeit.' *Evangelische Theologie* 28:445–58.

———. 1980. 'Weltgeschehen und Gottesvolk im Buche Daniel.' In *Kirche. Festschrift für Günther Bornkamm Zum 75. Geburtstag,* ed. Dieter Lührmann and Georg Strecker, 53–78. Tübingen: Mohr.

Stemberger, Günter. 1977. 'Die sogennante "Synode von Jabne" und das frühe Christentum.' *Kairos* 19:14–21.

———. 1991. *Pharisäer, Sadduzäer, Essener.* Stuttgarter Bibelstudien, vol. 144. Stuttgart: Verlag Katholisches Bibelwerk.

Stendahl, Krister. 1962. 'Biblical Theology.' In *The Interpreter's Dictionary of the Bible,* vol. 1, 418–32. Nashville: Abingdon Press.

Stern, Menahem. 1973. 'Zealots.' In *Encyclopaedia Judaica Year Book 1973,* 135–52. Jerusalem: Keter.

———. 1976. 'The Jews in Greek and Latin Literature.' In *Compendia* 1.2.1101–59.

Stibbe, Mark W. G. 1992. *John as Storyteller: Narrative Criticism and the Fourth Gospel.* Society for New Testament Studies Monograph Series, vol. 71. Cambridge: CUP.

Stoldt, Hans-Herbert. 1980 [1977]. *History and Criticism of the Marcan Hypothesis.* Macon, Ga.: Mercer U. P.

Stone, Michael E. 1984. *Compendia.* Section Two. Vol. 2. *Jewish Writings of the Second Temple Period: Apocrypha, Pseudepigrapha, Qumran Sectarian Writings, Philo, Josephus.* Philadelphia: Fortress; Assen: Van Gorcum.

———. 1987. 'The Question of the Messiah in 4 Ezra.' In *Judaisms and Their Messiahs at the Turn of the Christian Era,* ed. Jacob Neusner, William S. Green, and Ernest Frerichs, 209–24. Cambridge: CUP.

———. 1990. *Fourth Ezra: A Commentary on the Book of Fourth Ezra.* Ed. Frank Moore Cross. Hermeneia. Minneapolis: Fortress.

Stoppard, Tom. 1967. *Rosencrantz and Guildenstern Are Dead.* London: Faber & Faber.

Stowers, Stanley K. 1986. *Letter-Writing in Greco-Roman Antiquity.* Library of Early Christianity, vol. 5. Philadelphia: Westminster; London: SPCK.

Strack, H. L., and G. Stemberger. 1991 [1982]. *Introduction to the Talmud and Midrash.* Trans. M. N. A. Bockmuehl. Edinburgh: T & T Clark; Minneapolis: Fortress.

Strecker, Georg, ed. 1975. *Das Problem der Theologie des neuen Testaments.* Wege der Forschung. Darmstadt: Wissenschaftliche Buchgesellschaft.

———. 1983 [1966]. 'The Concept of History in Matthew.' In *The Interpretation of Matthew,* ed. Graham N. Stanton, 67–84. Issues in Religion and Theology, no. 3. Philadelphia: Fortress; London: SPCK.

———. 1988. *The Sermon on the Mount: An Exegetical Commentary.* Edinburgh: T & T Clark.

Streeter, B. H. 1930 [1924]. *The Four Gospels: A Study of Origins.* 2nd edn. London: Macmillan.

Strobel, A. 1961. *Untersuchungen zum Eschatologischen Verzögerungsproblem, auf Grund der spätjüdisch-urchristlichen Geschichte von Habakuk 2,2 ff.* Supplements to *Novum Testamentum.* Leiden: Brill.

Stroup, George W. 1984. *The Promise of Narrative Theology.* London: SCM.

Stuhlmacher, Peter. 1966. *Gerechtigkeit Gottes bei Paulus*. Forschungen zur Religion und Literatur des Alten und Neuen Testaments, vol. 87. Göttingen: Vandenhoek und Ruprecht.
——. 1977. *Historical Criticism and Theological Interpretation of Scripture: Towards a Hermeneutics of Consent*. Trans. Roy A. Harrisville. Philadelphia: Fortress; London: SPCK.
Sykes, Stephen W., ed. 1991. *Sacrifice and Redemption: Durham Essays in Theology*. Cambridge: CUP.
Talbert, Charles H. 1977. *What is a Gospel? The Genre of the Canonical Gospels*. Philadelphia: Fortress; London: SPCK.
Talmon, Shemaryahu. 1987. 'Waiting for the Messiah: The Spiritual Universe of the Qumran Covenanters.' In *Judaisms and Their Messiahs at the Turn of the Christian Era*, ed. Jacob Neusner, William S. Green, and Ernest S. Frerichs. Cambridge: CUP.
Tannehill, Robert C. 1985a [1977]. 'The Disciples in Mark: The Function of a Narrative Role.' In *The Interpretation of Mark*, ed. William R. Telford. Issues in Religion and Theology, no. 7. Philadelphia: Fortress; London: SPCK.
——. 1985b. 'Israel in Luke-Acts: A Tragic Story.' *Journal of Biblical Literature* 104:69–85.
Taylor, M. C. 1982. *Deconstructing Theology*. American Academy of Religion/Studies in Religion, vol. 28. New York: Crossroad.
Taylor, Vincent. 1933. *The Formation of the Gospel Tradition*. London: Macmillan.
Tcherikover, Victor. 1961. *Hellenistic Civilization and the Jews*. Trans. S. Applebaum. Philadelphia and Jerusalem: The Jewish Publication Society of America, The Magnes Press, The Hebrew University.
Theissen, Gerd. 1978 [1977]. *Sociology of Early Palestinian Christianity*. [English Title: *The first followers of Jesus*]. Trans. J. Bowden. Philadelphia: Fortress; London: SCM.
——. 1982. *The Social Setting of Pauline Christianity: Essays on Corinth*. Ed. & trans. John H. Schütz. Philadelphia: Fortress.
——. 1987 [1986]. *The Shadow of the Galilean: The Quest of the Historical Jesus in Narrative Form*. Trans. John Bowden. London: SCM.
——. 1991 [1989]. *The Gospels in Context: Social and Political History in the Synoptic Tradition*. Trans. Linda M. Maloney. Minneapolis: Fortress.
Thiemann, Ronald. 1989 [1985]. 'The Promising God: The Gospel as Narrated Promise.' In *Why Narrative? Readings in Narrative Theology*, ed. Stanley Hauerwas and L. Gregory Jones, 320–47. Grand Rapids, Mich.: Eerdmans.
Thiselton, A. C. 1980. *The Two Horizons: New Testament Hermeneutics and Philosophical Description with Special Reference to Heidegger, Bultmann, Gadamer and Wittgenstein*. Exeter: Paternoster.
——. 1992. *New Horizons in Hermeneutics: The Theory and Practice of Transforming Biblical Reading*. London & New York: HarperCollins.
Thompson, A. L. 1977. *Responsibility for Evil in the Theodicy of IV Ezra*. Society of Biblical Literature Dissertation Series, no. 29. Missoula, Montana: Scholars Press.
Tilley, Terrence W. 1985. *Story Theology*. Wilmington, Del.: Michael Glazier.
Tillyard, E. M. W., and C. S. Lewis. 1939. *The Personal Heresy: A Controversy*. London: OUP.
Torrance, Thomas F. 1976. *Space, Time and Resurrection*. Edinburgh: Handsel Press.
Toulmin, Stephen C. 1958. *The Uses of Argument*. Cambridge: CUP.
Tuckett, Christopher M., ed. 1983a. *The Messianic Secret*. Issues in Religion and Theology, no. 1. Philadelphia: Fortress; London: SPCK.
——. 1983b. *The Revival of the Griesbach Hypothesiˑ*. Society for New Testament Studies Monograph Series, vol. 44. Cambridge: CUP.
——. 1986. *Nag Hammadi and the Gospel Tradition: Synoptic Tradition in the Nag Hammadi Library*. Studies of the New Testament and its World. Edinburgh: T & T Clark.
——. 1987. *Reading the New Testament: Methods of Interpretation*. London: SPCK.
——. 1988. 'Thomas and the Synoptics.' *Novum Testamentum* 30:132–57.
——. 1989. 'A Cynic Q?' *Biblica* 70:349–76.
Tugwell, Simon. 1989. *The Apostolic Fathers*. In *Outstanding Christian Thinkers*, ed. Brian Davies. London: Geoffrey Chapman.
Tyrrell, George. 1963 [1909]. *Christianity at the Cross-Roads*. London: George Allen & Unwin.
Urbach, E. E. 1987 [1975, 1979]. *The Sages: Their Concepts and Beliefs*. Trans. I. Abrahams. Cambridge, MA., London: Harvard U. P.
VanderKam, James C. 1988. 'Jubliees and the Priestly Messiah of Qumran.' *Révue de Qumran* 13:353–65.

Vermes, Geza. 1973a. *Jesus the Jew: A Historian's Reading of the Gospels*. London: Collins; Philadelphia: Fortress.

———. 1973b [1961]. *Scripture and Tradition in Judaism*. 2nd edn. Studia Post-Biblica, vol. 4. Leiden: Brill.

———. 1977. *The Dead Sea Scrolls: Qumran in Perspective*. London: Collins; Philadelphia: Fortress.

———. 1987 [1962]. *The Dead Sea Scrolls in English*. 3rd edn. London: Penguin Books.

———. 1991. 'Josephus' Treatment of the Book of Daniel.' *Journal of Jewish Studies* 42:149–66.

Via, Dan O. 1967. *The Parables, Their Literary and Existential Dimension*. Philadelphia: Fortress.

———. 1975. *Kerygma and Comedy in the New Testament: A Structuralist Approach to Hermeneutic*. Philadelphia: Fortress.

———. 1965. *Old Testament Theology*. Trans. D. M. G. Stalker. Vol. 2. *The Theology of Israel's Prophetic Traditions*. New York: Harper & Row.

Wacholder, Ben Zion. 1983. *The Dawn of Qumran: The Sectarian Torah and the Teacher of Righteousness*. Monographs of the Hebrew Union College, no. 2. Cincinatti: Hebrew Union College Press.

Walasky, P. W. 1983. *'And So We Came to Rome': The Political Perspective of St. Luke*. Society for New Testament Studies Monograph Series, vol. 49. Cambridge: CUP.

Walsh, Brian J. 1989. *Who Turned Out the Lights? The Light of the Gospel in a Post-Enlightenment Culture*. Toronto: Institute for Christian Studies.

Walsh, Brian J., and J. Richard Middleton. 1984. *The Transforming Vision: Shaping a Christian World View*. Downers Grove, Ill.: IVP.

Wansbrough, Henry, ed. 1991. *Jesus and the Oral Gospel Tradition*. Journal for the Study of the New Testament Supplement Series, vol. 64. Sheffield: Sheffield Academic Press.

Warner, Martin, ed. 1990. *The Bible as Rhetoric: Studies in Biblical Persuasion and Credibility*. London & New York: Routledge.

Webb, Robert L. 1991. *John the Baptizer and Prophet: A Socio-Historical Study*. Journal for the Study of the New Testament Supplement Series, vol. 62. Sheffield: Sheffield Academic Press.

Wedderburn, Alexander J. M. 1987. *Baptism and Resurrection: Studies in Pauline Theology Against Its Graeco-Roman Background*. Wissenschaftliche Untersuchungen zum Neuen Testament. Tübingen: Mohr.

Weeden, Theodore J. 1985 [1968]. 'The Heresy That Necessitated Mark's Gospel.' In *The Interpretation of Mark*, ed. William R. Telford. Issues in Religion and Theology, no. 7. Philadelphia: Fortress; London: SPCK.

Wells, Colin. 1984. *The Roman Empire*. Fontana History of the Ancient World. London: Fontana.

Wenham, David. 1984. *The Rediscovery of Jesus' Eschatological Discourse*. Gospel Perspectives, vol. 4. Sheffield: JSOT Press.

Wenham, John W. 1991. *Redating Matthew, Mark and Luke: A Fresh Assault on the Synoptic Problem*. London: Hodder & Stoughton.

Westerholm, Stephen. 1988. *Israel's Law and the Church's Faith: Paul and His Recent Interpreters*. Grand Rapids, Mich.: Eerdmans.

White, Roger. 1982. 'Notes on Analogical Predication and Speaking About God.' In *The Philosophical Frontiers of Christian Theology: Essays Presented to D. M. MacKinnon*, ed. Brian Hebblethwaite and Stewart Sutherland, 197–226. Cambridge: CUP.

Whittaker, Molly. 1984. *Jews and Christians: Graeco-Roman Views*. Cambridge Commentaries on Writings of the Jewish and Christian world, 200 BC to AD 200, vol. 6. Cambridge: CUP.

Wilken, Robert L. 1971. *The Myth of Christian Beginnings*. London: SCM.

Wilder, Amos N. 1982. *Jesus' Parables and the War of Myths: Essays on Imagination in the Scriptures*. Ed. James Breech. London, Philadelphia: SPCK, Fortress.

Wilson, Bryan. 1982. *Religion in Sociological Perspective*. London: OUP.

Wilson, R. McL. 1968. *Gnosis and the New Testament*. Oxford: Basil Blackwell.

Winter, S. B. C. 1984. 'Methodological Observations on a New Interpretation of Paul's Letter to Philemon.' *Union Seminary Quarterly Review* 39:203–12.

———. 1987. 'Paul's Letter to Philemon.' *New Testament Studies* 33:1–15.

Wittgenstein, Ludwig. 1961 [1921]. *Tractatus Logico-Philosophicus*. Trans. D. F. Pears and B. F. McGuiness. London: Routledge & Kegan Paul.

Wolterstorff, Nicholas. 1979. *Works and Worlds of Art*. Oxford: Clarendon Press.
——. 1980. *Art in Action*. Grand Rapids, Mich.: Eerdmans.
——. 1984 [1976]. *Reason Within the Bounds of Religion*. 2nd edn. Grand Rapids, Mich.: Eerdmans.
Wrede, William. 1971 [1901]. *The Messianic Secret*. London & Cambridge: James Clarke; Greenwood, S. Carolina: Attic.
Wright, G. Ernest. 1962. *God Who Acts: Biblical Theology as Recital*. Studies in Biblical Theology. London: SCM.
Wright, N. T. 1986a. ' "Constraints" and the Jesus of History.' *Scottish Journal of Theology* 39:189–210.
——. 1986b. *The Epistles of Paul to the Colossians and to Philemon*. Tyndale New Testament Commentaries, new series. Leicester: IVP; Grand Rapids, Mich.: Eerdmans.
——. 1991a. *The Climax of the Covenant: Christ and the Law in Pauline Theology*. Edinburgh: T & T Clark; Minneapolis: Fortress.
——. 1991b. 'How Can the Bible Be Authoritative?' *Vox Evangelica* 21:7–32.
——. 1991c. 'One God, One Lord, One People: Incarnational Christology for a Church in a Pagan Environment.' *Ex Auditu* 7:45–58.
——. 1992a. *The Crown and the Fire: Meditations on the Cross and the Life of the Spirit*. London: SPCK.
——. 1992b. 'Romans and the Theology of Paul.' In *Society of Biblical Literature 1992 Seminar Papers*, ed. Eugene H. Lovering. Atlanta, Ga.: Scholars Press [forthcoming].
——, ed. 1978. *The Work of John Frith*. The Courtenay Library of Reformation Classics, vol. 7. Appleford: The Sutton Courtenay Press.
Yamauchi, Edwin. 1973. *Pre-Christian Gnosticism: A Survey of the Proposed Evidences*. London: Tyndale Press.
Yee, Margaret M. 1987. *The Validity of Theology as an Academic Discipline: A Study in the Light of the History and Philosophy of Science and with Special Reference to Relevant Aspects of the Thought of Austin Farrer*. Unpublished doctoral dissertation, Oxford University.
Young, Frances M. 1990. *The Art of Performance: Towards a Theology of Holy Scripture*. London: Darton, Longman & Todd.
Young, Frances, and David F. Ford. 1987. *Meaning and Truth in 2 Corinthians*. Biblical Foundations in Theology. London: SPCK.

INDEX OF ANCIENT SOURCES

6. Philo

7. Rabbinic works

Mishnah

9. Other Early Christian Works

INDEX OF MODERN AUTHORS

INDEX OF SELECTED TOPICS